That's Enough, Folks

Black Images in Animated Cartoons, 1900–1960

Henry T. Sampson

The Scarecrow Press, Inc.
Lanham, Md., & London
1998

SCARECROW PRESS, INC.

Published in the United States of America
by Scarecrow Press, Inc.
4720 Boston Way
Lanham, Maryland 20706

4 Pleydell Gardens, Folkestone
Kent CT20 2DN, England

British Library Cataloguing-in-Publication Information Available

Library of Congress Cataloging-in-Publication Data

Sampson, Henry T., 1934–
    That's enough folks : Black images in animated cartoons, 1900–1960
  / Henry T. Sampson.
       p.   cm.
  Includes bibliographical references and index.
  ISBN 0-8108-3250-X (cloth : alk. paper)
    1. Animated films—United States—History and criticism.   2. Afro-
  Americans in motion pictures.   I. Title.
  NC1766.5.A35S26   1998
  791.43′6520396073—DC21   96–49987
                                                          CIP

♾™ The paper used in this publication meets the minimum requirements of
American National Standard for Information Sciences—Permanence of
Paper for Printed Library Materials, ANSI Z39.48–1984.
Manufactured in the United States of America.

This book is dedicated with love to my two sons, Henry T. Sampson III and Martin T. Sampson.

CONTENTS

PREFACE

Revisionist history collapses,
like a house of cards,
when nudged by the truth!

Henry T. Sampson II
January 1997

Some of my fondest memories as a youngster growing up in Jackson, Mississippi, in the 1940s were Saturday mornings. My godfather, Mr. Patterson, who lived across the street, would pick up my brother and me in his immaculate 1939 Cadillac and drive us to the theater to see the Saturday matinee. For the price of six cents we saw a double feature, a newsreel, and what was the highlight of the morning's entertainment, a cartoon short. Laughter filled the air as the youngsters viewed the fast-paced antics of their favorite cartoon characters as they cavorted through six minutes of continuous action. Sometimes stereotypical black caricatures appeared on the screen, but we laughed anyway. Although the blacks were funny, they represented an image that also made me feel uneasy.

It was not until I began researching this book by viewing hundreds of cartoons made prior to 1960 that I learned that depicting black characters as derogatory stereotypes was the universal practice at all cartoon companies before 1960. Cartoon stories satirized and burlesqued almost every facet of the political, social, cultural, and religious activity of African Americans. Positive black images were a rare exception. Before starting this project, I was aware that, in general, cartoons derive a large measure of their humor from ethnic, political, and racial stereotypes. Historically, all ethnic groups have been the targets of animators' humor, including Jews, Irish, Italians, Native Americans, and Asians. But for these groups, there appeared to be boundaries defined by sexuality, criminality, religion, and patriotism that constrained story content and the depiction of characters. These constraints amounted to a type of censorship that was officially enforced by the motion picture code and unofficially enforced by distributors, exhibitors, and the general public (since children were a significant segment of the viewing audience). My research revealed that for black characters, animators had few such constraints. They created black female caricatures with pickaninny hair braiding who were physically unattractive and imbued with lascivious tendencies. The black male caricatures were slow walking, slow talking, lazy, unintelligent, with criminal or cannibalistic tendencies. Animators found humor in their concept of smiling blacks singing and tap dancing on the auction block of a southern slave plantation. But I believe showing smiling Europeans singing and dancing their way through the gate of a Nazi concentration camp would have been so abhorrent and raised so much public indignation that it would have resulted in certain financial ruin for any animation studio foolish enough to do it.

Animation historians have made scholarly attempts to rationalize the creation of black stereotypes and to explain away the motivation of their producers. But I believe the essential point is that not only were they created, but they were enjoyed by a vast majority of the movie-going audiences in the United States and abroad. An analysis of the psychological and sociological aspects of this mass behavior is well beyond the scope of this book. But results from studies by qualified scholars have shown that, in general, stereotyping of another race serves as an effective vehicle for others to enhance their own self-esteem and to acquire a sense of personal power and perhaps to reinforce their own feeling of inherent superiority. Within a multicultural society, cartoons can offer a convenient opportunity for the dominant majority to legitimately express many of their prejudices towards a less powerful minority. S. L. Gilam, in his book *Difference and Pathology: Stereotypes of Sexuality, Race and Madness (1987),* argues that human beings need to create stereotypes as a means of dealing with anxiety and their ultimate lack of control over the environment.

I soon discovered that inclusion of black stereotypes in a cartoon was not considered to be a detriment by newspaper film reviewers. Studios advertised all of their cartoons as good, wholesome family entertainment. This was expressed by Walt Disney in 1947 when he testified before the House Committee on Un-American Activities. He was asked, "Aside from those pictures you made during the war, have you any other pictures, or do you permit pictures to be made at your studio, containing propaganda?" Disney replied:

> We watch so that nothing gets into the films that would be harmful in any way to any group or any country. We have large audiences of children and different groups, and we try to keep them as free from anything that would offend anybody as possible. We work hard to see that nothing of that sort creeps in.

The cartoons in this book will demonstrate that the animation studios considered the collective sensitivities of African Americans to be insignificant.

Some white-owned segregated southern movie theaters catered to both white and black patronage using separate showings. I was surprised to discover that they often showed black cartoons to their white audiences but not to their black audiences. I was not able to find a plausible explanation for this practice.

I used 16-mm films, video tape, newspaper reviews, trade publications, and production company advertisements of the period to develop a title database and describe stories. Much of the dialogue was in so-called Negro dialect, which I transcribed phonetically. Finding illustration material including cartoon stills was very difficult. Stills were obtained at swap meets and at movie collector shows. The historical cartoon stills I have included in this book which show black stereotypes are used solely to complement the text and are in no way intended to defame or malign any past or present animator or animation studio.

The illustrations are located as one group in the middle section of the book. They are numbered and cross referenced to the corresponding stories in the chapters of the book.

The appendix contains a listing of all the cartoon titles and credits included in this book. For cartoons where black charac- ters make a cameo appearance, a brief description of the relevant gag(s) is also included.

Finally, I thoroughly enjoyed researching this book. Viewing hundreds of vintage cartoons and reading about their history was an informative and, for the most part, pleasurable experience. That they also brought laughter to millions of theater goers the world over for six decades is a stellar tribute to the hundreds of ingenious artists who created them. However, it is an enormous public loss that many of these brilliantly conceived and produced cartoon shorts cannot be shown today because they are forever marked with the ugly and indelible stain of racism. About these cartoons, African Americans of yesteryear must have collectively proclaimed, "That's enough, folks!"

ACKNOWLEDGMENTS

The author acknowledges the cooperation of the staffs of the following libraries: Academy of Motion Picture Arts and Sciences; UCLA Research Library and Film Archive; Motion Picture, Broadcasting, and Recorded Sound Division, Library of Congress; Doheny Library, University of Southern California; and Los Angeles City Library, El Segundo Public Library.

Also much thanks to the following companies and individuals: Turner Entertainment Corporation, Glenn Video Vistas, Urbanski Film and Video, Kit Parker Films, B. G. Phillips, B. McDaniel, C. Vesce, R. Lessard, C. Kellogg, and J. B. Sampson Jr.

Very special thanks to Mark Mayfield, whose vast knowledge of animation history and extensive collection of vintage cartoons were invaluable to this project.

Chapter 1

BLACK IMAGES IN ANIMATED CARTOONS:
HISTORICAL OVERVIEW, 1900–1960

On May 20, 1895, Woodville Latham, using his Pantoptikon projector, gave the first public showing of moving pictures on a big screen on the roof of Madison Square Garden in New York City. By April 20 of the following year motion pictures had attracted enough public attention that Koster and Bial's Music Hall began presenting Edison's Vitascope pictures as one of the "acts" on their variety bill. On December 12, 1897, William Randolph Hearst began publishing on the last page of the Sunday supplement of his *New York Journal* a new picture series called the comic strip. Within the following decade the cinematic technique of moving pictures would be combined with the artistry of comic strips to create a new art form—the animated cartoon. From the beginning the animated cartoon captivated movie audiences and propelled its producers into the forefront of the short-subject segment of the motion picture business. The *Motion Picture Herald* reported that cartoons won top honors for the moneymaking short subjects of 1939–1940, according to a vote of exhibitors. Cartoon characters such as Bugs Bunny, Mickey Mouse, Andy Panda, Donald Duck, Tom and Jerry, Popeye, Woody Woodpecker, and many others became known throughout the world, everywhere American motion pictures were played.

Historically black characters played a significant role in American comic strips before the advent of animated cartoons (fig. 1). The first real newspaper comic strip was "The Katzenjammer Kids" published in 1887. The strip was set in an imaginary country in Africa, and in addition to the featured characters, Africans were depicted as being unintelligent, lazy, or hostile, and as having cannibalistic tendencies. Winsor McCay's "Little Nemo" strip, created in 1905, included a black character called Impy, a cannibal who wears a grass skirt and utters gibberish like "google-geegle-gimpleg-bumble." Impy was not an original character, but became a regular after Nemo made a trip to a cannibal island. Black characters made frequent appearances in other popular strips, such as "Happy Holligan," "Poor Old Robinson Crusoe," "Prof. Hypnotiser," "Simon Simple," "Willie Cute," "Boots and Buddies," "Wash Tubbs," and "The Newfangles." Almost without exception, the black characters appearing in these strips were comic foils of the white characters. They were usually drawn with exaggerated features (big mouth, very thick lips), and they spoke in a heavy dialect.

In the years before World War I, several strips featuring black characters made their debut in the Sunday papers. One of the most popular was "Sambo and His Funny Friends," published between 1906 and 1910. "Sambo," a black boy, had all of the typical racial stereotypes except that the character was street-smart and usually outwitted his white friends who attempted to play mean tricks on him. Negro Raul was a black character published in a strip appearing in 1916 in a Buenos Aires newspaper. Raul was depicted as a victim who unsuccessfully tried to overcome the hostile and racist environment of the city. "Sunflower Street," published in 1904 for King Features Syndicate, was unique in that it depicted a complete black family—Susie, Granny, Lou, Pop Henry, Mr. Native, Cousin Bobo, and the children—Eeny, Meeny, Miney, and Moe. Other black comic strips of this period included "'Scuse Me Mr. Johnson," "And Sam Laughed," "Polly and Her Pals," and "Uncle Mose." "The Chocolate Drops" featured the characters Chocolate Eclair, Chocolate Sundie, Sweetbunch, and Cutey. In the introduction to the 1933 book, *Dark Laughter: The Satiric Art of Oliver W. Harrington* (Harrington probably being the most famous black newspaper cartoon artist), M. Thomas Inge commented:

> Throughout the history of comics, the artists were given to drawing racial stereotypes, whether the characters were Irish, Jewish, Asian, Italian or African American. For visual humor to be effective, as in editorial cartoons or comic strips, it tends to reduce the target of the satire or joke to a recognizable, generic image, which in turn unfortunately can become a negative stereotype.

During this period the artists targeted African Americans with their racial satire and jokes (fig. 2).

By the time animated cartoons made their debut in the second decade of motion pictures, the weekly comic strips had already imbued black characters with negative and degrading racial stereotypes. It is not surprising that these stereotypes were carried over into animated cartoons, since many of the pioneer cartoonists, including Pat Sullivan, Winsor McCay, John Randolph Bray, and Paul Terry, were recruited from the ranks of newspaper comic-strip artists. Throughout their history animated cartoons have included stereotyped representations of all ethnic and racial groups, especially black people.

Between 1900 and 1960, approximately seven thousand animated cartoon shorts were copyrighted in the United States. The relative production rates by decade for this period are compared in figure 1.1. Production increased significantly in the 1920s and 1930s:

> One of the most interesting phases of production since sound became an adjunct of the screen is the popularity and interest shown cartoon comedies. While cartoon comedies in the silent days were accepted as fillers and proved quite interesting, since sound was introduced they have been looked upon as a sort of necessity, filling the gap that had long been overlooked by producers.
>
> The cartoon comedy is one short subject that seems to have met with instant approval. While some are better than others, the standard of the average cartoon comedy so far shown on the sound screen has been along a more perfect tenor than any other of the various types of sound productions.

%

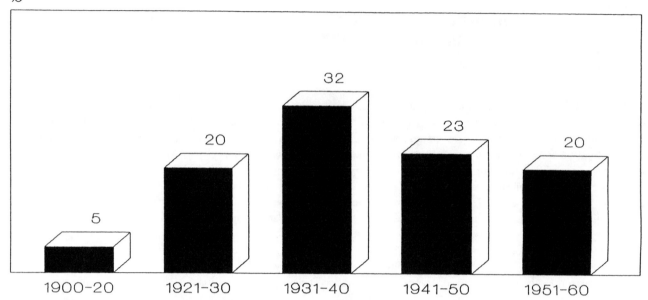

Fig 1.1. Production of animated cartoon shorts (copyrighted only), by decade, as a percentage of total production, 1900–1960.

With the demand for sound cartoons pouring into exchanges, numerous producers are preparing for new series during the year. . . . (*Billboard,* 15 February 1930)

Because of increasing demand, cartoon production peaked in the 1930s in spite of the fact that the cost of producing the average animated short had increased from about $4,400 in the silent era to $12,500. Production decreased during World War II due to a shortage of film stock and the war effort. Increasing production cost caused the rate to continue to decrease in the postwar years. Walter Lantz, in an article appearing in the December 26, 1952, issue of *Film Daily,* argued for increased rental rates, citing that it took from $35,000 to $40,000 to produce an animated cartoon, or about $65 to $75 per foot of film. Lantz also stated that production costs had gone up 165 percent, while rental rates had increased only 15 percent during the same period. By the late 1950s the major cartoon studios had begun to reissue earlier releases (fig. 3).

Many of the first cartoonists drew cartoon characters in black because it saved drawing a lot of outlines and made depicting motion easier. Mickey Mouse, Flip the Frog, Felix the Cat, Krazy Kat, and the first Oswald Rabbit were all drawn in black, but were not ethnically black. Between 1900 and 1960 ethnically black characters appeared in only about 8 percent of the cartoons produced in the United States. Figure 1.2 shows the distribution by decade of cartoons with black characters. Although the total production rate of cartoons increased by 12 percent between the 1920s and 1930s, the percentage of black characters increased by a factor of more than two. The principal reason is that sound cartoons gave the producers an opportunity to exploit the extraordinary popularity of black music and entertainers during the 1930s. Famous black stars of the stage, movies, and radio appeared in

cartoons either live or as human or animal caricatures of themselves. It is not by happenstance that several popular cartoon series featured black characters in starring or featured roles in their initial debut. Animated caricatures having the distinctive style of nightclub entertainers such as Cab Calloway, Louis Armstrong, Eddie "Rochester" Anderson, with his unique radio voice, and the lazy, slow-talking, dull-witted movie persona of Stephin Fetchit were instantly recognized by movie audiences wherever American cartoons were shown (fig. 4).

With few exceptions, no blacks were employed in an administrative or a creative capacity by any of the cartoon studios. A live-action tour of the Disney studio, seen in *The Reluctant Dragon,* showed no blacks involved as animators, technicians, musicians, cameramen, or anything else. *The Woody Woodpecker Show,* broadcast by ABC between 1957 and 1958, included cartoons as well as live sequences with Walter Lantz demonstrating how cartoons were made in his studio. Again no blacks were seen working there in any capacity. None of the cartoon studios recruited talented black cartoonists of the period such as E. Simms Campbell, Morrie Turner, Brumsic Brandon Jr., and Ted Shearer. As in the early minstrel shows and in vaudeville, where many whites performed in blackface, the voices of the animated black characters were most often provided by white actors speaking in an exaggerated form of "Negro" dialect. Exceptions to this practice included Roy Glenn as the voice of Scarecrow in the *Jasper* series, Lillian Randolph, the voice of Mammy Two-Shoes in the *Tom and Jerry* series, and Amanda Randolph, the voice of Mandy in the *Little Lulu* series.

During the postwar years the number of cartoons including black characters declined more sharply than cartoon production itself, due to successful efforts by civil rights organizations opposing negative stereotypes of blacks in motion pictures. It is

%

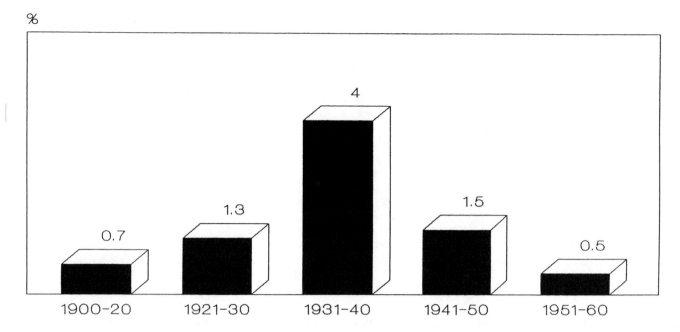

Fig. 1.2. Number of animated cartoons with black characters (copyrighted only), by decade, as a percentage of total number of all cartoons, 1900–1960.

unfortunate that these negative stereotypes were not replaced in equal numbers by positive cartoon images of black Americans.

The first black character to appear in an American cartoon was the smiling face of Coon, done on the screen in lightning-sketch fashion by James Stuart Blackton in 1907 in a short cartoon entitled *Humorous Phases of Funny Faces*. In 1911 Winsor McCay, recognized as one of the pioneers of American animation, brought *Little Nemo in Slumberland* to the screen. It included Impy, a black cannibal. In 1916 Henry Palmer produced *The Escapades of Estelle,* one of the first cartoons to feature a black character in the title role. Estelle, a heavyset black woman, steals some cloth to make herself a fancy dress. Thus in the first decade of animated cartoons black characters had appeared as a coon, a cannibal and a thief, thus establishing a trend for animated black stereotypes that continued well into the 1950s.

In 1915 Pat Sullivan created Sammy Johnsin, the first black character to star in his own cartoon series. At least nine of the *Johnsin* cartoons were produced between 1916 and 1918 for the Powers Film Company, headed by Pat Powers and released through the Universal Film Company (later Universal Pictures). *Johnsin* was the only ethnically black series created during the silent-film era. However, black characters made frequent appearances in many of the popular cartoons series, including Pat Sullivan's Felix the Cat, Paul Terry's Terrytoons, Walt Disney's Alice Comedies and Oswald Rabbit, J. R. Bray's Bobby Bumps, Police Dog, and Col. Heeza Liar, Wallace Carlson's Dreamy Dud, Bud Fisher's Mutt and Jeff, Max Fleisher's Out of the Inkwell, and others.

Bosko, created in 1929 by Hugh Harman and Rudolph Ising, was the first black character to be featured in a sound animated cartoon series. His sweetheart, Honey, was the first black female character in a cartoon series. The Bosko character inaugurated the long running and very popular Looney Tunes cartoon series, which helped make Warner Brothers one of the more profitable cartoon studios in the 1930s and 1940s. The only other cartoon series to feature a black character in the 1930s was *Li'l Eightball,* created by Walter Lantz and released by Universal. All three issues of this short-lived series were produced in 1939. The last and longest running black character featured in its own cartoon series was Jasper, created in 1942 by George Pal and released under the banner of his Puppetoon series by Paramount Pictures. Fifteen Jasper cartoons were released before the series came to an end in the late 1940s.

In March 1909 the National Board of Censorship of Motion Pictures was organized by the People's Institute of New York. One of the eight standards of judgement announced by the board included "the prohibition of blasphemy, by which is understood the careless or wanton or unnecessary offence against religious susceptibilities of any large number of people in the country." Two of the infamous eleven "don'ts" of 1927, which eventually made their way into the Production Code of 1930, included prohibitions against ridiculing clergy and willfully offending any nation, race, or creed. It was not clear whether the codes applied to animated cartoons, but the selection of acceptable subject matter was a concern for the producers of animated cartoons:

> Selection of subject matter has been developed to a high degree thru various stages of experimentation with the audience reaction and novelty of plot. Many are intended merely as mediums for song plugging, others for humorous program fillers and some even for advertising purposes. Occasionally suggestive matter is injected into the content, but public taste is

gradually eliminating this practice by protesting to exhibitors. It is reported that the public demands the producer keep cartoons clean because of their special appeal to children and minors. (*Billboard,* 12 July 1930)

The immense appeal that cartoons had for children was also recognized by producers, who realized that self-censorship would be good for business. In an article titled "Hollywood Censors Its Animated Cartoons," Leon Schlesinger, head and founder of the Warner Brothers animation department, wrote (fig. 5):

> We cannot forget that while the cartoon today is excellent entertainment for young and old, it is primarily the favorite motion picture fare of children. Hence we always must keep their best interest at heart by making our product proper for their impressionable minds. (*Look,* 17 January 1939)

At the time Schlesinger was producing forty-two cartoons a year.

Apparently the producers of animated cartoons did not feel that the above guidelines were applicable to black motion picture audiences, 25 percent of whom were made up of children under the age of sixteen. Black characters, in addition to being depicted as stupid and lazy were, more often than not, shown engaging in antisocial, illegal, or immoral behavior. Black religious customs were satirized in cartoons such as *Goin' to Heaven on a Mule* (1933), *Clean Pastures* (1936), and *Sunday Go to Meetin' Time* (1936). In the case of *Clean Pastures,* the censors deleted the words *De Lawd.* They had been included in the dialog of the black feature film *Green Pastures,* which was satirized by the cartoon. The black preacher was burlesqued in ways that were not acceptable for priests, rabbis, or leaders of any other religious group.

In other cartoons such as *Alice Cans the Cannibals* (1924), *Cannibal Capers* (1930), *Jasper Goes Hunting* (1944), and *Chew Chew Baby* (1958) black characters are shown engaging in cannibalistic behavior. *Uncle Tom and Little Eva* (1937), *Uncle Tom's Bungalow* (1937), and *Uncle Tom's Cabana* (1947), burlesqued the institution of slavery in the United States.

It would be hard to underestimate the negative impact that these stereotypical animated caricatures had on black audiences and especially on thousands of black youngsters who watched them at Saturday morning matinees in theaters all across the country.

From 1941 to 1945 the Hollywood animators produced many cartoons that had both entertainment and propaganda objectives. Cartoons such as *The Japoteurs* (1942), *The Ducktator* (1942), *Tokio Jokio* (1943), *Herr Meets Hare* (1945), *Bugs Nips the Nips* (1942), *Der Fuehrer's Face* (1943), *You're a Sap Mr. Jap* (1942) caricatured Germans, Japanese, and Italians, using some of the most vicious racial and national stereotypes ever seen in cartoons. This practice was acceptable to most of the film-going public because thousands of American men and women of all races were losing their lives in a life-and-death struggle against these nations. However,

producers continued to feature black stereotypes throughout the duration of the war effort, even as blacks were fighting and giving their lives for their country in the Atlantic and Pacific theaters of war. On the home front, the cartoon *Old Blackout Joe* ridiculed the efforts of a black air-raid warden to do his duty.

Neither the mainstream press nor the motion picture trade publications directed criticism against black stereotypes in cartoons. In fact, before the mid-1930s film reviewers commonly used terms such as *coon, darky, pickaninny,* and sometimes *nigger* when referring to black characters in their reviews. It was only after the end of World War II that the mainstream press in the United States began to take issue with some of the more blatant instances of racial stereotyping in cartoons.

In the 1950s cartoons that had originally been released in theaters were broadcast on television, a rapidly growing medium of popular entertainment. The Saturday morning matinee in the local theater was replaced by the morning cartoon show on television, which children watched in their homes. Rising costs had slowed the production of new cartoons, and the studios saw a golden opportunity to make a profit from their earlier releases then stored in film vaults. With the emergence of the civil rights movement in the late 1950s, many cartoons featuring black characters, including Li'l Eightball and Jasper, were judged unsuitable for broadcast because of their racial content. Some cartoons were edited to remove the objectionable stereotypes. A more notable example of this effort is represented in Walt Disney's feature-length cartoon, *Fantasia.* The original release included black stereotypes that were later edited out. The stereotypes were not included in the 16-mm format released for home viewing in the 1940s or in the video that was released in the 1990s. Similarly, in the theatrical and video release of *Little Nemo in Slumberland* in the 1990s, Impy, the black cannibal character, was not included. The voice of Mammy Two-Shoes, the black maid in the *Tom and Jerry* cartoon series, was replaced with an Irish-accented voice. Cartoons that featured all black characters, such as *Goin' to Heaven on a Mule, Sunday Go to Meetin' Time, Coal Black and De Sebben Dwarfs,* have never been shown on network television. One exception is the original Warner Brothers Bosko cartoon series, which has been shown regularly on cable television in the 1980s. Harman and Ising significantly toned down the racial characteristics of Bosko and his girlfriend, Honey, after the first few issues of the series. However, the M-G-M Bosko cartoons, in which Bosko and Honey are clearly depicted as two black youngsters, have not yet been released for viewing on network or cable television.

From Blackton's Coon sketch in 1906 to Mammy Two-Shoes of the *Tom and Jerry* series in the 1940s and 1950s, the statistical distribution of black character types in animated cartoons remained, for the most part, heavily skewed toward the same derogatory racial stereotypes that were being portrayed in feature motion pictures and on the stage and that permeated American society in general during this period. In recent times, self-imposed restrictions by the entertainment industry have prevented the public showing of most of these cartoons in their original form. A few were shown after the objectionable content was removed. Although done in a spirit of political correctness, these actions have resulted in a de facto revision of the true history of animation in the United States. The vast majority of people born after 1960 are probably not even aware that these racial cartoons were ever produced and exhibited publicly in the United States and abroad.

The remaining chapters of this book use detailed stories, trade reviews, and photographs about many of these cartoons to provide the reader with a detailed understanding of the content and extent of the racial stereotyping that was intentionally directed at African Americans by one segment of the movie industry during the first half of the twentieth century.

Chapter 2

Black Stars of Animated Cartoon Series

The October 24, 1957, edition of the *Motion Picture Herald* reported that "... eight of the top ten winners of the 1956 *Motion Picture Herald* fan poll of champion short subjects belong to the paint and brush set, including such favorites that are returning again this season as Bugs Bunny (the Champion of Champions), Mr. Magoo, Merrie Melodies and Looney Tunes, Popeye and Walter Lantz." Although cartoons were riding the crest of public popularity in 1957, the last black character to be featured in a theatrical cartoon series was terminated in 1952 when Mammy Two-Shoes was featured in *Push Button Kitty,* her last appearance in M-G-M's *Tom and Jerry* series. From the debut of Sammy Johnsin in 1916 to 1952, black characters, including Bosko, Li'l Eightball, Jasper, and Inki, were created during a period when ethnic humor was at the pinnacle of popular entertainment in the United States, especially in animated cartoons. But a growing and vocal civil-rights movement, combined with the rising popularity of television, placed increasing pressure on cartoon producers not to offend African Americans, a significant fraction of the moviegoing public. However, as cartoonists ceased to caricature black Americans as a race, they did not fill the void with new black characters devoid of the usual stereotypes, so that, in general, the appearance of black characters in American theatrical cartoons significantly decreased in the early 1950s, and black stars of theatrical cartoon series disappeared completely.

Sammy Johnsin (1916–1917)

In 1915 Pat Sullivan created Sammy Johnsin, the first black character to be featured in a cartoon series. Previously Sullivan had worked as a newspaper comic-strip cartoonist for William Marriner, creator of several popular strips, including *Wags, the Dog That Adopted a Man,* and *Sambo and His Funny Noises.* After Marriner died, Sullivan was hired by Pat Powers, head of the Powers Film Company, to draw a new cartoon series. Powers was one of the dominant pioneers of the independent motion picture producers. He owned over 40 percent of the stock of Universal Pictures before he sold out to Carl Laemmle in 1920. Sullivan adapted Marriner's black comic strip Sambo character to star in the series, but changed the name to Sammy Johnsin to avoid copyright problems with the Hearst Newspaper chain. He also employed Otto Messmer to do much of the drawing for the series. The first Sammy Johnsin cartoon was released in February 1916, and it was followed by twelve more under the banner of the Powers Film Company. The Johnsin cartoons were distributed in the United States by Universal Film Manufacturing Company, which also sold the rights for distribution in England and other European countries. Many of the cartoons were released on a split reel with another Powers short usually a travelog.

By mid-1916 Sullivan had lost interest in the Sammy Johnsin character and left most of the production work in the hands of Messmer while he created a new cartoon character, Charlie Chaplin, with the aid of the famous screen comedian of the same name who reviewed his work. In 1917 he created the short-lived Box Car Bill cartoon series before working for the U.S. Signal Corps until the end of World War I. After the armistice he produced *Origin of the Shimmy,* a cartoon featuring black characters, before teaming again with Messmer to create his most famous and successful cartoon character, based on a black cat named Felix, for the Paramount Pictures. Film historian Donald Crafton, in his book *Before Mickey* (1984), argues that the Sammy Johnsin character was a significant factor in the original conception of the Felix character:

> According to the accepted, humorously intended racism of the time, black children were portrayed as witty, wide-eyed waifs who experienced feats of the imagination presumably denied white children. Furthermore, blacks were frequently regarded as talented extroverts and as having innate advantages over whites as entertainers. Many of these same qualities were subtly transfused into the Charleston-dancing Felix, although he was never overtly identified as a black.

Felix was not drawn as an ethnically black character, but Sullivan imbued him with many of the stereotypical racial characteristics of Sammy Johnsin and the comic strip Sambo character that preceded him.

Sammy Johnsin Reviews

CUPID GETS SOME NEW DOPE (1917)

Company: Pat Sullivan, Powers Film Company, distributed by Universal Pictures
Characters: Sammy Johnsin, black washer woman

Review: *Moving Picture World,* 26 May 1917

Sammy Johnsin finds some love potion. He sees a black washer woman about to wake her lazy sleeping husband with a mallet. He squirts some of the potion over her head and she kisses her husband instead. Then he comes to a man proposing to a spinster. She is about to refuse him but some of the potion makes her accept him. There is a "Keep off the grass sign" and a nurse with a baby on the forbidden grass. A policeman is about to arrest her, but the potion makes him love her instead. At last, just as he thinks that he had reformed the world, Sammy wakes up and finds it a dream.

A DAY IN THE LIFE OF A DOG (1917)

Company:	Pat Sullivan, Powers Film Company, distributed by Universal Pictures
Type:	On same reel with *The Buried Treasure of Ceylon as Seen by Doctor Dorsey*
Character:	Sammy Johnsin

Review: *Exhibitors Herald,* 24 February 1917

Sammy Johnsin, reading a book about dogs, falls asleep and dreams he is a dog, but after an encounter with a cat he awakes and is glad that he is not a dog.

Review: *Moving Picture World,* 24 February 1917

Sammy Johnsin is reading a book about dogs. He goes to sleep and dreams that he is one. Many adventures happen to him, ending with a fight with a cat in which the feline has the best of it. Sammy wakes and decides that he does not care about being a dog after all.

Review: *Motography,* 24 February 1917

Having read a book about dogs, Sammy goes to sleep and dreams that he is one. He has many thrilling adventures and finally ends up in a fight with a cat, in which the feline has the best of it. Sammy wakes up and is mighty glad he's not a dog.

A GOOD LIAR (1917)

Company:	Pat Sullivan, Powers Film Company, distributed by Universal Pictures
Type:	On same reel with *In Monkeyland*
Characters:	Sammy Johnsin, war veteran

Review: *Moving Picture World,* 4 August 1917

Two pickaninnies follow an old veteran, and ask him how he won his medal. He tells them that back in '16, when he was a young private on sentry duty, the enemy attacked them in an aeroplane. He managed to overcome them, and then discovered a huge bologna sausage, which was the enemy's entire food supply. He reported his find to headquarters, saying that he was sending the food supply by wireless. It duly arrived at the tent of Gen. Delivery, from Private House. He was presented with the medal for this achievement. The boys say that he deserves a badge, and give him one with "Liar" on it. He is disgusted, and then tells them they don't know a real liar when they see one. (415 ft)

Review: *Bioscope* (London), 22 November 1917

Sammy Johnsin and his pal meet a hobbling old colonel. "Where did you get that medal, Colonel?" asks Sammy, and without delay we have an illustration of the colonel's story. "When I was a private, Haus," he begins. Lies, all lies, but, Munchausen like, the old boy is delightfully amusing. Clever drawing.

SAMMY JOHNSIN GETS A JOB (1916)

Company:	Pat Sullivan, Powers Film Company, distributed by Universal Pictures
Type:	Forth of the series; on the same reel with *Mexican Natural History*
Characters:	Sammy Johnsin, black cannibal girl

Review: *Moving Picture World,* 15 July 1916

Sammy asks his mother for a nickel, but she only tells him to get himself a job. He wanders out and sees a sign "Boy Wanted" outside a District Messenger office. He goes in and gets the job. Dressed in his A. D. T. uniform he is sent to a business man who wants a messenger. He is told to wait. He picks up a book called "Fiji Islands" and looks at the pictures. He falls asleep over it and begins to dream. He sees a cannibal girl eating a co-conut. A tiger comes after her, but he drives it away with one kick, and she is very grateful.

She is delighted to see him and rolls her eyes at him. They kiss each other and a big baboon comes down the tree and watches them. Sammy closes his eyes in enjoyment and while they are shut the girl walks away. The baboon comes down and takes her place and when Sammy starts to kiss again he finds himself gazing at the hideous baboon. It jumps up in the tree again and Sammy goes after the girl. He finds her just as a porcupine is coming up behind her. He tells her to take a seat. She does so and sits on the porcupine. She yells and Sammy laughs, but a big cannibal comes up and hits him over the head with his club. Sammy wakes to find the business man hitting him on the head with a ruler to wake him and gives him the letter.

Review: *Moving Picture World,* 15 July 1916

Animated funny pictures, by Pat Sullivan, showing the adventures of a small pickaninny who becomes an A. D. T. boy. These are clever and amusing.

Review: *Exhibitors Herald,* 15 July 1916

Sammy gets a job as a messenger boy. He falls asleep and dreams of rescuing a beautiful girl from tigers, cannibals and elephants. He dreams that a cannibal is beating him on the head with a club, and wakens to find the manager hitting him with a ruler.

Review: *Motography,* 15 July 1916

Pat Sullivan depicts his character as Sammy Johnsin in this cartoon comedy as having a curious dream in which he visits a land where cannibals abound. As usual with a dream, Sammy wakes at the crucial point and is brought rudely to earth.

SAMMY JOHNSIN AND HIS WONDERFUL LAMP (1916)

Company:	Pat Sullivan, Powers Film Company, distributed by Universal Pictures
Type:	Ninth of the series; on the same reel with *Majes-*

tic Ceylo as Seen by Doctor Dorsey

Characters: Sammy Johnsin, black cannibals

Review: *Moving Picture World,* **16 December 1916**

Sammy reads the story of Aladdin and the Wonderful Lamp. He decides that he must find one. So he searches the ash cans. He discovers a lamp and rubs it. A genie appears to do his will. He orders all sorts of things, but finally wakes to find it all a dream. (531 ft)

Review: *Bioscope* **(London), 22 November 1917**

Sammy Johnsin (the author and designer of this series is Pat Sullivan) having read the story of Aladdin, gets a magic lamp (small paraffin variety) and summons varieties of genie. He is transported to a new land, where the prehistoric camel drinks and drains the lake, robbing our hero of his bath. Sammy gives the camel a prickly pear, which punctures the water supply. In his car Sammy goes farther afield. Meeting a rhinoceros, he makes it dance, then an elephant throws him into the cannibal king's cauldron and then he wakes up. Delightful cartoon.

SAMMY JOHNSIN—HUNTER (1916)

Company: Pat Sullivan, Powers Film Company, distributed by Universal Pictures
Type: First in the series; on the same reel with *Fishing for Lamprey*
Characters: Sammy Johnsin, mammy

Review: *Motion Pictures News,* **21 January 1916**

A most amusing animated cartoon by P. Sullivan portraying the dreaming adventures of a colored boy who goes hunting. Just the right thing for children and highly amusing for old folks.

Review: *Bioscope* **(London), 20 April 1916**

A cartoon comedy, the drawing and animated effects being remarkably clever. The little black coon and his dog have hunting adventures with an ostrich, a skunk, and an elephant. A very funny dream story. (435 ft)

Review: *Moving Picture World,* **19 February 1916**

Animated cartoon showing the adventures of Sammy Johnsin, an indolent colored boy. Sammy's big mammy orders him to do some chores, but he is engrossed in reading a lurid periodical in which the capture of wild animals is the main theme. Sammy dozes off and dreams that he, too, is a mighty hunter. His dress takes him to the wilds of Africa, where he has many humorous encounters with lions, tigers, boa constrictors and untamed elephants.

Sammy, during his hunting expedition, comes upon an ostrich with its head buried in the sand and mistakes it for a coconut tree. He arouses the wily bird and meets with several harrowing experiences trying to capture it. Sammy gets from one difficulty to another with rapidity. Just as he is about to be devoured by a ferocious beast he is awakened from his adventurous dream by a well directed stream from a hose sprayed by his angry mammy.

SAMMY JOHNSIN—MAGICIAN (1916)

Company: Pat Sullivan, Powers Film Company, distributed by Universal Pictures
Type: Third of the series
Characters: Sammy Johnsin, Sammy's mother

Review: *Moving Picture World,* **1 July 1916**

Sammy's mother is making flapjacks while Sammy is fishing in the pond. She refuses his request for some when he arrives home. He finds an announcement of a magician's show and dreams that he has magic power. He conjures the flapjacks out of the frying pan into his mouth. He makes the duck lay him three eggs. They fly in the air and burst, letting out the full grown ducklings. The pig is made to dance on his tail. Sammy conjures a dog until it is small enough to be swallowed by a frog in the pond. A pelican eats the frog. A lady artist is frightened by a big snake, but Sammy charms the serpent and it rolls away like a huge hoop. The pretty artist then kisses him, but he wakes to find that the caress comes from the tongue of a big cow.

Review: *Exhibitors Herald,* **1 July 1916**

Sammy sees a magician's posters and falls asleep in the meadow. He dreams he is a magician and performs various feats. A lady artist is frightened by a snake, which Sammy conjures away. She then kisses him, when he awakes to discover that he is being caressed by a cow.

SAMMY JOHNSIN IN MEXICO (1916)

Company: Pat Sullivan, Powers Film Company, distributed by Universal Pictures
Type: Fifth of the series; on the same reel with *Creating Life from a Dead Leaf*
Characters: Sammy Johnsin, bandit

Review: *Moving Picture World,* **26 August 1916**

Little Sammy Johnsin was a foolish boy when he failed to heed the sign that was posted, warning the worthy denizens of Cartoon Land to keep away on account of blasting. So it happened that Sammy was given a free ride to the land of cactus and hot tamales. Upon his arrival Sammy procured a gun and set out to capture the bandit and thus win the reward offered to the man who brought him in dead or alive. Sammy found the bandit, but just as he was on the point of killing the dangerous character a little chicken flew across the path. Now when a colored man sees a chicken all his interests in bandits just naturally fades out. Sammy got neither and just as he was about to be killed by the ferocious Mexicans he awoke from his terrible dream. (517 ft)

Review: *Motography,* **26 August 1916**

In this comedy cartoon, Sammy, not heeding a warning of blasting, is blown into the land of cactus. Here he has many adventures trying to capture a bandit, finally being dissuaded from his purpose when a chicken crosses his path. The darky gets neither the fowl nor the bandit, but is nearly killed by ferocious Mexicans.

Review: *Bioscope* **(London), 15 November, 1917**

Sammy Johnsin, that delightful nigger mite created by the Powers cartoonist, sets forth to capture a Mexican bandit for the huge reward. He practices shooting in the desert, where birds of prey, testing on prickly pear, swallow his bullets with ease. At length he sights the bandit. "Hand up, Mistah Bandit,". . . "I ain't a bandit, I'm the new President," and a sadder and wiser nigger wanders into the unknown. Delightful.

SAMMY JOHNSIN MINDS THE BABY (1916)

Company: Pat Sullivan, Powers Film Company, distributed by Universal Pictures
Type: Sixth of the series
Characters: Sammy Johnsin, Sammy's mother, baby

Review: *Moving Picture World,* **4 November 1916**

Sammy Johnsin is told to mind the baby by his mother, and he goes in the fields with the child. But while there the wiles of old Morpheus are too strong, and he falls fast asleep. And the dream he dreams is one that is enough to make the hair of the most unemotional old maid stand on end. At last he wakes to find that after all it was only a dream, but the remembrance of the awfulness of it makes him a better boy for many weeks to come.

Review: *Motography,* **4 November 1916**

In this comedy cartoon, Sammy is told to mind the baby by his mother and he goes into the fields with the child. He falls asleep and dreams a dream that is enough to make the hair of the most unemotional old maid stand on end. At last he awakens to find that, after all, it was only a dream, but the remembrance of it makes him a better boy for many weeks to come.

SAMMY JOHNSIN AT THE SEASIDE (1916)

Company: Pat Sullivan, Powers Film Company, distributed by Universal Pictures
Type: Seventh of the series; on the same reel with *In and around Japan with Doctor Dorsey*
Character: Sammy Johnsin

Review: *Moving Picture World,* **25 November 1916**

Sammy Johnsin is a Character that is not new to the admirers of comedy cartoons of the films. He has appeared off and on the Universal program and now he is performing some of his comic antics at the seashore. He almost gets drowned and then plays the hero, but in the end he is happy as all the heroes of the films and those in real life ought to be.

Review: *Motography,* **2 December 1916**

Sammy Johnsin is a cartoon character that is not new to the followers of the Universal program. The picture sees him at the seashore. After being almost drowned he plays the hero, and the end is happy.

SAMMY JOHNSIN SLUMBERS NOT (1916)

Company: Pat Sullivan, Powers Film Company, distributed by Universal Pictures
Type: Tenth of the series; on the same reel with *Civilization in the Far East*
Character: Sammy Johnsin

Review: *Moving Picture World,* **30 December 1916**

Sammy needs a goodnight's sleep, as the cats of the neighborhood persistently keep him awake night after night. They sit on the fence outside and serenade each other. Sammy engages the services of a formidable bulldog, but that night the cats remain away. As soon as he dismisses the dog they return and make the night more hideous than ever. He tries in many ways to get rid of them. Finally they stay away for a time, and he enjoys his repose. Then one night they return, worse than ever. He looks out of the window and sees, not two cats, but a whole row of lusty kittens and their proud parents.

Review: *Motography,* **30 December 1916**

This is an animated cartoon which features the doings of two night howlers. Sammy has various experiences with the wailing cats on the back fence. As the pictures closes with showing of a new brood of kittens, relief for the future does not seem to be in sight.

SAMMY JOHNSIN—STRONG MAN (1916)

Company: Pat Sullivan, Powers Film Company, distributed by Universal Pictures
Type: Second of the series; on the same reel with *A Romance of Toyland* (cartoon)
Characters: Sammy Johnsin, Sammy's mother, black cannibals

Review: *Motography,* **18 March 1916**

A cartoon comedy by Pat Sullivan. Sammy sees an advertisement of "Bullo," a preparation which makes men as strong as bulls. This bases the subsequent dream which Sammy has, giving him power to pull up trees, subdue wild beasts, etc. But as Sammy is about to enjoy the sweet fruits of his daring, he awakens.

Review: *Bioscope* (London), 8 June 1916

An animated cartoon by Pat Sullivan. The drawing and animation are remarkably clever. Sammy is one of the most attractive of juvenile coons. A good film of this type. (545 ft)

Review: *Moving Picture World,* 18 March 1916

Sammy's mother was washing clothes and she called her son to carry home the basket. He was lost in contemplation of the advertisement of "Bullo," which makes men strong as bulls. He came, took the basket on his head and went back to rapt study of the fascinating poster. Then he began to dream. He drank a bottle of "Bullo" and the effect was immediate. Sammy is in the desert and he sees a giraffe enjoying a bunch of bananas hanging from a high tree. A little way off there is a bear who just cannot reach a bunch of the fruit. The doughty Sammy catches him by the neck and stretches it to the desired length.

Sammy comes to the hut of a cannibal, who is asleep under a tree, while his little daughter plays outside. A deep ditch separates Sammy from his charmer, but he pulls up a palm tree and makes a bridge on which to cross to her. The cannibal wakes and chases Sammy away, shooting after him with his bow and arrows. Sammy pulls them out, counting "He loves me, he loves me not." A hungry lion enters the hut and cries for help are heard. Sammy flies to the rescue, drives off the lion and claims the maiden. Just as he is about to enjoy the fruits of his daring he wakes to find his mother and the neglected basket of washing.

SAMMY JOHNSIN'S LOVE AFFAIR (1916)

Company:	Pat Sullivan, Powers Film Company, distributed by Universal Pictures
Type:	Eighth of the series
Characters:	Sammy Johnsin, Sammy's girl friend

Review: *Moving Picture World,* 2 December 1916

Sammy has a terrible time. He is in love with a little pickaninny, but she does not return his sentiments. He buys her all sorts of candy and other goodies, but in the end, after taking all these things, she turns him down in favor of the other fellow. So Sammy vows that never again will he fall for the fair sex.

Review: *Motography,* 2 December 1916

Sammy is in love with a beautiful little pickaninny, but she does not return his sentiments. He buys her candy, and all sorts of good things, but in spite of this she turns him down in favor of the other fellow. So Sammy vows he is done with the fair sex for good and all.

THE TRIALS OF WILLIE WINKS (1917)

Company:	Pat Sullivan, Powers Film Company, distributed by Universal Pictures
Characters:	Sammy Johnsin, Willie Winks

Review: *Motography,* 6 January 1917

Willie Winks is a friend of our old acquaintance, Sammy Johnsin. He has had an unfortunate experience with a goat, and goes to get his dog to chase the offending animal. The goat, however, chases the dog instead. Willie finds pressing business elsewhere, and warns his friend Sammy to look out for trouble. They are not quick enough in getting away, however, and the picture ends in a series of bumps.

Bosko the Talk-Ink Kid (1930–1938)

In 1929 Hugh Harman and Rudolph Ising created a new cartoon character and presented him to Vitaphone-Warner Bros. in a pilot film titled *Bosko the Talk-Ink Kid.* Between 1930, when Bosko made his cartoon debut in *Sinkin' in the Bathtub,* and 1938, when he made his last appearance in *Bosko in Bagdad,* a total of forty-six cartoons were made. The first thirty-eight were released under the banner of Vitaphone-Warner and the last eight by M-G-M (fig. 6).

In the previous year, 1928, Harman and Ising had worked for the Winkler Picture Company, headed by Margaret and George Winkler, making silent Oswald Rabbit cartoons. But when Walter Lantz arrived on the scene, they found themselves out in the cold as Lantz took over the Oswald character. Harman and Ising then set out to make *The Talk-Ink Kid,* a test film to show to prospective distributors. It was a one-reel film in which Ising sat at a drawing board and bantered with Bosko on the screen before him. This was probably the first cartoon in which actual dialog was synchronized with drawings. At the conclusion of the film Bosko says, "That's all, folks," which later became the well known ending for all *Looney Tunes* cartoons.

Harman and Ising tried unsuccessfully to make deals with several distributors before being steered to Leon Schlesinger, who owned the Pacific Title and Art Studio and later became head of the Warner Bros. cartoon division. Schlesinger became a middleman for Harman and Ising and sold their Bosko cartoons to Vitaphone-Warner Bros., which were marketed under the banner of new cartoon series called *Looney Tunes.* The first *Looney Tune, Sinkin' in the Bathtub,* opened in New York City on May 6, 1930, playing with another Warner Bros. feature film. Warner intended the new *Looney Tunes* series to compete with Walt Disney's *Silly Symphonies* cartoon series. An article titled "How Funny Looney Tunes Are Made" commented on the new cartoon series (fig. 7):

> . . . The first of the "Looney Tunes" Vitaphone cartoons is *Sinkin' in the Bathtub,* a take-off on Winnie Lightner's song hit in Warner Bros. musical revue, *Show of Shows.* The song is heard at intervals throughout the picture and now and then the characters are heard singing it. Bosko and his Honey,

the queer and attractive little characters introduced in *Sinkin' in the Bathtub* will appear in each of the series, all of which are to be based upon Vitaphone song hits from Warner Bros. and First National feature pictures.

The second number will be entitled *Congo Jazz* a burlesque on a First National Exhibitors Vitaphone picture song hit.

Leon Schlesinger is supervising the series of "Looney Tunes" for Vitaphone. The cartoons are by Hugh Harman and Rudolph Ising, with musical score by Frank Marsales and animation by I. Freleng. (*Variety,* 25 June 1930)

Not having seen the pilot film, reviewers were at first unsure of the ethnic or racial identity of Bosko and Honey or whether they were human. A review in *Billboard* referred to Bosko as a "monkey" after seeing him in *Sinkin' in the Bathtub.* He was referred to as a "mutt" and a "darky" in their respective reviews of *Congo Jazz* by *Variety* and *Billboard.* But Bosko's minstrel-show routine and southern accent in *The Talk-Ink Kid,* and Honey's pigtail hairstyle in her first appearance in *Sinkin in the Bathtub* clearly identified them as black stereotypes. The pigtail (tight braids) hairstyle, with coiled braids of hair sticking out of the head, was the most common cartoon depiction of young black females from the very beginning of animated cartoons.

Warner Bros. decided early on that the marketing strategy for their new cartoon series should emphasize the songs sung by Bosko and Honey, not their physical antics. Much of the music featured in the cartoons was taken from Warner Bros. and First National features that played on the same bill as the *Looney Tunes.* After the first two releases of the series, Harman and Ising had significantly downplayed the ethnicity of their new cartoon stars. This gave Bosko and Honey credibility in situations and locales not normally associated with black people. Bosko could play roles as diverse as a World War I doughboy, a French foreign legionnaire, a Dutchman, a cowboy hero, a lumberjack, and a Mountie with reasonable credibility. Similarly Honey could imitate such well-known white performers as Mae West, Helen Kane, Greta Garbo, and others.

By 1931 the popularity of Bosko and Honey, the stars of the *Looney Tunes* series, was so great that the Harman-Ising studio doubled its output and added a new series called *Merrie Melodies.* The new series had no continuing characters and was designed around music published by the Warner Bros. sheet music company with the aim of competing with Disney's *Silly Symphonies"* series. By 1934, however, Harman and Ising's business relationship with Schlesinger had become strained because he disapproved of higher budgets. So Harman and Ising decided to leave Warners and join M-G-M, taking the Bosco and Honey characters with them. At M-G-M the pair created a new series called *Happy Harmonies.* It was essentially a continuation of the *Looney Tune* series with emphasis on music, and it also introduced their first color cartoons. Bosko and Honey were drawn in their original forms in *Bosko's Parlor Pranks* (1934), *Hey, Hey, Fever* (1935), *Run Sheep, Run* (1935), the first three cartoons released by M-G-M. In *The Old House* (1936) Bosko and Honey made their debut as recognizably black children. This was the first cartoon in the series to be made in color. Honey made her last appearance in *Bosko's Easter Eggs* (1937),

and the series came to an end in 1938 with the release of *Bosko in Bagdad* (1938). The last three releases of the series were repetitious. In them Bosko is menaced by jazz singing, tap-dancing frog caricatures of Louis Armstrong, Fats Waller, Bill Robinson, the Mills Brothers, and Stephin Fetchit, who wants to take the cookies meant for Bosko's grandmother.

Bosko Stories and Reviews

AIN'T NATURE GRAND (1931)

Company:	Hugh Harman, Rudolph Ising, Vitaphone, Warner Bros.
Type:	Looney Tunes; Vitaphone Song Car-Tune
Character:	Bosko

Press Release: Vitaphone Corporation, 1931

Bosko becomes a disciple of Izaak Walton and goes a-fishing! The worm is so cute that he turns it loose, and the early bird chases the worm! But the worm turns on the unfortunate bird! Cheery Bosko sings and dances with the carefree denizens of the country who resent his intrusion! They get together and give him the works to the snappy tunes of popular music! Bosko is his usual happy self as he makes whoopie with nature's pests!

The tunes used in Bosko's last appearance in *Ain't Nature Grand* are: "Picolo Pete," "Telling It to The Daisies," "Kiss Waltz," the popular song hit from the Warner Bros. picture *Dancing Sweeties,* "Under the Sweetheart Tree," and "Don't Tell Her What's Happened to Me."

The "Looney Tunes" are as important to your program as the feature picture—bill them on your marquee! Popular songs featured in a novel way offer effective methods of exploitation!

The artists show their ingenious imagination in the seventh of the "Looney Tunes" series in a way that will bring laughs from everybody! *Ain't Nature Grand* will please them all!

BATTLING BOSKO (1932)

Company:	Hugh Harman, Rudolph Ising, Vitaphone, Warner Bros.
Type:	Looney Tunes
Character:	Bosko

Review: *Motion Picture Herald,* 6 February 1932

Bosko turns battler in this animated effort set to music of the modern mode. Bosko's opponent is a pugilist of mountain-like proportions in comparison. Just as the small lad's sweetheart reaches the ringside he is very surely counted out. This is number six of the series. (6 min)

BEAU BOSKO (1933)

Company:	Hugh Harman, Rudolph Ising, Vitaphone, Warner Bros.
Type:	Looney Tunes
Characters:	Bosko, Honey

Review: *Motion Picture Herald,* 21 October 1933

Bosko, of the Looney Tune cartoon comedies, takes his turn as a member of the Foreign Legion ordered to capture the desperate bandit. In the town he meets the belle of the harem, who is soon pursued by the bandit. He captures him in rather novel but universal cartoon style. Ranks a fair number. (7 min)

BIG HEARTED BOSKO (1932)

Company: Hugh Harman, Rudolph Ising, Vitaphone, Warner Bros.
Type: Looney Tunes
Characters: Bosko, Bruno the hound

Review: *Motion Picture Herald,* 16 April 1932

Little animated Bosko goes skating with his lop-eared hound, and finds a baby in a basket on the ice. They take it home, and try to quiet it. Their success is quite conspicuous by its absence, until they hit upon the musical jazz formula. The baby not only likes it but stands up in the cradle and joins in. Clever enough, amusing enough. (7 min)

BIG MAN FROM THE NORTH (1931)

Company: Hugh Harman, Rudolph Ising, Vitaphone, Warner Bros.
Type: Looney Tunes, Vitaphone Song Car-Tunes
Characters: Bosko, Honey

Press Release: Vitaphone Corporation, 1931

A he-man romance of a two-fisted country! Bosko of the Royal Mounted Police is ordered to get his man—a hard-boiled desperado with a peg-leg. After miles of musical mushing over the wasteless tracks of a chirping pack of hounds, he arrives at a log cabin saloon. He burns up the frozen North with a series of hot dances and funny capers with his sweetheart Honey. In the midst of gaieties, the Bad Man enters, armed to the teeth. Bosko get his man . . . and his woman! Frolicsome fun in the frozen North! With Bosko in a new and funnier role!

Four songs are travestied by Bosko in *Big Man from the North.* They are: "Looking for the Lovelight in the Dark" from the First National success *Top Speed,* "Chinnin' and Chattin' With May," "The Man from the South with a Big Cigar In His Mouth" and "I'm Needin' You."

Tie-ups with music scores are still a natural for the series of Vitaphone Song Car-Tunes. Popular song hits are a feature of the "Looney Tunes"—play them up!

The sixth of the "Looney Tunes" series . . . and each one better than the last! Bosko is a cartoon favorite! *Big Man from the North* will have them asking for more!

THE BOOZE HANGS HIGH (1931)

Company: Hugh Harman, Rudolph Ising, Vitaphone, Warner Bros.

Type: Looney Tunes, Vitaphone Song Car-Tunes
Character: Bosko

Press Release: Vitaphone Corporation, 1931

Life on the farm with the frolicking Bosko as a musical plowman extraordinary! Singing cows, pigs, and tuneful squeals, and a dancing chorus of happy ducks make the fourth of the song cartoon series a de lux musical comedy down on the farm! A bottle of liquor makes the animals perform many novel and laughable capers. Bosko is at his funniest in *The Booze Hangs High.*

Popular song hits from *Song of the Flame,* the First National musical extravaganza, are travestied in this cartoon comedy. The songs from the picture are "The Goose Hangs High" and "One Little Drink." Other tunes used are "Turkey and the Straw" and "Sweet Adeline."

The fact that the Vitaphone Song Car-Tunes use popular songs as a background throughout the series gives the exhibitor unlimited opportunities for tie-ups with music stores, radio broadcasts, piano rolls, phonograph records and sheet music.

The comic antics of Bosko and his animal friends in *The Booze Hangs High* provide plenty of laughs for young and old. "Looney Tunes" are still the most popular and entertaining of animated cartoons! "Looney Tunes" are blues chasers!

Review: *Variety,* 9 September 1930

Funny piece built around the song, "The Goose Hangs High," and latter's amusing lyrics that offer adaptation to the cartoon with good effect. Can be used anywhere for filler.

"Looney" and various kinds of fowl and animals tap, hop, and croon for laughs. Some of it's usual as the "Loon" using a horse's tail hairs for fiddle strumming. The music and the rhythm plus the synchronous voices make the subject entertaining. (6 min)

Review: *Motion Picture News,* 4 October 1930

Production value of this one rates high, but entertainment value is lowered because of the absence of originality in gags—a trait predominating in most of the cartoons of the current age. Here and there, we find in this "Looney Tune" a clever twist, easily recognized from the cut-and-tried material depended upon for laughs. Audience reaction was favorable. Vocal renditions helped tremendously, particularly those by the bass singer.

BOSKO AT THE BEACH (1932)

Company: Hugh Harman, Rudolph Ising, Vitaphone, Warner Bros.
Type: Looney Tunes
Characters: Bosko, Honey, Bruno

Review: *Variety,* 9 August 1932

Well-made and entertaining cartoon having to do with Bosko's day at the beach and a picnic party with his girl, plus a life-saving gag for a finish.

Considerable singing and dialog. Song double during picnic sequence very well worked up.

Cartoon has better pace than most. (7 min)

Review: *Photoplay,* October 1932

If you like the brisk antics of that clever little animated cartoon fellow, Bosko, you will enjoy this reel which shows him picnicking at the beach with his girl. It has good singing and dialogue, too.

Review: *Motion Picture Herald,* 5 November 1932

Little animated Bosko has an outing at the beach where he meets his sweetheart, is annoyed by his lop-eared hound and rescues her small brother in amusing fashion. Without being in any way an unusual cartoon, this is light enough and bright enough to fill in nicely on any bill.

BOSKO AND BRUNO (1932)

Company: Hugh Harman, Rudolph Ising, Vitaphone, Warner Bros.
Type: Looney Tunes
Characters: Bosko, Bruno

Review: *Motion Picture Herald,* 10 December 1932

An amusing cartoon number, in which young Bosko and his hound run into all sorts of difficulty on the railroad track, chase a chicken, are chased by the constable and finally are marooned aboard a runaway freight car with almost disastrous results. There is nothing outstanding about the short but is lightly amusing in its own fashion. (7 min)

BOSKO AND THE CANNIBALS (1937)

Company: Hugh Harman and Rudolph Ising, M-G-M
Characters: Bosko, Mammy, frog impersonations of Louis Armstrong, Mills Brothers, Fats Waller, Bill Robinson, and Cab Calloway

Story: The cartoon opens to the page of a book that reads, "Once upon a time little Bosko's mammy gave him a nice bag of cookies to take to his grandma. As he walked . . ." Bosko's mammy, a big woman wearing polka-dot stockings and house slippers, is standing at the front door of their cabin holding a bag of cookies in her hand and calling, "Bosko! Land sakes, I wonder where dat chile done got to now." Bosko sneaks up behind her as she says, "Oh Bosko! Now don't dat beat de all git out. Bosko where is you chile?" Bosko turns around to laugh, sees her turn, and she sees him. He hears her pat her feet, gets scared and turns and buries his head in her apron. She pats him on his head and says, "Mammy sho' did scare her little honey child dat time." She gives him the bag of cookies and tells him, "Now I want you to take dis bag of cookies to your grandma's. Now don't you go lackadaisin' on the way." Bosko says, "Yes, mammy" and heads off to grandma's chanting "straight to grandma's house I go to take these cookies to her front door" but soon finds himself lost

in the woods, which change into a swamp with the sound of frogs croaking all around him. He says, "Boy, here I is marooned in the middle of the Atlantic Ocean—on a cannibal island." Cannibals (frog caricatures) leap out of the jungle and carry him to the cannibal village where he is put before the cannibal chief who is seated on his throne. The chief says (Louis Armstrong voice impersonation), "Ya, ya, ya, what do you have there, boy? What do you have? Clutching his bag of cookies, Bosko answers, "Cookies." And the chief says, "Cookies?" Bosko says, "Ya and I'm taking them straight to my grandma's house." The chief laughs and walks over to Bosko and tells him, "Well, we're just a bunch of li'l ole' hungry cannibals. We ain't got no cookies and you've got cookies and we like cookies and we want cookies-Yah!" Bosko slowly backs away saying, "These here cookies?" and the chief answers, "Yes, those cookies." Four cannibals (Mills Brothers caricatures) appear from behind their shields and sing, "I like jam on whole wheat toast/Blackeyed peas and chicken roast/Everything that grows from coast to coast/But we all like grandma's cookies most." Another cannibal (Fats Waller caricature) is playing a piano and asks Bosko, "Hey boy, what you got in that sack there? Well, looks like your have good news. Or maybe you hadn't got good news. Well, what do you say Bosko boy?" as he picks him up and sits him on the piano. Bosko looks at him and says, "Well, what do you have to say, Mr. Piano Man?" The cannibal answers, "What do I say? I want cookies . . ." Bosko answers, "Not these. They just stay in this bag." Another cannibal (Bill Robinson caricature), wearing a derby hat, comes on the scene and tells Bosko, "I want cookies" while doing a tap dance. Bosko tells him, "You can't have cookies," and the dancing cannibal says, "OK, keep those things." Then the cannibal playing the piano says, "What's the matter with him?," before singing "I like great old Irish stew, sweet potatoes, and corn bread too, but if I don't get those cookies I might eat you." Meanwhile another cannibal (Cab Calloway caricature) leads a band while singing "hi-dee-ho." Bosko tries to escape but is captured by the cannibal chief who holds him suspended on the end of a large fork. Chief asks him, "Now what you say there little man? Do we does or does we do get those cookies?" Bosko answers, "No! Those cookies go straight to grandma's." The chief then tells him, "All right then. We gonna march you right up to that ol' boiling pot" as he marches Bosko up to the top of a ladder and onto a catwalk suspended over a pot of boiling water. Just before Bosko walks off the end and falls into the boiling pot, he rescues himself by tap dancing. The rhythm of his taps incites the cannibals to make music and dance. While they are dancing to a frenzy of fast music, Bosko, holding his bag of cookies, escapes from the cannibal village and finds himself back in the forest. Frightened by the croaking of a frog he hears behind him, Bosko takes off running to his grandma's house, leaving a cloud of dust behind him as the cartoon ends.

Review: *National Exhibitor,* 2 August 1937

Again this series scores with a lightning-fast cartoon. Bosko is told to take some cookies to his grandmother's. He is stranded on a lily pad, imagines he meets up with some frog-like cannibals who act strangely like Cab Calloway, Fats Waller, Bill

Robinson, others. They want his cookies, show him plenty of swing, try to cook him for a mulligan stew, but he wakes up in time. This is the same order as *Old Mill Pond, Swing Wedding.* It should play anywhere. Excellent.

Review: *Selected Motion Pictures,* 1 November 1937

Bosko on an errand to his grandmother's meets a colony of cannibal frogs. The musical interpretation of the antics of the frogs is facinating. Family.

BOSKO THE DOUGHBOY (1931); also released as War Daze

Company: Hugh Harman, Rudolph Ising, Vitaphone, Warner Bros.
Type: Looney Tunes
Character: Bosko

Story: The cartoon opens on a World War I battlefield. Shells are flying through the air, bombs are bursting, and soldiers are marching off to battle while big cannons are firing at the enemy. Bosko is in his trench eating a meal as an incoming shell makes a direct hit and blows away his pot of beans. Hungry and homesick, Bosko reaches into his pocket and pulls out a large photograph of his sweetheart, Honey, as the background music plays "Am I Blue" (Ethel Waters's song hit of the 1930s). Another shell burst blows a hole through Honey's image and an angry Bosko attempts to climb out of his trench to charge the enemy lines. But a stream of bullets knocks him off the ladder and he falls on the ground. His pal arrives on the scene and cheers him up by playing a hot tune on the harmonica. Bosko dances and has a good time before his trench is blown up by a direct shell burst. The enemy soldiers prepare to charge as Bosko and his pal come under air attack. In the end Bosko saves the day and his pal.

BOSKO THE DRAWBACK (1933)

Company: Hugh Harman, Rudolph Ising, Vitaphone, Warner Bros.
Type: Looney Tunes
Character: Bosko

Review: *Film Daily,* 21 April 1933

A Looney Tune, with Bosko the hero starring in the football game, scoring a couple of sensational touchdowns. He encounters tough opposition with the entire rival team trying to put him out of commission. But by employing some ingenious tricks he manages to outwit them. Plenty of action and excitement that will please the kids.

BOSKO IN BAGHDAD (1938)

Company: Hugh Harman, M-G-M
Type: Happy Harmonies
Characters: Bosko, Mammy (voice characterization by Lillian

Randolph), frog caricatures of Bill Robinson, Fats Waller, Louis Armstrong, Stephin Fetchit

Story: The cartoon opens at Bosko's home, where his mammy is baking cookies. Bosko says, "Ooh ooh, those cookies sho' does smell scrumptious." His mammy takes the cookies out of the oven and places them in a bag that Bosko is carrying. She tells him, "No Bosko, you go straight to grandma's and don't you go eatin' none of those cookies, Bosko." Bosko answers "Yes, Mammy." His mother also tells him to "go along now and don't let your imagination go percolating on any wild goose chases." Bosko leaves carrying the bag full of cookies in one hand and a kerosene lantern in the other hand. It is dark and as Bosko skips along he sings to himself, "Straight to grandma's house I go. Take the cookies to her front door." But before long the forest gets darker, and he hears a hooting sound that causes him to drop the cookies and the lantern. Bosko says, "Who dat?" and he hears a voice answer, "Who dat?" Bosko says, "Who dat say who dat when I say who dat?" A frog hops up to Bosko, who says, "Doggone frog. I wish I done had me a flying magic carpet so I wouldn't have to walk through these dark old woods." Suddenly the smoke from his lantern materializes into a genie who has a trumpet and talks like Louis Armstrong. The genie tells Bosko, "Ya, ya. You talk about you wants a carpet. You want a magic carpet. You want an Arabian carpet. You want a flying carpet. Well boy you got one right now." A magic carpet appears on the ground at Bosko's feet, which Bosko and the genie climb aboard. The genie blows his trumpet, and he and Bosko fly away on the magic carpet and land in Baghdad. The genie tells Bosko, "I will take you to the sultan, and he will be glad to see you and your cookies." They arrive at the palace and knock on the front door. Inside, a servant with a Stephin Fetchit demeanor walks slowly, scratching his head and saying, "Well, hold on. There's always somebody coming to see the sultan just when I git busy in my sleep." The genie opens the door first, slamming the servant against the wall. The servant asks, "Who's there?" The genie says, "Never mind who's there. He's got cookies." Bosko tells them, "I'm taking these cookies to my grandmother." They met the sultan, who resembles Fats Waller and is playing the piano. The genie says, "He has cookies" and the sultan says, "Offer him a harem for his cookies." The genie follows instructions, but Bosko refuses him. The sultan claps his hands loudly, summoning beautiful dancing girls. The curtain then opens on a dancing frog that resembles Bill Robinson. Robinson does a nifty tap dance and offers Bosko a big red apple and an orange for his cookies, but Bosko refuses. Next Robinson grabs a big watermelon, polishes it, then cuts a big slice and offers it to Bosko. Bosko smiles and tastes the juice but again refuses to trade his cookies for the melon. Frustrated, Robinson throws the melon into the air. The sultan and the genie say, "What's the matter with that boy?" The melon lands on the head of the sultan and the angry sultan asks Bosko, "Is you is or is you ain't gonna give us those cookies?" Bosko refuses and the sultan pulls a lever. Then Bosko is carried away on a conveyor belt to a torture chamber, where a huge bottle of castor oil is poured into a large spoon. But before Bosko can be forced to drink the castor oil, he breaks out into a tap dance and the music starts to play hot jazz. Meanwhile the genie and the sultan are so frustrated that they begin to tear up the place while Bosko has the whole palace jumping with his hi-dee-ho singing and tap dancing. The sultan and the genie find themselves on the conveyor belt where they bang into each other. Finally the sultan catches up to Bosko and is about to grab him. But a puff of smoke envelops Bosko, and when the air clears he is back in the forest. Bosko says, "Shucks." They can't have my grandma's cookies." He hears a hooting sound and he runs to his grandmother's house as fast as he can. Arriving there, he goes in and slams the door shut as the cartoon ends.

Review: *Selected Motion Pictures,* 1 February 1938

Fantastic color cartoon in which Bosko is taken on a magic carpet to frogland Baghdad. Amusing. Family and Junior Matinee.

Review: *National Exhibitor,* 2 January 1938

Bosko takes the cookies to Grandma but before he does so he lets his imagination run wild in a patch of woods leading to Grandma's house. He imagines the magic Genie takes him to Baghdad where giant frogs looking suspiciously like "Fats" Waller, Bill Robinson, et al, entertain him lavishly to get the cookies. When he still won't give them they take him to a Castor Oil machine. But the works go wrong, "De Sulton" lands in the machine. Everything ends all right when Bosko gets back to reality, runs screaming to Grandma's door, with cookies still safe. A rather elementary story with few humorous touches, this still entertains through ingenious fantasy. Good.

BOSKO IN DUTCH (1933)

Company: Hugh Harman, Rudolph Ising, Vitaphone, Warner Bros.
Type: Looney Tunes
Characters: Bosko, Honey

Review: *Variety,* 7 February 1933

Shade above average for cartoon filler. In this release, as noted of late, in other series of its kind, is a predilection toward dubbed-in-singing. Apparently that had to come, with sound effects and music alone not sufficing.

Offscreen singing adds something that will increase the flavor and value of cartoon series, most of which have suffered from sameness through synchronization of music with character actions as principal bid.

Skaters in Holland, with Bosko and his girl doing a song double and same number (plus voices applying to a cat couple) figure in this one with a drowning rescue for a finish. (7 min)

BOSKO THE MUSKETEER (1933)

Company: Hugh Harman, Rudolph Ising, Vitaphone, Warner Bros.

Type: Looney Tunes
Characters: Bosko, Honey

Review: *Motion Picture Herald,* 21 October 1933

Not particularly outstanding among animated cartoons, this number is nonetheless reasonably amusing. Bosko visits his sweetie, and falls into day dreams of himself as D'Artagnan, the Musketeer, wielding his sword and saving his girl from the bad man. The youngsters will like it, no doubt, and the oldsters will find it enjoyable of its kind. (7 min)

BOSKO IN PERSON (1933)

Company: Hugh Harman, Rudolph Ising, Vitaphone, Warner Bros.
Type: Looney Tunes
Characters: Bosko, Honey

Review: *Film Daily,* 24 March 1933

A clever Looney Tunes cartoon, with Bosko and his sweetheart, Honey, doing a personal stage appearance. They do a series of impersonations of stage and screen celebs that are knockouts. Those of Chevalier and Jimmy Durante will click in a big way anywhere. Here is a new slant on the animation that is bound to meet with popular approval.

Review: *Motion Picture World,* 13 May 1933

The animated youngster, Bosko, and his sweetheart Honey, equally perform on the vaudeville stage, and via the cartoonist's pen, give rather amusing, apt impersonations of several of the more noted stars of the screen. Chevalier, Durante and others come in for a bit of play, done in amusing fashion. (7 min)

Review: *Film Daily,* 29 September 1933

This is one of the best turned out by the Harman-Ising studio. Bosko puts on a "personal appearance" act with a girl partner. Routine includes imitations of Maurice Chevalier, Jimmy Durante and other celebs by Bosko, while his partner mimics Greta Garbo and others. Action is lively, the musical numbers are tuneful, and the job as a whole makes snappy entertainment of its kind.

BOSKO AND THE PIRATES (1937)

Company: Hugh Harman, Rudolph Ising, M-G-M
Type: Happy Harmonies
Characters: Bosko, Mammy (voice characterization by Lillian Randolph), frog caricatures of Louis Armstrong, Fats Waller, Mills Brothers, Bill Robinson, Cab Calloway

Story: The cartoon opens with Mammy telling little Bosko, "Hey, hey mammy's little honey chile. Now you take these cookies straight to grandma's house. Git along now." Bosko takes the bag of cookies from his mother and starts off through the woods for his grandma's house. He skips along and raps, "Straight to grandmother's house I go. Take these cookies to her front door." Along his way he passes a woodpecker tapping on a tree. Hearing this Bosko, jumps on a log and does a tap dance in time with the bird's tapping. Bosko's path leads him to a pond where he jumps into a barrel and starts to paddle. He picks a bottle out of the water and pretends it is a spyglass. Looking through the bottle he sees a wrecked ship, which he imagines is a pirate ship flying the skull and crossbones on its mast. The ship fires its cannon, and the shell lands so close to Bosko's boat that it causes a huge wave that lifts up Bosko's boat and lands it close to the pirate ship. On board the ship, the captain (Louis Armstrong frog), lifts Bosko onto the deck of his ship. He tells Bosko, "Say boy, what you got there?" Bosko answers, "I'm going to my grandmother's house." But the captain persists, saying, "You wouldn't mind looking in that bag now would you?" Bosko tells him, "You can't have these cookies." The captain says, "We ain't got no cookies 'round here." The word that there are cookies on the ship spreads rapidly among the crew. The captain insists that Bosko give up his cookies, and the Mills Brothers frogs sing, "We can't have no grandma's cookies today." Bill Robinson frog shows up on the scene and does a tap dance, but Bosko still refuses to part with his grandmother's cookies. By now the captain is very frustrated and asks Bosko, "Is you gonna give up those cookies or is you ain't?" Bosko shakes his head no. The captain tells Bosko that he must walk the plank. As he forces Bosko to walk out on the plank, he counts one, two, three . . . seven, eight. But when Bosko reaches the end of the plank, he begins to count backward and do a tap dance. The crew starts to play music, Bosko starts to dance, and the captain pulls out his trumpet and starts to play hot jazz. Cab Calloway frog comes on the scene singing in his scat style but falls into the ship's hold. Bosko picks up Calloway's baton and does an imitation of him, shaking his hair as he leads the band. Fats Waller frog joins in the fun and sings "Those Cookies, those cookies, I love 'em" while playing the piano with his hands and feet. Bosko taps so fast that his shoes heat up and burn a hole in the deck. Bosko falls through the hole down into the cargo deck and lands in a bucket of gun powder, which explodes. Bosko is propelled high into the air and lands in his little boat on the pond. Reaching shore, Bosko starts off for grandma's house singing, "Straight to grandma's house I go. Take these cookies to her front door" as the cartoon ends.

Review: *Motion Picture Herald,* **8 May 1937**

Quite a while back the Harman-Ising cartoon people turned out a sensationally successful subject called *The Old Mill Pond,* if memory serves, in which frogs impersonated, or whatever the word for that might be, various colored musical stars. This is a natural follow-up on that subject and is like it, yet different enough as one blues song is like another. Cab Calloway, Bill Robinson, the Mills Bros. and Louis Armstrong are among the personalities seen in froggish caricatures, and heard in action. The subject merits and will stand up under special billing. (8 min)

Review: *Selected Motion Pictures,* **1 September 1937**

Bosko dreams that he is captured by pirates. Clever Family and Junior Matinee.

BOSKO AT THE ZOO (1932)

Company: Hugh Harman, Rudolph Ising, Vitaphone, Warner Bros.
Type: Looney Tunes
Characters: Bosko, Honey

Review: *Motion Picture Herald,* **5 March 1932**

When Bosko and his feminine friend wend their animated way to the animated zoo, they find excitement and entertainment. The audience should experience the latter emotion at least. When the six tentacles of the octopus are used as the arms of the may-pole, the patrons at a New York neighborhood house had an enjoyable few moments. (7 min)

BOSKO THE SHEEPHERDER (1933)

Company: Hugh Harman, Rudolph Ising, Vitaphone, Warner Bros.
Type: Looney Tunes
Character: Bosko

Review: *Motion Picture Herald,* **12 August 1933**

Bosko, as the shepherd, has a gay time minding his flock while one particularly inquisitive lamb, gamboling over the green, gets himself into all sorts of difficulties until he meets a wolf in sheep's clothing. He is nearly done for, when the neighboring birds and beasts come to the rescue to vanquish the wolf. Entertaining for the youngsters and a light few minutes for the elders. (8 min)

BOSKO SHIPWRECKED (1931)

Company: Hugh Harman, Rudolph Ising, Vitaphone, Warner Bros.
Characters: Bosko, black cannibals

Story: Cartoon opens on a stormy ocean to claps of thunder and flashes of lightning. A sailing ship is tossed around on huge waves. On board the ship Bosko is clinging to the helm as the old captain shouts orders from the upper deck. Finally the ship disappears under a large wave. The next scene shows Bosko lying unconscious on the beach of a tropical island. Two monkeys climb out of a tree to take a close look at the stranger on their island. They take Bosko's derby and climb back up the tree. One of the monkeys puts on the hat, and they both jump up and down happily on the limb of the tree. They shake the egg out of a bird's nest, which falls and breaks on Bosko's face. Bosko wakes up and looks around and asks, "Where am I?" A parrot viewing the scene in a tree laughs and tells Bosko, "The joke's on you." The parrot laughs so hard that he falls out of the tree and Bosko laughs at him. But his laughter is interrupted by a huge lion that arrives on the scene. The lion chases Bosko, but he escapes when he jumps up in a tree and the lion runs under him into the river where he is swallowed by a crocodile. Bosko finds a boat and rows across the river. Arriving on the other side, Bosko throws an anchor into the water. But it gets stuck in the backside of a huge hippo. The hippo jumps out of the water and pulls Bosko and the boat behind him until he falls into a hole. Bosko is tossed out of the boat and lands on the ground where he rolls over and over before rolling into a large cooking pot sitting on a fire in a cannibal village. Bosko's backside is burned by the flames and he screams and jumps into the air. Bosko's screams are heard by a black cannibal who runs out of a grass hut. The cannibal has thick white lips, wears a grass skirt, and has two bones tied in his hair. The cannibal takes one look at Bosko and yells and then pulls the bones out of his hair and uses them to beat his chest like a drum. The drumbeats summon all of the other cannibals, who run screaming out of their huts and quickly surround Bosko while waving their spears in the air. A skeleton wearing a stovepipe hat rises out of the cooking pot and tells Bosko, "Come on in—the water's fine, ha-ha-ha" before sinking back into the pot of boiling water. On one side sits the cannibal chief, a fat man wearing a crown and sitting on a throne that is a soapbox. The chief commands his guard to bring Bosko to him, saying, "Goopa-goopa-ugh, and make it snappy." The guard, who has arms so long that his hands drag the ground like an ape's, brings Bosko to the chief, who shouts, "Boil him!" But Bosko says "stop," pulls out a gun, aims it at the chief, and fires—a cork! Bosko yells and runs off followed by the angry cannibals who shake their spears in the air as they yell and chase after him. Bosko reaches the beach and jumps into what he thinks is a rowboat. When he tries to row away, the boat does not move. Then he discovers that he is sitting in the mouth of a huge rhino. The rhino shuts his mouth, trapping Bosko inside. But Bosko climbs out of the trapdoor on the rhino's back as the animal swims out to sea. He pulls the horn off the animal's nose and uses it to play music. He pauses and smiles as he looks back at the angry cannibals on the island as the cartoon ends.

BOSKO THE TALK-INK KID (1929)

Company: Hugh Harman/Rudolph Ising Productions
Type: Combination live action and animation
Characters: Rudolph Ising (as himself), Bosko

Story: Cartoon opens with live action as Rudolph Ising draws the figure of Bosko on a sheet of paper. Bosko comes to life and says, "Well, here I is and I sho' feel good." The cartoonist says, "Oh, you feel good, do ya?" Bosko says, "Yeah. I's just out of de pen. Ha-ha." The cartoonist then says, "OK Now that you are here, what can you do?" Bosko answers, "What can I do? Hah. What I can't do ain't." The cartoonist says, "Well, who are you?," and Bosko says, "Who is I? I's Bosko, that's who. I ain't nobody else except but." The cartoonist says, "Bosko, eh. All right Bosko, show me what you can do." Bosko says, "OK Boss.

Watch dis heah." He starts to dance but stops and looks out of the paper and asks, "Who's all dem folks out there in the dark?" The cartoonist says, "Why, the audience Bosko. Can you make 'em laugh?" Bosko ponders the question as he taps one foot and scratches his head. He gets an idea and asks, "Got a piano?" The cartoonist says, "Yes. Here you are," as he sketches a piano on the paper. Bosko plays the piano and sings, "Where dere is gray skies, I don't mind de gray skies, I still has you Sonny Boy." As Bosko slides off the piano stool, his head, attached to one end of a spring, separates from his body. Bosko looks down and says, "Boy where is I at? Man, I's regressin'. " Bosko manages to pull himself together and sings "Sonny Boy . . ." but the cartoonist has heard enough and sucks Bosko back into his pen, squirts the black ink back into the ink bottle, and puts the cap back on the bottle. But Bosko pushes himself halfway back out of the bottle, tips his derby hat to the audience, smiles, and says, "See y'all later." He turns to the cartoonist and sticks his tongue out at him before diving back into the ink bottle as the cartoon ends.

BOSKO'S DOG RACE (1932)

Company: Hugh Harman, Rudolph Ising, Vitaphone, Warner Bros.
Type: Looney Tunes
Characters: Bosko, Bruno

Review: *Motion Picture Herald*, 9 July 1932

Bosko and his lop-eared hound are both hungry, and the dog is entered in the big dog race with a large sum at stake. It is only when a nest of bees light on the dog's back that he has enough incentive to win. Not unusual, this animated cartoon is nevertheless entertaining. (8 min)

BOSKO'S EASTER EGGS (1937)

Company: Hugh Harman, Rudolph Ising, M-G-M
Characters: Bosko, Honey, Bruno (fig. 9)

Story: Bosko, wearing a straw hat, is carrying a basket of Easter eggs in one hand and pulling Bruno by a rope with the other hand. He skips down the road singing, "Now takin' Honey some Easter eggs. The basket's full if dey don't drop out. And I'll step real soft so de shells don't crack. If she don't like 'em I can take 'em back." Bosko trips over the rope and falls down, but the eggs don't break. He tells Bruno, "Doggone Bruno! How come ya always gotta stop so much?" Bosko gets up and picks up the basket of eggs saying, "Now you come on. Now I'm takin' Honey some Easter eggs. De one is green and de other is blue." Meanwhile Honey is in the henhouse looking after her hen, Betty, who is sitting on her eggs waiting for them to hatch. Honey sets a bowl of water in front of the hen and says, "Come on Betty, drink. Look like dis" as she takes a drink from the bowl. The hen gets the idea and takes a drink of water. Honey tells her, "That's it. Now I'm gonna get you some nice corn and you gonna sit real still and you gonna hatch out a whole bunch of little Easter chicks. Now you be sure to sit tight on dem eggs." Then she leaves the henhouse. Meanwhile Bosko walks along singing, "Now Easter time is de time for eggs and de time for eggs is de Easter time." He decides to walk on top of a fence and says, "And praise de Lord as I climb de fence dat I ain't gonna ruin my Sunday pants" as he slips and falls to the ground and the basket of eggs lands on top of his head. Some of the eggs break, and the yolks run down his face. Meanwhile Bruno pays a visit to the henhouse and teases Betty. But she scares him and he runs so fast that he bumps into Bosko, breaking the rest of the eggs. Bosko says, "Now dog-gone Bruno. See what ya done? You've ruined de Easter time." But Bosko gets an idea where to find more eggs and pays a visit to the henhouse. Slowly he walks in front of Betty and says, "Well hello dere Mrs. Chicken. You sho' is lookin' mighty scrumptious today." Bosko looks at the eggs under Betty and says, "Well, just look at dem eggs! You sho' is powerful uncomfortable sittin' on all those eggs. Now you better jes let me kinda get in here and help you." He reaches under the hen to get the eggs, but Betty is angry and chases Bosko. He runs as fast as he can down the road then stops and turns around and says, "De Easter time is de time for eggs and the time for eggs is de Easter time." He decides to have another try at the eggs and goes back to the henhouse, telling Betty, "Hello dere Mrs. Chicken. You sho' lookin' mighty scrumptious today. How 'bout you eatin' some of dis here corn and makin' your self all nice and fat cause de Easter time is de time for eggs and de time for eggs is de Easter time." Bosko lays a trail of corn along the ground that leads Betty away from the henhouse and into a cage where she is locked up. Bosko paints Betty's eggs in different colors and carries the basket of Easter eggs to Honey, who is watering her flowers. Bosko says, "Honey, oh Honey," and Honey says, "Oh Bosko! For me?" Bosko says "Yes! Fo' you," as he sets the basket of eggs on the ground. Honey says, "Oh Bosko! I think they're just simply, absolutely—abdominal. Where did you get such lovely . . ." as she takes a closer look and suspects that they are Betty's eggs. Honey puts her hands on her hips and says, "Bosko, where did you get dem eggs? Where did you get 'em?" Bosko says, "I—I—jest passed by . . ." and Honey says, "Yes, jes passed by and took poor Betty's eggs. That's what you done." At this time they hear a cracking sound coming from the basket of eggs as they begin to hatch. Honey grabs the basket of eggs and they both run to the henhouse where Honey says, "Oh, she's gone. Now Betty is gonna miss the maternity ward and she's . . ." Bosko tells her, "You put the eggs in the nest. Bruno will keep dem warm." He runs and gets Bruno and brings him back to the henhouse, saying, "Come on Bruno! You're gonna be a mama." He sets Bruno on the nest and Honey puts a bonnet on his head and a shawl around his shoulders. Honey and Bosko leave to find Betty and Bosko tells Bruno, "Ya, ya. We made de bed. Now you lay in it." Betty has managed to escape from the pen, and she runs back to the henhouse where she finds Bruno sitting on her eggs. She chases Bruno. The dog runs head-on into a fence, and Betty pulls his tail. Bosko and Honey hear the noise and Honey runs back to the henhouse and Bosko runs to rescue

Bruno from the hen. But Betty chases Bruno and Bosko back to the henhouse where the eggs have hatched and chicks of all colors are seen. Honey says, "The Easter chickens! Oh, Betty look! Isn't this simply . . . Oh Betty! Now we got a whole bunch of little Easter chickens. Oh, they are just so cute." Bosko and Bruno walk over to take a closer look at the chicks, but Betty angrily flaps her wings and they both hide under the egg basket. Bosko peeks from under the basket and says, "Now de Easter time is de time for eggs. But the hen got loose and cooked our goose" as he and Bruno smile at each other and the cartoon ends.

Review: *National Exhibitor,* 20 April 1937

Bosko, stealing the hen's eggs so he can present them as Easter eggs to his sweetie. When the eggs hatch they are brightly colored. But the hen gets after everybody; she picks mostly on Bosko's dog, Bruno. She chases Bosko, poor Bruno plenty. This isn't original nor are the gags funny. The color work is nice as in all Harman-Ising stuff. Fair.

Review: *Film Daily,* 25 April 1937

Two pickaninnies and a pup get mixed up with a hen trying to hatch her eggs. The boy is trying to get his Easter eggs to his little sweetheart, but meets with a spill, so he borrows the eggs from the hen and colors them for Easter. The girl makes him return them, and the pup is put to work to keep them warm til the hen returns. When she does, there is the dickens to pay, and the enraged fowl makes the pickaninny and the pup sorry they ever mixed in. Done in Technicolor, with plenty of clever technique. (8 1/3 min)

Review: *Motion Picture Herald,* 3 April 1937

A combination of some clever comic situations, brightly colored animations and a bit of a catchy tune makes the subject gay and diverting. Bosko, a cute pickaninny, is in high spirits as he carries along with him a basket filled to the top with tinted Easter eggs. But, as accidents will happen, the eggs become broken and Bosko is forced by devious and underhand methods to use a few of the freshly laid eggs of Miss Chicken. This scheme does not meet with the unqualified approval from the little lady and things grow exciting as Bosko and Miss Chicken enter into a lively contest to outwit each other.

Review: *Motion Picture Reviews,* 3 April 1937

Both drawing and color are delightful in this episode of a small darky who steals the eggs from a mother hen and dyes them to present to a little girl for an Easter gift. The action however is a bit noisy and helterskelter, showing comic strip influence.

Review: *Selected Motion Pictures,* 1 May 1937

Bosko robs the hen's nest to make Easter eggs for his best girl, but he is discovered and the trouble begins. A passable colored cartoon suitable for the family.

Review: *Motion Picture Reviews*, May 1937

Both drawing and color are delightful in this episode of a small darky boy who steals the eggs from a mother hen and dyes them to present to a little girl for an Easter gift. The action however is a bit noisy and helter skelter, showing comic strip influence.

BOSKO'S FOX HUNT (1931)

Company: Hugh Harman, Rudolph Ising, Vitaphone, Warner Bros.
Type: Looney Tunes
Characters: Bosko, Bruno, black fox

Story: The cartoon opens in the country, where Bosko and Bruno are on a fox hunt. The black fox is ahead of the hunters, who include a group of animals on horseback followed by Bosko who is riding a white horse. The fox is too smart for his pursuers and manages to elude them by covering up his tracks and running through streams. Bosko's horse breaks down. His back is so bowed that Bosko's feet drag on the ground. Bosko stiffens the horse's back by inserting a tree trunk in him and then continues the hunt. Bosko's horse stops at a wide ditch, and Bosko removes the log from the horse and uses it as a bridge. Meanwhile the fox thinks that he is well ahead of pursuers until he hears a horn sounded by an elephant that blows through his trunk. The fox hides in a log and all of the hunters pass by him, except a very long dachshund that has picked up his scent. But he manages to wrap his long body around the log so that he smells himself, and the fox crawls out of the log right in front of Bosko who is trailing the others. The fox is on the run with Bosko not far behind. When the horse jumps a fence and lands in a muddy puddle placed there by the fox, he becomes so disgusted that he pulls off his harness and leaves Bosko. Bosko pulls out his shotgun, and he and Bruno resume the chase. The fox tries unsuccessfully to elude Bosko and Bruno by hiding behind a tree, then in a hole in the ground, and then by running into the lair of a wild boar. Bosko reaches into the lair, pulls on a tail, and pulls out a wild boar, which chases Bosko and the dog into a cave where there is a wild fight. Bruno rushes out first and keeps on going. Black fur comes flying out of the cave followed by a victorious Bosko. But he is clubbed on the head by Bruno, who expects the fox to come out. Bruno tries to make up by licking Bosko on his cheek as the cartoon ends.

Review: *Variety*, 11 November 1931

Very funny cartoon dealing with a bunch of animals that go fox hunting. Compares with the best of the kind.

Considerable repetition, probably explaining the running time, but that's more than made up for by laughs and originality of some of the action. One gag of a dog smelling around for the fox, and finally smelling himself after going around in circles, is a pip as a laugh shaker. Looney Tunes turned it out.

BOSKO'S HOLIDAY (1931)

Company: Hugh Harman, Rudolph Ising, Vitaphone, Warner Bros.
Type: Looney Tunes no. 11
Characters: Bosko, Honey

Press Release: Vitaphone Corporation 1931

Popular song hits which compose the musical score for *Bosko's Holiday* include "I Can't Give You Anything but Love, Baby," "Hullabaloo," "Funny Little You," "Doing the Sigma Chi" and "Tie a Little String Around Your Finger."

North America, China, Japan, Brazil, New Zealand, Australia, the Federated Malay States, the Dutch East Indies, Egypt, Syria, Palestine and most European countries are playing these patron and profit getting shorts! This international cartoon figure will do the same for you. Get the exhibition lobby card on this issue. It's a curiosity arouser.

Bosko, the funniest, happiest character in animated cartoons, continues his merry makings in *Bosko's Holiday,* the eleventh of the ever popular "Looney Tunes" series, carrying laugh explosions and much good humor in his wake! This one is a peach! Filled with merriment and plenty of funny gags. It's a little subject full of big laughs!

Bosko, the chief character in all these Looney Tunes, and Honey, his inspiration in all of his adventures, are the hero and heroine in this, the funniest animated cartoon travesty on sweethearts on a holiday.

The story is told in a simple manner. The opening scene shows Bosko being awakened by everything in the room including the anxious alarm clock and telephone, which, through the generosity of the animators, are given a pair of hands. Honey, on the other end of the wire, invites Bosko to the picnic. At the picnic ground, Honey refuses to kiss Bosko. He tempts her by eating a delicious sandwich under her nose. As she turns to ignore this tempting delicatessen, the puppy which accompanied them to the grounds, licks Honey on a ticklish spot. What takes place after this will keep the audience roaring. This Vitaphone short should prove effective competition to feature pictures!

Intricate action and background, plot and animation and sound synchronization are very well worked out! The laugh qualities in this short makes it well worth a number one spot on any exhibitor's program!

Bosko's Holiday is a fast-moving and original cartoon comedy with plenty of laughs and a clever idea. It should prove a welcome delight on any bill! Keep your theatre out of the red with this clever cartoon series!

Review: *Motion Picture Herald*, 9 May 1931

The Looney Tune featured player, Bosko, the animated cartoon star, has a great deal of fun himself, and pleases the audience. This number is no exception. Clever drawing through the story, of course, means little or nothing. Good for a light spot almost anywhere.

Review: *Bioscope* (London), 27 May 1931

The imp, very much in love phones his inamorata and arranges a trip. Tyre troubles cause delay, but amorous transports follow.

Review: *Variety,* 1 September 1931

"Looney Tunes" entertaining for more than half way and then winds up so suddenly artist may have fallen short of a good finish idea. Makes it ordinary and for lesser programs.

Opening is good, having the telephone telling the alarm clock to awake Bosco. After Bosko hits for his picnic with his sweetheart the comedy runs about even and then weakens at the finale. (7 min)

BOSKO'S KNIGHT-MARE (1933)

Company: Hugh Harman, Rudolph Ising, Vitaphone, Warner Bros.
Type: Looney Tunes
Characters: Bosko, Honey

Review: *Film Daily,* 6 September 1933

An adventure of Bosko, who dreams that he is a knight at the ancient court of King Arthur, where he pulls his modern stuff on the Knights of the Round Table. There is plenty of excitement when the villain knight abducts the fair heroine. Bosko awakes in the middle of a hot fight to find that it's all a dream. The modern treatment of the knights in armor is clever and has plenty of laughs. (7 min)

BOSKO'S PARLOR PRANKS (1934)

Company: Hugh Harman, M-G-M
Type: First cartoon of the M-G-M Bosko series
Characters: Bosko, Honey, Bruno, Wilbert

Story: As the cartoon opens, Bosko and his dog, Bruno, are walking along toward Honey's house. Bosko is happy and turns toward the audience and says, "Hi ya!" Honey is attempting to coax Wilbert, a boy who is depicted having a tail, to practice on the piano. Wilbert does not want to practice and shouts that he wants an ice cream cone. Bosko arrives. Honey lets him in and he says, "Hello Honey! How do you do." Honey says, "Hello Bosko. Toodle-le-do." Wilbert asks Bosko, "Hey, did you bring me an ice cream cone?" Bosko smiles at him and then walks to the piano where he plays a jazzy tune that inspires Honey to dance. Bosko stops playing but the music continues while he and Honey tap-dance until they are interrupted by Wilbert shouting "Hey, I want my ice cream cone." Honey decides to buy Wilbert some ice cream and asks Bosko to take care of Wilbert while she is gone. Bosko answers, "Oh sure. We'll have lots of fun, won't we, Wilbert," patting Wilbert on his head. Honey looks into a mirror while she pats powder on her face, and then she puts the powder puff inside her dress. She pulls down the dress and then leaves. Bosko tries to amuse Wilbert by

relating his adventures from several of his Warner Brothers cartoons, including *Bosko's Knight-mare, Battling Bosko, Ride Him, Bosko,* and *Bosko the Musketeer.* In between stories, Bosko blows up a long white balloon that he attaches to his nose. He is transformed into a whiteface caricature of Jimmy Durante But, Wilbert is not amused and shouts for ice cream. Just then Honey arrives home. When she walks through the door, the ice cream cone she is carrying is knocked out of her hands by a sword swung by Bosko as he relates his adventures as a musketeer. The ice cream cone lands on top of Bosko's head. Bruno runs inside and licks the ice cream off Bosko's face, and Honey laughs as the cartoon ends.

BOSKO'S PARTY (1932)

Company: Hugh Harman, Rudolph Ising, Vitaphone, Warner Bros.
Type: Looney Tunes
Characters: Bosko, Honey, Bruno

Review: *Motion Picture Herald,* 7 May 1932

Bosko gives a surprise party in this number of the Looney Tunes. It all goes well in an animated fashion until Bosko's dog gets his tail caught in a mouse trap and finally lands in the dead center of the birthday cake. The youngsters, especially, will like it. (7 min)

BOSKO'S PICTURE SHOW (1934)

Company: Hugh Harman, Rudolph Ising, Vitaphone, Warner Bros.
Type: Looney Tunes
Characters: Bosko, Honey

Review: *Motion Picture Herald,* 13 January 1934

There is much cleverness, not a little amusement in this number of the Looney Tunes animated cartoon series in which the little hero puts on a picture show. Cleverly caricatured are the various stars in burlesqued versions of their pictures of today. The adults will enjoy this subject even more than the youngsters. A good number. (7 min)

BOSKO'S SODA FOUNTAIN (1931)

Company: Hugh Harman, Rudolph Ising, Vitaphone, Warner Bros.
Type: Looney Tunes
Character: Bosko

Review: *Motion Picture Herald,* 11 November 1931

Bosko has a lively time at and away from his soda fountain in this cartoon. When the little imp of a piano pupil doesn't like the vanilla ice cream cone and throws it into Bosko's face, the pursuit is on. Bosko meets one reverse when the youngster swings on a pendulum of the clock and administers a vigorous kick on the return swing. He also takes a humping ride down the bannister when the "villain" pulls off the rail. (7 min)

Review: *Bioscope,* **(London) 9 March 1932**

Only in spasms does the artist here show an originality, though he does not fail to include just those vulgar strokes in which the majority of American cartoonists love to indulge. A useful program filler.

BOX CAR BLUES (1931)

Company: Hugh Harman, Rudolph Ising, Vitaphone, Warner Bros.
Type: Looney Tunes, Vitaphone Song Car-Tune
Character: Bosko

Press Release: Vitaphone Corporation, 1931

The adventurous Bosko joins the ranks of hoboes! More fun and snappy tunes as Bosko rides the rails with a hippopotamus for a pal! The ever popular cartoon character is taken for a long and hilarious ride on the trickiest of choo-choos! Up hill and down dale, and through treacherous tunnels, Bosko coaxes ingratiating tunes from a willing guitar! The fifth of the song cartoon series presents Bosko at his merriest!

Two popular song hits are burlesqued by Bosko in *Box Car Blues*. There are: "Highway To Heaven," the song hit from *Oh Sailor Behave!,* the Warner Bros. musical comedy success, and "Cryin' for the Carolines" from the First National picture, *Spring Is Here.* Bosko plays other tunes on his guitar, among them "Alabama Bound."

Exhibitors have many means of exploitation in the Vitaphone Song Cartoon series. Both the picture itself and the featured song hits offer unlimited exploitation angles. Tie-ups with music stores are a natural for "Looney Tunes"!

Bosko is still the most entertaining of animated cartoon characters! *Box Car Blues* is the answer to the exhibitor's prayer! There is fun for all in "Looney Tunes"!

CIRCUS DAZE (1937)

Company: Hugh Harman, M-G-M
Type: Happy Harmonies
Characters: Bosko, Honey, Bruno

Story: Opening scenes show a crowd entering a circus tent and the various acts preparing to perform. Honey and Bosko come on the scene. Honey has a balloon, and is all excited with a big smile on her face. Bosko is pulling his reluctant dog, Bruno, on a leash. They stop to watch two small monkeys playing in a cage. Bruno teases the monkeys and gets so excited that he falls into a barrel of water. Bosko pulls him out and tells him to sit and be still. While backing away, Bosko falls into the same barrel of water. This makes Honey laugh and she asks Bosko, "What's the difference between you and a fish?" Bosko answers that he doesn't know and Honey says, "A fish is all wet." Bosko

says, "Well, I's all wet." Honey says, "Well, there ain't no difference" and has a big laugh. At this point one of the caged monkeys reaches through the bars and takes Honey's balloon. While Bosko and Honey try to retrieve the balloon, Bruno slips away for a little exploring on his own. He runs into a flea that he tries unsuccessfully to catch. The small flea leads him to the flea circus, and Bruno ends up covered with fleas. Meanwhile Bosko has pulled Honey's balloon away from the monkeys, but it floats him through the air until he falls among the band. The balloon becomes stuck on the end of a trombone which, as it is played, causes the balloon to expand and rise again, carrying Bosko along for the ride. Bruno arrives on the scene carrying the fleas who begin to fly off in all directions. The fleas cause pandemonium to break out, completely disrupting the circus. Finally Bosko and Honey manage to get away and Bosko wonders where Bruno is. Just then Bruno is seen being kicked out of the circus tent as the cartoon ends.

Review: *Selected Motion Pictures,* **1 March 1937**

Color cartoon. Honey and her boyfriend have a fine time until Bruno falls into the flea circus. Family.

Review: *National Board of Review of Motion Pictures,* **1 January 1937**

Color cartoon in which Bosko and Honey take their dog to a circus, and get involved with the flea circus.

CONGO JAZZ (1930)

Company: Hugh Harman, Rudolph Ising, Vitaphone, Warner Bros.
Type: Looney Tunes
Character: Bosko

Story: The cartoon opens in the African jungle where Bosko is on a big-game hunt. He is unaware that he is being stalked by a huge Bengal tiger. When he turns and sees the tiger, he literally melts in his pants with fear. He recovers and fires his shotgun at the tiger, but the bullet only dribbles out of the gun. Bosko turns and runs with the tiger close behind him. He soon realizes that he cannot outrun the tiger, so he stops and pulls out his flute and plays music that enchants the tiger. It meekly follows Bosko to the edge of a high cliff and then is pushed off. Continuing his hunt, Bosko next encounters two small monkeys playing leapfrog. One runs off, and when Bosko tries to make friends with the other one, it rejects him by spitting in his face. An angry Bosko then grabs the monkey and pulls down its pants to spank it. But the monkey's father, a huge ape, comes on the scene. Bosko quickly drops the baby monkey and attempts to show the ape that he intended no harm to his baby. But the angry ape is not convinced, so he rolls up his sleeve and prepares to smash Bosko. Bosko quickly offers the ape a package of chewing gum. He pulls out a stick and shows the ape how to chew. The ape forgets that he is mad at Bosko as they chew together and pull strands of gum out of their mouths and pluck them to make music. The hot rhythm soon attracts the other animals, who join in the fun playing and dancing to the music with Bosco doing the conducting. The music is so hot that a co-conut tree begins to sway, causing some coconuts to drop off and fall on Bosko's head to the delight of the other animals as the cartoon ends.

Press Release: Vitaphone Corporation 1930

With Bosko in Africa! Thrills, chills and laughs with the inimitable Bosko becoming the Pied Piper of the Congo! The second of the song cartoon series finds the popular character hunting wild animals in the jungle! Pursued by a ferocious tiger, Bosko tames him with song. Trapped by a giant ape, Bosko uses his wits and his voice in escaping. One of the funniest scenes on the screen is the chorus of songs and dances by gathering of jungle beasts. Even the trees sway to the tunes of the enchanting melodies initiated by Bosko.

Congo Jazz, the second of the "Looney Tunes" series, is based on numerous song hits from feature pictures.

Once again, exhibitors are given the opportunity of making effective tie-ups through radio broadcasting, phonograph records, piano rolls, and sheet music. The melodies in *Congo Jazz* will catch the fancy of audiences and have them whistling the tunes after the show!

The second of the series is even more hilarious entertainment than the first. The antics of Bosko are the last word in laughs! Give the patrons "Looney Tunes"—and keep them laughing!

Review: *Variety,* 8 August 1930

If the picture cartoonists ever run short of idea men, they can always drop in at the nearest nut asylum for a supply. For if the cartoon shorts as they are now progressing don't wind up in the bughouse for ideas, the idea men will.

The current idea for screen cartoons is to outdo the last one and the other fellows in just being crazy. *Congo Jazz* of the Looney Tunes series isn't as nutty as others seen around, but it'll do. It has a mutt or what looks like a mutt in the jungle on a wild game hunt. The mutt finally has the whole jungle tribe in jazz band formation with the elephant using his own trunk for a trumpet, the giraffe as a bagpipe, etc. Even a coconut tree does a cooch, and pretty good.

With these cartoons it's possible to distort human actions by applying them to pen and ink animals and to make them grab a laugh or two. But the boys have started to repeat themselves and the sameness makes them all look alike. All, however, manage to be more or less interesting through the ridiculous action when effectively scored and synchronized. (9 min)

Review: *Motion Picture News,* 30 August 1930

Congo Jazz is the second of the Vitaphone song cartoon series produced by Leon Schlesinger. It is a good synchronization of animal antics and meaningless tunes that will be good for a couple of laughs from the audience. It also incorporates a num-

ber of those vulgarities which are bringing the cartoons more and more to the attention of censor boards across the land. The drawings are by Hugh Harman and Rudolph Ising. Musical score by Frank Marsales.

Review: *Billboard,* 6 September 1930

Congo Jazz is the second of the Vitaphone song cartoons drawn by Hugh Harmon and Rudolph Ising, produced by Leon Schlesinger, with a musical score by Frank Marsales. The reel is not unlike many other similar animated, except in the main caricature of the big-lipped darky who motivates all the action of the short. The darky is shown with a wide grin, stealthily walking thru the jungle, hunting tigers with an elongated shotgun. He is totally unmindful that a tiger is actually tracking him down from the rear, and when he does discover it he saves the day by offering the beast some chewing gum. After a bit of chewing and a few games of ring-around-the-rosy the pickaninny sees a cute pair of baby monkeys playing leap-frog. On approaching them he is given the well-known razz, whereupon he spanks one, only to be confronted by the gigantic mother ape, saving the day again with his trusty chewing gum.

Kangaroos and ostriches are seen doing complicated dances, and a jungle orchestra offers hot rhythm which makes the palms sway and the leaves shimmy. There are numerous laughs hidden in the antics of the cartooned characters and on the whole it is a pleasant short.

DUMB PATROL (1931)

Company: Hugh Harman, Rudolph Ising, Vitaphone, Warner Bros.
Type: Looney Tunes, Vitaphone Song Car-Tunes
Character: Bosko

Press Release: Vitaphone Corporation, 1931

Happy landing! Bosko takes a flyer in the front line trenches! The merry little fellow and his tricky airplane do some nonsensical cavorting to the staccato tune on the machine gun fire. Blown up by a German air ace, Bosko lands in the home of a captivating French damsel where he does some more frolicking. But the villain again appears and Bosko mounts his trusty plane. The battle in the air is one of the fastest and funniest of its kind ever seen! *Dumb Patrol* is an adroit burlesque of the picture success *Dawn Patrol,* and will have patrons rocking the theatre with laughs!

The melodies used in the ninth of the "Looney Tunes" series are: "Get Happy," "Madelon," "Under The Moon It's You," "Shuffle Your Feet," "Living a Life of Dreams," "Nine Little Miles From Ten-Ten-Tennessee," "Here Comes My Blackbird," and "When Love Comes in the Moonlight."

Give your feature program the proper support—play a "Looney Tunes" short! *Dumb Patrol* will make every movie fan a Bosko fan!

Hugh Harman and Rudolph Ising, the originators of this musical cartoon are one of the cleverest pairs of cartoonists in the field! *Dumb Patrol* is grade A entertainment in every inch of film.

HEY HEY FEVER (1935)

Company: Hugh Harman, Rudolph Ising, M-G-M
Type: Happy Harmonies
Characters: Bosko, Bruno, Mother Goose characters, black child (cameo appearance)

Story: Bosko and his dog, Bruno, walk down a country road while an offscreen choral group sings, "All the birds were singing so merrily and all the world was so gay, while Bosko and Bruno were strolling along on a beautiful sunny day." Bosko says, "Well, Bruno, shall we stop and eat our last sandwich?" The song continues, "Little Bosko was sad and blue, weary and hungry too; Bosko felt sorry for Bruno and wanted to make him feel gay, so Bruno got all of the sandwich and Bosko went hungry all day." Bosko sees a billboard behind him advertising Mother Goose pies and says, "Gee, Bruno, how would you like a piece of Mother Goose goodies with cream and sugar?" Bosko sits under the billboard to take a rest, when the sign comes to life and Mother Goose herself comes out of her house and tells Bosko, "My my there, little man. You must be awfully tired." Bosko says, "Oh, Mother Goose! Sure we're tired and hungry too." She tells him that she has no food to offer but will join him in the search for a good meal. Their first stop is at Mother Hubbard's house where she tells them that her dog ate the last bone. At their next stop they are greeted by a woman who has many small children hanging on her. Bosko says, "Are you the old woman who lives in a shoe?" The woman answers, "Yes, I have so many children I don't know what to do." A white child says, "We haven't any butter and we haven't any bread" and a black child peeks out from under the old woman's dress and says, "And we don't get no supper befo' we go to bed." Bosko is sad that the big family is hungry and decides to go and see the king. The others follow him to the castle. The drawbridge is lowered and Bosko crosses and enters the castle. He finds the king, dressed in his underwear, ironing his own clothes. Bosko asks him, "Sir are you really the king?" The king replies, "Sure. I'm old King Cole, a merry old soul." When Bosko asks, "Are you poor too?" the seven old dwarfs answer, "Why, he's so poor he hasn't even got a pot to cook in." Disappointed at not having found a meal, Bosko leaves the castle but gets an idea and tells the others, "The farm is just the place we oughta be" and they all follow him to find a farm. On the way Bosko sings, "I've got hay hay fever. That city smoke fills my eyes with tears, hey-hey." He and the others dance and sing on down the road to the rhythm of the music. They arrive at a farm and Bosko asks the farmer, "Are you the farmer in the dell?" He answers yes but tells them that his crops have failed and there is no food. Bosko and the others go to work plowing the soil and planting seeds. After the first spring rain they harvest a bountiful crop. It is time to celebrate and a feast is prepared. Jazz music fills the air as Bosko holds his hat over his head and says, "Is everybody happy?" as the cartoon ends.

Review: *Selected Motion Pictures,* 1 February 1935

Musical color cartoon. The depression in Mother Goose land is routed by a strenuous use of the plow. Good. Family. Junior Matinee.

HOLD ANYTHING (1930)

Company: Hugh Harman, Rudolph Ising, Vitaphone, Warner Bros.
Type: Looney Tunes, Vitaphone Song Car-Tunes
Characters: Bosko, Honey

Press Release: Vitaphone Corporation, 1930

The popular Bosko as a jolly riveter! Gasps and laughs mingled with snappy tunes with the happy Bosko at work on the house that Bosko built! The third of the song cartoon series presents the favorite cartoon character building a skyscraper. Hilarious fun as Bosko gets music from steel girders, brick walls and hoisting ropes. He meets his sweetheart Honey and serenades her with tantalizing tunes coaxed from the keys of a musical typewriter! A trick goat takes Bosko for a merry ride among the clouds!

Well-known song hits from feature pictures are burlesqued by the cartoon comedy pair, Bosko and Honey, in *Hold Anything,* the third of the "Looney Tunes" series.

Radio broadcasts, piano rolls, sheet music and phonograph records will serve as effective means towards popularizing the cartoon. The melodies in *Hold Anything* are tuneful and popular!

The adventures of Bosko and Honey among the skyscrapers are a series of tuneful nonsense and spontaneous laughs that will please adults and children alike. "Looney Tunes" are the most popular and entertaining of song cartoons! Hold everything for *Hold Anything!*

THE OLD HOUSE (1936)

Company: Hugh Harman, Rudolph Ising, M-G-M
Characters: Bosko, Honey, Bruno

Story: The cartoon opens on a dark and stormy night. Flashes of lightning illuminate a sign showing the title of the cartoon. Bosko is introduced and he says, "The goblins gonna get you if you don't watch out." Honey is introduced and she says, "Aw, who's afraid of spooks anyhow?" Finally Bruno is introduced. The story opens with Bosko reading a ghost story to Bruno. He reads, "As he passed the haunted house they grabbed him. . . . The biggest piece they ever found was just his little head. . . . The goblins gonna get you if you don't watch out." Bruno is scared but Honey, hiding behind a tree, shouts "boo!" Bosko and Bruno run and hide in Bruno's doghouse. Honey laughs at them and says, "Bosko, I'm ashamed of you. You're a scaredy-cat. Sure I will go to grandma's house with never any fear. There ain't no such thing as goblins and spooks. Goblins never bother me." Bosko comes out of the doghouse and says, "What if you would meet a ghost?" Honey says, "Ha-ha. I'll bet he gets scared the most. I ain't afraid of spooks because there ain't no spooks no where." She skips off to grandma's house but does not get far down the road before dark clouds gather, followed by wind and rain. Honey passes the old haunted house and decides to take shelter there. The door opens and she walks inside. It closes behind her. She tries to convince herself that she is not afraid until she hears weird noises. She can't control her fear and screams for help. Bosko hears her and runs to her rescue. He enters the house but soon gets covered by a white sheet. Thinking that he is a ghost, Honey hides from him while he runs around the house and looking for her and trying to dodge a skeleton. They eventually escape from the house and all ends well.

Review: *National Exhibitor,* 20 September 1936

Bosko, Little Honey and their dog, Bruno are caught in an old haunted house with Honey scoffing at "spooks" till their own imagination and the tricks of wind and fright make them run from the house almost scared white. There are some laughs and the color and draftsmanship are excellent. Good.

Review: *Selected Motion Pictures,* 1 October 1936

Happy Harmonies series. Two little darkies caught in a ramshackle house are frightened by spooky noises. Family and Junior Matinee.

SINKIN' IN THE BATHTUB (1930)

Company: Hugh Harman, Rudolph Ising, Vitaphone, Warner Bros.
Type: First of Looney Tunes series, Vitaphone Song Car-Tunes
Characters: Bosko, Honey

*Press Release: Vitaphone Corporation, 1930

"Looney Tunes" is a new series of animated cartoons—the funniest cartoon creation of the talking screen! No happier, no more mirthful animated characters than Bosko and his sweetie, Honey, have been created for the delectation of fans since the advent of talking pictures.

The antics of this comic pair are presented with a burlesque background of popular tunes from Vitaphone feature pictures' successes—songs that have already become national hits through the showing of the productions, through radio broadcasting and the sale of sheet music, phonograph records and piano rills. Film patrons are prepared to welcome these animated parodies of the songs with open arms.

Sinkin' in the Bathtub, the first of the series, is a travesty of Winnie Lightner's song "Singing in the Bathtub," in the Warner Bros. mammoth revue in Technicolor, *Show of Shows.* That tune runs through most of the cartoon accompanying the antics and adventures of Bosko and Honey.
*Note: The Vitaphone press releases spelled the main character's name as "Bosco" in numbers 1 through 9 of the series. After that the name was changed to "Bosko."

The cartoon opens with Bosko in the bathtub singing

snatches of Miss Lightner's song, after which the bathtub does a rakish dance to the same strains. Then Bosko gets into the trickiest automobile in all filmdom, calls for Honey and the happy pair become involved in a series of laughable adventures that provide a riot of fun. The theatre-going public demands song cartoons—supply the demand with "Looney Tunes" and cash in!

Review: *Billboard,* 31 May 1930

As the first of Warner Bros. animated cartoon series dubbed Looney Tunes, this short makes a good impression as far as animation and synchronization are concerned. Yet the selection of subject and comedy bits evidences considerable poor taste, and those handling that end of it will have to exercise greater care. The effective musical score comprises a travesty on "Singing in the Bathtub" from a Warner special. Hugh Harman and Rudolph Ising directed.

Takeoff of short has an animal, seemingly a monkey, warbling while in the bathtub. He gets out of the tub to go into a spring dance, using a lavatory accessory instead of the customery flowers. Followup has him going out into the yard for his car, which comes out of one of those "little houses in the back of big ones." He goes to meet the girl friend, and the rest of the short is given over to the trouble they have with the car. The finish has them landing in a lake, singing in a bathtub again.

Might book this as a filler if your audience is not inclined to fastidiousness. (9 min)

Review: *Motion Picture News,* 10 May 1930

Launching a new series of Vitaphone Varieties which will be extremely popular if the pace is maintained, *Sinking in the Bathtub* is decidedly clever and original; resulting in plenty of laughs.

Idea incorporates cartoon action in rhythm to musical accompaniment of popular tunes in Warner and First National features. In this case, "Singing in the Bathtub" and "Tip Toe through the Tulips" were used.

Action opens with lady love in bathtub when boy friend calls, to strains of the first named number. It's a laugh riot. Then they swing into the second melody with the orchestra, and comedy action is built around the tune for more laughs. Finale brings the characters into the open for a fast-tempo chase.

For laughs and originality, this one ranks with the best of cartoon comedies.

Good subject for any bill anywhere, especially where positive laughs in large numbers are required.

Review: *Boxoffice,* 14 May 1930

Very amusing short comedy cartoon, with that its value, of course. For this short may be especially placed on a program where a laugh is called for, as it guarantees that laugh.

As the first of a series contemplated by Warners' Vitaphone Varieties, WB has something worth a lot here if the series can commence to hold up to its start.

The cartoon is a sort of parody, as signified by its title, on

Sinkin' in the Bathtub, on the song, "Singing in the Bathtub" in *WB Show of Shows.* Its brief story is the travels of the bathtub, its mishaps, all the while containing Bosco or his sweetie, Honey, or both. Placed to open the show at the premiere of Warners' *Song of Flame,* at the $2 Warners, New York, the class audience at that opening found this comedy most enjoyable. It will strike any audience the same way.

While original in reason as here, to burlesque songs in Warner pictures, it's not original in conception, but is in sketching.

Leon Schlesinger is supervising the series, with the cartoons by Hugh Harman and Rudolph Ising; musical score by Frank Marsales, and animation by Isadore Freleng.

The score is but another arrangement of "Singing in the Bathtub," cued to the cartoon, and again this became a continual plug for the song proper, since its melody in one way or another is played throughout the short. That this picture has been generally released for some time may lose the strength of the plug, but to bring a cartoon of this character out on top of the picture itself and to follow the next week would no doubt lend itself easily to a real plug.

Regardless of the song itself or the other values it may contain, "Looney Tunes" has made a flying comedy start.

TREES' KNEES (1931)

Company: Hugh Harman, Rudolph Ising, Vitaphone, Warner Bros.
Type: Looney Tunes, Vitaphone Song Car-Tunes
Characters: Bosko, Honey

Press Release: Vitaphone Corporation, 1931

Bosko does wonders in the woods with the aid of the animators' magic pens! Laughs and guffaws follow each other rapidly as the inimitable Bosko becomes a wandering woodchopper in the twelfth of the song cartoon series. The producer has hit upon a new subject of an animated cartoon and has taken full advantage of its comedy possibilities.

The antics of Bosko and the almost human trees provide a gale of merriment as they plead with Bosko, the heartless woodsman, to spare their trunks.

One of the funniest and most exhilarating scenes on the screen is the chorus of songs and dances by the gathering of young forest trees. Even the branches sway to the tunes of the enchanting melodies initiated by Bosko.

Trees' Knees is based on numerous song hits, with DeSylva, Brown and Henderson's "Trees" the featured musical number.

The melodies in *Trees' Knees* "have been popularized over the air, on music sheets, piano rolls, and phonograph records.

Exploitation! Invite school teachers—use as many lobby cards as you possibly can—stage a letter-writing contest on what your patrons think of "Looney Tunes." Form a "Looney Tunes" club! Offer a prize for the best Looney Tune in rhyme form! Devise and distribute "Looney Tunes" buttons for kiddies! Employ a youngster to parade among the streets in Bosko's clothes! Hold a contest on your stage and offer prizes for kiddies wearing the most original "Bosko and Sweetie Honey" costumes! Give prizes for the best original drawings! Cash in on this series for a series of new profits!

UPS 'N' DOWNS (1931)

Company: Hugh Harman, Rudolph Ising, Vitaphone, Warner Bros.
Type: Looney Tunes, Vitaphone Song Car-Tunes
Character: Bosko

Press Release: Vitaphone Corporation, 1931

They're off! From hot dog stand to race track stand! Jolly Bosko turns jockey in the funniest sweepstakes ever seen. His mechanical horse develops engine trouble at the post, but Bosko is a great veterinary! He rides neck and neck with the favorite whose villainous jockey tries to put him out of the race. But tricky Bosko pulls a fast one and wins by the stretch of a neck! Ingenious fun with Bosko at his merriest. Novel situations that are screamingly nonsensical and funny!

The melodies used in the eight of the "Looney Tunes" series, *Ups 'n' Downs,* are: "Lady Luck," "Reuben," "Dutch Warbler," "Sonny Boy," "Nobody Cares If I'm Blue" and "Tiger Rose."

Bolster up your program with a "Looney Tunes"—the funniest animated musical cartoons series in the market! The latest of the series, *Ups 'n' Downs,* offers an excellent tie-up with sporting goods stores.

Hugh Harman and Rudolph Ising, the creators of Bosko, show their skill as imaginative cartoonists in the latest of the "Looney Tunes" series. *Ups 'n' Downs* packs a full reel of laughs—any way you look at it!

Review: *Bioscope* (London), 25 March 1931

A horse race, won by Bosko on a mechanical mount of great flexibility, is the theme. The fun is fast and should earn its laughs from even the hardest hearted audiences. (793 ft)

YODELING YOKELS (1931)

Company: Hugh Harman, Rudolph Ising, Vitaphone, Warner Bros.
Type: Looney Tunes, Vitaphone song Car-Tunes
Characters: Bosko, Honey (fig. 10)

Press Release: Vitaphone Corporation, 1931

Bosko becomes a yodeler! Thrills! Chills! Laughs galore with the inimitable Bosko becoming the snappiest yodeler of Switzerland! The tenth of the song cartoons series finds the popular character wooing his sweetie Honey in the Swiss Alps. Misjudging his skiing space, he starts sliding down the mountain, carrying Honey with him. Bosko uses his wits and a St. Bernard dog in rescuing her! One of the funniest scenes on the screen is the chorus of songs and dances by the mountain goats, bears, and a lonely owl! Even the mouse, which plays a golf game on a piece of Swiss cheese using a part of a noodle as a putter, utters a yodel to the tunes of the enchanting melodies initiated by Bosko. Laughs at the beginning! Laughs all the way through! And laughs when you think of it days afterwards!

The scintillating melodies of *Yodeling Yokels* will catch the fancy of audiences and have them whistling the tunes after the show. Live exhibitors are once again given the opportunity to cash in by making effective and profitable tie-ups through radio broadcasting, phonograph records, piano rolls, sheet music. The nearest music dealer will gladly cooperate.

The tenth of the series is even more entertaining than the previous numbers. The antics of Bosko are the first and last word in laughs! Give the patrons something new in laughs— "Looney Tunes"—and you give the box-office something over which to gloat.

Li'l Eightball (1939)

Walter Lantz was a veteran cartoonist when he created his stereotypical black cartoon character, Li'l Eightball, in 1939. He had broken into the animated cartoon business in 1916, at age sixteen, when he got his first job with Gregory LaCava in New York City. During the next few years he worked on several popular cartoon series, including *The Katzenjammer Kids, Happy Hooligan,* and others. Around 1918 he joined the famous J. R. Bray Studio, were he created and directed such cartoon characters as Pet the Pup, Dinky Doodle, and the most famous of them all, Col. Heeza Liar. Shortly before the Bray studio closed, Lantz moved to Hollywood, where Carl Laemmle offered him the job of running Universal's animated film department, where he supervised production of the Oswald the lucky rabbit cartoon series. After Laemmle left Universal in 1936, Lantz set up his own studio in a building on the Universal lot, and Universal distributed his cartoons. When the Bosko series ended at M-G-M in 1938, there was no black character series. Lantz decided to create a new one featuring Li'l Eightball, a steroetypical black boy similar to Sammy Johnsin and Bosko. Only three were produced, all in 1939. Lantz abruptly terminated the series in favor of his new and most famous character, Woody Woodpecker, who made his debut in 1940. Although Eightball was a short-lived series, Lantz managed to drag in all of the usual black stereotypes such as superstitiousness, fear of ghosts, and using mules instead of horses. This depiction consistent with other Lantz cartoons, such as *Robinson Crusoe Isle* (1935), *Voodoo in Harlem* (1938), *100 Pygmies and Andy Panda* (1940), *Scrub Me Mama with a Boogie Beat* (1941), *Boogie Woogie Bugle Boy of Company B* (1941), *Cow Cow Boogie* (1943), and *Jungle Jive* (1944) (fig. 11).

Compared to Lantz's other characters, as well as other cartoon characters of the period, Li'l Eightball has languished in relative obscurity. An excellent book on animated cartoons published in the United States, Charles Solomon's *Enchanted Drawings: The History of Animation* (1989), mentions Eightball briefly in a section dealing with ethnic humor. Perhaps many historians would prefer to forget Eightball, but, like it or not, Eightball is part of the true history of American animation.

After the cartoon series ended in 1939, the Li'l Eightball character and stories continued to appear into the early 1940s in *New Funnies* comic books published monthly by Dell Publishing. Although Lantz was a pioneer of animated cartoons, creating Woody Woodpecker and other favorite cartoon characters, he also contributed significantly to the long legacy of black stereotypes in motion picture cartoons.

In response to questions submitted to him by Chris Buchman, animation historian, regarding his black characters, Walter Lantz replied, "I never had any problem with black organizations or minority groups." In another response to a question about Li'l Eightball, Lantz replied, "Li'l Eightball was a cute black boy, directed by Burt Gillett."

In his later years, Lantz deeply regretted ever having created Li'l Eightball. In 1944 he claimed to oppose cartoon stereotypes:

> The Hollywood Screen Cartoon Producers' Association headed by Walter Lantz of Universal studio, assured the *Pittsburgh Courier* that they planned to seriously consider at an executive meeting to be held this week, the subject of harmful caricatures of minority races of American citizens. Previously, Mr. Lantz had requested from the publisher's Pacific Coast bureau, a specific letter in which he asked that such protests concerning the Negro be contained therein and suggested plan of correction be outlined.
>
> Listed among members of the association are Universal, Walt Disney Productions, MGM, Paramount, Warner Brothers, Twentieth Century Fox, RKO, and Columbia.
>
> Lantz also expressed himself as being personally opposed to any alleged derogatory treatment and promised to use his good offices for cooperation in the future. ("Film City Cartoonists Act to Correct Race Caricatures," *Pittsburgh Courier,* 7 October 1944)

The sincerity of Lantz's remarks is questionable because he was still featuring his Li'l Eightball as a prominent character in his *New Funnies* comic books when he made the above statement to the *Courier.*

Li'l Eightball Stories and Reviews

A HAUNTING WE WILL GO (1939)

Company: Burt Gillett, Walter Lantz, Universal Pictures
Characters: Li'l Eightball (voice characterizations by white actors), ghosts

Story: The cartoon opens in an old haunted mill. Floating out of the mill is a small, smiling ghost looking for someone to haunt. He smiles as he says, "I'm a ghost, I'm a ghost, just a little bitty ghost, scaring people from coast to coast." The little ghost finds his way to Li'l Eightball's cabin where he flies through the window and finds Eightball in bed asleep. The ghost makes a haunting noise that wakes up Eightball. He looks at the little ghost, says "boo," and the ghost falls to the floor. Eightball laughs and says "Hello!" The ghost replies, "Aw shucks! I was supposed to scare you." When Eightball asks why, the ghost replies, "'Cause I'm a ghost." Eightball laughs and says, "I don't believe you are a ghost. You can't scare me, big boy." The ghost replies, "But I'm confident I can." Laughing, Eightball tells him, "Your confidence is commendable. But it is a lot of bull to me, Boy." The ghost grabs Eightball's shirt and pulls him through the window and back to the haunted mill. The little ghost calls for his father ghost and tells him, "Hey Pop, he says you can't scare him." Pointing to Eightball, he says, "He says he don't believe in ghosts." Father and son ghost have a big laugh. Then the father ghost whistles, summoning a group of ghosts who arrive and salute father ghost in military fashion. Father ghost picks up Eightball and tells the others, "Hey fellers he says he don't believe in ghosts." The others laugh. Eightball raises his hands for quiet and tells them, "Quiet, quiet. Now listen you night-shift jitterbugs. In this enlightened age we chillun do not recognize ectoplasmic figments of the imagination. I refuse to be terrified by such a phantasmic audience." Papa ghost shakes his head and tells the others, "What will we do with him, boys?" The other ghosts confer in the back of the room before saying, "Give him the works!" Papa ghost says "OK, the works" and the others dance in a circle around Eightball before disappearing. Eightball says, "This here nonsense don't scare me." The the room gets dark except for beams of headlights and sounds of automobiles driving around the room. Eightball is momentarily scared but he recovers and says, "They can't scare me with that stuff." A hand picks up Eightball and puts him in an invisible taxi that drives around the room at high speed before crashing into the wall. This scares Eightball, who runs out of his shoes and later tries to dive through a locked window. Eightball runs into another room, slamming the door behind him, and calls out, "Leave me alone you bedsheet aberrations." The ghosts shrink the room to the size of a dice, which a ghost picks up to play craps. The room then expands, allowing Eightball to run through the door and into another room where he falls through a trapdoor but manages to hang on to the ceiling. The little ghost arrives and asks Eightball, "Ha, ha, are you scared now?" Eightball replies, "Why you invisible half pint phantom! This exhibition of supernatural claptrap don't affect me in the least. Scram!" The little ghost responds by opening a panel in the wall through which fly several ghosts who pull Eightball from the ceiling and toss him around the room while claps of thunder and flashes of lighting are heard and seen. Eightball is chased out of the mill and runs toward his house, while the ghosts stand at the door laughing at him. The little ghost says to his father, "Hey Pop, I think you scared him all right." But then Eightball returns and tells them "I . . . I . . . I ain't scared yet—much" before he runs back home where he dives through the window and into his bed, throwing the bedsheet into the air. He says, "Still I'm not scared," as the bedsheet falls on top of him, scaring him again as the cartoon ends.

Review: *Motion Picture Herald,* 15 July 1939

A juvenile ghost unable to frighten Little Eight Ball kidnaps him and takes him to the haunted house inhabited by the Ghost family. Still unafraid, the ghosts really go to town on the colored boy. Many amusing situations develop and Eight Ball flees home but still claims to be unafraid. An amusing Walter Lantz cartoon. (7 1/2 min)

Review: *Motion Picture Herald,* 11 February 1950

This Walter Lantz Cartoon stars Li'l Eightball in his adventure with the ghosts. When a spook appears, our little dark-skinned hero stoutly maintains his fearlessness, but when a group of spirits gang up on him his chattering teeth beat an accompaniment to the ghost's laughter.

Review: *Selected Motion Pictures,* 1 September 1939

Lantz cartoon. Little Sambo has some weird experiences in a haunted house. Good. Family.

Review: *Motion Picture Exhibitor,* 12 July 1939

Little Eight Ball is visited by a baby ghost who drags him to a haunted mill where the grown up ghosts put on their best scary act. Some good fantastic cartooning in this one should go over with the kids. Good.

Review: *Exhibitor Servisection,* 23 November 1948

In this re-release, Sambo, troubled slightly by a baby ghost from a nearby mill which is supposedly haunted, brags in five syllable words that there's no such thing as a ghost. Taken aback, and angered, the young ghoul grabs Sambo, and flies to the mill with him, calling upon his pop to frighten the wits out of this unbeliever. The father ghost calls upon all his ethereal friends to decide what should be done about Sambo. After putting their heads together, the ghosts decide to give Sambo "the works." Through it all, Sambo seems unperturbed but finally he breaks down, and dashes home to hide in the bed-covers convinced that there are ghosts after all. Fair.

SILLY SUPERSTITIONS (1939)

Company: Burt Gillett, Walter Lantz, Universal Pictures
Characters: Li'l Eightball, his dog, Mammy (voice impersonations by white actors)

Story: The cartoon opens with Li'l Eightball and his dog rushing out of his cabin to play in the yard. His mammy, a heavy-set woman with a bandanna tied on her head, stands on the front porch and calls out to him, "Eightball! Eightball!" As Eightball stops playing, he hears his mammy say, "Now you all remember today is Friday the thirteenth." Don't walk under no ladders and don't break no mirrors and don't let no black cats run cross your path or you have bad luck. Now run along and play." Eightball chuckles at his mother's advice and tells his dog, "Ladders, black cats and mirrors etc, etc.—that's just superstition. I don't believe in superstition. Do you?" The dog shakes his head affirmatively, and Eightball tells him, "Well, I'm surprised. An individual of your mental caliber should comprehend that superstition is just a lot of hooey. I'll demonstrate. See that ladder over there?" Eightball walks across the street and stands next to a ladder leaning against a wall. Bowing up and down, he says, "O ladder on the wall. I ain't scared of you at all." Eightball then walks under the ladder while his dog holds his fingers over his eyes. The dog is happy after seeing nothing bad happen to Eightball, who tells him, "You see, I didn't have any bad luck. Now let's see you try it." Seemingly full of confidence, the dog starts to walk under the ladder. Then he has second thoughts and stops. Eightball tells him, "Don't be afraid. I'll fix it so you won't be scared." And he ties a blindfold over the dog's eyes. The dog runs under the ladder and continues to run up a fire escape all the way up to the top story of a building under construction. The building collapses and the dog falls, but is caught by Eightball before hitting the ground. Eightball asks his dog, "Now do you believe in superstition?" The dog nods yes. Eightball then tells him, "Ummm, I was afraid of that. I will demonstrate again." His dog trembles with fright at the very thought of another demonstration. Eightball walks over to a black cat and says, "Pardon me. I wonder if I could interest you in helping to prove the age-old tale that if you cross my path I'll be subject to a mess of bad luck." The cat agrees and proceeds to cross Eightball's path two times. Eightball says, "You see, I didn't have any bad luck," as a large lion appears on the scene behind Eightball. The black cat runs away and the dog tries to warn Eightball, who he is saying, "There's nothing to be afraid of. It's people like you who always think things are gonna happen. Is you a dog or a mouse? What's the matter little baby? Don't let a little thing like that scare you. Be brave like me." Eightball turns and sees the lion behind him. As he slowly backs away, the lion follows. A police car, siren wailing, arrives on the scene, and the officer tells Eightball that a ferocious lion has escaped from the zoo before he speeds away. Eightball trembles and says to himself, "Keep goin' feet and take me with you." Eightball tries to escape with the lion chasing him before he stops and asks the lion, "Now, now, now, just a minute! Is you chasin' me because its Friday the thirteenth or just because you're a lion?" The lion answers with a loud roar and Eightball starts to run, saying, "That's all I wanted to know." The chase continues until the lion gets his tail wrapped around a fire hydrant. The dog feels brave and puffs himself up larger than the lion, who is so frightened that he runs back to the zoo and gets back into his cage. Meanwhile Eightball has climbed a lamppost, and is happy to see his dog when he arrives on the scene. Eightball asks him, "Now do you believe in superstition?" The dog nods his head yes. Eightball shakes his hand and says, "Well, brother so do I!" as the cartoon ends.

Review: *Motion Picture Herald,* **23 September 1939**

The thesis of this Lantz laugh effort is to prove that superstitions are silly stuff. Aside from the incredibility of such far

fetched beliefs, the cartoon effort in debunking the popular potents of ill luck as the black cat, walking under a ladder and the fateful day of Friday, the 13th, partakes of the silliness of superstitious slogans. Although logic is the last factor to be asked in the composition of cartoons the business of the miniature effects of a boomerang on its avowed purpose and the results of the action would seem to postulate the conclusion that there may be some ounce of reality and reason in the saying that ill luck follows the breaking of superstitious canons. Anyway Little Blackball ventures forth on a Friday with the avowed purpose of making faces at misfortune. The laughs and jokes fall on the rash lad and the finish of the argument and the subject may lead the credible cartoon customer to believing that there may be something in this superstition stuff. (7 min)

Review: *Boxoffice,* **23 September 1939**

Little Black ball tries to convince his dog that it is foolish to be superstitious even though it is Friday the 13th. What transpires is meagre program fare.

Review: *Selected Motion Pictures,* **1 October 1939**

Sambo has a difficult time when he tries to defy a current superstition. Fair. Family.

Review: *Motion Picture Exhibitor,* **20 September 1939**

Little Eight Ball isn't afraid of superstition but when a lion almost gets him he changes his mind. Fair.

THE STUBBORN MULE (1939)

Company: Burt Gillett, Walter Lantz, Universal Pictures
Characters: Li'l Eightball, mule

Review: *Moving Picture World,* **12 August 1939**

In the latest Walter Lantz, Little Eight Ball cartoons, the colored lad runs into a difficulty with a stubborn mule which he has received as a gift from a fruit peddler. After using every possible means to make the mule move from the spot he gives up, exclaiming "that only a bolt of lightning would do any good. Conveniently, lightning strikes, and the mule races back to the peddler ready to work again. (7 min)

Review: *Boxoffice,* **12 August 1939**

Fairly routine animation although the kids won't be disappointed. Little Eight Ball, new pickaninny character, employs a heap of ruses to get a stubborn mule off its haunches. There's a lot of effort but little action until a bolt of lightning does the trick. (7 min)

Review: *Motion Picture Exhibitor,* **9 August 1939**

Li'l Eight Ball attempts to tame a stubborn mule, but gives up, only to find that lightning does the trick. This is just run-of-the-mill. Fair.

Jasper (1942–1947)

In 1934 George Pal, a Hungarian artist, created and produced his first three-dimensional *Puppetoon* cartoon of cigarettes marching in and out of their packages as a commercial for a cigarette manufacturer in Paris. When World War II broke out, Pal left Holland with his wife and son for Hollywood, where he founded his own cartoon studio, George Pal Productions. He produced cartoons using carved wooden figures and released them under the banner of *Puppetoons* and *Madcap Models* by Paramount Pictures. Pal's cartoons had a unique three-dimensional quality that was obtained by photographing approximately nine thousand carved wooden figures with a stop-motion technique.

In the fall 1971 issue of *Cinefantastic* George Pal is quoted as saying that he created Jasper because he "had long been attracted to the folklore of the American Negro and believed it to be the richest and the most colorful in American history." Pal may have succeeded in bringing black folklore to the public, but he also helped perpetuate all of the negative racial stereotypes that he found when he came to the United States. The stereotypes including chicken stealing (*Jasper Goes Hunting*), shooting craps (*Jasper and the Choo-choo*), fear of ghosts (*Jasper and the Haunted House*), black cannibalism (*My Man Jasper*), watermelon eating (*Jasper and the Watermelons*), the minstrel show (*Jasper and the Minstrels*), shoeshine boy (*Shoe Shine Jasper*) and a burlesque of the black church (*Jasper Goes Fishing*). By the end of War War II, Pal received increasing criticism from both white and black publications regarding his Jasper character (figs. 12 and 13).

> "Pictures help form children's minds," says Mr. Pal. "The creator has a responsibility to all children." But it is precisely this responsibility that he betrays in his Puppetoon series "Jasper," in which he presents the Negro stereotype that Negroes resent. Jasper himself is a colored puppet boy, wide-eyed, musical, childish, lovable. But the "scarecrow" who appears in the pictures, and the black crow perched on his shoulder, are braggarts-in-dialect, Amos and Andy caricatures at worst. The adventures of Jasper as in *Jasper and the Watermelons* and *Jasper and the Haunted House*, perpetuate the misconceptions of Negro characteristics. When we are building a democratic world in which all races should have a chance for full development, it is libelous to present the razor totin', ghost-ha'nted, chicken stealin' concept of the American Negro. (*Hollywood Quarterly*, July 1946)

Similar sentiments were expressed in an article that appeared in *Ebony* magazine:

> Pal's best known Puppetoons are the Jasper series. Jasper, a Negro boy with a wide, white mouth, romps and scurries through adventurous tales like *Jasper and the Watermelons, Jasper's Close Shave, Jasper and the Haunted House, Jasper and William Tell.*
>
> While Pal says "Little Jasper is the Huckleberry Finn of American folklore in my opinion," his Puppetoons have been criticized by Negro and white newspapers, organizations, and notables as perpetuating the myth of Negro shiftlessness, fear, and childishness.

> Pal himself is unable to understand this criticism. He "doesn't want to hurt anyone, especially now." As a European not raised on race prejudice, he takes America for what he finds in it. To him there is nothing abusive about a Negro boy who likes to eat watermelons or gets scared when he goes past a haunted house. But to American Negroes attempting to drown the Uncle Tom myth that Negroes are childish, eat nothing but molasses and watermelons and are afraid of their own shadow, Jasper is objectionable. Paul does not use, as other cartoonists do, white actors that talk "like Negroes." He employs the finest Negro talent available.
>
> Most objection to the Little Jasper series is directed against Professor Scarecrow and his friend Black Crow, who talk in Amos 'n' Andy dialogue. Pal recently took them out of the Jasper pictures but some white audiences objected. ("Little Jasper Series Draws Protest from Negro Groups," *Ebony*, January 1947)

Pal was stunned by the criticism of his "Jasper" character and objected to it as unjustified. He felt that his representation of the Negro boy was well within the accepted theatrical tradition of bringing black folklore to the American screen. Furthermore he felt that Jasper was depicted as an honest, respectful boy who obeyed his mother. The Scarecrow and his friend the Crow were immoral characters who introduced the young, naive, and innocent Jasper to dice shooting and chicken stealing. They also attempted to con him out of his possessions. Pal did not understand that although the Scarecrow and the Crow always came out on the short end for their deeds against Jasper, it was the close association of negative stereotypes with the black characters that was objectionable to blacks and others.

Near the end of the series Pal attempted, with limited success, to counter objections to his *Jasper* series by changing the story content and toning down the traditional racial stereotypes in such cartoons as *Jasper Tell, Jasper in a Jam, Jasper and the Beanstalk, Jasper's Close Shave*, and others. He also produced other Puppetoons with black characters that he considered to be nonsterotypical, such as *Date with Duke,* the latter combining the live action of the famous composer–conductor Duke Ellington with puppet animation. In 1946 Pal produced *John Henry and the Inky-Poo,* an adaptation of the legendary tale of the black folk hero John Henry, which was narrated by the accomplished screen actor Rex Ingram and featured the singing of the Carlyle Scott chorus.

Unlike most of the cartoons of the period, which relied primarily on sight gags for laughs, the humor of the *Jasper* series was, for the most part, derived from the verbal repartee between the Scarecrow and the Crow. In developing this type of humor, Pal relied heavily on verbal contests called "signifying" that were a popular pastime among black youth. Two contestants exchange personal or parental insults, usually in rhyme. The game was always played in the presence of others. The winner was the contestant who got the last word and the most laughter from the onlookers by demonstrating superior verbal dexterity and imagination. In his book *On the Real Side: Laughing, Lying, and Signifying* (1994), Mel Watkins sums up this type of verbal repartee as follows:

Shuckin' and jivin', talkin' and testifyin', dippin' and grippin', slappin' and clappin', or simply dissin' are all vernacular descriptions for African-American inner-community verbal play. . . . They describe the core verbal interaction that defines one of the fundamental attributes of African-American humor.

In the *Jasper* series the Crow put down the Scarecrow with humorous verbal insults spoken in rhyme. The Scarecrow usually responded by threatening the Crow with physical harm, which the Crow ignored. Usually Jasper furnished the straight line that initiated these verbal exchanges.

The voice characterization of the Scarecrow was provided by the very versatile and talented character Roy Glenn Sr. Glenn, who made his film debut in 1937 in the all-black cast of the film *Dark Manhattan,* was born in Kansas in 1911. He began his professional career as a singer in Los Angeles, later switching to acting in stage productions, among them the highly acclaimed all-black version of *Macbeth.* He is remembered best for his role as Sammy Davis's father in the spectacular Broadway production of *Golden Boy.* His feature motion picture credits include *Guess Who's Coming to Dinner, Sweet Bird of Youth, Lydia Baily, Man in the Grey Flannel Suit,* and *A Raisin in the Sun.* Glenn died in Los Angeles March 12, 1971.

In 1944 the Academy of Motion Picture Arts and Sciences presented Pal with an honorary award for his "development of novel methods and techniques in the productions of short subjects known as puppetoons." The overall production quality of the *Jasper* series remained excellent until the end. The technicolor was vivid and brilliant and was combined with excellent background music furnished by black choral groups. The series was terminated in 1947 when rising production costs rendered the distribution of puppetoons unprofitable.

Jasper Stories and Reviews

HOTLIPS JASPER (1944)

Company: George Pal, Paramount Pictures
Type: Puppetoons
Characters: Jasper, Scarecrow (voice characterization by Roy Glenn), Crow

Story: The cartoon opens showing a truck, bearing a sign that reads Louis Strongarm, moving at excessive speed along a winding road that passes Jasper's house. Jasper is sitting on a fence watching it pass by, when a case falls off the truck onto the road. He calls out, "Hey mister! You dropped something off the truck. Come back!" Meanwhile, standing in a nearby corn field, the Scarecrow says, "What in the world is that boy yelling about?" Perched on the Scarecrow's shoulder is his friend the Crow, who says, "They dropped something off the truck." The two hurry over to Jasper to investigate as the Scarecrow says, "It might be something valuable—something that I should take care of for him." The crow says, "You mean just take," and the Scarecrow says, "Be quiet, Blackbird!" Jasper tells them, "I'm

going to take this case home to my mother because she says to never keep anything that isn't yours." The Scarecrow agrees but tells Jasper, "Let's just open it first just to see what's inside." They open the package and find a gold trumpet and a note written on the inside of the case which reads, $100 for returning the horn if lost. Only the Scarecrow reads the note but doesn't tell Jasper as he closes the case and hurries off to give it to his mother. The Scarecrow tells the Crow that "$100 will buy an awful mess of spareribs, sweet taters, and corn" before calling after Jasper "Come here, boy! If you let me have that horn, it will make you a star in Hollywood. I know all the movie stars and great directors at Paramount Studies, including Mr. DeMille." The scene changes to a Hollywood location where the Scarecrow, the Crow, and Jasper are driving through the gate at Paramount Studios in a long limousine. The Scarecrow assumes the role of a Hollywood film director and takes Jasper to the star dressing room. He is about to direct a big extravaganza about the buzzing of the bumble bee and shouts, "Lights! Soundman! Cameraman! Quiet!" Jasper arrives on the scene dressed as a bumblebee and playing "The Flight of the Bumble Bee" on his trumpet. Jasper walks up to a beehive as the sound of his music lures out a swarm of bees. They follow Jasper to a garden of blooming flowers, where the bees take honey before Jasper leads them back to the hive. They arrive as Jasper is ending his trumpet solo, and the Scarecrow shouts, "Cut! Cut!" The Scarecrow tells Jasper that "you will be the sensation of the country" as the sound of a police siren is heard. This jolts them back to reality. The police arrive at Jasper's house and ask the Scarecrow, "Where did you get that horn?" He answers, "It ain't mine" before he looks at Jasper. The policeman takes the horn from the Scarecrow and then tells Jasper, "You are getting a reward for finding the horn." Jasper is delighted and runs off to tell his mother. Meanwhile, the Scarecrow is dumbfounded. Just as the Crow opens his mouth to make a wisecrack, the Scarecrow tells him, "If you open your mouth to make one crack . . ." as the cartoon ends.

Review: *Motion Picture Herald,* 23 December 1944

As Jasper is day-dreaming he is rudely interrupted by the rumblings of an approaching truck. He is barely able to read the sign, which says Hairy James Orchestra. Jasper picks up an instrument case that drops from the truck. The Scarecrow decides to investigate the disturbance and opens the case and finds a gold trumpet. He also sees a notice of $100 reward for its safe return, but he manages to keep this from Jasper. They imagine they are musicians in Hollywood. But as the story finishes the Scarecrow grabs the instrument from Jasper. At this moment a police car approaches and the Scarecrow returns the trumpet. Whereupon the other officer hands the $100 reward to Jasper. (8 min)

Review: *Boxoffice,* 30 December 1944

The reel is easily in keeping with the high standards of this superior series. In the charming style of phantasy, which is the hallmark of Jasper's stories, a musical interlude featuring "The Flight of the Bumblebee" is played on a hot trumpet by the talented Jasper. Color is magnificent and the three-dimensional effects add wonderful realism to the proceedings.

Review: *Motion Picture Exhibitor*, 13 December 1944

Jasper finds a trumpet which falls off a truck. The Scarecrow spins for him a phantasy of what he can do for him as a star in a Paramount Pictures phantasy if he can master the instrument. This is interrupted when Jasper gets a reward for finding the horn. The Technicolor and miniature effects are marvelous, as is the expert off screen playing of the "Flight of the Bumble Bee" as a trumpet solo by Ralph Mendez. Excellent.

JASPER AND THE BEANSTALK (1945)

Company: George Pal, Paramount Pictures
Type: Puppetoons
Characters: Jasper, Scarecrow (voice characterization by Roy Glenn), Crow, magic harp (Billie Holiday caricature)

Story: The cartoon opens on a tranquil scene in the country. Jasper's little cabin is seen sitting on a hill. The sound of music is heard as Jasper, playing his Jew's harp, comes out of the door and skips along down the road where he passes a cornfield where the Scarecrow, with the Crow perched on his shoulder, is asleep. The Scarecrow wakes up and points to Jasper and says, "Hey you! Come here." Jasper walks back to him, and the Scarecrow says, "How would you like to turn in that beat-up Jew's harp for a new sports job? One like Jackson got himself." Jasper asks, "Jackson?" The Scarecrow says, "Yeah, you remember Jackson and the beanstalk—how he plants a bean and up jumped a stalk that grew clear out of this world. Dat's where he got his harp, Jasper." Jasper says, "But they wasn't real beans" and the Scarecrow says, "Neither are these boy. These is black magic beans. You take 'em home and bury them and don't say nothin' to nobody. Dig me?" Jasper gives the Scarecrow his harp and takes the beans and runs home as fast as he can. The Scarecrow and the Crow look at each other and say, "Black magic beans—ha-ha—and he gonna bury them too. That was a killer, ha-ha." Inside the house Jasper plants the beans in a small pot before getting into his bed and going to sleep. During the night the beans begin to sprout and grow, lifting Jasper and his bed out of the house and through the clouds before coming to rest in a strange kingdom in the sky. Jasper wakes up and looks around. A huge bee flies near him and says, "What's buzzin', cousin?" Jasper answers, "I's lookin' for the magic harp." The bee tells him, "E:I-yi-yi. That belongs to the giant." Jasper walks off and soon arrives at the giant's castle. Soft music is heard inside. He opens the door and sees the magic harp in a cage on the table. The giant is sitting in a chair and resting his elbows on the table while he sleeps. The magic harp is a beau-

tiful girl dressed in an elegant gown singing a blues song a la Billie Holiday, "Ain't goin' no place, ain't got no place to go. Ain't goin' no place, ain't got no place to go. I'm just sittin', hopin', prayin', for some good man to show. I'm no good without one, can't move it from my mind. But you know when he wants me I'm not hard to find." Meanwhile Jasper has walked over to the cage where he asks the beautiful harp, "What you in for? How come you're fenced in?" The harp replies, "Shhh! Don't wake him; he's a murderer. Unlock the door, honey chile, and let's get out of here." Jasper says, "OK, but keep on singing" while he bends a piece of wire and uses it to pick the lock. Meanwhile the harp sings, "Only got one thing to say, I gotta make my plans for movin'. If you can't do one thing right, I'm gonna head for rack and ruin." Jasper opens the door, and they both walk across the table. But then they stumble over a fork, and the noise wakes up the giant. He sees them and says, "Hey boy! Drop that girl! Drop her!" But Jasper manages to elude the giant and carry the harp back down the beanstalk. Then he takes an ax and chops it down. It is now morning. In the field the Scarecrow wakes up smiling, and the Crow asks him, "So what's funny?" The Scarecrow says, "Ha-ha! Don't you remember? These are not real beans—they are magic beans." He and the Crow have a big laugh but stop when they hear the sound of harp music coming from Jasper's cabin. The Scarecrow asks, "What's that?" The Crow answers, "It must be music, I think." They walk over to investigate. When they look in the window, they see Jasper playing the magic harp while she sings, "Listen to me baby. Don't ever stop what you're doin'. Man, you kill me with your wooin'. If you just stay home and do right, I'll never head for rack and ruin." The Scarecrow throws up his hands in disbelief, and the Crow says, "Boss, she is the most terrific lie you ever did tell." The harp touches Jasper on his head and tells him, "I'm glad you brought me home, baby" as Jasper smiles and the cartoon ends.

Review: *Motion Picture Herald*, 27 October 1945

In this variation of "Jack and the Beanstalk" of nursery-rhyme fame, the Scarecrow trades Jasper a handful of beans for a mouth organ. Jasper climbs up the huge beanstalk that eventually grows, and at the top finds a beautiful girl in a golden cage playing a golden harp. Jasper rescues the girl from the giant, takes her out of the cage and brings her down the beanstalk and so spends the rest of his life happily dancing to the tunes his girl friend plays on the beautiful harp. In Technicolor. (8 min)

Review: *Boxoffice*, 6 October 1945

This is a variation on the Jack and the Beanstalk theme and ranks with the better George Pal subjects of past years. Jasper swaps his Jew's-harp for some "magic" beans given him by the Scarecrow. In a dream, he is transported to the beanstalk that rises into the sky. He finds a beautiful damsel playing a harp while singing some lively jive. Jasper awakens the next morning to find the Scarecrow laughing at the joke he has played on him. (8 min)

Review: *Besa Shorts Shorts,* **22 October 1945**

Jasper's juice harp is keyed high on a swell arrangement of "That Old Black Magic" as he goes scampering down the pathway from his home. Of course, old Scarecrow and friend are available for trickery which involves giving Jasper an alleged Black Magic bean. Jasper relinquishes his harp for the legumes, plants same, and up comes a monstrous beanstalk which towers to the Giant's place where Jasper discovers and rescues a siren with a sultry song.

Review: *Motion Picture Exhibitor,* **3 October 1945**

The mischievous Scarecrow and Crow trade in Jasper's Jews-harp for some mystic beans that grow very high. That night Jasper dreams that the planted beans grow up to the sky. He climbs to the top, and discovers a castle, a giant, and a beautiful girl playing a magic harp. While the giant sleeps, Jasper rescues the girl and the harp, brings them down to earth. The next morning, as the Scarecrow laughs at his trick, he sees the harp and girl and sadly takes a taunting of the Crow. Excellent.

JASPER AND THE CHOO-CHOO (1942)

Company: George Pal, Paramount Pictures
Type: Madcap Models
Characters: Jasper, Scarecrow (voice characterization by Roy Glenn), Crow, Mammy

Story: The cartoon opens with a view of Jasper's small cabin sitting on a hillside surrounded by cornfields. Through a broken windowpane piano music is heard. Jasper's mammy tells him, "Jasper, here's that nickel for cleaning up the yard. Now get on with you. And remember chile you don't git nothin' fo' nothin'." Jasper answers, "All right, Mammy. Good-bye." He walks out of the house and skips down the road flipping his nickel in his hand. He passes the Scarecrow standing in a nearby cornfield with the Crow perched on his shoulder. The Scarecrow calls out, "Hey there, Boy! Where you goin' with dat nickel?" The Crow says, "Yeah, where you goin' with dat dough?" Jasper stops and says, "My mammy done give it to me," and then walks away. The Scarecrow says, "That's a powerful lot of money for a boy like you to be totin' 'round. You liable to lose dat." The Crow adds, "Yeah. You'd better let us keep dat for you." The Scarecrow says, "Be quiet, Blackbird! Say Boy, how would you like to liquidate dat nickel into some foldin' money?" Jasper stops and says, "You mean a whole dollar?" The Crow says, "Yeah. You heard what the man say." The Scarecrow walks closer Jasper and tells him, "Why Boy, you is talkin' to a man who what knows big numbers. Why we is liable to change it into more than a dollar. We liable to ride up high as 85¢." Jasper says, "85¢? How you gonna do dat?" The Scarecrow says, "Why Boy, that's easy. Dis certainly is your lucky day. I's gonna let you play some African golf— some cow pasture pool." He pulls out a pair of dice, and the Crow bends down and takes a close look at them. He shakes his head and says, "Boy, you is in for some education." The

Scarecrow tells the Crow, "One of dese days I's gonna radicate me a blackbird" and then tells Jasper, "Now Boy, you just put the nickel on the stump while I rolls out dese jungle jitterbugs. You sees, if I rolls a seben, den I win. And if I rolls some other number, you lose. But first I sets the indicator." The Scarecrow then sets the dial on the loaded dice to roll seven. The Scarecrow shakes the dice, saying, "Now hit me! Baby needs shoes. Here we go. Get that Jasper boy's nickel. Then he rolls the dice. The dice roll around and around the tree stump as Jasper's eyes get wide watching them. The Scarecrow says, "Look at dem gallopin' dominos." The dice come to rest with one showing one and the other showing one before flipping to six. The Scarecrow says, "Well shut my mouth wide open! A seven!" The Crow says, "That certainly is a coincidence, ain't it." The Scarecrow tells Jasper, "You done lost. Well, I tells you what . . ." He starts to pick up Jasper's nickel but stops as the dice suddenly grow in size and come to life. One of the dice tells the Scarecrow, "Don't you touch dat boy's money!" The other dice says, "What you mean cheatin' dat boy." Suddenly the Scarecrow, Jasper, and the Crow are surrounded by huge dice. Before they can escape, they find themselves trapped inside one of them. The dice rolls around and the Scarecrow cries, "Help me!" The dice pops open and the trio fly out and through the air. After they land on the ground, they run along a road but are stopped by a railroad crossing arm with an eightball on the end of it. They can hear a train's whistle in the distance. Two huge dice roll toward them and say, "Yeah man" as jazz music plays in the background. Jasper, the Scarecrow, and the Crow jump over the crossing arm just as a dice train arrives. The train chases them as they run around the huge dice before they are trapped in a deck of playing cards and shuffled, leaving the trio flat as pancakes. After they return to normal size, they jump inside a pinball machine and are chased by the ball as the machine lights up. They are ejected through the coin slot and run back to Jasper's farm. The Scarecrow sees Jasper's nickel on the tree stump and attempts to pick it up, but Jasper beats him to it saying, "Gamblin' never pays, you cheater," as he pulls the Scarecrow's hat down over his head and twists the Crow's head around and around his neck before running back into his cabin as the cartoon ends.

Review: *Besa Shorts Shorts,* **15 December 1942**

Lil Jasper has been given a nickel by his mammy. On his way that same old Scarecrow equipped with running chatter Crow, stops Jasper and lures him into a dice game. Jasper loses but the dice themselves become so irate at the Scarecrow's crooked tactics that they come to life and escort Jasper, the Crow, and Scarecrow through a terrifying excursion through a land made up of gambling devices.

Review: *Motion Picture Herald,* **30 January 1943**

Jasper has earned a nickel and a lecture from his mammy on the subject of working for what you get, but he still falls for the crow's smooth line about a get-rich-quick dice game. The dice, however, have a conscience, and afford both players an impressive lesson. The immediate cause of all this trouble is almost forgotten, but Jasper runs back in time to reclaim his nickel from the crow who was about to pocket the prize. (7 1/2 min)

JASPER DERBY (1946)

Company: George Pal, Paramount Pictures
Characters: Jasper, Hi-Octane the horse

Story: Cartoon opens on a tranquil setting in the countryside as sounds of soft music are heard. It is Jasper sitting on a fence, playing "Golden Earrings" on his violin. In the barn, Hi-Octane, a broken-down old race horse, listens to the music, which brings tears to his eyes. Then Jasper speeds up the tempo of the music, and old Hi-Octane bolts out of his stable and runs at high speed around the meadow until he collapses with exhaustion in front of Jasper. He says, "Please, no more. Somebody stop the music. Please, no more." Jasper asks him, "What's the matter? Don't you like music?" The horse answers, "I's mighty fond of it son, but that last fiddlin' around—it done somethin' to me. It gimme de gallops, and I ain't as young as I used to be. Like when I was burnin' up dem race tracks." Jasper asks him, "Wus you a race horse?" Hi-Octane replies, "Sho' nuff." Jasper continues, "A champeen like Man of War? Like Sea Biscuit?" The horse says, "Amateurs, amateurs. Come on, Jasper. I'm gonna show ya the scrapbook full of my fancy goin's on when I was pretty big." Jasper turns to a page and reads, "Three-week-old miracle colt Hi-Octane thunders to victory." As the background music plays "My Old Kentucky Home," Jasper turns a page and reads, "Hi-Octane wins Derby; captures Manila." Hi-Octane says, "And come next May what am I, son? Nothin' but the champeen. That's all—nothin else." On the next page they read, "Hi-Octane top money winner—Breaks Track Record." Looking at his photo, Hi-Octane says, "I was as pretty as a petunia bud. Look at that head of hair. Look, no stomach, no double chin." Jasper says, "Gee! You sho' must be a rich horse." Hi-Octane shakes his head and responds, "No, no! I haven't got a red cent to my name, son. Yes sir! Dere's an old sayin'—A fool and his money are soon parted. And I'm just a plain old fool" as tears fall from his eyes. Jasper tells him, "Oh, come now. After all, you can do it again." Hi-Octane asks, "Do what, Son? Jasper says, "Win another race." Hi-Octane says, "At my age?" And Jasper says, "You sho' wuz puttin' on a powerful lot of speed over yonder." Hi-Octane says, "I was only messin' around cause y'all was playin' that fast stuff." Jasper tells him, "I can play it again, any place, any time." And the horse says, "Any place like Louisville?" Jasper answers, "Yes sir." Hi-Octane asks, "At any time like the Kentucky Derby?" Jasper says yes and Hi-octane says, "Great day—the Kentucky Derby" as the scene shifts to a racetrack. The track announcer says "Yes sir, ladies and gentlemen, it's a great time at Kentucky Downs. The stands are packed with a colorful crowd gathered here to witness the sixty-seventh running of the thrilling Bluegrass Classic." Jasper sits atop Hi-Octane, holding his violin. As he lines up at the starting gate with the other horses, he asks the horse, "How does you feel, old fella?" Hi-octane replies, "I's just as fit as yo' fiddle." The bell rings and the horses take off, leaving Jasper and Hi-Octane at the starting gate. But Jasper begins to play a fast tune, and Hi-Octane takes off like a streak of lightning, passing all the other horses. Despite the fact that Jasper falls off his mount several times, Jasper and Hi-Octane are in the lead. But then the strings on Jasper's fiddle break one by one. Hi-Octane collapses and the other horses pass them by. But Hi-Octane lifts his tail and tells Jasper to use it as a bow, thereby putting them back in the race. They win and are showered with flowers and receive the gold cup. With their winnings they buy a large house, where Jasper is playing soft music. Relaxing on a sofa beside him is Hi-Octane, who says, "Play on Jasper, play on. But no mo' of the fast stuff—only the slow" as he smiles and the cartoon ends.

Review: *Motion Picture Herald,* 22 June 1946

The Kentucky Derby, in all its color and pageantry, is the scene of "Jasper's Derby." Jasper befriends an old racehorse and provides a violin solo causing the horse to win the race of races. The final scene shows the horse enjoying the fruits of his victory-mint-julep. (8 min)

Review: *Film Daily,* 3 June 1946

Jasper befriends an old nag, Hi-Octane, and learns that he once was a great race horse. He learns also that his violin playing inspires the horse to great bursts of speed. Jasper persuades the horse to enter the Derby, which they win, despite the fact that the going gets a little rough when Jasper's violin strings break at the crucial moment. Po' Lil' ol' Jasper is sure to soften the hardest heart as he and Hi-O ride to victory.

Review: *Boxoffice,* 18 May 1946

Striking Technicolor and skillful manipulation of puppets are combined to make this an outstanding one-reeler. In addition there is the amusing story of the violin playing Jasper who discovers that his music can reconvert a retired broken down race horse into a Kentucky Derby winner. The horse, Hi-Octane, not only wins the Derby, but earns enough money in that race to provide Jasper and himself with a comfortable home and long, cool mint juleps.

Review: *Motion Picture Exhibitor,* 29 May 1946

Jasper finds that Hi-Octane, former race horse, now a fair plug, is pushed to great bursts of speed when he plays his fiddle. Jasper convinces the old horse to enter the derby once more, and in a fast comic sequence, with Jasper sawing away on his fiddle, old Hi-Octane comes through, and wins the derby. Excellent.

JASPER GOES FISHING (1943)

Company: George Pal, Paramount
Type: Puppetoons
Characters: Jasper, Scarecrow (voice characterization by Roy Glenn), Crow

Story: Opening credits are superimposed on Jasper fishing on a large lake as a black choral group sings in the background. The cartoon opens on a Sunday morning on Jasper's farm with the trees in bloom. Standing near a road is a ramshackle church with the Crow perched on top of the steeple. He is fast asleep and snoring when the church organ begins to play. The front door of the church opens, and the preacher walks out and rings the bell. The ringing wakes up the Crow who holds his hands over his ears before flying away and landing on the shoulder of the Scarecrow who is asleep standing in a nearby cornfield. The Crow is out of breath as he wakes up the Scarecrow who says, "What's the matter?" The Crow says, "The bell . . ." and the Scarecrow says, "They ringin' dat thing again. It's gettin' so a person can't sleep no mo' on a Sunday." The Crow says, "Naw, you can't sleep." The Scarecrow turns his head and says, "Now what's that?" as Jasper walks past them reading a book and singing, "No more cotton, no more pickin' cotton. We're goin' to the river." The Scarecrow calls out, "Hey dere Boy! What you mean yellin' dat way dis early in de mornin?" as he walks over to where Jasper has stopped in the road. The Crow says, "Is that necessary?" Jasper answers, "I's practicin' my songs fo' Sunday school" and continues on his way. The Scarecrow calls after him, "Come back heah, boy" and Jasper walks back. The Scarecrow asks him, "Do you like to fish?" Jasper smiles and nods his head yes. The Scarecrow says, "Why Boy, I knows a place where dere is de best fishin' in all de world." Jasper answers, "You does!" The Scarecrow continues, "And de fish—they's just swimmin' 'round beggin' fo' somebody to come and catch 'em." The Crow says, "Dere ain't no such place" and the Scarecrow says, "Will you button up dat big lip." He tells Jasper, "And boy dey is the biggest fish you done ever seen. Why, some of them is dis big" as he stretches his arms out like rubber to twice their length. The Crow shakes his head and says, "Dis is a bigger lie than dat man told in the last picture." The Scarecrow tells the Crow, "How would you like to be in a pie with a big crust over your head?" The Scarecrow continues, "Why boy, dere's so many fish dat they done drafted the ones without dependents." At this, the Crow shakes his head and says, "I don't know why I hangs around him anyway." The Scarecrow tells Jasper, "Come on Boy, I'll show you where dis good fishin' is" as he leads Jasper past the church. The Scarecrow says, "When I was a boy, we'd go fishin' everyday and twice on Sunday. And some of the fish we caught was so big . . ." as they arrive at the shore of a beautiful lake surrounded by tall mountains. They carry fishing poles on their shoulders and the Scarecrow says, "Well, here we are. Ain't that scrumptious." He tells Jasper, "Now you just stand there and count 'em while I haul 'em in." The Scarecrow throws his line into the water, and the

hook settles to the bottom of the lake. On the bottom the fish are holding a Sunday prayer meeting. The deacon fish stands before the congregation and sings, "Goin' to the river fo' to meet the comin' day! Goin' to de river not the legal way! Everybody's goin', goin' to the river. I'm goin' to the river, waitin' fo the comin' day. Are you goin'?" The congregation answers, "Sho' we're goin', goin' to the river to meet the comin' day." At this point the Scarecrow's fishhook comes to rest in front of the deacon's face. He looks up and shouts, "Who dat up dere disruptin' dese here services?" The congregation says, "Yeah deacon, there's a sinner up dere fishin' on the Sabbath. What dey mean droppin' dat hook dat way?" The deacon says, "Dey ain't supposed to be fishin' on a Sabbath day," and the congregation says, "What you say, Deacon? Yeah Deacon, what you say?" The deacon says, "Get after 'em, boys. And make 'em pay" and the others say, "Yeah man." The deacon yanks hard on the Scarecrow's line and on shore the Scarecrow says, "Lawdy me! We got a biggin'. Hold on, Jasper, we's got a holy mackerel." At the lake bottom the fish say, "Pull 'em in, Deacon." The deacon gives a hard pull on the line which yanks the Scarecrow, Jasper, and the Crow into the water. The trio sinks to the bottom of the lake and the Scarecrow says, "If you asks me, I'd say we were submerged." And the Crow says, "Not only dat, we is underwater." They look around and find themselves surrounded by hostile fish and try to run away. The deacon calls out, "Git 'em, boys" and the fish take off after them. They run in and out of the mouth of a giant fish and are attacked from above by a flying fish as the Scarecrow says, "Lawdy me! Flyin' fish!" and the Crow says, "Yeah, dive bombers." The fish drops a large bomb on the trio, but they keep running until they are stopped by a wall. A large sword sticks through the wall and the Scarecrow says, "What's dat?" The Crow answers, "It ain't no bread-and-butter knife." The sword cuts a door in the wall and a knock is heard. The Scarecrow says, "Come in," and the door opens and a giant swordfish swims through it. The fish chases them, and they hide in the barrel of a large cannon on a wrecked ship. The deacon fish lights the fuse on the cannon, saying, "Praise de Lord! We's got the ammunition." The cannonburst propels Jasper, the Scarecrow, and the Crow to the surface of the lake. They land on the ground near the small church. Jasper runs into the church, sits down, and smiles as the deacon says, "And that's the end of the lesson of the prodigal son who returned to the fold." The deacon closes the book and says, "Now sisters and brothers, we're all gonna go and get in some real good fishin'." Jasper's eyes pop out of his head and his face turns white with fear. He faints and falls flat on the floor as the cartoon ends.

Review: *Motion Picture Herald,* 13 September 1943

George Pal induces his animated models to tell an amusing moral in this Technicolor description of what happens when a little pickaninny, Jasper, goes fishing on Sunday. He has some narrow escapes from weird underwater creatures before he wakes up to find himself dreaming in the pew. (9 min)

Review: *Boxoffice*, 28 August 1943

One of the finer of the George Pal series is the latest in which Jasper meets temptation on the way to Sunday School when he confronts the Scarecrow and his blackbird. The height of imaginational fantasy is reached when Jasper and the Scarecrow cast their lines into the sea of fish observing the Sabbath. At Deacon Fish's behest they haul the fish line to the bottom with Jasper and the Scarecrow on the end of it, to teach them a lesson. Chastened, Jasper rushes to church to hear the preacher say "Now we're all goin' fishin'."

Review: *Besa Shorts Shorts*, 11 October 1943

It's that Scarecrow and Crow again out to tear down the morals of little Jasper, who is on his way to Sunday School. After all Jasper is just a lad and he can't withstand the fascinating fish stories told by the Scarecrow and goodness knows they are whoppers—so off they all go fishing while church is being held across the way. Way down at the bottom of the sea—so are the fish attending services and they don't like this Sunday fishing business so they teach Jasper and the rowdy Scarecrow a thing or three and you can darn well bet that Jasper is awful glad to be able to sneak into church and out of trouble.

JASPER GOES HUNTING (1944)

Company: George Pal, Paramount Pictures
Type: Puppetoon, Madcap Models
Characters: Jasper, Scarecrow (voice characterization by Roy Glenn), Crow, Mammy, Bugs Bunny

Story: The cartoon opens with an overview of Jasper's small farm. Standing next to the chicken coop, Mammy, wearing a polka-dot dress and a bandana on her head, has finished counting her chickens and says, "Well, I declare to goodness! Everytime I counts dem chickens there's another one missin." Standing in the cornfield nearby, the Scarecrow, with the Crow perched on his shoulder, is smacking his lips as he eats a chicken drumstick. He says, I sho' loves my chicken," and the Crow says, "You means you love your stomach." Ignoring him, the Scarecrow says, "Well, after all I'm just a growin' boy." The Crow says, "Yeah, with an appetite." The Scarecrow finishes his chicken and throws the bone at his feet where it lands on top of a pile of chicken bones. Meanwhile, in the house, Mammy is telling Jasper (who is holding a rifle), "Now Jasper, if you see anybody messin' 'round with dem chickens while I's gone, just chase 'em away." Jasper answers, "I will Mammy," as she leaves the house. Jasper imagines that he is a soldier all dressed up in a uniform and calling out drill cadence as he marches around the room. The Scarecrow and the Crow, looking through a window, observe him a few seconds before the Scarecrow says, "Hey dere, Boy." Jasper turns around and points the gun at them. The Scarecrow ducks and says, "Hold it! Put, put, put that gun down, Boy" The Crow says, "We gives up." Rising up, the Scarecrow says, "Don't ever point dat thing like dat, Boy. It's liable to go off." Then the Scarecrow enters the room, takes the gun from

Jasper, and says, "Let me see dat gun." He breaks the gun down and says, "Dat sure is a mean-lookin' thing. Reminds me when I hunted big game." The Crow says, "He means crap game—come seven, baby needs new shoes, little Joe, hot dog . . ."as the Scarecrow shouts at him, "Hold it." Continuing his story, the Scarecrow says, "Why I remembers as it wuz yesterday. It was in the Belgian Congo," as his clothes change to those of a big-game hunter. He says, "And right there, where their chair is, was a synthetic rubber tree," as the chair changes into a rubber tree. Next he says, "And right over there, where dat table is, was a great big rock" as the table turns into a rock. Continuing, the Scarecrow says, "And there was jungle all around—full of wild animals" as the room changes into an African jungle and the roar of lions is heard. Pointing to the ground, the Scarecrow says, "Look dere, Boy—feet prints" as they see the tracks of a large animal. They follow the footprints as the Scarecrow says, "'Course you know we ain't gonna shoot none of this little stuff. We is just goin' for the big one. The bigger they are, the better I's likes 'em. I shot an elephant one time, and he was so big, I raised my old .88 and drew a bead smack on him. And then I . . . "as the Crow looks behind them and sees a big elephant following close behind them. He tells the Scarecrow, "And you say you like the big ones?" The Scarecrow answers, "Yeah." The Crow says, "Well, that ain't no hummin' bird behind us" and they look behind them before running off and climbing to the top of a coconut tree. Sheepishly, the Scarecrow says, "Did you see that, Smarty? And the Crow says, "Yeah, you gonna run him to death." They continue to follow the animal prints when they come upon a hole in the ground. The Scarecrow looks down and says, "I sees you. Come on out and fight like a man. I got you covered. You can't get away." Out of the hole pops Bugs Bunny who looks around and says, "Eh, what's up, Doc?" as he chews a large carrot. The Scarecrow says, "Well, what do you know—Bugs Bunny." Bugs looks at him and says, "Hey, I'm in the wrong picture" and after waving good-bye dives back into the hole. The hunt resumes and Jasper asks the Scarecrow, "When is you gonna shoot an elephant? The Scarecrow answers, "Now don't worry, Boy. We'll run across one pretty soon." Just then they bump into the backside of a huge elephant. The Scarecrow shushes Jasper and sets the sights on his gun. He is about to shoot when a spear, thrown by one of three natives hiding behind a nearby rock, strikes the elephant in the rearend. They try to escape the angry elephant but it catches them on the end of its tusk and throws them high into the air. The Scarecrow and the Crow land back in Jasper's mammy's chicken coop. As they sit on the ground, eggs fall on their heads and break. Mammy, hearing the noise, goes to the chicken coop carrying her gun. She looks inside and sees the Scarecrow and Crow and tells them, "So you's the ones who's been stealing my chickens. I's got a good mind to call the police." The Scarecrow smiles and says, "Aw, they can't put you in jail for snitchin' a little chicken" as the scene changes to a jailhouse where the Scarecrow, dressed in prison stripes, looks sadly out of the barred window. The Crow, also a prisoner, looks out of his smaller cell and says, "I gotta write my congressman" as the cartoon ends.

Review: *Motion Picture Exhibitor,* 23 August 1944

Jasper's Mammy knows that someone is stealing her chickens, and she gives him a gun while she goes off to town. The Scarecrow, and the Blackbird, the real thieves, spot Jasper with the gun and the Scarecrow tells him of his big game hunting experiences. When the Scarecrow finishes the Mammy comes home, and finds him in the chicken coop trying to snatch another hen. He winds up in jail along with the Blackbird as the reel closes. Fair.

Review: *Boxoffice,* 26 August 1944

The excellent models precipitate in an amusing story of chicken theft, and a flight into fantasy of big-game hunting. In color, conception and execution of this short is decidedly superior and a novel introduction of Bugs Bunny, way off limits from his own stomping grounds, is the highlight of the reel.

Review: *Besa Shorts Shorts,* 15 November 1943

For the first time in screen history a cartoon star is being loaned to a rival studio. Bugs Bunny is going to guest star in George Pal's forthcoming Puppetoon, *Jasper Goes Hunting.* Bugs will make his appearance and after a suitable performance turn to the audience and shout "Hey, I'm in the wrong picture."

JASPER AND THE HAUNTED HOUSE (1942)

Company: George Pal, Paramount Pictures
Type: Madcap Models
Characters: Jasper, Scarecrow (voice characterization by Roy Glenn), Crow

Story: As the title and opening credits roll, a black choral group sings about how a gooseberry pie is made: "First I bakes the crust so it gets good and brown. Then I pares the berries—gooseberries. Get's 'em even with the brim-um mo' berries. Covers the top with flaky dough. There's some powerful eatin' in a gooseberry pie." The opening scene is a close-up of a freshly baked pie. The aroma of the pie drifts out over the cornfield where the Scarecrow is standing with the Crow perched on his shoulder. Scarecrow says, "What's that fumigating the atmosphere?" The Crow ways, "Yeah! What's that smelling up the landscape?" Just then they see little Jasper walking down the road carrying a large pie. When Jasper reaches a fork in the road, he is greeted by the Scarecrow, who asks him "Boy, where you takin' that gooseberry pie?" Jasper answers, "My mammy done told me to fetch it over to Deacon Jones." The Scarecrow lifts up one edge of the crust and says, "Say, that's a powerful lot of gooseberries." And the Crow says, "That pie is really stuffed." The Scarecrow asks, "You don't think the deacon would miss a few of them, do you?" Jasper replies, "I'd better get going" as he walks off in the direction of the deacon's house as directed by a road sign. The other direction points to a haunted house. The Scarecrow switches the two signs and then calls Jasper back. "Boy, Deacon Jones don't live down that way. He done dispossessed those premises. He done moved

down this way," pointing in the direction of the haunted house. Jasper replies, "But there ain't nothin' down that way but that haunted house." Scarecrow replies, "Oh, that house ain't haunted no mo'. Them hants, they's all been drafted." The Crow says, "They was all 1-A." Jasper replies, "Well, thank-you, Mr. Scarecrow, for sending me the right way." Jasper arrives at the old, deserted-looking haunted house and knocks softly on the door. Hearing no response, he pounds on the door, which mysteriously opens by itself. He cautiously enters a deserted room, holding the pie is both hands. The door slams and locks behind him. As Jasper passes a large standing clock, it opens and the Scarecrow yells out, "Put that pie on the table." Scared, Jasper throws the pie into the air and runs over to a piano and hides inside it while the pie lands on the table. The Scarecrow with the Crow on his shoulder walks over to the table, looks down at the pie, and says, "I sho' got one mess of a pie." The Crow says, "We sho' has, don't we?" He turns his head to look at the Crow and says, "We? What you mean 'we?'" The crow replies, "Well, we's we ain't we?" Meanwhile, a hidden panel in the wall behind the two opens and a knife floats out and over to the table where it cuts a large slice out of the pie. Knife and slice then disappear back into the wall. The Scarecrow turns around and sees that a piece of the pie is missing. He turns to the Crow and says, "Did you snitch that piece of pie?" The Crow says, "No, I didn't take no piece." The Scarecrow says, "Listen Blackbird, that was a whole pie here just a minute . . ." before he turns and sees that the whole pie is gone. It disappeared into the hidden panel on the wall when their backs were turned. They both turn toward the wall and see the panel open and an empty pie tray fly out and land on the table in front of them. They hear a voice say, "There you are, boys. Get your refund later." The frightened Scarecrow with the Crow jumps into the piano where Jasper is hiding. Next, footprints appear on the floor walking over to the piano where the mysterious voice says, "There's nothing like a little music." The piano stool rises, and a hot boogie-woogie tune is played by invisible hands. The voice says, "Yeah Man! Hot Cha!" The music gets so hot that it throws Jasper, Scarecrow, and Crow out of the piano, through the roof, and through a large billboard sign, which reads, Next time try Spooks' gooseberry pie. With their heads poking out of the large pie painted on the sign, Jasper asks, "What I'm I gonna to tell my mammy about that pie?" The Scarecrow tells him, "Don't you worry about that, Boy" as he gives Jasper the empty pie tray. Jasper takes the tray and repeatedly hits Scarecrow on the head with it as the cartoon ends.

Review: *Boxoffice,* 14 November 1942

Very Good. Jasper is delivering a gooseberry pie to Deacon Jones. He is misdirected and lured to a haunted house by a scarecrow. There follows some smart business with ghosts and weird atmosphere. These subjects are very well done. The artistic creativeness is readily apparent. Every segment of the audience will respond. (7 1/2 min)

Review: *Besa Shorts Shorts,* 2 November 1942

In beautiful Technicolor and very clever opening, little Jasper is found on his way to deliver a gooseberry pie to Deacon Jones. On the way there is the old Scarecrow with the black crow perching on his shoulder. They both confer on what is the best way to separate pie and Jasper. They decide on giving him the wrong directions to the Deacon's house, so little Jasper lands in the awful haunted house followed by the greedy Crow and Scarecrow. A ghost talks and walks and just about scares the living daylights out of Jasper but he gets away safely. Cunning little character, stunningly done with excellent negro dialect for them all.

JASPER IN A JAM (1946)

Company: George Pal, Paramount Pictures
Type: Puppetoons
Characters: Jasper, policeman (voice characterization by Roy Glenn), black female vocalist (voice characterization by Peggy Lee), background music Charlie Barnett and his orchestra

See fig. 14. Story: It is a cold and stormy night, and Jasper is lost in the big city. He huddles in the doorway in front of a pawn shop. A flash of lightning reveals that Jasper is inside the shop. It is a very scary place, and at first the only sound is the ticking of the many clocks on the walls around him. The clock strikes twelve, and the sound of music is heard. A doll is transformed into a black female vocalist who sings "Old Man Mose Is Dead." Musical instruments begin to move around, and a clarinet rolls to where a frightened Jasper is standing. As Jasper picks it up and begins to play a hot tune, the other instruments join in. Jasper seems to be having a good time when a wooden Indian suddenly starts to throw tomahawks at him. Jasper manages to duck all of them but is grabbed by a wooden statue and held tight. Jasper appears to be doomed until a loud knocking on the front door is heard and a voice calls out, "What's going on in there? Open the door!" The policeman manages to force his way in, not seeing Jasper as he speeds out the door past him. The policeman wakes up Moe, the night watchman, who tells him that all was quiet until he came along, as the cartoon ends.

Review: *Boxoffice,* 13 December 1946

Guaranteed to please all age groups with no let down in the entertainment provided by these newest adventures of Jasper. This time Jasper is forced to spend midnight in a pawn shop, and all the musical instruments and a cigar store Indian come to life. Charlie Barnett's orchestra provides top instrumental, and Peggy Lee does a rhythmic job on "Ole Man Mose Is Dead." The Technicolor is highly effective. (7 min)

Review: *Film Daily,* 27 September 1946

Charlie Barnett, his orch., and vocalist Peggy Lee provide the aural interest in this fantasy of Jasper and his adventures in a pawnship, while taking refuge from a storm. The musical instruments come alive and fascinate the boy. Probably cast a spell over the audience too, which should really like this one.

Review: *Motion Picture Herald,* 5 October 1946

The jam in this Technicolor short is the jam and jive of Charlie Barnett and his orchestra, plus the hot vocalist, Peggy Lee. The instrumental story takes place in a pawnship where, just as the clock strikes midnight, every musical instrument in hock comes to life. Miss Lee sings "Old Man Mose Is Dead." Charlie plays "Pompton Turnpike," and then everybody gets together for "Cherokee" while Jasper dreams he is trapped by a totem pole.

Review: *Motion Picture Exhibitor,* 2 October 1946

This fantasy shows off the band of Charlie Barnett and the voice of Peggy Lee. Jasper seeks refuge from a storm and goes into a pawn shop. At the stroke of midnight, all the musical instruments come to life. Peggy Lee is heard singing "Ole Man Mose Is Dead," and then Charlie Barnett and his band play "Pompton Turnpike" and "Cherokee." A policeman knocks on the door, and disturbs the pawnbroker who tells the officer that everything is quiet, and to go away. Good.

JASPER TELL (1945)

Company: George Pal, Paramount Pictures
Type: Puppetoons
Characters: Jasper, Scarecrow (voice characterization by Roy Glenn), Crow, Mammy

See fig. 15. Story: Cartoon opens in a field near Jasper's cabin where the Scarecrow, with the sleeping Crow perched on his shoulder, yells, "Hey!" and wakes up the Crow who says, "What's the matter?" The Scarecrow says, "Well, it's about time for breakfast. I could go for some ham and eggs, some sausage, and some toast and coffee, waffles, cantaloupes." Just then Jasper walks past them carrying a big red apple in his hand. The Crow asks the Scarecrow, "Would you settle for an apple?" The Scarecrow sees the apple and says, "Kinna makes my mouth water." The Crow says, "You is a drip, allright." The Scarecrow protests, "Can't we go through one picture without you makin' them insulting remarks?" The Crow pulls out the script and says, "I've got the script and it says right here . . ." as the Scarecrow reads the script. The Scarecrow says, "How come you get all the good lines?" before he calls out to Jasper, "Hey there Boy! Where you goin' with that apple?" Jasper says, "I'm takin' it to my teacher and she is gonna read us the story of William Tell" as he holds up a book. The Scarecrow says, "Oh, William Tell" as he takes the book from Jasper and begins to read the story. As the Crow looks on, the Scarecrow says, "If there's anything I hate its somebody reading over my shoulder." He then continues to read and then says, "Dis ain't the way it happened. They have got it all wrong." Jasper says, "They have?" and the Scarecrow tells him, "Sho' dey have. Give me the apple and I'll tell you how it really happened" as he takes Jasper's apple and places it on top of the boy's head. The Scarecrow then says, "Now once upon a time, long, long ago, maybe as much as a hundred years ago . . . " The scene changes to show the planet earth. The Scarecrow continues, "Way on the other side of the world there is a place by the name of Switzerland, which was full of hills and mountains and all that stuff." The scene changes to a small village surrounded by tall mountains. The Scarecrow continues, "There was a ruthless tyrant by the name of Jestler" as the scene shows Jestler dressed in Swiss clothing standing before his subjects. The Scarecrow continues, "On this particular day he had an announcement to make. Turning to one of his men, he tells him to read the proclamation." The man pulls out a scroll and reads, "It is hereby declared that all men will bow to Jestler's hat sittin' on top of the pole up there. Anyone failing to do so shall be seized and thrown into the dungeon of death." The Scarecrow continues his story. "Everybody looked up at the hat and started bowin' and bowin' for they knew that this was the law. While that was goin' on, there appeared on a nearby mountain a proud and noble man by the name of William Tell" as the scene shows William Tell (Scarecrow look-alike standing on a mountain with his bow and arrow and the Crow perched on his shoulder). The Scarecrow says, "Now William Tell liked to stand on the mountain and sing to his little boy." William Tell yodels and his son (Jasper look-alike standing on top of another mountain) answers him with a yodel of his own. Then William Tell and his son climb down their respective mountains and walk off toward the village together. The Scarecrow continues his story, "Now dis Jestler did not like to hear his people singin' and he told his soldiers to arrest that Alpine Sinatra." The soldiers seize William Tell and take him before Jestler who demands, "How come you ain't bowin' befo' de hat and how come . . . What's this?" He pauses to read the inscription on the medals pinned to William Tell's coat; It reads "Sharpshooter— Bow and Arrow." Jestler says, "So you're a sharp shooter, eh?" William Tell says, "Well, I didn't win these playin' gin rummy." This answer makes Jestler angry and he says, "Well, I'll give ya a chance to show how good ya are." He walks over to Tell's son and places an apple on top of his head and commands Tell to "shoot the apple off the boy's head." A hush comes over the crowd as William Tell makes ready with the bow and arrow and then takes careful aim while his son shakes with fear. But the son calms down and tells his dad, "Do your stuff, Pop." This was all William Tell needed to hear as he pulled his bow back and shoots the arrow. Everybody turns to watch the arrow as it flies to its target. The tyrant watches. William Tell watches as the arrow strikes the apple's dead center a few inches above his son's head. The crowd cheers, but Jestler can't believe his eyes. Then he calls to one of his men and says, "Fetch me dat hat from the top of the pole and fill it full of the biggest apples in the kingdom. William Tell is presented the hat full of apples as the scene changes back to the field near Jasper's cabin where Jasper watches the Scarecrow eat his apple as he says, "And that's the way it really happened." The Scarecrow finishes eating the apple and puts the apple core on the top of Jasper's head, saying, "Yes sir, Boy" as Jasper's mammy's voice calls out,

"Jasper, Jasper." Jasper answers, "Yes Mammy" and his Mammy says, "You bring dat apple right back here. It's all full of worms." Hearing this, the Scarecrow puts his hand over his mouth and his face turns green as Jasper runs home and the cartoon ends.

Review: *Motion Picture Herald*, 6 January 1945

Jasper has an apple for a teacher which is promptly appropriated by the scarecrow who distracts the boy with a modern version of the story of William Tell. Jasper is completely wrapped up in the tale of the arrow and the apple, the father and the son, played out again with the chalets, mountain yodelers and a bit of William Tell Overture. (8 min)

Review: *Boxoffice*, 7 April 1945

This attractively-Technicolored novelty maintains the standard established by George Pal, its producer. Utilizing to amusing effect the three previously established Puppetoon characters of Jasper, the scarecrow, and the blackbird, it parodies the story of William Tell and his son. In this version the scarecrow waylays Jasper and tells him about the Swiss archer in order to get the apple he (Jasper) is taking to his teacher. A surprise ending furnishes one of the best laughs in the picture. Picturesque Alpine backgrounds and an artistic musical accompaniment augments the entertainment value of the production.

Review: *Motion Picture Exhibitor*, 13 December 1944

Jasper is taking an apple to his teacher in school. The Scarecrow tells him a new version of William Tell, meanwhile eating up the apple. The Technicolor and miniature work are tops as the age old Swiss phantasy is re-created by the Pal technique. The William Tell Overture is played softly as background music, and a Yodeling chorus is another off screen feature. Excellent.

Review: *Besa Shorts Shorts*, 28 December 1944

It is down at Jasper's little house on the hill. Scarecrow and Crow are just waking up when along skips Jasper on his way to school, fortified by a big shiny apple for the teacher. The greedy Scarecrow wants that apple, immediately sets about to scheme Jasper out of it. He tells the story of William Tell and that little sharpshooting act of his. The story unfolds and has Jasper playing the role of the fearless son on an apple-shooter. It's a charming little yarn and ends with Scarecrow chomping on the apple. Jasper's mother calls to advise the cute little pickaninny that the apple was full of worms anyway.

JASPER AND THE WATERMELONS (1942)

Company: George Pal, Paramount Pictures
Type: Madcap Models, Puppetoons
Characters: Jasper, Scarecrow (voice characterization by Roy Glenn), Crow

See fig. 16. Story: The opening credits of the cartoon are super-imposed on a big watermelon, which fills the screen. The opening scene finds Jasper, a bug-eyed little black boy with thick white lips, taking a stroll through the family watermelon patch as the background music plays a jazzed-up version of "Shortnin' Bread." His mammy calls out to him from their little shack on the hill, "Jasper, Jasper! Don't go too far." He answers, "I won't, Mammy." As he looks at the melons and licks his lips, he stops, taps one, decides that it's ripe and that it will fit in his stomach. He is about to eat it when he hears his mammy's voice telling him, "Jasper stay outta dem watermelons! Does you all want to come down with the colic again?" Jasper walks away but soon runs back and is about to take a melon when he hears the Scarecrow say, "I wouldn't do dat if I were you. Jasper, didn't you hear what your mammy said?" The crow, perched on his shoulder, adds, "Yeah didn't you?" The Scarecrow says, "She don't want you messin' 'round dis melon patch" and the Crow adds, "Naw, she don't want you messin' 'round." The Scarecrow tells Jasper, "But I knows some place where dere's big ripe watermelons full of juice dat just trickles down your chin." Jasper smiles as the Scarecrow says, "They're luscious and they're all layin' 'round loose, just free for the takin'." The Crow protests, "Dere ain't no such place." Jasper asks, "Is dere all I can eat dere?" The Scarecrow tells him, "All you can eat! Why listen, Boy. Dat place is infested with watermelons and they's the biggest watermelons in the world. And some of 'em is even bigger than that." Jasper asks, "Is dey bigger den dese?" as he points to the ones in his patch. The Scarecrow tells him, "Bigger den dese. You ask me bigger den dese" and the Crow says "Yeah, you heard what he said." The Scarecrow says, "Go 'way, Blackbird. You bother me." He tells Jasper, "Why Boy, at this place I'm tellin' you 'bout, the roads is paved with watermelons." The Scarecrow and Jasper then find themselves in Watermelonland. The Scarecrow continues, "And dese ain't trees—they's big watermelons. The mountains, they ain't mountains—they's great big watermelons. And when it rains, it rains sweet watermelon juice. Why de rivers, they runs full up to the brim with pink watermelon juice." And the Crow adds, "Yeah, except for the seeds." Scarecrow tells him, "One of these days I's gonna radicate me a blackbird." Continuing his description of Watermelonland, the Scarecrow says, "What did I tell you? Look, just feast your eyes on this congregation." And they look at the gigantic watermelons all around them. The Crow says, "I don't believe it," and the Scarecrow tells Jasper, "But you ain't seen nothin' yet. I got plenty to show you befo' we gits outta this Watermelonland. Of course, you know you ain't supposed to eat any of 'em." Scarecrow hears a noise behind him and sees Jasper sitting on the ground beside a broken melon. The Scarecrow asks him, "You didn't eat any of dat, did you?" Jasper shakes his head no, but watermelon seeds fly out of both ears. The Scarecrow throws up his arms and says, "Lord's me! We's in fo' it now. Look a' dere" as he points to giant melons that come to life before their eyes. The melons are angry and sing, "There's gonna be trouble in Watermelonland today." Another melon says, "Sho' is." The melons repeat the song as they crowd around the Scarecrow and Jasper. They tell them, "You shouldn't have done it no

how. Whoever told them they could eat us melons? We'll fix that Jasper. Dat Scarecrow man caused all the trouble." Jasper and the Scarecrow run for their lives and after several narrow escapes, Jasper exits Watermelonland and returns to his farm, crying "Mammy, mammy" as he runs into his cabin and throws his arms around his mammy's waist. She pats him on his head and tells him, "Dere-dere child. Don't you cry 'cause your old mammy won't let nothin' hurt you. She picks him up in her arms and seats him at the table while telling him, "Mammy's got a surprise for you." She places a big slice of watermelon on the table in front of him. Jasper says "Oh" as he shakes his head. Outside, the Scarecrow is telling Jasper's pet dog, "I wouldn't be diggin' in this melon patch if I were you. Now I knows a place where dere's great big juicy ham bones full of marrow what just trickles down your chin" as the dog smiles. The Scarecrow continues, "They is the crunchiest bones in the world." The Crow adds, "Yeah, but dere ain't no meat on 'em." The Scarecrow says, "The trees, they's . . ." as a slice of watermelon thrown by Jasper hits him on his face and the juice drips from his chin. As the Crow laughs, a slice hits him in the face and the cartoon ends.

Review: *Motion Picture Herald,* 31 January 1942

This is a fantasy about a little colored boy, Jasper, whose desire for big ripe watermelons leads him into the fabulous watermelonland, where he meets with adventures that make him happy to be back again in the security of his mammy's arms. (10 min)

Review: *Time,* 9 March 1942

Jasper and the Watermelons is a new departure in the field of U.S. animated cartooning: it substitutes carved puppets and miniature sets for the drawn figures and backgrounds of the customary animated cartoon. Jasper, sixth of a series of ten-minute shorts which Paramount calls Puppetoons, is the first to enter successfully the animated cartoon's best realm-fantasy.

Jasper is a little Negro boy who can't stay away from the forbidden land of his mammy's melon patch. Hearing of a country where melons are free, he goes there with his scarecrow informer. But the melons aren't free, after all, and after he eats one of them, the other melons run him straight back to his mammy. Moral: don't talk to scarecrows.

This brief fantasy is keyed to a novel background score performed by a 50-piece symphony orchestra, to some Grade-A Negro choraling of "Shortnin' Bread" and "Nobody Knows the Trouble I've Seen," and to some very solid jive. The result is a colorful, intriguing, three-dimensional cartoon whose smooth animation is the result of considerable and clever technique.

Review: *Hollywood Reporter,* 9 February 1942

Jasper and the Watermelons opens a new field for the future of George Pal's clever Puppetoon creations. Frankly more of a fantasy than any of the previous five shorts Pal has turned out for Paramount release, "Jasper" gives promise of unlimited subject matter for the series, now in a second year. The smooth animation of the little wooden figures shows constant improvement of technique; for example, the amazing grace of Mammy's black hands when she comforts her mischievous pickaninny.

Jack Miller and Cecil Beard wrote the story of the troubles that beset Jasper when the little boy is tempted by his insatiable appetite for watermelons. He follows a live scarecrow, upon whose shoulder perches a blackbird with a Southern accent, into a land that has the biggest melons in the world, "some of dem even bigger dan dat." But the melons resent being eaten, and turning on Jasper and his companions, chase them home.

The picture gains splendid advantage from it's Technicolor photography, the high-grade musical scoring by William Eddison's symphony orchestra and the rich singing by the Carlyle Scott negro chorus in such selections as "Shortnin' Bread," and "Nobody Knows." It all adds up to another engaging Pal entertainment that will be talked about on any bill.

Review: *Time,* 9 March 1942

Jasper and the Watermelons (Pal:Paramount) is a new departure in the field of U.S. animated cartooning: it substitutes carved puppets and miniature sets for the drawn figures and backgrounds of the customary animated cartoon. "Jasper," sixth of a series of ten-minute shorts which Paramount calls Puppetoons, is the first to enter successfully the animated cartoon's best realm-fantasy.

"Jasper," is a little Negro boy who can't stay away from the forbidden land of his mammy's melon patch. Hearing of a country where melons are free, he goes there with his scarecrow informer. But the melons aren't free, after all, and after he eats one of them, the other melons run him straight back to his mammy. Moral: don't talk to scarecrows.

This brief fantasy is keyed to a novel background score performed by a 50-piece symphony orchestra, to some Grade-A Negro choraling of "Shortnin Bread," and "Nobody Knows de Trouble I've Seen," and to some very solid jive. The result is a colorful, intriguing, three-dimensional cartoon whose smooth animation is the result of considerable and clever technique.

JASPER'S BOOBY TRAP (1945)

Company: George Pal, Paramount Pictures
Type: Puppetoons
Characters: Jasper, Scarecrow (voice characterization by Roy Glenn), Crow

Story: Cartoon opens as sounds of work are heard coming from Jasper's little workshop. The door is closed and a sign on the shack reads Man at Work. Jasper exists the shop and walks by the Scarecrow, who is asleep with the Crow perched on his shoulder, holding a cooked chicken on a tray. The sleeping Scarecrow smells the aroma from the chicken and says, "Roast chicken," as his fingers walk down his shoulder toward the Crow who says, "Well, get him. He's walkin' in his sleep." The Scarecrow grabs the Crow and says, "Sho' does smell scrumptious" before he stuffs him into his mouth. Crow yells, "Wake up, Boss! You're havin' a nightmare. Wake up, I tell you!" The Scarecrow wakes up saying,

"What's goin' on? What's the matter? Why can't you keep your big mouth shut?" He notices that the Crow has turned white with fear. The Scarecrow says, "Man, you is de whitest blackbird I ever did see." Meanwhile Jasper spreads his picnic cloth on top of a well and places the roast chicken on it. The Scarecrow tells the Crow, "Pull yourself together, Jackson," as he fans the Crow with his hat and the Crow's color changes from white to black. The Crow says, "Don't you ever do a thing like that again, or so help me, I'll break every straw in your body." The Scarecrow says, "Simmer down feathered friend. I only wants to know what's cookin'." The Crow says, "Well, don't look at me. Look over there," pointing to the roast chicken. The Scarecrow says, "Get a load of that. My, My! Indeed a timely tidbit," as he pulls out his carving knife and begins to sharpen it. Jasper, hiding behind a tree, rings the dinner bell and the Scarecrow and Crow say, "Well, what are we waiting for?" before running to get the chicken. The Scarecrow leaves the Crow behind and dives on top of the chicken and falls into the well. The Crow sits on the side of the well and says, "There's somthin' screwy goin' on around here" as the Scarecrow's voice is heard calling for help and a splash of water rises from the well and hits the Crow in his face. Next Jasper is sitting under a tree removing bullets from a box and wrapping them into candy wrappers as the Crow watches him. After finishing, he rings the dinner bell. The Scarecrow runs to the candy and eats all of it before the Crow can warn him. When he finishes, the Crow says, "I wouldn't have eaten them things if I was you. That candy was tainted." The Scarecrow says, "Tainted?" and the Crow says, "Tampered with." The Scarecrow says, "Tampered with?" and the Crow says, "Don't look now but you've been booby-trapped." The Scarecrow says, "Booby-trapped!" as he hiccups and a bullet fires out of his mouth. The Crow says, "That should give you a vague idea" as the Scarecrow hiccups and another bullet shoots out of his mouth. The Scarecrow says, "Who would tamper with a poor starvin' Scarecrow's vittles?" The Crow says, "Well, if you stop shootin' off your trap, I'll tell ya." The Scarecrow asks, "Was it that Jasper boy?" and the Crow says, "Yessuh. Takes yuh life in yuh hands with every mouthful" as he points to a table loaded down with food. He looks at the food and says, "Well, what do you know—a blockbuster smorgasbord. Calamity a la cart. Misery on the half shell. Yo sho' nuff was right. Everything has been tampered with." The Crow then says, "Well, why don't you turn the tables?" The Scarecrow asks, "How?" The Crow says, "Well, make him eat his own booby traps." Jasper rings the dinner bell and the Crow says, "Steady, Boss. This is it." The Scarecrow says, "I'm gonna teach dat boy a lesson he'll never forget" as they walk over to the table piled high with food. Jasper offers the Scarecrow turkey and the Crow says, "Careful, it's a trap." So the Scarecrow says, "No thanks, Boy. But you go ahead. You can eat it yourself." The Scarecrow and the Crow laugh while Jasper eats all of the turkey with no ill effects. Next Jasper offers them a juicy porterhouse steak. The Scarecrow says, "I am sure . . ." before he is interrupted by the Crow who says, "It's a land mine smothered in onions." The Scarecrow tells Jasper, "Well, I guess not. It's a little early in the day for a steak" and then whispers into the Crow's ear, "Are you sure you aren't givin' me a wrong steer?" Jasper finishes the steak and the Crow says, "He's just lullin' you into a false sense of security." One after another Jasper offers them fruit salad, crepes suzette, and strawberry tarts, all of which they refuse. Jasper eats them all with no problem. All of the food is gone and Jasper says "Excuse me please. Good-by." As he leaves, the Scarecrow looks at the bare table with tears running down his cheeks and says, "Gone, gone, everything gone. Not a single morsel to sustain me, not a scrap, not a miserable little crumb. Food, food! I must have food, food, food. I must have food. What cruel fate has dealt me this foul blow." Pointing to the Scarecrow, the Crow says, "Get that ham," as they walk away. The Scarecrow says, "Ham, ham. Where, what voice mocks me in my misery? Food, food! I must have food" as he sees a single olive sitting on a plate. The Scarecrow says, "glory be, an olive!" and the Crow says, "You'll be sorry" as he flies away. The Scarecrow says, "But I must have it, must . . ." and he picks it up and puts it into his mouth and is blasted into the sky, as if by a rocket. Meanwhile the Crow lands on Jasper's head, sees the cigar on the table, and says, "One cigar for a gentleman." Jasper picks up the cigar and its explodes, blowing him and the Crow all the way back inside Jasper's workshop. The walls of the shop collapse around them and the Crow, sitting on Jasper's head, as white as snow, says, "I'm not gonna say it. I'm not . . ." as the cartoon ends.

Review: *Motion Picture Exhibitor,* 30 May 1945

Jasper, knowing the tremendous appetite of his friend, the Scarecrow, sets some fancy food, such as roast chickens, steaks, etc. out in front of the Scarecrow with boobytraps attached, but after the first one the Scarecrow refuses to touch any food. Then Jasper sits down and polishes off the entire supply. The olive remains, and the Scarecrow reaches for it when it proves to be a super boobytrap. Jasper gets a cigar which is loaded, and everybody has an explosive time. Good.

Review: *Boxoffice,* 16 June 1945

Jasper turns a potential feast for the starving Scarecrow into a miniature blitz by planting a series of booby traps in a picnic lunch of tempting delicacies. Blackbird warns the Scarecrow to be wary, and he allows Jasper to gorge himself with no disastrous results. A charged olive proves Scarecrow's undoing, and Jasper is awarded a big black exploding cigar. (8 min).

Review: *Besa Shorts Shorts,* 25 June 1945

Finally, after all the times that Scarecrow and Black Crow have outwitted little Jasper, the little black boy starts to get even. He puts luscious looking food all around for Scarecrow to eat some. Scarecrow tries to eat but every time finds he has been tricked. Determines not to touch any more of Jasper's tainted food and passes up one whole table of the stuff, and watches Jasper wolf it down with no ill effects. Finally succumbs to the beckoning charms of a plain little olive and is blown sky high.

JASPER'S CLOSE SHAVE (1945)

Company:	George Pal, Paramount Pictures
Type:	Puppetoons
Characters:	Jasper, Scarecrow (voice characterization by Roy Glenn), Crow

Story: The cartoon opens in Jasper's cabin, where Jasper is looking at himself in the mirror. When he sees that a hair is growing on his face, he jumps up and down and says, "Bless my britches! I got whiskers. I need to shave. Hooray! Hooray! I need a shave." He shakes fifteen cents out of the piggy bank he keeps under his mattress and runs outside to find the Scarecrow as he calls out "Oh, Professor Scarecrow, I've got whiskers." He climbs over the fence and runs to where the Scarecrow is sleeping with the Crow perched on his shoulder. He shakes the Scarecrow, saying, "Wake up! Wake up! I gotta talk with Professor Scarecrow. I gotta, I gotta . . ." The Crow says, "Whom shall I say is calling?" Jasper says, "It's me—it's Jasper." The Crow says, "And, uh, what is the nature of your business?" Jasper says, "Whisker business, that's what. It's about my big, long, fuzzy-wuzzy beard." The Crow looks closely at him and says, "Boy, barbers cost money—lots of money." Jasper asks, "Even more than fifteen cents?" as he shows the Crow the coins he is holding in his hands. The Scarecrow wakes up and asks. "Uh, what fifteen cents? You mean fifteen cents? Who's talkin' that high finance?" The Crow replies, "The little shaver has got fifteen cents." The Scarecrow says, "Umm, let me see now. Barber man, shave, fifteen cents" as he counts on his fingers. "It all adds up. Boy, step right up in the chair. You done picked yo' self the right shop." The Crow says, "Yeah, the right shop to get clipped." Jasper asks, "Is you an honest-to-goodness, cross-my-heart shavin' barber sho' nuff?" The Scarecrow says, "Is I a barber, the gentleman asks." He turns and whispers, "Make like a barber pole" in the Crow's ear. The Crow changes his color to red and white stripes and then turns around and around. The Scarecrow tells Jasper, "Of course, there is a slight cover-up charge. This is the the cover-up." He wraps a cloth around Jasper as he sits on a tree stump. The Scarecrow tells Jasper, "My assistant will accept the fifteen cents" as Jasper drops his coins into a slot on top of the Crow's head. The Scarecrow says, "Yes sir, You'll really get wrapped up in my work on account that I'm a whiz on turnin' out gentlemen" as he continues to wrap the cloth completely around Jasper's head and body. Then he pulls hard on the end of the cloth, causing Jasper to spin so fast that he is propelled from the stump like a rocket. He lands in a glass barber chair in a strange place that looks like a fancy barber shop. A sign on the wall reads Barber of Seville and the background music plays a selection from the opera of the same name. The Scarecrow appears dressed in costume as if he were playing the title role. The Crow, perched on his shoulder, is also dressed in costume. The barber sings as he mixes shaving cream and approaches the chair where Jasper is sitting. He smears the cream on Jasper's face, and then strops his razor. Jasper is scared and cries out, "Professor Scarecrow, is you sho' you knows yo' business?" The barber answers, "Do I know my business? Boy, I's givin' you de business." Meanwhile the Crow flies over to Jasper and shines his toes with a cloth. The barber wraps a hot towel on Jasper's head, uses a hot iron to curl a single hair sticking out of Jasper's head, and then squirts him with cologne. The Crow lands again on the Scarecrow's shoulder and says, "Blow your top! Blow your top!" The barber slaps the Crow off his shoulder and attempts to shave Jasper. Jasper jumps out of the chair and hides behind the barber pole. The barber chases Jasper around and around the shop before they both wind up back on the farm. Jasper, his face covered with shaving cream, sits on the stump turning around and around while the Scarecrow attempts to shave him. Jasper jumps up and runs back inside his cabin where he washes the cream off his face and head. He looks into the mirror and discovers that his head has been shaved clean and says, "Jeepers! He shaved my head." He picks up a bar of soap and throws it through the open window. It lands in the open mouth of the Scarecrow, who is still singing. He then gets his gun and fires it at the fleeing Scarecrow and Crow as the cartoon ends.

Review: *Motion Picture Herald,* 4 August 1945

The great moment in Jasper's life comes with his discovery of whiskers. Off he goes with 15 cents for a shave, but in some fashion the Scarecrow lures him into a clip joint where, to the tunes from "Barber of Seville," he gets just what he doesn't want. Scarecrow plays Figaro with additional appropriate lyrics and with great flourishes shaves the hair off Jasper's head. (10 min)

Review: *Boxoffice,* 28 July 1945

Even better than the high standard usually maintained by George Pal is this fast moving one-reeler. It is backed with an exceptionally fine musical score—much of it from "The Barber of Seville"—and presented in lavish settings. The picture boasts more production value than is usually found in this type of film. The plot deals with the Scarecrow's efforts to remove Jasper's newly discovered beard and 15 cents, the usual shaving charge for one hair whiskers. Characteristically the Scarecrow clips Jasper in more ways than one.

Review: *Besa Shorts Shorts,* 16 July 1945

Mr. George Pal has the courage to have moppet Jasper think he is growing a beard in this one. In his thatched cottage in front of his mirror, Jasper convinces himself that there are some evidences of a chin stubble. With fifteen cent jingle-jangling in his pockets he dashes out to the sophisticated Scarecrow for barbering. The crafty Scarecrow realizes that he can get that fifteen cents. With his stooge, the Black Crow, he takes the hopeful Jasper on a shaving tour that is something to behold.

Review: *Motion Picture Exhibitor,* 8 August 1945

The famous "Barber of Sevelle" aria inspires this amusing cartoon of little Jasper's first shave. With 15 cents, he goes in

hunt of a barber who can do the job, and meets up with the Scarecrow and pal, the Blackbird, who convince him that they are experienced barbers. While singing the "Figaros" and wielding a tremendous razor, the Scarecrow starts the shave. When all is done Jasper, who was mortally afraid, finds that his head, not his beard, was shaved. Good.

JASPER'S MINSTRELS (1945)

Company: George Pal, Paramount Pictures
Type: Puppetoons
Characters: Jasper, Mammy, Scarecrow (voice characterization by Roy Glenn), Crow

Note: The Georgia Minstrels, mentioned in this cartoon, referred to the first black-owned minstrel company, managed by Charles Hicks. The company toured the United States and abroad between 1865 and the 1880s. "Carry Me Back to Old Virginny" was written by James Bland, songwriter and black-minstrel man who also wrote "Oh Dem Golden Slippers."

Story: The cartoon opens as Jasper is having a good time in his yard swinging on his swing, as "Dixie" plays in the background. Jasper's mammy comes out of the front door of their little shack on the hill, calling out, "Jasper! Jasper Hawkins!" Jasper answers, "Yes, Mammy." She tells him, "You git down there off of dat swing dis here minute and come in dis house." But Jasper keeps on swinging and says, "Ah, just when I was havin' so much fun." Then Mammy shouts, "Jasper!" and he jumps off the swing, saying, "And all I was doin' was just sittin' there havin' a good time." Reluctantly he walks into the house where Mammy tells him, "Now you take this coat over to Deacon Jones right away." Jasper replies, "All right, Mammy." As he leaves the house carrying the deacon's coat, Mammy tells him, "You don't get no dirt on it" as the background music plays "Swanee River." In a cornfield the Crow, perched on the shoulder of a sleeping Scarecrow, taps him on his stovepipe hat and says, "Hey, hey, wake up! Look a there! Look!" The Scarecrow wakes up and says, "What's goin' on? What's the matter?" The Crow tells him, "Look at what's goin' down the road," and the Scarecrow sees Jasper carrying the coat. He says, "Dat's a mighty fine sharp lookin' coat dat boy is carryin' there. Now ain't dat a coincidence, I was just thinkin' this old shirt was gettin' a little frayed." The Crow tells him, "A little frayed—it's scared to death." The Scarecrow tells the Crow, "Why must you always open dat sassy mouth." The Scarecrow calls out to Jasper, "Just a minute there, Boy" as he walks toward Jasper and then says, "What do you have there?" Jasper replies, "It's the deacon's coat." The Scarecrow takes a close look at the coat and says "That sho' is a fancy number. And look at dem tails. Hot dog! You know dat coat looks just like the one I wore when I was with Dixie Wheeler's Georgia Minstrels. I was an interlocutor—you know, the emcee." The Crow says "Yeah, M-C. Mostly con." The Scarecrow replies, "Quiet, Blackbird." He takes the coat away from Jasper saying, "Hey, gimmie dat coat, Boy, and I will show you how we used to put on a minstrel show." He puts the coat on and finds that it is a tight fit. Jasper asks him, You ain't gonna hurt it, is you?" The Scarecrow says, " 'Course I won't" and then describes his minstrel days. "Well first, Boy, I gives them the patter out in front," as the scene changes to the front of a theater where the Scarecrow is welcoming the patrons, saying, "Hurry, hurry, hurry! Step right up and get your tickets to the Dixie Minstrels. The show is just about to start folks, so hurry, hurry!" As the audience applauds, the curtain rises and the show begins with a vocal duet of the song "Polly Wolly Doodle All Day." Next the Scarecrow says, "Gentlemen be seated." He plays the straight man in a comedy routine with Mr. Bones and Mr. Tambo. Next the Scarecrow introduces the Dixieland Quartet, which sings "Carry Me Back to Old Virginny." This is followed by a final act, "Dixie," sung by the entire company with the Scarecrow playing the banjo. The curtain falls, and the Scarecrow walks stage front and stands before the footlights and bows to the audience as a ripping sound is heard. The scene changes back to Jasper's farm where Jasper, seeing the rip in the deacon's coat, says in a loud voice, "You went and ripped the deacon's coat." His Mammy, who is sweeping the front porch, hears him and says, "So fibbin' again, tellin' Jasper tall tales" as she walks to the Scarecrow. She hits him repeatedly on his head with her broom saying, "Take dat and dat and dat!" as the cartoon ends.

Review: *Film Daily,* 3 March 1945

A frock coat which Jasper is delivering to the deacon is the object of the Scarecrow's desire. To get Jasper to part with the garment, the villain regales him with a story of his days as a minstrel. That leads to a fanciful and highly entertaining flashback picturing a minstrel show of which the Scarecrow is interlocutor. The Technicolor item ends with Jasper's ma chasing the Scarecrow for tearing the frock coat. Excellent. (9 min)

Review: *Motion Picture Herald,* 17 March 1945

Jasper is again waylaid by the Scarecrow, this time on his way to the deacon with a black frock coat. It reminds the Scarecrow of his minstrel days, which he re-creates with jokes and soft shoe routines for an entranced audience of one. Scarecrow, in a black coat, bows to applause at the end and a harsh tearing sound spoils the whole effect. Mammy is wielding her broomstick as the curtain falls. (9 min)

Review: *Motion Picture Exhibitor,* 27 March 1945

Jasper passes the Scarecrow on his way to deliver a black coat to Deacon Jones. The Scarecrow tells the boy about the time he was in a minstrel show, and puts on the Deacon's coat. Then follows a sequence in which the Scarecrow plays the part of the interlocutor. Typical minstrel acts including jokes, quartet singing, soft shoe dancing, etc. wind up this reel. Good.

Review: *Besa Shorts Shorts,* 12 May 1945

Jasper Hawkins is yanked from his swinging pleasures down under the old tree by Mammy and sent to deliver the Deacon's coat. You know who stops him on the way—Scarecrow and Crow. The big whopper told this time by Scarecrow is about the time he was a star in the Dixie Minstrels. This allows for some

very handsome production as the cartoon goes into a minstrel show including many George Pal characters. Songs of the deep south abound and the color and music are swell. The ending comes with the Deacon's coat being ruined by Scarecrow. Jasper is absolved from blame by Mammy's broomstick.

Review: *Boxoffice,* 24 March 1945

Jasper, passing a cornfield on his way to deliver a coat to Deacon Jones, is stopped by the Scarecrow who tries to talk him out of the coat. He tells Jasper he used to be with a minstrel show, and dons the coat in order to illustrate some old minstrel routines. Ensues a sequence wherein the scarecrow, as Intelocutor, takes part in an old times Dixie minstrel show. The company has an all Scarecrow cast. Following the minstrel show's finale, the Scarecrow takes a bow-and rips the Deacon's coat. At end, he gets his own coat tails fanned by Jasper's irate Mammy.

JASPER'S MUSIC LESSON (1943)

Company:	George Pal, Paramount Pictures
Type:	Puppetoons
Characters:	Jasper, Scarecrow (voice characterization by Roy Glenn), Crow, Mammy

See fig. 17. Story: The Cartoon opens outside Jasper's cabin. The sound of a piano can be heard through a broken window. Jasper is practicing his lessons. Standing in a nearby cornfield is the sleeping Scarecrow with the Crow perched on his shoulder. The music wakes them up, and the Scarecrow says, "Dat is probably the sorriest playin' I done ever heard. The Crow adds, "Yeah. Makes your blood curdle." The Scarecrow says, "We gotta stop that ruckus." The Crow answers, "Yah, we gotta ration dat stuff." The Scarecrow says, "Come on" as they go to the window and see Jasper picking the piano keys with his fingers. The Scarecrow shouts through the window, "Hey, Boy, what you doin' with dat piano?" The Crow says, "Yeah, what you pounding on dat thing?" Jasper says, "My Mammy says I got to practice my lessons to play good like him" as he points to a bust of Chopin sitting on top of the piano. The Scarecrow and the Crow walk inside Jasper's cabin and take a look at the bust. The Scarecrow says, "You mean choppin'?" and the Crow says, "Naw, that's Chopin, you dope." The Scarecrow looks at the Crow and tells him, "One of these days I's gonna radicate me a blackbird." Jasper says, "He wrote all dem classics." The Scarecrow responds, "Aw, who wants to play all dem classics? 'Course I ain't got nothin' against all dem boys like Chopin or ugh . . ." The Crow says "Kelly" and the Scarecrow says "Kelly." The Crow says "Or Wilki" and the Scarecrow says "Wilki" and the Crow says "or Joe Louis" and the Scarecrow says "Or Joe . . . Will you keep that big claptrap shut." The Scarecrow tells Jasper, "Why boy, let old maestro at the piano so I can give you a real music lesson." Jasper climbs down from the piano stool, dusts it off, and says, "You mean you can play the piano?" Jasper turns the stool to adjust the height but the top comes off, leaving the sharp point of the screw for the Scarecrow to sit down on. But before the Scarecrow sits all the way down, Jasper replaces the top of the stool. The Scarecrow says, "You lookin' at a man what knows all the keys and the black ones too. "First I gets comfortable." He plays a few notes before saying, "Say, ain't that pretty." Jasper nods his head yes. As the Scarecrow plays the white keys, he says, "Now look here Boy, dese white keys is all right for dem scales. But you gotta get up on the black ones for the real hot stuff." He begins to play boogie-woogie music on the black keys. Jasper's eyes get big and he smiles as he listens to the music. The Scarecrow pauses and says, "See what I mean?" Jasper nods his head yes. The Scarecrow turns the page of the sheet music and says, "Now you take Chopin, your friend up there" as he begins to play classical music. He continues, "Chopin is all right, but I sneaks in the pinsecata to fuzzy it up like dis" as he changes to playing hot boogie. When he says "dere you are," the music gets so hot that the piano shakes and the bust of Chopin falls and breaks on the floor. The Crow says, "What's he blowin' up about?" The Scarecrow says, "Well, I will never forget the night I played for de king." Jasper asks, "A real king?" and the Scarecrow answers, "They brought me into court . . ." and the Crow says "Yeah, and they gave you thirty days." The Scarecrow says, "Quiet, Blackbird!" before he continues. "And dere all prettied up in my tails" as the scene changes to show the Scarecrow dressed in formal clothes. "And instead of a box like dis—I was seated in front of a great big grand piano" as Scarecrow appears seated in front of a big grand piano. The Crow, wearing a top hat, says, "That's the biggest lie that man ever told." The Scarecrow continues, "And where dem windows is was a great big elegant plush curtain" as a big curtain appears in front of the window in Jasper's cabin. The Scarecrow continues, "Instead of a little old boy like you standin' there, there was a very distinguished audience" as the scene changes from Jasper's room to a concert hall filled to capacity with people. The audience applauds as the Scarecrow takes a bow, tips his hat before sitting before a large grand piano and starts to play the classics before quickly changing to boogie-woogie. The audience, all looking like Jasper, sways back and forth in time with the music. The Crow plays the keys with his beak as the Scarecrow's piano playing gets so fast that the piano begins to smoke. The Crow says, "Look at dat man burn up dat piano" as flames shoot out of the piano. From the outside of Jasper's cabin smoke is seen coming out of the broken window. At this time Jasper's mammy, wearing a bandanna on her head and carrying a basket of groceries, arrives back home. She hears the music and sees the smoke and says, "Well, I declare to goodness! What dat boy up to?" She hurries to the front door where she drops her basket and picks up a broom. As she opens the door and says "Jasper," the interior scene changes back to Jasper's cabin. Mammy says, "And for dat Scarecrow man, I hit him over the top of the de head with dis broom. Get on with you!" As she rushes inside she says, "Git out of dis house! Skat and take dat and dat" as she hits the Scarecrow with the broom. The Scarecrow and the Crow jump out the window as Mammy says, "Take dat blackbird with you and don't you ever let me catch you 'round dis house again." Next she points at Jasper and

tells him, "And you, Jasper, you git back to yo' lesson dis very minute." Jasper starts to play the scales slowly before he changes to boogie-woogie. His mammy sits nearby and taps her feet to the music and she says, "Now dat's it, Jasper. You stick with dem classics and you'll be a great piano player like Patrophristie" as Jasper plays hot boogie. Mammy smiles and laughs "hah-hah" as she taps her feet and the cartoon ends.

Review: *Motion Picture Herald,* 29 May 1943

Jasper is working away at his piano practice when the Scarecrow and Crow appear with views of their own about music. Classics are all right in their place, but boogie woogie's the thing. The Scarecrow gives a demonstration while Jasper dreams up the setting, but his mammy arrives with a broom and Jasper's back with his music lesson. (8 min)

Review: *Boxoffice,* 29 May 1943

Humor, boogie woogie and good strong material abound in this short which is packed to the brim with wholesome entertainment. Little Jasper, the Scarecrow, and the Crow play some hot licks on the piano, so that, in fact, a figure of Chopin is blasted to pieces. The boogie woogie is such to put average audiences in the groove for the balance of the show.

Review: *Besa Shorts Shorts,* 24 May 1943

With magnificent color, music, and an incomparable Pal technique, the little puppetoon starts its story with Jasper doing his scales as per his Mammy's instruction. Outside the discords annoy Mr. Scarecrow and his little chum, the Crow. They proceed to the house to put a stop to it. But Mr. Scarecrow gets so involved in a session of boogie that they linger. Jasper wants more boogie woogie than even before and there are miracles of camera work in Mr. Scarecrow's yarn which the old Crow says is the biggest lie one ever heard. While the tempo grows more torrid, comes Mammy to rout the intruders and put Jasper back to his practicing which this time turns into boogie woogie.

JASPER'S PARADISE (1944)

Company: George Pal; distributed by Paramount Pictures
Type: Puppetoons
Characters: Jasper, Scarecrow (voice characterization by Roy Glenn), Crow, gingerbread man (voice characterization by Joel Fluellen), heavenly voice (voice characterization by Joel Fluellen)

Story: The Cartoon's opening finds Jasper skipping along a country road, carrying a freshly baked gingerbread man cookie in his hands and saying, "I've got a gingerbread man that my mammy baked for me." Along the way he passes the Scarecrow, asleep in a nearby field with the Crow perched on his shoulder. The Crow jumps up and down and cries out, mocking Jasper, "I've got a gingerbread man. I've got a gingerbread man my mammy baked for me." He wakes up the Scarecrow who tells him to be quiet. But when he smells the aroma of Jasper's cookie, he says, "Ummm, ummm. That Jasper boy done got himself a cookie. Hey there Boy, What you got there?" as he walks over to Jasper. Jasper answers, "It's a gingerbread man. But I ain't gonna eat 'em. I's always gonna keep him just the way he is." The Scarecrow says, "Let me see him, Boy. I won't hurt him." Jasper replies, "No, no, no. I won't do it. You always takin' everything I get. But you ain't gonna take my gingerbread man" as he runs down the road. The Scarecrow, shaking his head, says, "Why is it nobody ever trusts me?" the Crow replies, "Well, if you ask me . . ." But the Scarecrow cuts him off by saying, "Don't answer that." Meanwhile Jasper sits down under a tree to take a rest and soon falls asleep. The gingerbread man comes to life and calls out, "Jasper." When Jasper does not wake up, the gingerbread man grows larger and pats Jasper on the shoulder saying, "Wake up there, Sonny." Jasper wakes up and the gingerbread man asks him, "Aren't you the boy who doesn't eat gingerbread men?" Jasper nods his head in the affirmative and the gingerbread man continues, "Well, you just come along with me. I've got a big surprise for you." He takes Jasper by the hand and leads him to a flight of stairs that stretch into the sky. They both climb the stairs, but the gingerbread man stops. Jasper asks him, "Aren't you gonna go with me?" The gingerbread man replies, "No, you go ahead Jasper," and Jasper continues to climb. He disappears into the clouds and reappears wearing a white robe, with a pair of angel wings on his back and an halo over his head. At the top of the stairs Jasper finds a large gate and he says, "Oh boy!" The gate opens and a heavenly voice tells him, "Come in, Jasper. Come on, Boy. There's nothing to be afraid of." Jasper walks through the gate as the voice tells him, "That's it. Now look here, Boy, all those luscious cakes all free for the taking." Jasper smiles and his eyes get big as the voice tells him what he can have. "Now here, Boy, is a chocolate layer cake." Jasper walks over to the cake, takes a taste, and says, "For me?" The voice answers, "Yes, you can have all you can eat." The voice continues, "Over here there's a honey drippin' angel food cake and by the way Boy, do you like bananas?" Jasper nods his head yes and the voice says, "Well, feast your eyes on this luscious banana cream cake. How about a piece of golden lemon cake? A sweet juicy strawberry short cake? Whipped cream? There's all kinds here, Boy, and they are all yours." Jasper smacks his lips as he sees a large white cake with a big red cherry on top. Jasper reaches for the cherry but stops when the voice tells him, "Now wait a minute, son. There's one thing I forgot to tell you. You mustn't touch that cherry!" Jasper turns to walk away but is stopped by the Scarecrow, who materializes from a puff of smoke. The Scarecrow, who has a long tail and horns on his head, tells Jasper "I am the devil, ha-ha." The Crow, perched on his shoulder, tells him "Oh boy, what a ham!" The Scarecrow tells Jasper, "That's a mighty pretty cherry there, Jasper. You can eat it if you want to." Jasper asks him, "Do you really think it's all right? The Scarecrow replies, "Of course it's all right if I say so. Go ahead." The Scarecrow laughs and disappears in a puff of smoke. Jasper

walks to the cake and is about to take the cherry when the heavenly voice tells him, "Un-uh, Jasper. Remember what I tells you." Jasper stops but the Scarecrow reappears and tells him, "Pay no attention to him. Go ahead and take it." Again the heavenly voice says "Jasper, you is messin' with the forbidden fruit." The verbal tug of war between good and evil continues with Jasper in the middle until the Scarecrow takes the cherry off the cake and puts it in Jasper's mouth. Immediately claps of thunder are heard and the ground begins to shake. All of the cakes start to crumble, and Jasper and the Scarecrow escape by sliding down the ladder to the ground where Jasper wakes up from his dream. It is raining, and he discovers that his gingerbread man is missing. In the distance he sees the Scarecrow holding the gingerbread man and about to eat it. Jasper says, "Oh, my gingerbread man" and runs over and grabs it from the Scarecrow and runs home. The Scarecrow says, "What's the matter with that boy? He acts like he mad at me. All I was gonna do was keep it for him." Immediately he is struck by bolts of lightning as he runs off and the cartoon ends.

Review: *Motion Picture Herald,* 20 October 1944

Jasper resists temptation and falls asleep with his gingerbread man intact. He dreams of a paradise filled with huge cakes, all his to eat except the cherry, which he is forbidden to touch. In the steps of his early ancestors he heeds the promptings of the Scarecrow, reaches for the cherry, and is exploded from paradise by a terrific clap of thunder. He wakes up, once more under the tree. (7 1/2 Min)

Review: *Boxoffice,* 7 October 1944

This is a marvelous combination of the superlative talents of the originator of this series. It is a delightful flight into fantasy, recounting the tale of what happens to Jasper when he falls asleep and finds himself in a veritable paradise of delectable cakes, a reward for not eating a gingerbread man. The color and conception are outstanding and should continue the reputation established for this cartoon.

Review: *Besa Shorts Shorts,* 16 October 1944

Jasper's Mammy has given him a gingerbread man and of course old Scarecrow wants it. Jasper refuses to give it up—indeed he will not even eat it himself. He naps beneath a tree and dreams that his gingerbread man comes to life and leads him to a paradise of giant luscious cakes which he can have. But there's a catch in the cakepile. He must not eat a certain cherry. Scarecrow appears as a Satan and persuades him to eat it and down comes the cakes, Jasper and all.

MY MAN JASPER (1945)

Company:	George Pal, Paramount Pictures
Type:	Puppetoons
Characters:	Jasper, Scarecrow (voice characterization by Roy Glenn), Crow, cannibals

Story: The cartoon opens as Jasper, wearing the Scarecrow's hat, is trying to do the Scarecrow's job but is surrounded by crows. He says "Shoo, shoo! Go away! Mr. Scarecrow, what am I gonna do? Dese birds don't scare easy." The Scarecrow, resting under a shade tree and holding the book *Robinson Crusoe* before him, says, "You gotta work harder, Boy, if you wants your book back." Jasper answers, "Yes sir." The Scarecrow tells the Crow, "Now feathered friend, read on." The Crow reads, "So Robinson Crusoe latches on to the island and Jack he is solid. He digs himself a mellow mess of dims and das . . ." The Scarecrow interrupts, "Don't read me that jive talk, chickadee, just read what the book says." The Crow then reads, "It was on ye fair isle that ye Robinson Crusoe spendeth a score of years in idle bliss mid exotic flowers heavy with lush perfume." The Scarecrow says, "Man, that's for me, Shangri-la with built-in music and flowers. You know I'd make a solid sendin' Crusoe" as the scene changes and the Scarecrow is lying in a swing under a palm tree on an island surrounded by palm trees. The Scarecrow continues, "Yes, we just la la there smack in the lap of luxury—and you, chickadee, makin' like the parrot bird given' out with that swooning stuff." Playing a ukulele, the Crow sings, "Night and you and blue Hawaii, the night is heavenly, and you is heaven to me. Lovely you and blue Hawaii, with all this loveliness there should be love. Come with me while the moon is on the sea. The night is young, and so is we." Sipping a cool drink, the Scarecrow says, "Birdie, peel me a grape." The Crow says, "Yes suh, comin' right up" as he peels a grape and flips it into the Scarecrow's mouth. The Scarecrow says, "Grape me again," but the crow says, "Boss, if you can dispense with my services, I would like to fetch myself one of them seafood specials" as he walks to the seashore. But he stops short when he sees footprints in the sand. "Hey Boss! Wake up, Boss! We's been invaded." Then he beats a big drum to sound the alarm. The Scarecrow wakes up, saying, "What's goin' on? What's the matter? What do you mean 'invaded?'" The Crow says, pointing to the footprints, "Invaded by strange feetprints." The Scarecrow says, Hey, chickadee, dat man Friday made that feet print just like the book said." The Crow says, "Friday, come on, I wants to know what he's doin' out on Monday." He and the Scarecrow follow the footprints, which lead them to a rock on which words are written. The Scarecrow asks, "What's that writing say?" and the Crow says "You is kordiality invited to come for dinner immediately. Friday." The Scarecrow says, "That's nice" and the Crow says, "That is really kind of the old boy." Just then they are surrounded by cannibals and thrown into the cooking pot. They are placed on trial as the judge (Jasper) plays the drums and the Scarecrow says, "Look at that—a floor show." The judge, speaking in rhyme, calls the court to order and asks the prosecutor if he is ready. He answers, "I's ready to distort the truth." The judge asks if the jury is hip to the jive, and another cannibal says, "They tried nine hundred men and not one is alive." The judge says, "The case is open and ready to start. Dish up de defendants a la carte." The Scarecrow is found guilty of stealing Jasper's book, his Jew's harp, his trumpet, his roller skates, his slingshot, his ice cream, and his apple. For each guilty verdict the judge orders more logs to be thrown on the fire under the cooking pot.

The cannibals obey while chanting, "Hurl on de log, turn on de hot feet, eight to the beat, all reet." The Scarecrow pleads, "Now cool down, Judge. All I asks for is a little mercy. Please, I appeals to ya." The judge says, "To be perfectly frank, I don't even like you." The jury tells the Scarecrow that his goose is cooked and the Crow says, "I objects, Your Honor. I resents that fact. I was never a goose. I's a stool pigeon." The fire is getting hotter and the flames rise up around the pot. The water begins to boil and steam rises from the pot as the Scarecrow wakes up—it was all a dream. The Scarecrow says, "I's cookin'! Let me out of here" as he runs over, retrieves all of the things that he has stolen from Jasper, and lays them at his feet. He fans Jasper and says, "That's all there is. So help me, there ain't no more. And I ain't gonna do that to you no more. Boy, is there anything else I can do for you?" Jasper smiles and tells him, "Yeah, chickadee. Peel me a grape" as the cartoon ends.

Review: *Motion Picture Herald,* 23 March 1946

The Scarecrow and the Crow trick Jasper into parting with his various possessions. The Crow reads to the Scarecrow from Jasper's book. Then the Scarecrow falls asleep and has a nightmare in which he dreams he is on trial for the theft of Jasper's property. In Technicolor. (8 min)

Review: *Boxoffice,* 16 March 1946

The nefarious Scarecrow appropriates Jasper's playthings, including a copy of *Robinson Crusoe* and forces the boy to take his place in the cornfield. Scarecrow falls asleep while pursuing the novel and dreams he and his sidekick, the Crow, are attacked by cannibals on a desert island. Before the heat is put on the community kettle, Jasper and a jury appear and demand a full confession to the accompaniment of "jivey" jungle rhythms. He is pronounced guilty, awakes with a start and returns Jasper's belongings.

Review: *Motion Picture Exhibitor,* 12 December 1945

The Scarecrow and the Crow are reading *Robinson Crusoe,* while Jasper is forced to scare off crows. While reading, they imagine that the Scarecrow is Crusoe. Jasper, head of a tribe of man-earing savages, captures the Scarecrow and Crow, and puts them into a pot to boil. The flames are getting closer and closer when they wake from their reverie. Jasper sees the Scarecrow immediately returning all the things he has stolen from him, and begging forgiveness. Good. (7 Min)

Review: *Besa Shorts Shorts,* 8 October 1945

Jasper is besieged with petit black crows, who swam all over him whilst his old and constant enemy, the Scarecrow, reads his swiped copy of Robinson Crusoe. His ill-gotten pastime brings him dreaming of being on a lush island with its swinging breezes and beauties and he is having a heck of a nap until cannibals come and scare him back to wakefulness with urges to seek Jasper's forgiveness.

OLIO FOR JASPER (1946)

Company: Greorge Pal, Paramount Pictures
Type: Puppetoons
Characters: Jasper, Scarecrow (voice characterization by Roy Glenn), Crow

Story: Cartoon opens outside Jasper's home where Jasper is polishing his yo-yo and singing to himself. He is overheard by the Crow, who is perched on the shoulder of the Scarecrow. The Crow says, "That boy! He done has got a funny tremble or he got a yo-yo." The Scarecrow responds, "Let's go over and look at that yo-yo." They walk out of the field to Jasper, and the Scarecrow says, "Boy, why don't you give me that yo-yo?" Jasper says, "No! And I will fight to keep it." So the Scarecrow and the Crow cook up a scheme to get Jasper's yo-yo. They decide to elicit his sympathy, and a tearful Scarecrow tells Jasper a sad story about his hard life as a child. Jasper is curious and asks the Scarecrow, "Did you have a mammy?" The Scarecrow quickly puts a bandanna on his head and says, "This is how poor Mammy looked." Then he tells Jasper the story of his childhood. The scene changes to the city many years previous where the baby Scarecrow is held in the arms of his poor mammy, who is begging on the street. Finally she abandons her baby on the doorstep of a rich man's home and falls over, dead from sorrow. The cries of baby Scarecrow are heard by a butler who opens the front door, picks him up, and carries him into the house. But the master of the house is heartless and tosses the baby back into the snow-covered streets. Three months pass, and the baby Scarecrow gets a job as a whistle for a peanut vendor. But he is fired after his voice becomes hoarse and he can't whistle. More time passes, and the Scarecrow is a young man in his apartment. Opportunity literally knocks at his door in the form of a door to door salesman with the Opportunity Loan Company who begs the Scarecrow to take some money. The Scarecrow accepts a nickel which he takes to Wall St. where he invests it in the stock market and soon makes a fortune. As a rich man, the Scarecrow soon becomes an investment banker and occupies a big office on Wall St. But his fortunes quickly reverse after the market crashes, leaving him penniless. The scene changes back to the present as the Scarecrow says to Jasper "That's how a poor, broke Wall St. magnet became a Scarecrow." He then begins to cry and says, ". . . And you stand there in your silks and satins askin' me how come I is like is" The Scarecrow becomes so angry at Jasper that he chases the boy in circles around a tree as the cartoon ends.

Review: *Motion Picture Herald,* 15 February 1946

Jasper gets tough with the scarecrow when that villain attempts to steal Jasper's yo-yo. But the scarecrow, trying a new angle, tells the sad story of the poverty of his boyhood—he was too poor ever to own a yo-yo, he reports. But the scarecrow works himself into such a state of violence that Jasper runs away, taking the yo-yo with him. In Technicolor. (7 min)

Review: *Boxoffice,* 13 April 1946

George Pal has produced a Puppetoon up to the usual high standards. This is entertaining aplenty for young and old. The Scarecrow, using a phony story about his childhood poverty, tries to gain possession of Jasper's Yo-Yo. Convinced of his imaginary sufferings he frightens Jasper, who flees . . . with the toy intact.

Review: *Motion Picture Exhibitor,* 7 August 1946

Jasper sits under a tree playing with a small gimmick when the Scarecrow comes up, and tries to take it. Jasper refuses and the Crow gives him a heart rending story that winds up in a fight between the Scarecrow, Jasper, and Father Time. Good. (8 min)

Review: *Besa Shorts Shorts,* 1 April 1946

Professor S. Crow and his inky pal, Crow, are out to high pressure poor little Jasper out of his toys. The Professor tells a whopper this time and goes dramatic just to break Jasper down. Clever dialogue and situations come about in the story telling and put this one in the top drawer for the George Pal Puppetoons.

PACKAGE FOR JASPER (1944)

Company: George Pal, Paramount Pictures
Type: Puppetoons
Characters: Jasper, Scarecrow (voice characterization by Roy Glenn), Crow

See fig. 18. Story: The cartoon opens in front of Jasper's house near the mailbox. A hand appears, which opens the box and pulls out a package. It's Jasper's hand, and he pulls out a package addressed "To Jasper Jefferson, Cabinville, Alabama." Jasper grins as he opens the package and finds the harmonica he ordered. He says, "Gee! Ain't that super!" He opens the instruction book, "How to Learn the Harmonica in Five Easy Lessons." He eagerly starts his first lesson and rapidly progresses to lesson 5, playing a tune. In a nearby cornfield the Crow is perched on the shoulder of his friend, the Scarecrow, who is sleeping. The Crow hears Jasper's harmonica music and says, "Wake up, wake up!" The Scarecrow, hears the music and says, "That Jasper boy done got himself a harmonica." The pair hurry out of the cornfield to Jasper, and the Scarecrow says, "Boy, what's that you got?" Jasper replies, "I have my harmonica." The Scarecrow says, "This harmonica is a concert model just like the one I used to play." He quickly snatches the harmonica out of Jasper's hand and takes a closer look at it. Jasper says, "Mr Scarecrow, can you play a song?" The Crow says to himself, "That boy is asking for trouble by asking him that." The Scarecrow proceeds to tell Jasper about his last harmonica concert at Kornegie Hall, and the scene changes to a concert hall where a huge crowd awaits the start of a harmonica concert. On stage stands the Scarecrow dressed in formal attire, about to begin his solo harmonica performance. Jasper walks on stage carrying a solid gold harmonica and gives it to the Scarecrow. He begins to play, and soon he is playing several other instruments before switching to the harmonica again. The Crow shakes his head and says, "He blows in it so sweetly, and it comes out so sour." The concert is being broadcast over the radio, and the Scarecrow is asked to speed up the tempo before the program goes off the air. He finishes just in time. The sound of a whistle is heard as the scene changes back to the front of Jasper's house where the mailman has arrived carrying a package. The mailman says, "Package for Jasper." Jasper opens the package and pulls out a tuba. The Scarecrow says, "Say Boy, did I ever tell you about the time . . ." But an angry Jasper doesn't let him finish. He hits the Scarecrow on the head with the tuba, knocking him to the ground. The Scarecrow rubs his sore head as he sits on the ground next to Jasper looking at the bent tuba as the cartoon ends.

Review: *Motion Picture Herald*, 29 January 1944

Jasper, the Scarecrow, and the crow, are featured in another George Pal Puppetoon. It turns into quite a musical presentation when Jasper receives a harmonica by mail and is interrupted in the six easy lessons by the Scarecrow. As he boasts of his reputation on the instrument, the scene shifts to Kornegie Hall for a concert before hundreds of admirers. The postman's whistle calls him back to reality. It's another package for Jasper, but this time the story is different. (7 1/2 min)

Review: *Boxoffice*, 1 January 1944

George Pal has worked out a little story with a lively harmonica band musical background. Jasper gets an harmonica by mail, tries his skill, and gets assistance from the scarecrow and the crow kibitzer. The color work is very good and the music is swinging.

SAY AH, JASPER (1944)

Company: George Pal, Paramount Pictures
Type: Puppetoons
Characters: Jasper, Mammy, Scarecrow (voice characterization by Roy Glenn), Crow

Story: The cartoon opens with Jasper running home calling for his mammy and holding his jaw. He runs past the Scarecrow, standing in the field next to the road, with the Crow perched on his shoulder. He tells the Crow, "Dat Jasper boy certainly is in a powerful hurry." The Crow answers, "Yes, he came by here like a P-38." Jasper arrives at his small cabin and runs into the house, closing the door behind him. With tears running down his cheeks he tells his mammy he has a toothache. His mammy ties a white bandage over his head and under his jaw as she tells him, "Well, dis 'll take care of it. I'm goin' to the store and get you some medicine. Just keep that on until I gits back." As she leaves she tells him, "That's a good boy—good honey lamb." Jasper's tooth is aching so bad he can't wait for the medicine, so he decides to take action to get rid of the tooth. He ties one end of a string to it and the other end to the doorknob and sits down

to wait for someone to open the door. He nods and falls asleep. The Scarecrow calls him through the window and says, "Hey there, Boy." Jasper wakes up and the Scarecrow tells him, "That ain't no way to extricate a tooth." The Crow asks him "What do you know 'bout it?" The Scarecrow says, "Go on! Take off, Blackbird, you bother me." He tells Jasper, "Son, you better let me take a look at that." As he walks around the house to the front door he says, "I don't know what this family would do without me." He tries to pull open the door, but the door handle is pulled out by the string attached to Jasper's tooth. The Scarecrow tells Jasper, "There you are. What did I tell you. You can't pull no tooth that way. Let's see that tooth." He walks over to Jasper and asks him to say "ahhh." The Scarecrow looks into his mouth, shakes his head, and tells him, "Just as I thought "A discombobulation of the perturbulence. That's Latin for 'bad tooth.'" The Crow responds, "That's a hyperbolical fabrication." The Scarecrow asks, "What's that?" The Crow answers, "That's English for a big lie." The Scarecrow tells the Crow, "One of these days you gonna regustitate my patience." To Jasper he says, "Now look here, boy. We better get you to a real dentist." Jasper asks him, "Will it hurt?" The Scarecrow tells him, "Naw, it won't hurt. Why it's just like pattin' you on the top of the head." As he pats Jasper's head, the Crow says, "Yeah, with a blackjack." The Scarecrow tells him, "Will you keep that flytrap shut" and slaps the Crow on his head. He then tells Jasper, "Come on, Boy. I knows a dentist who's the greatest in the world." As they all leave the house and get in the back of an ambulance, the Scarecrow tells Jasper, "Why some of the teeth he done fixed is the biggest you ever seen." The ambulance speeds toward the city with sirens on. It stops in front of a tall building where Jasper and the Scarecrow get out. The Scarecrow says, "Yes, dis is the place. Go right in, Sucker—ah, I mean Jasper." Jasper enters the building and arrives at the dentist's office. The sign on the door reads Dr. Scarecrow, D.D.S.—Dentistry Done Snappy. Jasper enters and takes a seat in the waiting room, which is crowded with other patients. The Scarecrow opens the door to the operating room and says, "Next!" All of the people get up and run out of the room, leaving Jasper alone. Walking over to Jasper, the Scarecrow says, "Well, well, well, is you the lucky one!" He pulls Jasper into the operating room and seats him in the chair. He then shows Jasper all of his equipment, saying, "This machine is for ordinary teeth, and this one is for teeth that are a little stubborn." Jasper asks, "Which one of dem are you gonna use on me?" The Scarecrow walks over to a wall and pushes a button. From the ceiling is lowered a big box with wheels on the bottom. The front of the box opens to reveal a mechanical monster. Jasper is frightened, but before he can get out of the chair, Scarecrow pulls another lever. It straps Jasper's arms and legs to the chair, and a large metal tank is placed over his head. The Scarecrow then places a mask with a tube attached to it over Jasper's face and says, "Fust I turns on the gas." He does not know that the other end of the tube, which is attached to a tank of laughing gas, has a knot in it. The gas pressure breaks the tube and gas escapes. The Scarecrow is driving the large machine toward

Jasper, but as he inhales the gas fumes he begins to giggle and finally laughs uncontrollably. Even the machine he is riding begins to laugh while trying to pull the mask off Jasper with its mechanical hand. Then Jasper wakes up, for it has been a dream. His mother is trying to open the front door, which is pulling the cord attached to Jasper's tooth. She says, "Just what's the matter with dis door?" She pulls harder and it opens. She walks over to Jasper and tells him, "Chile, I got some medicine for that ol' nasty tooth," as Jasper shows her that his tooth was pulled out when she opened the door. She says, "Well, I guess we don't need dis no more" while showing him the two bottles of medicine she bought for him. But Jasper grabs one of the bottles from her hand and says, "Oh yes we does." He tosses the bottle out of the open window and it hits the Scarecrow squarely on the head, knocking off his hat and spilling medicine all over his face. As the Scarecrow wipes his face, the Crow laughs at the funny sight, just before another bottle of medicine thrown by Jasper knocks him off the Scarecrow's shoulder as the cartoon ends.

Review: *Boxoffice,* 18 March 1944

Jasper, who has an achin' molar, decides to do something about it himself by tying the traditional string to the door knob. Then follows a dream sequence in which the scarecrow takes Jasper to the imaginary dental office equipped with all kinds of gadgets. This is the most engaging scene of the short, filled with the whims and delightful imagery. When he regains consciousness, Jasper comes to the realization that his tooth had been pulled meanwhile and all is well. (8 min)

Review: *Motion Picture Herald,* 18 March 1944

Jasper is dozing off hopefully on a stool by the door, although his tooth is aching, when the Scarecrow appears to boast of this former prowess in dentistry. The scene shifts to his office where an overdose of laughing gas affects doctor, patient and implements alike. But Mammy's arrival breaks into the dream and accidentally pulls the tooth. (8 min)

Review: *Besa Shorts Shorts,* 3 April 1944

Little Jasper has a very bad tooth ache. He rushes home to Mom who rushes out for medicine. Meanwhile Jasper decides to use the old reliable open door method of tooth yanking. He prepares and waits for someone to come and yank on the door. He also has a nightmare in which the Scarecrow and the Black Crow take great part. After some harrowing experiences, Jasper finally comes thru and the tooth comes out.

SHOESHINE JASPER (1946)

Company: George Pal; released by Paramount Pictures
Type: Puppetoons
Characters: Jasper, Scarecrow (voice characterization by Roy Glenn), Crow

Story: Cartoon opens on Jasper, an employee at Joe Scarecrow's Shine Parlor, busy at work shining shoes. Standing by watching him work is the Scarecrow who says to himself, "You know this work is too confining. I's 'bout to break out all over with a nervous breakdown. The trouble with me is I works too hard." He pauses a few seconds then says, "Well, I wonder how my investment is coming" and turns on the radio. Out of the radio the loud sound of a trumpet calling the racehorses to the starting post is heard. This wakes up the Crow, who has been sleeping nearby, and he tells the Scarecrow, "Turn that thing off. Do you have to do that? Why is you always startin' somethin'? Is that horn necessary? You can be the biggest pest." Then the program is interrupted by an announcer who says, "We interrupt this program to bring you a special announcement. Tune in tonight for the biggest colossal jitterbug dancing contest. And the prize is not ten dollars, not one hundred dollars, but one thousand dollars for the best jitterbug dancer. And you'll dance to the hottest band in town—Hot Shot Morgan and His Fiery Five." Hearing this, the Scarecrow says, "Hot dog! I's gonna go and take the first prize." The Crow flies over and perches on his shoulder and tells him, "Yeah, and they gonna make you put it back too." The Scarecrow answers, "Now is that any way to talk in front of this fine, upright, intelligent man?" He points to Jasper, who is busy shining shoes. The Scarecrow says, "Come on, let's go and win that thousand-dollar prize" as he and the Crow walk away. Jasper calls after them, "Mister Scarecrow! Can I go to the dancin' contest too? I can dance, see" as he stands up and demonstrates some fancy dance steps. "Can I go, huh?" The Scarecrow is not impressed and says, "You just stay here and finish your work." Jasper tells him, "But I am finished." The Scarecrow opens a door on the shoebox, and many pairs of dirty shoes fall out on the sidewalk. He tells Jasper, "You see that? See that this is all done when I get back" and walks away. The Scarecrow arrives at the dance hall, where hot jazz music is playing and the dance floor is crowded with contestants. The Scarecrow walks to the center of the floor, holds up his hands for quiet, and announces, "Y'all can all go home and forget your jive because the great champion has just arrived." A hush comes over the crowd just before notes from a boogie-woogie piano introduce a hot tune. The Scarecrow begins his dancing exhibition with splits, turns, and high leg kicks. Back at the street corner, night has fallen and Jasper is still shining shoes. There are tears on his face because of his disappointment at not going to the dance contest. Suddenly a beam of light appears before him, and the voice of his fairy godmother says, "Jasper, be content with what you are. So listen, shoeshine boy. In all the world it's you upon whom I choose to bestow these golden shoes. I promise you they will serve you well, if you but obey their magic spell." The beam of light disappears and before him Jasper sees a pair of golden shoes. He puts them on and hurries to the dance hall where the Scarecrow is just finishing his dance routine, which has impressed the judges. They are about to award him the prize money when Jasper arrives on the scene and goes into his torrid dance routine. He turns cartwheels, does hand flips, and displays some fancy footwork. He wins the first-place prize of one thousand dollars to thunderous applause from the audience. Jasper is now the proud owner of a new business, Shoeshine Jasper. He relaxes while the Scarecrow, his employee, shines shoes and wipes the sweat off his brow as the cartoon ends.

Review: *Motion Picture Herald,* 8 February 1947

Little Jasper is working at shining shoes when a mysterious fairy godmother visits and leaves him a pair of golden slippers. He tries them on and is immediately turned into a wonderful dancer. Wearing the shoes he visits a dance palace and wins first prize in a dancing contest over the Scarecrow.

Review: *Film Daily,* 27 January 1947

Po' Lil ol' Jasper is awfully sad when his boss, the Scarecrow, goes off to a big jitterbug contest and leaves him with mountains of shoes to shine. A fairy godmother comes upon the scene and gives Jasper some of dem dere golden slippers with which he wins the contest. He pockets the prize money, buys an ultra-modern shoe shine emporium and has the Scarecrow working for him. This Puppetoon has plenty of life and should sell well.

Review: *Boxoffice,* 15 February 1947

Jasper is forced to shine a huge pile of shoes while his lazy employer. Scarecrow, goes off to a jitterbug contest. A mysterious fairy god mother gives him a pair of golden slippers. Jasper reaches the contest just as the judges are about to award the $1000 prize to Scarecrow. His routine so impresses the judges that he wins the contest and is able to open his own shoe shine parlor with the money (7 min)

Inki (1939–1950)

In 1939 Chuck Jones, an animator who worked for several animation studios, including Ub Iwerks, Warner Bros., and M-G-M, created a new cartoon character for Warner Bros. named Inki. Inki was a little African boy who wore a bone in his hair and lived in the jungle. Even though he was a boy, neither his parents nor other members of his family nor friends were seen in the series, which consisted of four releases and ended in 1950. One unique feature of this series was that there was no spoken dialog. The comedy stemmed entirely from sight gags. All Inki cartoons consisted of the same plot elements: (1) Inki goes out to hunt, (2) Inki encounters the lion, (3) the lion chases Inki, (4) minah (mynah is an alternative spelling) bird saves Inki, and (5) minah bird humiliates Inki and the lion at the end. In each cartoon the mysterious minah bird created by Jones stole the show from Inki. In reality a minah bird is a tropical bird found in Southeast Asia. Jones imbued his character with a deadpan expression and a funny, offbeat hopping walk accompanied by the music of Mendelssohn's Fingal's Cave Overture. The minah bird's appearance was always preceded by a loud noise produced by mountains shaking or by some other commotion in the jungle, that made all of the other animals

take flight. His appearance was timed to rescue Inki from the lion, but the minah bird always remained aloof and gained the upper hand at the end of the cartoon.

The Inki cartoons were devoid of the usual stereotypes that animators of the period usually associated with black characters. Although he wore a bone in his head, there was nothing to suggest that Inki was a cannibal. After *Caveman Inki* was released, Jones refused to continue the series. That was probably just as well because the series had become repetitive and had lost its funniness.

Inki Stories and Reviews

CAVEMAN INKI (1950)

Company: Chuck Jones, Warner Bros.
Type: Looney Tunes; excerpts shown on the *Porky Pig and His Friends* show broadcast nationally by the ABC television network (1964–65) and sponsored by the makers of Tootsie Rolls candy
Characters: Inki, minah bird, baby dinosaur, baby lion, old man on the mountain

Story: There is not much plot to this cartoon, which opens in a prehistoric jungle where little Inki cautiously comes out of his cave to hunt. The cries of prehistoric animals can be heard all around him in the jungle. He whistles, calling his pet—a baby dinosaur—out of the cave. They set off on a hunting trip, on which they fail to snare a kangaroo and an angry honey bee. Then they are chased back to Inki's cave by a large dinosaur. A loud roar is heard all over the jungle, which frightens all of the beasts. A huge mountain splits in half and the little minah bird walks out with his hippity-hop walk. When he passes by Inki's cave, Inki decides to hunt him. He is soon joined by a baby lion, who wants the bone on Inki's head. The lion chases Inki up the mountain where they run past an old man with a white beard, knocking over his cooking pot. The chase continues until they again encounter the minah bird. Inki chases the bird and the lion chases Inki. Again they run up and down the mountain before being joined by the big dinosaur, who takes over the lead. The dinosaur catches the minah bird, and they engage in a rough-and-tumble fight that the minah bird wins, leaving the dinosaur tied up in knots. Meanwhile the old man on the mountain has snared Inki and the lion in a rope trap, where they hang upside down by their legs. The minah bird appears on the scene and walks away wearing the old man's hat as the cartoon ends.

Review: *Motion Picture Herald,* 20 January 1951

Inki and the Minah bird are at it again. This time the setting is the prehistoric days of the dinosaur. To complicate matters further for the native boy, a tough nasty lion is included.

Review: *Exhibitor Servisection,* **8 November 1950**

A decidedly pleasant number, this has Inki as a little caveman in prehistoric days with the ever present bird with the odd walk unperturbed at what is going on. Inki tries to be tough but no one is a match for the bird, with even the dinosaurs terrified. All in all this makes a clever entry. Good.

INKI AND THE LION (1941)

Company: Chuck Jones, Warner Bros.
Type: Merrie Melodies
Characters: Inki, minah bird, lion

Story: The film opens showing a monkey running for his life and finally hiding in a tree. Little Inki the hunter shows up on the scene carrying his spear and looking for the monkey. Suddenly a coconut thrown by the monkey lands on Inki's head and knocks him down. Inki gets up and throws his spear at the tree, but the monkey throws it back at him. Inki continues on his hunt and is startled by a loud noise coming from a bush. Frightened, Inki hides behind a tree and peeks out only to see the strange minah bird emerge from the bush. The bird ignores Inki and walks away with his strange gait, three steps and a hop. Inki decides to make the bird his next prey and starts to follow him. He launches his spear at the bird but misses, and the spear sticks in a tree trunk. The bird calmly perches on the spear and disappears into a hole in the tree. Inki reaches in, trying to pull the bird out, but what he finds is a skunk that he quickly puts back. Inki resumes his hunt and comes upon a small lion cub. Just as Inki is about to launch his spear, it is pulled out of his hands by a huge lion standing behind him. Inki makes a hasty retreat with the lion close behind him. He crawls into one end of a hollow log. When he emerges, the lion sees him, and the chase is on again. Inki hides in a hollow tree stump and eludes the lion. When he climbs out of the stump, he is surprised to find the minah bird perched on his head. The minah bird continues on his way with Inki following him, but the native boy does not realize that the lion is close behind him. The minah bird walks into a cave, and Inki blocks the entrance with large boulders. He grabs the last boulder and is about to push it in place but is surprised to find out that he has grabbed the lion's rear end. He frantically removes the boulders from the entrance and dashes into the cave for safety, only to see another pair of eyes inside the dark cave. He believes that the eyes belong to the lion, so he runs outside again and blocks the entrance with boulders. He thinks that he is safe at last but when he turns around, he sees the lion behind him. The lion hypnotizes Inki and uses the spell to pull Inki toward his mouth. But suddenly the boulders begin to fly away from the entrance of the cave, and the minah bird walks out and breaks the spell on Inki. Inki is about to run away and the lion is about to pounce on him, but the minah bird grabs the lion by his tail, which he ties to a tree trunk. Inki is grateful that the minah bird has rescued him from the lion and extends his hand to shake the bird's hand. The minah bird grabs it, but then jerks Inki off his feet and whirls him around in the air before slamming him onto the ground. Inki is lying on the ground as the Minah bird hops away and the cartoon ends.

Review: *Film Daily,* **18 July 1941**

These Merrie Melodies cartoons just keep on rolling along with happy abandon and swell animation. Nothing much to the tale, but many a laugh, which has a little native boy hunting a lion. Inki faces many perilous situations but a cute cartoon character, the Minah Bird, saves him. It is good program material. (7 min)

Review: *Boxoffice,* **20 September 1941**

Inki, a native boy, about three years old, is hunting in the jungle. He has many escapes from violent death at the fangs of a lion and at length is rescued by a comic bird. Good for kids.

Review: *Motion Picture Herald,* **3 June 1950**

Little Inki, the jungle native, provides a hilarious situation when he discovers that the Lion he is hunting is stalking him. Inki is saved by the little Minah Bird as the lion is about to trap him.

Review: *Motion Picture Herald,* **9 August 1941**

Little Inki sets out hunting wild animals and comes across a ferocious lion. As the lion is about to trap Inki, Inki is saved by the little Minah bird. (7 min)

Review: *Motion Picture Exhibitor,* **6 August 1941**

Inki, a small cannibal, meets the lion, with the crow with the hopping walk coming to his aid. The crow has possibilities as a character in the series. Good.

Review: *Exhibitor Servisection,* **26 April 1950**

Inki, a small cannibal, meets the Lion, with the crow with the hopping walk coming to his aid. This was first reviewed in the *Servisection* of August 1941. Good.

INKI AND THE MINAH BIRD (1943)

Company: Chuck Jones, Warner Bros.
Type: Merrie Melodies
Characters: Inki, minah bird, lion

See fig. 20. Story: The cartoon's opening scene shows a snake moving down a jungle trail. Suddenly a spear comes out of nowhere, almost hitting him. He is surprised but not afraid. Then Inki shows up on the scene. The snake lets out a roar so loud that it causes Inki to spin like a top. Next the brave little hunter sees a butterfly. He throws his spear at it but misses. The butterfly also lets out a loud roar, and frightened little Inki runs for his life. Then the minah bird shows up with his weird, hopping walk. Inki decides that the bird is his next victim and casts his spear at the bird but misses it. The minah bird continues on its way. When Inki goes to retrieve his spear, he finds to his dismay that it is impaled on one of the huge claws of a gigantic lion. Inki runs home, with the lion giving chase. Inki runs into his house, pulls a large steak out of his icebox, and tosses it to the lion. The lion opens his mouth, but the minah bird, who is in its mouth, catches the steak and eats it. The bird then hops out of the lion's mouth and walks away. At first the lion begins to cry, but then decides to chase the minah bird. The minah bird hides in a clump of loose grass. When the lion catches up with the moving clump, the minah bird is gone. The frustrated lion again finds Inki and chases him home. Inki thinks he has found safety in a dark closet, but it turns out he is actually in the lion's mouth. Inki jumps out of the lion's mouth so fast that he carries the lion's huge teeth with him. The lion chases Inki and finally catches him and gets his teeth back. The lion continues chasing Inki, who jumps in a barrel to hide only to discover that the lion is also inside. They go around and around in the barrel before little Inki jumps out, followed by the lion. Just then the minah bird shows up and chases the lion away. Inki and the minah bird shake hands, but the lion returns. This time the bird grabs the lion by the tail and twirls the lion so fast that the lion loses his teeth. In the closing scene the lion is looking for his teeth. Then the minah bird opens its mouth to smile, displaying the lion's lost teeth.

Review: *Motion Picture Herald,* 20 November 1943

Inki is a nut-brown, pint sized native of the jungles who sets out on his usual hunting trip. He is met, however, by a highly unusual lion also looking for game. The match is an unequal one until the Minah bird joins the losing side. (7 min).

Review: *Film Daily,* 12 November 1943

Leon Schlesinger has done a swell job with the story of a lion's encounter with a little jungle native (Inki) and a minah bird, a mysterious sort who remains silent throughout. Inki runs into the lion while out hunting. He is almost done for when the bird comes to the rescue. The Technicolor is superb.

Review: *Boxoffice,* 20 November 1943

The subject is notable for the reappearance of the cartoon character the Minah Bird, which appeared in several previous Merrie Melodies and has been absent much too long. This critter is a pantomimist who can cook up the screwiest schemes in alliance with Inki to cope with the lion. Film audiences certainly would like to see many more of this little fellow's antics in this or any other series.

Review: *Motion Picture Herald,* 3 September 1949

Little Inki is out hunting small game, when deep in the jungle he meets a ferocious lion who sets out to annihilate him. At the crucial moment, the mysterious Minah Bird forms an alliance with Inki, and amazes the live native with his dextrous defeat of the lion. (7 min)

Review: *Motion Picture Exhibitor,* 17 November 1943

Inki is a little colored character while the Minah bird is a now-you-see-him, now-you-don't-creation. Inki, while out hunting, arouses a huge lion with false teeth and tries to bribe his way out of a ticklish situation by feeding him a steak, but the Minah bird gets it instead. The bird succeeds in infuriating the

lion and he can't do a thing about it. After a furious chase, he finally captures Inki, but when he tries to eat him, the Minah bird comes to the rescue. This is silly. Fair.

Review: *Besa Shorts Shorts,* 15 November 1943

Inki with this spear does his best to kill a worm, butterfly and such. On one attempt the spear is caught by a lion, who reacts with an Edgar Kennedy slow burn. Action begins with the lion chasing Inki, until the Minah Bird enters the picture and causes Mr. L. quite a bit of trouble.

INKI AT THE CIRCUS (1947)

Company:	Chuck Jones, Warner Bros.
Type:	Merrie Melodies
Characters:	Inki, minah bird, dogs

See fig. 19. Story: There is little plot to this cartoon. All of the action takes place at a circus where little Inki is billed as the dangerous African Wild Man. Two rival dogs want the bone that is tied to the hair on Inki's head. They chase Inki through the circus tents and on the high wire, but neither dog gets the bone. The strange minah bird arrives on the scene and finally hops away with Inki's bone attached to its head.

Review: *Boxoffice,* 5 July 1947

There are plenty of chuckles as Inky, the little African boy, tries to live up to his billing as the circus wild man. Two dogs are after a bone ornament he wears in his hair. The three of them, Inki, and the two dogs, have a hectic time scampering through the circus.

Review: *Film Daily,* 14 August 1947

Little Inki is billed as a ferocious wild African at a local circus. The bone he wears in his hair attracts two pups who decide to steal it. The chase leads through various midway concessions with the Minah bird thrown in for good measure. Good cartoon entertainment.

Review: *Motion Picture Exhibitor,* 11 June 1947

Inki, and the dog, visit a circus, spot an African Specimen sporting a luscious looking bone on his head and proceed to give chase. He receives competition from another canine, and is joined by a bird who joins very distinterestedly. After lots of swinging from the trapeze, etc. the bird winds up with the bone. Fair.

Review: *Motion Picture Herald,* 30 August 1947

Inki, the little African native boy, is billed at the local town circus as a ferocious wild man. The bone he wears in his head dress as an ornament attracts the attention of a pup which shows Inki's audience that Inki isn't the wild man he is supposed to be. (7 min).

Review: *Motion Picture Herald,* 19 February 1955

Inki, a little African native boy, is billed as a ferocious wild man in the local circus. He wears a bone in his head dress as an ornament which attracts the attention of a mongrel pup and another mutt. Both dogs take after Inki, who leads them a merry chase through the various midway concessions.

LITTLE LION HUNTER (1939)

Company: Chuck Jones, Warner Bros.
Type: Merrie Melodies
Characters: Inki, minah bird, lion

Story: In the opening scene a beautiful parrot is seen flying around and coming to rest on a tree branch. Out of nowhere a spear whizzes by, narrowly missing the bird. Little Inki is out hunting again. In short order he unsuccessfully attempts to snare a giraffe and a butterfly. As he continues on his hunt, Inki hears a loud noise and sees a disturbance in a bush. Just as Inki is poised to launch his spear, the minah bird comes out of the bush, walking with his strange gait—three steps and a hop. Inki decides to follow the bird and when his intended victim crawls into a hollow log, Inki reaches into the hole in an attempt to retrieve him. He grabs something, but is surprised to find that he has captured a skunk. Next Inki sets his sights on a turtle who happens to wander by. He launches his spear and narrowly misses the turtle, which runs away and hides in a hollow log. Inki crawls into the log to follow the turtle. When he emerges from the other end, he is surprised to find the minah bird perched on his head. As the minah bird walks away, little Inki follows him to the top of a tall tree. As Inki's head emerges from the uppermost branches, Inki is startled to find the pesky bird again perching on his head. In the ensuing tussle, Inki is thrown from the tree and hits the ground with a thud. He decides to track the bird by putting his ear to the ground. He hears a loud sound and feels the ground tremble as a large animal approaches. Inki feels a tap on his rear end and turns around to see a large lion. Inki beats a hasty retreat with the lion at his heels. Inki tries to elude the lion by hiding in a tree stump, but the lion finds him. Just as the lion is about to pounce on little Inki, the minah bird emerges from the tree stump. The lion forgets Inki and attacks the bird. A tremendous struggle between the minah bird and the lion ensues. The bird emerges the victor, the lion having received a terrific beating and his tail having been tied to a tree. The minah bird then beckons Inki to come out of his hiding. The little boy is very grateful to have been saved again. When Inki turns around to see what has happened to the lion, the minah bird gives Inki a swift kick in the rear end and slowly walks away from the scene as the cartoon ends.

Review: *Motion Picture Herald*, 16 March 1946

Little Inky decides to go on a lion hunt but once he enters the jungle, it develops that the hunter becomes the hunted. The lion is just about to catch Inky when the Minah bird rescues him in the nick of time. (7 min)

Review: *Boxoffice*, 23 March 1946

Top-notch animation and the appealing Little native, Inky, prove dialog is not an essential for good cartoon production. In this reel the dusky hunter sets out single-handed in search of game. He tangles with a passing lion, but is saved in the nick of time by the blase Minah Bird, who is unimpressed by Inki's hunting prowess.

Review: *Selected Motion Pictures,* 1 November 1939

An impudent bird saves a little black hunter from the jaws of an angry lion. Fair. Family.

Review: *Motion Picture Exhibitor,* 4 October 1939

Massa Schlesinger strayed from his wise-cracking cartoon path to present this drama of the black moppet who went a-hunting. The bird he was chasing nabs the lion that was ready to nab the hunter. It is okay stuff for the kids. Good.

Review: *Motion Picture Exhibitor,* 3 April 1946

Little Inky decides to go hunting, and comes across such ferocious animals as the Minah Bird, turtle, and butterfly. He finally comes across a lion, but the match is too great. Inky is getting the worst of it when the Minah Bird comes to his aid and outwits the big bad lion. Good.

Review: *Besa Shorts Shorts,* 25 March 1946

Inki, charming baby savage of the latest Blue Ribbon Merrie Melody, starts with a handful of darts to do the day's hunting. A mynah bird, a possible victim, becomes disgusted with Inki's no-bulls-eye technique. When a lion starts stalking the little hunter, the Mynah bird ties said lion up in knots and gives Inki a kick in the pants as a slight critical gesture.

Mammy Two-Shoes (1939–1952)

In 1939 William Hanna, formally a journalist and an engineer, collaborated with Joseph Barbera, a former accountant, to create a new cartoon series for M-G-M. The first release, *Puss Gets the Boot* (1939), introduced a cat named Jasper and a mouse with no name. In subsequent releases of the series the cat became Tom and the mouse was Jerry. The series also introduced the character of Mammy Two-Shoes, a black maid who appeared in nineteen releases, making her last appearance in *Push-Button Kitty* in 1952. By the time *Mouse for Sale* was released in 1955, the maid character had been changed to a white woman. Recently several early cartoons, including *The Framed Cat* (1950), were edited to substitute the voice of the stereotypical black maid character with the voice of an Irish woman so that the cartoons could be shown on TV.

By having her speak in dialect and use broken grammar and by stereotyping her physical appearance and dress, the cartoonists ensured that movie audiences would not mistake Mammy

Two-Shoes for the owner of the house in which she lived with Tom and Jerry. The owners of the house rarely appeared in the series, and when they did, only off-screen voices were heard. *Busy Bodies* (1956) included the first full views of the white owners.

Although Mammy Two-Shoes was only the maid, she exercised control over the house and held absolute authority over the two main characters. She also served as their foil, which generated most of the gags. More often than not, she stole the scenes in which she appeared with Tom and Jerry. She was depicted as a heavyset woman and was usually dressed in a colorful flower-patterned dress or house robe. She cooked meals and cleaned the house wearing a long baggy dress, polka-dot stockings with patches at the heels, and house slippers on her feet. With two exceptions, audiences were not allowed to see the part of Mammy's body above her waist. In *Part Time Pal,* the back of Mammy's head, her hair covered with a bandanna, can be seen while she is sleeping in bed. In *Mouse Cleaning* her full-length silhouette is seen as she chases Tom down the road at the end of the cartoon. Fred Quimby, the producer of the series, explained that Mammy's head was not seen because "Tom and Jerry were the stars of the pictures, and we did not wish to do anything that might distract attention from them."

Mammy Two-Shoes provided the only spoken dialog in the cartoons. By speaking with a southern drawl, using incorrect grammar, and mispronouncing and misusing common words, she generated the comedy as she alternated from being the victim of Tom and Jerry's practical jokes to being a stern mistress who often punished the two by kicking them out of the house. The Mammy Two-Shoes character fit well with the stereotypical depictions of black women in cartoons, which were already well established by pioneer animators years before Hanna and Barbera created their Mammy character. They merely chose to conform to the well-established cinematic status quo.

With the possible exception of *Puss Gets the Boot,* the voice characterization of Mammy Two-Shoes was provided by a versatile black actress of the stage, screen, and radio—Lillian Randolph. Lillian Randolph was born in Cleveland, Ohio, and made her professional stage debut in a black show, *Lucky Sambo,* in 1927. Later she went to Detroit where she was selected to sing with a group on WJR radio and later on WXYZ radio where she was in the cast of *Lulu and Leander,* which was on the air for two and a half years. Between her radio appearances she filled nightclub singing dates at the Palm Cafe. She came to Los Angeles in 1935 to take a singing job at the famous Club Alabam on Central Avenue. Later she was seen by Ralph Cooper, who selected her for his musical and comedy revue at the old Burbank Theatre. During this period she became a contract actress with M-G-M, playing maid roles in feature films. She also went back to radio, playing the part of Mammy on the *Al Jolson Show.* Then followed fifteen weeks on the *Al Pearce and His Gang* radio show. Later she played the part of the widow on the *Amos 'n' Andy* radio show.

In 1954 Lillian Randolph had a short run as the star of her own radio show, *The Lillian Randolph Show,* which had its first broadcast on Friday, October 18, at 11:00 A.M. over station KOWL in Los Angeles. The show featured homemaking hints, music, and a potpourri of chatter and interviews with famous black celebrities.

The radio characters that she was most remembered for was Birdie the maid on *The Gildersleeve Show* in the 1940s, the same time she was providing the voice for Mammy Two-Shoes in the *Tom and Jerry* cartoon series. Her major motion picture credits include *That's My Baby, Wonderful Life,* and *Once More My Darling.* She also made many commercials for TV before her death in Los Angeles on September 12, 1980.

Mammy Two-Shoes Stories and Reviews

DOG TROUBLE (1942)

Company: William Hanna, Joseph Barbera, M-G-M
Characters: Tom cat, Jerry mouse, Mammy Two-Shoes (voice characterization by Lillian Randolph)

Story: The cartoon opens as Tom is toying with Jerry. He holds on to the mouse's tail as he tries to run away. After several narrow escapes Jerry manages to run back into his hole in the wall. Tom arrives and knocks on the wall. Then he hides around the corner and waits for Jerry to come out to eat the cheese in a mousetrap. But the mouse exits through an electrical outlet. After trying unsuccessfully to put Tom's tail into the electric socket, Jerry catches Tom's tail in a large mousetrap. Tom chases Jerry who stops short as he runs past the open front door where a large bulldog is sleeping. Tom arrives on the scene and bumps into the dog, waking him up. The dog chases Tom around the house as Jerry observes from a distance. Tom climbs to the top of a floor lamp to escape the dog. Jerry is laughing at Tom, but when the dog sees the mouse he starts to chase Jerry who escapes by hiding in a cuckoo clock. The dog alternately goes after Tom and Jerry, they both wind up on top of the clock, where Jerry has an idea how they can cooperate to rid themselves of their common enemy. Tom occupies the dog's attention while Jerry climbs down from the clock and uses a yarn of wool to weave a net by walking under tables and in and around other furniture. Then Jerry kicks the dog and the dog chases Jerry, becoming entangled in the yarn and pulling plates off a table, which crash to the floor. Mammy Two-Shoes, wearing house slippers with holes in the soles and stockings with patches in the heels, hears the noise and enters the kitchen and sees the mess all over the floor. She says, "Land sakes! What's goin' on in heah?" She sees the dog wrapped up in yarn and tells him, "You overstuffed Pekingese hound, you! What you doin' in heah wreckin' up the house?" Mammy grabs the dog by the collar and pulls him out of the house, saying, "Get out of here you old pug-nosed good for nothin'. You know darn well you ain't allowed heah in the house no how." Tom and Jerry, with smiles on their faces, wave good-bye to the dog. Tom wipes the sweat off his face just as the mousetrap snaps on his tail. He looks at Jerry who shakes his head and pretends that he did not do it. But Tom is not buying it and chases Jerry as the cartoon ends.

Review: *Boxoffice,* 19 July 1952

With the family bulldog on the warpath, Tom and Jerry unite to defeat the common enemy. They play scores of tricks on the dog, and each time he gets Tom or Jerry in a corner the other comes to the rescue. Victory is achieved when Tom, beleaguered, on top of the cuckoo clock, is liberated by Jerry unraveling the mistress's knitting, winding it around the furniture until it forms a spider's web pattern. Then enticing the bulldog into the middle. The resultant clatter as things go crashing to the floor brings the family's "help," who promptly drags the defeated dog into the yard where he belongs.

FRAIDY CAT (1942)

Company: William Hanna, Joseph Barbera, M-G-M
Characters: Tom cat, Jerry mouse, Mammy Two-Shoes
             (voice characterization by Lillian Randolph)

Story: As the cartoon opens, Tom is listening to a radio program. The announcer is saying, "Once again the phantom is around. Trapped in the lonely town, the girl can hear its mocking laughter echo louder up the staircase. Then a claw-like hand pulls heavily upon the latch. Slowly the door creeps open . . . " Tom is scared and trembles at what he hears. Jerry comes into the room and laughs when he observes Tom's fear. The radio program continues, "The ghostly form drifts through the blackness of the chamber. The helpless girl feels her hair stand on end. Icy chills race down her spine. Her heart leaps into her throat . . . " Tom can't take it any more and leaps into a flowerpot to hide. The program ends as the radio announcer says, "And that, my dear children, concludes this evening's witching hour." Relieved, Tom sticks his head out of the flowerpot as the announcer says, "But you do believe in ghosts don't you?" Tom nods his head yes. Jerry decides to have some fun by scaring Tom. He plays various tricks on the cat, such as using a vacuum cleaner to inflate a white dress to look like a ghost. Tom is really scared until he finds out that it is Jerry who is playing tricks on him. He chases the mouse around the house, making noise as furniture is knocked over. The noise awakens Mammy Two-Shoes, who walks on the scene carrying a rolling pin in her hands and wearing a white gown and house slippers. She says, "Man dat sounds like a burgla' problem. If you's lookin' for trouble burgla' man, heah I come," as she backs into the room. Tom, seeing Mammy's backside, thinks it's Jerry playing ghost again and jumps on her back and bites her on her rear end. Mammy screams and says, "Thomas, you no good cat! Attackin' from de rear, eh? Well, take dis, dis. Get out of heah, you good-for-nothin', moth-eatin' mousetrap" as she chases Tom out of the room. Meanwhile Jerry has fallen into a box of flour, and when he gets out he is white as a ghost. He gets the idea to scare Tom

again. But he when he looks at his own reflection in a shiny dish, he scares himself. He runs back into his hole in the wall as the cartoon ends.

Review: *Boxoffice,* 7 February 1942

Tom and Jerry have another session of chase. This time Tom gets the creeps listening to a horror tale on the radio. Jerry makes his blood run cold with imitations of ghosts, weird sounds, and stuff. Tom learns too late. Cook (Mammy) trounces him. Jerry falls into a flour canister and his reflection scares him back into his hole.

THE LONESOME MOUSE (1943)

Company: William Hanna, Joseph Barbera, M-G-M
Characters: Tom cat, Jerry mouse, Mammy Two-Shoes
             (voice characterization by Lillian Randolph)

Story: The cartoon opens as Tom lies on the floor near the fireplace sleeping with a smile on his face. Jerry, standing on the mantelpiece above him, pushes a large vase off the edge, which falls down and breaks on Tom's head, waking him up. The noise is heard by Mammy Two-Shoes, who enters the room wearing house slippers on her feet and saying,"Thomas, you no-good cat! Dat's sabotage." She grabs Tom by the back of his neck and tosses him out of the house saying, "Out you go!" Tom flies through the door, bounces down the steps, and slides into a fence. Jerry looks out the window, very happy that Tom has been kicked out. He then proceeds to dance around the room to the tune of "Happy Days Are Here Again." He hangs a For Rent sign on the wall near his hole and then proceeds to help himself to the food. But soon he becomes bored and begins to miss Tom. As he looks out the window at Tom, his conscience tells him, "I bet you never thought you'd miss that cat, did you? Feeling kind of lonesome? Look at him. You know you could get that guy back in here if you really wanted to. Why don't ya?" Jerry agrees and leaves the house, makes peace with Tom, and then tells him of his plan to get him back into the house. Tom agrees and Jerry proceeds to put the plan into action. He goes into the house where he finds Mammy in the kitchen washing dishes and singing, "I like New York in June. I like a Gershwin tune. I like potato chips, pork chops, and motor trips . . ." Jerry slips up behind her and pulls her garter, stretching the rubber before letting it go. It snaps back and Mammy screams before turning around to see Jerry making funny faces at her. Mammy is frightened and jumps onto a stool, which Jerry then rocks. Mammy sways back and forth, and various objects fall out from under her dress, including hairpins, coins, a pair of dice, and a barber's razor. Jerry uses the razor to cut off one leg of the stool. Mammy crashes to the floor and screams, "Tom! Get in heah! Save me!" Tom rushes onto the scene and pretends to angrily chase Jerry all over the house, pausing to eat food and wreck furniture. At one point they pass Mammy, who is sitting on top of the stove. Jerry turns on the gas burner, and the flames cause Mammy to jump into the air and scream. At another point they find Mammy hiding under the sink with her large rear end sticking out. They both poke her with forks while Mammy screams. Later Mammy stands on a chair holding a broom. As the two run by, Mammy calls out to Tom, "Chase him in here Thomas!" Mammy swings the broom at Jerry but hits Tom several times as they run in circles around her. Finally Tom grabs the broom from Mammy and breaks the handle in half before giving the pieces back to her. Jerry crawls under the carpet while Mammy slams the broom on top of the carpet trying to hit him. Jerry crawls out from under the carpet and Tom slides a big red tomato under it. Mammy thinks the tomato is Jerry and slams the lump. Then she says, "Did I get him?" Tom looks under the carpet and pretends that he sees a smashed Jerry. He cries out in sorrow before replacing the carpet and laying flowers on top of it to a musical background of Taps. Satisfied that the mouse is dead, Mammy gives him a whole pie to eat while saying, "Yes sir, Thomas. You is a hero. Here's a reward for gittin' rid of that mouse, heh-heh." She pats him on his head and then leaves. Tom smiles and is about to eat his pie, but Jerry, thinking that he has been doublecrossed, pushes Tom's head into it. Jerry walks away with a frown on his face saying "Why that dirty, doublecrossin', too timin'. . ." as the cartoon ends.

Review: *Motion Picture Herald,* 5 June 1943

The continuing feud between Tom and Jerry, MGM's cat and mouse team, takes a surprising twist in this latest appearance but only for a time. Tom has been evicted from the house by Mammy and all the sympathies of his mortal enemy are aroused. But his efforts to reinstate the cat are interrupted and old traditions reassert themselves. (8 min).

Review: *Boxoffice,* 5 June 1943

Particularly entertaining because it reverses the role of the hunter and hunted in the case of the mouse and cat. After the cat has been banished from the house the mouse gets lonesome and figures out a way to get him back under a flag of truce. It's highly diverting action both for the kids and grown-ups.

Review: *Motion Picture Herald,* 11 February 1950

When Tom is evicted from the house, Jerry finds that time hangs heavy indeed. He thinks up all kinds of excuses and maneuvers to get his adversary back into the scene once more.

Review: *Motion Picture Exhibitor,* 16 June 1943

Tom and Jerry, cat and mouse, chase each other through the house until the cat is blamed for some breakage and is evicted by the cook. The mouse feels lonely without any one to annoy and attempts to get the cat back in the house. He so scares the cook that she calls the cat in to catch the mouse. After a con-

vincing chase the cat is permitted to stay. Once he is reinstated both revert to type and the race between them is resumed. Good. (8 min)

Review: *Besa Shorts Shorts,* 24 May 1943

Tom and Jerry are at it again in an amusing skit that offers lots to laugh at and much swell music to enjoy. It seems that Mandy ousts Tom from the house for some mischief which was strictly Jerry's doings. The friendly enemies seem to have come to a parting of the ways, but Jerry is a softie and regrets his part of the situation and promises to get Tom reinstated. He goes about it in a very rowdy manner and Tome gets a chance to pay him back for what he has done. Jerry continues his streak of wrecking the place thinking all the time that Tom is on the level, but it is Tom who gets the special dish from Mandy and it is disgruntled little Jerry who fades out for the end.

Review: *Exhibitor Servisecion,* 21 December 1949

Jerry, the mouse, is lonesome in this hilarious issue after he manages to get Tom, the cat, ousted from the house. He collaborates with Tom to get the latter back in by scaring the maid, taking a beating, and then hiding, and then Tom pretends to have killed him. However, the old cat and mouse relationship is resumed when Tom hogs his reward of a creamy pie. So Jerry pushes his face in it, and disgusted, walks away. Excellent.

MIDNIGHT SNACK (1940)

Company: William Hanna, Joseph Barbera, M-G-M
Characters: Tom cat, Jerry mouse, Mammy Two-Shoes (voice characterization by Lillian Randolph)

See fig. 21. Story: The cartoon opens in a kitchen late at night. The only light that can be seen is coming out of an open icebox from which Jerry is removing a huge slice of cheese. He manages to get the cheese out of the icebox, but Tom sees him. Tom then plays a trick on Jerry by piling a plate, a saucer, and a flowerpot on top of the cheese, which Jerry is carrying on top of his head. The increased weight causes Jerry to fall, and he is caught by Tom. But Tom is hungry and decides to raid the icebox. He places a flatiron on Jerry's tail to hold him and goes to the refrigerator and eats the food until he picks up a piece of cheese that he smells and then throws away. The cheese breaks the glass plate on a cupboard, making a loud noise. The sound of a voice is heard calling out "Thomas" as Mammy Two-Shoes, wearing house slippers and striped stockings, is coming fast down the stairs. Mammy says, "Thomas, if dat cat's in dat kitchen . . ." Tom gets an idea and puts Jerry in the icebox. He slams the door shut and then hides out of sight. Mammy enters the kitchen and says, "Cat, if you're been in dat icebox, start prayin'." She opens the icebox door, sees Jerry inside, and jumps on top of a stool. She pulls her five petticoats up tight around her legs and says, "Thomas, Thomas! Git in here, big boy, and get dis mouse!" Meanwhile Jerry slides down a string of spaghetti to the floor and is chased by Tom who gets wrapped around the legs of the stool Mammy is standing on, causing it to fall over. Mammy falls to the floor, landing on her backside. She gets up and runs out of the kitchen, saying, "Man, dis here is no place for a lady." The chase is on. Jerry manages to evade capture and finally turns the tables on Tom when he gets his tail caught in an ironing board. Jerry jabs him in the rear so hard that Tom skids across the floor into the icebox, the door closing behind him. Mammy enters the kitchen, sees pots and pans all over the floor, and thinks that Tom has chased Jerry away. She says, "Thomas, man dat mouse sure did git demobilized." She gets Tom's bowl, opens the icebox for some milk, and Tom falls out on the floor in front of her with food all over him. She says, "Thomas, why you two timin', doublecrossin' cheat! Get out! Skat! Go! You moth-eaten mousetrap . . ." Jerry smiles and eats a piece of cheese as the cartoon ends.

Review: *Motion Picture Herald*, 26 June 1948

Ordinarily a midnight snack is considered a peaceful enterprise but when Tom & Jerry attempt it, bedlam breaks out. (7 min)

Review: *Boxoffice*, 15 May 1948

Another clever cat vs mouse cartoon in Technicolor. The mouse-hungry Tom lies in waiting to pounce upon Jerry when the tiny rodent emerges from the refrigerator with a huge hunk of Swiss cheese. He holds the mouse by the tail while he further tortures him by making a feast out of the icebox goodies. But the cook (Mammy) arrives and chases Tom with a broom.

Review: *Exhibitor Servisection*, 31 March 1948

Jerry is caught trying to get away with his cheese by Tom and the latter gives the Mouse plenty of trouble. However, the windup has Jerry getting back at the wise cat who takes a tremendous beating from his mistress while the little fellow comfortably munches away at the cheese. Fair.

Review: *Motion Picture Exhibitor*, 6 August 1941

The old story of the cat and the mouse, with the latter again victorious over the cat who winds up in the refrigerator. Some byplay is humorous. Fair.

Review: *Boxoffice*, 16 August 1948

The cat and mouse story again. Here it is done tastefully and at length. Tom and Jerry are cat and mouse, respectively. Jerry caught at the icebox turns the trick on Tom who then gets his lumps at the hands of a cook (Mammy). (9 min)

Review: *Motion Picture Herald*, 23 August 1941

Tom and Jerry, cat and mouse, respectively, spend an evening chasing each other around the kitchen and cutting up a good deal. As Mammy, the maid, enters Tom makes it appear that Jerry is to blame, but Tom is later found to be the guilty party and he is made to suffer. (9 min)

Story: *MGM Shorts Story,* August 1941

The same Cat and Mouse who were so well received in their first Metro-Goldwyn-Mayer cartoon *Puss Gets the Boot* are back again, by popular demand, in another co-starring vehicle titled *Midnight Snack.*

Supervised by William Hanna and Joe Barbera, the Technicolor one-reeler opens on Jerry, a little mouse, loaded down with a big slice of cheese, struggling away from the ice-box. He looks cautiously as he staggers forward making sure that he isn't being followed by Tom, the cat. However, the cat has spotted the mouse and creeps stealthily after him.

As the mouse continues on, Tom puts an occasional dish, pot, and pan on top of the cheese, and the mouse begins to collapse under the load. Dodging out ahead, the cat grabs a rollingpin and puts it directly in the mouse's path and puts down slices of bread to form steps leading to the rollingpin. The mouse struggles up the steps and onto the rollingpin. He loses his balance and crashes to the floor amid pot, pans, and dishes and cheese.

The mouse struggles to his feet and starts off again with the cheese. Now the cat drops a flatiron on Jerry's tail, takes the cheese away, and returns it to the icebox. However one of the dishes slips and falls to the floor. The cat hears the maid coming. He grabs the mouse, shoves him into the ice box, and then ducks out of sight. The maid opens the box and finds the mouse cowering in a corner.

Jasper comes running out and immediately sets out after the mouse. Jerry manages to trick the cat into chasing him around the legs of a chair and by doing so Jasper ties himself into a knot. The mouse slips into an electric toaster by mistake and after simmering for a few seconds is catapulted out by the automatic release.

The little mouse then runs up the venetian blinds and the cat jumps after him, misses, and lands on the end of an ironing board attached to the wall. The board teeters and the cat struggles to hold on.

Swinging down the blinds cord, the mouse grabs a fork. Then swinging wide, Jerry, with fork pointed, jabs the cat and Jasper sails through the air and crashes into the open icebox. Needless to say, the contents are destroyed.

Again the maid enters the room, this time thinking that Jasper has eliminated the mouse. She looks into the icebox and there she finds Jasper shivering in the corner. Tom is immediately thrown out of the house and then when all is quiet the little mouse returns to the icebox to enjoy his pieces of cheese in comfort, quietude and peace of mind.

MOUSE CLEANING (1948)

Company: William Hanna, Joseph Barbera, M-G-M
Characters: Tom cat, Jerry mouse, Mammy Two-Shoes (voice characterization by Lillan Randolph)

See fig. 22. Story: Cartoon opens as Mammy, wearing house slippers, is mopping the kitchen floor. She finishes, straightens her back, and says, "That's that. The whole house is clean. And brother, it better stay that way." Meanwhile Tom, while chasing Jerry out in the yard, falls into a mud puddle and tracks mud into the house as he follows the mouse inside. He does not see Mammy as he runs around the room and splatters mud on the floor and walls. He runs into Mammy who pins him to the floor with her mop and says, "Hold on there, you no-good cat! Just look what you have done to my clean floor! Get up heah" as she jerks him up. She continues, "Take this mop. Now start cleanin'." She give the mop to Tom and he begins to clean the floor. Mammy, dressed up in dress shoes, gloves, and an overcoat, prepares to leave the house and says, "And furthermore if I finds one spot of dirt in the house when I gets back we is gonna be minus one cat around heah. Understand?" Tom nods yes and Mammy says, "Well get on with that cleanin'" as she leaves the house, slamming the door behind her. After she is gone, Tom makes faces in her direction but stops when Mammy opens the door and points her finger at him and says, "And keep it clean!" Then she shuts the door. Tom works hard and cleans every speck of dirt from the floor and even wipes up sweat that falls from his face. Meanwhile Jerry has decided to make life difficult for Tom, spreading dirt all around while Tom frantically cleans up behind him. Tom finally manages to run Jerry out of the house and lies down to take a nap. Jerry sneaks back inside and applies black ink to the bottom of Tom's feet. Tom wakes up and chases Jerry around the house before he realizes that he has left his footprints all over the floor and walls. Tom throws Jerry down the laundry chute into the basement and rapidly cleans up the mess, just as Mammy is returning home carrying two sacks of groceries. Meanwhile the coal delivery truck has arrived. Jerry arranges to have the load of coal dumped into the living room where Tom is waiting for Mammy. Mammy opens the door and is carried backward by a flood of coal flowing out of the house. She digs herself out of the pile of coal and says, "When I get a hold of that low-down, good-for-nothin' . . ." Tom, with his face covered by black coaldust, and his hair standing on end, pops up from the pile of coal. Mammy says, "Hey you! Has you seen a no-good cat around heah?" Tom says, in a Stephin Fetchit demeanor, "There ain't no cat, no place, no how" as he shuffles down the road. But Mammy recognizes him and shouts at him as Tom runs as fast as he can. Mammy throws chunks of coal at him that miss. Tom stops to make a face at Mammy and starts to run again before the last chunk of coal hits him on the head, knocking him out as the cartoon ends.

Review: *Motion Picture Herald,* 12 May 1956

Tom is under orders to keep his house clean or find a new home. When Jerry hears the news, he couldn't be happier, and as usual provides Tom with a peck of trouble. Tom, as usual, fights a losing battle. (7 min).

Review: *Boxoffice,* 12 December 1948

This is a repeat performance of a common film cartoon gag but

amusing nevertheless. Tom, the cat, is ordered not to mess up the house under pain of eviction, so Jerry the mouse goes to work with buckets of paint while Tom tries to clean up after him. The ending shows a truck dumping tons of coal into the parlor. (8 min)

Review: *Exhibitor's Servisection,* 8 December 1948

Just as the colored housekeeper finishes house cleaning, Tom tracks in mud while in the process of his usual chase after Jerry. She admonishes him, and tells him if the house gets dirty again she will hold him responsible, and make him clean it up. This affords Jerry a golden opportunity to make the place dirty as fast as Tom cleans it up. Finally Jerry switches a coal chute from the cellar window to the parlor window, and just as the housekeeper returns, the coal pours into the house, burying both her and Tom who, of course, gets all of the blame. Fair.

A MOUSE IN THE HOUSE (1947)

Company: William Hanna, Joseph Barbera, M-G-M
Characters: Tom cat, Jerry mouse, Mammy Two-Shoes (voice characterization by Lillian Randolph)

See fig. 23. Story: The cartoon opens as Mammy-Two Shoes, wearing a house robe and slippers, walks into the kitchen carrying an alarm clock while the background music plays "Shortnin' Bread." She sees the breadbox open and says, "Lands sakes! Dat pesky mouse been havin' a jam session right here in my breadbox." She then notices the open icebox door and scraps of food on the floor and says, "And look at my raided refrigerator!" She sees that big bites have been taken out of her cake and says, "And the nibbling on my chocolate cake. Boy, what is this? A holiday for mice? And me with two cats in the house." As she walks out of the kitchen and into the dining room she says, "Boy when I lays my hands on those good-fo'-nothin'-lazy . . ." She stops in front of Tom and his friend, a black cat, who are lying among dirty plates. Mammy says, "Well, gentlemen, glad to see you is enjoyin' your little siesta" as both cats smile and nod their heads in agreement. Mammy continues, "You comfortable, ain't you?" Again the cats nod their heads. She then says, "And is you both gettin' plenty of nice fresh cream" as Tom tastes some milk in a dish on the floor. Mammy then says in a loud voice, "Well, I'm glad you's satisfied because I ain't." Both cats jump up and back up against the wall. As they stand in Mammy's shadow and hold each other, Mammy says, "There's a mouse in the house, and there's two cats. But there's only gonna be one in this house in the mornin'. And that's the cat that catches that mouse. Now get goin'!" Both cats run out of the room and begin a frantic search for Jerry. Jerry sees them and decides to give them a hand. They soon discover him and chase him around the house. After they catch him, they first fight a duel with toy pistols and then engage in a boxing match to decide who gets to take the mouse back to Mammy. But Jerry escapes by hiding in the oven. Tom closes the door and turns on the gas, and then both cats look inside to find Jerry. While they have their heads in the oven, Jerry, who has climbed out, lights the gas and the oven explodes in a cloud of black dust. When the the cats pull their heads out, their faces are covered in black soot. They are depicted as two black stereotypes with thick lips and pigtail hairstyles. The black cat manages to capture Jerry, while Tom dresses up in Mammy's clothes and wraps a bandanna around his head. The black cat enters the kitchen to bring Jerry to Mammy as "Shortnin' Bread" is heard in the background. Tom hits the black cat on his head, snatches Jerry out of his hands, pulls off Mammy's clothes, and runs out of the kitchen. Later the black cat, dressed in Mammy's clothes, tricks Tom into giving the mouse to him. Eventually Jerry escapes. Mammy hears the noise and says, "I think I'd better go peek in on dem two cats." Tom sees Mammy and thinks that it's the black cat trying to trick him. The black cat sees Mammy and thinks that it is Tom trying to trick him again. As Mammy stops and looks through the kitchen door, both cats sneak up behind her and hit her on her backside with a dustpan and skillet, respectively, with their eyes closed. Mammy screams, and when the cats open their eyes and see each other they stop, realizing that they have made a terrible mistake. They both turn to run away, but Mammy grabs their tails and says, "Hold on there, you crazy cats." Jerry looks on with delight as Mammy beats the two cats, saying, "Take this, good-fo'-nothin'. . ." She throws them both out of the house as Jerry opens the door for her. Jerry, smiling, turns around and finds an angry Mammy standing in front of him, tapping her foot. He sheepishly smiles and backs out of the house as the cartoon ends.

Review: *Exhibitor Servisection,* 17 September 1947

A mouse, Jerry, is discovered in the house, and Tom, the cat, his best friend, is given strict orders to capture him. This is easier said than accomplished, however, as Jerry is not one to give up very easily, in fact, the tiny mouse gets the better of the deal all around. Good.

NIT-WITTY KITTY (1951)

Company: William Hanna, Joseph Barbera, M-G-M
Characters: Tom cat, Jerry mouse, Mammy Two-Shoes (voice characterization by Lillian Randolph)

Story: The cartoon opens in the kitchen, where Mammy and Tom are trying to catch Jerry. Tom chases Jerry in circles around Mammy as she says, "Tom, chase him over here. Get him around here, Tom. Not that way, but this way." Mammy is holding a broom and is trying to hit Jerry as she continues, "Move there, Tom. I'll get him." She swings the broom, missing Jerry but hitting Tom squarely on his head. Tom is dazed, and when he regains his senses, he makes squeaking sounds like a mouse's. Mammy looks at him and asks, "Tom, what's the matter with you? What's come over you? Get away from me, Thomas." She hops on a chair and says, "Shoo! Go away!" Tom pulls the chair over, sending Mammy crashing to the floor. She gets up and runs screaming out of the room while Tom laughs. Tom gets some cheese from the refrigerator and offers a piece to

Jerry, who is standing by the entrance to his home, a hole in the wall. Jerry does not know what to make of the situation, and he walks into his hole. Tom squeezes through also and jumps into Jerry's tiny bed, which collapses under Tom's weight. Jerry is more puzzled than ever when he overhears Mammy making a phone call. She is saying, "Yes, Doctor. That's right Doctor, he's acting just like a mouse. He's even eatin' cheese." Jerry walks out of his hole to listen. Mammy says, "He's got what? Amnesia? Is that bad, Doctor? Never had, Doctor." Tom also comes out of the hole. She says, "Here he comes . . ." and tries to run away on a pair of stilts. But Tom knocks them out from under her, sending Mammy crashing to the floor. Tom goes back into Jerry's house and relaxes on the bed eating cheese while Jerry finds a medical encyclopedia and looks up "amnesia." He reads, "A temporary state of forgetting. Memory is sometimes restored by a sharp blow on the head." Armed with this knowledge Jerry tries various tricks to deliver a blow to Tom's head, including a baseball bat, a piano, an anvil, and a bowling ball. All are unsuccessful. Then Tom offers Jerry a small piece of cheese, which Jerry tosses away. The cheese knocks over a vase that rolls into a plate that falls off the mantelpiece onto a basket of clothes and bounces onto the floor and rolls until it hits a latch that opens a door out of which falls an ironing board that hits Tom on the head, curing his amnesia. Jerry jumps for joy and gives Tom a big kiss before running inside his hole. Tom stops outside the hole and falls asleep. Meanwhile Jerry is relaxing on his bed and eating a piece of cheese when he hears Mammy's footsteps approaching. He hears her as she reads from the encyclopedia, "It say here, a sharp blow on de head is sure cure for amnesia." Jerry exits his hole and sees that Mammy is holding a baseball bat preparing to hit Tom while saying, "Dat's what he gonna get." She hits Tom who turns into a mouse again and goes into Jerry's house again and jumps into the bed, pushing a disgusted Jerry onto the floor as the cartoon ends.

Review: *Exhibitor Servisection,* 20 September 1951

Tom, accidently hit in the head, begins acting like a mouse. The disturbed Jerry consults a book on psychiatry and learns that Tom is suffering from amnesia, and that a blow on the head should get him back to normal. Tom returns to his normal mouse-hating self. However the maid comes along, and gives the cat another blow on the head, and Jerry's problem starts all over again. Good.

OLD ROCKIN' CHAIR TOM (1948)

Company: William Hanna, Joseph Barbera, M-G-M
Characters: Tom cat, Jerry mouse, Mammy Two-Shoes (voice characterization by Lillian Randolph)

See fig. 22. Story: The cartoon opens in the kitchen as Mammy, holding her dress up to her knees, is standing on top of a stool while Jerry rocks it from side to side. She screams, "Help, Thomas, save me! Go on, mouse. Shoo shoo! Git away from heah. You quit tryin' to scare me, Thomas." Tom runs to her aid but fails to get rid of Jerry, who is chopping at one leg of the stool with an ax. Tom takes the ax from Jerry and swings it at him, but he chops off the leg of the stool. Mammy falls feet first on top of Tom's head, and they both tumble downstairs into the basement. Mammy says, "Thomas if you is a mouse catcher, I is Lana Turner, which I ain't. The trouble with you is you is gittin' too old to catch mice." She walks up the stairs out of the basement, and Tom follows her. She tells him, "So I is decided to bring in a new younger cat. Step up heah and meet a real mouse catcher." She calls out, "Oh Lightnin'," and an orange cat speeds into the room, catches Jerry and kicks him out of the house into the street. He runs back to Mammy and kisses her hand. She says, "Boy, you is a gentleman and a mouse catcher." Jerry tries to sneak back into the house through the mail drop, but Lightnin' catches him and kicks him out again. Lightnin' then pastes white cotton onto Tom's head and onto the bottom of his chin and gives him a walking stick to lean on. Mammy laughs and says, "That's right, Lightnin'. Take good care of old Uncle Tom. Well, good night Lightnin'. See you in de mornin'." As she leaves the room, Lightnin' runs past her and opens the door for her. Mammy says, "Hee hee Love dat cat." As soon as she has gone, Lightnin' runs to the icebox, opens it, and eats the food. A bottle of milks drops onto the floor, and Mammy hears the noise. She says, "Thomas, is dat you in de icebox?" Lightnin' puts the blame on Tom by stuffing Tom's head in a watermelon and placing food all around him. Mammy enters the kitchen and says, "Thomas, has you been in dat icebox?" Lightnin' shakes Tom's head up and down. Mammy then tells Tom, "You has. Then out you go." And she grabs him by his neck. But Lightnin' stops her and kicks Tom out of the house and into a trash bin. Jerry tries to enter, but when he realizes Lightnin' has seen him he kicks himself out and into the same trash bin where Tom is sitting. Both are puzzled as to what to do next when Jerry whispers an idea into Tom's ear. They enter the house with Tom carrying a powerful horseshoe magnet and Jerry carrying a flatiron. Jerry holds the flatiron in front of Lightnin' while he pulls his mouth wide open. Tom, standing behind Lightnin', uses the magnet to pull the flatiron inside Lightnin', and it comes to rest at his rear end. Tom and Jerry have great fun with the helpless Lightnin', pulling him back and forth with the aid of the magnet. Mammy hears all the noise and decides to investigate. She comes into the kitchen and says, "What in de world goin' on in heah?" Jerry runs to her and snaps her garter belt. Mammy screams and jumps on top of the stool and says, "Lightnin'!" But Lightnin' is held against the wall by the magnet. As Jerry shakes the stool, Mammy clasps her hands together in prayer and screams, "Thomas!" Tom lets go of the magnet and grabs Jerry and takes him outside where he pretends to beat him. Mammy says, "Good boy, Tom." Mammy picks up Lightnin' and is about to kick him out but Tom takes him away from her. He hurts his foot on the flatiron when he kicks him in the rear. Tom, with his foot bandaged, relaxes on a bed of pillows, as Mammy tells him, "Thank-you, Thomas. And I sincerely hopes you will accept my apologies and dis small token of

gratitude." She gives him a big lemon pie in a metal pie pan. Tom takes a slice and puts the pie down on the floor beside him. Jerry uses the magnet to pull the pie to him, and he eats a slice and smiles as the cartoon ends.

Review: *Exhibitor Servisection,* 4 September 1948

When mouse Jerry terrorizes the housekeeper, and cat Tom's efforts to catch him are ineffectual, she gets a new fast cat, Lightnin'. Younger and faster, the latter gets rid of Jerry and than raids the ice box, so that Tom is blamed, and he is thrown out too. Tom and Jerry join forces, and, with the aid of a flat iron and a magnet, succeed in slowing Lightnin' down so that Jerry can again terrorize the housekeeper. Tom arrives for the rescue, and he is reinstated handsomely. The cat sees Jerry share in the reward. Good.

Review: *Film Daily,* 13 October 1948

With Jerry the mouse making merry over the plight of a colored maid who is scared of mice, Tom is not around to give chase and another cat, a red lightning-fast feline, is brought in. But Tom and Jerry being old pals from way back, something must be done. Jerry does it. At the finish the red cat is booted out. It's a frisky, diverting Technicolor frolic. (7 min)

PART TIME PAL (1947)

Company: William Hanna, Joseph Barbera, M-G-M
Characters: Tom cat, Jerry mouse, Mammy Two-Shoes (voice characterization by Lillian Randolph)

Story: The cartoon opens as Mammy Two-Shoes, holding a broom and wearing house slippers and a robe, shakes her finger in Tom's face as she tells him, "And this, Mr. Thomas, is yo' last and final chance. Either you keep that mouse outta dis icebox or you goes out. Understand?" She shoves the broom into Tom's hands and tells him, "You's is on guard. Understand?" Then she walks out of the kitchen. Tom puts the broom on his shoulder and marches around the room as Jerry watches him from a distance. The mouse takes the cover off the floor heating duct, and Tom falls through the hole into the basement. Jerry takes a big chicken drumstick out of the icebox, but Tom snatches it out of his hand. Tom chases Jerry around the house before tripping and falling down the stairs into the basement, landing in a barrel of cider. Tom drinks his fill of cider and climbs out of the tank dead drunk. He is now Jerry's friend and leads him back to the kitchen, where he opens the icebox and offers Jerry food. But Jerry is too confused to eat it. Tom pulls a shelf out of the icebox, and it crashes on top of his head. The noise is heard by Mammy, who is upstairs in the bedroom. She puts on her robe and walks down the stairs, saying, "Lands sakes! What's goin' on down there?" Jerry pulls Tom away from the food and they hide behind the door just before Mammy enters the kitchen, saying, "Thomas, Thomas, if you messin' 'round with that ice box, I'm gonna skin you alive." Mammy comes in and sees the mess and says, "Well, slap my face if dis ain't a mess! Now ain't dis somthin'. When my back is turned dat low-down, good-fo'-nothing' feline is up to somethin'." As she talks, Tom sneaks up behind her and is about to kick her on her rear end but Jerry stops him. Mammy says, "Boy, when I lays my hands on that no count cat, I'll make it plenty hot for him." Jerry stops Tom as he is about to give Mammy a hot foot with a lighted match. Tom hiccups, and Mammy turns and says, "Is that you, Thomas?" Mammy walks out of the kitchen, saying, "Boy, will I mop this flo' with his ornery hide." After Mammy leaves, Tom, still drunk, leads Jerry back to the icebox but trips and falls, knocking a bottle of seltzer off a shelf, which falls into his open mouth. The cold drink sobers up Tom, who starts to chase Jerry again. Tom chases Jerry into the bathroom where he trips and falls, knocking over a bottle of Bay Rum shaving lotion, which falls into his mouth. He drinks the lotion and it makes him drunk again. Tom and Jerry are friends again and go back into the kitchen where he seats Jerry and then himself at the dinner table and then rings the bell for the cook. But Mammy lies asleep in her bed snoring. She is wearing a bandanna on her head (only scene in the entire series that shows her head). Next Tom staggers to the bottom of the stairs, gives out a loud whistle, and then beats on the bannister with an umbrella. Jerry tries to stop him, but Tom pushes him away and climbs up the stairs and kicks open the door before entering Mammy's bedroom, where he sees Mammy's bare feet sticking out from under the sheets. He grabs a pitcher of water and is about to throw it on Mammy, saying, "One for the money, two for the show, three to make ready, and four to go." At the bottom of the stairs Jerry hears Mammy scream and sees broken chairs and tables flying out of Mammy's bedroom before Tom runs out with his head in the pitcher. Mammy chases him with a broom that she uses to break the pitcher as Tom runs down the stairs. Mammy follows but jumps down the stairs and crashes loudly on the floor. Jerry watches out of the front door as Mammy chases Tom down the road and the cartoon ends.

Review: *Motion Picture Herald,* 29 March 1947

A funnier-then-the average cartoon with a new twist. The mouse sets the cat drunk and for happy while the two become pals, with the cat committing all the crimes usually ascribed to the mouse. Swaying tipsily, the cat robs the icebox and then proceeds to wake the maid. The fleeing cat, hotly pursued by the infuriated maid, makes for a hilarious fade-out. (8 min)

Review: *Motion Picture Herald,* 28 May 1955

Another Tom and Jerry cartoon where the famous feud between the mouse and the cat starts with a bang, continues with fists flying here and there and ends with the idea that there is no such thing as a "part time pal."

Review: *Boxoffice,* 3 May 1947

Tom Cat is assigned to guard the refrigerator from the marauding Jerry Mouse. The rodent tries to distract the cat's attention, and in the ensuing chase, Tom falls into a barrel of cider. He emerges thoroughly inebriated, and in a gesture of friendship opens the refrigerator and offers Jerry some tempting delicacies. He sobers up long enough to realize the damage he has done, and the chase is on again.

Review: *Film Daily,* 11 April 1947

Tom Cat and Jerry mouse are battling again, with Tom usually on the losing side. He is guarding the ice box with full intent of keeping Jerry away from its contents. Under the influence of cider, he collaborates with Jerry, forgetting the feud, till he sobers up and the chase is on again. Good for lots of laughs.

Review: *Exhibitor Servisection,* 1 March 1947

Tom, the cat, is instructed by the cook to make sure that Jerry, the mouse, doesn't get into the refrigerator; but during a chase the cat winds up in the cider barrel and emerges drunk with the result that he helps the mouse raid the ice box. Once he sobers up the chase is on again, until he accidently drinks some bay rum after-shave lotion, and once more is a pal to Jerry. The cook wakes up, and chases Tom over the horizon. Good.

POLKA-DOT PUSS (1949)

Company: William Hanna, Joseph Barbera, M-G-M
Characters: Tom cat, Jerry mouse, Mammy Two-Shoes (voice characterization by Lillian Randolph)

The cartoon opens as Tom plays with Jerry, using him like a yo-yo. When he hears Mammy's voice say, "Thomas, oh Thomas," he tucks Jerry under the cushion of a chair and lies down on a rug in front of the fire. Mammy, wearing a housecoat and slippers, enters the room and says, "Oh, there you are. Well come on, Tom. It's time you was put out for the night." Tom looks out of the window and sees that it is raining hard outside. Mammy opens the door and says, "Thomas, hurry up and get on outside. Land's sake if I stand here by an open door like this I'm goin' to catch my death of a cold." Tom starts to sneeze and Mammy says, "Why Thomas, is you catchin' a cold?" Tom nods yes and sneezes. Mammy says, "You poor little thing. I better let you stay inside the house tonight." Meanwhile Jerry is disgusted that Tom will not be put out. Mammy leads Tom back in front of the fire and lays him down and puts a blanket on top of him and a hot water bottle under his head. She says, "Yes sir, if you got a cold you better curl up here by the fire." Then she points her finger at him and says, "You is tellin' the truth about that cold ain't yuh?" Tom nods yes and crosses his heart. She says, "If I thought you wasn't tellin' the truth, I'd wash out your mouth with soap. Well, good night." She walks out of the room, closing the door behind her. As soon as she is gone, Tom jumps up and runs to the chair, reaches under the cushion, and grabs

Jerry. Jerry sticks a bar of soap into Tom's mouth and washes it before running away. Toms settles down for a good night's sleep and Jerry gets an idea. Using a can of red paint, he covers Tom's face with red dots. Tom wakes up to find Jerry reading a newspaper story: "Measles epidemic hitting the nation: Sneezing and sniffles first symptoms." Jerry places a mirror in front of Tom, who is convinced that he has the measles. Consulting a book entitled *Dr. Quack's Home Remedies,* Jerry administers various cures, including hot and cold treatments. After a cold shower Tom sees himself in a mirror and realizes that all the red spots have been washed off his face. He has been tricked, and he confronts Jerry with a sword. But now Jerry's face has broken out in red spots. He has a real case of the measles. The house has been quarantined for measles and both Tom and Jerry, covered with red spots, look out the window as the cartoon ends.

Review: *Exhibitor Servisection,* 13 March 1949

Tom, the cat, in order to avoid being sent out in the cold for the night, feigns a cold, and is allowed to remain. However, Jerry, the mouse, up to his usual mischief, dabs spots on the cat's puss, and almost convinces him he has the measles until the paint washes off. The climax comes when both wind up with the real thing. Fair. (8 min)

Review: *Boxoffice,* 9 April 1949

Good. This Technicolor subject tells very amusingly how the mouse paints the sleeping cat's face to make it believe it has the measles, then, consulting a medical tome by Dr. Quack, puts the cat through a number of drastic treatments that include freezing in the refrigerator and baking in the oven. In the end both animals fall victim to the measles. Drawing and animation are top quality.

PUSH-BUTTON KITTY (1952)

Company: William Hanna, Joseph Barbera, M-G-M
Characters: Tom cat, Jerry mouse, Mammy-Two Shoes
              (voice characterization by Lillian Randolph)

Story: The cartoon opens as Mammy Two-Shoes, wearing house slippers, is sweeping the floor as Tom lies in front of Jerry's hole in the wall. Mammy wants to sweep under Tom's feet and says, "Sorry to disturb you Mr. Tom," as Tom lifts his feet. Mammy says, "Thank you so much." Jerry walks out of his hole and Mammy says, "Don't look now Tom, but a mouse just walked by." But Tom rolls over onto his other side. Jerry walks back into his hole carrying a piece of cheese and Tom does nothing. Mammy says, "Dat's right, enjoy yo' self. It's later than you think." The front doorbell rings and Mammy opens the door. She says, "Oh, thank you. I been waitin' fo' dis" as she receives a package. She opens it to find a remote-control mechanical cat. Mammy reads the instructions: "Mechano, the cat of tomorrow. No Feeding. No Fussing. No Fur. Clean, Effi-

cient, Dependable." Mammy says, "Thomas, oh Thomas, come in heah and see what I've got." Sleepy-eyed, Tom walks into the room and yawns. Mammy says, "Thomas, meet Mechano. Mr. Mechano heah is takin' yo job as mouse catcher." Tom slaps his knee and laughs and so does Jerry who sees what's happening. Mammy says, "Is ya through laughin', Tom? Den watch dis." She turns the remote control from off to on. Mechano snaps to attention and rolls over to Jerry. Its head opens, a mechanical arm extends, and it hits Jerry on his head with a club. Jerry is knocked cold, and Mechano sweeps him into his mouth and carries him out of the house where he is deposited in the street. When Mechano returns, Mammy laughs and says, "OK if I laugh now Tom?" A dejected Tom leaves the house as Mammy tells him, "But dat's how it is, Tom. De machine age and stuff like dat dere. But don't worry, maybe you can find an old-fashioned house dat needs an old-fashioned cat." Tom walks away from the house and Mammy returns inside, saying, "Dat's my Mechano. No feedin', no fussin', no fur. Just remember all you has to do is git dat mouse outta de house." She chuckles and walks away. Jerry wants back inside and tries all sorts of tricks to return home. They all fail until he releases several mechanical mice into the house. Mechano, while chasing Jerry and the mice, knocks over furniture and breaks dishes. Mammy, hearing the noise, arrives to investigate. Mechano runs by her, chopping holes in the floor with an ax as he tries to hit a mechanical mouse. Mammy says, "What in de world goin' on in here? Mechano, put down dat ax! Mechano!" As the mouse runs by her, Mammy screams, "Help, Thomas!" With the mouse following her and Mechano following the mouse, Mammy and mouse run into a closet and close the door behind her. Mechano crashes through the door and knocks off his head in the process. Tom arrives on the scene and sees a blind Mechano chasing the mechanical mice before bumping into a table and completely breaking apart. Mechanical parts fly everywhere. The electric motor winds up in Tom's mouth and he swallows it. Mechano is gone, and Mammy is happy to see Tom. She says, "Thomas! Am I glad to see you." She shakes his hand and says, "Boy, dey can have dat new-fangled Mechano. All I want's is a plain old-fashioned cat." Meanwhile Jerry has seen Tom swallow the electric motor and decides to play a trick on Tom. He turns the remote control to on, and immediately Tom stands to attention and his tail lights up. Mammy says, "Thomas, don't do dat" as Tom chases one of the mechanical mice and destroys more furniture in the process. Mammy shouts for Tom to stop as he runs over her, knocking her flat on the floor as the cartoon ends.

Review: *Exhibitor Servisection,* 2 January 1952

The maid throws Tom out of the house when she purchases a mechanical cat, which gets rid of Jerry without any trouble. When Jerry brings in some mechanical mice, the latter goes berserk, and wrecks the place, bringing in the call for Tom, who proceeds to swallow the mechanical cat's mechanism. This puts him in the same spot as the mechanical cat. Good. (6 1/2 min)

Review: *Boxoffice,* **1 November 1952**

A new mechanical wonder—an electronic mouse chaser—is introduced to plague Tom Cat in this live cartoon in Technicolor. Tom has become so lazy that he allows little Jerry Mouse to run riot so the housekeeper busy a new gadget which works wonders in chasing out the mouse. However, Jerry sends some wind-up mice into the house and the mouse-chaser goes wild and all but wrecks the place.

PUSS GETS THE BOOT (1940)

Company: Rudolph Ising, M-G-M
Type: First in the Tom and Jerry series
Characters: Jasper the cat (name later changed to Tom), Pee-Wee the mouse (name later changed to Jerry), Mammy Two-Shoes (voice characterization by Lillian Randolph)

Story: The cartoon opens as Jasper is tormenting Pee-Wee by holding onto his tail as he tries to run away to background music, "Three Blind Mice." Jasper plays all sorts of tricks on the little mouse, including painting a fake hole on the wall, complete with a sign reading Home Sweet Home. Pee-Wee, trying to escape Jasper, runs into the wall, knocking himself silly. Later while chasing the mouse, Jasper knocks over a flowerpot and sends it crashing to the floor. Mammy Two-Shoes, the black maid who is cleaning on the second floor, hears the noise. She calls out, "Jasper, Jasper! That no good cat." She comes downstairs holding a broom in her hands and wearing house slippers on her feet. Jasper tries to run, but she pins his tail to the floor with her broom and says, "Just a minute you good-for-nothin' fur coat." She picks him up by his tail and says, "Now, would you jes' look at dat mess you made." She drops Jasper on the floor and tells him, "Now understand this Jasper. If you breaks one more thing, you is goin' out. O-W-T—out. Dat's clear, ain't it? One more breakage and you is goin' out. Now get outa my sight befo' I gets mad." She hits him with her broom. Meanwhile Pee-Wee has heard the conversation and is pleased. As soon as the maid leaves, Jasper is after Pee-Wee again but stops short when the mouse threatens to drop a wineglass from the table. Meanwhile Mammy is carrying a dustpan filled with broken glass, saying, "Any more breakage and dat cat's goin' out of here." Pee-Wee drops the wineglass and whistles for Jasper to take a look. Jasper catches the glass barely before it hits the floor. Pee-Wee has a good time throwing glasses, plates, and bottles. He watches Jasper catch them before they break. Jasper finally gets the idea of covering the floor with soft pillows. Pee-Wee runs away and as he goes dishes roll off the mantelpiece. Jasper catches them before they land on the table. Dishes pile up higher and higher in Jasper's arms, and Pee-Wee throws one more dish, which crashes to the floor. Mammy hears the noise and rushes downstairs, carrying her broom and saying, "Jasper, Jasper! Man, you is practically out now." Meanwhile Pee-Wee and Jasper, who is sweating as he holds a large stack of dishes, hear her coming. Just before she arrives, Pee-Wee hits Jasper on his rear end with a mallet, sending the dishes crashing to the

floor. Pee Wee runs into his hole just before Mammy passes and hears the sound of her hitting the cat with the broom. As he looks out of his hole, Pee-Wee sees Mammy dragging Jasper by his tail behind her, saying, "And when I says out, I means O-W-T—out." Pee-Wee comes out of his hole, waves bye-bye to Jasper, and places the Home Sweet Home sign on the wall above his hole as the cartoon ends.

Review: *Motion Picture Exhibitor,* **6 March 1940**

Puss teases the mouse but when the latter learns that breakage in the house will lead to Puss being thrown out, the fun begins. Windup has the crockery crashing, the mouse victorious, Puss getting the boot.

Description: *Metro-Goldwyn-Mayer Short Story,* **January/February 1940**

Since Eve evolved from Adam's rib, cats have waged constant war against mice. Now comes a one-mouse revolution brought on by a cat, which ends in victory for the mouse.

The story, as told in Rudolph Ising's latest M-G-M cartoon, *Puss Gets the Boot,* relates how the one small mouse, taking advantage of one large cat's shortcomings, subdues the larger warrior in a battle of wits and with the aid, or course, of circumstances.

Ising's cat feels particularly wicked this day. Before putting an end to the mouse of his choice, he decides to toy with it. As the mouse pokes his head out of his hole, friend cat grabs him with his tail, flips him in the air, and lets him fall to the floor. The cat then dips his paw into some ink and draws a false hole in the wall for the mouse. As soon as he awakes, the mouse makes a dash for his hole, runs into the solid wall and is knocked unconscious again. This time, when he awakes, he is angry. With great courage he strolls up to the cat and punches him right in the eye.

Furious, the cat runs after the mouse, and dashes right into a pillar that supports a beautiful vase. The vase falls to the floor, crashes into a thousand pieces, and the cat, Jasper, by name, is in for it. Immediately the housekeeper chases after Jasper with a broom, beats him, and warns him that if anything else is broken in the house, he will be thrown into the street.

Now the mouse, named Pee-Wee, knows how to handle Jasper. If Jasper tries to hurt him again, he'll break something and blame it on the cat. The next time Jasper chases Pee-Wee, the mouse runs to the edge of a table, grabs one of a set of cocktail glasses, and defiantly shouts that he will drop the glass if the cat comes any closer. For each of Jasper's lunges, Pee-Wee threatens to drop the glass, which Jasper catches before it breaks, by the skin of his teeth. Another glass and still another comes hurtling down with Jasper catching each before it hits the floor. Now Jasper cat is wise and places soft cushions all over, so that even if Pee-Wee does drop the glasses, they won't break.

Jasper moves towards Pee-Wee, who threatens to drop another glass. Jasper laughs, the mouse drops the glass and it falls on the pillows and doesn't break. Immediately, Pee-Wee is in Jasper's tail, being tossed up and down like a ball of cork. But Jasper flips Pee-Wee a bit too high. The mouse catches on the ledge of a mantel on which there are many valuable plates. Immediately he starts throwing these to the floor. The cat dashes around madly, catching each dish until his arms are full.

Calmly, Pee-Wee comes down from the mantel, and kicks Jasper right into next week. Up in the air goes every dish and down they come. The housekeeper catches the cat and banishes him from the house forever. Calmly, and with great confidence, Pee-Wee strolls back to his hole, sighing, "Home Sweet Home."

PUSS 'N' TOOTS (1942)

Company: William Hanna, Joseph Barbera, M-G-M
Characters: Tom cat, Jerry mouse, Mammy Two-Shoes
             (voice characterization by Lillian Randolph)

Story: The cartoon opens as Tom amuses himself with Jerry, who is trapped inside an empty glass flower vase. Tom hears the doorbell ring and Mammy Two-Shoes say, "Just a minute. I's a comin'." Tom hears Mammy walking his way and quickly pulls Jerry from the flower vase and hides him in a desk drawer, filing him under the letter *M*. The bell rings again and Tom hears Mammy say, "I's comin'!" Then he ducks behind a corner as Mammy walks by. He hears her open the door and say to a visitor, "Well, How de-do, Ma'am. Of course I'll take care of her. Lands sakes, she ain't no trouble at all. Are you honey? Now you just take yo' time, Ma'am Good-bye." After Mammy leaves the scene, Tom discovers that "she" is a cute female white cat with a bow tied around her neck and another on top of her head. Tom quickly grooms himself before he approaches the visitor and tries to make friends by offering her the goldfish and then the pet canary. When she rejects both of these, Tom gets Jerry out of the desk drawer and offers him to her. Jerry manages to escape, and the chase is on all over the house. Tom tries to catch the mouse who usually manages to turn the tables on him. After Tom gets trapped in a phonograph player, Jerry sees his chance and gives the cute girl cat a big kiss. He enters his hole with a smile on his face as the cartoon ends.

SATURDAY EVENING PUSS (1950)

Company: William Hanna, Joseph Barbera, M-G-M
Characters: Tom cat, Jerry mouse, Mammy Two-Shoes
             (voice characterization by Lillian Randolph)

Story: As the cartoon opens, Mammy Two-Shoes is grooming herself for a night out with her girlfriends. She puts on flashy jewelry as Tom peeks around the corner. After she puts on her coat and leaves the house. Tom invites some of his alley cat friends over for a party. His friends arrive, and Tom turns on the phonograph while another cat plays the piano and another smaller cat beats on a xylophone. Tom decides to prepare some food and raids the icebox. He makes sandwiches and stuffs them into the open mouths of his friends. Jerry is in his hole but can't sleep because of all the noise the cats are making. His body is bouncing up and down in bed in time to the rhythm of the music. When, he can tolerate the situation no longer, he walks out of his hole and confronts Tom, shouting for him to be

quiet. But the music is so loud that Tom doesn't hear him. Jerry climbs on top of a table and shouts directly into Tom's face. Tom ignores him and pushes him toward one of his friends, who shoves Jerry into the phonograph's needle holder. Jerry is angry as he climbs out of the container, rubbing his rear end. He breaks the tone arm of the phonograph and then slams the piano cover on the fingers of the black cat who is playing the piano. Now the cats are angry and dash after Jerry, who runs back into his hole. They lure Jerry out again by turning on the phonograph. The cats catch him when he becomes caught when he becomes entangled in the venetian blinds. They tie him to the blinds and then resume the party. Jerry manages to wriggle to the telephone and place a call to Mammy. Mammy is at a friend's house playing cards with her girlfriends when the phone rings. Mammy answers the phone, and Jerry tells her that the cats are having a wild party at the house. Mammy slams down the phone saying, "A party! Excuse me!" She runs out the door and dashes down the street, leaving a trail of dust behind her. She arrives at the house and pushes the door open in front of her. Seeing the door, Tom opens it, and Mammy says "Thomas!" Tom slams the door in her face before she can say anything else. But Mammy breaks the door down and grabs Tom by his tail. She tosses him and his cat friends out of the house into the street. Mammy says, "Doggone cats! Mess up my whole evenin'! Well, might as well relax and play myself a little soothing, red-hot music." She puts a record on the phonograph and turns it on. The jazzy music is so loud that Jerry vibrates as he lies in bed as the cartoon ends.

Review: *Motion Picture Herald,* 25 March 1950

While the maid's away, the cats play, and Tom invites his alley cat friends in for a jam session. Jerry can't sleep and although he manages to eliminate Tom and his friends, it is to no avail as the maid returns and continues the jam session on the record. (7 min)

Review: *Film Daily,* 16 February 1950

When Beulah, the maid, steps out to her Saturday night social, Tom, the cat decides to throw a shindig for the rest of the gang. This disturbs Jerry, the mouse, who tells Beulah—who hurriedly stops the party. Marvelous cartoon.

Review: *Exhibitor Servisection,* 4 January 1950

This Technicolor frolic has Tom staging a party for his cat friends when the family goes out. Jerry is annoyed by the noise and the blasting of the jazz since he wants to sleep. When he protests, the cats really do him in until he is forced to get back at them by telephone to the maid who comes home and breaks up the cats' frolic. Alas, there is no rest for Jerry as she starts to play all the jazz recordings. Good.

Review: *Boxoffice,* 4 February 1950

Good. The sleep of Jerry, the mouse, is disturbed by a wild cat party, so he tries to break it up. He inflicts various kinds of punishment on the celebrants, such as slamming the piano lid down on the player's fingers, but finally gets run out. Jerry then phones the mistress to come home. As he is settling down for sleep, she puts on a noisy jazz record. In Technicolor.

SLEEPY-TIME TOM (1951)

Company: William Hanna, Joseph Barbera, M-G-M
Characters: Tom cat, Jerry mouse, Mammy Two-Shoes (voice characterization by Lillian Randolph)

Story: The cartoon opens on the street just as dawn is breaking. Tom and his three alley-cat friends are winding up a night on the town. They are singing tipsily when they arrive at Tom's house, where he leaves them. He is very sleepy and yawns before he attempts to climb through a window. He falls asleep lying on the window sill. His snores are heard by Mammy Two-Shoes, who walks into the room wearing house slippers on her feet, stockings with patches at the heels, and an apron around her waist. She shouts, "Thomas!" He jumps and becomes entangled in the venetian blinds at the window. Mammy shakes the blinds and Tom falls to the floor with a sleepy look on his face. Tom gets up as Mammy tells him, "Well, Mr. Playboy, while you is our partyin' all night, I has to keep dat mouse out of the refrigerator." Half asleep, Tom leans on her as she says, "Dat's yo' job, not mine." Tom slides off Mammy onto the floor and Mammy says, "Get up! Now get in there." Toms crawls into the kitchen, where he falls asleep again. "Is you asleep again?" Mammy walks in the kitchen with her hands on her hips and says, "Is you awake?" Tom snaps to his feet, stands at attention, and nods yes. Mammy tells him, "Listen heah, night owl! If I catch you asleep on the job, you is goin' out—understand?" Meanwhile Jerry sticks his head out of the cookie jar and overhears Mammy's orders. Mammy leaves the kitchen, slamming the door behind her. Tom looks around for Jerry and sees that the mouse has prepared a bed on a table for him using a loaf of bread as the pillow. Tom climbs in the makeshift bed and pulls the covers over him then goes to sleep and starts to snore. But he is awakened by Mammy's voice saying, "Thomas! Is dat you sleepin'?" Tom realizes that Jerry has tricked him and chases him until he trips and falls on the floor and goes to sleep. Mammy hears Tom's snores and says, "Thomas!" Immediately Tom is awake and chasing after Jerry again. Tom catches Jerry on a table but goes to sleep again after Jerry tunes in soft music on the radio. Tom falls asleep and slides to the floor where he lies asleep on Mammy's feet. Mammy taps her foot, which wakes up Tom. He snaps to attention before he chases Jerry, who hides in his hole in the wall. Tom stakes out Jerry's hole holding a baseball bat in his hand waiting for him to come out. He tries to keep awake by drinking cup after cup of coffee, but he falls asleep while he stands and holds the coffeepot in his hands. Mammy walks on the scene again and takes the pot out of his hands and says, "Were you sleeping, Tom?" Tom smiles and shakes his head no. Mammy walks away, saying, "You hadn't better be." Tom tries unsuccessfully to keep his eyes open by first propping them up with toothpicks and then by taping them open. As a last

resort, he paints a false eyeball on the lid of each eye before falling asleep standing up. When Mammy again arrives on the scene to check on him, she thinks he is awake and says, "Well Tom, glad to see you is wide awake. Keep up the good work." Then she leaves again. But Jerry is not fooled and is determined to get Tom thrown out of the house. He decides to paint road signs (a la Burma Shave highway signs of yesteryear) that read Are You Sleepy? Want a Bed? Solid Comfort, and Straight Ahead. They lead Tom directly to the bedroom where he falls asleep in bed. Mammy hears him snoring and runs into the room saying, "Thomas, git out of dat bed" before she tosses him out of the house and into the street where he falls asleep again lying on the sidewalk. His three cat buddies walk around the corner singing and stop when they see Tom. One of them says, "Well, look! It's Tom. Come on boys, we got a big night tonight." They pick him up and drag him, still sleeping, along with them as the cartoon ends.

Review: *Exhibitor Servisection,* 28 March 1951

When Tom, out all night, comes home, and tries to sleep, his slumbers are disturbed by the maid and Jerry, who helps make life miserable. His efforts to sleep comes to naught, he winds up, much against his will, goes out for more carousing with the cats. Fair.

Review: *Boxoffice,* 2 Jun 1951

Tom goes home after a night out with the fellow night-cats with just one aim—to sleep. But the maid orders him to keep Jerry out of the pantry. Tom does his best but every time he is about to catch Jerry, he falls asleep. Finally, when he manages to escape from the maid and get a few winks, his pals pick him up and drag him off to another sleepless night.

TRIPLET TROUBLE (1952)

Company: William Hanna, Joseph Barbera, M-G-M
Characters: Tom cat, Jerry mouse, Mammy Two-Shoes (voice characterization by Lillian Randolph), three little kittens

Story: The cartoon opens as Tom is having fun at Jerry's expense. Jerry is tied to one end of a long rubber rope. The other end is tied to a flat bat that Tom is holding. Tom whacks Jerry on his rear end, and Jerry springs back to be hit again. Tom is laughing when the sound of the front door buzzer is heard then followed by the voice of Mammy Two-Shoes saying, "Just a minute." Tom hears her approaching, and he hides Jerry in a desk drawer just before Mammy walks by wearing an apron around her waist and house slippers on her feet. Her stockings are patched at the heels. The door buzzer again rings and Mammy says, "I's comin', I's comin'." Tom hears the front door open, and then Mammy says, "Well look a here! Ain't dey cute! Why 'course we'll take care of 'em. Dey won't be no trouble at all. Good-bye." Tom hears the front door close and then sees Mammy enter the room with three little kittens—one black, one orange, and the other grey—cuddled in her arms. She says, "You is de sweetist things." She puts them down on a stuffed couch and tells them, "Three little fluffy kittens." She then turns her back on them and calls out, "Thomas, oh Thomas, come see what we's got." While her back is turned, the orange kitten prepares to give her a "hot foot" by placing a lighted match under one of her feet. The black kitten sticks a huge firecracker in the folds of her apron, and the gray kitten aims his slingshot at her. Tom arrives on the scene, and the kittens quickly remove the firecracker, and the burning match, seating themselves with innocent looks on their faces. Mammy turns back to face them and tells Tom, "Ain't dey cute, Tom?" Tom looks them over and nods his head yes. Mammy then says, "And you gits to take care of 'em. You be good to them until I return." They watch Mammy leave the room and the kittens place the firecracker and lighted match on Tom. The firecracker explodes, his foot is burned, and he is hit by the slingshot. He jumps in the air and yells. Then two of the kittens grab his arms and one of his legs while the other pulls a long knife and prepares to cut off his arm. He takes the knife and is about to give them a beating, when he hears Mammy shout "Thomas" as she walks into the room carrying a broom. She is dressed smartly, wearing a full-length fur-lined topcoat, gloves, and matching high-heeled shoes. She hits Tom on the top of the head six times before telling him, "What's de matter with you pickin' on dem po' little kittens? If you don't take good care of dem little angels while I's gone, I'll pulverize you to pieces. You heah me?" Covering his head with his hands, Tom, nods his head yes while the kittens sit on the couch cuddling each other. Mammy pats them on the head and tells them, "Good-bye my little darlin's." Then she leaves the room. Tom makes sure that Mammy has left the house before he prepares to attack the kittens. He stops when they pretend to make up to him by kissing his hand and rubbing against this legs. Just as Tom thinks that they want to be friends, two kittens attach rollerskates to his feet and push him across the room so that he crashes into a door. Meanwhile Jerry is having a good laugh as he sees Tom being the victim of the kitten's practical jokes. Tom chases the kittens, but they hide under the desk where Jerry is. Tom can't find the kittens, and after he walks away Jerry tries to congratulate them. However, the frowns on their faces, indicate to him that they plan to make him their next victim. Tom laughs when he sees Jerry being chased by the kittens who eventually throw him out of the window into the yard. The kittens then turn their attention to Tom, and eventually he too is tossed through the window into the yard. Satisfied, the kittens drink a bowl of milk while Tom and Jerry look angrily at them through the window. The cat and mouse decide to work together, and they develop a plan to rid themselves of the kittens. They successfully implement their plan, which results in the kittens' being removed from the house tied to a revolving clothes line in the yard. They hang suspended in the air as they slowly turn around and around while Tom and Jerry spank their rear ends. The kittens are partially covered by white sheets that resemble wings on their backs. Meanwhile Mammy arrives home, carrying a bottle of milk in her hand. As she enters the house, she says, "Well, here I is with de cream for dose three little angels." She hears the

sound of a spanking and looks out the window to see her three little angels with red rear ends flying through the air in circles while being spanked as the cartoon ends.

Mandy (1944–1948)

In 1944 Seymour Kneitel adapted Little Lulu, the popular cartoon character created by Marjorie Henderson and published in the *Saturday Evening Post,* to a new series of animated cartoons. The series was produced under the banner of Famous Studios and distributed by Paramount Pictures. Mandy, the black maid, appeared in a number of the cartoons. Mandy worked in Lulu's house and served as a comic foil for little Lulu, a little white girl who was usually involved in mischievous but harmless episodes. But she did not discipline Lulu. That role was always left to her father. Unlike Mammy Two-Shoes, Mandy was depicted in full view as a buxom house servant who wore a full-length dress and an apron around her waist and a bandanna on her head. Like the black maids in other animated series, she spoke in heavy dialect, using incorrect grammar and misusing common words.

LITTLE LULU CARTOON SERIES OPENING SONG

"Little Lulu, Little Lulu with freckles on your chin,
Always getting in and out of trouble, but mostly in.
Using daddy's necktie for the tail of your kite.
Using mommie's lipstick for the letters you write.
Though the clock says seven thirty, it's really after ten.
Looks like Little Lulu has been repairing it again.
Though you're wild as any Zulu and you're just as hard to tame
Little Lulu, I love you you just the same."
Written by Fred Wise, Sidney Lippman and Buddy Kaye

The brilliant comedienne Amanda Randolph, older sister of Lillian Randolph, provided the voice characterization for Mandy. Randolph who appeared in several of Oscar Micheaux's films of the 1930s, including *Lying Lips* and *Swing.* She was born in Louisville, Kentucky, and began her stage career in Cleveland, Ohio, at the age of fourteen. In addition to appearing on the stage, she also sang in nightclubs. Her first real break came in 1925 when she appeared in the black musical revue *Lucky Sambo* as part of a singing trio that also included Hilda Perleno and Berlena Banks. Between 1926 and 1932 she appeared in many hit stage productions, including *Joy Cruise, In the Alley, Chili Peppers, Fall Frolics, Radiowaves,* and *Dusty Lane,* opposite Dusty "Open the Door" Richard. In the 1930s she toured Europe with a show headed by the two famous minstrels Scott and Whaley. In 1932 Amanda and Catherine Handy (daughter of the famous composer W. C. Handy) were billed as the Dixie Nightingales and sang in several shows, including Glenn and Jenkins "Re-vue." She also made many radio appearances and succeeded her sister, Lillian, in the role of the housekeeper on *The Great Gildersleeve* radio show and the in title role on the *Aunt Jemima Show.* Her television roles included the maid on the *Danny*

Thomas Show, and also the mother-in-law on the *Amos 'n' Andy Show.* Her major film credits include *No Way Out,* and *She's Working Her Way Through College.* Amanda Randolph died in Los Angeles in 1967.

In 1948 Famous Studios/ Paramount Pictures decided to replace Little Lulu with another cartoon character, Little Audrey, a freckle-faced, red-haired white girl. The cartoons were based on a comic book character and included a black maid in several of the releases of the series, which ended in 1958.

Mandy Stories and Reviews

BUTTERSCOTCH AND SODA (1948)

Company: Seymour Kneitel, Famous Studies; released by Paramount Pictures
Type: First in Little Audrey series
Characters: Little Audrey, black maid

Story: The opening shows Little Audrey sitting on a sofa in her home eating candy. Meanwhile the black maid, a large, heavy-set woman with a red bandanna tied on her head, has just come home from grocery shopping. As she walks through the kitchen she sees that Little Audrey did not eat her lunch, which is on the table. The maid shakes her head and says "Dat Little Audrey ain't done eat her lunch again." The maid looks around and says, "I wonder if . . ." Little Audrey hears the maid calling her and wraps up her bag of candy in a towel. She cradles it like a baby as the maid enters and snatches the candy from her saying, "Eating candy again!" Dragging Little Audrey behind her, the maid takes her to the kitchen and seats her at the table and says, "Now you sit right down and eat your lunch and no mo' candy." The maid turns and begins to put up the groceries, saying, "I just can't understand a child eating candy forty-eight hours a day." Meanwhile Little Audrey is seated at the table with a fork in one hand that she is using to eat candy from a bag she has hidden under the table and with the other hand feeding her lunch to the dog sitting on the floor behind her. The maid discovers what Audrey is doing and says, "It's just candy, candy, candy . . ." She pulls Little Audrey to her room and seats her on the bed, saying "Now you gonna stay right here in your room 'til you is ready to eat food." The maid opens the window and discovers that Audrey has tied bags of candy, one for each day of the week, to a string hanging out of the window. The maid takes the bags and tells Little Audrey, "You gonna stay here for the whole weekend if necessary" and leaves the room. After the maid leaves, Audrey remembers that she has hidden candy in the room and searches for it frantically. Unable to find it, she feels dizzy and suddenly finds herself in a strange land where everything is made of candy. Delighted, Audrey begins to stuff candy in her mouth and into a large bag that she pulls behind her. She passes a sign that reads I'd Walk a Mile for a Caramel. Suddenly she begins to feel ill and drops her bag of candy. It turns into a large, ghostlike figure that hovers over her singing, "You've got the tummyache blues from eating all the candy you did." Little Audrey tries in vain to escape but soon all of the candy surrounding her, in-

cluding five licorice-drop heads with stereotypical black features that hover over her singing, "You've got the tummyache blues. The look on your face is telling the news." Next she becomes stuck in a lake of sticky candy, and later she is tied to a chair and candy is stuffed into her mouth. Finally she wakes up. It has all been a dream. The maid is washing her face with cool water and saying, "Honey chile, you is alive. Here is all the candy you want." She gives her a bag of candy, but Little Audrey runs to the kitchen. When the maid looks through the door, she is astonished to see the dog sitting at the table eating Audrey's candy with one paw and using the other one to give food to Little Audrey who is eating her lunch while seated on the floor behind him as the cartoon ends.

EGGS DON'T BOUNCE (1943)

Company: I. Sparber, Famous Studios; released by Paramount Pictures
Characters: Little Lulu, Lulu's dog, Mandy (voice characterization by Amanda Randolph)

Story: Cartoon opens with two large eyes that fill the screen. Next seen is the face of Mandy, the black maid, wearing a red and white polka-dot bandanna on her head. She is standing outside the house looking up and down the street, calling, "Lulu!" She is wearing a long dress, red polka-dot stockings, and house slippers on her feet. Meanwhile Lulu is down the street playing with her dog and doing good deeds. In a short time she pacifies a crying baby and cuts the hair away from the eyes of a large sheepdog before she skips home licking a large piece of candy. When she arrives home, Mandy is waiting and tells her, "Lulu, you is never 'round when I needs you. Now you'all go to the store and get me a dozen eggs. Now be careful not to disintegrate 'em." Lulu goes to the store and buys a bag of eggs. Then she and the dog walk home. After dodging cars while crossing a busy street, Lulu and the dog sit down on a park bench to rest. But the bench breaks, throwing the eggs and the dog into the air. Despite the efforts of the dog to save them, the eggs are broken when they hit the sidewalk, which makes Lulu very sad. She wonders what Mandy will do to her. She has a daydream that she is in Eggland running over a sea of eggs with an angry Mandy hovering over her and singing, "Now you've done it, Lulu. You shouldn't have broken them eggs. You're in trouble now. Now you've done it." Lulu continues to run and break the eggs under her feet, and Mandy continues to sing, "Now you've done it. You done, done, done it. You gonna catch it good 'cause you didn't behave the way that you should." Now swimming in a sea of broken eggs, Lulu is pulled into a whirlpool created by a giant eggbeater. She sinks into egg hell where two deviled eggs tell her that she's in trouble. Her next stop is at the North Pole. Santa Claus scratches her name off his list of good little girls. Mandy continues to sing, "You've got yourself in a mess now, ain't that a shame. You wouldn't take my warning. My, is your face red! When you woke up this mornin', you should have stood in bed. You've done done it. Didn't take you long. When you done what you done, you sho' done it good." Sitting on the curb, Lulu stops daydreaming. She and her dog get up and slowly walk toward home. On the way Lulu hears the clucking sound of a hen, and she and the dog get an idea about where they can "borrow" some eggs. They arrive at the henhouse and try unsuccessfully to buy and then to steal eggs from Henrietta, the hen. Next Lulu, dressed in overalls and in blackface makeup, pretends to be the black farmhand. Carrying a large ax, Lulu walks by the hen and says, "My mouth is waterin' for some fried chicken, umm, umm!" She carefully looks at the frightened hen and says, "Let me see now! What part of de chicken does I eat fust? De leg, wing, or de neck?" Lulu pulls a feather out of the tail of the chicken and cuts it on the blade of the ax. The hen runs for her life. Lulu and her dog return home with a bag of eggs that are broken when Lulu trips and falls on the front steps. Little baby chicks come out of the egg shells as Mandy comes out of the door, reviews the scene, and says, "Is that you Lulu?" She lets out a big chuckle as the cartoon ends.

LUCKY LULU (1944)

Company: Seymour Kneitel, Famous Studios; Paramount
            Pictures
Characters: Little Lulu, Mandy (voice characterization by
            Amanda Randolph)

Story: The cartoon opens as Little Lulu writes an entry in her diary for Tuesday: "Because I saved a horse from starving, I got a spanking." The following scene is a flashback showing that she fed the sway-backed horse by allowing it to eat apples loaded on a wagon it was pulling, much to the consternation of the owner. Her Wednesday entry in her diary says that she got a spanking for winning first prize in a hobby contest. Her hobby was raising a hive of bees that chased all of her fellow contestants and the judges from the building. On Thursday she writes that she got a spanking for putting out a fire. Mandy, wearing a bandanna on her head, brings in a flaming dessert from the kitchen and places it on the table in front of where Lulu and her father are sitting. Lulu uses a fire extinguisher to put out the flames, ruining the dessert. On Friday Lulu writes, "Resolved: Today I'm going to be a good girl." Mandy tells her, "If you wants to keep dat resolution you better git yo'self some good luck cause today am Friday the thirteenth. What you need is a lucky charm to keep you out of trouble." Lulu says, What is a lucky charm, Mandy?" Mandy explains, "There are a lot of lucky charms—let me see now. There's de fo' leaf clover, and there's de rabbit's foot, and de horseshoe, Dat's it, horseshoe. You find yourself a horseshoe and your luck will change." The scene changes to a farm in the country where a horse is eating oats. Lulu is inside a barrel, with a fishing pole sticking out of the top. She slowly sneaks up on the horse. A magnet is tied to the end of a fishing line, and Lulu uses it to pull the shoe off one of the horse's hoofs. She says, "Wait till Mandy sees my good luck charm." But the horseshoe is now magnetized, and on the way back home Lulu manages to pull the metal handcuffs off a policeman, destroy a storefront mannequin, and spill a load of watermelons, one of which rolls into a manhole and hits a street worker on his head. Arriving home, she greets Mandy, saying, "Mandy, look my good luck charm" while holding up the horseshoe. Mandy says, "You is gonna need good luck 'cause you's got visiters in dere." Lulu sees

the policeman, the store owner, the delivery driver, and the street worker sitting in the next room. Mandy says, "They is waitin' fo' yo' daddy to come home." The sound of a closing door is heard, and Mandy says, "Heah he comes now. If you wants good luck, you better kiss dat horseshoe and throw it over your left shoulder." Lulu follows Mandy's instructions, but the horseshoe flies through the air and wraps itself around her father's neck, pinning him to the door. Lulu writes in her diary, "P.S. My daddy doesn't believe in good luck charms, so . . ." She lies across her daddy's lap and receives her spanking as the cartoon ends.

LULU GETS THE BIRDIE (1944)

Company: I. Sparber, Famous Studios; released by Para-
            mount Pictures
Characters: Little Lulu, Mandy (the black maid), a black
            crow (voice characterization by Lillian Randolph)

Story: The Cartoon opens with Mandy, the black maid, arriving home. As she comes through the door, she is so shocked by the mess in the kitchen that she turns white and her pigtail hair stands straight out of her head. There are pots and pans all over the table and empty milk bottles all over the floor. She says, "For lands sakes. My, my! Somebody has been makin' sabotage in my kitchen." She sees fingerprints on the icebox and says, "Dem fingerprints looks mighty familiar." When she opens the icebox door, she sees inside a big pile of ice cream and says, "Just what I thought. Lulu's been reconnoitering around here again. I don't know what I's gonna do with that Little Lulu. I wonder where she could be? Well, I guess I gotta eat all that delicious ice cream myself." Lulu, with ice cream on her face, pops out of the dresser drawer. Mandy shakes her finger in Lulu's face and tells her, "Lulu, you sho' pulled a Lulu in this here kitchen." Lulu asks, "How did you know it was me, Mandy? Mandy answers, "I always knows when you done wrong." Lulu asks, "How do you know?" Mandy answers her, "A little birdie done told me. That's right, a little birdie done told me." A puzzled Lulu looks through the window and sees a bird's nest in a tree in her yard. Lulu is about to shoot the red bird sleeping on the nest with her slingshot when she asks, "Are you the little birdie that's been talking about me?" At this moment a little red bird appears and Lulu says, "Beat it, small fry. I want to converse with your mother." The mother awakes, sees her baby in danger, and snatches it under her wing. Lulu asks her, "Did you tell Mandy on me?" The mother bird kicks the nest, which falls down over Lulu's head. Then she flies away with her baby as Lulu says, "I guess red birds can't talk." Next Lulu confronts a woodpecker and asks, "Have you been poking your nose into my affair?" The woodpecker responds by chopping the handle off Lulu's slingshot before he flies away. Discouraged, Lulu sits down on a stump and says, "Mandy's been telling me fibs. Birds can't talk." She hears a voice behind her saying, "You wouldn't be bettin' any money on that statement, would you?" The voice is coming from a black crow perched on a straw scarecrow. Lulu answers, "I don't bet. But I know birds can't talk." The crow says, "Oh yes, they does talk." Lulu replies, "Oh no they don't." Again the crow replies, "Oh yes they does" as Lulu looks around and sees him. Lulu says, "So you can talk." The crow replies "Yowassa, I's probably one of de few winged linguists in de world." Lulu then says, "You must be a tattletale bird too?" The crow answers, "Yowassa." Lulu pulls out her slingshot and aims it at the crow, who ducks and tells her, "No! Put that lethal weapon down, gal! I ain't no tattletale bird. I'm just a scared crow. Why, I's known lottsa other birds dat talks." Lulu says, "Name one," and the crow replies, "Well he's about so big" while stretching out his wings. Lulu asks, "Is he black?" The crow answers, "Ya got it—black." Lulu aims her slingshot at the scared crow who has beads of sweat dropping from his beak and says to her, "No, no, no. What am I saying. He's big and blue. Blue as the sky." He looks up and sees a big bluebird holding a slingshoot aimed at his head. The crow says, "Did, did, did I say big and blue? Count that out and make it little and red." Lulu answers, "Little and red," and imagines she sees the little red bird whispering into Mandy's ear. Lulu decides to capture the little red bird using an apple to lure it through the window of her garage. But before she can get it, the bird is captured by a black cat who plans to eat it. Lulu rushes to the rescue. She enters the garage and ties cans of paint to the cat's tail before chasing it away. Lulu sits down on the steps of her house, the outside of which is covered with spots of paint. From inside she hears Mandy's voice saying, "Lulu, what's all dat racket 'bout?" Lulu grabs a book and pretends to read as Mandy comes out the door and sees spilled paint all over the house. She says, "Pains my soul. We been blitzkrieged." She asks Lulu, "Did you done dat?" Before Lulu can answer the little redbird crawls out from under the garment Lulu is wearing. Mandy says, "Well, a little birdie! Tell me, little birdie, did Lulu make all dat mess? The little bird shakes its head and Mandy says, "Well, dat does it. Just wait till your daddy hears what dat little birdie done tell me." The next scene shows Lulu lying across her daddy's knee for a spanking. She is reading a book on first aid. Daddy's hand rises to strike Lulu's bottom but stops in midair. A sign is pinned to Lulu's drawers, "Fragile, Handle with Care," as the cartoon ends.

Review: *Box Office,* 13 May 1944

Swell. The high standard of cartoon fun established by Little Lulu in her past two efforts is maintained in the third number of the series. Lulu has a winsome charm which is fully exploited by the animators. Here she gets angry at a little red bird for carrying tales, and almost causes its sudden at the hands of a greedy cat. However, her conscience balks, and Lulu sets things alright.

LULU'S BIRTHDAY PARTY (1944)

Company: I. Sparber, Famous Studios; released by Paramount Pictures

Characters: Little Lulu, Mandy (voice characterization by Amanda Randolph)

Story: The cartoon opens in the kitchen where numerous notes with "Sept. 2" written on them are tacked to the walls. Mandy, the black maid, a heavy woman wearing a bandanna on her head, polka-dot stockings, and house slippers, enters the kitchen as one of the notes floats through the air and lands on her face. She reads the note, which says, "September 2nd. Today is my birthday, Lulu." Mandy looks around and sees the notes, laughs, and says, "Well, fan my pure Virginia body. Dat little Lulu puts dem birthday remembrances in de funniest of places." She does not see the note that is pinned to the back of her dress. She opens a book entitled *Birthday Party Recipes* and says, "Dat little angel gonna be historical with joy when she finds out what's perculatin's today." Meanwhile Lulu, with her pet frog, Quincy, sitting on top of her head, decides to go to the kitchen. Mandy is busy making the cake saying, "Sho' 'nuff I'd better quit dis bakin' done befo' Lulu finds out what's cookin'." Mandy hears Lulu coming and hastily hides the cooking utensils and replaces them with an ironing board. Lulu enters the kitchen and says, "Good morning, Mandy." Mandy says, "Is that you, little angel?" Lulu replies, "Yes Mandy, me and Quincy." She points to her pet frog. Mandy takes a close look at the frog and says, "Well shut my mouth wide open." When the frog croaks, Mandy screams and jumps on top of the icebox and says, "Lulu, you put dat leapin' dinosaurian out of here. What you tryin' to do—make a nervous wreck outta me?" Lulu opens her pocket and the frog jumps into it. Mandy then pushes Lulu out of the kitchen with her broom, saying, "Now get outta here with dat jumpin' jack befo' I makes a frog fricassee out of him." Then she closes the door. But Lulu sticks her head in another door and says, "But Mandy, don't you know what day this is?" Mandy says, "Don't bother me chile. Now preambulate your body right out of here." Lulu says, "But is it gonna be . . ." Mandy tells her, "You heard what I told you. Now go on and play like a good little girl." Outside Lulu tries several times to peek through the window, but each time Mandy pulls down the shade. Finally Lulu plays hopscotch with her frog, who jumps through the window into the kitchen. Mandy screams and calls for Lulu to come help her. Lulu enters the kitchen and says, "A birthday cake!" She sees Mandy standing on a stool holding the birthday cake over her head. Mandy says, "Lulu, get that vicious crocodile out of heah!" The frog jumps on Mandy's back and crawls under her dress, and Mandy jumps up and falls on the floor. The cake lands on top of her head. Lulu asks her, "Mandy, am I gonna have a party? Huh?" Mandy says, "Chile, the answer is N-O-U-H—no!" Lulu says, "That's what I suspected" as she slowly walks out of the house into the yard and sits under a tree. She says to the frog, "The day started off to be a perfect one. And me and Quincy were oh so glad. But I had to go and be the nosey one and spoil the best time I almost had at my birthday party." She daydreams of a land high in the clouds where it's her birthday. The mountains are made of ice cream and the rivers flow with lemonade. She climbs high atop a birthday cake and is about to light the candle when she is awakened by the sound of Mandy's voice calling, "Lulu, Lulu, come here!" Lulu rushes home, and when she opens the door she sees that the room is full of her friends who have come to her birthday party. Mandy tells her, "Congratulations, Lulu. Now make a wish and blow out the candles" as she puts the birthday cake on the table. But Lulu uses a bellows, which creates a jet of air so strong that it blows the candles and icing off the cake and onto the faces of her guests. They all smile and say, "Happy birthday, Lulu" as the cartoon ends.

LULU'S INDOOR OUTING (1944)

Company: I. Sparber, Famous Studios; Paramount Pictures
Characters: Little Lulu, Mandy (voice characterization by Amanda Randolph), tall ghost (Jimmy Durante caricature), Junior the short ghost

Story: The cartoon opens in a forest where there is an old haunted house. Inside are two ghosts—a tall one and a short one. The short ghost cooks an old leather boot in the fireplace while saying, "Oh boy! What I wouldn't give for some roast turkey with cranberry sauce, mashed potatoes . . ." The tall ghost says, "Shut up! You're talkin' about turkey and we haven't eaten in fifty years." As the scent of roast turkey floats in through the window, the ghosts look outside and see Mandy and Lulu having a picnic. Lulu cooks the turkey on a grill while Mandy, a large black woman with thick white lips who wears a bandanna on her head, striped stockings on her legs, and house slippers on her feet, says, "Dat sho' am luscious smellin' turkey." The ghosts look at each other and say, "Turkey!" The tall ghost decides on a plan to get the food. They trick Lulu and Mandy into believing there is a storm by flying over them and sprinkling them with water while beating a drum to imitate thunder. Mandy, holding the basket of food on her head, runs for cover as she says, "Wait a minute, Lulu! You gonna get drenched to the bone." But Lulu hides under the basket of food and runs while licking her lollipop. They arrive at the haunted house where Mandy says, "Whew! Dat weather done changed its mind in a hurry." Lulu says, "Let's have our picnic in here, Mandy. It's nice and dry." She opens the front door and they both go inside. Mandy is nervous as she looks around her and says, "I got a feelin' dat dis here house is haunted." Lulu tells her, "Aw, Mandy. You're afraid of your own shadow." As she cuts the cake, Mandy tells her, "Ghosts and me just don't get along." She puts the basket of food on the floor. Then Junior appears in front of Mandy. Her eyes open wide and she screams as she runs through the wall, out of the house, and down the road, leaving a trail of dust and her oversized polka-dot bloomers behind her. Lulu, looking through the hole in the wall, calls out, "Mandy! Come back here. There ain't no such thing as ghosts." Then Junior and the tall ghost appear in front of her. Junior says, "Boooooo" and Lulu places a mirror in front of them. They see their reflection and are scared and run into the next room as Lulu snorts, "Scaredy cats." Junior looks through the keyhole and sees Lulu eating the food. He turns to the tall ghost and says, "We can't scare her. Now who's goin' to get the food?" The two ghosts try all sorts of means to get the food from Lulu, but they are unsuccessful. Lulu eats the last of the food, packs the dishes into the basket, and walks out of the

house. The ghosts see her leave and throw their arms around each other and say, "It's all gone." They begin to cry. Lulu hears them and walks back to the house and signals with her finger for them to follow her. Back at Lulu's house the two ghosts are feasting on a table full of food. Mandy has fainted and is lying in a corner while Lulu fans her and says, "There ain't no such things as ghosts" as the cartoon ends.

SONG OF THE BIRDS (1949)

Company: Bill Tytla, Famous Studios; released by Paramount Pictures
Type: Noveltoons
Characters: Little Audrey, black maid

Story: The characters portray the story in pantomime. The sound of birdsong superimposed on the background music is heard throughout the entire cartoon. The cartoon opens as Little Audrey is having great fun with her rifle, taking target practice inside her house. She exhibits expert marksmanship as she hits a skillet tied to the wagging tail of her dog. Then she hits the mechanical cuckoo bird as it pops in and out of the clock. Next she sneaks up on the black maid, who is fast asleep in a rocking chair. The maid is wearing a bandanna on her head and house slippers on her feet. Audrey places a tomato on the top of the maid's head and then backs away. She takes aim and shoots the tomato. The sound of the shot causes the maid to wake up with her mouth and eyes wide open. She wipes the red tomato juice from her face and thinks it is blood. She is convinced that she has been shot, and her face turns white with fear before she faints and slumps back into her chair. As Audrey laughs, the maid wakes up and grabs her shoulder. She pulls her out of the house and into the street. Standing in the front door, she shakes her fist at Audrey and gestures to her to never shoot her rifle in the house again. Audrey is angry for being thrown out of the house but quickly turns her attention to other targets of opportunity. Her first victim is a squirrel. She shoots a walnut out of his paws before he dives back into his hole in a tree trunk. Meanwhile, high in a tree, a mother robin is coaxing her baby bird to take its first flying lesson. Just after the little bird has learned to stay aloft on his own, he becomes Audrey's next target. She fires several shots at him. He dodges the bullets, but becomes so frightened that he faints in midair and falls to the ground. Audrey and the mother bird think that the baby bird is dead. Audrey goes home and has a nightmare about the little bird's funeral. She wakes up when it it begins to rain and when she looks out of her bedroom window, she sees that the raindrops, falling on the baby bird's face, have revived him. He was not dead after all. He opens his eyes and his happy mother takes him into her wings and flies back to their tree home. Audrey is so happy that she runs outside to be with the baby bird, but is rejected by the other birds. She sadly walks away with her head down. But the little bird feels sorry for her and flies out of the tree to perch on her shoulder. They smile at each other and quickly become good friends as the cartoon ends.

Buzzy the Crow (1947–1954)

In 1947 Famous Studios/Paramount Pictures introduced a new character—Buzzy the black crow (see fig. 24). Buzzy had the demeanor of Kingfish of the *Amos 'n' Andy* radio and television shows and a voice like Eddie "Rochester" Anderson's of the *Jack Benny* radio and television shows. Buzzy turned the tables on a dull-witted cat, who attempted to eat him to cure common ailments such as hiccups, baldness, toothache, and insomnia. In this series the voice characterization by Buzzy was probably performed by a white actor, a common practice for cartoons of the period.

Buzzy the Crow Stories and Reviews

AS THE CROW LIES (1951)

Company: Seymour Kneitel, Famous Studies, Paramount Pictures
Type: Noveltoons; later distributed as Harveytoons
Characters: Buzzy the crow, Katnip the cat

Story: The Cartoon opens with the sound of hiccups. On the kitchen table are standing several bottles of medicine. Katnip has the hiccups and looks at a calendar on the wall, saying "Thirty days . . . and I still got the hiccups." When the alarm clock rings, he says, "My goodness! It's time for my pill—the last one. It's just gotta work." He tries to swallow the pill, but it slips out of his mouth and bounces into a fishbowl and is swallowed by a small fish. Katnip grabs the fish out of the bowl and tells him, "Gimmie that pill." The fish spits out the pill, which rolls on the floor before dropping through the grating of a heating vent. Katnip says, "There goes my only hope" as he bumps into a bookcase, spilling a pile of books on the floor. Katnip picks up one book and says "Wow! What do you know about that—a cure for hiccups." Katnip reads it aloud, "If hiccups you've got, and you want them to go away, there is one sure cure: eat freshly caught crow!" Katnip says, "That sounds logical," as he hears the sound of music outside of his window. The music is coming from a treehouse. Buzzy is inside playing a tune on the piano and singing, "Listen to the mocking bird, listen to the mocking bird—a chick that's got a boogie-woogie beat." Katnip cuts down Buzzy's treehouse and is carrying it home when he hiccups and shakes the house so much that Buzzy thinks it's an earthquake. He tries to fly away, saying, "Here I goes, as the crow flies." Buzzy is captured by Katnip who carries him into his house and ties him up. Sweating with fear, Buzzy begs him, "Please tell me this is just a bad dream and you ain't no cat." Katnip looks at him and says, "Meowwww!" Buzzy turns white with fear. Katnip reads the recipe for crow sandwich. "Use two slices of bread, (hiccup) no more or no fewer, (hiccup), eat the crow in between them, (hiccup) and your hiccups will be cured." Buzzy observes the situation and says to himself, "That cat has a bad case of hiccups. That's all I needs to know." Katnip unties Buzzy, puts him between two slices of bread, and opens his mouth to take a bite. Just

then Buzzy says, "Boss! Boss! Now Boss, I hates to interrupt you while you're eatin', Boss, but I knows of a sure cure for the hiccups." Katnip says, "Really?" Buzzy says, "Yeah Boss, hiccups doctor is what they calls me." Buzzy sits Katnip in a chair and places a paper bag over his head, tying it tightly around Katnip's neck. "Now all you has to do is breathe deeply." Katnip says, "That sounds logical." Buzzy flies to the front door and he is about to exit the house through the mail slot, saying "Don't stop! Inhale, exhale, inhale . . ." Katnip follows the instructions, but his breathing is interrupted by a big hiccup that sends him flying across the room where he lands on the floor, knocking the bag off of his head. He tells Buzzy, "It didn't work." Buzzy replies, "Didn't work. Now Boss, a sure enough cure is to count to ten and to drink a glass of water between each count." Katnip begins to count, "One, two . . ." Buzzy gives him glasses of water, each one larger than the preceeding one. By the time Katnip has counted to nine, the water has swollen his stomach to twice its normal size. As he reaches the count of ten, Buzzy gives him a beer keg full of water. He drinks it as Buzzy again tries to escape. Then Katnip hiccups, and the water he drank exits his mouth, creating a flood. Katnip tells Buzzy, "It just didn't work." Buzzy says, "Now don't get discouraged, Boss. The only genuine sure cure is the shock treatment." Katnip says, "That sounds logical." Buzzy places Katnip on the bed, covers him with an electric blanket, plugs it into an electrical socket, and cuts the cord, which burns like a fuse back to the blanket, which burns up. Katnip jumps out of the bed and yells in pain, but Buzzy tells him, "Step right this way for the cold treatment." As he holds open the door of the refrigerator, Katnip runs into it. Buzzy slams the door shut and finally exits through the letterdrop while saying, "So long, stupid!" Katnip hiccups, the refrigerator opens, and a block of ice containing Katnip slides out across the floor and into a fireplace. The fire melts the ice, exposing Katnip to the flames. He gets such a burn that he leaps up the chimney into the air, where he catches Buzzy who is flying away. He tells him, "This time I'm doing what the book says." Katnip is about to take a bite of his crow sandwich when Buzzy pops up, "Boss, Boss, let's not jump to concussions. We still didn't try the scare treatment." Buzzy flies to a closet and enters, closing the door behind him. Katnip pulls the door open and is frightened when he sees a skeleton standing in front of him. The skeleton is painted on an ironing board, which falls on Katnip's head. Next Buzzy pushes a bomb with a lighted fuse under Katnip, who is so terrified that he jumps up and clutches the ceiling so hard that his claws penetrate the roof. On the roof Buzzy nails Katnip's claws down and then saws a circle around him. Katnip falls to the floor as the bomb explodes. On the roof Buzzy says, "Well, I guess dat cures his hiccups for good." He sees cat angels floating through the hole in the roof. He counts them one by one as the cartoon ends.

Review: *Film Daily*, 6 February 1951

A cat plagued by hiccups reads that a sure cure is tasty, fresh crow. He finds one but the crow talks him into a series of the cures, none of which work. Lots of laughs. (6 min)

Review: *Motion Picture Herald,* **8 February 1951**

What is the cure for hiccups? The cat in this subject decides it is to swallow a fresh crow. He is about to down the crow, Buzzy by name, when the bird succeeds in convincing him that there are better remedies. Buzzy demonstrates the remedies for the cat, but they are more calculated to kill than cure. (6 min)

Review: *Exhibitor Servisection,* **20 June 1951**

Buzzy, the crow, is about to be eaten by a cat with hiccoughs when he thinks of some remedies to stop the attack. None of them works, and the windup finds cat going to a cat's heaven, all nine lives of him. Fair.

Review: *Boxoffice,* **28 July 1951**

An amusing cartoon about Buzzy, the crow, and his arch-enemy, the big cat. A cat has a bad case of hiccups until he reads in a medical book that the best cure is "fresh crow must be eaten." He spies Buzzy and puts him between two slices of bread but the crow gets out of this predicament by promising the cat the perfect cure. He then puts him through all sorts of horrible experiences until all nine lives are used.

THE AWFUL TOOTH (1952)

Company: Seymour Kneitel, Famous Studios, Paramount Pictures
Type: Noveltoons
Characters: Buzzy the crow, Katnip the cat

Story: The cartoon opens inside Katnip's house, where he is in pain. He has a toothache and says, "This stupid tooth is killing me." Inside his mouth tiny workers are drilling one of his teeth with a jackhammer. He hears singing coming from outside and he looks out of his window to see Buzzy the crow sitting on his front porch, fishing. His line extends from his house high in a tree down to Katnip's birdbath. Katnip decides to catch himself a meal, and he removes a stuffed swordfish hanging on the wall and ties it to the end of Buzzy's line. Buzzy thinks he has caught a fish, but the cat pulls on the line and Buzzy is pulled into the house. Katnip prepares to make crow stew as Buzzy looks around and says, "Oh man, what have I got myself into?" Katnip is chanting to himself. "Confucius say, when toothache drives you loco, catch a black crow. Stew it like chow mein. Slowly eat now, good for pain." On hearing this, Buzzy says to himself, "This feline has a bad toothache. That's all I needs to know." Katnip raises his knife and is about to chop Buzzy into pieces, when Buzzy says, "Boss! Boss! I is the sole living soul that has the formula for curing that toothache. And Boss, if I die, the secret dies with me." Katnip pauses and says, "Secret—what secret?" Buzzy tells him, "The secret of freezing the nerves, Boss." Katnip says, "That seems logical." Buzzy tells Katnip to put his head into the freezer of the refrigerator. Instantaneously Katnip is frozen stiff as a board. Buzzy attempts to get away while singing "Small fry struttin' by the pool room." But he is also frozen solid as he walks across the cat's back. Katnip sneezes so hard that it blows both of them across the room. Buzzy slams into a door, which knocks the

ice off him. Katnip lands on the steam-heater vent, and the ice melts off him. Katnip grabs Buzzy and tells him that his tooth is still hurting. Buzzy tells him, "Think nothing of it, Boss. The only perfect cure is my old home remedy." He then ties one end of a string to Katnip's tooth and the other end to a doorknob. He tells the cat, "Boss, when you slam the door, no more toothache." But before he slams the door, Buzzy ignites a stick of dynamite and ties it to the door handle. Buzzy slams the door, pulling the cat to the door where he swallows the dynamite, which explodes in his mouth. Smoke flows out of Katnip's ears, and when he opens his mouth, all of his teeth fall out, except the one that is hurting. Katnip is frantic and runs out of the house calling for a doctor. Katnip arrives at the dentist's office, where he finds Buzzy dressed as a dentist and pretending to be Dr. Tapalong Cavity. Katnip tells Buzzy, "Hurry up Doc! I can't stand the pain." Buzzy tells the cat to get in the chair and open his mouth wide. Katnip obeys and Buzzy grabs a bag of plumber's tools and walks across Katnip's outstretched tongue into the cat's mouth. Inside the cat's mouth, loud sounds of banging and welding are heard. Buzzy walks out and says, "See Boss, a new bridge!" A bridge with cars traveling on it is seen in Katnip's mouth. Buzzy tells him that he will put in fillings and then he pours concrete into the cat's mouth. The concrete keeps on flowing until the cat is so heavy that he falls through the floor. Buzzy quickly pulls off his uniform and starts to walk away, saying, "Your troubles are over, Boss. So long." He doesn't go far before he hears a voice say, "Hey Doc." Katnip appears pushing a concrete statue of himself and says, "My filling fell out." He then looks at Buzzy and says, "Hey, you're no dentist." He chases Buzzy round and round the room. Buzzy plays tricks on him at every turn: throws dinner plates into Katnip's mouth, telling him, "Boss, you have upper and lower plates"; throws a gold pot into Katnip's mouth, saying, "Boss, you need a gold inlay." Buzzy finds a piano and tells Katnip, "Boss, come over this way for a new set of ivories." He ties rubber bands to each end of the piano, and they snag Katnip as he runs by. Katnip continues to run, stretching the rubber bands. Katnip runs into the wall and the piano is pulled into Katnip's mouth, which knocks him silly. Buzzy flies out of the house back up to his treehouse and grabs his fishing pole, saying, "You ain't the biggest catfish in the sea" as the cartoon ends.

Review: *Motion Picture Herald,* **24 May 1952**

The cat, suffering from a toothache, gets out his remedy book, which recommends eating a crow. To make matters simple, a crow is sitting right outside the window fishing and singing. The simplicity stops there. The crow pulls all sorts of tricks on the suffering cat, leaving him at the end without a tooth. (7 min)

Review: *Motion Picture Exhibitor,* **4 April 1957**

An aching wisdom tooth is driving the cat mad until he reads a remedy that calls for crow to be eaten. The cat captures a crow, which immediately goes to work on him with substitute remedies, until the crow has the cat helpless, and he returns to his fishing. Fair.

Review: *Exhibitor Servisection,* **23 April 1952**

An aching wisdom tooth is driving the cat mad until he reads a remedy that calls for crow to be eaten. The cat captures a crow, which immediately goes to work on him. First, he has the cat freeze the tooth by placing his head in the refrigerator. The crow then tries the string-on-door technique, which results in the cat losing all teeth but the right one. After a few more experiments the crow has the cat helpless, and he returns to his fishing. Fair.

Review: *Boxoffice,* **31 May 1952**

A little crow makes matters miserable for a cat whose aching wisdom tooth is driving him crazy. The crow suggests freezing the nerves by pushing the cat into the refrigerator, and then he pushes a bridge into the feline's mouth—only the bridge is one with cars, trucks, and buses. At last the crow puts in a new set of ivories—the keys of a piano.

BETTER BAIT THAN NEVER (1953)

Company: Seymour Kneitel, Famous Studios, Paramount Pictures
Type: Noveltoons
Characters: Buzzy the crow, Katnip the cat

Story: The cartoon opens as Katnip walks toward the pier with a fishing pole on his shoulder. When he arrives, he sees a No Fishing sign. Lying on the ground nearby, is the guard dog, taking a nap. Katnip ignores the sign and walks quietly around the dog, baits his hook, and casts his line into the water. A fish sees Katnip's hook sinking to the ocean bottom and cuts his line. Feeling a tug on the line, Katnip pulls it up and discovers it has been cut. Not to be outdone, the cat replaces the line with a metal wire and casts it again into the ocean. This time an electric eel wraps himself around the steel line, which sends an electric current up the line. The shock knocks Katnip flat on his back. Unsure about what to do next, Katnip pulls out his "Angler's Guide" and reads, "Bass, snapper, trout, or snook go for crow bait on a hook." At this point he hears singing coming from the top of a nearby tree. It's Buzzy the crow, relaxing in his treehouse and singing "Listen to the mockin' bird, listen to the mockin' bird. She's a chick that's got the boogie-woogie beat." Buzzy dives off his porch, aiming at a birdbath below. But he lands in a net held by Katnip instead. While Buzzy wonders what happened, he reads the page from Katnip's book and says, "Man! Looks like I's gonna be food for the fishes." Buzzy gets an idea and says, "Boss, you is done made a mistake. I ain't no crow. I's a seagull." But Katnip ignores him and takes him out of his net and ties him to the end of his fishing hook. Buzzy tries again saying, "Go ahead, put in the hook. But if I dies, the secret dies with me." Katnip hesitates and asks, "What secret?" Buzzy says, "Well, secrets like catching a fish, which any moron can learn. And you is no exception." Katnip frees Buzzy, and the crow shows Katnip the correct way to bait his hook and how to cast his line. After Katnip has followed Buzzy's instructions and has cast his line into the water, the crow sneaks behind him,

pulls his hook out of the water, and ties it to a hair in the fur on the cat's back. Buzzy then tugs on the line and Katnip, thinking he has a bite, reels in his line, pulling the hair and unraveling the fur on his body. Realizing what has happened, Katnip quickly throws down his pole, pulls out his knitting needles, and proceeds to knit the fur back onto his body. But Buzzy has substituted fishing line for his hair. When the cat has finished, he discovers he has knitted a checkerboard pattern on his back. Next Buzzy lights the fuzz on a huge stick of dynamite and then jams it into the mouth of a stuffed fish mounted on a nearby pole. Buzzy then attaches the stuffed fish to Katnip's hook and throws it into the water. He tells Katnip, "Look Boss! Marlin! Grab the line!" Katnip rapidly reels in his line and unhooks the stuffed fish. Buzzy grabs a camera and tells him, "Boss, pose for a picture." But when Buzzy snaps the camera, the dynamite explodes in Katnip's face. Next Buzzy pretends to be Captain Billy, a guide for sport fishermen. Buzzy straps Katnip into a chair bolted to the pier and says, "Boss, you will catch a genuine swordfish." Buzzy casts Katnip's line into the sea and immediately a huge swordfish is hooked on the end of it. Katnip reels in his catch as Buzzy detaches his chair from the pier. The cat is pulled off the pier, over the water, and into the mouth of the huge fish. Buzzy looks on and says, "Well, that's one that won't get away." He then turns away and walks off the pier, singing "Listen to the mocking bird—a chick that has a boogie-woogie beat." But he doesn't get far before Katnip reaches out of the water and grabs his tail feathers and ties him back on the fishing hook, saying, "This time I will do it by the book." Before he can cast his line, Buzzy frees himself and ties the hook to the tail of the sleeping dog. Katnip thinks he has a bite and reels in his catch, which is a very angry dog. The dog chases Katnip round and round a tree while Buzzy relaxes in his treehouse with a large glass of cool drink in his hands as the cartoon ends.

Review: *Motion Picture Herald,* **13 June 1953**

A big, lazy cat doesn't seem to be having much luck on a fishing expedition, so he consults a book on fishing methods. The book suggests the use of live crow for bait. Naturally the crow doesn't particularly care for this method and puts up a number of substitute articles to use for the bait and gets the better of the cat. (7 min)

Review: *Exhibitor Servisection,* **1 July 1953**

A sunny day brings a lazy cat to the docks for a fishing expedition. The fish are not biting, and to remedy the situation the cat takes out a book, "How to Fish," where he reads that crows make the best bait. A crow approaches, and the cat is about to hook him up on his line. The crow persuades the cat to use various kinds of bait all intended to catch the fisherman instead of the fish. The crow leads the gullible cat into a number of unbearable situations, ending up in the jaws of a dog. Fair.

Review: *Boxoffice,* **15 August 1953**

A mildly amusing cartoon dealing with a big, lazy cat who gets set for a good day's fishing, but reckons without Buzzy, the crow, who refuses to be used as bait. First, the crow uses a weighty anchor to pull the cat into the sea and then he uses a stick of dynamite. Finally the cat gets his "bite" when he lands in the jaws of a monstrous bulldog.

CAT-CHOO (1951)

Company: Seymour Kneitel, Famous Studies, Paramount Pictures
Type: Noveltoons
Characters: Buzzy the crow, Katnip the cat

See fig. 25. Story: The cartoon opens on a winter scene, showing a small house surrounded by a snow-covered landscape. From inside the house the sounds of sneezing are heard. It's Katnip the cat who is suffering from a bad cold as he consults his medicine book. He learns that he has all the symptoms of a cold, including watery eyes and a runny nose. On a page entitled "Hot Tips for Colds" he reads, "Starve a fever and feed a cold. But a remedy for cats like you, it's best to eat some fresh crow meat cooked in a deep-dish stew." He says to himself, "That sounds logical." Then he hears music coming through an open window. It's Buzzy the crow, who is ice skating on the frozen birdbath, singing, "No worries for me. I just feels like a crow on the wing. I's just glad I'm alive. In this weather cats have cold feet." Using a large magnet to attract the metal skates on Buzzy's feet, Katnip pulls the crow inside his house. Inside, the surprised Buzzy looks around and says, "How did I get into this situation?" He sees Katnip and says, "Sorry I can't join you for dinner, Boss. But I have a previous engagement." Katnip sneezes and blows Buzzy near the book. He figures out that the cat is suffering from a cold. Katnip grabs Buzzy and is about to shove him into a hot oven, when Buzzy shouts, "Boss! Boss! I's got a sure cure for the cold. The best way to cure a cold is to use an inhalator." Katnip says, "That sounds logical." Buzzy quickly mixes sneezing powder before pouring it into Katnip's inhalator. Katnip takes a deep breath and inhales the powder, which makes his sneeze so hard that the jet of air out of his mouth propels him through a window into the snow outside. But before Buzzy can leave the house, Katnip crawls back inside through an air vent, saying, "The inhalator didn't work." Buzzy tells him, "You discourages too easy, Boss. I'm going to make you my grandmother's favorite cold cure." He proceeds to mix together tabasco sauce, mustard, chili powder, and red pepper in a drink. Katnip drinks Buzzy's concoction, which makes his head turn red and then change into a blowtorch that shoots a flame out of his mouth. The cat bounces off the walls and the ceiling before calling for a doctor. Buzzy opens the door and walks back inside, wearing a doctor's uniform and carrying a black medical bag. He says, "Did you call a physician, Boss? What's the matter? Now open your mouth so I can have a close look." Buzzy climbs inside the cat's mouth with a magnifying glass and says, "I can't see anything for all this stuff." He then proceeds to toss various things out of the cat's mouth, including chains, tires, and other pieces of hardware. Buzzy prescribes a shot for Katnip and then pulls a shotgun out of his medical bag and places the barrel of the gun in Katnip's mouth. Katnip bites down on the barrel just as Buzzy pulls the trigger. The gun backfires and blows off Buzzy's disguise. Katnip grabs Buzzy, telling him, "You tricked

me." Buzzy tries to escape but runs right into the cat's open mouth, from which he says, "I'm sorry to interrupt you while you is eating, Boss. But your pilot tooth is missing." Buzzy then pries open the cat's mouth, runs out, and attempts to hide in a closet. When Katnip sticks his head inside, Buzzy hits it with a huge club, knocking him out cold. Buzzy grabs the cat's tail and pulls him under a heatlamp, saying, "This is a sure cure for a cold." Next Buzzy smears mustard plaster all over Katnip's body and then turns on the lamp. The radiant heat bakes the cat and he becomes so hot that he jumps out the window into the snow to cool off. The snow melts and freezes again, trapping the cat inside a block of ice. Buzzy sings a song as he skates on the ice frozen over Katnip's body and the cartoon ends.

Review: *Film Daily,* 25 October 1951

A cartoon cat has a cold. Crow pie is indicated. Immediately a crow is caught and from that point on the cat regrets, but plenty. After a vivid series of revenge cure attempts, the cat winds up frozen with the crow using the surface for ice skating. (7 min)

Review: *Exhibitor Servisection,* 23 October 1951

Looking for a cure for his cold, the cat reads that eating a fresh crow will turn the trick. He spies a crow skating, and prepares to cook him. Not relishing the idea of being eaten, the crow tells the cat that he has a sure cure for colds. First, he gives the cat an inhaler full of pepper. The cat almost sneezes himself to death. The crow brews a drink made of tabasco sauce and mustard. The cat turns into a blazing fireworks display. Next, the crow places the cat under a stove with a sun lamp blazing. The burning cat rushing out into the snow, which melts, and then freezes over. Good.

Review: *Boxoffice,* 20 October 1951

A cat reads that fresh crow will cure his cold. An ice-skating crow is caught by the feline. The crow convinces the cat that he knows a sure remedy for a cold. He administers an inhalator full of hot pepper. It isn't long before the crow has the cat right where he wants him—under the ice he's skating on.

CAT O'NINE AILS (1948)

Company: Seymour Kneitel, Famous Studios, Paramount Pictures
Type: Noveltoons
Characters: Buzzy the crow, Sam the cat

Review: *Motion Picture Herald,* 21 February 1948

Sam the Cat is a hypochondriac, living for each moment when he can swallow a pill to cure some imaginary ailment. Buzzy the blackbird sizes up the situation and, disguising himself as a doctor bird, the proceeds to minister to Sam. His diagnosis includes a number of dread diseases, all aptly illustrated. In the end he paints Sam's throat with red paint and when he gets through Paramount's trade mark is found emblazoned on a billboard in the cat's throat. (7 min)

Review: *Boxoffice,* **24 January 1948**

Sam, the cat, is a pitiful hypochrondriac who swallows quantities of pills every hour in the day. Buzzy, the blackbird, sizes up the situation and disguises himself as a doctor. His diagnosis includes pneumonia, measles and bats in the belfry. Buzzy finally paints the cat's throat with the Paramount trademark. (7 min)

Review: *Film Daily,* **4 February 1948**

Buzzy the Blackbird, playing doctor, decides to treat Sam the Cat, a hypochondriac, to a few pills. His diagnoses include pneumonia, measles, and bats in the belfry. Excellent cartoon with a barrel of laughs.

HAIR TODAY GONE TOMORROW (1954)

Company: Seymour Kneitel, Famous Studios Paramount Pictures
Type: Noveltoons
Characters: Buzzy the crow, Katnip the cat

Story: The cartoon opens as Katnip is sleeping and dreaming that he is with his girlfriend, who is admiring his hair. The alarm rings and he wakes up, gets out of bed, and goes into the bathroom where he stands in front of a mirror and combs his hair. He is shocked when bunches of hair come out, leaving him with a bald spot on top of his head. He seeks a solution and pulls a book off the shelf and reads, "A pomade made from fresh crow, when rubbed on the scalp, will make hair grow." Katnip smiles and says, "That sounds logical." Meanwhile Buzzy the crow, in his house high up in a tree, is preparing to take a swim in Katnip's birdbath below. He dives off his porch into the water. But Katnip siphons the water out of the bath and draws Buzzy into his house. Surprised, Buzzy says, "How did I get suckered into this?" Buzzy sees the cat mixing hair pomade and realizes the cat has a balding problem. He says, "Boss, Boss, I'm the only living mortal what knows the secret of curing baldness." Katnip says, "What is your secret?" Buzzy says, "Boss, my secret is regrowing hair. Just leave your head in my hands." Buzzy massages Katnip's scalp, saying, "I have a secret hair tonic handed down by my sacred granny." Buzzy then pulls balls of cotton stuffing from the upholstery of a couch and glues them on top of Katnip's head. After finishing, Buzzy holds a mirror in front of Katnip's face, the cat is happy to have his hair back, but as Buzzy is about to leave the scene, metal springs pop out of Katnip's head. He stops Buzzy, saying, "My hair has come out again." Buzzy says, "Boss, your hair is a rare type. It needs a mudpack." Buzzy packs mud from a flowerpot on top of Katnip's head and then adds grass seed and water. In no time grass grows out of Katnip's head. Katnip is happy with green hair as Buzzy tells him, "There you are, Boss. Who says grass won't grow on a busy street?" Suddenly flowers pop up and when the cat picks them, he pulls out all of his new hair. Again Buzzy is headed out the door when Katnip stops him saying, "It came out again." Buzzy says, "No wonder Boss. You got to get rid of

that dandruff." He pours salt on Katnip's head before shoving him into a barber's chair. Next Buzzy pours benzene on the cat's head then sets it on fire. Next he fries an egg on top of Katnip's hot head before jacking the chair up in the air so high that he goes through the roof. Buzzy attempts to leave again, but Katnip, covered with bandages, appears again and grabs him. The cat prepares to chop him up, but Buzzy fights back. They stop fighting and Buzzy holds up a mirror and tells the cat, "Look Boss. Genuine natural hair." Sure enough, Katnip sees real hair on his head, and he leaves to show it to his girlfriend. As he walks off, a big bald spot is seen on his back. Buzzy smiles and winks as he holds up a pair of scissors as the cartoon ends.

Review: *Motion Picture Herald,* **27 March 1954**

Buzzy, the wise-guy Crow, is up to his old antics again. This time he makes Katnip, the cat, believe he is curing his baldness. The subject, in color by Technicolor, has Buzzy resort to a variety of trucks to get his point across.

Review: *Exhibitor Servisection,* **10 March 1951**

Katnip, the cat, having fears of approaching baldness, is afraid he will lose his girl if it continues. Consulting a remedy book, he learns that the application of freshly caught crow might help his condition. However, Buzzy, the Crow, realizes his predicament and goes about creating fantastic remedies to placate the cat. After much manipulation, Katnip finally gets a good head of hair, but doesn't know that it is transplanted from another part of his exterior. Good.

Review: *Boxoffice,* **20 March 1954**

Katnip is the sucker in this amusing bit of slapstick. Buzzy, the wise-guy crow, learning that Katnip has been told the application of a freshly caught crow is a cure for Katnip's baldness, gets to work fast with a number of ludicrous remedies of his own but they don't prove effective for long. Finally, the application of dirt and grass seed seem to do the trick.

NO IFS, ANDS OR BUTTS (1954)

Company: I. Sparber, Famous Studios, Paramount Pictures
Type: Noveltoon
Characters: Buzzy the crow, Katnip the cat

Story: The cartoon opens as black smoke pours from every room of Katnip's house. Inside Katnip takes a puff on a cigar, coughs, and says, "I been feeling punk lately. I wonder why." His radio is on and the announcer says, "Good afternoon, friends! This is Doctor Nicotine bringing you your daily little hints on health. Are you a chainsmoker? Does your tongue feel like leather? Do you suffer from throat scratch? Do you have a palpitating heart?" Katnip indicates yes to all of the questions, and the announcer says, "Brother, you've got about two minutes to live . . . unless you stop smoking immediately. All you have to do is send for a free copy of my *Sure Cure for Smoking*

Habits. My address is Tobacco Road, Smoky Mountain, Tennessee. Hurry! Hurry!" Katnip writes a letter to order the book, runs outside, and puts the letter in the mailbox as the mail truck arrives and the letter carrier gives him a package. It's the book he ordered. Back inside the house Katnip, smoking a cigar, opens the book and reads, "If the smoking habit you must beat, then eat a salad with fresh crow meat." He says, "That sounds logical." At this moment Buzzy lands on the windowsill and says, "Hi Boss! Got a light?" Buzzy lights his cigar using Katnip's cigar. Buzzy tries to fly away, but Katnip grabs him and rolls him in a leaf of lettuce, saying, "If the smoking habit you're trying to beat, then eat a salad with fresh crow meat." Buzzy says, "Dat cat is a tobacco smoking fiend. Dat's all I has to know." Katnip cuts his salad, but Buzzy dodges the knife blade and says, "Wait a minute! Who says you gotta quit smoking. Maybe your brand is too strong. Let's make a test." Katnip says, "That sounds logical." Buzzy put a blindfold over Katnip's eyes and puts a cigarette in his mouth. Buzzy says, "First we lights up my brand." Then he lights the cigarette and Katnip takes a deep puff. Then Buzzy takes the cigarette out of his mouth and replaces it with a stick of TNT, saying, "Now we tries your brand." Buzzy lights the TNT and it blows up in a cloud of smoke, leaving Katnip's face covered with soot. Buzzy says, "Now what is the difference between the two brands?" Katnip says, "Ah, your brand is milder." Buzzy says, "You is abso-tively right." Katnip grabs him and says, "I've still got the habit." Buzzy says, "Now listen Boss! The real sure cure is to use willpower." Katnip says, "Willpower? That sounds logical." Buzzy seats Katnip in a chair and tells him, "Now all you got to do is to keep sayin' willpower, willpower, and you will break the habit for sure." Buzzy waves a smoking cigar under Katnip's nose and then flies across the room and places the cigar on an ashtray. Katnip can't resist, and the fumes lure him to the cigar, where Buzzy drops a five-hundred-pound weight on his head. Katnip is smashed flat as a pancake and Buzzy tells him, "Congratulations, Boss! You is cured." Buzzy flies through a window and lands in the yard and walks away singing, "My heart is a hobo, loves to roam the whole world over. I was born to be a rover . . ." But he is caught by Katnip who says, "The sure cure is crow salad." He takes Buzzy back into the house and stuffs Buzzy into his mouth. Buzzy pulls a gun and blasts a hole in catnip's teeth. Then he flies to the roof of a building. On the roof is a large sign with an image of a man smoking a cigarette. Buzzy flies through the hole in the man's mouth, and when catnip tries to follow him, he falls to the street below. Buzzy slips a rocket under Katnip. Buzzy lights the rocket, and Katnip is shot high into the sky before the rocket explodes in a cloud of smoke. Meanwhile Buzzy walks down the street smoking a very long cigarette. He smiles and says, "Ahhh! King size" as the cartoon ends.

Review: *Motion Picture Herald*, 30 April 1955

To stop smoking, the cat plans to try a new remedy, guaranteed to break the habit. The remedy is a salad, the principal ingredient of which is crow meat, whereupon Buzzy the Crow conveniently appears. In the ensuing chase, the cat eventually wears Buzzy down and is just about to capture Buzzy when Buzzy offers the cat a "milder" smoke. The cat accepts gratefully. It turns out to be a stick of dynamite. (6 min)

Review: *Exhibitor Servisection*, 9 February 1955

A cat, frightened by continuous warnings against the dangers of cigarettes, consults a remedy book which suggests eating a crow meat salad to cure the smoking habit. Buzzy, the Crow, suddenly appears and the cat makes a grab for the bird, who evades his pursuer. However, when Buzzy is cornered, he talks the cat into trying a milder smoke which proves to be a stick of dynamite that explodes. Good.

Review: *Boxoffice*, 5 May 1955

This Noveltoon in Technicolor kids the current cigarette scare. The cat, frightened by continuous warnings against the dangers of cigarette smoking, is told to eat a salad composed of fresh crow meat. When Buzzy, the crow, shows up, the cat makes a grab for him but he persuades him to try a milder smoke instead. But the mild smoke proves to be a stick of dynamite—with the usual explosive results.

SOCK-A-BYE KITTY (1950)

Company: Seymour Kneitel, Famous Studios; Paramount Pictures
Characters: Buzzy the crow, Katnip the cat

Story: The cartoon opens to a close-up of a book entitled *How to Cure Insomnia*. Lying on a nearby bed is Katnip the cat, who cannot fall asleep. He says, "This not being able to sleep is keeping me awake." He twists and turns before finally falling off the bed. He picks up the book and reads, "If you can't get to sleep, just plug up your ears. With no noise to disturb you, you will sleep well for years." He says to himself, "That's sounds logical." He puts earplugs in his ears but still can't sleep because he hears water dripping from a faucet. He opens the book again and reads another cure: "The only sure way to get any rest is to get a blackbird fresh from the nest. Eat him in pie, Crow-Quettes or in a stew, and you'll sleep like a top. Pleasant dreams!" The cat says, "A blackbird . . ." He hears Buzzy the crow preparing to go to bed in his birdhouse, singing, "Good night ladies, good night ladies, I's gwine to call it a day. Good night fellows, good night trees, good night everyone, I'se gwine hit the hay." He jumps into bed and falls asleep. The cat takes the birdhouse, with the sleeping Buzzy inside, to his house and follows the directions for making a crow sandwich. "First, toast two pieces of bread." He puts the bread in the toaster and turns it on. The toaster makes a ticking noise that wakes up Buzzy, who thinks that it is his alarm clock. Buzzy breaks the clock but still hears the ticking. He looks around to see the cat catching the two pieces of bread as they pop out of the toaster. The cat continues to follow instructions: "Butter the toast and add some spice if you like Crow-Quettes tasty and nice." Buzzy is frightened and says, "Uh-oh, dis Crow is gonna be a dead duck." Buzzy reads a page in the book and says, "Dat man's got insomonia. Dat's all I needs to know." The cat picks him up, places him between the two slices of bread, and is about to take a bite when Buzzy says, "Boss, Boss, eatin' at dese late hours is de worst thing you could do. It'll keep you awake all night." The Cat says, "Awake? But I ain't slept for weeks." Buzzy tells him, "The best way to get some sleep is to start by countin' sheep." The cat says, "That sounds logical," as Buzzy puts him to bed. Buzzy says, "And I's gwine to be the little lambies" as he takes his hat off and replaces it with sheeps' wool. The cat begins to count "one, two . . ." Buzzy says "bahh, bahhh" as he cuts a circle in the floor underneath the cat's bed. The cat falls through the hole in the floor and Buzzy says, "Sleep tight, Boss." As he attempts to leave the house, the cat bounces out of the hole on the bedsprings and blocks Buzzy's exit, telling him, "But I didn't sleep a wink." Buzzy says, "Dat's a gross misunderexaggeration, Boss. Look, you was sawin' wood so hard that you went right through the floor." They look at the hole in the floor. Buzzy tells the cat, "Now look, if you wants to get sleepy, you gotta relax in a good hot bath." He puts the Cat in a bathtub filled with hot water. The cat says, "That sounds logical." Buzzy places logs of wood underneath the tub and says, "Now Boss, ain't that cozy! Soon you will feel dozy." He sets fire to the logs and flies away. The fire boils the water, and the cat jumps out of the tub and flies across the room where he runs into a foldaway bed that Buzzy pushes into the wall. Buzzy escapes from the house singing, "Good night pussy, sleep tight, kitty, You's gwine to leave you now." But he runs into the cat, who is waiting for him. The cat picks him up by the neck and says, "This time I'm doin' what the book says." He carries him back inside and prepares to eat him. Buzzy says, "But Boss, I can explain everything." He gets away from the cat who chases him until Buzzy hits him on the head with a bag of sand, saying, "Hey Boss! Here come de sandman." Buzzy jumps into a stack of hay and when the cat jumps in after him, he hits his head on an anvil. Buzzy says, "It's time to hit the hay, Boss." The chase continues and Buzzy stretches a rubber tube across the doorway and says, "It's time to retire." The cat runs into the tube, which stretches before flinging him out of the house where he lands on a clothesline and slides across to a tree where he ends up suspended on a limb. Buzzy looks up at him and sings, "Rock-a-bye kitty on a treetop. When the wind blows, the cradle will rock. When the rope breaks, the cradle will fall, and down will come kitty—cradle and all." The cat tries to get loose but falls to the ground and is knocked out. Buzzy pries the cat's eyes open and reads "good-night" written on his eyeballs. Buzzy smiles and says "boy, what a mess" as the cartoon ends.

Review: *Film Daily,* 22 January 1951

Buzzy, the crow, helps an insomnia-ridden cat fall asleep by pulling one fast trick after another, practically killing the cat in the process. Lots of laughs.

Review: *Film Daily,* 25 February 1951

An insomnia-ridden cat hears that eating a crow is a sure-fire cure. Buzzy the crow is available but changes his mind on the method he should use to fall asleep. Splendid, lively action cartoon.

Review: *Motion Picture Herald,* 30 December 1950

The cat has insomnia and finds that a sandwich made of crow-quetts is a sleep inducer. Luckily, Buzzy, the crow, is available and is trapped. Buzzy advises him that eating before he goes to bed is bad for his health, and guarantees to put the cat to sleep, which he does after a few fast tricks. (7 min)

Review: *Exhibitor Servisection,* 17 January 1951

A cat troubled by insomnia reads that by eating a blackbird he will go to sleep. He catches a blackbird, and is just about to eat him when the bird convinces him there are less drastic ways to cure insomnia. The blackbird proceeds to punish the cat with a variety of amusing "sleep inducing" tricks, with the cat being finally knocked unconscious. Good.

Review: *Boxoffice,* 17 March 1951

A funny Technicolor cartoon dealing with a common ailment, insomnia. Kitty, who is tossing in misery, decides to try one remedy, eating crow-quettes. Buzzy, the crow, pleads with the cat to spare his life and he will promise to put him to sleep. He practically kills the cat in the process.

STUPIDSTITIOUS CAT (1947)

Company: Seymour Kneitel, Famous Studios, Paramount Pictures
Type: Noveltoons
Characters: Buzzy the crow, Katnip the cat

Story: The cartoon opens in Katnip's bedroom. He is asleep in bed. His good luck horseshoe sign hangs on a wall over his bed. He wakes up and starts to get up when he realizes he is about to get up on the wrong side of the bed. He says, "Get up on the wrong side of the bed—for that you could be dead." Next he breaks a wishbone in two and makes a wish, thinking that this will be his lucky day. Suddenly he hears singing coming from high in a tree near his house. He says, "If you whistle before breakfast, you'll fry before dinner." In his treehouse high above, Buzzy the crow stops singing and decides to take a swim in Katnip's birdbath on the ground below. Buzzy dives off his porch and into the bath, but Katnip removes the top of the birdbath and carries it into his house. Buzzy is surprised as he looks around and says, "How did I get in here?" He tries to get out of the house, saying, "Man, you'd better straighten up and fry right." But Katnip catches him in his butterfly net. Buzzy see the cat put two slices of bread in the toaster and says, "Looks like I's been invited to dinner." Katnip is about to make a Crow sandwich on toast when he stops to look down at a pin and says, "See a pin, pick it up, and all day you will have good luck." Buzzy says, A superstitious cat, that's all I wants to know." Katnip opens his mouth wide to take a bite of his sandwich when Buzzy says, "Hey Boss, I hate to interrupt you when you is eating, but you done spilled the salt." Katnip drops his sandwich and throws a saltshaker over his shoulder. When he picks up the sandwich again, he finds that Buzzy has gone, leaving a sign—Out to Lunch. Katnip looks for Buzzy and finds him standing under a ladder. Katnip informs Buzzy that "if he stands under a ladder, his days will grow sadder." Buzzy says, "Thank-you for the information Boss" and reaches out his hand to Katnip. Katnip reaches for Buzzy's hand but grabs an umbrella that lifts him up and carries him under the ladder. Later he floats down on top of a mousetrap. Katnip springs up, and his head collides with the top of the ladder, which collapses and crashes to the ground. Now Katnip is angry and chases Buzzy who hides under a bookcase. When Katnip lights a match to see if he can find Buzzy, the crow uses it to light three cigars. Katnip cries, "Three on a match." Then Buzzy says, "And you wind up in the booby hatch." The three cigars explode in Katnip's face, and he is propelled into a chair. Katnip throws the chair at Buzzy, but the crow places a full-length mirror directly in its path. Katnip is unable to keep the mirror from being broken and says, "This is hard luck." Buzzy tells him, "That's right—seven years hard luck." Katnip lunges at Buzzy but only succeeds in spilling a bottle of black ink all over himself. He looks in the mirror and says, "Yipes, a black cat" and runs through a wall to the outside of the house and away down the road. Buzzy chuckles and says, "Man, ain't he superstitious!" Buzzy looks around and discovers a calendar that shows that it is Friday the thirteenth. With a worried look on his face he rapidly grabs a horseshoe and a rabbit's foot as the cartoon ends.

Review: *Motion Picture Herald*, 19 April 1947

Superstition proves to be the downfall of the cat in this color short. Buzzy the wise-guy bird saves himself from being devoured by the cat by creating a number of supernatural situations. He finally escapes, but just as the film ends a black cat crosses his path, throwing fear into his heart. (7 min)

Review: *Boxoffice*, 12 May 1947

A superstitious cat captures Buzzy, the wise-cracking crow, with the intention of having him for breakfast. Once the bird realizes the cat is superstitious, he plays on the feline's weaknesses by leading him under a ladder and forcing him to crash through a mirror. Buzzy wards off the cat, but when the bird realizes it is Friday the 13th, he proceeds to throw salt over his shoulder and rub a rabbit's foot.

Review: *Film Daily*, 13 May 1947

A superstitious cat catches Buzzy, a flippant bird, who knows the feline's weakness. Everytime the cat gets ready to devour him, Buzzy brings on another omen or charm which panics the cat and frees him. Switch at the end proves that the wise-guy is not always so smart, and the audience gets the last laugh.

Review: *Motion Picture Herald*, 27 March 1954

In color by Technicolor, the cartoon presents the antics of a superstitious cat who is very hungry and Buzzy, the wise-guy crow, who has to resort to a variety of clever devices to keep himself out of the way.

Review: *Motion Picture Exhibitor*, 30 April 1947

The very superstitious cat wakes up, makes sure that he gets up on the right side of the bed, and starts looking for some breakfast. He spots Buzzy, the bird, captures him, puts him between two slices of bread, and prepares to eat him. Buzzy, however, has different ideas. Knowing the cat to be superstitious, Buzzy purposely spills the salt, calls the cat's attention to it, so that he will have to release him, and throw the salt over his back. This goes on for some time, the bird using these angles to escape the clutches of the cat. The fade-out shows the cat fleeing after seeing an animal of his own nature, only black. Good.

Chapter 3

Way Down in the Jungle: The Animated Safari

In a very popular genre of early animated cartoons the main character was thrown into a cooking pot by black cannibals and served for dinner. These cartoons were of the same genre as the Tarzan and Jungle Jim motion pictures popular in the 1930s and 1940s. In virtually every one of these films the heroine and hero were white (or animal stars in a cartoon series), but the cannibals were always black. All of the popular cartoon heroes, from Col. Heeza Liar, Felix the Cat, and Walt Disney's Alice of the silent era to Bugs Bunny, Porky Pig, Andy Panda, and Hanna and Barbera's Tom and Jerry, encountered the threat of savage black cannibals in one or more cartoons of their respective series. All the cartoons of this type shared a similar plot. The main character turns up stranded in Africa or shipwrecked on an island and is captured by a tribe of cannibals. They take the prisoner to their village and throw him into a cooking pot. The cannibals are hostile and have a hearty appetite for white humans. But they drop their spears and go into a dance at the first sound of the rhythmic beat of a drum.

One has to question the motives of the animators who selected black as the characteristic color of cartoon cannibals. In one of a very few serious studies, "On Cannibalism" (published in London in 1926 by Scottiswood and Co.), Fiske discusses the practice of cannibalism in relation to ethnology. He points out that cannibalism has been practiced by all races of people and nations during certain periods in their history. Evidence of cannibalism has been discovered in the early history of Belgium and Scotland, for example. Similar evidence has been discovered in Africa, Asia, North and South America, and on the New Zealand islands. In short, Fiske found that throughout ancient history cannibalism has been practiced by people of all races–white, black, yellow, and brown. But the cartoon animators always depicted their cartoon cannibals as blacks.

Filmmakers have always struggled with how to treat cannibalism as the central plot of a film without offending the public. Guidelines for appropriate film subjects are provided in the Motion Picture Production Code: "No picture shall be produced that tends to incite bigotry or hatred among peoples of differing races, religions, or national origins . . . and should be avoided." Apparently the code was not rigorously applied to cartoons depicting black cannibals, and the majority of white audiences of yesteryear were amused, not offended. Even though they treated cannibalism in a burlesque manner, these cartoons could not have created a favorable image of blacks and probably reinforced the image of all Africans as savage and uncivilized people in the minds of the millions of people who viewed them as entertainment. Even if these cartoons did not directly incite bigotry, they certainly encouraged disrespect for people of African descent and therefore tended to reinforce the justification of the continued colonization of Africa by Europeans in the minds of the moviegoing public.

In cartoons that do not involve cannibals, black natives are usually depicted at the other extreme as being childlike and docile. They are easily led by the whites who invade and take over their territory. The hunter on a safari employs natives to carry his supplies on their heads. Needless to say, the natives are frightened of every animal that lives in the jungle and depend completely on the white hunter for their safety and well-being.

Animators drew cannibal characters with exaggerated facial features, such as extremely long or flat lips that they used for everything from playing table tennis to playing music. Usually they wore human bones tied to the hair on their heads and sometimes a single bone in their noses. The cannibal chief, usually depicted as a fat man, sat on a crude throne, smiling, licking his lips, and rubbing his fat stomach while the other cannibals danced around the cooking pot. The chief would be the most intelligent cannibal, but in the end he would inevitably be outwitted by the white hero. The hero, using his superior intellect, would trick the cannibals either into allowing him to escape or into making him their chief. In several cannibal cartoons, the hero's escape is facilitated by the assistance of the cannibal chief's fat daughter, who falls madly in love with the white man. But in the end she is rejected by him. In one cartoon a white man prefers to jump into the cooking pot and be boiled rather than be married to the cannibal chief's daughter. Another popular plot of the cannibal cartoons loosely followed the storyline and the characters taken from the classic novel *Robinson Crusoe,* in which the hero is befriended by a native who becomes his devoted servant, or Man Friday (fig. 26).

Jungle Stories and Reviews

AFRICA (1930)

Company: Bill Molen, Walter Lantz, Universal Pictures
Characters: Oswald the rabbit, Africans

Review: *Motion Picture News,* 29 November 1930

Oswald the rabbit visits the dark continent and has some fun with camels, lions, dancing girls, mummies, etc., etc. There are a few novel bits of business, but there is too much noise emanating from the horn. This series is far from what it used to be. (6 min)

AFRICA SQUEAKS (1932)

Company: Ub Iwerks Celebrity Pictures; distributed by M-G-M
Characters: Flip the frog, black cannibals

Story: The cartoon opens with Flip the frog in Africa on a big-game hunt. As he searches for wild animals, he does not realize that he himself is being stalked by a large rhinoceros, a giraffe, an elephant, a monkey, and a small bird. When Flip feels hot breath on his neck, he reaches behind and feels the nose of the rhinoceros. He turns around, swallows hard, and fires his rifle into the air. Finally working up his nerve, Flip aims his gun at the animal but finds that it is empty. Flip runs away with the rhinoceros and the other animals in hot pursuit. He escapes them by placing a detour sign in the road, which directs the animals the other way. Flip's next encounter is with a Lion. He sets up his gun like a camera and asks the lion to smile and watch the birdie. When he fires his gun, the bullet misses the lion and it runs away. Flip gives chase and thinks that he spots the animal behind a rock. Flip aims his gun and fires, but the bullet hits a black cannibal hiding behind the rock. The cannibal, wearing a bone in his hair, is angry and approaches Flip. He tries to escape but is surrounded, and the cannibal tribe takes him to the village. Flip appears before the cannibal king, a fat man wearing a crow on his head. The king takes one look at Flip and smiles as he reaches out his hand and feels Flip's arms. The king licks his lips and rubs his stomach. The cooking pot walks on the scene and sits down on a stack of firewood. Flip believes that he is being invited to dinner. He puts a napkin around his neck and says to the king, "Well, when do we eat?" The king replies, "Right now," and he pulls Flip over to the cooking pot and throws him in. The king tries unsuccessfully to light two matches before Flip gives him a cigarette lighter, which he uses to start a fire under the cooking pot. Meanwhile the cannibals are dancing, each holding a knife in one hand and a fork in the other. They smack their lips while they dance in anticipation of a good meal. They smile as they dance past Flip, who is still puzzled at their strange behavior. As the water in the pot gets hotter, Flip begins to sweat. He looks under the pot and sees the fire and realizes that he is the dinner. Finally he figures out how to extricate himself from the mess he's in. He pulls a flute out of his pocket and starts to play. The flames under the cooking pot keep time with the music. The flames move toward the cannibals, who run away. The chief is the last to leave as flames burn his grass skirt. Flip jumps out of the pot and starts to walk away when four female cannibals show up on the scene. They fall in love with Flip, and each one gives him a big kiss. They carry him back to the village and put him on the throne, placing the king's crown on his head. Rather than marry the cannibal women, Flip takes off the crown and runs back to the cooking pot and jumps in. He uses his lighter to start the fire and ducks his head under the water as the cartoon ends.

Review: *Motion Picture Herald,* 9 January 1932

To the dark continent of Africa goes animated Flip the Frog, and has adventures there are of the stuff that makes the youngsters laugh and oldsters chuckle. When Flip is in the kettle and about to be boiled, the cannibal King cannot get the match to ignite. Flip hands him his cigarette lighter. Cleverly drawn, and with good synchronization, the short is amusing. (8 min)

AFRICA SQUEAKS (1940)

Company: Robert Clampett, Warner Bros.
Type: Looney Tunes
Characters: Porky Pig, African natives, caricatures of Kay Kyser and Spencer Tracy

Story: The cartoon opens on a scene of a map of Africa. An off-screen narrator says, "Africa, land of mystery and adventure. Truly the dark continent of the world. To the rhythmic chant of the native safari we start our journey to the very heart of darkest Africa." The scene shifts to the jungle where we see the white hunter, Porky Pig, leading a safari of chanting African natives carrying bundles of supplies on their heads. One turns to the camera and says, "We don't know where we are going, but we're going." Porky stops and reads a sign on a tree: Welcome to Africa—The Lion's Club. Suddenly a strange white man comes along the trail and stops and asks Porky, "Dr. Livingstone, I presume?" Porky tells him that he is Porky Pig, and the safari continues on its way, passing many interesting animal species. An ostrich is asleep with its head resting underground on a pillow. Two lions are eating a pile of animal bones and deciding to make a wish on a wishbone. A mother monkey is taking her baby for a ride in a stroller while swinging on a vine in a tree. A native hunting for food wins a dart-blowing contest at a carnival. On the third day out they see a large gorilla backing out of the bush. The narrator describes the animal as the most feared fighter in the jungle. When the gorilla turns, he is seen to have the face of the heavyweight prize fighter "Two Ton" Tony Galento, who fought and lost to heavyweight champion Joe Louis. Tony holds a mug of beer and says, "I'll murder de bum." Night falls and Porky makes camp but can't sleep for the noise of the jungle. Meanwhile Stanley is looking under rocks for Dr. Livingstone. The next day the safari passes a sign that reads Los Angeles City Limits. On another road they pass a picture of a white man on a sign that says, "Reelect the king of the Jungle. Thirty Coconuts Every Thursday." Next the safari passes a jungle boardinghouse, where the landlady is evicting an elephant for nonpayment of rent. The landlady tells the elephant, "I warned you time and again. I simply can't put up with this sort of thing. Now get out and stay out. And until you pay your rent I'm going to keep your trunk." She takes the elephant's trunk and goes into the house, slamming the door behind her. Outside the elephant turns and sadly says, "Keep my trunk. Oh, and it's got all my things in it too, darn." A giant condor circles overhead and spots three baby deer grazing below. The narrator says, "It's a giant condor, deadly bird of prey. Despised attacker of the weak. The jungle's most ruthless killer." The bird dives to attack, but the deer run into the bush. Suddenly the bush parts and the deer are seen manning an antiaircraft gun. One sounds the air-raid siren, while the other two fire shells at the diving condor. The bird is hit and falls to the ground with a thud. Meanwhile an excited native scout appears and informs Porky that a strange white man is living in the jungle. The narrator asks, "What strange, compelling reason can a white man have to thus isolate himself so completely from the outside world?" Porky finds Stanley and drags him to the village and places him in front of the strange white man. Stanley asks him, "Dr. Livingstone, I presume?" The strange white man pulls off his beard and says, "That's right, you're wrong. I'm Cake Icer (Kay Kyser), the old professor, ain't that right students?" A large billboard reads, "Cake-Icer's Kollage of Musical Knowledge." The professor then calls out to the animals. "Now come on, you elephants and antelopes, gorillas and giraffes, roll out the barrel. Tinkle your toes. Twirl your tails. Make the jungle jump, jitter and jingle. What I mean is come on chillun', let's dance." An animal band plays hot swing music and everybody dances, including Porky and Stanley. A gorilla grabs a microphone and croons, "You're the greatest discoverer since 1492." A pair of fat natives do a shimmy dance. The professor tells all, "That's it, chillun'. Now we're Looney Tunes." The party ends and we see Porky and his safari starting for home. The narrator says, "After a pleasant stay in the interior our safari reluctantly starts the long, weary trek toward home." The natives sing "California Here I Come" while the scene shifts to the map of Africa. The narrator says, "So we say good-by to the dark continent. Africa farewell." A giant black face with big white lips superimposed on the map grins and says good-bye as the cartoon ends.

Review: *Motion Picture Herald*, 20 February 1940

This time porcine Porky is a leader of a safari into the darkest regions of the Black Continent. Particularly productive of funny bone tickling in the spoofing of the Stanley search for Dr. Livingstone. There are additional sights of the strange behavior of animals and natives. In fact, the whole fun and frivolity piece is good. (7 min)

Review: *Boxoffice*, 3 February 1940

Play this one by all means. It is composed of the stuff that shakes the rafters and fairly blows the roof off when the laughter starts to whip around. Porky goes to Africa on a safari. What occurs when he does a little exploring was cooked up by the fertile brain that injected the right touches of unusual caricature and bang-up comedy to give 'em the shrieks. And there is an ending that will knock 'em right out of their seats.

Review: *Motion Picture Exhibitor*, 7 February 1940

One of the best of the Leon Schlesinger series, with Porky as the hunter invading the Darkest Continent. He meets, among other things, an explorer who looks strangely like Spencer Tracy looking for Doctor Livingstone, and finds the Doctor who turns out to be a version of Kay Kyser. The belly laughs are many, and the gags good. Excellent.

THE AFRICAN HUNT (1915)

Company: Lubin Film Manufacturing Company
Type: On the same reel with *Susie's Suitors*
Characters: White hunter, black Africans

Review: *New York Dramatic Mirror*, 4 August 1915

A split-reel animated cartoon drawn by Stewart C. Whitman, which shows a hunter leaving by balloon for darkest Africa and his amusing adventures with various large and savage denizens of the jungle.

AFRICAN JUNGLE HUNT (1957)

Company: Connie Rasinski, Paul Terry, Twentieth Century-Fox
Type: Terrytoons
Characters: Phoney Baloney, black Africans

Story: The cartoon opens as Phoney Baloney, carrying a small briefcase, enters the tent of the manager of the Circus Sideshow Attractions. He tells the manager, "I have here the greatest attraction on earth, and I got it at the risk of life and limb. My adventure started one evening while I was enjoyin' a quiet cruise in tropic waters." As the scene changes, Baloney is seen at the helm of a ship being tossed about by high waves on a stormy sea. The storm ends, and across the calm waters Baloney can see the coast of Africa. A high wave lifts him off his boat and deposits him on the shore, where he lands on the seat of his pants. He sets off to explore the land and encounters many wild animals, including a lion, an elephant, a gorilla, and a hippo, but he is not harmed. Next he encounters an African native with thick white lips who wears a grass skirt and holds a long spear. Baloney tries to get away but is captured and carried by the native on the end of his spear. They cross a river by walking underwater. When they emerge on the other side, the African has been replaced by a large alligator who smacks his lips while carrying Baloney on the end of the spear. Baloney gets away from the alligator and decides to continue his exploration. After resting and eating his last meal—his own shoe—he encounters a white pygmy elephant. He captures it but it later frees itself and flies away. He chases it but stops short at the point of a spear held by one of a band of pygmies. He tries to escape but is captured and tied up before being carried to the pygmy village. The natives dance in a circle around him, holding their spears over their heads and wearing war masks on their faces. They keep time to the rhythm by beating his head like a drum. The scene changes back to the circus tent where Baloney is finishing his story. "I'm tellin' you it was awful." The manager asks him, "And then what happened?" Baloney says, "They shrunk me." He opens the briefcase and pulls out a shrunken replica of himself. Then he says, "And it's myself in this condition that I'm offerin' for your sideshow." The manager kicks him out of the tent and Baloney lands on the ground. His smaller self says, "Baloney you're an awful liar." Baloney shrugs his shoulders as the cartoon ends.

ALICE CANS THE CANNIBALS (1925)

Company: Walt Disney; distributed by M. J. Winkler
Type: Animation combined with live action
Characters: Virginia Davis as real live Alice, black cannibals

Story: The cartoon opens with Alice joyriding through the countryside in an automobile driven by her black cat. Alice becomes frightened as the car goes too fast and shouts stop as the car approaches the edge of a cliff overlooking the ocean. Too late, the body of the car, with Alice and her cat, goes over the cliff and falls into the sea, where it floats like a boat. Alice asks the cat, "How are we gonna get to shore?" The cat gets an idea. He uses a rope to lasso a large fish swimming nearby and attaches the rope to the car-boat. Then he baits a hook with a worm and dangles it in front of the fish. This causes the fish to swim forward, pulling the car-boat and its passengers through the water. Alice and the cat sleep through a stormy night and awaken the next morning to find themselves just off shore of the Cannibal Islands. They are surrounded by sharks who attack their boat, so the cat uses the spare balloon tire to float them into the air and out of danger. However a large bird flying by, thinking that the balloon is a large doughnut, pecks it. The balloon bursts, and Alice and the cat fall out of the sky and land on a tall palm tree. Alice looks down and sees a pond just below them, so she tells the cat, "Let's dive. . . ." Meanwhile a thirsty elephant has arrived and sucks all of the water from the pond, and Alice and the cat land in the mudhole. They both climb out covered with mud, which the elephant washes off by spraying water on them. A group of black cannibals shows up on the scene, led by their chief. Alice is frightened, but the ingenious cat uses the trunk of a rubber tree as a slingshot and propels rocks at the cannibal tribe. The flying rocks hit cannibals and knock them down. But the chief becomes angry and throws a rock that hits Alice and the cat, knocking them both down. They attempt to run but are followed by the cannibals who are now throwing spears at them. Alice and the cat find their escape blocked by a high cliff, but they use the spears stuck in the cliff as a ladder to climb to the top. Out of danger, they think of ways to attack the cannibal tribe. The cat finds a nest of old ostrich eggs that he uses to bombard the cannibal tribe below. The eggs stun the cannibals, but when they recover they begin to climb the ladder of spears to the top of the cliff. Again the cat gets an idea. He throws a spear with a long rope attached at one end at the cannibals. Pulling the rope behind it, the spear travels through the nose ring of each cannibal and hooks them together before it is embedded in the rear end of a large hippo. The hippo dives in the lake, pulling the roped cannibals along with him. Only the cannibal chief is left. He is scratching his head and wondering where all of his tribe has gone. Alice and the cat laugh at him before Alice throws another spear, which hits the chief in the backside as the cartoon ends.

Review: *Motion Picture News,* 10 January 1925

This novel animated cartoon should prove an entertaining contribution. It is novel in that it combines the usual pen and ink sketches and a human figure which is accomplished by a double printing process. A number of cannibals, perceiving in Alice the basis of a wonderful feast, try to ensnare her but are foiled in their attempt due to her fleetness of foot and to the methods she adopts in defending herself in which she is assisted by her companion the "cat." There is an abundance of comedy

and novel effects interspersed throughout the action, which is kept at high speed. (one reel)

Review: *Moving Picture World,* 3 January 1925

Each one of these Walt Disney cartoons, which are being distributed on the independent market by M. J. Winkler, appears to be more imaginative and clever than the preceding, and this one is a corker. A real little girl portrays Alice, and she is pictured in various experiences with cartoon characters. This combination of photography and cartoon work is exceedingly well done. In this number, Alice and her pal the cat land on a cannibal isle and finally through the ingenuity of the cat they succeed in killing off all of the tribe of cannibals who attack them.

ANDY PANDA GOES FISHING (1940)

Company: Burt Gillett, Walter Lantz, Universal Pictures
Characters: Andy Panda, black cannibals

Review: *Exhibitor Servisection,* 9 May 1951

While fishing, Andy Panda meets his turtle friend who has a very unique way of fishing. Against the turtle's warning he makes friends with an electric eel. Suddenly a tribe of natives hunting for pandas arrives, and the chase is on. Although the turtle does his best to help, it is the electric eel who finally chases off the hunters. Good.

Review: *Boxoffice,* 19 May 1951

Another amusing Technicolor cartoon dealing with the panda and his friend, the turtle. The turtle shows Andy some new methods of fishing, none of them requiring labor. Then the turtle tells Andy that some cannibals are chasing him, but after a wild chase, he finally eludes them.

AROMA OF THE SOUTH SEAS (1926)

Company: Bud Fisher, Fox Films
Type: Komocolor, silent with sound track added later. Title is a takeoff of 1926 Paramount feature, *Aloma of the South Seas,* starring Warner Baxter and Gilda Grey
Characters: Mutt, Jeff, black cannibals

Story: The cartoon opens with Mutt and Jeff on a tiny raft in the middle of the sea. Tall and skinny Mutt, looking through binoculars, tells short and fat Jeff that he sees land ahead. They land on the shore and immediately set out to explore the island. Mutt tells Jeff, "Let's go over there." They walk over to where they see two pairs of black footprints in the sand. They are puzzled and both kneel down and smell them. The stinky odor given off by the footprints knocks both of them unconscious. After they recover, they walk away holding their noses with their fingers. The footprints they leave behind begin to move and are attached to legs that come out of the ground, followed by the bodies of two black cannibals, each carrying a club. One cannibal looks in the direction of Mutt and Jeff and licks his lips with his long tongue. Then they both run off to capture them. Mutt and Jeff see them coming and run away. Mutt says, "Hey Jeff, I think they're right behind us." They stop, and the cannibals dive into a bush. Jeff says, "I think they're in there but I'm not sure. I'm going to take a look." He looks under a branch and says, "Naw, I don't see any thing. I wonder what happened." While he is talking, the bush grows into a tall palm tree. Jeff pushes on the trunk of the tree, the top bends down, and a cannibal rises out of the branches and hits Mutt on the head with his club. Jeff asks Mutt, "What happened to you?" Before Mutt can answer, both cannibals jump out of the tree. After a fierce battle Mutt and Jeff are subdued and tied up with ropes. They are put on a large circular tray and covered with a lid before being carried back to the cannibal village. Meanwhile in the village, the cannibal chief, a big fat man with a crown on his head, sits on his throne. Mutt and Jeff arrive and are displayed before the chief, who smiles and licks his lips with his long tongue, which wraps around his head. The chief holds Jeff in his arms and smiles while he looks him over. He pats Jeff on the head and says, "Nice, nice." He is satisfied that the chubby Jeff has enough meat on his bones to make a fine meal. Jeff is placed on the cooking pan and carried away by a cannibal. He dumps him into a big cooking pot resting on a fire and then puts the lid on the pot. Meanwhile the chief is looking Mutt over, but decides that he is too skinny after feeling his arm and leg. The chief orders that Mutt be carried away and locked up. The water in the cooking pot is getting hot, so Jeff lifts up the lid and sticks his head out to cool off. He is trying to put out the fire under the pot as the cannibal chief's daughter arrives on the scene. She is a fat woman with pigtail braids sticking straight out from her head. She takes one look at Jeff and falls in love with him. She gives him a big smile but Jeff tells her, "Aw, go on!" She literally throws him a big wet kiss that lands on his face. But Jeff pulls it off and throws it on the ground. To show her affection she tickles Jeff's chin with her toes. Jeff holds his nose so he can't smell the odor from her stinky foot. Jeff tries to hide by putting the lid on the pot, but she manages to blow him another wet kiss which he blocks, using the lid as an umbrella. Not discouraged, she pulls him out of the pot and into her arms while Jeff kicks and screams, "No! Let me go!" When she gives him wet kisses on his face, he jumps out of her arms onto the ground. He spits out her wet kisses before pulling out his toothbrush and brushing his teeth. Jeff tells her, "Keep away from me, will you? Keep away!" Then the cannibal chief arrives on the scene. The female cannibal asks the chief if she can marry Jeff, and the chief gives her his approval. She smiles, waves her hands, and dances with joy before picking Jeff up, giving him another wet kiss, and dropping him and walking away. Later, in her hut, the bride-to-be is preparing herself for the wedding as she stands looking into a large mirror. She picks up a can of black shoe polish and smears it all over her face. She rubs her face with a cloth, giving it a bright shine. She squirts lotion on her face from a large bottle and then directly into her mouth. When she is finished, she uses a funnel to spit the liquid back into the bottle to use again next time. Next she places a barrel over her body and then calls her servant, who arrives with a tow

truck. She uses the towing arm to pull the barrel around her mistress's body, drawing it tight like a corset. The bride-to-be then puts on a dress over her now shapely body. Meanwhile the chief sits on his throne with Jeff at his side. The cannibal bride arrives, and the chief nods his approval. But he and Jeff are surprised when several more would-be brides show up on the scene. While the chief is trying to figure out the situation, Mutt is in his cage trying to escape. Finally he cuts the bars with his teeth. As he goes to the village to help Jeff, a cannibal, tosses some old clothes right into his path. This gives Mutt an idea to save Jeff. He picks up the clothes and makes himself a dress that he uses to impersonate a white woman. Jeff and the others run away when they see Mutt coming, but the chief is curious and remains to greet him. The chief is pleased at what he thinks is a comely female. He sits Mutt on the throne beside him, but Mutt rejects all of the chief's amorous advances. When the chief closes his eyes and tries to kiss him, Mutt picks up the dog and the chief kisses it instead. The chief is pleased until he sees Mutt's trousers underneath the dress and realizes he has been tricked. He becomes angry and runs after Mutt, who makes a hasty retreat. Mutt is joined by Jeff, and the chief is joined by the rest of the cannibal tribe, and the chase is on. As spears fly over their heads, Jeff says, "Run for your life, Mutt! Run for your life!" They manage to stay ahead of the angry cannibals, but Jeff is hit in the rear end by several spears. Mutt pulls them out and uses them to build a raft on which they escape after they reach the ocean shore. The angry and frustrated chief and the other cannibals stand on shore and wave their spears at them as the cartoon ends.

AVIATION VACATION (1941)

Company: Tex Avery, Warner Bros.
Type: Merrie Melodies
Characters: Offscreen narrator, black Africans

Story: This travelog cartoon opens at an airport. The narrator says, "Attention! Attention! Plane number 4 now leaving California on world tour. Passengers board ship immediately. Attention, pilot! Ceiling five thousand feet, weather clear, track fast." The passengers rush aboard the plane, and it takes off. After flying over "sunny" California, it passes over Mount Rushmore where the four faces of past presidents and the 1941 presidential nominees, Franklin D. Roosevelt and Wendell Willkie, are seen carved in rock. As they fly over Ireland, Patrick sings a tenor solo, "When Irish Eyes Are Smiling." The narrator says, "And we are approaching the interior of darkest Africa" as the sky turns from day to night. Drum beats are heard as the overhead view shows three Africans in a village. Two beat the tom-toms while the other stands by, holding a spear in his hand. The narrator says, "The primitive beat of the tom-toms to send messages from one village to another is still used by the natives." The camera pans over the landscape where the natives beat drums, relaying the message from one village to another until it is heard by the chief. He is a fat man with thick white lips, a bone in his nose, and a crown on his head. He is sitting on a bamboo throne. The chief looks at another African, who is sitting on the ground beside. This one has long white lips and wears a bone in his hair. The chief says, "What do he say?" The other African says, with a Stephin Fetchit demeanor, "He say boop-tiddy-boop-tiddy-boop-ti-boop." The chief gives him a puzzled look and says "oh." The scene changes and the narrator says, "The natives of this savage tribe use blow guns for weapons. They can shoot poison darts a great distance with great accuracy. Watch." An African with a painted face and thick white lips wears a skirt and holds a blowgun in his hand as he appears from behind a bush and walks over to a tree. He puts a dart in his gun and blows it at a target. The dart hits the target but misses the bull's-eye. Another African looks at the target and says, "Terrible shot, Joe." The overhead tour continues as the narrator points out ostriches and a tropical butterfly. As the sun sets, the narrator says, "And with a heavy heart we bid a reluctant farewell to these foreign lands of enchantment and beauty as we head homeward to the good old USA." When the plane arrives home, New York is covered by fog. The plane finally lands anyway. When the fog lifts, the plane is seen attached to a carnival ride as the cartoon ends.

BAFFLED BY BANJOS (1924)

Company: Pat Sullivan, distributed by M.J. Winkler
Characters: Felix the Cat, black natives

Review: *Moving Picture World*, 23 April 1924.

This is one of the very best of the Felix the Cat Cartoons distributed by M. J. Winkler. The idea of this picture is a thoroughly humorous one and one that will strike home to a large number of persons. Felix, annoyed by the continual strumming of a ukulele in the apartment overhead, tries to get away from it. He goes to the South Sea Island and finds the natives have the habit; diving to the bottom of the ocean, he discovers the fish engaged in this pastime. Discouraged, he seeks peace by inhaling gas, but on reaching Paradise his spirit soon discovers that even the angels have substituted ukes for harps. There are a lot of laughs in this comedy and it should be universally popular.

BETTY BOOP'S BAMBOO ISLE (1932)

Company: Dave Fleischer, Max Fleischer, Paramount Pictures
Characters: Betty Boop, Bimbo, Royal Samoans Band (live action), black natives

Story: The cartoon opens in Hawaii where the Royal Samoans play music and dance the hula. The scene shifts to Bimbo playing a ukulele in a small motorboat traveling across the open sea. His route takes him around North Africa and through the Panama Canal before he finally winds up on an island in the South Seas. When his boat hits the shore, he is tossed out and lands in a canoe carrying Betty Boop. They travel together down the river, Bimbo serenading Betty with

his ukulele. Their boat carries them over a waterfall, and they are thrown onto dry land. Before long Bimbo sees a group of black natives carrying spears. Bimbo decides that they are hostile, so he decides to disguise himself as a native. He puts a bone in his hair and blackens his face with dirt. When the natives come on the scene, they are tricked into believing that Bimbo is one of the tribe. They take him back to their village, where they make him king and Betty his queen. One native gives Bimbo a large black cigar. He lights it with a match that he strikes on the rear end of a native. The native dancers entertain Bimbo, and when they are finished Betty tells him that he ain't seen nothing yet. She then does a hot hula dance. Just as she finishes, the rain begins to fall and washes the blackface makeup off Bimbo's face. The natives turn hostile and chase Bimbo and Betty. The two manage to run to the seashore and jump into Bimbo's motorboat, barely escaping the pursuing natives as the cartoon ends.

THE BIG FLOOD (1922)

Company: Paul Terry, Pathe Film Exchange
Type: Aesop's Fable, released in 1929 with added sound track by RKO
Characters: Farmer Al Falfa as Noah, black cannibal

Story: Captain Noah comes out of his house on crutches. His foot is throbbing, so he thinks that it will rain soon. He looks through his spyglass, and off in the distance he sees a big storm approaching. He calls his black cat, Paul Revere, and instructs him to go and tell all the animals to come to the ark as soon as possible. Paul says, "aye-aye, Captain" and rides off on his black horse to spread the captain's message to all the animals. Soon they are seen running to the ark as the storm gets closer. Just as they and their provisions are loaded on board, a tidal wave sweeps the ark out to sea. The ark is towing a small boat carrying a family of skunks. Huge waves cause the ark to toss and turn, but eventually the storm subsides. On board the ark Noah and the animals celebrate. Noah plays the piano while two small black mice do a torrid dance to the delight of the animal audience. The skunks hear the music, and two of them climb on board the ark. Noah then stops playing and says, "Gas, gas! Beat it, boys!" All the animals scatter. They are chased around and around the boat before the animals dive overboard. In an effort to escape the skunks, Noah climbs to the top of the ship's mast and grabs the sail. A gust of wind breaks the sail away from the mast, and Noah flies through the air. Somehow the skunks run through the air and follow him. Noah releases the sail and falls to the ground, landing on an island. As he gets up and looks around, he is confronted by a black cannibal carrying a sword who appears from behind a rock. Noah tries to run, but the cannibal captures him. Noah can see himself in the cooking pot when the cannibal tastes his hand and smiles. Noah thinks he is doomed when the two skunks fall out of the sky, hitting the cannibal on top of the head. One of the skunks chases the cannibal away. Noah expresses his gratitude to the other skunk with the moral of the story—"It's an ill wind that blows nobody good." The moral flashes on the screen as the cartoon ends.

Review: *Moving Picture World,* 30 September 1922

Paul Terry has used his keen imagination with amusing effect in the Aesop's Film Fable depicting the great flood. He has indicated the reaction which Noah and his menagerie had to the news that the storm was approaching. It is a highly original number, starting in with the rainfall literally of cats and dogs and ending with the comic parade of all the animals into the ark except the skunks. (Released in 1929 with sound track.)

Review: *Film Daily,* 1 October 1922

Built around the idea that it is an ill wind that blows no one good, this cartoon reel holds interest in good fashion. It includes several amusing bits of business, one touch being especially funny. That is a play on the popular expression, "It's raining cats and dogs." During the flood which causes Noah to embark in his boat, innumerable little cats and dogs are seen mingled with the rain drops. It should get a laugh.

BOLA MOLA LAND (1939)

Company: Frank Tipper, Dick Marion, Walter Lantz, Universal Pictures
Characters: Black cannibals

Story: The offscreen narrator guides the audience through this cartoon travelog. Before leaving the United States on the Crack Pot Travel liner it is suggested that the passengers see the scenic views of the United States but the view is blocked by billboards advertising beer, liver pills, razors, etc. The ship sails under the Golden Gate Bridge, and the voyage is underway. The first stop is the Hawaiian Islands, where an active volcano is blowing smoke rings and doing the hula dance. The ship then sails around and through the horn, a large tuba. Many interesting sea birds appear, including a level-headed blue jay, and a cradle puss pelican, a rare bird that rocks itself to sleep in its own bed. A flock of birds overhead is flying backward because the birds don't want to see where they are going. They only want to see where they have been. They pass three wandering buoys—Big Buoy, Little Buoy, and Baby Buoy. They pass by an island where they see many strange trees including two whispering pines softly talking to each other, and a lonesome pine that is crying because it's so lonely. A rubber tree is seen blooming with tires, hot water bottles, boots, etc. Many strange animals appear, such as two living alligator bags, bridge-playing kangaroos, and canary birds that sing bass. They sail on to Bola Mola Land but stop by Venice, where they see a street band playing under water. They next take a trek across the black belt of Africa until finally they reach Bola Mola Land. The captain looks through his spyglass and sees natives dancing with spears in their hands. Above them is a sign: Well-Fed Tourists Welcome. The tourists make a hasty retreat and sail for home as the golden sun sinks into the sea with a splash as the cartoon ends.

Review: *Motion Picture Herald,* 27 May 1939

The Walter Lantz cartoon, a satire on travel cruises, takes the patrons from California to the imaginary "Bola Mola Land." In a typical sequence the boat goes through a bass horn when rounding the "Horn." Arriving at Bola Mola the travelers are met with hostile natives and sign proclaiming that "well fed tourists are welcome." (6 min)

Review: *Boxoffice,* 10 June 1939

Being a fairly cute satire on travel cruises, and this being the vacation-planning season, the material in this cartoon should make for general amusement. The cruise ship takes off and makes some strange-looking spots, properly "seasoned" by a barker. After passing through most of the world's most renowed countries, the ship arrives at its destination. When the tourists see a hungry-looking band of natives waiting for some fresh tourist meat, the ship makes a hasty departure.

Review: *Selected Motion Pictures,* 1 June 1939

Walter Lantz cartoon. An utterly ridiculous but funny burlesque of a cruise to "Bola Mola Land." Good. Family.

BOYHOOD DAZE (1957)

Company: Chuck Jones, Warner Bros.
Type: Merrie Melodies
Characters: Ralph Phillips, black Africans, Dr. Living-Son, Martians

Review: *Motion Picture Exhibitor,* 21 August 1957

This shows the vivid creation of Ralph, a little boy sent to bed for being naughty. First he is Dr. Living-Son, African explorer hero, rescuing his parents from savages; Next a jet ace, saving his country from Martians. The ultra-modern drawings are excellent, but this is not very funny. Good.

BUDDY IN AFRICA (1935)

Company: Ben Hardaway, Vitaphone, Warner Bros.
Type: Looney Tunes
Characters: Buddy, African natives

Review: *Moving Picture World,* 6 February 1935

An amusing Looney Tune number, in which Buddy is an African trader. He trades with the natives, with results which are amusing judged by cartoon standards. When a small monkey tries to steal something, Buddy hits him and the little one brings his gorilla father. But when they both get the worst of it, the gorilla joins Buddy in chasing the young one. The youngsters should enjoy it especially. (7 min)

Review: *Philadelphia Exhibitor,* 1 May 1938

Buddy is a trader, manages to sell the savages all his merchandise, nearly runs into disaster when a monkey's pup gets excited.

BUDDY OF THE APES (1934)

Company: Ben Hardaway, Vitaphone, Warner Bros.
Type: Looney Tunes
Characters: Buddy, black cannibals

Story: The cartoon opens with a scene of Buddy, the ape man, in his treehouse high at the top of a coconut tree. Buddy beats his chest and yells like Tarzan before leaving his house, swinging from vine to vine until coming to rest on the back of an elephant that is drinking water from a small pond. Buddy slides down the elephant's back, and the elephant gives Buddy a shower by spraying him with water from his trunk. After he has had his shower, Buddy plucks a water plant from the pond and uses it to brush his teeth. Meanwhile a mother chimpanzee has left her baby unattended. The baby rocks his cradle out of the tree, and it falls into a river. The mother runs to Buddy, who is drinking coconut juice for breakfast, and asks him to rescue her baby, who is about to plunge over a waterfall. Thinking fast, Buddy ties one end of a long vine to his knife. Holding the other end of the vine, he throws the knife, which sticks in the baby's cradle just before it goes over the falls. Buddy pulls the baby to shore and becomes a hero for saving the baby chimp. While he and the other animals are celebrating, they are sighted by a black cannibal who is sitting atop a tall tree. The cannibal smiles and licks his lips before sliding down the tree and running off to his village. After hearing the news the fat king, who is sitting on his throne, rings a bell that is stuck through the nose of another cannibal. When they hear the alarm, all the cannibals stop what they are doing. The cook throws away the newspaper he is reading, *The Nudist Times,* and rushes off to the king. Two female cannibals, who are swinging a baby on a rope tied between rings in their respective noses, drop the baby and hurry off to see the king. Two others stop their game of ping pong, in which they use their long, wide lips as paddles. After they have all gathered around the king, he orders them to capture Buddy for their dinner. The king goes with them, riding in a bathtub carried by two cannibals. Meanwhile Buddy is playing tic-tac-toe with a little monkey when a spear passes close by his head and sticks in a tree. Buddy sees the cannibals coming, so he lifts the small monkey onto his back before swinging back up to his tree house on a vine. Buddy expresses no fear as the cannibals surround him, and he beats his chest and lets out a Tarzan yell to summon the other animals to his aid. Hearing Buddy call, the elephant fills his trunk with rocks and propels them like machine-gun bullets in the direction of the cannibals. Three of the cannibals are dispatched. Buddy catches one of the spears thrown at him and hurls it back toward one of the cannibals. The spear hooks the nose ring of a cannibal before becoming embedded in a tree, leaving the cannibal dangling with his feet off the ground. A kangaroo comes along and boxes the hapless cannibal. The cannibal's little son tries to help him by kicking the kangaroo on the leg, but a baby kangaroo comes out of his mother's pouch and hits the little boy cannibal on the head, knocking him out cold. Monkeys are loading large stones into the mouth of a hippopotamus. After they finish, another monkey swings out of a tree and kicks the hippo on the rear end, which propels the rocks out of the hippo's mouth like cannon balls. The projectiles make quick work of the cannibals except for the king, who is trying to escape. As the king is carried in the bathtub, Buddy swings out of the treehouse and attacks him. When the dust clears after the fight, Buddy is seen standing with his foot on the head of the fallen king. Buddy beats his chest and gives the Tarzan yell as the cartoon ends.

BUSHY HARE (1950)

Company: Robert McKimson, Warner Bros.
Type: Merrie Melodies, Bugs Bunny special
Characters: Bugs Bunny, black native

Review: *Motion Picture Herald,* 30 June 1951

Through a mix-up, Bugs Bunny is delivered by the stork to a mother kangaroo. Bugs is reluctant to be considered a kangaroo baby and protests. A native arrives to menace Bugs and the kangaroo, but Bugs leads the native through a series of misadventures, disposes of him and makes peace with his new-found "mother." (7 min)

Review: *Film Daily,* 22 July 1950

In a stork mix-up, Bugs Bunny is delivered to a kangaroo in Australia. In trying to rid himself of his new "mother," B. B. runs into trouble in the form of a local bushman. Wonderful cartoon for all ages.

Review: *Exhibitor Servisection,* 8 November 1949

Bugs Bunny, transported to Australia by a stork, is deposited in the pouch of an expectant kangaroo mother. Anguish causes Bugs to allow himself to be adopted. He becomes a target for a caveman, and is rescued by the kangaroo, whose real child arrives on time. Both Bugs and the baby kangaroo are then transported to the U.S. Fair.

Review: *Boxoffice,* 18 November 1950

Good. This is a wealth of imagination and is really funny. A stork delivers Bugs Bunny to Australia by mistake and Bugs is adopted by a motherly kangaroo. Bugs doesn't like being kept in her pouch, but when a dangerous bushman with spear and bommerang arrives, he really appreciates "mother."

CANNIBAL CAPERS (1930)

Company: Burt Gillett, Walt Disney, Columbia Pictures
Type: Silly Symphony, later released as silent cartoon *Zulu Jazz* by Hollywood Film Enterprises.
Characters: Black cannibals

Story: The cartoon opens in a jungle where the tall, skinny, black trunks of coconut trees sway in the wind. The tree trunks are in fact the long, skinny legs of black cannibals with big thick lips and wide mouths wearing grass skirts. The scene changes to a cannibal village with grass huts. The beat of drums is heard in the background. Four black cannibals dance while others look on. The cannibal cook, wearing a bone in his nose, stands near a large black cooking pot that sits on a fire. Human skulls attached to the end of long poles stand near spears and shields that lie near the huts. A cannibal beats human skulls as drums and plays others as castanets. Other cannibals dance the shimmy. Everybody joins in the merriment while the cook uses the long tongue of another cannibal to sharpen his meat cleaver. He smacks his lips and rubs his stomach before running over to two turtle shells lying on the ground. A cannibal is hiding under one shell, and a turtle is under the other. The cook can't decide which one to turn over, so he says "Eeney-meeney-miney-mo" to decide which one to select for dinner. He chooses the one covering the cannibal and carries it and the cannibal back to the cooking pot while all the others crowd around and smile. The cannibal is tossed into the boiling pot but pops right back up and fans his rear end with a shield. Suddenly a huge lion shows up on the scene, and the cannibal dives back into the pot while the other cannibals scatter in all directions. The cook is left behind as he tries to decide which way to run. Finally the others pull him into a grass hut while the lion emits a loud roar. The lion walks over to the cooking pot, sniffs the aroma, smiles, and then stirs the pot. He tastes the liquid and decides to add more salt and pepper to the brew. The lion then dips the ladle into the pot, pulls out the cannibal, and tries to swallow him. But the cannibal is still in the ladle when the lion takes it out of his mouth. The lion tries unsuccessfully several more times to swallow the cannibal. The cannibal manages to get away, but the lion chases him, catches him, and bites him on the rear end, and has his teeth pulled out of his mouth. The cannibal puts the lion's teeth in his own mouth and makes a loud roar that frightens the lion, who tries to run away. The cannibal catches him and bites the lion on his rear end and pulls the lion's fur off him. But the lion continues to run in his underwear. The cannibal bites the lion again on his rear end as the cartoon ends.

Review: *Film Daily,* 13 July 1930

One of Walt Disney's best "Silly Symphonies" to date. After the little band of cannibals have disported awhile in highly amusing fashion, a ferocious lion turns up and the whole gang takes to its heels. The cannibals' victim, however, jumps out of the boiling pot and gives the lion the run-around, winding up by getting hold of the lion's false teeth and using them to scare the jungle beast out of his skin.

Review: *Billboard,* 19 July 1930

Plenty of laughs to this animated cartoon of the Walt Disney Silly Symphony series. The conveying of numerous by-plays sparkling with originality and cleverness, is a big factor in mirth producing, tho there's no overlooking the skillful animation. Catchy music is used along with the laugh bits, thus making the short stronger in its appeal. Recording of the music and sound effects are good.

Cannibalism is played up in the short, showing the people of the jungle going in for dancing and music. The hoofing is amusing enough, but a choice piece of business is the one playing up the versatility of the drummer in the native band. Strongest risibility tickler is the battle between a lion and one of the cannibals. Lion first chases the black-skin around, but soon the worm turns and the fellow has the battle won.

Book this to give your audience laughs. (5 min)

CANNIBAL ISLAND (1928)

Company: Kinex Studios
Type: Kodax Cinegraph, puppet stop-motion animation
Characters: Snap the gingerbread man, Snap's dad, black cannibal

Story: The cartoon opens as Snap and his dog are flying high over the ocean in their single-engine airplane. Suddenly they see land below, and Snap looks down through his binoculars and sees a fat black cannibal stirring a huge cooking pot. The cannibal has thick white lips and bushy hair, and he wears a grass skirt. The cannibal picks up a white bone from the ground and takes a close look at it before throwing it into the pot. He stirs the stew in the pot before tasting some of it. He smiles and licks his lips with his tongue. Meanwhile Snap loses his balance and falls from the plane. As he falls, he opens his umbrella, which allows him to float gently down. He lands in the cannibal's stew and raises his head out of the liquid, but the cannibal pushes his head down again. Snap manages to jump out and is chased around and around the pot by the cannibal who holds a spear in his hand. Snap escapes and then hides in a hollow log. The cannibal arrives on the scene and looks around but can't find Snap. The cannibal then looks in the log, sees Snap, and crawls in after him. As the two struggle inside, the log rolls from side to side. Snap is the first to crawl out. Snap picks up a huge club and then climbs up on the log to wait for the cannibal to crawl out. The cannibal pokes his head out, and Snap hits him with the club, which knocks the cannibal out of the other end of the log. The cannibal is stunned as stars fly around his head, but he recovers quickly and grabs his spear and chases Snap around the log. He catches Snap and they struggle on the ground behind the log. Snap gets up and runs away, but the cannibal runs after him. Meanwhile Snap's dog looks down from the plane and sees that Snap is in trouble. The dog lowers a rope with an anchor tied to the end of it. Spot grabs the anchor, and the dog pulls Snap up to the plane. Snap looks down and smiles at the frustrated cannibal who shakes his fists in the air as the cartoon ends.

CARTOON OF MR. PAUL RAINEY'S AFRICAN TRIP (191?)

Company: No data
Characters: Paul Rainey, black cannibals

Story: The cartoon opens as Mr. Paul Rainey, a gentleman dressed in a suit, a derby hat, eyeglasses, and spats, stands on the deck of a ship and looks down into the ocean. The waves rise high and the captain reads, "When the waves gave a slight exhibition of a fervent wave's greatest ambition, Granpa got as wet as anyone yet on the day before real prohibition." A large wave rises and washes Rainey off the deck and into the ocean, where he swims to save his life. The caption reads, "On the crest of a wave in the ocean came a whale with a deuce of a notion. He cavorted and swam like a gamboling lamb with a hermit slithering motion." Rainey jumps into a barrel that floats by him and then grabs the tail of a black whale who pulls him through the water. The caption reads, "Though a barrel's not much for protection, 'twas welcome at least in this section. So grabbing the tail of the gyrating whale, he raced like one bent on election. There's a spot on a continent distant which the explorer sought most persistent. So he landed once more on shore; we swear that the place is existent." Arriving on the beach of an island, Rainey jumps out of the barrel and waves to it before turning around and walking off to explore the island. The narration reads, "Behold! Nature's sweeter creation, the national bird of the nation. Her featherless legs are smooth like the eggs that she lays without rest or cessation." An ostrich sits down and lays an egg and then gets up and walks away. The screen reads, "Now the egg of his wonderful creature has a patented copyright feature. 'Twill swell up and grow in a minute or so. (Children! Verify this by your teacher.)" The small eggs grows to fifty times its size as Rainey arrives on the scene and jumps on top of it. Suddenly an angry lion sticks his head from behind a rock and roars. The egg hatches into an ostrich that runs away carrying Rainey on his back with the lion chasing them. As they run by a tall cliff, a human figure on top of the cliff throws down a rope and lassoes Rainey and pulls him to the top. The screen reads, "Deprived of his afternoon tiffin, the lion is weeping and sniffing. When a wonderful bird in the offing is heard, who chased the poor beast like a griffin." The ostrich chases the lion and grabs his tail and flings him into the ocean, where he is swallowed by the black whale. Meanwhile Rainey is being held in the arms of the black female cannibal. She has thick white lips and wears a short grass skirt. She has bare feet and wears rings in her ears and nose. She takes a close look at Rainey and smiles before licking her lips with her tongue. She rolls her eyes and whispers into Rainey's ear, "Boss, you am just in time fo' de wedding' feast." Meanwhile the chief and several other cannibals are at the village, where they stare into a pot of boiling liquid with sad looks on their faces. The chief wears a stovepipe hat and earrings. The female cannibal arrives on the scene carrying Rainey in her arms, which brings smiles to the faces of the chief and the others. She sits Rainey on the ground and then tells the chief and others, "Ladies, everything am ready. Let de ceremony begin." Rainey asks, "Where's the bride?" The female cannibal says, "Here come de bride now" as she points in her direction. Rainey then asks, "But where is the bride groom?" They all smile and say, "You am g'wine to be de groom!" The chubby face of the smiling cannibal bride appears. She has braids in her hair that resemble coils of steel wire. The bride-to-be smiles and rolls her round eyes, but Rainey runs off and the spear-carrying canni-

bals chase him. Rainey runs back to the seashore and jumps into the barrel, which is floating near the beach. He sticks his head out of the barrel and thumbs his nose at the angry cannibals who have arrived on the scene and are jumping up and down, shaking their spears in the air. Rainey then smiles and tips his derby hat at them as he slowly floats away in the barrel and the cartoon ends.

CHEW CHEW BABY (1958)

Company: I. Sparber, Famous Studios, Paramount Pictures
Type: Noveltoon
Characters: Chew Chew the black pygmy cannibal, Harry the white tourist

Story: The cartoon opens on a scene somewhere in Africa as Harry and his friend are riding in their jeep on a jungle trail. They encounter a group of pygmies and decide to take a picture of one, Chew Chew, who is in front of the group. The pygmies have small bodies, large heads, very large mouths, and long sharp teeth. They stop the jeep and Harry says, "Ha-ha, cute little fella. With pygmies you never know what they are thinking." Whereupon Chew Chew imagines Harry cooking in a pot of boiling water. Harry raises his camera, points it at Chew Chew, and asks him to smile. Chew Chew shows a wide smile that resembles a slice of watermelon. As they prepare to leave, Harry tells Chew Chew, "Well, its been nice knowing ya. If you ever get to Cincinnati look me up. Ha-ha!" He jabs his partner in the ribs and says, "Funny, funny." Back home Harry is presenting a slide show of his trip to Africa to group of his friends. As he projects a picture of Chew Chew on the screen, he narrates, "He was the cutest little fellow, that pygmy with a great grin from ear to ear. Lived all of his life in one village. Never been more than two hundred yards away from his home in his life. So I said something very very funny, ha-ha. He turns on the lights and continues, "Now what was it I said . . ." as the doorbell rings. Harry walks over and opens the door, looks back at the group, and says, "Oh yes. Just as I was leaving . . ." He pulls the door open, "I shook hands with the little guy and I said to him," as Chew Chew enters and walks behind Harry and takes a seat. Harry, still talking, says, "I know you don't do much travlin', but if you ever get to Cincinnati, look me up, ha-ha." When Chew Chew laughs, Harry turns around and sees him, wondering how he got there. The guests have departed, and Harry and Chew Chew are in the bedroom. Harry climbs into bed and says, "Good night." Chew Chew sits on the floor by the bed and yawns, revealing two rows of large, sharp teeth. Chew Chew goes to sleep and dreams of Harry sitting in a pot of boiling water. Chew Chew's stomach begins to growl. He wakes up and walks to the bed and smears catsup on Harry's hand. As Chew Chew opens his mouth to take a bite, Harry wakes up and asks, "What's eating you?" Chew Chew points to one of his teeth. Harry tells him, "Ahh, you have a toothache." Chew Chew nods yes. Harry tells him, "Well, relax. I know the best dentist in Cincinnati." They arrive at the dentist's office and Harry tells the dentist, "Doc, this is Chew Chew. Comes all the way from Pygmania to have his teeth fixed." Sitting in the dentist's chair, Chew Chew is asked to open his mouth and say ah. The dentist asks Chew Chew, "Open wider, wider. Ah that's fine." He sticks his head into Chew Chew's mouth. Outside in the waiting room Harry is seated reading a paper when a loud noise comes from the operating room. The door opens and Chew Chew walks out, but the dentist is nowhere to be seen. As they are walking home, Harry tells Chew Chew, "You must be starved, Chew Chew. Let's put on the feed bag" as he carries Chew Chew to an automat restaurant. Harry makes his food selection from the automated food compartments, but Chew Chew selects the cook as his meal. Walking home, Chew Chew observes a policeman directing traffic. The cop sticks out his hand to give directions and disappears. Chew Chew has had another meal. They pass a clothing store with a male mannequin in front, which disappears. Chew Chew's stomach begins to ache, so he spits out the mannequin into a trash can. Harry and Chew Chew catch a crowded bus on which all of the seats are occupied. Chew Chew looks at two passengers seated nearby and they disappear. Chew Chew tells Harry that a seat is vacant, and they both sit down. Harry says, "First seat I've had on this bus in thirty-two years." Chew Chew smiles and rubs his stomach. They get off at the next stop where Fred, a friend of Harry's, is standing. Harry tells Chew Chew, "I want you to meet Fred. Fred and I went to school together." Next thing Harry knows is that Fred disappears. Harry throws up his hands and tells Chew Chew, "Oh no! I said meet him, not eat him!" Harry sticks his head inside Chew Chew's mouth and calls out, "Hey Fred, are you there?" Harry pulls his head out just before Chew Chew snaps his jaws shut. Harry is frightened and runs home with Chew Chew chasing him. Harry arrives home, slamming and barricading the door behind him. But Chew Chew chews his way in, bites Harry on the rear end. He hangs on as Harry runs up to the bedroom and slams the door shut, knocking Chew Chew off him. Harry phones the police, telling them, "Help! I've got a cannibal in the house . . ." as Chew Chew breaks in and bites him again. The chase around the house continues until Harry gets his hunting rifle and aims it at Chew chew. He becomes meek as a pet cat, purring and rubbing against Harry's leg. But when Harry puts away his rifle, Chew Chew bites him again and the chase is on. Harry runs out of the house and into the street, where he is hit by a truck. While he is lying in the street, an ambulance arrives. The medic decides to give him a blood transfusion just as Chew Chew arrives on the scene. The medic transfers Chew Chew's blood into Harry, who wakes up and finds that he has big sharp teeth and an appetite for human flesh. Chew Chew looks at him and tries to run away. Harry chases Chew Chew, opens his mouth wide, and is about to bite the pygmy on the rear end as the cartoon ends.

Review: *Motion Picture Exhibitor,* **1 October 1958**

Featuring modernistic drawings, this concerns an American hunter in Africa who tangles with a small native who comes to

America and turns out to be a purple people eater. The cannibal finds the loud mouthed hunter. There is an accident. The hunter is given a blood transfusion from the cannibal, and this makes him a people eater, too. Fair. (7 min)

COLONEL HEEZA LIAR'S TREASURE ISLAND (1923)

Company: Walter Lantz, J. R. Bray Studio; distributed by Hodkinson and Selznick Pictures
Characters: Col. Heeza Liar, black cannibals

Review: *Film Daily,* **4 February 1923**

This is a clever little reel combining the little cutout cartoon of Colonel Heeza Liar with the actual photographs of the artist and the staff of the art department. The little figure is exceedingly real and the manner in which the entire action is handled makes extremely interesting material. The Colonel hears the boys reading about a desert island that contains treasure and gets himself radioed to the nearest ship from which he sails to the island in a bottle. The cannibal chief tries very hard to cook him but the Colonel escapes and dives off a cliff only to be swallowed by a fish which after a supposed lapse of time is caught by the artist and his friend who are on a vacation. They are much surprised to see the Colonel and hear about his adventures. (one reel)

Review: *Bioscope* **(London), 16 August 1923**

Hearing that Robinson Crusoe's Island is about to be discovered, Col. Heeza Liar arrives on the spot by wireless in a really dramatic manner. He is received by negroes, who are puzzled by the indestructibility of the mannequin, and he returns to his master via a fish. Full of original ideas and irresistible humour, this admirable production provides a novelty that will have very general appeal.

Review: *Moving Picture World,* **10 February 1923**

In this reel, the Colonel hearing of the discovery of the location of a treasure has himself sent by radio to a desert island and meets with a unique adventure at the hands of cannibals.

CRAZY CRUISE (1942)

Company: Tex Avery, Robert Clampett, Warner Bros.
Type: Merrie Melodies
Characters: Offscreen narrator, black cannibals

Story: This travelog cartoon starts out at a tobacco plantation in old Kentucky with brief pauses in Havana, Cuba, the Swiss Alps, and Egypt before reaching the African jungle. The narrator leads us across Africa, pausing briefly at "Veronica Lake," which is shaped like a woman. The narrator continues, "Then on into the interior. Now we come to the most dangerous territory in the Congo. This land of mystery is feared by natives, for it is said that herein dwells a tribe of ferocious giant cannibals. Here we see two of the world's most famous big-game hunters about to brave this unexplored jungle. They plan to capture a couple of these giants alive." The scene shows two white hunters being led by a black African who has thick red lips and wears a bone in the hair on his head. They are walking along a jungle trail when they disappear behind some bushes. A loud noise is heard, and the bushes shake. Then the excited black native runs out, shaking his hands in the air. He says "Look! They got 'em. They got cannibals." Two giant black cannibals are seen. They have painted faces and wear rings in their ears and noses. The tall one holds the two shrunken explorers in the palm of his hand. The white men are in the shape of two cigarettes. The large cannibal smiles, showing a single gold tooth. He says, "Ummm. King size." The shorter cannibal leans on a rock and smiles. A flock of black buzzards is seen attacking some bunny rabbits as the travelog leaves the jungle. The rabbits deploy antiaircraft guns and fire at them. Bugs Bunny, wearing a steel army helmet, smiles and says, "Thumbs up, Doc!" as the cartoon ends.

Review: *Motion Picture Exhibitor,* 8 April 1942

A burlesque cartoon, this pokes fun at all things held sacred by serious travel cruises. High spots are a land of ferocious cannibals known as the Hut Sut tribe and a battleship camouflaged so perfectly that only men aboard are visible. It's vivisection of more pompous travel films. Good.

DR. DOLITTLE'S TRIP TO AFRICA (1928)

Company: Lotte Reiniger, Deutscher Werkfilm (Berlin)
Type: Animation done in silhoutte. Originally released in three parts: *The Trip to Africa, Cannibal Land, The Lion's Den*
Characters: Dr. Dolittle, his animal friends, black cannibals

Story: The opening shows Dr. Dolittle taking off his hat. Letters fly out of it and spell "I am Doctor Dolittle." Next he introduces his animal friends—a duck, a dog, a monkey, a pig, and a parrot. The cartoon opens on a winter scene in Dr. Dolittle's homeland. Snow covers the ground and the roof of a large two-story house by the sea, where Dr. Dolittle is preparing a cup of hot tea. The caption reads, "Here, they tell, upon a time, lived the hero of our rhyme." Meanwhile a man leading a sick horse approaches the house, stops at the front gate, and rings the doorbell. Dolittle lets the man and horse inside and learns that the horse is sick. Dolittle examines the horse and prescribes a pair of eyeglasses, which he puts on the horse. The horse and the man leave the house very happy. Next the caption reads, "Clever pets with willing paws daily do the household chores." Dolittle's animal friends are seen doing the chores: the duck cooks a sausage, the monkey washes dishes, the dog dusts the stairs, the pig fetches water from the outside well, and the parrot cleans the doctor's eyeglasses. When they finish, they all sit around the fire as Dr. Dolittle reads to them. The captain reads, "See them reading at evening time stories of a foreign clime." Meanwhile a swallow is nearing the end of a long journey as he

flies down and rings the doctor's doorbell. The dog opens the door, and the swallow flies inside and perches on the doctor's hand. The doctor gives the cold, tired bird a sip of hot tea. Then the bird says to him, "Doctor, come and help us quick! The monkey folks have fallen sick!" All the animals are excited, but Dolittle is sad as the caption reads, "There's no cash to pay his fare." He explains to the others that he does not have enough money to make the trip to Africa. Then he puts on his coat and hat and goes for a walk in the snow. While walking he observes a small boy fall into some icy water. Dolittle rescues him and his grateful father, a sea captain, tells Dolittle, "You have snatched him from the grave. How can I reward you, sir, I crave?" Dolittle says, "Captain, I must cross the seas. Help me find a vessel, please." The captain tells him, "In the harbor lies my ship. Take her, Doctor, for your trip." Dolittle goes back home and tells the others of his good fortune. Shortly they are all packed and leave the house and board the sailing ship as the caption reads, "Hear their nautical hurrah! All aboard for Africa." On the way the swallow flies ahead, telling Dolittle, "Steer your course along my flight. I will guide you day and night." After a long voyage the monkey climbs the mast and looks off into the distance and says, "Land ahoy!" But there is a storm and the ship is tossed about on the sea as the caption reads, "Then the winds began to roar. Mountain high the billows soar!" The ship is wrecked on the rocky shore of Africa, but Dolittle and his friends get off and climb ashore before the ship sinks. The caption reads, "Every danger is safely passed. They're in Africa at last." Dolittle loses his hat in the water, but the swallow retrieves it. The caption reads, "Here's our doctor and his band journeying into Monkey-land. Come to cure their dire disease all the way from overseas."

Dolittle and his friends set off to find Monkeyland but are stopped when they are confronted by a black cannibal who wears a tall headdress and short skirt. He is accompanied by other cannibals carrying spears. The cannibal says, "Pomkwau-molle-molle!" Dolittle doesn't understand the language, which makes the cannibal angry. The cannibal then says, "jolliginki," but Dolittle is still puzzled. The cannibal then moves his frowning face close to Dolittle and says, "No admittance" and immediately jumps on top of Dolittle. Dolittle manages to get free. He and his friends try to run away but they are captured and taken to the cannibal village, where Dolittle is tossed at the feet of the fat cannibal chief. The chief sits on a throne. Dolittle bows to him and extends his hand to shake the chief's hand, but this angers the chief and he shouts, "Paleface spies. Lock them in the dungeon cell!" Dolittle and his friends are locked in the dungeon, and a cannibal removes the key from the lock. The parrot flies out through the bars of the cage and follows the cannibal, who gives the key to the chief. The chief goes into his grass hut and hangs the key on the wall before he relaxes in bed. Meanwhile outside of the chief's hut the parrot engages another cannibal in a game of racquetball. The bird knocks the ball through the window of the chief's hut, breaking the glass. The angry chief rushes outside, and the parrot hides in a tree while the chief chases the cannibal up a tree and spanks his rear end. The parrot takes this opportunity to fly through the broken window into the hut where he grabs the key and then flies back to the dungeon. He unlocks the door and allows Dolittle and the others to escape. The chief discovers that they have gone, and he quickly beats on a large drum, which summons the rest of the tribe. He orders them to catch Dolittle, and they all run off carrying spears. They chase Dolittle and his friends up and down the sides of mountains. Dolittle tries unsuccessfully to stop them by blocking the jungle trail with a large boulder. Finally they arrive at the border of Monkeyland as the caption reads, "See the monkey envoys stand on the borders of their land." Dolittle gives one of the monkey envoys his medicine bag, which the monkey carries away. The other monkey envoys tell Dolittle to follow him, but the cannibals also follow close behind. Dolittle and party manage to stay ahead of the cannibals until they are stopped at the edge of a wide canyon. The monkeys on the other side see that Dolittle is in danger from the cannibals and says, "Boys, the foe is on the trail. Bridge the chasm head to tail!" The monkeys form a living bridge that allows Dolittle and the others to cross over to the other side of the canyon. The monkeys then pull back quickly, preventing the cannibals from crossing over. Dolittle doffs his hat at the cannibals and then thumbs his nose at them as the angry chief and the other cannibals look at them from the other side. The monkey chief tells Dolittle, "Sir no human ever saw the famous monkey bridge before." The caption reads, "Doctor mops his heated brow. Soon he'll cure his patients now! After the monkeys are cured and Dolittle and friends narrowly escape a huge lion, they safely make the trip back home as the cartoon ends.

DREAMY DUD IN THE AFRICAN WAR ZONE (1916)

Company: Wallace Carlson, Essanay Film Co.
Characters: Dreamy Dud, Dunk (Harry Dunkinson live action), black cannibals, colored washerwoman

Review: *Moving Picture World,* 21 October 1916

This is another split reel in which Cartoonist Carlson has worked out his humorous incidents by combining, through excellent double exposure, his human figures with his well-known pen and ink characters. Dreamy Dud, Dunk and the dog put out to sea. The captain orders the cook to quit boiling cabbage. The cook produces an alibi and Dunk's cigar is found to be the offensive smell. Before the captain can finish his argument a battleship opens fire on them, the gunners having orders to get the fat fellow. Dud and the dog delight in Dunk's dodging of fourteen-inch shells. Then a gigantic whale lifts the three off the boat and sends them whirling into space, Dud coming down right through a newspaper in which a cannibal chieftain is reading the latest movie news. "Spoila pictura Hank Walthall," says the chief angrily. Dud is chased over the desert and caught, but the chief's daughter pleads for his life. He awakens to find the

colored washerwoman telling him to get up, while Dunk and the dog laugh.

Review: *Moving Picture World,* 4 November 1916

A split reel sharing animated cartoons and scenic views. The novelty cartoons by Carlson are funny, and they embrace some good double exposure work which brings into the action a human character-Harry Dunkinson. Dud, Dunk and the dog put out to sea, and their adventures are numerous and humorous.

Review: *Motography,* 21 October 1916

This is another split reel in which Cartoonist Carlson has worked out his humorous incidents by combining through excellent double exposure, his human figures with his well-known pen and ink characters.

DREAMY DUD IN KING KOO KOO'S KINGDOM (1915)

Company: Wallace Carlson, Essanay Film Co.
Type: On the same reel with *The Grand Canyon*
Characters: Dreamy Dud, Africans

Review: *New York Dramatic Mirror,* 14 July 1915

Wallace Carlson continues his animated dreams of Dreamy Dud, which besides being funny in the way these drawings usually are, are a good deal like the dreams of a child.

DREAMY DUD JOYRIDING WITH PRINCESS ZLIM (1916)

Company: Wallace Carlson, Essanay Film Co.
Type: On the same reel with *Apache Trail*
Characters: Dreamy Dud, African princess

Review: *Moving Picture World,* 2 December 1916

Dreamy Dud finds himself in Africa, the reluctant escort of Princess Zlim, the ebony lady of pronounced pulchritude. She invites him to take a ride in the Royal Jitney Bus and after cranking the elephant's tail, they climb aboard. Gasoline is taken on for the elephant and after drinking it he becomes unsteady and engages in various fights with the animals, making it extremely hard for the Princess to make love to Dreamy Dud. The resultant adventures give Dud a thrilling time, but he soon wakes up to find his mother calling him.

FARMER AL FALFA'S REVENGE (1916)

Company: Paul Terry, J. R. Bray Studio, Pathe Film Exchange, Thomas Edison Film Co.
Characters: Farmer Al Falfa, Sir Henry Bonehead, black porter

Story: The cartoon opens as Sir Henry Bonehead, dressed as a white hunter on safari, strolls through the forest carrying a long hunting rifle. Following behind him is his black porter, who carries a sack on his back. The porter turns toward the camera, smiles, and gives a salute before continuing on. Meanwhile Bonehead has come upon a hole in the trunk of a tree. He blows smoke from his pipe into a hole in the tree trunk. He looks up and sees the smoke blowing out another hole near the top of the tree. Soon a cat, overcome by the smoke, walks out of the hole onto a limb. It collapses and falls down to the ground dead. Bonehead says, "Some pipe, believe me." Bonehead continues his hunt and soon reaches the shore of a lake. On the other side he sees two pair of feet sticking out of the water and takes a shot at them. The feet belong to Al Falfa, who is taking a swim. When he sticks his head out of the water, Bonehead shoots again. Al Falfa jumps out of the water and tries to escape, but Bonehead swims across the lake and runs after him as he shoots his gun. Al Falfa decides to give up. He jumps on a tree stump and holds his hands up. Bonehead arrives on the scene and uses his spyglass to take a closer look at Al Falfa's face and says, "My word! I thought you were a goat." Then he walks away. But Al Falfa is angry. He picks up a rock and throws it at Bonehead. The rock strikes Bonehead on his head so hard that he drops his pipe and is propelled through the air, landing in the bag held by his black porter. The porter throws the sack over his back as Al Falfa arrives on the scene and shows him Bonehead's pipe. He then asks the black man, "Pardon me little 'Inkspot.' But is this your master's pipe?" Al Falfa holds the pipe under the porter's nose. When the porter unhales the smoke, it knocks him off the ground and he lands in the sack with Bonehead. Al Falfa throws the pipe into the sack turns toward the camera and smiles as the cartoon ends.

FELIX THE CAT IN NONSTOP FLIGHT (1927)

Company: Pat Sullivan, M. J. Winkler, released by Pathe Film Exchange and Educational Pictures
Type: Later released by Bijou Films with added sound track
Characters: Felix the cat, black cannibals

Story: The cartoon opens as Felix lies sleeping on the floor, which the maid is sweeping. She sweeps the dirt into a pile and then into a dustpan. She tosses the dust out of the window where it falls into a trash barrel sitting on the ground near the house. Felix is swept up with the dirt and lands in the barrel. Angrily he climbs out of the barrel and decides to leave town. He walks down the road before stopping near a sign that reads 478 Miles. He then picks up a newspaper from the ground and reads, "To Timbuctoo—$50,000 Prize-Winner—First to Arrive Wins Prize." Felix decides to enter the contest but doesn't know how to travel there. While pondering a solution to this problem, he get an idea when he sees a man walking by smoking a pipe. He is wearing a stovepipe hat and a two-piece billboard sign that covers the front and back of his body. The sign reads, "Eat at Joe's Lunchroom." Felix tricks the man into falling into an open manhole in the street. He then takes the sign and uses it to fabricate an airplane by attaching the boards,

which are the wings, to the side of a trash barrel. When the man sticks his head out of the hole in the street, Felix grabs the pipe out of his mouth and uses it as the plane's propeller. He takes off, and in no time he is flying over the ocean on his way to Timbuctoo. His plane carries him through the air and under the sea. En route he encounters many dangerous situations including a storm with lightning bolts that nearly strike him, a flock of angry birds that chase after him, a large whale that tries to swallow him, and a school of shark police who try to arrest him for exceeding the underwater speed limit. Finally he arrives safely at Timbuctoo but is prevented from landing by a group of attacking jungle animals, including elephants, hippos, and a lion. Finally he lands his plane—in the middle of a tribe of black cannibals! The cook, wearing a chef's hat and apron around his waist, holds a large knife that he waves at Felix. Nearby the fat cannibal chief sits on a rock wearing a stovepipe hat and holding a long spear in one hand. Seated on the ground near him are cannibal women who all have thick white lips and braided hair that sticks out of their heads. The cannibals smile and lick their lips as they anticipate dining on Felix for dinner. But Felix quickly realizes that he is in danger and tries to escape by running away. He is chased by the cannibal cook. Felix stops in front of a sleeping elephant. Felix grabs the animal's trunk and pulls it so hard that he pulls the elephant's hide off its body. Next he blows air into the trunk, inflating the hide so that it takes the shape of a large balloon. Felix blows and blows, and the balloon grows larger and larger until it floats off the ground with Felix hanging on to the trunk. As Felix floats away high in the air, he smiles as he looks down below and sees the angry cannibal cook standing on the ground looking up and waving his knife at him as the cartoon ends.

FELIX THE CAT IN STARS AND STRIPES (1927)

Company: Pat Sullivan, released by Pathe Film Exchange and Educational Pictures
Characters: Felix the cat, black porter

Story: The cartoon opens as Felix lies on top of the roof of a house sleeping. He is awakened by the cries of a baby standing in the yard below. Felix climbs down and tries to quiet the baby by amusing him with tricks. But the baby wants the striped pole standing in front of a barber shop. Felix steals the pole but is arrested and thrown into the penitentiary, where he is put to work breaking rocks. He and another prisoner manage to escape by tunneling under the walls, but are seen by a guard who chases the pair. When they run past a mule standing in a farmyard, Felix gets an idea. He pulls the striped suit off his prison buddy and puts it on the mule. Then he pulls the clothes off a scarecrow and puts them on the prisoner. The prison guard is fooled, and the prisoner escapes while Felix and the mule walk away. Meanwhile a black man dressed in a porter's uniform grooms an elephant standing near a circus tent. The porter turns around and sees Felix and thinks the mule is a zebra. He says "Well, doggone. 'At zebra got loose!" The black man walks over to the mule and pulls its tail, saying, "Git back in yo' cage!" But the mule resists, so the black man ties a rope to it and pulls the mule into a cage, locks the door, and walks away. Felix decides to help the mule escape. [The ending of the cartoon is missing from the author's copy of it.]

FELIX DOPES IT OUT (1925)

Company: Pat Sullivan, distributed by M. J. Winkler, Educational Pictures and Pathe Film Exchange
Characters: Felix the cat, black cannibals

Story: The cartoon opens as a bored Felix walks around in circles with his hands behind his back. Meanwhile two men are seated on a park bench. One of them has a big red nose. The other man takes a cigarette out of his pocket and turns to the man with red nose and says, "Gotta match?" The red-nosed man shakes his head no. The man with the cigarette lights it on the other man's red nose before leaving the scene. The red-nosed man is angry, but Felix is amused. The red-nosed man yawns and falls asleep. When he wakes up, he sees a beautiful young lady who has arrived on the scene. The red-nosed man runs over to the woman and says, "Darling!" The woman turns her back and ignores him. Next the man kneels and says to her, "Will you marry me?" The woman shakes her head no before taking a mirror out of purse and holding it in front of the man's face. He looks at his reflection and sees his big red nose. She laughs and gives the man a powder puff, which the man uses to brush white powder on his nose. But it remains red. The woman laughs at him before walking away. The man is so embarrassed that he pulls a gun out of his pocket and holds it to his head as tears roll down his cheek. Felix runs to him and says, "Stop! What's the matter?" The man answers, "My nose is a jinx!" Felix shakes his head no and then pulls a sheet of paper out of his pocket and holds it in front of the man's face. The man lowers the gun from his head and reads the paper, which says, "The only known cure for red noses is in the possession of H.R.H., the king of Boola Boola Land, an island of the south seas." The red-nosed man says, "What will I do?" Felix says, "Leave it to me!" Felix goes to a house and finds a washtub and clothes drying on a line in the backyard. He uses the tub as a boat and a nightgown for a sail. Then he takes his boat to the seashore and launches off toward Boola Boola Island. On the way the manages to escape man-eating sharks and a swordfish that punches a hole in the bottom of his boat. He walks ashore on the island but can't find the king, and so he paces back and forth on the edge of a cliff. Meanwhile two monkeys are playing baseball with a coconut. One of them hits the coconut, which flies through the air and hits Felix on the head, propelling him through the air. Meanwhile a cannibal cook is standing near a large black cooking pot, which is near the "royal mess kitchen," wearing a chef's hat and an apron around his waist. He scratches his head and looks at the menu, "Royal menu— turtle soup, oysters, fish," as Felix lands on the ground behind him. He turns around, sees Felix, and changes the menu by substituting *cat* for *fish*. Felix smiles and shakes the cannibal's hand and asks him, "Where is his majesty?" The cannibal answers,

"I'll take you right to him!" He reaches out to grab Felix, but Felix runs away. The cannibal chases after him, but Felix manages to elude him before he arrives at the front door of "his majesty's palace." He looks inside and sees the fat cannibal king sitting in a chair, fast asleep. The king wears a crown on his head and white spats on both of his bare feet. Felix walks inside and sneaks past the king. He goes into the "treasure room" where he finds the "Boola Boola royal treasury" locked in a large safe secured with a combination lock. Felix picks the lock, opens the safe, and looks inside, but is surprised by a large cobra, which crawls out and chases Felix out of the room to where the king is still sleeping. He finds a flute and places the instrument in the king's open mouth. Instead of snoring, the king blows a tune on the flute, charming the snake which begins to sway back and forth to the the music. Felix runs back to the open safe where he removes a scroll. Then he quickly runs back to the seashore, jumps into the water, and swims all the way back home. He finds the red-nosed man, who asks him, "Did you get the formula?" Felix nods his head yes, pulls the scroll out of his pocket, and gives it to the man. The man unrolls the scroll and reads it: "Cure for a red nose—keep on drinking and it'll turn blue." Felix is embarrassed and lowers his head and turns his back on the man but soon tries to run away as the angry man chases after him as the cartoon ends.

FORBIDDEN FRUIT (1923)

Company: Vernon Stallings, J. R. Bray Studios, released by Hodkinson and Selznick Pictures
Type: Animation combined with live action
Characters: Col. Heeza Liar, black cannibals

Story: Opening shows the skyline of New York City, over which appear the words, "Yes, we have no bananas." In the next scene three Jewish men are having a conversation. The on-screen caption, which changes from Yiddish to English, reads, "Yes, we had some bananas, yes!" Next is shown a close-up of a crying white baby with the caption, "We ain't dot no bananas." The scene then shifts to the interior of a cartoon studio, where two men are talking. One says to the other, "I got a banana." He pulls one out of his pocket and peels it, revealing the cartoon character Col. Heeza Liar. The man grabs the colonel and throws him onto the surface of a large white screen attached to a nearby wall. When both live-action men sit down to talk to each other, Col. Heeza Liar says to them, "That reminds me of the time that I ended the great banana famine in 1923." The two men turn to listen and ask, "What did you do?" The colonel replies, "Well, it was like this . . ." and begins to tell them the story of his adventure. The colonel leaves his homeland in a small boat that is pulled across the ocean by a rope attached to a pelican flying overhead. Eventually he arrives at the Ba-na-na Islands. A sign reads, "Americans keep off." Going ashore, the colonel walks on round, black rocklike objects protruding out of the shallow water. One of the rocks turns out to be the top of the head of a large black cannibal wearing a grass skirt and carrying a spear. He stands up with the colonel on top of his head. The cannibal rolls his eyes, licks his lips, and jabs the colonel with the tip of his spear. The colonel gives the cannibal a hard kick, knocking him down into the water, and walks on shore. At the cannibal village the chief is telling his people, "An' de fust pusson ah ketch swipin' bananas shall be confiscated, cremated, and epitaphed!" Meanwhile the colonel, who is exploring the island, arrives at a grove of banana trees. A snake tells him, "Go on, take one." After looking around to see if anybody is watching, the colonel picks a banana, which comes alive and squirms out of his hand and starts to slither away on the ground. The colonel gives chase to the banana and tries unsuccessfully to shoot it and lasso it with a rope. Chasing the banana, the colonel runs into a large black hippo, who then chases the colonel. Meanwhile at the village the cannibal queen, a large black woman with a crown on her head and her hair braided in pigtails, is seen rubbing her stomach as if she has missed a meal. Still trying to escape the hippo, the colonel hides between the legs of the queen, who picks him up and says, "Whadda yo mean by approachin' de Queen like dis? I's got a pedigree what goes back to Louis Quince!" The colonel replies, "I've got a pianola that goes back to Louis Cohen." The hippo arrives and gives chase to the two of them until it gets its horn stuck in the trunk of a palm tree. The colonel takes his hammer and bends the tip of the hippo's horn so that it cannot free itself. The queen is so impressed with the colonel's quick thinking that she picks him up, gives him a loving kiss, and tells him, "Yokin have anything yo little heart craves." The colonel answers, "Bananas," and the queen responds, "Consider yo'self craved." Next the colonel is standing on the deck of a large steamship as it is being loaded with bananas for the trip back home. The colonel waves good-bye to the cannibal queen standing on shore, who responds by blowing him a kiss. The colonel throws her a banana, which hits her on her head and knocks her down and out. On the way home the ship survives a terrible storm. Continuing his story, the colonel says, "But I finally arrived home by the skin of the bananas." The ship arrives at pier 10, and the colonel turns to the two men and asks, "And whadda you think of that?" Both men laugh in disbelief at the colonel's tall tale and ask him, "And what did you do with all those bananas?" The colonel replies, "I took them to the traders on Wall Street." The men say, "*Did you?*" to which the colonel replies, "I'll say, they *did* me!" One of the men takes a bottle of black ink and throws it at the colonel. The bottle lands upside down on the colonel's head, spilling ink all over him as the cartoon ends.

HALF-PINT PYGMY (1948)

Company: Tex Avery, M-G-M
Characters: George and Junior (two bears), black pygmies

Story: The cartoon opens in a city park, where George, a small bear wearing a derby hat, is reclining on a park bench reading a newspaper. Beside him, sitting on the ground playing jacks, is Junior, a large bear who is not too smart. George says, "Hey Junior, take a look at this," as he shows Junior an article in the

paper that reads, $10,000 Reward for the capture of the world's smallest pygmy." George puts down the paper and tells Junior, "For ten thousand bucks, you and I are headed for pygmy country." The scene changes to an African jungle trail where George and Junior are riding atop an elephant. Suddenly the elephant stops and sticks his trunk straight out, pointing in the direction of pygmies. George and Junior dismount and walk over and stop at the entrance of a small grass hut. George shakes the hut while telling Junior, who is holding a big club, "Now when the littlest one comes out, you smack 'em." George shakes the hut and the pygmies, with big white lips and wearing bones on their heads, come out one by one, each being smaller than the preceding one. Finally when George thinks the smallest has come out, he says, "Let him have it." But Junior misses the pygmy and hits George on the head. Junior meekly hands the club to George, who takes it and hits him on the head before they both run after the tiny pygmy. The wild chase is on, but the pygmy evades being caught—even when he is lured out of a cave by a big slice of watermelon. Finally the pygmy lays a trap for the two bears but is knocked cold when it backfires. They capture him and George, holding the pygmy in his hands, says, "Hey Junior, look! We got the world's smallest pygmy." But the pygmy shakes his head and tells him, "Sorry, boys." He points to a grass hut and calls for "Uncle Louie." Out of the hut walks a tiny pygmy wearing a bone in his hair that is twice as big as he is. The pygmy walks past the astonished George and Junior and then out of sight. George and Junior hold guns to their heads as the cartoon ends.

Review: *Motion Picture Herald,* **20 November 1948**

Into darkest Africa where the pygmies dwell goes cartoon director Tex Avery. He brings the sad story of a pygmy with a inferiority complex. (7 min)

Review: *Boxoffice,* **9 October 1948**

Two half-human creatures read an advertisement offering a reward for the smallest pygmy in the world and immediately make tracks for darkest Africa. There after superhuman efforts, that include encounters with lions, tigers, elephants, giraffes and other fauna, they finally capture a tiny pygmy—only to learn that there is another still smaller.

Review: *Film Daily,* **1 October 1948**

With a $5000 award in sight, a couple of animal characters hop to Africa and after a harum scarum time in which a number of new animation twists are worked up they locate their objective. They pursue him at length and when he is finally captured it seems they come still smaller. It has snappy, ingenious handling. In Technicolor.

HIS DARK PAST (1919)

Company: William Noland International Film Service; distributed in America by Educational Film Exchange; distributed in England by John D. Tippet (London)

Type: Pussyfoot Cartoon
Characters: Happy Hooligan, cannibals

Review: *Bioscope*, 9 October 1919

Friend Fly is rescued from flypaper danger by the Mouse, which reminds Happy Hooligan of one of his famous adventures. Wrecked on a South Sea isle, he meets Princess Koko, and later on the huge and hungry Prince Polo. The Prince wants to boil and eat him, but the Princess yearns to love and sing to him. Happy Holligan prefers death, but tries an escape first. And his Mouse again saves him in the most original fashion.

Laughable and original cartoon. (450 ft.)

HIS MOUSE FRIDAY (1951)

Company: William Hanna, Joseph Barbera, M-G-M
Characters: Tom cat, Jerry mouse, black cannibals

See fig. 27. Story: The cartoon opens as Tom is adrift at sea on a small raft. He is out of food and water and even tries to eat his shoe. He sights an island in the distance and then is carried to it on top of a large wave and is thrown on the beach. Desperate for food, Tom tries unsuccessfully to crack open a coconut. Then he tries to eat a turtle, but cracks his teeth on its shell. Jerry shows up on the scene dressed as a native holding an umbrella over his head. Tom decides that Jerry is his meal and chases him until Jerry finally ends up in a frying pan heating over a hot fire. Jerry manages to escape by hitting Tom in the face with the pan. Tom chases Jerry to a native village, where Tom skids to a halt and nervously looks around him. Jerry beats a drum and the sound frightens Tom, he jumps into a bush and hides. Meanwhile Jerry runs over to a large cooking pot sitting on wood logs in the middle of the village. Jerry pretends to be a cannibal to frighten Tom even more. He smears black soot on his face, puts on a grass skirt and a bone in his hair, and grabs a spear. As Tom cautiously walks out into the clearing, Jerry jabs him in the rear end with his spear and says, "Ja bah wah. I's de bulah of yaa azusa. Neck bone connected to de . . ." Jerry marches Tom at the point of his spear to the cooking pot and forces him to jump in, saying, "Hop in. Hop in pot here." He then fetches an armload of various vegetables and dumps them in a pile near the pot. He orders Tom to "cut da potato," and Tom takes a knife and cuts the potato. The slices fall into the pot. Tom follows similar instructions and cuts up other vegetables while Jerry laughs and lights a fire under the pot with a match. Tom begins to feel hot, drops of sweat falling from his brow and steam rising from the water. Tom tastes the water before shaking his head and adding more salt. Jerry continues to walk around the pot, but his grass skirt falls off. Tom sees this and realizes that Jerry has been playing a trick on him. Tom jumps out of the pot and chases Jerry, but comes to a sudden halt in front of the bare feet of several large black cannibals. The cannibal chief, who has a bone stuck in his

nose, licks his lips and looks down at Tom and says, "Barbeque cat." Tom runs away with the cannibals running close behind him. Jerry laughs at Tom until he is jabbed in the rear end by a spear held by a small cannibal. The little cannibal, with a smile on his face, licks his lips and says, "Umm, barbeque mouse." Jerry runs away with the cannibal running close behind him as the cartoon ends.

Review: *Film Daily*, 11 September 1951

Tom and Jerry—cat and mouse—parody Robinson Crusoe and his man Friday. Their own antics are accentuated by a desert island setting with cannibalistic natives on the scene. A pert parody. In Technicolor. (7 min)

Review: *Exhibitor Servisection*, 25 April 1951

Tom, adrift on a raft, finally lands on an island where Jerry is having a pleasant time. Tom tries to make Jerry serve as his meal but the latter turns the tables, posing as a cannibal. When Tom learns of the deception, real savages come around, and both take it on the lam. Fair.

HOOLA-BOOLA (1941)

Company: George Pal, Paramount Pictures
Type: Puppetoons
Characters: Jim Dandy, Sarong Sarong, black cannibals

Story: The cartoon opens on a close-up of the tuning dial of a radio as Hawaiian music plays softly in the background. Jim Dandy is relaxing on his raft, which is sailing on the ocean pulling several other rafts loaded with supplies. Jim Dandy looks out his window and says, "Ah-ha, an island." The rafts land on the island and skid to a stop on the beach. The equipment spills out and assembles itself into a furnished log cabin. In no time Jim Dandy, dressed in Hawaiian clothes, is playing his ukulele as he strolls along a beach lined with beautiful flowers and coconut trees. He pauses briefly to look at a beautiful waterfall before continuing on his way. He discovers footprints in the sand and follows them, saying, "Seems that I'm not alone." Suddenly he hears a voice say "hello." He looks up and sees a beautiful brown-skinned native girl dressed in a short skirt. She says hello again and winks an eye at him. Then she asks him, "You want to hula? Me teach you how to hula. Me teach you how to dance the hula." Dandy takes off his cap and says, "I'm Jim Dandy—just Jim to you. You must be Langston, I presume." She says, "No, me Sarong Sarong." Dandy says, "I'm charmed to make your acquaintance, Mademoiselle" as he bows and kisses her hand. Suddenly, off in the distance, a native chant is heard. A war canoe loaded with black cannibals approaches the island. The chief sits in the stern wearing a derby hat and holding an umbrella over his head. The canoe arrives at the island and the cannibals, who have big red lips and wear bones in their hair, land on the beach. They look fierce and carry spears as they start off toward Jim Dandy and Sarong Sarong. Sarong Sarong manages to escape capture by climbing to the top of a tree, but Jim Dandy is finally captured by the cannibals. They lock him in a cage and carry him back to the chief. From a distance Sarong Sarong watches as tears roll down her face. Jim Dandy looks out of his cage and waves to her and says, "So long, Sarong Sarong." Sarong Sarong says, "My little Jim Dandy—I don't see him no more." Meanwhile at the cannibal village the chief sits on his throne, which is located inside the mouth of a huge stone idol shaped like the head of a black cannibal. The rhythmic beat of drums is heard before he strikes a large gong beside him. The witch doctor appears on the scene wearing a full-length grass outfit that covers his head. He dances to the top of a rock and looks up at Jim Dandy in the cage. The witch doctor says a strange chant, and Jim Dandy's cage opens and he slides down a chute into a cooking pot filled with water. The cannibal chief and cook smile while the others cheer. Then the chief laughs and rubs his fat stomach and says, "Yum-yum." The cook puts chopped vegetables into the cooking pot when a flash of lightning appears and the sound of thunder is heard. A new character appears wearing a full-length mask. The cannibals are frightened as the strange person dances to the beat of the drums. The chief throws up his hands and cries out, "Spooks!" Soon all the cannibals are so terrified that they run out of the village and down to the beach where they get in the canoe and row away. Jim Dandy is also scared as the strange creature approaches him and pulls him out of the cooking pot and seats him down. Suddenly beautiful flowers spring up all around Jim Dandy, and the music changes to the hula. The creature pulls off its mask, and it is Sarong Sarong. She dances close to him and they touch noses as the cartoon ends.

Note: Many of the cannibal scenes in this cartoon were taken from *The Little Broadcast* (1939).

Review: *Motion Picture Exhibitor,* 9 July 1941

Here is another of those little gems from the George Pal Studio. Jim Dandy gets shipwrecked on a tropical isle where he meets Sarong Sarong, beautiful native girl. Soon however, local cannibals seize Jim, performing a weird witch-dance before the meal. But Sarong enters in a horrific disguise. The man eaters are dispersed and love finds a way. Puppet technique is used again to the fullest advantage in color medium resulting in an entertaining, lovely-to-look-at short. Excellent.

Review: *Boxoffice,* 16 April 1941

This is another George Pal adventure of Jim Dandy done in the diverting puppet technique. Jim is stranded on a desert island. He meets alluring Sarong-Sarong. They run afoul of cannibals. Jim is headed for the pot. Sarong-Sarong in a neat bit of whimsy, rescues Jim. Art work is compellingly evident in good Technicolor.

I AIN'T GOT NOBODY (1932)

Company:	Davie Fleischer, Max Fleischer, Paramount Pictures
Type:	Screen Song; combined live action and animation
Characters:	Mills Brothers (live action), lion, black cannibals

Story: The cartoon opens with the Mills Brothers singing and on-screen graphics that read, "Presenting for the first time on the screen, radio's greatest sensation—the Mills Brothers. Note! The music throughout this cartoon is furnished by the Mills Brothers quartet. They employ no musical instruments of any kind except the guitar. There is no tuba, no bass, only their voices." The animation begins in a house where a lion is tuning a television set. The first program he gets is a Chinese man doing a Russian dance. The second picture is a scene showing a black cannibal dancing near a pot in which sits a white man who is tied up. The third picture is a Mexican man, and the fourth is an American Indian chief. He finally tunes the set to the Mills Brothers, and they sing a scat version of "Tiger Rag" while the lion dances. After the song ends, the lion stands in front of the TV and says, "When the Mills Brothers ask you to sing, you must sing along." The Mills Brothers appear on screen again and sing, "We are just four singers who sing like a real live band. If you like to join us, won't everybody sing along using your hands. Don't use a cornet or violin. If you sing the notes, you're sure to win. Sing "I Ain't Got Nobody." They finish the song and then sing "Tiger Rag" again in the background as the animation shows a tiger rug coming to life and chasing the lion and TV set through the wall of the house, out into the yard, and down the road as the cartoon ends.

Review: *Variety,* 7 June 1932

Mills Brothers are of considerable, if recent, radio prominence, and as a short constitute a name. Managers will be the best judges of what they mean on the radio in various communities and how much they're worth on the marquee and billing. Where shown, Mills boys should be given display type in ads. Don't waste this short as a filler or in the agate afterthoughts. It's an attraction as well as an entertainment.

Max Fleischer has had a number of celebs to carry along the white dancing ball that accents the syllables in the lyrics. This particular release is built around "I Ain't Got Nobody," which is appropriately lowdown for the negroid harmonies of the Mills quartet. Usually cartoon nonsense is interpolated. These shorts have displayed considerable showmanship and progressive notions over a period of time and are reputed audience favorites.

Put on the preferred list. (7 min)

I'LL BE GLAD WHEN YOU'RE DEAD, YOU RASCAL YOU (1934)

Company:	Dave Fleischer, Max Fleischer, Paramount Pictures
Type:	Combined animation and live action
Characters:	Betty Boop, Louis Armstrong and his orchestra, Ko-ko the clown, Bimbo, black cannibals

Story: The cartoon opens with live action as Louis Armstrong fronts his orchestra playing the title song. Then the scene changes to animation. Betty, Bimbo, and Ko-ko are on a jungle safari as Armstrong and band provide the musical background. Betty, Bimbo, and Ko-ko are surrounded by cannibals who carry off Betty, leaving Bimbo and Ko-ko dazed on the ground wondering which way they carried Betty. They see prints of bare feet on the ground, which they follow. But soon they find themselves captured by cannibals, who place them in a pot of boiling water while they dance around it holding knives and forks in their hands. Ko-ko and Bimbo escape from the pot and climb to the top of tall palm trees, which they use as stilts to walk out of the village. They continue to search for Betty as the head of a large cannibal (Louis Armstrong caricature) hovers over them, singing the title song. The animated cannibal head changes to Louis Armstrong and then back to his caricature and finally to a cannibal who chases Ko-ko until Bimbo hits him with a rock. The cannibal turns into four large trash cans. Bimbo and Ko-ko finally arrive at the cannibal village. They see Betty tied to a tree and the cannibals dancing around her to the rhythm of jazz music. Meanwhile the cook, a smiling female cannibal, stirs a large cooking pot. The face of the cannibal cook dissolves into the live-action face of the smiling drummer in Armstrong's band before changing back to the face of the cook. Bimbo and Ko-ko rescue Betty by catching a porcupine, pulling out his sharp spines, and then throwing them at the cannibals. Betty manages to free herself as the cannibals dodge the porcupine spines. Along with Bimbo and Ko-ko, she runs out of the village followed by the angry cannibals. They run up and over a large volcano, which explodes as the cannibals follow them. The cannibals are blown high into the air as the scene changes back to live action. The Armstrong orchestra plays while Louis Armstrong sings, "I'll be glad when you're dead you rascal you" and the cartoon ends.

THE ISLAND FLING (1946)

Company: Bill Tytla, Paramount Pictures
Characters: Popeye the sailor, Olive Oyl, Bluto (as Robinson Crusoe), Friday, his wife Saturday, and his children Sunday and Monday

Story: The cartoon opens with an offshore view of an island on which stands a two-story jungle house. As the camera zooms in for a close-up, the sound of singing is heard coming from the house. "O Robinson Crusoe, O Robinson Crusoe. No one needed a gal like he did. He wanted to woo so . . ." Outside there is a Post No Bills sign and two mailboxes—one labeled "Robinson Crusoe" and a smaller one labeled "Friday." Inside the house Friday, a black man one front tooth visible between thick pink lips, wearing a short skirt, and a bone in his hair, is cleaning the house while singing, "His faithful man Friday—that's me. Kept everything tidy, yet his sign post shows hi-dee-ho-oh Robinson Crusoe." Friday sweeps dirt under the carpet, but a mouse walks out from under the carpet and sweeps the dust back out again. Friday looks out the front window and suddenly stops cleaning. He runs to the telephone and calls Robinson Crusoe who is lying on the bed reading a book entitled *Lovey Dovey Stories*. Crusoe picks up the phone, hears Friday say, "Hey Boss, hey Boss!" Crusoe asks, "Who is it?" Friday says, "Is you kiddin', Boss? There's only the two of us on this island. Look, there's a raft on the horizon." Crusoe says, "Bring

me my telescope." Friday, who is standing near him, gives the telescope to Crusoe. As Crusoe looks out the window, his eyes literally jump out of the telescope. He sees a raft with Olive Oyl standing next to Popeye, who is seated. Olive wears a skirt and a halter top. As he stares at Olive, Crusoe says, "Ahh dem fems sure bowls me over." With his mind on Olive, he puts down his telescope, runs to his "Hope" chest (which sits in front of his "Crosby" chest), and pulls out various items that he needs for entertaining her—a book entitled *Etchings*, pillows for the sofa, a bucket containing champagne on ice and glasses. Next he looks at two bottles of cologne labeled "Night in Paris" and "Morning in Brooklyn" before spraying on another labeled "Channel no. 49." Crusoe is now ready to greet his guest, so he jumps out of the window and lands on a spiral chute and slides down and lands in the backseat of his convertible car. He raises an umbrella over his head and shouts, "Hurry up, Friday!" Friday shouts, "I'm jumpin', Jackson." He jumps out the window, slides down the chute, and lands on top of Caruso's umbrella. He bounces off it and lands in the front seat. Friday rotates the sign on his hat, which first reads "Stooge," then "Cook," then "Washer," then "Dishwasher," and then "Chauffeur" where it stops. Crusoe's car has no motor and is propelled by Friday's bare feet, which touch the ground. They drive from the house but stop when they see Popeye and Olive walking out of the water onto the shore. Popeye smiles and says, "Oh boy, human inhabitants" as he rushes forward with his hands extended to meet Crusoe. Crusoe jumps out of the car and rushes forward with his hand extended, saying, "Welcome to the island of Robinson Crusoe." But Popeye, with his head down, walks past Crusoe and grabs the hand of a monkey that is hanging by his tail from a tree. The monkey kisses Popeye, who quickly realizes his mistake. He looks back and sees Crusoe kissing the hand of Olive who smiles and says, "Mr. Crusoe, you must be Smoocho." Popeye jumps between them and says, "Popeye's the moniker. Shake!" Crusoe grabs Popeye's hand and slams him to the ground, and Popeye says, "A real friendly handshake." Meanwhile Friday, wearing a chef's hat, walks out of the house and rings the dinner bell. He shouts, "Come and git it!" Inside the house Crusoe seats Olive at the table. He wants to make love, but Olive is hungry and wants to eat. He tries and tries, but each time he gets close he is interrupted by Popeye. He tries to get rid of Popeye by persuading him to go big-game hunting and mining for gold, but each time Popeye arrives back on the scene. Finally Crusoe gets frantic and chases Olive, but Popeye comes to her rescue after eating a can of spinach. Popeye knocks Crusoe high in the air, and he lands at the feet of a huge black female ape. The ape smiles and says, "Oh, a man. And a live one at that." Crusoe runs from her, saying, "You ain't goin' to make a monkey out of me." Meanwhile Popeye sits next to Olive in Crusoe's car, which they are using as a boat to sail away. Olive says, "From no on it's Coney Island. No phoney island for me." Friday's voice is heard saying, "How we doin', Boss?" They look back where Friday is seated and using his feet to turn a paddle wheel that propels the boat. Popeye says, "It's Friday," and a black female sitting next to Friday says, "I'm Saturday." The head of a black girl with braided hair pops up and says, "I'm

Sunday," and the head of a black boys says "I'm Monday." The four blacks sing "And always . . ." as the cartoon ends.

ISLE OF PINGO PONGO (1938)

Company: Tex Avery, Vitaphone, Warner Bros.
Type: Merrie Melodies
Characters: Black natives, caricatures of the Mills Brothers and Louis Armstrong

Story: This travelog cartoon opens as the offscreen narrator says, "Pingo Pongo, the pearl of the oyster islands" as the scene shows the oceanliner SS Queen Minnie of the Half Dollar Lines at the pier making ready to start off on an ocean cruise. The narrator says, "Boarding the luxury liner Queen Minnie, we bid bon voyage to New York. We're off at last to the adventurous island of Pingo Pongo" as the ship slowly sails away from dock 13 with the skyline of New York City in the background. The narrator says, "On the high seas we set a direct course for Pingo Pongo" as the scene shows a zigzag course superimposed on a map of the south seas. The narrator says, "Steaming through the calm waters of the Pacific ocean, our ship passes many interesting islands" as the scene depicts several islands, including the Canary Island, where canary birds sing from cages hanging from trees on the island; the Sandwich Island, which is shaped like a huge hot dog; and the Thousand Island, on which stands a huge bottle of salad dressing. The narrator continues, "And on the tenth day out we spot the island of Pingo Pongo, which rises suddenly out of the distant horizon." The island appears and the narrator says, "As we slowly approach the island, the passengers throw coins in the crystal-clear water for the native divers." A woman on deck throws coins in the water, and several of the passengers dive into the ocean after them. The narrator says, "Finally, we dock" as the passengers leave the ship. The last passenger off is a man dressed in a derby hat and carrying a violin case. In a stuttering voice he says, "Now, now, now Boss?" The narrator says, "No, not now." The passengers walk along the jungle trail toward a village, and they encounter many beautiful birds, elephants, and several more animal species native to the island. Again the man with the violin case appears and says, "Now, now, now Boss," and the narrator answers, "No, not now." Next they encounter a white polar bear being fed by an Eskimo. The narrator says, "Hey, what are you fellows doing here in the tropics?" The bear and the Eskimo answer, "We're on a vacation." When the narrator says, "The islanders are skilled hunters," a black native holding a spear runs by chasing two antelope. They disappear behind some bushes, and when they reappear, the antelope are carrying the hunter, bound, between them on a sling. The narrator continues, "As we near the village, we hear the primitive beat of the jungle tom-toms as we come upon a group of savage natives beating out a rhythm that is old as the jungle itself." The black natives, who have thick lips and bones in their noses, look menacing as they beat the drums. Other natives holding spears dance around in a circle. Suddenly a quartet of natives get up and

sing, "I'll Be Coming 'Round the Mountain" in country and western style while another plays a guitar. The narrator then says, "And here we find the typical aborigine—completely untouched by civilization and totally ignorant of our presence" as a black native with a Stephin Fetchit demeanor slowly walks by and then suddenly pulls out a camera and aims it at the audience. Next the passengers stop at a grass hut with a sign that reads, "Eat at the Dark Brown Derby." Inside the natives are seen having a good time eating and drinking while a fat native cook serves two fried eggs and potatoes on a large flat plate. But the plate is really the large flat bottom lip of another native who eats the food. Next the narrator says, "The common beverage of the island is the milk of the coconut" as another native sticks a spigot into a coconut and drinks the juice by wrapping his long lips around the fruit. The drink intoxicates him, and he hiccups. The narrator continues, "The typical sport of the island is a game similar to our American football." The natives line up along the scrimmage line as a big, fat native standing in the backfield calls out the signals "22-46-24-24-26." Then another native rises up and says, "Bingo! That's mah number." The narrator continues, "Filling the air with vibrant jungle rhythm, a jungle celebration gets on the way." First the natives are seen dancing the minuet. Then the beat of the music changes to hot jazz, and a short, fat native wearing a derby hat and smoking a cigar comes on the scene and says, with a Fats Waller demeanor, "Swing it, Gates!" The natives do the jitterbug to the tune of "Sweet Georgia Brown" played by the native band and sung by a native quartet (Mills Brothers caricature). At the same time a chorus line of shapely black girls dressed in short skirts (caricature of Cotton Club chorus line) dance the "shim sham shimmy." The music gets fast and furious before it ends, and the scene changes back to a jungle setting as the narrator says, "But all good things must come to an end. With the soft, sweet strains of the native music still lingering in the air, we say farewell to this isle of enchantment as the sun sets slowly in the west." The scene shows the sun, which is not setting. The narrator repeats, "As the sun sinks slowly . . ." again and again but still nothing happens. Suddenly the little man in the derby hat with the violin case suddenly appears and says, "Now, now, now . . . Boss?" This time the narrator answers, "Yes, why not?" The little man opens his violin case, pulls out a shotgun, and shoots the sun, which then slowly sinks into the ocean as night falls on the island. The little man laughs as the cartoon ends.

Review: Selected Motion Pictures, 1 June 1938

Merrie Melodies cartoon. A cleverly amusing burlesque of an imaginary South Seas Island tour. Family and Junior Matinee.

Review: National Exhibitor, 2 May 1938

Amusing take-off on the cruise-ship type of travel short, with some very funny tropical animals, island birds, natives shown. It should raise laughs anywhere. Up to the high Schlesinger laugh standard. Excellent. (8 1/2 min)

Review: *Motion Picture Exhibitor,* 23 August 1944

A revival of a hilarious cartoon, this shapes up well with plenty of gags, offered during a cruise around the world, landing in Pingo Pongo. This still packs plenty of laughs. Good.

Review: *Besa Shorts Shorts,* 7 August 1944

The Blue Ribbon version of a Merrie Melodie which kids the pants off the travel subject. The big vacation liner pulls away from New York harbor with the Statue of Liberty directing the traffic. Once underway, all sorts of destinations are covered until the Isle of Pingo Pongo is reached and then the camera dwells on the flora and the fauna with the narrator doing a fine job. Native dances go from their hula to hotcha and the ending comes with a setting sun as we reluctantly take our leave for beautiful Pingo.

IT HAPPENED TO CRUSOE (1941)

Company: Columbia Pictures
Type: Fables
Characters: Robinson Crusoe, Westchester (Friday), cannibal king, black cannibals

See fig. 29. Story: The cartoon opens in a jungle village where cannibals dance around the cooking pot while two native women play a game of Ping-Pong, using their large flat lips to hit the ball. The king, sitting on his throne, tells his son, in a voice like Fred Allen's, "Westchester, my boy, you're a terrible disappointment to your old pappy. For years I'd hoped you would follow in my footsteps—the champion meat eater of our tribe. Instead you turn out to be a softie, a lowly vegetarian." Westchester, with a Stephin Fetchit demeanor, and a voice similar to Rochester's, says, "Pappy, I just can't see myself dancin' around like a jitterbug. So I'm a wallflower—I hates meat and I love vegetables. So what?" His father throws a tomato at him, hitting him on the head, and says, "Well then, go. Go and never darken my door again." Westchester leaves the village, saying, "Meat, meat, blah! String beans, peas, carrots, umm." Westchester arrives at the grass hut of Robinson Crusoe, who walks out of the front door and is greeted by his pet parrot saying, "Hi-ya, Buck! Hi-ya." Crusoe answers, in a voice like Jack Benny's, "Hello Andy!" He picks up his violin and begins to play. The music is so bad that the parrot cries out, "Stop, stop!" Crusoe puts his violin away and walks into the hut, saying, "All right, it's not my fault if you don't appreciate good music." Westchester reads a sign on the door: Help Wanted—Man Friday. He knocks on the door and Crusoe walks out, takes one look at Westchester, grabs his gun, and points it at him. Westchester says, "Hi-ya, Boss. When do I start?" Crusoe replies, "Oh, you want the job. You're positive you're not a cannibal?" Westchester says, "I's strictly vegetarian." Crusoe says, "OK, the job is yours. We'll start in right now on a little tiger hunt." Looking worried, Westchester, "Little tiger . . . See ya later, Boss. Call me Friday" as he walks away. Crusoe says, "Where are you going?" Westchester replies, "Today is Thursday. You go huntin' alone. I'll call back Friday." Crusoe tells

him, "No, no. Friday will be your name." Westchester says, "Friday will be the end of me if we go huntin' Thursday." The hunting trip has started as Westchester drives Crusoe's jalopy with Crusoe riding beside him. Westchester asks, "Boss, did you ever hunt tigers befo'?" Crusoe answers, "Tigers? Why yes, I've killed lots of 'em." Westchester then says, "You know I once met up with a tiger. He was all set to pounce on me, but I couldn't shoot him because he just didn't have the right expression on his face for a rug." Just then a big tiger hops in the backseat of the car. Crusoe says, "You sure got away lucky. Tigers love meat you know," as the tiger blows the car's horn. Westchester glances in back of him at the tiger, and he starts to sweat. He says, "Oh, oh! Meat, meat. Say Boss, is there any vegetarian tigers?" Crusoe answers, "I guess not. They all love meat." Westchester says, "I hates meat. Meat is no good for nobody. Now take vegetables. They is the healthiest food anybody could eat." Crusoe decides to play his violin. The music is so bad that the tiger faints and falls off of the back of the car. Then Westchester faints, and the car runs off the road and crashes into a tree. They are immediately surrounded by a band of fierce-looking cannibals. One of them says, "Greetings, Westchester. I see you got a prize captive, and single-handedly too." He looks Crusoe over and says, "A little thin, but not bad. Let's go. We'll keep him covered." Then they march off toward the village. The cannibal king is sad, but he smiles when he sees his son arriving with Crusoe. He says, "Westchester, my son" as he kisses Westchester and sits him on his lap. He then says, "You've come back with a captive too. Good for you. Meat on the table." But Westchester hops off his father's lap and says, "Oh, oh. Here's where I go again." Crusoe says, "Look here, Friday. Didn't you tell me Thursday? You, you say you belong to this tribe?" Westchester answers, "Yes, Boss." The king looks at Crusoe and says, "Mr. Livingstone, I presume." Crusoe says, "No just plain Robinson Crusoe." The king says, "Oh Crusoe, eh? You sound like a certain radio comedian." Crusoe says, "Do I? Well right now I wish I was him. I wouldn't be here now. Say, you sound like someone on the radio too. No, no, it couldn't be. He could never get that sunburned." The king says, "Come on boys, tie him up," and the cannibals tie Crusoe to a tree just as the tiger walks into the village. All of the cannibals run away and Westchester, from the top of a tree, calls Crusoe and says, "Hey Boss, play, play." Crusoe unties himself and plays his violin, causing the tiger to faint. All the cannibals are happy, and Crusoe is a hero and is appointed the new king. Crusoe sits on the throne with the crown on his head as the cannibals bow down before him. Crusoe smiles and says, "Well, this is more like it." The former king says, "Now you're king, what would you like to feast on tonight?" Crusoe looks at the tiger, now tied up, and says, "Tonight my friend we shall have meat." Westchester throws both hands in the air and says, "Meat, meat! I may be a vegetarian but I sho' brought home the bacon" as he smiles and the cartoon ends.

Review: *Moving Picture World,* 17 May 1941

The King of the cannibals disowns his son, Westchester, because he is a vegetarian and refuses to follow the old cannibalistic traditions. Westchester leaves the tribe and trudges through the jungle until he arrives at Robinson Crusoe's hut and becomes his man Friday. Friday's first task is to drive Crusoe in his old jalopy on a tiger hunt. Soon they are captured by cannibals and brought before the King, who recognizes his son and holds Crusoe prisoner. The King praises his son for his single-handed capture. Just as Crusoe is being tied up for execution, a tiger appears and all the cannibals scatter. Crusoe plays his violin, which agonizes the tiger to such an extent that he is easily subdued by the cannibals, who then make Crusoe King of their tribe. (6 min)

I'VE GOT TO SING A TORCH SONG (1933)

Company: Tom Palmer, Vitaphone, Warner Bros.
Type: Merrie Melodies
Characters: Caricatures of various entertainers, including Ed Wynn, Boswell Sisters, Bing Crosby, George Bernard Shaw, Wheeler and Woolsey, black cannibal

Story: The opening scene is a group of hands tuning radios and finally tuning in a health program as the announcer repeats, "One, two, one, two . . ." Meanwhile various people are seen exercising in time with the instructions. A man pulls his wife's corset tight, another man rocks two babies and their cradles, a Russian does a dance, and George Bernard Shaw, wearing boxing gloves and boxing trunks, punches a globe of the earth. Meanwhile at the radio the announcer of the "Early Bird Hour" program is fast asleep while a recording of "one, two . . ." is played over the air. Ed Wynn arrives on the scene wearing a firefighter's hat and riding a toy horse. He announces, "When you hear the gong it will be eight o'clock, whether you like it or not." Meanwhile Bing Crosby in a bathtub covered with soapsuds croons "Why Can't This Night Go On For Ever" while an old lady hugs and kisses her radio and two little blackbirds chirp to the music. Then the radio announcer says, "See your dentist once a day and brush your teeth once a year," and his teeth fall out. Ben Bernie, the old maestro, conducts the music all over the world. In China, the Shanghai police are being pulled in a rickshaw while listening to the broadcast. In Africa a black cannibal adds ingredients to a cooking pot containing two white men while listening to his radio made from a human skull. He sings, "Add a little mustard, a dash of salt, and stir well before serving." At the North Pole an Eskimo fishing on a floating block of ice and listening to the radio hooks a black whale. The whale tries to swallow the Eskimo, but manages only to swallow the ice and the radio with the antenna sticking out of his blowhole. In Arabia, a sultan is bored by his belly dancer and switches on the radio to hear the *Amos 'n' Andy* program. Back at the radio station Ed Wynn again comes on the scene and says, "At the sound of the gong, it will be eight o'clock," and he strikes the gong. The Boswell Sisters sing the title sing while a safecracker uses a blowtorch to open a safe while singing, "I got to sing a torch song. I gotta have the dough." When he breaks

the safe open, a policeman comes out and puts him in jail. Back at the station Zasu Pitts, Mae West, and Marlene Dietrich take turns in singing the chorus of the title song. Ed Wynn arrives on the scene, and this time he is pulling a cannon. He calls out, "Last call for eight o'clock," and he fires the cannon. There is a big explosion that propels Wynn through the air. He lands in a bed with his wife and children.

JINGLE, JANGLE, JUNGLE (1950)

Company: Seymour Kneitel, Famous Studios, Paramount Pictures
Type: Screen Song, "Civilization" (Bongo, Bongo, Bongo)
Characters: Circus manager, black cannibals

Story: Cartoon opens with a close-up of a map of Africa as the slow beat of drums is heard in the background. The offscreen narrator says, "Africa, once known as the dark continent, is no . . ." As the screen darkens, only several pairs of eyeballs are seen, which develop into several black African women with thick white lips. Next the scene changes to show a desert as the narrator says, "And in Africa is the Sahara, the greatest desert in the world." The scene changes to show a desert region in the shape of a slice of toasted bread. Crossing the desert on foot is a white hunter carrying a pack on his back and wiping sweat off his face. The narrator says, "Breaking the monotony of the desert is the oasis where the weary traveler can stop for a rest and a cool drink." A desert oasis is seen. Inside a mixed group of blacks and Arabs are seen eating hot dogs and popcorn, and drinking soda. Meanwhile two blacks carry the white hunter on a sling between them as the narrator says, "On his travels the hunter faces many hardships. While being carried through the jungle many rivers must be crossed . . ." The natives cross a river, walking under water and carrying the hunter. When they surface on the other side of the river, the hunter has been replaced by a large alligator with a fat stomach who seems to be pleased after having eaten a tasty meal. The narrator says, "The hunter, while searching for big game, must be always on the lookout for cannibals," as the scene shows a white hunter carrying his gun and looking for big game. A black cannibal with a bone on his head appears suddenly from behind a rock and rings the dinnerbell he holds in his hand. The cannibal calls out, "Come and get it!" The hunter drops his gun and tries to escape, but he is captured by another cannibal who throws him into a cooking pot. The cannibal places a lid on the pot and screws it down so that it becomes a pressure cooker as it sits on a large fire. The scene changes as the narrator says, "There are also peaceful tribes in the jungle, such as the Ubangis." Two natives are seen playing Ping-Pong, using their huge flat lips to hit the ball back and forth across the net. Next the narrator says, "The natives are communicating with each other across the impenetrable jungle, cleverly sending messages by rhythmically beating tom-toms." The screen shows a native chief sitting on his throne with his stenographer sitting in front of him writing down the message of the drum beats on a stone pad. The message ends and the chief says, "What he say? What he say?" The stenographer lets him read the message: "Boom-tid-dy, boom-tid-dy, boom-tid-dy." Following scenes of various types of birds and a group of elephants, the lion, king of beasts, is seen sitting on his throne wearing a crown on his head. A white messenger rides in on the scene and gives the lion an invitation to join the circus. The lion shakes his head no and says, "I don't want to leave the jungle, and this is the reason why, now all sing along . . ." The words of the song are flashed on the screen over a map of Africa. The first verse is "Bon-go, bon-go, bon-go I don't want to leave the Con-go, oh no, no, no, no. Bin-go, ban-go, bungle I'm so happy in the jungle, I refuse to go. Don't want no bright lights, false teeth, doorbells, landlords. I make it clear that no matter how they coax me, I'll stay right here . . ." The songs ends as a beautiful, shapely lioness comes on the scene and lures the lion out of the jungle and across the ocean to an American city where the "Famous Circus" is playing. There she lures him into a cage and exits the other end, closing the gate behind her and trapping the lion inside. Then the lioness pulls off her costume to reveal that she is really the circus manager, who laughs at his successful effort to capture the lion. The lion then reaches through the bars of the cage, pulls the manager inside, and eats him. Afterward he lies on his back in the cage with a full stomach and a smile on his face as the cartoon ends.

Review: *Motion Picture Herald,* **3 June 1950**

There is plenty of melody and madcap humor in this zany tour through darkest Africa. The Congo River flows to a rhythmic conga beat, hunters turn up on the dinner menus of crocodiles and cannibals, and strange jungle creatures frolic about. It's all in fun and the audience joins in singing the popular "Civilization" to the beat of the bouncing ball. (7 min)

Review: *Film Daily,* **25 May 1950**

A madcap tour of darkest Africa with a humorous slant on the jungle hi-jinks and jive. The bouncing ball interrupts to lead a community sing in a catchy song, "Civilization." Full of bounce for a lively, sing-a-long audience.

Review: *Boxoffice,* **17 June 1950**

Good. There is plenty of madcap humor and wisecracks in this entertaining Technicolor cartoon. The sun toasts the desert until it looks like a slice of toast and the Congo river flows to a conga beat as pink lemonade is sold by the natives at a desert oasis. Then along comes the bouncing ball to guide the audience into singing the catchy "Civilization," rather an old song by this time. (7 min)

JUNGLE DRUMS (1943)

Company: Don Gordon, Paramount Pictures
Characters: Superman, African natives, Lois Lane

Review: *Motion Picture Herald,* **24 April 1943**

Superman's latest struggle with the Axis occurs in their secret broadcasting station inside a huge idol in the jungle. Lois is being tortured by natives to reveal the location of papers describing an Allied convoy, when Superman arrives with the speed of lightning. The Axis agents are overpowered, their submarines are sunk by American dive bombers and the convoy proceeds safely. (8 min)

Review: *Film Daily,* **29 April 1943**

Here's the latest of the Technicolor-hued Superman epics, with the mighty man hurtling down from a plane to rescue the captive Lois, prisoner of a Nazi, jungle-based band of agents and wild natives who are plotting to destroy an American convoy. As Lois is being tortured by fire before a weird, gigantic pillar, the saving hero, in tights and cape, snatches her from death, makes short shrift of her tormentors, and saves Uncle Sam's ships from destruction. It's all wild, woolly, and in two words, in credible!

Review: *Boxoffice,* **1 May 1943**

The kiddies Saturday Matinee trade should "go" for this one. Superman helps U.S. bombers to sink Axis submarines lurking in wait for a convoy. All is saved through his intervention.

Review: *Motion Picture Exhibitor,* **24 March 1943**

Axis agents operating in the midst of a jungle are trying to locate a large American convoy. The location is contained in important papers carried by a pilot ferrying Lois Lane. The plane crashes in the jungle near the Axis base. The pilot passes the papers to Lane before he dies, and she, in turn, hides them before she is captured. The Nazis threaten to burn her if she doesn't reveal the location of the documents. She refuses, and is turned over to natives to be sacrificed. Superman (Clark Kent), flying to meet the convoy, spots Lois's predicament, and parachutes to earth, mops up the Axis agents as well as their headquarters and rescues Lois, who radios for the American bombers which blast the group of enemy submarines. Fair.

Review: *Besa Shorts Shorts,* **3 April 1943**

Lois, the girl reporter, in this chapter is captured by Nazis deep in the heart of what seems to be the Egyptian Jungle. One Nazi makes like the ghost of Ptolemy, rising from a pyramid tomb which hides a radio sending set. He lures Miss Lois inside and she tries to message the American convoy approaching Africa. All is discovered and she is about to be burned to death by the Nazi rascals when conveniently overhead floats Superman. A couple of swoops and the situation is in hand.

JUNGLE JAM (1931)

Company: John Foster, George Stallings, Van Beuren; released by Pathe Film Exchange
Characters: Tom and Jerry, black cannibals

Story: The cartoon opens as Tom and Jerry are enjoying a sailing trip on the ocean. Tom rows the small boat while Jerry sits in back and enjoys the sights. They pass a group of hippos that raise their heads out of the water near the boat. Finally they arrive on the shore of an island where they see a trio of monkeys dancing. They join in but narrowly escape the jaws of two large alligators as they attempt to follow the monkeys across a river. Back on shore they find themselves surrounded by black cannibals, who appear from behind rocks. The cannibals have monkeylike faces and hold spears as the beat of drums is heard in the background. Tom and Jerry try to run away, but are trapped by a wall of spears that stick in the ground around them. The cannibals, wearing grass skirts, march Tom and Jerry to the village. Meanwhile at the village the cannibal chief, wearing a crown on his head, sits on his throne and sharpens his large razor using a leather strop. He is surrounded by human skulls. He is interrupted by a small cannibal wearing a bone in his hair who arrives on the scene and excitedly jumps up and down and speaks gibberish while pointing in the direction of the approaching prisoners. The cannibals arrive on the scene and dump Tom and Jerry on the ground in front of the chief. Jerry is not afraid as he looks up at the chief and says, "Hello." But Tom is so frightened that he can't make a sound. When he opens his mouth to speak, the chief grabs his tongue, stretches it out of his mouth, and then uses it to sharpen his razor. When he finishes, he pulls a single strand of hair from Tom's head and splits it with his razor. The chief rings a bell as sweat pours from Tom's face. The cannibal cook arrives on the scene. He is a short, fat man wearing a chef's cap. He has various cooking utensils tied to a belt around his waist. Jerry is not impressed as he taps the utensils and makes music while he yodels a song. Tom pulls out a horn and joins in. The chief is not impressed as he watches their performance with a frown on his face. After they finish, the chief sticks his tongue out at Jerry and then commands his cook to pick up Jerry so he can have a closer look at him. A button pops off Jerry's shirt to reveal the tatoo of a shapely female on his chest. Jerry wriggles his chest, causing the tattoo to dance. The chief is delighted, and when the dance is finished, the chief smiles and kisses Jerry on his cheek. Jerry first frowns but then smiles and says, "Oh gee." The chief summons the rest of his tribe and commands them to play music. Using various types of musical instruments, they produce jazzy music that causes the chief to dance. Soon everybody, including Tom and Jerry, is dancing to the music. Tom and Jerry grab two female cannibals and dance with them. Tom has a tall, skinny one and Jerry a short, fat one. Their hair resembles coils of wire sticking out of their heads. Another tall, fat female cannibal cuts in and dances while holding Tom in one hand and Jerry in the other. She has five coils of hair sticking out of her head. Suddenly the music stops. The female cannibal drops Tom and Jerry at the feet of the chief as a dark cloud appears in the sky over the village. Lightning bolts from the cloud strike the ground. The cannibals are terrified, and they all drop to their knees and kiss the ground. Tom and Jerry are not afraid and are puzzled at the cannibals' behavior. Jerry takes advantage of the opportunity and kicks the chief in the rear before they both run off. The

chief howls, and in no time he and the rest of the cannibals are of running out of the village after Tom and Jerry. Tom and Jerry reach the seashore, but their boat is gone. Meanwhile a fleet of U.S. Navy battleships is steaming nearby. The captain looks through his binoculars and sees Tom and Jerry waving for help. He orders his ships to the rescue. The ships stop, and the captain is rowed to shore in a small boat. As he nears land, the cannibals arrive on the scene. The captain takes one look at them and makes a hasty retreat. As they sail over the horizon. Tom and Jerry find themselves abandoned, so they jump into the ocean and swim away. Spears thrown by the cannibals land in the water around them as music plays "Dixie" and the cartoon ends.

JUNGLE JAZZ (1930)

Company: John Foster, Harry Bailey, Van Beuren, released
             by Pathe Film Exchange
Type: Aesop's Sound Fables
Characters: Waffles the cat, Don the dog, black cannibals

Story: The cartoon opens in a jungle where Waffles Cat and Don Dog are on a safari. They are attacked by a huge black ape who jumps on Waffles. As Waffles falls to the ground, the gun he is holding fires straight up in the air. As the ape is about to finish off Waffles, a dead bird falls from the sky and hits the ape on its head and knocks him silly. Waffles and Don escape. As they continue to explore, they encounter many strange-looking animals, including an ape who carries a golf bag on his back. The ape holds a golf club that has a human skull attached to the end of it. Next they are chased by a huge python. They run inside a mission hut to escape. The snake follows them inside, where he is changed into a shapely Arabian dancing girl by music played by Waffles on an organ-piano. Waffles and Don hear humans outside the hut. It's a group of black cannibals, each one wearing a bone in his hair, a short grass skirt, and a nose ring. They carry spears and shields, except for one who looks inside the hut and sees Waffles and Don. Waffles is very scared and his knees shake. Don remains calm, standing with his arms folded and a smile on his face. They are captured, taken to the cannibal village, and thrown into the cooking pot full of water. The cannibals dance around the pot, chanting and shaking their spears, before one walks over to the pot and attempts to use his cigarette lighter to ignite the logs under the pot. He tries several times but is unsuccessful. Don, smiling, watches him before striking a match and giving it to the cannibal who uses it to start the fire. The cannibal smiles and shakes Don's hand and says "toodleloo" before joining the other cannibals. The water is getting hot, and sweat drips from Waffles's face as two cannibal cooks arrive on the scene and blow their trumpets. Then they shout "Attention, please! The king!" As they all bow down, the king arrives. He is a fat man wearing a crown and smoking a big black cigar. The king stops in front of the pot and looks at Don, who smiles at him. Don grabs his nose and makes a weird sound that scares away all of the cannibals, including the king. Don and Waffles jump out of the pot and shake hands. Then they pick up sticks and beat on the pot as an animal quartet sings "The Honeymoon is coming to Jungle Town" as the cartoon ends.

Review: *Billboard,* 26 July 1930

Aesop Sound Fable, showing the adventure of Waffles Cat and Don Dog in Africa. Just as is the case with many of these animated cartoons, music occupies much of this short's attention. It's excellent music, too, the kind processing catchy tunes. Along with it is clever animation, revealing the animals going in for dancing and engaging in other delightful nonsense.

The two adventurers trek the wilds of Africa, meeting up with gorillas, apes, and other ferocious animals, but manage to come out alive. A python gives them much trouble, but an organ solo from Waffles Cat makes it become an Oriental dancer. However, the two meet up with a cannibal bunch, and are placed in the cooking pot. Don Dog scares the King of the cannibals, though, and both make their escape. An amusing finish is the animal quartet singing "Jungle Town." Good harmony there. Can't go wrong in booking this short. (8 min)

JUNGLE JITTERS (1938)

Company: I. Freleng, Vitaphone, Warner Bros.
Type: Merrie Melodies
Characters: White salesman (Willie Whopper persona), black cannibals

See fig. 30. Story: The cartoon opens in a cannibal village, where a celebration is taking place with music and dancing. Three cannibals beat tom-toms. All have thick red lips and wear rings in their ears. One wears a stovepipe hat. Other cannibals dance in a circle and wave their spears in the air. Another cannibal keeps the beat with his feet by dancing on a large drum and slapping his backside with his hand. He wears a grass skirt over polka-dot briefs. Meanwhile a fat female cannibal is amusing herself by jumping back and forth through a large ring in her nose. Suddenly the circle of dancing cannibals turns into a merry-go-round with the cannibals trying to grab the nose ring of another cannibal who is standing close by. One manages to grab the ring, which stretches the neck of the other cannibal like a spring. Another cannibal with a Stephin Fetchit demeanor, too lazy to dance, relaxes under a persimmon tree. He eats a persimmon and says, "For goodness sakes," as his long lips shrink to the shape of a little round hole. One cannibal, who is a look-out, straps toilet plungers to the bottom of each foot and uses them to climb to the top of a tree where he looks all around. In the distance he sees Willie Whopper, a strange-looking salesman knocking on the door of a grass hut in the cannibal village. Willie says, "I guess nobody's home—I hope, I hope, I hope." His demeanor is like that of Elmer Blunt (a character created by comedian Al Pearce for his radio show, which was broadcast over NBC and later ABC in the 1940s). Willie is unsuccessful at trying to talk to a cannibal until he gets the idea to knock on all of the doors. He sticks his foot in one of the doors before a cannibal can close it and says, "Good morning Mama sir. Is the lady

of house due home? I have here a fine assortment of a sort of useful, useless, utensils. They are all designed to take the work out of housework, ha-ha-ha." Meanwhile a group of frowning cannibals peer over the top of the fence at Willie. But then they smile and lick their lips as they imagine Willie in the form of big roasted turkey. Willie continues his sales pitch, saying, "We are giving away absolutely free for twenty-five cents each one, a better beating, beat better, egg beater." Suddenly he is snatched away by the cannibals and thrown into a huge pot of boiling stew. The fat female cannibal cook, wearing a chef's hat, smiles as she sprinkles salt into the pot. She is about to pour some cut-up onions into the pot, but stops when Willie holds up a sign that says Hold the Onions. Meanwhile the cannibals have opened Willie's sample case and are puzzling over what they find. One accidently turns on a vacuum cleaner that sucks the grass covering off his hut. Another carries a car battery into a hut, screws a light bulb into each ear, and sits on the battery. Both bulbs light up. She then covers her head with a tub like a lamp shade and reads a magazine. Meanwhile Willie is slowly heating up in the cooking pot as steam begins to puff out under his hat. But the cannibals are getting hungry and make noise by banging their knives and forks on top of the dinner table. Meanwhile at the hut of the cannibal queen there is a sign posted that reads, The palace (temporarily) is moving to more palatial quarters June 1." Inside the hut the queen, a white character who has a birdlike face and wears eyeglasses, sits on her throne and is guarded by two mean-looking black cannibals. She hears the noise outside and asks, "What's the matter out there?" One of the guards answers, "We are having a salesman for dinner." The queen says, "A man—bring him in." The two guards carry Willie inside and dump him on the floor in front of the queen. For the queen it's love at first sight. She smiles and says, "What are you doing here, young man?" Willie opens his case, pulls out a toaster, and begins, "Now Lady, I have here a marvelous device that you can't afford to not to afford." He turns the toaster on, and it automatically toasts and butters a slice of bread. Willie says, "Too marvelous, too marvelous for words. Oh yes indeed Mama, it's guaranteed to answer every household need." As he is speaking, the queen imagines him as Clark Gable and then as Robert Taylor. Willie continues, "And it's wonderful. I just can't find the words to say enough, sure enough, to tell you that it don't cost much. No, no, no, it shouldn't squeeze you. And you'll find that our payment plan will please you, I hope, I hope, I hope. So I'm giving you a demonstration free to show you that it's marvelous, too marvelous to me." Meanwhile the frowns on the two cannibal guards' faces change to smiles as they lick their lips and imagine Willie as a big roast turkey. But the queen has other plans for Willie. She rises to her feet and says, "We'll get married right away." She ducks behind a curtain, changes into a bridal dress, and grabs a bunch of flowers. She leads Willie to the front of a portable altar, which has rolled into the room. The cannibal preacher says, "Does you all take this man to be your wedded husband or don't yah?" The queen, with a coy smile on her face, says, "Oh, this is so sudden." The preacher asks Willie, "You take this woman to be your wedded wife or don't yah?" Willie hesitates but mumbles yes after he is prodded in the rear end by a guard's spear. The preacher then says, "I now sentence you to be man and wife. Now kiss the bride. That will be two dollars, please." The queen puckers her lips and waits with her eyes closed for Willie to kiss her. But Willie runs outside and dives headfirst into the pot of boiling stew. He sticks his head out and says, "I hope you all get indigestion, I hope, I hope, I hope." He then grabs his nose and ducks his head back under the liquid as the cartoon ends.

Review: *Motion Picture Herald,* 5 February 1938

A cleverly designed and executed cartoon that is also entertainment, this subject invades the radio field, more particularly the Al Pearce program, for voices. Located in the African jungle, the story concerns the adventure of a salesman set upon by natives who start to prepare him for dinner. The cannibals' queen decides to spare the salesman and take him for a husband. The salesman decides he would rather be cooked for the cannibals' dinner. *Jungle Jitter* sets a fast pace in action and comedy and keeps it up throughout. (7 min)

Review: *Film Daily,* 31 January 1938

Producer Leon Schlesinger goes to darkest Africa in this one with a highly amusing set of characters. A supersalesman attempts to sell his wares to the cannibals, but finds himself in the stew pot as the result of his efforts. The spinster queen hears of this stranger, and decides she will marry him. He is removed from the pot and the wedding ceremony starts, but the salesman takes one look as his prospective wife, flees the ceremony, and jumps back in the stew pot. There are some very funny sequences and gags, with the characterizations very amusing. The cartoon is in Technicolor. George Manuel provided the story and Phil Monroe the animation, with I. Freling supervising.

Review: *National Exhibitor,* 1 February 1938

The salesman who looks like the Goofy in Disney's shorts, but is twice as goofy, tries to sell his household gadgets to the savages who prefer white meat. The spinster white queen marries him to save him from the boiling pot. But when she tries to kiss him, he jumps back into the pot, hoping they'll all get indigestion. It sounds forced to say that this is better than the best so far, but that is what one must say about a series that improves continually. This is full of cute little touches that will be best appreciated by a class audience, but will still have the masses chuckling. Excellent.

KANNIBAL KAPERS (1935)

Company: Manny Gould, Columbia Pictures
Characters: Krazy Kat, black cannibals

Story: The cartoon opens showing Krazy afloat on a rubber innertube on a calm sea. He is pushed so hard by a friendly whale that he flies through the air and he lands on an island on the top of a coconut tree. A small monkey who is also in the tree scratches his head in wonder of who this strange visitor is as Krazy slides

down the tree. Meanwhile at the bottom of the tree a black cannibal is seen stirring a pot of boiling liquid. He looks up and sees that Krazy is about to land in the pot, and he licks his lips and smiles. As Krazy is about to land in the pot, the cannibal catches him and puts him on a roasting pan and puts the top over him as he rubs his stomach and smiles. The cannibal cook carries the roasting pan off in the direction of another cannibal playing rhythmic sounds on two drums. It turns out to be the drummer of the crowded Coconut Grove night club. The hot jazz music is played by a cannibal band with a fat cannibal leader. Outside the club more cannibals are arriving and are greeted by a doorman in a top hat. Some arrive on foot while others are brought by the Hippopotamus Cab Company. The cook arrives and places the roasting pan containing Krazy at the king's feet and removes the lid. When the king sees Krazy, he licks his lips and feels Krazy's leg. He and the cook smile. But Krazy is not afraid. The cat stands up and starts to dance with the music and sing in a skat style made popular by Louis Armstrong. Meanwhile a fat female cannibal comes on the scene, walking and talking like Mae West. She joins in the music signing in hi-de-ho style made popular by Cab Calloway. She sits down at the king's table before a slow walking cannibal with a Stephin Fetchit demeanor brings them a coconut cocktail. Krazy comes over to the table and serenades the lady cannibal. She is so impressed that she takes him in her arms and tells him, "Big boy, you got me." Krazy then takes over as leader of the band, and the music gets so hot that Krazy finds himself being tossed from instrument to instrument while the musicians never miss a beat. Finally the cannibals tire of Krazy, and the king tosses him back out to the sea as the cartoon ends.

Review: *Boxoffice,* 18 January 1936

This is a fairly amusing cartoon that depicts Krazy Kat's adventures on a cannibal isle. His chances of escaping the cook's dinner-plate seem very slim until the band, which is entertaining the assembled islanders in a cabaret, gets hot and arouses the terpischoren instinct in Krazy. He starts strutting his stuff with the belle of the place, but makes the mistake of getting too familiar with the musicians. Once on the band-stand he gets blown from one instrument to another until in sheer desperation one of the players toots him right back to the ocean whence he came. (7 min).

Review: *Motion Picture Review Digest,* 10 June 1936

This pictures the feline on a cannibal isle, embellished with a Cocoanut Grove, where night club entertainment is in vogue. It is poorly done and not recommended.

Review: *Selected Motion Pictures,* 1 February 1936

Antics of Krazy Kat on a cannibal island. Fair entertainment, clever in spots. Family.

Review: *National Exhibitor,* 3 January 1936

Krazy, as a castaway, lands on an island inhabited by savages who run a night club, "Coconut Grove." In the absence of any interesting plot Mintz has savages run through various dance forms and the hot-cha orchestra displays the versatility with instruments that only a cartoon will allow. Result so-so. Fair. (7 min)

KING KLUNK (1933)

Company: Bill Nolan, Walter Lantz, Universal Pictures
Characters: Pooch the pup, African natives

Story: The opening shows a newspaper headline that proclaims "Pooch Braves the Jungle." Next we see Pooch and his girl walking through the jungle, exploring it. Some black Africans are preparing a sacrifice to King Klunk, but the chief is worried because the pot is empty. A native sounds the dinner bell and King Klunk, a huge ape, enters and is so hungry its mouth is dripping. Angry because the natives have not presented him with a sacrifice, he grabs the chief and is about to devour him. Just then he sights Pooch and his girlfriend walking nearby. The ape grabs the white girl and replaces her with a native girl. When Pooch turns around, he is surprised to see the black girl beckon to him with loving eyes. Pooch makes a hasty getaway with the native girl close behind. The ape is about to eat Pooch's girlfriend, when he is struck by cupid's arrow and instantly falls in love with the girl. Still being chased by the black girl Pooch runs up a hairy hill, and when he reaches the top he finds that he has climbed the ape's back. The ape blows Pooch into the air, and he lands in a pond on the top of an alligator's head. The alligator chases Pooch out of the river but stops when he sees the ape holding the white girl. The alligator attempts to make a meal of the girl, and he and the ape get into a terrific battle. In the end the ape wins, and Pooch decides that he will rescue his girlfriend. Pretending to be Tarzan, he swings from limb to limb until he is close enough to grab the girl from the ape. Pooch and the girl flee to the top of a large mountain, where they find a huge egg. The ape starts to climb up after them. When he is almost at the top, Pooch pushes the egg down the mountain. It hits the ape on the head, and he falls to the bottom of the mountain stunned. Next we see Pooch and the girl in a boat on the ocean towing the ape, who is tied in chains from head to foot. When they arrive back home, they open a night club with King Klunk being billed as the sixth wonder of the world. The ape is seen strapped to a chair on the stage. He is very sad. Out of nowhere comes cupid's arrow and strikes him. Again he is madly in love with the girl. He breaks his straps and is soon chasing Pooch and his girlfriend, who are running for their lives. The ape catches them, knocks Pooch away, and takes the girl and climbs to the top of a tall building in an effort to escape the police. Meanwhile Pooch has found a plane. He takes off and flies over the ape and shoots at him with a cannon. But the cannonball just bounces off the ape's chest. Pooch then fires his machinegun at the ape, who falls to the street dead. Pooch lands his plane on top of the building and leans over to kiss the girl. At this instant the native girl pops up out of the plane, and Pooch kisses her instead at the fade out.

Review: *Motion Picture Herald*, 23 September 1933

Pooch the Pup and his girl are in Africa, when a giant ape captures the girl. Pooch rescues her, and they bring back the ape to exhibit in a sideshow. Everything goes well until the ape breaks loose, captures the girl again and escapes to the top of a skyscraper with her. Pooch effects another rescue, via a cartoonist's idea of an aeroplane and destroys the monster. It is an amusing takeoff in cartoon form on *King Kong*. (9 min)

KONGO ROO (1946)

Company: Howard Swift, Columbia Pictures
Type: Phantasy Cartoon
Characters: Fuzzy-Wuzzy, cannibals

Review: *Motion Picture Herald*, 29 June 1946

Fuzzy-Wuzzy finds out in this reel that getting mixed up with cannibals is no sport for any man. Hunting the cannibal on his pet ostrich, the Fuzzy-Wuzzy meets him, to his regret. (6 min)

Review: *Film Daily*, 8 July 1946

Fuzzy-Wuzzy goes huntin' for cannibals astride his favorite ostrich. Unfortunately, things do not work out as F–W wishes. This is a pleasant comedy which will please most.

Review: *Motion Picture Exhibitor*, 26 June 1946

Fuzzy-Wuzzy, aboard his pet ostrich, goes hunting a kangaroo. They find one, and, after a number of monkey shines, the native and the kangaroo whittle each other down to minute size whereupon the ostrich eats both of them unknowingly. Fair.

Review: *Besa Shorts Shorts*, 6 May 1946

In black and white, there are some new characters here. They are the hunter, Fuzzy Wuzzy, and the hunted, a kangaroo who can do a lot of funny things. As Fuzzy stalks his prey atop a fascinating ostrich in the bush country, there are many clever gags and much fast action.

KORN PLASTERED IN AFRICA (1932)

Company: Features Film Company
Characters: Kernel Korn (voice characterization by Uncle Don, a radio personality who was fired for saying at the conclusion of his children's radio program, "That oughta take care of the little bastards for another week!"), black cannibals

Story: The cartoon opens with Kernel Korn, an elderly man with a white beard, standing in the yard of his farm smoking a pipe. The sign on the fence reads Trader Korn. He says, "Hello, everybody! I went to Africa to get away from civilization and radio crooners. But you'll see from my map . . . wait just a minute." He pulls out his map of Africa, and the scene shifts to somewhere in

Africa where Kernel Korn is walking on stilts in the jungle. He says, "I walked on stilts so the natives would think I was far above them." He sees a group of small monkeys playing and says, "Monkey business is one of the leading industries in Africa. There's a lot of that going on in our part of the world." Next he observes a tiger and comments, "Now this is Minnie the moocher. At first Minnie was shy before the camera. But she felt much more at home after she ate the cameraman. You know, Minnie ran away from the circus to join the jungle." As the Kernel says "the heart of darkest Africa," a huge beating heart is superimposed on a map of Africa. In the distance the sounds of native drums can be heard, and Kernel sees the cannibal chief and his band of fierce-looking natives. A page from the diary of Kernel Korn reads, "December 10, 1923. S'long . . . we're not afraid." He sets up camp in a grass hut where two natives are sleeping. The Kernel says, "One night the jungle was quiet. You could hear a cough drop. Suddenly I heard buzzin'—it was a snozzola. Snozzolas are like the usual skeeters." A snozzola, looking like a mosquito with a very long proboscis, is seen about to attack the cannibal chief inside the hut. The next day Kernal Korn is sailing down the river in his boat with half a beer keg. He passes a group of cannibals on shore and says, "They would have eaten me, but they found that I wasn't kosher." On shore the natives are dancing, and the chief wears an empty tincan as a crown. The Kernel remarks, "You know cannibals eat their meats rare. They ain't got no stove." The cannibals hold a mass meeting to plan how to defend themselves against an invasion of the snozzolas. The Kernel sees them and says, "Once again the blackbottom dancers." Meanwhile the snozzolas are holding a meeting to plan their attack on the cannibals. They decide to tie all the cannibals from end to end, then they fly off saying, "Can the cannibals!" Back at the village the cannibals are ready to fight. The Kernel remarks, "But the cannibals are ready to fight. They just had a bottle of beer and some cold missionaries." The cannibals run off to war while the Kernel remarks, "The cannibals are hopping to the battle front. They hop around this way for hours. When they get enough hops, they make beer. Then they grab a tree by the roots and make root beer." As the cannibals run to meet the snozzolas, a black bug sounds the alarm to the other insects— "Black cannibals are coming; the cannibals are coming!" The cannibals defeat the snozzolas and then attack the Kernel, who is now riding a unicycle and wearing a World War I army uniform. The Kernel says, "Suddenly I realized my life was in great danger." The cannibals cry out, "Let's get Korn! Let's have Korn on the cob!" Kernel responds, "Those hungry maniacs. They will eat anything." The Kernel crashes into a grass hut and falls into a deep hole. He falls for a long time before he lands on a seat inside a car of the Bronx subway. He looks around at the other passengers and remarks, "I fought my way out of the jungle and soon I'll tell you how I fought my may out of the subway" as the cartoon ends.

THE LION HUNT (1938)

Company: Mannie Davis, Paul Terry, released by Educational Pictures

Type: Terrytoons, also released under title *African Daze*

Characters: Papa mouse, mama mouse, children mice, black natives, white hunter, lion

Story: The cartoon opens on a jungle scene. A king cobra snake is playing hot jazz music, and all the animals, including monkeys and elephants, dance and sing hi-dee-ho, imitating Cab Calloway. The mighty lion, trying to sleep inside his den, is disturbed by the music, so he comes out and gives a loud roar. The music stops and the frightened animals quiet down. As soon as the lion goes back inside, the music starts up again. The lion comes back out and roars so loudly that all of the animals run away. The lion is pleased and walks around with a smile on his face. In the meantime a mouse family is taking a vacation. Papa mouse is driving a car pulling a house trailer that has mama mouse and the children in it. The lion takes a nap with his tail lying across the road. The mouse drives along and runs over it. The angry lion catches the mouse, pulls him out of the car, and threatens to eat him on the spot. Papa mouse's cries for help are heard by mama mouse, who comes out of the trailer, together with her children, and rushes to papa's aid. Mama mouse, holding her baby in her arms, looks up at the lion and sings a blues song: "You got our daddy in the palm of your hand, ya-ya-dee-ho. Won't you let him go because we need him so. We ain't got doses and we ain't got deeses and we ain't got clothes and we ain't got cheese." The song makes the lion so sad that he drops papa mouse and wipes tears from his eyes. "One of the children pulls on her dress, saying, "Stop, Ma. He can't take it." The mother continues to sing, "Just 'cause we haven't got a daddy, jes 'cause we haven't got a man. Please let him go." The lion says, "Stop! Stop! You're breaking my heart." Papa mouse thanks the lion and tells him, "I'll do as much for you some day." Then he and his family drive away. The lions hears the sounds of a safari led by a white hunter riding an elephant. His native helpers, who wear bones in their hair, are on foot. The hunter sees the lion and shoots at him. At first the lion is not afraid and roars at the group, hoping to frighten them away. Then the hunter fires more shots, and the lion decides to escape. The hunter and the natives, who are throwing spears, chase the lion and succeed in knocking him down and out with a well-thrown spear. The lion is lying flat on his back at the side of the road when the mouse family drives by. Papa mouse sees the lion and stops. He revives the lion with smelling salts and they all, including the lion, get into the trailer and drive away with the natives giving chase. They drive across a rope bridge that spans a deep, wide canyon. On the other side the mouse gets out of his car and uses his sharp teeth to cut the rope so that when the natives are halfway across, the bridge breaks and they fall to their deaths. The grateful lion shakes the hand of papa mouse and tells him, "Thank you, Pal" as the cartoon ends.

Review: *Motion Picture Exhibitor,* 1 January 1938

This is encouraging because it presents a few gags that indicate these might take a turn for the better. The lion and the mouse fable is presented, with the commentator assisting in the narration. The sepia tone is no longer present but if the gags improve no one will care. It will be interesting to see what the future will bring. Good.

Review: *Motion Picture Herald,* **15 January 1938**

Not only does the elephant never forget, if the adage holds, but it would seem that this tiny but fearsome bugaboo, the mouse, is one equally well gifted with a fine memory. At least, that is the implication one would gather from this recent Terry-Toon. For, when the lion spares the life of a little rodent at the tearful, wifely plea of Mrs. Mouse, the two animals become friends. Later on, as the big beast is being pursued by a band of savages and a hunter, the mouse remembers the good turn done him by the lion and saves his life, however, the narration of this good deed fable is not very comically or imaginatively told. (8 min)

Review: *Selected Motion Pictures,* **1 February 1938**

Paul Terry-toon cartoon. An ingenious and amusing version of the old fable Lion and Mouse. Excellent. Family and Junior Matinee.

THE LION'S FRIEND (1934)

Company: Frank Moser, Paul Terry, released by 20th Century-Fox and Educational Pictures, also released as *The Big Game Hunt*
Type: Terrytoon
Characters: Farmer Al Falfa, black cannibals

Story: The cartoon opens on a jungle scene with Farmer Al Falfa as a big-game hunter riding on an elephant and carrying a hunting rifle. Along the way he encounters many friendly animals, including a trio of dancing monkeys and a group of monkeys playing tiddly winks with the spots of a leopard. He meets a rhino who puts up a fight until rapid-fire shots from the farmer's gun and cannon balls shot from the elephant's trunk drive him away. Next the Farmer chases away a large gorilla who runs headfirst into a large coconut tree. The impact shakes a group of wild-looking black cannibals out of the tree. They throw spears at the farmer as he tries to escape. He is captured and taken back to the cannibal village. He is placed in a large cooking pot and he sits there as the cannibals dance around him to the sounds of jungle rhythm. The fat cannibal chief, wearing a top hat with a bone stuck through it, sits on his throne and keeps time with the music. He is smoking a big black cigar and has a wide smile on his face. The cannibals make music with unusual instruments, including using the teeth of a rhino as a piano and the tails of several monkeys as a harp. Meanwhile the farmer sits in the cooking pot as a cannibal approaches and tries to light a match. Seeing that he is having trouble, the farmer gives him his cigarette lighter, which the cannibal uses to light a fire under the pot. A big lion arrives on the scene, and all of the cannibals run away. The farmer jumps out of the pot and also runs as the lion chases him. The farmer finds a suit of leopard skin that he puts on and then beats his chest and yells like Tarzan. The lion stops in his tracks and decides to make friends rather than war. He walks over and shakes the farmer's hand. With their arms around each other, both give out a loud roar as the cartoon ends.

Review: *Selected Review of Motion Pictures,* **1 April 1937**

Farmer Alfalfa, hunting in Africa, is captured by cannibals and rescued by a friendly lion. Family.

LITTLE BLACK SAMBO (1935)

Company: Ub Iwerks, Pat Powers, Celebrity Productions
Type: Comi-Color
Characters: Little Black Sambo, his mother, and his dog

Story: The cartoon opens on Sambo's mother bathing her little boy in a washtub filled with soapy water while his dog looks on. Sambo's mother then takes him out of the tub, dries him, sprinkles black talcum powder on him, and dresses him in nice clean clothes. She tells him, "Now run along and play, honey chile. But watch out for that bad old tiger. That old tiger sho' do like dark meat." Sambo's dog overhears this and decides to play a trick on little Sambo. Sambo leaves home to play in the woods. The dog starts to follow him, but stops at a freshly painted fence. He rubs the wet black paint on his body to resemble the stripes of a tiger. He puts the steel jaws of an animal trap into his mouth to simulate tiger fangs. When he looks into the mirror to admire his disguise, the tiger image is so real that he frightens himself. He does not realize that the image he sees is a real tiger standing behind the glassless mirror. The dog runs off to find Sambo, who is skipping merrily along in the woods. When Sambo's dog catches up with him, the boy is convinced that it is a real tiger and climbs a tree to escape. From the top of the tree Sambo throws down coconuts that hit the dog's head. The dog is stunned and decides to end his masquerade. Meanwhile Sambo disturbs a large monkey who throws Sambo out of the tree. His dog licks Sambo's face, and Sambo forgives him. Then they play a game of fetch the stick. Sambo throws the stick, but when the dog is about to bring it back the tiger shows up and the dog runs back to Sambo. The tiger chases boy and dog back to Sambo's house. They barricade the door from the inside moments before the tiger arrives. The tiger knocks hard on the door but can't break in. He rigs up a large rock attached to a rope so that it swings like a pendulum, knocking on the door at each swing. Thinking the tiger is at the front door, Sambo and dog relax. But tiger goes around to the back of the house and finds an open window through which he enters the house. He surprises Sambo, who manages to elude the tiger and is chased around and around the house. Finally little Sambo manages to succeed in throwing a large pot over the head of the tiger. Sambo then spreads thick, sticky molasses on the floor, and the tiger's feet become stuck in it. While he is immobilized, Sambo hits him on the backside with a hot skillet he has taken off the stove. The sharp pain causes the tiger to jump through the roof of the house. He lands on the side of a hill with the floorboards attached to his feet. He slides downhill until he lands in a mudhole. When he climbs out, he is so embarrassed by his experience that he runs off back into the forest. Back home Sambo and his mother are dancing around to celebrate ridding themselves of the dangerous tiger. The dog gets an idea to play another trick on Sambo. He sneaks out the back door of the cabin, goes around to the front door, and sets the rock on the string in motion again. Hearing a knock at the door, Sambo and his mother are frightened, thinking that the tiger has returned. The dog comes in the back and pretends that he is not afraid to open the door. He does and is hit on the head by the rock. The joke is on him as the cartoon ends.

Review: *Boxoffice,* 25 May 1935

Entertaining Comi-Color reel of a Little Black Sambo and his faithful dog. Sambo is warned by his mother to watch out for the tiger. Not heeding the warning, the two wander into the woods where they run smack on to the tiger—then the fun follows as they seek escape, finally pulling a fast one and capturing the beast. Good fun throughout. (8 min)

Review: *Film Daily,* 25 April 1935

The tale of a pickaninny's adventures as he wanders off into the jungle with his faithful pup. They encounter a ferocious tiger, who gives chase, and they escape to the shelter of the cabin. The tiger breaks in, but the pickaninny and the pup pull a fast one, and get rid of him. Done with a swell comedy technique by Iwerks, and the color treatment is very good.

Review: *Motion Picture Herald,* 11 May 1935

An entertaining cartoon of the Powers Comi-Color series, this recounts in amusing fashion the adventures of little Sambo, who is warned by his mother to beware of the tiger. His dog, to frighten him, dons stripes, but they both get more than the dog bargained for when the real tiger appears, bent on a good meal. The day is saved, and the tiger is routed, but not until Sambo and the dog have had plenty of excitement.

Review: *Philadelphia Exhibitor,* 1 May 1935

Swell color; swell drawing; satisfactory comedy, music not too good. All about Little Sambo, mother warning him against the big bad tiger, family dog overhearing, deciding to play tiger, notion of them receiving scare from real tiger. Pleasant.

THE LITTLE BROADCAST (1939)

Company: George Pal; released by Paramount Pictures
Type: Madcap Models, Puppetoons
Characters: Orchestra conductor, Jim Dandy, black cannibals

Story: The cartoon opens as an orchestra conductor, carrying a violin case, approaches a concert hall where he reads the posted billing, "Madcap Models—Composed and Produced by George Pal." He enters the hall by way of the sewer. He takes his place in the orchestra pit, and the lights dim. The announcer walks out and in a stereotypical Italian accent introduces the first act: Jim Dandy joins a gypsy group and plays a swing version of a gypsy song on his violin. The act concludes, the audience applauds, and the announcer tells the audience, "Now we have a treat for you. A group of natives from a faraway island

have Jim Dandy for dinner." The curtain opens on the scene of a cannibal village. In the center is a cooking pot in which Jim Dandy is sitting. The cannibals dance to the rhythm of drum beats and the chief, sitting on his throne, smiles and rubs his stomach and says, "Yum-yum." The conductor arrives on the scene and makes a loud noise that is heard by the witch doctor, who cries out "Spooks!" All of the frightened cannibals run out of the village to the seashore where they climb into their boats and row away from the island. The curtain falls to the applause of the audience as the cartoon ends.

THE MAJOR LIED 'TIL DAWN (1938)

Company: Frank Tashlin, Warner Bros.
Type: Merrie Melodies
Characters: Major Twambe, Freddie, black Africans

Story: The cartoon opens in the trophy room of Major Twambe's house as he and little Freddie stand by the fireplace. The stuffed heads of various wild animals are mounted on the walls of the room. Freddie looks up at him and says, "I say, Major Twambe, I say, you have an awfully fine collection of heads there, you know." The Major answers, "Yes Freddie, quite so. Definitely, so to speak. You know what I mean." Freddie says, "I say, Major, do tell me about some of your adventures hunting big game in Africa." The boy looks up at the stuffed head of a lion and says, "I say, that ferocious-looking fellow up there. Was he stuffed when you got him?" The major laughs, slaps his hands on his knees, and says, "Oh no . . . oh golly . . . I don't get it. He looks at a map of Africa and says, "You see, ol' boy, in Africa on my third expedition we had just left Bela Bela in Somaliland . . ." The scene shifts to the African jungle as colorful birds fly through the air. The major continues, "Naturally, I was leading the safari atop my favorite elephant, Tallulah." The major is seen riding his elephant seated in a chair and drinking from a glass. The major continues, "Most extraordinary animal. Travels quite extensively, you know." Travel stickers are seen pasted to the elephant's trunk. The major continues, "I even had my man Tiffany along." His butler, Tiffany, is seen riding on a trailer being pulled by the major's elephant. The major says, "As well as the usual contingent of native baggage boys, gun bearers, and all that sort of of rot." A line of African natives carrying bags of supplies on their heads is seen walking in single file behind the major. Next to the last in line is a skinny native with a Stephin Fetchit demeanor. Behind him is a another native who partially peels a banana and then stuffs it whole into his mouth. Behind him walks a large native woman wearing a polka-dot dress as the music plays "It Don't Mean a Thing If You Don't Got that Swing." She opens her wide mouth and reaches inside to wind up a phonograph. Meanwhile one native walks in front of the group and crosses a river. He becomes completely submerged, with only the bag he is carrying on his head sticking out of the water. When the bag reaches the other side of the river, it is on the head of a big alligator that walks out of the water smiling and rubbing its fat stomach, having eaten the native. They continue and along the way encounter many animals, including an elephant who is trying hard to remember something. The major continues his story, "We soon found ourselves in lion country." The safari arrives at a sign that reads Lion's Club. The major says, "My boys were beating the bushes" as the natives are seen walking along making loud noises. The major says, "I was poised and ready to pop anything they scared up." Suddenly a lion is flushed out of the bushes and the major fires a shot at it. The recoil from his gun sends him spinning over the elephant's back. The lion escapes, and the major dismounts and continues to track him on foot, using his butler like a hound dog to track the lion's scent. They sight the lion, who is standing in a boxing ring wearing boxing gloves. The lion beckons the major to climb into the ring for a prize fight. While the major is climbing into the ring, the lion slips a horseshoe in each boxing glove. The lion and the major fight, and the major is knocked out of the ring. But then he eats a can of spinach, which gives him added strength. He reenters the ring with bulging muscles and defeats the lion. He smiles as he stands over the fallen lion. But his victory angers a Tarzan-like character who beats his chest and yells to all of the animals, who arrive on the scene and attack the major. He defeats them all, and the scene changes back to the house. The major is saying, "And here I am as fit as a fiddle." The boy says, "Yes, yes, Major. Most interesting. But what about the elephant? Tell me what about the elephant." He tugs on the major's arm. The major says, "Oh yes, the elephant. Yes. Quite so. The elephant is seen in the jungle still trying to remember something. The elephant says, "What am I supposed to say? If I can only remember that." After a short pause he smiles and says, "Wait a minute. Yeah, that's it. I got it, I got it." As a trumpet sounds in the background the elephant says, "That's all, Folks" as the cartoon ends.

MICKEY'S MAN FRIDAY (1935)

Company: David Hand, Walt Disney; released by United Artists
Characters: Mickey Mouse, Friday, black cannibals

Story: Mickey Mouse is sailing the ocean alone on his small boat when a storm wrecks it on an island. Only a few of his possessions are saved. He soon discovers footprints in the sand, and in the distance he sees a group of cannibals about to push a helpless black native into a huge cooking pot. Mickey decides to rescue him. He makes himself a witch doctor's costume by painting an empty barrel. He pulls the barrel over his body, puts on a stovepipe hat, and then goes to rescue Friday. The cannibals are so frightened by the sudden appearance of this strange-looking man that they run to the beach, jump into their canoes, and row away from the island. The grateful native gets on his hands and knees and bows to Mickey and agrees to be Mickey's servant. Mickey tells him, "OK, my boy. You be my Man Friday. Savvy?" Mickey places the top hat on Friday's head and then tells him, "You Friday and me Mickey." Friday points to Mickey and then to himself before saying, "You Friday and me Mickey." Mickey laughs at him and then gives Friday a hatchet. Together they build themselves a fort with a wall around it for protection in case the cannibals decide to return to the island. They are assisted in

the work by a long python snake that strings the logs together. Meanwhile Friday does a tap dance on the back of a huge turtle that is nailing the walls in place with wooden spikes. Their fort is finished in no time, and they hoist a flat over it, proclaiming it to be Fort Robinson Crusoe. Soon they discover that the cannibals have again arrived on the island and immediately run to the fort. On the way they trip over a bell that rings an alarm, warning Mickey and Friday that they are in danger. Mickey is lifted to the top of their lookout tower by Friday who powers the manual elevator by running on a treadmill. On top of the tower Mickey pulls a rope that closes the gate before the cannibals can get in. Next the cannibals try to scale the wall using a tree trunk as a makeshift ladder. But Mickey activates a battering ram that knocks the cannibals off the walls. Finally Mickey and Friday find themselves overrun when the cannibals break down the gate. Mickey and Friday try to escape by jumping into a large basket that is suspended on a rope stretched between two trees. They ride the basket down, but the cannibals cut the rope. Mickey and Friday are tossed out of the basket and fall to the ground, where they run to the shore. There they jump into their boat and leave the island just before the cannibals arrive on the scene and the cartoon ends.

Review: *Boxoffice,* 26 January 1935

A fast-moving and plenty lively Mickey Mouse short. This time Mickey is shipwrecked on an island. Here he prevents the cannibals from eating a prisoner, who becomes Mickey's slave to repay him for saving his life. The reel concerns the hot and humorous battle that takes place between the cannibals and Mickey and his "Man Friday." (7 min)

Review: *Motion Picture Herald,* 9 February 1935

The latest exploit of Mickey, Mr. Disney's cheerful and energetic rodent, finds him a veritable Robinson Crusoe. Marooned on a desert isle, he saves a native, who becomes his Man Friday. Together they fashion a home of no mean proportions with the gadgets which stand them in good stead when the natives attack. All the novelty of the cartoonist's art is here as the attack is repulsed and Mickey sails away. An entertaining subject.

Review: *Motion Picture Reviews,* August 1935

An Ingenious, imaginative cartoon in which Mickey and his man Friday rout cannibals. Very entertaining, all ages.

Review: *Selected Motion Picture,* 1 March 1935

A Walt Disney cartoon. A very amusing animated cartoon with Robinson Crusoe flavor. Family.

Review: *Philadelphia Exhibitor,* 1 April 1935

Mickey rescues a native, attaches him to his retinue as his man Friday, fights off the cannibals, escapes safely. No Minnie this time. Fair.

MIGHTY MOUSE IN SWISS CHEESE FAMILY ROBINSON (1947)

Company: Mannie Davis, Paul Terry, 20th Century-Fox Pictures
Type: Terrytoons
Characters: Mighty Mouse, black cannibals

Review: *Exhibitor Servisection,* 18 February 1947

While Mighty Mouse relaxes on the Florida shore, the victims of a shipwreck, a family of mice floating on a raft of cheese, reach an island loaded with cannibals, after setting a rescue note free in a bottle in the ocean. The father, mother, and daughter are captured, and are about to be boiled when Mighty Mouse receives the note, makes his dash through space, and arrives in the nick of time to save them. The island is then turned into an amusement park. Good.

Review: *Motion Picture Herald,* 10 April 1948

Mighty Mouse, basking on the sands of Miami Beach, does not realize that the ship-wrecked Family Robinson is out on the ocean somewhere, tossed about by the waves. A turtle tries to help them, but they land on an island inhabited by cannibals. At the last moment, Mighty Mouse streaks from the sky in a fast and funny climax.

Review: *Boxoffice,* 6 March 1948

Mighty Mouse again comes to the rescue of some unfortunate rodents in a novel cartoon subject. The victims of a shipwreck toss a bottle with a message into the sea. They land on a desert island and are almost devoured by cannibals before the message reaches the mouse relaxing on the sands of Miami Beach. Of course he dashes to the rescue and vanquishes the cannibals.

MILD CARGO (1934)

Company: Van Beuren; released by RKO-Radio Pictures
Characters: Cubby Bear, black Africans

Story: The cartoon opens in the African jungle. All of the animals are looking at a newspaper headline, "Cubby Bear Returns to Bring 'Em Back Alive." The animals are frightened, and some run away while others hide themselves. A huge ape, however, is not afraid and decides to investigate this great hunter who is invading his jungle. The great hunter Cubby Bear arrives on the scene riding on the back of an elephant. He is followed by black Africans walking behind carrying huge sacks of supples on their heads. Cubby makes camp before setting out on foot with the natives to trap wild animals. They stop and dig a deep pit that they cover with a cloth. For bait Cubby uses a beautiful bird. After Cubby and the natives leave the scene, a lion arrives is lured into the pit by the bird. Cubby has the natives put the lion in a cage before they continue their trek through the jungle. They stop and Cubby lays out a full-course dinner, which they use as bait to catch a tiger. The huge ape suddenly arrives on the scene

and decides to follow Cubby and his party surreptitiously. Next Cubby fabricates a huge trap made of concrete reinforced with steel beams. But instead of catching big game, they trap a tiny mouse that Cubby decides to keep. He sets the trap again and the ape, who has grown fond of Cubby, decides to let himself be caught in it. But Cubby decides to release him, and the ape begins to cry. But Cubby and his party decide to move on, and before long they are stalking a hippo that tries to get away by diving into a pool of water. Cubby tries to lasso the hippo using a rope, but he catches the ape instead. Again Cubby lets the ape go before returning to camp, where the natives guard several cages containing the animals they have captured. When Cubby blows a whistle, the cages open and the animals come out chained together in single file. Cubby leads the animals to the harbor where they are loaded onto his ship for the voyage home. Following behind them is the smiling ape, who attaches himself to the end of the group of animals as the cartoon ends.

MOLLY MOO-COW AND ROBINSON CRUSOE (1936)

Company: Burt Gillett, Van Beuren, RKO-Radio Pictures
Type: Rainbow Parade
Characters: Molly Moo-Cow, black cannibals

Story: The cartoon opens on a stormy sea as Molly Moo-Cow's boat is being tossed about. A huge wave sweeps the boat to the shore of an island, and Molly is tossed onto the beach. She decides to explore the island. Meanwhile Robinson Crusoe, who lives on the island, is taking a stroll through the jungle. With rifle in hand he sings, "I'm all my myself and happy to be that way because I'm Robinson Crusoe." He stops suddenly when he sees footprints in the sand. Then a spear flies by, just missing his head. He runs away and hides behind boulders until he runs into Molly Moo-Cow. They frighten each other and run their separate ways. Later Molly decides to make friends with Crusoe and attempts to get close enough to him to lick his face with her tongue. But Crusoe rejects her, saying, "No cow is going to kiss me." Molly is very sad, and with her head down she slowly backs away. Crusoe walks away, and Molly follows him to his jungle hut, which is protected by a high wall all around it. Seeing the lonesome cow, Crusoe lets her in his compound but tells her, "Now look, you're a nice cow. I like you, but this place is only big enough for one of us. Now get off this island." He chases Molly down to the seashore, where she gets into her boat and rows away from the island. Suddenly black cannibals show up on the scene, capture Crusoe, and carry him back to their village on the tips of their spears. On the way Crusoe cries out for help, while the happy cannibals sing and dance a jazzy rendition of "Diga Diga Doo Doo." They arrive at the cannibal village and throw Crusoe into a large cooking pot sitting on a fire. Hearing Crusoe's cry for help, Molly has turned her boat around and paddled as hard as she can back to the island. After she arrives on shore, she runs to Crusoe's house and ties three of his hunting rifles to her tail. She carries them to the cannibal village, and when she is close, she slings the guns off her tail high into the air. When the guns come down and strike the ground, they all discharge and make the sound of a machinegun blasting away. The noise frightens the cannibals, and they run to the shore and leave the island. A happy Crusoe stands up in the cooking pot and says to Molly, "All right, you can stay. But what will I do with you?" Molly takes some black soot from under the cooking pot and uses it to blacken her face. The sight of a blackface cow makes Crusoe laugh. He looks at Molly and shouts "Friday." Molly gives him a big kiss and the cartoon ends.

Review: *National Exhibitor,* 5 January 1936

Molly, the cow with horns, is cast off on Crusoe's island. He doesn't want her, shoos her away with a shotgun. But when she rescues him from savages, he is grateful. A few laughs; color is nice. (8 min)

ON THE PAN (1933)

Company: Van Beuren, RKO-Radio Pictures
Characters: Little King, black cannibals

Story: The cartoon opens on a scene in the castle of the Little King. He is preparing to leave for Africa to go big-game hunting. His servants pack his bag with clothing and with the animals that he is planning to hunt, including a lion and some monkeys. Little King drives away in his car as the queen and the servants wave good-bye. But two of the servants tell the queen that the king forgot to take his rubbers (shoes). The queen gives the rubbers to the king's little dog, telling him to fetch them to the king. At the dock the ship is loaded with the king, his car, and his servants. The dog arrives just as the ship is pulling away from the dock, so he jumps into the ocean and swims after it. On board the servants tell the king that he should do some target practice. A target is set up, and the king hits the bull's-eye. The ship arrives in Africa, and the servants carry the king, car and all. They decide to stop and shoot their first animal. The servants lay down a red carpet, and the king steps out of the car. A servant takes a small bird in a cage out of the car and places it in front of the king, who aims a cannon at it. Realizing that he is the target, the small bird, manages to escape the cage an instant before the king fires the cannon. The cannon backfires, and the king tries to outrun the cannonball. He swings up on a large vine, and the cannonball passes under him. But the vine turns out to be a large python. The king lets go of the snake and falls at the feet of a strange-looking bird. The king pulls his gun and aims it at the bird. At this moment the head of the bird is transformed into the head of Jimmy Durante and says, "Why, I'm sitting here minding my own business, then what happens. A guy comes along and pulls a .44 on me. Why, it's a lotta nerve, that's what it is." Meanwhile the king's dog has arrived in Africa and starts off to find him. The king continues his hunt and sees footprints that he follows as drumbeats are heard. The king comes face-to-face with a cannibal and tries to escape. But

then the cannibal tribe arrives and captures him. As they walk along taking him back to their village, they lick their lips and smile. At the village the king is brought before the cannibal king. He orders that Little King be taken to the cook house, where the female cook lays him out on the roasting pan and arranges vegetables around him. She starts a fire under the stove as outside the witch doctor and three shapely native girls dance to the beat of the drums. Meanwhile Little King's dog has seen the cannibal footprints and is following them to the cannibal village. The cook prepares a frosting mix that she uses to write Happy Birthday on Little King's chest. She places a lid over the roasting pan and leaves the cook house to take the menu to the cannibal king. The menu reads, "King with french-fried potatoes." While she is gone, Little King's dog enters the cook house and gives him his rubbers. The cook returns and places the roasting pan on the fire. Outside the drums beat and the cannibals await their meal. Finally the main dish is done and the cook brings the roasting pot to the cannibal king. When he lifts the lid, he finds a pair of roasted rubbers. He takes two big bites from one of the rubbers and starts to swell up like a balloon. The other cannibals eat the rubbers and also become inflated. Little King and the dog see their chance to escape, but are chased by the floating cannibals as they run away. They throw their spears in the direction of Little King and his dog. He stops and catches the spears in his hand and then places them in the barrel of his cannon. He fires the cannon and the spears hit the cannibals, deflating them so that they shrink into small balls and disappear. At this time the bird with the Jimmy Durante head lands next to Little King and tells him, "King, you're a fighter after me own heart. Congratulations." Meanwhile the bird has laid an egg. It hatches, and out pop several small birds that say "ah, shut up" as the cartoon ends.

Review: *Selected Motion Pictures,* 1 September 1939

An Englishman and his butler go lion hunting. Fair. Family.

Review: *Motion Picture Exhibitor,* 14 June 1939

The Colonel and his butlers go Africa, where they get neither lions nor laughs.

100 PYGMIES AND ANDY PANDA (1940)

Company: Alex Lovy, Walter Lantz, Universal Pictures
Type: Animation with a brief live action sequence
Television Distribution: Shown on the *Woody Woodpecker Show* broadcast by the ABC television network in 1957–1958; sponsored by Kellogg cereals
Characters: Andy Panda, Daddy Panda, postman, black pygmies

Story: The cartoon opens in the jungle, where Andy Panda lies on the ground reading a book near daddy, who is sleeping in a hammock suspended between two coconut trees. Andy stops reading and calls out, "Daddy, Daddy." His father, with his eyes closed, responds, "Please, Andy, let daddy sleep." Andy frowns and continues to read. Meanwhile, at the mailbox the postman, a turtle named Whipple Tree, has arrived with a package addressed to Andy Panda. He calls out, in a voice similar to Amos of the *Amos 'n' Andy* radio show, "There's a delivery for ya. Andy, come and get it, Andy!" Andy shouts, "Boy, it must be my magic set. Whoopie!" He runs to the turtle and opens his package. Inside is a magic wand and a book about magic. Andy throws the book to the postman and asks, "Read it. What does it say?" The turtle reads, "Wave the magic wand and say the magic word—alagazam." He continues, "That's what it says, but I don't believe it." Andy waves the wand at the turtle and says the magic word. Immediately white bunny rabbits crawl out of the turtle's shell, and one from under his cap. Andy smiles and says, "It works! It works! Let's try it on Daddy." As he waves the wand at daddy and says the magic words, his sleeping father levitates off the hammock into the air. The turtle shakes his head and says, "My, my." Andy calls out, "Daddy!" His father, eyes closed, says, "Andy, please." Andy says, "Look at my magic wand." Daddy says, "There ain't no such thing as magic," and Andy replies, "Are you sure, Daddy?" Daddy answers, "Yes, sure. Now let me sleep." As he rolls over on his stomach, Andy says, "Well, Daddy, what's holding you up there?" Daddy looks down and then rolls around in the air, shouting, "Help! Help! Put me down. Help me. Please Andy, do something. Put me down, please." As Andy smiles and says the magic word, his father falls flat on the ground, making a hole. Meanwhile at the pygmy village, there is a sign on the door of a hut: Witch Doctor. Hours 3 to 4. Prescriptions Filled. Stamps, Cigars, Newspapers, Candy, Magic. The witch doctor wears a bone in his hair, has thick white lips, and his holding his magic wand—an empty tin can nailed to the top of a stick. He is standing near a huge cooking pot. Hanging on the wall over the pot is a magic mask of the voodoo god—a black man with thick white lips and big white nose. Attached to the wall over the mask are a human skull and cross bones. The doctor says, "Magic mask upon the wall, am I not more powerful than all?" The eyes of the mask open, and it answers, "Andy Panda has a magic wand. And you're playing second fiddle now." With a surprised expression on his face, the witch doctor says, "You mean he got mo' magic power den I's got?" The mask answers, "The mask speaks only the truth." The witch doctor says, Well, I don't believe it." The masks retorts, "Well, if you don't believe it, go see for yourself." The witch doctor says, "Well, OK." He grabs the mask off the wall, puts it on his face, and says, "Take me to Andy Panda." Then he disappears is a puff of white smoke. Meanwhile Andy is still playing with his magic wand and says, "Now do you believe in magic, Daddy?" His father says, "No. It's just a trick." Suddenly a puff of white smoke suddenly appears and then clears, revealing the witch doctor with his magic wand. The turtle says, "Dr. Livingstone, I presume?" The witch doctor looks at Andy and his wand and says, "Me witch doctor. Who You?" Andy says, "Andy Panda," and the witch doctor tells him, "Me got mo' magic than you." Andy says, "Really?" The witch doctor says, Yeah, really." He points his wand at daddy, and a top hat appears in daddy's hand. As

Daddy looks in the hat, boxing gloves spring out of it and hit him in the face. Andy says, "OK, Bogey Man, watch me." He waves his wand at daddy, and a chicken flies out of the hat and drops an egg, which breaks on daddy' head. Not to be outdone, the witch doctor waves his wand at daddy and causes him to shrink so much that the hat completely covers him except for his feet. Daddy shouts, "Help! Let me out! Andy, do something." Using his wand, Andy conjures up a pair of hiking boots that chase the doctor away, kicking him in his rear end as he is running. But the boots get tired and stop with their tongues hanging out. The witch doctor blows his whistle, summoning the pygmy tribe. They arrive carrying spears and wearing bones in their hair. The turtle hears their war cries and says, "Here dey come, Andy. Run fo' your life." He retreats all the way into his shell and covers the opening with a steel door that has a sign: Pygmy Proof Door. Andy tries to run away, but is captured. The witch doctor says, "I got it" as he holds up Andy's magic wand. He points the wand at Andy and says "Ala, Ala, Alabama." The pygmies disappear and are next seen running through the countryside and dodging automobiles in the city (live action) as they run to Alabama. Andy picks up his wand and uses it to return his father to his normal size. Daddy yanks the wand from Andy and bends it over his knee before throwing it away. He says, "I've had just about enough of this magic business." The wand lands at the feet of the turtle. He picks it up and straightens it out, saying, "He sho' fixed this magic wand. It's the end of that alagazam." Then he disappears in a puff of smoke. He reappears riding on top of a barrel that is about to go over Niagara Falls. He calls out, "Andy, get me out of here! Do help me. Hurry, hurry!" as the cartoon ends.

Review: *Motion Picture Herald,* 11 May 1940

Andy Panda in his newest colored cutup becomes mixed with matters magical. Andy finds a magician's wand and demonstrates with startling and amusing effects the wonders of his find upon his friend, the tortoise. Andy's fame with the stick makes the local witch doctor envious and he tries to capture the wand. Papa destroys the charm instrument and it is supposed that Andy will return to normalcy. A highlight of the magic demonstration by the Walter Lantz animators is the contest of hijinks between Andy and the witch doctor. (7 min)

Review: *Film Daily,* 9 May 1940

There are several good laughs in this cartoon. Young Andy Panda gets delivery of a magic set his father has bought for him. Waving the magic wand and mumbling the magic word, Andy immediately starts confusion on a wholesale scale. Andy has trouble with the local witch doctor, his father and several other people, including the doctor's pygmies, before the end of the reel.

Review: *Boxoffice,* 11 May 1940

It does not make sense, but Andy Panda's adventures with his magic wand are diverting enough as cartoon material. The excitement arises over the jealousy of a witch doctor who summons 100 pygmies to catch Andy.

Review: *Motion Picture Exhibitor,* 1 May 1940

Andy gets a magic wand, runs into trouble with the jungle magic man, is attacked by the pygmies, but beats them off, all of which includes some good gags, excellent color and good cartoon all told. Good.

Review: *Exhibitor Servisection,* 8 September 1951

Andy Panda, overjoyed when his magic wand set is delivered by the postman, tries out the magic wand on his father and leaves him hanging in midair. The power of the wand is discovered by a witch doctor, who goes to Andy, and gets into a contest to see whose magic is stronger, with Andy's father always getting the worst of it. The witch doctor calls 100 pygmy helpers but they are sent flying, and Andy's father breaks the wand. Good.

THE ORIGIN OF THE SHIMMY, OR GETTING A STORY (1919)

Company: Pat Sullivan, J. R. Bray Studio; released by Goldwyn Pictures
Type: Goldwyn-Bray Pictograph
Characters: Newspaper reporter, sailor, white and black natives

See fig. 32. Story: The cartoon opens as a newspaper editor sticks his head out of his office door and tells a reporter, "And if you don't get a story, you lose your job." The worried reporter stands with his hands in his pockets saying to himself, "A reporter's life is a tough one," as he walks away. Meanwhile a sailor is sitting on a park bench, reading a magazine. The reporter shows up on the scene, sits on the bench next to the sailor, and scratches his head, wondering what to do next. He thinks to himself, "Gee! If I could only get a story." The sailor stops reading, turns toward the reporter, and asks him, "Wot's the matter, Buddy?" The reporter answers, "I'm a reporter and if I don't get a good story, I'll lose my job!" The sailor tells him, "Listen! I'll give you a story. Get ready." The reporter pulls out his notepad and a pen as the sailor begins, "My name is Solomon. I was a sailor on a Swiss liner!" Over his head appears a scene of a ship sailing on the ocean. The sailor continues, "And a submarine strolled along . . ." as the scene changes to a submarine with its periscope sticking out of the water. The German captain sights the ship through his periscope and gives the order to fire a torpedo. It hits the ship, blowing it out of the water and throwing the sailor into the air. The sailor continues his story, "I landed on an island inhabited by white Negroes." He is shown falling down on a beach with coconut trees all around him. He looks around and sees a grass hut with a King Kookoo sign." He enters the hut and finds a white native wearing a crown on his head and sitting on a box. The native is deep in thought, and the sailor asks him, "Wot's the matter, Kink?" The king answers, "All my subjects are rubbing themselves thin

trying to keep clean." The sailor looks out of the window and sees the white natives scrubbing themselves with soap and water. The king says, "Gosh! I which we were black!" The sailor walks in circles around the room with his head down and his hands behind his back and thinks for a few moments. Then he tells the chief, "Don't worry, Kink. I'll try and help you out." The sailor walks out of the hut as the scene changes back to the park bench, where the sailor tells the reporter, "One day while looking for a sail . . ." As the scene changes back to the island, the sailor is seen standing on a hill and looking out at the ocean through his spyglass. He sights the wreckage of a ship near the shore. On the beach are several boxes that have been washed ashore. One box is labeled Indelible Black Ink and the other box is labeled Mohair Underwear. The sailor runs down to the beach, picks up the box of ink, and carries it back to the village. The sailor tells the reporter, "Then I treated each native, one by one." The natives are seen entering the chief's hut, obtaining a bottle of ink from the sailor, and then drinking it. Then their color changes from white to jet black. The sailor continues his story. "The king was tickled to death." The king is then seen drinking a bottle of ink and turning black. The king tells the sailor, "You're King now. And you have the choice among three fat wives." Three fat female natives wearing grass skirts are seen grooming themselves, and the king continues, "Or six skinny ones." Six skinny native women are seen in a hut. The sailor looks inside and sees the skinny women and puts his hands over his eyes. He says, "I'll take those. But how about clothes for them?" He runs back to the beach and gets the box of mohair underwear, which he brings back to the village. He gives the underwear to the women and tells them, "Say! Put these duds on." When the women put on the underwear, the fabric tickles their bodies and they begin to wiggle. The sailor says, "The wiggles that the natives called Boola Shimmy." Soon all of the natives are doing the shimmy. The sailor continues his story. "This was more than enough for me, though" as he runs out of the village and stops near a rubber tree on the beach. Just then a large steamship passes near the island. The sailor grabs the trunk of the rubber tree and bends it down so far that it springs back and flings him into the air. He lands on the deck of the ship. The sailor finishes his story and the reporter jumps up and says, "Great! Wait 'till I get back." He runs back to the editor's office of the *Morning Milk*—Hicksburg's only and greatest newspaper. He finds the editor sitting at this desk, and he tells him, "Boss, I have the story of stories." The editor says, "Good! Let's get a picture." They both run out of the building as the cartoon ends.

PLANE DUMB (1932)

Company: John Foster, George Rufle, Van Beuren, RKO-Radio Pictures
Characters: Tom and Jerry, black Africans

Story: The cartoon opens with Tom and Jerry in a small airplane flying over the ocean. Tom says, "If we make this flight to Africa, we will be heroes." They look down and see the African continent, but their hazardous flight is not yet over. Jerry says that they want to be safe in Africa. Tom tells him that they will disguise themselves. He takes out a jar of blackface makeup, and he and Jerry blacken their faces. They turn to each other, shake hands, and say "Well, I'm sho' glad to see you again." Their plane goes into a nosedive and crashes into the ocean. Tom and Jerry climb onto one of the wings and escape by flying over the octopus and sharks before landing on the shore of Africa. When they are attacked by wild animals, they run into a dark cave to hide. Inside the cave nothing but their eyes can be seen, and they both wonder who is touching them. Suddenly four skeletons with black bones appear, singing, "I'll be ready when the great day comes." Tom and Jerry run out of the cave and are immediately attacked by a group of spear-throwing Africans. Tom and Jerry run for their lives as the cartoon ends.

POP-PIE A LA MODE (1945)

Company: I. Sparber, Famous Studios; released by Paramount Pictures
Characters: Popeye the sailor, black cannibals

See fig. 33. Story: The cartoon opens as Popeye, floating on a small raft in the middle of the ocean, rubs suntan oil on himself and says, "Whew! Boy, if I don't get out of this hot Specific Ocean, I'll look like a poached Popeye on a raft." A black native with thick lips paddles by on a small boat. There is sign on his back: If Shipwrecked Try Joe's—Reasonable Rates. Popeye yells, "At last! Some land at last." He looks through his spyglass and sees a small island on which is Joe's Always Inn. Popeye propels himself to shore and winds up inside the hotel. He rings the bell at the front desk and says, "Service, service! Where's the manager?" Through a hole in a door an eye peeps out. It belongs to Joe the manager, who is a big, fat cannibal wearing a top hat with a bone stuck through it. He says, "Ah, there's a man of my feast," as he imagines Popeye as a slice of roast ham. Joe walks out of his office and says, "Welcome to Joe's Always Inn. I'm Joe, of course." Popeye says, "How ya, Joe. What do you know? Ha-ha. I wants me a room with meals." Joe says, "Ah, meals. Why, I'll be happy to serve ya." Popeye says thank-you as Joe calls for the bellboys. They put Popeye on a stretcher and Joe tells them, "Take good care of dis customer. He is de specialty of de house." Popeye is carried away as Joe reads a book entitled *How to Serve Your Fellow Man* by I. M. A. Cannibal. Joe turns to a page and says, "Ah, here it tis. All about the fatin' diet treatment." He imagines Popeye as a fat man. Meanwhile Popeye lies on a hammock while a cannibal stuffs large bowls of various potato dishes into his mouth—mashed, french fried, boiled, baked—followed by more starches, ice cream, and cake. After Popeye is finished eating, Joe holds a bowl of water and Popeye washes his hands. A pygmy cannibal arrives on the scene and smears mustard on Popeye's leg before placing it between two hamburger buns. He opens his mouth wide and is about to take a bite with his one long tooth, but Joe grabs him and says, "Ain't I told you to never eat between meals." Then he throws the pygmy down. Joe tells Popeye, "And now suh, we has

cooked up somethin' special for you. You is gonna be initiated into the secret Order of the Midnight Bath." Later that night the cannibals dance and play the drums. Popeye is led to a bathtub filled with hot water. Popeye climbs into the tub, saying, "Oh, this is embarrassing. I ain't done nothin' like this since I lost a bet in poker." Two cannibals remove the sides of the tub to reveal that Popeye is really sitting in a large cooking pot. The cannibals start a fire under the pot, and soon Popeye starts to sweat and to fan himself. The pygmy cannibal arrives and makes a sandwich of Popeye's arm. He takes a bit as Popeye screams and says, "Hey, what kind of an initiation is this? You'd think these guys was cannibals." He looks around him and sees that the smiling cannibals are all carrying World War II meat ration books, and the pygmy cannibal is holding a sign: I Get the Neck. When the cannibal cook rings the dinner bell, all of the cannibals rush Popeye and tie him up. Then they stand him on a block of wood. Two cannibals club him on the head repeatedly until he is as flat as a thick steak. All the while they sing, "You take the high ribs and I'll take the low ribs, and I'll get the white meat befo' ya." They throw him into a large frying pan and flip him high into the air. Popeye manages to open his can of spinach midair and swallow it. When he lands, he regains his normal size, beats his chest with his fists, and yells like Tarzan. He beats up all of the cannibals and ties them up with their own spears. Joe runs to his inn and fires cannonballs at Popeye. Popeye catches them and forms the shells into a blockbuster bomb that he throws at Joe's inn. When it explodes, Joe is blown into the ocean, where he sees two sharks and decides that they would make a good meal. He swims after them holding a knife and a fork in his hands. Meanwhile Popeye is now king and sits on the throne as all of the cannibals bow down before him. He smiles but then yells. He looks down to see that his leg has been bitten by the pygmy cannibal, who smiles and says, "I loves dat man" as the cartoon ends.

Review: *Besa Shorts Shorts,* 2 July 1945

Opening with Popeye floating on a raft on the sea, he makes his way to a tropical isle inhabited by cannibals, as he sorrowfully finds out. They get him real fat so's he'll be tastier, then pop him in a pot of boiling water. Comes his spinach to the rescue and Popeye beats 'em all up and zooms out of there in nothing flat.

Review: *Motion Picture Herald,* 9 June 1945

The sailor is marooned on a cannibal isle without quite realizing what's up. The natives feed him well, perhaps too well, and he takes some fat on his long thin frame. Then he is offered a hot bath in a large kettle, but the purpose begins to dawn on him. With his last can of spinach he whips up enough strength to dissuade the cannibals from their dinner and take over rule of the kingdom. (8 min)

Review: *Boxoffice,* 16 June 1945

Our sailor hero, shipwrecked on the Specific ocean, drifts to a lush tropic island inhabited by a cannibal tribe. He is unaware that the royal treatment he receives is intended to fatten him to pig-like proportions. When it becomes apparent that he is to be the main course for a native feast, he fortifies himself with spinach and escapes. However he cannot convince a juvenile cannibal that Popeye on rye should not become a national dish.

Review: *Motion Picture Herald,* **12 May 1951**

Popeye sights land, disembarks from his raft and enters a cafe. He orders a meal, which the manager is glad to give him as he is a cannibal chief. Later Popeye finds himself being cooked for dinner but with the aid of his can of spinach, escapes. (6 min)

Review: *Motion Picture Exhibitor,* **5 May 1945**

Sailor Popeye is marooned on an island where cannibals still get their meat where they can find it without red points. He is welcomed, and since he is a bit on the thin side, his hosts stuff him until he is fat. Next a nice hot bath which turns out to be a cooking pot, is in order, but, when Popeye discovers what's cooking, he digs up his last can of spinach, and takes over as King of the isle. Good.

POPEYE'S PAPPY (1952)

Company: Seymour Kneitel, Famous Studios, King Features Syndicate, Paramount Pictures
Characters: Popeye, Pappy, black cannibals

Story: The cartoon opens at the seashore, where a small boat, SS Popeye, is tied to the dock. Popeye walks into the scene carrying his knapsack and listening to his tearful mother saying, "And son, when you were a young infant, your pappy went to buy you some spinach. He never returned." Popeye puts his arm around her and says, "Don't worry, I'll finds me pop. Or I ain't Popeye." He holds up a picture of his pappy's smiling face as a young man with a black beard. The face in the picture dissolves and reappears as an older Pappy with a gray beard. He is sitting on a throne with a king's crown on his head. He is smiling as he smokes his pipe while two beautiful, brown-skinned servant girls wearing grass skirts stand on each side of him and fan him with palm leaves. A long red carpet leads to the throne. On each side of the carpet black cannibals kneel on ground, chanting in unison, "King-pop rag-mop be-bop." Meanwhile Popeye, in his boat, is nearing the island when he looks through his spyglass and says, "Well blow me down! Pappy! He sees Pappy being served coconut juice by one of the native girls. Suddenly Pappy is interrupted by the sound of a voice saying, "Pappy, Pappy." Arriving on the scene, Popeye lifts Pappy off his throne and says, "I'm your son—Popeye." But Pappy says, "I hate relatives. Scram, you swab." Popeye says, "I'm taking ya home to Mom." Pappy kicks him away, saying, "Shove off!" But Popeye grabs him and throws him over his shoulder. "I says I'm taking you home." As he carries him off, the angry Pappy shouts, "Blast ya! Put me down! Ya ugly-lookin' brat!" As they walk past a python lying coiled on the ground, Pappy reaches

down and grabs the snake's tail. They walk behind a rock, and when they reappear Popeye is carrying the coiled-up python on his back instead of pappy. The snake coils itself around Popeye who says, "No snake can sneak up on me." Then he blows hot flames from his pipe into the open mouth of the snake. The flames travel the length of the snake's body and blow out through its tail. The snake drops off Popeye, and he sees Pappy sitting on his throne eating a banana. Popeye sneaks behind him, lifts up the throne, and carries it on his back. Pappy hangs on the throne and kicks Popeye with his feet. Popeye is knocked through the air and lands inside the mouth of a huge alligator resting in a shallow pond. The alligator slams its mouth shut, trapping Popeye. But Popeye delivers a tremendous blow to the inside of the alligator's mouth. It flies through the air and crashes into a tree before breaking up into several pieces of luggage. Popeye punches his way out of one of the bags and sees his Pappy entertaining himself by playing a ukulele. Native girls dance in front of him as he sings, "Oh how I love this life. Who needs a wife? Girls by the score, who should ask for more." Popeye disguises himself as a shapely dancing girl and joins the other girls. Noticing the new "girl," Pappy likes what he sees and says, "Say, you're new around here." Pappy follows Popeye back to the ship, but along the way Popeye's dress is ripped off when it gets snagged on the branch of a tree. Pappy discovers the trick and kicks Popeye through the air before heading back to his throne. But Popeye snags him on the end of a spear and carries him off again. Pappy blows his pipe, and the sound summons the angry band of cannibals. The chief, who has a sergeant's insignia tattooed on his arm, shouts, "Ungo bogo bop save king pop" as they all run off carrying spears. They all throw their spears, which fly through the air and pin Popeye to the side of a wall. The cannibals throw Popeye into a large cooking pot sitting on a fire. The cannibal cook carries a basket filled with carrots on his head and is followed by a pygmy cannibal carrying a huge basket of potatoes on his head. They dump the vegetables on the head of Popeye, who says, "Oh, these guys must be cookin' up somethin'." Meanwhile Pappy, sitting on his throne, observes the happenings. He has second thoughts and says, "Holy gosh! Me own flesh and blood" as he sees a vision of baby Popeye in his arms. Meanwhile the cannibal cook adds salt to the stew, and uses an outboard motor to stir the pot. This scene is too much for Pappy. He slams his fist on his throne and says, "That's all I can stand, I can't stand this no more." Then he runs off to rescue his son. Pappy arrives on the scene and jumps on the cannibal cook, shouting "release my baby" as he hits the cook in the face. The cook throws Pappy through the air, and he slams into a tree. Picking himself up, Pappy sees a can of spinach inside a fire-alarm box. Pappy breaks the glass with an ax, opens the can, and eats some of the spinach. It gives him super strength, and he grabs a vine and swings through the air, shouting like Tarzan. He grabs the pot off the fire and swings through the air and lands on the beach. He lifts Popeye, who has a rope wrapped around his body, out of the pot, saying, "My son." But the angry cannibals arrive on the scene. Pappy uses the pot like a bowling ball and knocks over the cannibals, but others quickly arrive. Pappy gives Popeye the rest of the spinach. Popeye eats it and uses his extra strength to snap his bonds. The cannibals throw waves of spears, but Popeye and Pappy knock him back and they get stuck in a line on the wooden wall. As the cannibals attack, Popeye and Pappy knock them through the air and the unconscious cannibals wind up hanging on their own spears. As they depart the island, Pappy hangs a sign, Cheaper by the Dozen, on the cannibals. As they sail away, Pappy stands in the boat with his arms around Popeye and sings, "I am very happy that I'm your pappy." Popeye joins in and together they sing, "I'm Popeye the sailor man." They both toot their pipes as the cartoon ends.

Review: *Exhibitor Servisection,* 13 February 1952

Popeye goes off in search of his long missing father, and finds him entrenched on a tropical island and where, surrounded by beautiful dancing girls and an easy carefree life, he refuses to go back with Popeye. Determined to bring his pappy back, Popeye uses force, but the cannibalistic natives take a hand, and Popeye finds himself stewing in a pot. The sight of this brings out Pappy's love, and with father and son filled with potent spinach they quickly mop up the natives, and sail for home. Good. (7 min)

Review: *Boxoffice,* 29 March 1952

Popeye's theme song in this zippy zany cartoon is "Father, Dear Father, Come Home With Me Now." Father refuses to leave his tropical island paradise, but changes his mind when cannibalistic natives capture Popeye—who promptly gets into a stew pot. After rescuing his son from the dinner cauldron, Pappy, realizing that blood is thicker than coconut milk, agrees to accompany Popeye and go home to Ma. Technicolor.

PORKY'S ANT (1941)

Company: Charles Jones, Warner Bros.
Type: Looney Tunes
Characters: Porky Pig, black African pygmy, pygmy ant

Story: The cartoon opens as Porky Pig is on an African safari. He walks along a jungle trail reading a book about rare bugs while a pygmy native walks behind him carrying a huge pile of supply boxes on his head. The African has thick white lips, wears a long skirt, and has a huge bone in the hair on his head. Porky is looking at a page of the book that reads, "Pygmy ant of central Africa. Extremely rare. One specimen valued at approximately one hundred thousand dollars ($100,000)." There is a picture of the rare pygmy ant who wears an African costume. Meanwhile a live pygmy ant pops up out of the bushes and begins to follow the pair. The ant wears a small bone in the hair of its head and admires the big bone in the black African's hair. The African turns around and is so surprised to see the ant that he walks into Porky, who has stopped in front of him and is bending down to look for tracks on the ground. The African crashes into Porky and sends the pile of boxes down, burying

both of them. When Porky digs himself out of the pile, he sees the ant and starts to chase after him. He tries unsuccessfully to trap him using a piece of candy placed on the ground behind a sheet of sticky flypaper. But the ant jumps over the flypaper, grabs the candy, and escapes. Porky is so frustrated that he throws the sheet of flypaper into the air. It comes down on the face of the African. The angry African pulls the paper from his face as Porky sees the ant run and hide behind a bush. He chases after him, running over the African who gets the flypaper stuck on his face again. Porky reaches under a bush to grab the ant but pulls his hand back when he feels the claws of a sleeping lion. Porky makes several attempts to capture the ant without waking up the lion but fails. Eventually the lion wakes up and walks away, and the ant runs away while Porky chases him. Meanwhile the African manages to lift the flypaper from his face and is surprised to find himself face-to-face with the angry lion. He drops the paper on his face and blindly runs away, chased by the lion. He runs into Porky, who is looking behind a rock for the ant. The flypaper falls off the African's face, and they both run and hide as the lion arrives on the scene. But the brave ant is not afraid and places the flypaper on ground. When the lion runs over it, the paper sticks to his paws and causes him to tumble over the ground and crash into a tree, knocking him senseless. Porky is so grateful that he says, "G-G-G-olly. Thanks. You've saved our lives. Is there anything I can do to repay you? Anything?" The ant nods his head yes. The next scene shows the little ant walking behind Porky and the African. The ant has a big smile on its face. Tied to the hair on its head is the African's big bone as the cartoon ends.

PROFESSOR BONEHEAD IS SHIPWRECKED (1917)

Company: Emil Cohl (Paris), released in U.S.A. by Gaumont American, Mutual Film Exchange
Characters: Professor Bonehead, black cannibals, black bear

Story: The cartoon opens as a bottle of black ink tips over and the cap comes off. The spilled ink materializes into Professor Bonehead, a partially bald man who wears glasses. The scene changes to a windswept ocean. Bonehead is riding the waves seated at a dinner table that sits on a small raft. Aboard is an insect net that Bonehead plans to use to catch rare insects. A large wave upsets the raft, and Bonehead is tossed into the ocean and narrowly escapes being swallowed by a huge whale. He surfaces, spits water out of his mouth, and then discovers a huge egg. He climbs on top of it and floats to the beach of an island. He carries the egg from the beach to a small coconut tree where he sets it on the ground and is puzzled what to do next. Suddenly the egg begins to shake. It breaks open and a strange-looking creature that has the body and face of white man, but the bill of a goose for a nose, walks out. Bonehead tries to run away, but the creature follows him. Bonehead dives over a sand dune and into a huge cooking pot sitting on a fire. Seated around the cooking pot are four fat black cannibals. They have big thick lips and are naked except for short grass skirts around their waists. At first the cannibals look sad, but then surprised when they see the white man fall into the pot. They finally smile after they look into the pot and see their dinner. But Bonehead leaps out of the pot. His body turns into a kind of wheel, and he rolls away followed by the angry cannibals who carry spears. Bonehead rolls down the steep side of a canyon, rolls through the river below, and then rolls up the wall on the other side of the canyon. The cannibals fall into the canyon, and only one of them manages to climb up the other side to continue chasing Bonehead. Bonehead climbs to the top of a coconut tree and throws down a coconut that hits the cannibal on the head and knocks him out cold. As the cannibal lies on the ground, Bonehead climbs down from the tree to the ground where he decides to take a nap sitting next to the cannibal. A huge black bear arrives on the scene and licks the sleeping Bonehead's face. Bonehead wakes up and makes a hasty retreat, followed by the bear. Bonehead slides into a hollow log, and the bear follows him. The log rolls downhill, bounces into the air, and tips on its end. The log comes down over the head of the strange creature before coming to rest at the bottom of the hill. The creature and the bear come out at one end of the log, and Bonehead sticks his head out the other end. The bear runs back up the hill, and Bonehead says, "If we had some wheels, we'd have an automobile." The creature says, "That's easy." Immediately four automobile wheels roll down the hill and attach themselves to the log. With Bonehead sticking his head out the front end and the creature steering the car from on top, they drive back up the hill as the cartoon ends.

THE PYGMY HUNT (1938)

Company: I. Freleng, M-G-M
Characters: The captain, the inspector, black pygmy

See fig. 34. Story: The cartoon opens showing a map of Africa. On the map is traced the trail of a safari that ends in pygmy country. The next scene shows a campsite in the jungle. There is a large van with the words "African Expedition—I Bring 'Em Back Alive" painted on its side. The captain is seen preparing to go out and hunt a pygmy. Nearby there are cages containing a lion, an elephant, and a hyena. The captain picks up his gun and calls to the inspector, an old man who has a long white beard and wears a top hat. He is holding one end of a chain, the other end of which is tied to the captain's hound dog. Hearing the sound of the captain's voice, the dog runs off and drags the inspector behind him. The three begin the pygmy hunt with the dog leading the way as he sniffs the ground. The dog picks up a scent and runs off. The captain and the inspector follow only to find out that the dog has found a flower, not a pygmy. The captain tells the inspector, "Der dumb ox. He doesn't know a pygmy from a petunia." The hound picks up the trail again and sees footprints made by a little pygmy walking along carrying a spear and wearing a bone in the hair on his head. The

hound catches the pygmy and chews the bone on his head. The angry little pygmy pulls his bone out of the dog's mouth, kicks the dog out of sight, and continues on his way. But the dog follows and catches him again. The dog carries the bone in his mouth while dragging the pygmy to a spot where he digs a hole and attempts to bury the bone and the pygmy. Meanwhile the captain and the inspector catch sight of the dog before he has finished burying the bone. The captain says to the inspector, "Look! Der pooch, he got a pygmy." The captain calls out to his dog, "Hold on, we're coming," as he and the inspector run off in the direction of the dog. But the hound sees them coming and takes off in the opposite direction. The captain tells the dog, "Drop him, I say." The dog obeys him and drops the pygmy. While waiting for the captain and the inspector to arrive on the scene, the pygmy sneaks away. They all chase him. The captain manages to catch the pygmy, but the little native overpowers the captain and tosses him high into the air. The captain falls and hits the ground with such impact that trees are knocked down, several falling on the hound and the inspector. The chase is on again as the pygmy runs off followed by the hound, the inspector, and the captain. The pygmy runs to his hut and hides inside. The dog manages to get in before the door is locked. The captain bangs on the door, and out walks the pygmy, dragging the dog by the tail. He slams the dog on the ground and runs back into the hut, locking the door after him. The dog decides to tunnel under the door and succeeds. But when he reaches the inside of the hut, the pygmy hits him on the head, and the dog makes a hasty retreat. The captain and the inspector decide to use a large tree trunk as a battering ram to knock down the door. They each grab one end of the log and are about to charge the door when they find that the pygmy is sitting on the log. The pygmy runs back into his hut, and the hound decides to try to the tunnel trick again. But this time he wears a teapot on his head as a hard hat. He manages to tunnel into the hut again, but this time the pygmy removes the top of the teapot before hitting the dog on the head with a skillet. The dog again runs off, and the captain and the inspector decide to trick the pygmy into leaving his hut. The captain announces in a loud voice that they are leaving, but he hides by the front door and the inspector goes around to the back door. Loud sounds come from the hut, and when the door opens, the captain sees a figure wearing the inspector's coat and hat walk out. The captain is puzzled, but as the figure walks away, a tree branch knocks off his hat, revealing that it is the pygmy, not the inspector. Meanwhile the inspector comes out of the hut wearing the pygmy's grass skirt and a bone in his hair. The pygmy jumps out of the inspector's clothes and runs away with the hound chasing him. The hound and the Pygmy run out of sight, but soon the hound runs back with cans tied to his tail. Behind him is an angry tribe of pygmies carrying spears. The dog, the captain, and the inspector run to their van and speed off, with the pygmies in hot pursuit. The inspector and the hound stand on the back of the van and watch the pygmies, who are being left behind. The inspector removes his hat to wipe his brow, and the dog sees that he still has the pygmy bone in his hair. The dog jumps on the inspector and takes the bone from him and is seen holding it in his mouth as the cartoon ends.

Review: *Motion Picture Exhibitor*, 1 September 1938

Not up to standard of other Metro shorts, this can only earn a fair rating. The Captain, Inspector, dog go after pygmies, find plenty, ending with a chase. Fair.

PYGMY TROUBLE (1939)

Company: Alex Lovey, Walter Lantz, Universal Pictures
Type: First of Andy Panda series, Also released as *Life Begins For Andy Panda*
Characters: Andy Panda, his father, black pygmies

Story: The cartoon opens in the forest where a bluebird, perched on the limb of a tree, speaks into a microphone and announces that the giant pandas have been blessed with a bundle of joy early that morning—a baby boy. All of the animals hear the announcement over the Finchell Broadcasting Radio Station. The news spreads rapidly, and soon all of the animals hurry to visit the new arrival in the Panda family. Bringing up the rear is a black turtle who has a voice like Andy of the *Amos 'n' Andy* radio show. The animals suggest a name for the baby, but the parents name him Andy. Time passes, and Andy is a young panda of six years. His father decides to take him for a walk in the forest to teach him all about Mother Nature. As they walk along, Andy pulls out his slingshot and fires a shot into a hole in a tree trunk. This angers his father. He takes the slingshot from Andy just as a squirrel emerges from the hole rubbing a big lump on his head. The squirrel kicks Andy's father on his leg because it assumes that he fired the shot. As Andy and his father continue their walk, Andy goes ahead of him and is about to walk out of the forest. His father quickly runs after him and warns him never to leave the forest or he will be captured by animal hunters. They will take him away and he will appear in newsreels. As his father runs after him, he is caught in a panda trap. The sign on the trap reads, "You have been captured by the pygmy panda hunters." Andy tries to free him, but a group of fierce-looking black pygmies show up on the scene. The pygmies ignore Andy's father and run after little Andy. The news is flashed over the radio by the announcer, "Emergency! The pygmies are after Andy." Upon hearing the news, all of Andy's animal friends rush to the rescue, including the slow-walking and slow-talking turtle. One pygmy is about to grab Andy, but the turtle shows up and allows Andy to hide in its shell. While the pygmy looks for Andy, the little panda rises partly out of the shell and shoots the pygmy with his slingshot. The pygmy is so angry that he kicks the turtle and knocks Andy out from under the shell. The pygmy then jumps into the shell and fights the turtle. The turtle wins the fight and tosses the pygmy out of his shell. The turtle is about to run away when another pygmy jumps into its shell. This time it is the turtle who is tossed out of the shell. The turtle runs after the pygmy in an effort to retrieve his shell. Meanwhile Andy is

running away from another pygmy. Andy cries out, "Help! Pygmies have daddy!" His mother hears his cries for help and runs out of the house carrying her frying pan in her hands. She arrives on the scene and quickly dispatches a group of pygmies who are threatening little Andy. Andy runs off, chased by another pygmy. A kangaroo sees Andy and allows him to jump into her pouch and hide. The kangaroo grabs the pygmy by his hair and holds him while Andy punches him in his face. Two more pygmies arrive. One grabs a plank of wood and smacks the kangaroo on its rear end so hard that the blow knocks Andy out of the pouch. Andy is on the run again. Andy runs into a cave that is the home of a skunk. He pulls the skunk out and uses it to shield himself from the pygmies. The skunk lifts his tail, and the scent chases the pygmies away. Then the animals cheer Andy for saving his father. His father is so grateful that he tells Andy that he can have anything he wants. Andy replies that he wants to be in the newsreel movies. This reply angers his father, and he grabs Andy to spank him. But he changes his mind and hugs him instead. Meanwhile the turtle is still chasing the pygmy who took its shell as the cartoon ends.

ROBINSON CRUSOE (1933)

Company: Frank Moser, Paul Terry, Educational Pictures
Type: Terrytoons
Characters: Farmer Al Falfa, black cannibals

Story: The cartoon opens with Farmer Al Falfa and his pet parrot in a small boat being tossed about by waves on a windswept sea. A huge octopus swims under the boat and lifts it out of the water on his head. The wise farmer decides to take advantage of the situation and grabs the boat's mast and uses it to hook the octopus. He lifts the octopus out of the sea and spreads its body out like a huge sail. The wind catches the makeshift octopus sail, and their speed increases. Finally the wind increases so much that it lifts the boat out of the water. The body of the octopus begins to spin like the blades of a large helicopter, and they are propelled to the shores of an island where they land on the beach. Meanwhile a black native with big thick lips plays a banjo and sings to a group of dancing animals. The native sings, "Friday's my name, and I'm plenty free—no one to bother me." He rolls his eyes to the music and then smiles, revealing his white teeth. Meanwhile the farmer is strolling along the beach carrying his rifle on his shoulder with the parrot perched on the barrel of the gun. They are unaware that they are being trailed by huge, hungry alligators swimming in the sea next to the shore. Suddenly one of the alligators crawls out of the water and attacks the farmer, who kills it with one shot from his rifle. Continuing on their way, they discover footprints in the sand and decide to follow them. The tracks lead them to a hole in the sand. When the farmer stops to look down into the hole, he is attacked by a lion that arrives on the scene. The lion wants to look in the hole and pushes the farmer away. They get into a fight. The farmer pulls out his gun, but the barrel is bent into a U shape. The lion sees this and pushes the farmer backward. The parrot grabs the gun and fires at the lion, but the bullet goes backward and hits the farmer. The scene shifts to a large coconut tree where a native lookout is sitting. The native sees the farmer and signals his cannibal tribe that food is on the way. The chief calls his tribe around him and sends out the command, "Calling all cars." Car 23 shows up and speeds off toward the place where the farmer was seen with a group of angry cannibals carrying spears following him. They find the farmer, tie his hands, blindfold him, and lead him back to the village. When they arrive, a white lady is seen being held in a bamboo cage. They lead the farmer to the chief, who sees him and proclaims him to be Robinson Crusoe. They untie the farmer's hands and remove his blindfold and release the white lady. The last scene shows everybody having a grand time singing and dancing. Everybody is happy in Zululand.

ROBINSON CRUSOE ISLE (1935)

Company: Walter Lantz, Universal Pictures
Characters: Oswald the rabbit, black cannibals, Robinson Crusoe

Review: *Boxoffice*, 12 January 1935

Packs of originality in this cartoon. Oswald is washed ashore with his radio. Robinson Crusoe hires him for his Man Friday, the 13th; the other 12 having been eaten by cannibals. What Oswald and his radio do to the cannibals when they come after him is mighty amusing. Before the reel ends, the goat that swallowed the radio is sitting on the Chief's throne and Oswald is giving orders on the island. There is a catchy vocal score, too. (9 min)

Review: *Film Daily*, 4 February 1935

Crusoe wants another Good Man Friday, so Oswald applies. Cannibals make it difficult on the Island. Luckily, Oswald's goat swallows his radio, and the cannibals are so fascinated by the rhythm that they honor the goat with the throne of their chief. Music is catchy. Tale is simple enough for the smallest tot.

Review: *Motion Picture Herald*, 2 February 1935

An entertaining Oswald cartoon, in which our hero, cast upon Crusoe's isle, becomes his Man Friday, the predecessors having ended in a savage soup pot. He is enjoying life with his radio, when his goat swallows it. When the savages start to boil Oswald and the goat, the radio goes into the action, and Oswald is supreme on the cannibal isle.

Review: *Selected Motion Pictures*, 1 February 1935

Oswald cartoon. Oswald plays the part of Friday (the 13th) when he is shipwrecked on Robinson Crusoe's Island. Very amusing. Family and Junior Matinee.

ROBINSON CRUSOE JR. (1941)

Company: Norman McCabe, Warner Bros.
Type: Looney Tunes

Characters: Porky Pig, his Man Friday, Friday's family, black cannibals

Story: The cartoon opens as passenger Porky stands waiting on the deck of a ship while cargo is loaded in preparation for a long voyage. A call is heard, "All ashore, going ashore." All the mice on board pack their belongings and hurriedly leave the ship except one couple. The mouse tells his baby, "Come on, Snooks. We got to get off." Snooks asks him why, and he says, "The ship will sink." Porky overhears this remark and says to himself, "What do mice know anyway?" The ship sails out of the dock and the voyage gets under way. Weeks later Porky reads a sign nailed to the planking on the ship: This Ship Is Guaranteed. He says to himself, "I wonder if the guarantee is good for a hurricane." Almost immediately the ship is hit by a major storm. A huge wave carries it to an island, and it crashes on the beach. Porky is greeted by Friday, a black native with thick white lips who is wearing a black stovepipe hat. Friday carries a sign reading Welcome Robinson Crusoe, and he says to Porky, "Hello, Boss. What kept ya?" In a short time Porky and Friday have constructed a treehouse with all the comforts of home, including an elevator. Friday is Porky's servant and cleans house before making hot coffee while singing "Java Jive" (a takeoff on a hit song by the Ink Spots quartet). The song is so catchy that many jungle animals, including three elephants and a turtle, dance to the rhythmic beat of the music. Meanwhile Porky reasons that since Monday is Friday's day to wash, he will explore the island. He puts on his safari hat, grabs his hunting gun, and leaves the house via the elevator. Soon he is walking through the jungle. On his way he encounters a parrot and asks the bird, "Polly want a cracker?" The bird replies, "I'm waiting for the sixty-four-dollar question." Next Porky spots a group of wild animals at a waterhole. He approaches, they scatter, and it is revealed that they were drinking from an office watercooler. Next Porky sees monkeys playing. One monkey tries in vain to climb a tree on which a sign, Slippery Elm, is posted. Resuming his exploration, Porky sees human footprints in the soil and decides to follow them. They lead him to the entrance of a cave. Summoning all of his courage, he enters the cave. Soon he comes running out, followed by a group of bloodthirsty black cannibals carrying spears and yelling. The cannibals chase Porky in the direction of his tree house. From the porch of the tree house Friday sees Porky running for his life just ahead of the cannibals. Friday posts a For Sale sign on the house and makes a hasty departure. Porky manages to reach the seashore ahead of the cannibals. There he uses his ax to chop a log into a boat, complete with a motor. Friday arrives, and they both jump in the boat and sail away a few seconds before the cannibal tribe arrives on the scene. Standing on the beach, the frustrated cannibals hurl their spears at Porky and Friday. Porky raises a large American flag at the stern of the boat, and the spears stop in midair before falling into the water. Porky and Friday smile, and Friday waves a *V* for victory banner in the air as the cartoon ends.

Review: *Motion Picture Herald,* **15 Novembers 1941**

Porky Pig in this Looney Tune cartoon portrays the character of Robinson Crusoe in a travesty on the familiar old classic. (10 min)

Review: *Film Daily,* **31 October 1941**

As the title suggests, Porky Pig is cast away on a desert island with only his friend Friday to help. Cartoon is a series of gags which register in varying degrees of humor. Porky Pig's adventures are climaxed when a group of savages chase him.

Review: *Motion Picture Exhibitor,* **12 November 1941**

Porky enacts a burlesque of the Robinson Crusoe story. Gags and laughs are plentiful and good for an above-average subject. High spot comes when Porky and man Friday, escaping from the savages by a speed boat, turn away the onrushing spears by displaying the American flag on their ship. Good.

ROBINSON CRUSOE'S BROADCAST (1938)

Company: John Foster, Paul Terry, Educational Pictures
Type: Terrytoons
Characters: Farmer Al Falfa as Robinson Crusoe, Friday his
            black servant, black cannibals

Story: The cartoon opens as Robinson Crusoe is in the studio of a radio station telling the story of his adventures as a sea captain. The scene shifts to a small boat where Crusoe and his pets, a parrot and a cat, are being tossed about on the crests of huge waves on a stormy sea. As the boat begins to sink, Crusoe and friends climb to the top of the mast. After the boat sinks, they find themselves swimming in the ocean. By chance a raft carrying an animal floats nearby. They all climb aboard and throw the animal overboard. Later they are cast upon the shore of a desert island where they build a hut that promptly falls apart, leaving only the door standing. Crusoe next decides to build a raft, and they begin to chop down a huge tree. But the work is interrupted by a fierce storm that rains buckets of water. They run back to the remains of the hut and crawl under the logs to get out of the rain and find some sleep. The following morning finds Crusoe and his animal friends exploring the beach. They come upon footprints in the soil and decide to follow them. They are led to a black native who is literally combing the beach with a comb. Crusoe says, "There's something fishy about this fellow" so he decides to name him Friday. Friday gives Crusoe his comb, and they both begin to comb the beach, uncovering a two-wheel push cart. Friday says, "Ain't dat something'." Crusoe climbs on the cart and Friday begins to push it. As Friday pushes, a large ape sneaks up behind him. When Friday turns his head and sees the ape, he makes a hasty retreat, leaving Crusoe behind. The ape replaces Friday behind the cart and pushes it all the way up a tree, where he dumps out Crusoe. A monkey grabs Crusoe and swings him from limb to limb before he manages to escape and find his way back home. He is shocked to find his home occupied by black cannibals.

The cannibal chief tells Crusoe, "Mr Crusoe, the boys would like to have you for dinner." Crusoe replies, "I am flattered to have the invitation." Meanwhile at the village a group of cannibals are pouring water into a huge black cooking pot sitting on a fire. Crusoe and the other cannibals arrive on the scene, and the chief asks Crusoe, "How much meat is required to serve all these people?" Crusoe answers, "About 176 pounds." The chief says, "That's right. And how much do you weigh?" Before Crusoe can answer, the dinner bell rings. The chief picks up Crusoe and carriers him in his arms to the cooking pot, followed by the other cannibals. The chief stands Crusoe on a platform hanging over the pot and Crusoe, still believing that he is the guest of honor, makes a brief speech. After he concludes his remarks to the cannibals, they dump him into the pot. Finally he realizes that is the dinner. Every time Crusoe tries to climb out of the pot, the cannibals push him back down in the boiling water. The scene changes back to the radio station where Crusoe is concluding his story. The announcer asks Crusoe, "What did you do?" Crusoe answers, "What could I do? They ate me." He kicks the announcer in his rear end as the cartoon ends.

Review: *Motion Picture Herald,* **23 April 1938**

A Terry-Toon, this is a burlesque on the Robinson Crusoe radio broadcasts. Crusoe as pictured here is a tough Irish seafaring man with a decided accent who describes how his ship sailed from Plymouth, upside down, around the world and after all hands, but a parrot and himself, were lost in a storm they found land where a cannibal tribe drops him into the cooking pot. When questioned by the radio announcer as to what happened then the Crusoe character replies "they ate me of course." (6 1/2 min)

Review: *Film Daily,* **21 April 1938**

A small novelty cartoon with plenty of laughs. A radio station presents Robinson Crusoe, a tough old salt, to tell his adventures. Crusoe speaks throughout in a rich Irish brogue, and his comments are as funny as the action, The tough Irish sailor is seen being washed ashore after the vessel is wrecked on the desert island. The vessel has sailed upside down around the world.

Review: *Boxoffice,* **23 April 1938**

Audiences will be quick to spot the clever dialogue and original business that has gone into this cartoon. In flashback, a weather-beaten Irishman is telling a radio audience about his seafaring days. His experiences have received the full range of an imaginative artist's stuff. In and around his various escapades with storms, beach-combers, cannibal conventions, etc, there is a wealth of humorous gags, admirably timed.

Review: *Selected Motion Pictures,* **1 May 1938**

Terry-toon cartoon. An excellent cartoon is which Robinson Crusoe gives an illustrated lecture over the air relating his adventures on sea and land. Family and Junior Matinee.

Review: *Motion Picture Exhibitor,* 1 May 1938

Crusoe, in a voice reminiscent of Captain Bob Morrissey's, relates on a broadcast his adventures on the desert island. On the island, he overcomes the climate, the hardships; wins Friday as a servant; but is finally chucked into a boiling pot by some savages who invited him to dinner. There are some farcical touches here, indicative of the improvement lately in these cartoons. Adults, as well as kids, will like it. Good.

SPEAKING OF THE WEATHER (1937)

Company: Frank Tashlin, Warner Bros.
Type: Merrie Melodies
Characters: Popular radio and screen stars of the day, black
            cannibals

Story: There is not much plot to this cartoon, which opens at night with the skyline of a large city. The hands on a large clock tower show midnight. Inside the Rx Drugstore the characters depicted on magazine covers come to life. These include Ed Wynn, Bob Burns, Ted Lewis, Leopold Stokowski, Charlie Chan, William Powell, and Walter Winchell. A band of angry black cannibals chase an escaping criminal near the end of the cartoon.

Review: *Motion Picture Herald,* 21 August 1937

This probably will be acclaimed as one of the finest jobs yet accomplished in the animated cartoon field. It will richly deserve this distinction for it is vastly entertaining and the product of a most fertile mind. All the action takes place in a magazine store, after hours. The magazine comes to life, and the result is decidedly pleasing to watch. It is in color. (7 min)

Review: *Motion Picture Herald,* 30 June 1945

The locale of this cartoon is a stationery store where racks of popular magazines take on individual personalities. The villain is a gangster from the cover of detective magazine who tries to rob a safe in full view of the other live reading matter. While he makes his getaway, the others join forces to track him down. (7 min)

Review: *Selected Motion Pictures,* 1 November 1937

Characters on magazine covers come to life and present a vaudeville show in a novel way. The title song is one of a group furnishing the musical continuity. Family.

Review: *Motion Picture Exhibitor,* 15 August 1937

The pictures on the covers come to life. The Thug on the gang magazine cover robs the bank on "Wall Street Magazine," is jailed on "Life," breaks jail from "Liberty," is pursued and captured by a mob of characters from other magazines. The ideas are funny, the color excellent, the pace fast. The take-offs on some popular characters are hilarious. Excellent.

SWING MONKEY SWING (1937)

Company: Manny Gould, Columbia Pictures

Type: Color Rhapsody
Characters: Monkeys, black choral group (offcamera)

Review: *Motion Picture Herald,* 2 October 1937

A "Color Rhapsody" invasion of monkeyland and the infusion of swing music arouses the jungle inhabitants to outdo each other in rhythmic dances in this cartoon. The prolific monkeys are adept at playing all instruments. In the background a chorus of negro voices sing a new arrangement of the "St. Louis Blues." (7 1/2 min)

Review: *Boxoffice,* 23 October 1937

A group of monkeys get swing and cavort around on an island to the accompaniment of a jazz band. A feature is a new arrangement of "St. Louis Blues" sung by a group of colored voices. A wild dance in which the trees, ocean and jungle inhabitants catch "swing" fever and join in brings the festivities to a close. Below average and contains little audience appeal.

Review: *Motion Picture Herald,* 19 December 1948

Swing hits monkey-land in this one-reel Technicolor short. The "Saint Louis Blues" form the background for the sopranos and the chorus.

Review: *Boxoffice,* 3 November 1948

Monkeyland specializes in swing music in this melodious Technicolor short. The monkeys go in for orchestrations, choruses and dancing to the tune of "St. Louis" rendering many variations on the always popular song. It is well done and the work of the musicians is excellent. A sure audience pleaser.

Review: *National Exhibitor,* 1 October 1937

A summary of what happens when swing comes to monkeyland allowing free play for good color, draftsmanship, and some ingenious ideas. No real laughs here but on the whole enough for most. Good.

TEA FOR TWO HUNDRED (1948)

Company: Jack Hannah, Walt Disney, RKO-Radio Pictures
Type: Shown 1 January 1997, on Disney Cable Channel, from 1950s Disneyland TV series narrated by Walt Disney. Nominated for Academy Award
Characters: Donald Duck, black pygmy ants

Story: The cartoon opens to somewhere in Africa, where Donald Duck is camping near the rim of a canyon surrounded by tall cliffs. There is a river far below. His tent is in a clearing surrounded by trees. Donald comes out of the tent wearing a safari hat on his head and carrying a coffee pot in one hand and a cup in the other. He says, "Oh boy, oh boy, oh boy. Hot stuff" as he sits down on a sheet on the ground to have a cup of coffee. Meanwhile a long line of black pygmy ants marches from a nearby bush, each carrying a large bean on its head. They all wear rings around their necks, and the chief who leads them wears a bone on its head. The chief

... He turns to

suddenly orders them to stop and stand at attention. He turns to an ant with a Stephin Fetchit demeanor and shouts at him in gibberish because he is not carrying anything on his head. The Stephin Fetchit ant bows his head and gives a slow-talking reply. Then the chief orders the others to resume the march. Donald sees them as they pass by and decides to have some fun with the smallest ant, which is bringing up the rear. First he tries to stop the ant by pushing down on the bean that it is carrying on its back. When this fails, he piles more and more food, including a banana, a can of soup, a sandwich, a link of sausage, and a cup of coffee. But the little ant continues to walk, even carrying all of these items on its back. Next Donald places a large wooden box in the ant's path, but the ant climbs to the top of the box still carrying its load. The little ant walks with its head down and does not see that Donald is playing tricks on it. Next Donald manages to stick a pole in a hole in the box and ties a string to one end of the pole and holds the other end of the string in his hand. The little ant marches up the pole and across the string. Donald pulls the string, causing it to vibrate, and the ant loses its balance. Its load falls to the ground, and the ant lands in the middle of a huge custard pie. When it pokes its head out of the pie, it looks up and sees Donald laughing. Donald says, "What's the matter, big boy, stuck up?" This makes the ant angry, and it jumps out of the pie to the ground. Then it licks the custard off its face and suddenly realizes that it is surrounded by food. It rushes off to tell the others, who are carrying the beans into the anthill. It finally gets their attention, and another ant beats out a drum message on the tops of several toadstools. The drumbeat summons hundreds of black ants from the surrounding anthills. The ant army returns to Donald's campsite, where the ants tie up the sleeping Donald and carry him on their backs to the edge of the canyon and push him off. Donald falls into the river below and wakes up angry. When Donald arrives back at this camp, he sees his food being carried into the anthill. He makes several unsuccessful attempts to stop them and finally reaches into the anthill to grab his food. But the ants pull off his clothes. Donald puts a barrel over his head and then stuffs many sticks of dynamite into the anthill. The dynamite produces a huge explosion, and Donald laughs. But the blast has cracked the edge of the cliff on which Donald is standing. It breaks off, carrying Donald to the bottom and into the river again. But the ants are not killed by the explosion and return to the camp to take the last of the food, a cake topped with white icing and a big red cherry. The ants quickly devour the cake from the bottom up, as the smiling little black ant sits on top eating the cherry as the cartoon ends.

TEE TIME (1930)

Company: Pat Sullivan, Jacques Kopfstein, released by M. J. Winkler, Pathe Film Exchange, and later released in 16mm format by Copley Pictures with sound track added
Characters: Felix the Cat, black cannibals

See fig. 35. Story: The cartoon opens with Felix practicing the piano. He is an unwilling pupil and dreams of playing golf while his father in the next room urges him to continue to play. Felix gets an idea on how to skip practice. He captures a pair of grasshoppers and puts one each in a pair of gloves. They make music as they hop up and down on the piano keys. Felix is pleased with himself, and his father is happy too because he believes that Felix's playing is improving. Felix arrives at the golf course, where his caddy, a mouse, waits for him with his golf bag and clubs. Felix tees off. His first shot flies through the air, and the ball hits the ground and rolls before coming to rest on the nose of a sleeping policeman. Felix tees off the nose of the policeman, and the ball lands on a gong where it get stuck. Each time Felix tries to hit the ball, he hits the gong, which happens to be the town's fire alarm. The firemen arrive on the scene but are angry when they see that it is a false alarm. They turn their water hose on Felix, and the jet of water propels him across the ocean to a cannibal island where he lands on top of a drum. As Felix bounces up and down on the drum, the beat is heard by a black cannibal who carries a spear in his hand and wears a grass skirt. The cannibal sounds the alarm, and soon the other cannibals are chasing Felix. Felix climbs to the top of coconut tree and throws a coconut down on the head of a cannibal who stands under the tree. The coconut bounces up and down on the cannibal's head, driving him like a nail into the ground. A smiling Felix climbs down from the tree but finds that he is confronted by four more cannibals. Then a leopard arrives on the scene. Felix knocks him out and removes his spots, which he throws at the cannibals like rocks. The cannibals throw daggers at Felix, which he ducks, but one dagger hits a hippo in the rear end. The angry hippo chases Felix all the way back to his house. Arriving before the hippo, Felix looks inside through the window and sees that his father is very angry, having discovered the grasshoppers in the gloves trick. The hippo arrives on the scene, but Felix pulls his jaws over his head and plays his teeth like a piano. Felix is playing the piano as his smiling father looks at him through the window as the cartoon ends.

Review: *Motion Picture News,* 5 April 1930

In a desperate effort to prove that a cartoon comedy can be just as versatile as a sound feature, and create just as much noise, the producers of this "Felix The Cat" offering lost their sense of humor somewhere along the way, and the laughs are few and far between. The main idea was to get a musical note out of every object pictured, from a convertible rhinoceros-piano to a golf ball, but it doesn't click.

Play it if you have to, but it's not up to par. Needs strong support.

TRADER MICKEY (1932)

Company: David Hand, Walt Disney, United Artists
Characters: Mickey Mouse, Pluto, black cannibals

Story: The cartoon opens with Mickey Mouse standing in his small boat playing a banjo. The small boat is loaded down with goods and a flag that says Trader Mickey. Mickey's dog, Pluto, turns the boat's paddle wheel with his feet. They land on an unnamed shore and are immediately threatened by a group of angry alligators who had been sleeping on the beach. Mickey grabs his gun, and he and Pluto set off to explore the jungle. Pluto sniffs with his nose to the ground and picks up a scent that leads him to a bush where a black cannibal is hiding. Pluto rushes off to warn Mickey, but they are soon surrounded and captured by the cannibal tribe and carried on the tips of their spears back to their village. Meanwhile the fat cannibal chief is seen sitting on his throne reading a copy of "Ballyhood Magazine." Human skulls are piled all around him. As the cannibals arrive with Mickey and Pluto, the cannibal cook is seen stirring a large cooking pot. Mickey stands before the chief, and the cook comes over and touches his leg. He then licks his finger and smiles. The chief does the same and licks his lips before ordering that Mickey and Pluto be cooked for dinner. Mickey is thrown in the cooking pot as the cook slices vegetables and puts them in the pot. Pluto is put in a roasting pan with an apple in his mouth. Meanwhile the Mickey's boat is brought before the chief, and the goods in it are dumped out. The chief and the other cannibals open the boxes, and they are puzzled by what they find. The chief finds a woman's corset and places it on his head. A female finds a pair of suspenders and uses them to strap her four babies on her back. The other cannibals find various musical instruments, which they attempt to play in all the wrong ways. They blow into the wrong ends of trumpets and tubas. The chief finds a cuckoo clock, and when the bird comes out to sound the hour, he pulls it off the clock, sprinkles salt on it, and swallows it. The cook uses a saxophone to stir the pot that Mickey is sitting in. When Mickey takes the saxophone and starts to play jazz music, the cook dances to the music. The other cannibals start to play music, even though they use the instruments improperly. Meanwhile Mickey has climbed out of the pot and is playing a harmonica while the king laughs and claps his hands. Mickey gives the harmonica to the king, but when he puts it into his mouth and attempts to blow it, he swallows it. Mickey tickles the king's stomach and when the king laughs, he blows the harmonica he has swallowed to the tune of "St. James Infirmary Blues." Mickey and the chief do a cakewalk dance to the music of "Darktown Strutter's Ball." The music is so hot that the whole cannibal village is jumping. The king gets so excited that he slips on some logs and stumbles and falls into the cooking pot. Mickey and Pluto rush over and try to pull him out. The king has a big grin on his face as the cartoon ends.

TRAVEL SQUAWKS (1938)

Company: Harry Love, Louis Lilly, Columbia Pictures
Characters: Krazy Kat, black Africans

Story: The cartoon opens as Krazy Kat, riding on his flying carpet, flies high over the white clouds. He smiles and says, "Hello, folks. This is Krazy Kat, the flying vagabond, inviting you to come along on a tour of this great big, wide, wonderful, beautiful, safe world." As he finishes, he looks down and see bombs exploding all over the large city below him. He turns his carpet

and says, "Pardon me while we stay clear of civilization. Now let's go from a ridiculous to a colder climate." Krazy makes a quick change into winter furs. The cold wind blows as his carpet flies him to the North Pole. There he sees penguins sledding down a mountain on the back of a seal and two seal teams, the Hudsons and the Christmases, playing softball. The game ends in a dispute with the umpire as Krazy flies his carpet to Holland. There he observes a man shaving himself with the revolving blade of a windmill and villagers doing a clog dance in their wooden shoes.

Next Krazy says, "Let's fly to the place where rhythm was born." He looks below him and sees a group of black natives gathered together in village and chanting to the slow beat of a drum. A trial is about to take place but the chief, an elderly man wearing a top hat with the top missing, falls asleep standing at the podium. He is also the judge and the jury in this place. Krazy says, "There they are. Let's keep still and see what's goin' on down there." Nearby, a monkey climbs to the top of a tree and drops a coconut on top of the chief's head. He wakes up, pounds his gavel, and shouts, "Ordah, ordah in de court. Bring in de prisoner—bring her in de court." A shapely female defendant walks in wearing rings around her long neck. She has thick lips and only four front teeth. She wears a tight dress and high heels and carries a box of candy in her hands. She walks in keeping time with the background music. Walking close behind her are two guards armed with spears. The woman says, "I's comin', Judge. Hallelujah, Your Honor. Will you have a piece of fudge?" She holds a piece of candy in her hand. The male jury chants, "She's acomin! She's acomin! She may be guilty, but that baby is a wow!" The chief looks at her, smiles and chants, "She may be guilty, but that baby is a wow." The chief bangs his gavel and says, "Stop, stop. Proceed with the case." But the defendant seats herself and says, "Wait a minute, Judge, while I powder my face." As she does so, the prosecutor says, "Your Honor, dis woman is stallin' you." The defense lawyer answers, "Your Honor, I object!" The chief says "objection overruled" as he hits the defense lawyer on the head with his gavel. The prosecutor continues, "The woman is guilty, just as true as day. Penalize her, Judge, and make her swing." The defense lawyer answers, "Your Honor, I object." The chief says "Objection is overruled" before hitting him again. The prosecutor says, "Attah boy, Judge. You is cool." The chief looks a the defense lawyer and says, "The prosecutor claims she ain't got rhythm." The defense, slamming his hands together, answers, "We'll prove to you she has got rhythm. Go on, Baby. Give 'em, give 'em." The jury starts to play hot jazz, and the defendant smiles and begins to tap her feet. Then she rises from her chair and starts to do a shim-sham-shimmy dance to the delight of the chief and the others. As the music and dancing continue another native with large, flat lips stands in front of a radio microphone and flaps his lips, making a sound like a tobacco auctioneer. Meanwhile Krazy looks down from his flying carpet and says, "Looks like an auction to me. Solid! The rhythm has got me." He stands up and starts to dance and snap his fingers to the music. The carpet carries Krazy down to the villagers. The defendant starts to dance with

Krazy before she suddenly stops and stares at him with a frown on her face. The music stops, and the drums start to sound a slow beat. A close-up of another native shows a bone stuck through his nose and war paint on his face as he rolls his eyes round and round and makes growling sounds. The crowd begins to chant as they advance toward Krazy who says, "Don't leave now, Folks. We'll get out of here." The carpet takes off with Krazy and the defendant standing beside him. After they reach cruising altitude, Krazy tells her, "Gosh, lady. We can't take you with us." Then he pushes her off the carpet. She falls down and lands in the lap of the smiling chief. Meanwhile Krazy smiles and says, "So long, Folks. I'll see you next time" as the cartoon ends.

Review: *Motion Picture Herald,* 25 June 1838

Krazy Kat on his magic carpet goes visiting in this cartoon. His stops include the North Pole where the Penguins cavort on the snow, and ice; Holland, where the Dutch are shown smoking enormous pipes and Africa, where cannibals are holding a mock trial to determine if the accused native is guilty of not having a sense of rhythm. (6 1/2 min)

Review: *Selected Motion Pictures,* 1 October 1938

Krazy Kat visits the North Pole, Holland and Africa on his magic carpet. Fair. Family and Junior Matinee.

Review: *National Exhibitor,* 2 June 1938

Krazy is a commentator traveling on a flying rug, taking the audience to North Pole, Holland, finally Africa where he immediately becomes a candidate for the next meal—but he gets away. Good. (6 1/2 min)

WHICH IS WITCH (1949)

Company: I. Freleng, Warner Bros.
Type: Looney Tunes
Characters: Bugs Bunny, pygmy witch doctor

Story: The cartoon opens in a village deep in the jungle. A grass hut is seen with a sign over the door: Dr. I. C. Spots—Witch Doctor. Inside a black pygmy witch doctor, wearing a grass skirt and a black stovepipe hat, is mixing a brew in a large cooking pot sitting on a wood fire. There is a sheet of paper pinned to the wall that reads, "Rx prescriptions, lizard tongues, fish eyes, gnat's eyeballs . . ." He shakes these items from bottles into the cooking pot. Then he smiles, picks up his spear, and dances around the pot. He continues to add ingredients to the pot, including a jigger of XXX, one dozen bee stingers, five leopard's spots, and finally frog's legs and sauteed rabbit. When he discovers that he has run out of rabbit, he becomes very angry and jumps up and down. Meanwhile Bugs Bunny, exploring the jungle, stops at a crossroads and wonders if he should go to Huba Huba, which is one mile away, or to Kuka Munga, which is also one mile away. After flipping himself, he decides to go to the latter. Along the way he en-

counters the pygmy witch doctor, who is hiding behind a tree as Bugs passes by. Bugs sees him out of the corner of his eye and says, "Mice." Bugs arrives at the native village where the witch doctor jumps in front of him. He says, "It must be Halloween in these parts. Eh, what's up doc?" as he eats a carrot. The witch doctor says, "How did you know me doctor?" Bugs replies, "Doctor, did you say doctor?" Bugs rapidly changes to a white hunter's safari costume and asks the pygmy, "Dr. Livingstone, I presume. Put it there, doc," as he shakes hands with the witch doctor. Bugs tells him, "Gee, doc, this is quite a momentous histerical occasion you know. We gotta preserve if for posterity." Bugs sets up a camera in front of the pygmy and says, "Now give us a big smile." And the doctor smiles. Bugs tells him, "Let's skip it [the smile]. Now watch for the birdie. That's it." He pinches the pygmy's nose and walks away, saying, "You'll have to wait a few days for the proofs." The witch doctor realizes that he has been tricked and points his spear in Bugs's direction and says, "Now keep you eye on the bull's-eye." He catches up to Bugs and sticks him in the rear end. Bugs says, "Hey, what's the idea? Gimme that dart." He takes the spear and bangs the tip against a rock. He gives the spear back to the doctor, saying, "And don't let me hear about you playin' with matches either." The pygmy examines the bent tip of his spear before saying, "Push, pull, click, click." As he snaps off the bent blade of the spear and snaps on a new one. He catches Bugs again and orders him back to the village by jabbing him with the tip of the spear. Bugs says, "I got a notion—to do what you said." They arrive at the village where Bugs enters the doctor's hut, takes one look at the cooking pot, and says, "A hot bath—oh how thoughtful." He kisses the surprised doctor on top of the head. Bugs jumps in the pot, saying, "To think I had the little mutt all wrong." The water is hot and Bugs sits slowly down, saying, "Oooh, ahhh. Easy does it, ahhh . . ." Meanwhile the doctor is placing more logs under the pot. Bugs looks down, points his finger, and says, "Eh, a little more over here on the right." The doctor closes the lid on the pot and screws it down tight. Bugs is now in a pressure cooker and says inside the pot, "Hey, what's goin' on here? What is this—a steam cabinet?" Bugs smells the vapors from the simmering water and says, "Hey, what's cookin'?" When he realizes that he is cooking, he screams and says, "Hey, let me out of here!" Meanwhile the doctor continues to fuel the fire, and the pressure in the pot is increasing. The pressure gets so high that Bugs is blown through the valve on the lid by a jet of steam. Bugs runs out of the tent, followed closely by the doctor. Bugs eludes the doctor by hiding in a grass hut. When he sees two native women with long, skinny necks and big, flat lips pass by, he decides to impersonate a native woman to trick the doctor. He pushes coiled springs over his head and around his neck, stretching it. He stuffs two large dinner plates under his bottom and top lips, stretching them out. He walks outside and joins the women, but the spring comes off his neck and the doctor discovers he has been tricked. Bugs escapes from the village and runs to the river where he sees a paddle-wheel steamer sailing by. He jumps in the river, narrowly escapes the jaws of a large alligator, and climbs on board the boat. Bugs waves at the witch doctor on shore, saying "so long" in French, Spanish German, and Hawaiian, and finally English. The angry doctor jumps into the river and swims under water, only the tip of his hat breaking the surface. When the hat gets near the boat, Bugs sees that it is on the head of an alligator that smiles and picks its teeth. Bugs says, "Hey, where is the little guy at?" The alligator rubs it stomach. Bugs tells him, "Why, you grinning lug. Come on, cough him up." But the alligator shakes its head no. Bugs then grabs a club and says, "Oh yes you will." The alligator ducks under the water and Bugs dives off the boat into to the river after him. There is a furious underwater struggle before all become calm. A piece of alligator luggage springs from the water and lands on the deck of the boat. Bugs climbs back aboard, shakes his head, and says, "Too bad. At least I got something for my trouble." As he opens the bag of luggage, the doctor jumps out and says, "Me too." The pygmy is wearing alligator high heels and is carrying an alligator handbag. Bugs looks at him and says, "Very becoming, short stuff. Gives ya that new look" as the cartoon ends.

Review: *Motion Picture Herald,* 31 December 1949

Dr. Ugh, the village Witch Doctor, finds that he must have "one live rabbit" as an ingredient in a cure-all concoction he is brewing. He sets out to find a rabbit, and comes across Bugs Bunny. As any Bugs fan knows, Bugs is not a bunny that can be pushed around, which the medico soon learns.

Review: *Film Daily,* 1 January 1950

When Dr. Ugh, Witch Doctor extraordinary for a tribe of little people, decides he needs a rabbit for his cure-all concoction, Bugs Bunny decides it's time to leave. The jungle medico learns he can't split the hare, and B. B. emerges victorious once more. Wonderful cartoon. (7 min)

Review: *Exhibitor Servisection,* 23 November 1949

Bugs Bunny, cast in the role of a jungle explorer, is beset by a pygmy cannibal when the latter runs out of something made only from a rabbit. Tossed into a kettle of boiling water with a pressure cooking lid, Bugs forces his way out through the steam outlet. Chased by the cannibals, Bugs jumps into a river in the path of a boat and a crocodile. When the crocodile and Bugs battle, the former is somehow turned into an alligator bag, and both are tossed aboard the boat. Thinking that he is now safe, Bugs opens the handbag and out pops the pygmy wearing alligator accessories. Good. (7 min)

WHO'S COOKIN'? (194?)

Company: Canadian Production
Characters: Sailor, black cannibals

Story: Cartoon has background narration by the sailor, as well as on-screen sound effects. As the cartoon opens, a sailor hangs onto a log in the open sea while his ship slowly sinks in the background. He says, "When the good Mary Ann was wrecked, the sole survivor was me. For twenty days and twenty nights I floated upon the sea with nothing to eat and nothing to drink on that wet, wavy sea. And then I spied southeast by east a lovely tropical land." He waves his hat in the air and with a smile on his face paddles toward the island as he says, "I paddled with joy across the waves until I stepped on the land." He comes ashore, looks around, and says, "There was nothing to eat and nothing to drink on that hot and horrible island." He decides to catch some fish and says, "Balmily I was on the same island where Robinson Crusoe was wrecked. So I slips a safety pin on a length of line and a rod, and I throws it into the blue lagoon till I catches a cod." The sailor sits down in the sand, smokes his pipe, and soon gets a bite to eat. He says, "My very first meal in twenty-one days—that slippery, slimy cod." When he pulls the line out of the water, the fishing line flies over his head to the other side of a hill where the fish, hook, line, and sinker land in the open mouth of a sleeping black cannibal. The cannibal has thick white lips and hair like coiled springs. The cannibal is dressed in a grass skirt and wears rings in both his ears and his nose. The cannibal swallows the fish, wakes up, and rubs his stomach with a smile on his face. He spits the hook out of his mouth as the sailor, on the other side of the hill, says, "That codfish had wings, he did. That slippery, slimy cod flew way across the island, he did. I would have let him go but that little devil took me safety pin with him. And a safety pin, why that's a sailor's best friend. Besides, the particular pin brings me luck wherever I go." He puts down his fishing pole and climbs up the hill to look over to the other side. Meanwhile the cannibal climbs up the other side of the hill to find out where the fish came from. The sailor and the cannibal meet at the top of the hill. They look at each other and the sailor says, "A little fat native boy shows up who takes me by the hand." The cannibal licks his lips, grabs the sailor by the hand, and pulls him down the hill, where he calls the chief and two other cannibals. The sailor says, "We runs to find his little fat friends and play in the sand. The game we plays is an odd game. They peel my clothes with a woof. They hang them on a branch to dry and sticks me into soup." Hanging on the same tree with the sailor's clothes are the clothes of other sailors and captains. The sailor sits in the soup pot with a smile while the cannibals light a fire under him. The chief puts on a chef's hat, tastes the soup, and smiles. The sailor says, "The chief was a first-class chef with a first-class taste for stew. He was bringing me up to a first-class boil while I figured out what to do." The sailor he taps his finger on his head, deep in thought. He gets an idea and sits on the side of the pot and rocks it back and forth so the soup splashes out of the pot, putting out the fire under it. The sailor says, "How could I explain I wasn't right for his recipe? Why, you could boil me for a year and a day and I'd still be tough as shoe leather." Meanwhile three cannibals try to relight the fire by blowing on the embers. The sailor continues, "And then I had a horrible thought. Suppose the cannibals wanted to boil me and make me skin into a pair of shoes? The sailor gets an idea and says, "I takes some soot and one, two, three, black magic! I became as black as I had to be to join them cannibals and their horrible, terrible, extra indecent, highly carnivorous game." While the cannibals keep trying the light the fire under the pot, the sailor, in blackface, jumps out of the pot and grabs some leaves and makes a skirt to wrap around his waist. Finally the cannibals restart the fire before discovering that the sailor has mysteriously vanished. The sailor says, "And when they found I'd disappeared, the chief looked round and round. He had his boys pour out the soup to see if I had boiled down." The cannibals pour the soup through a strainer held by the chief and still can't figure out where the sailor went. The cannibals all look sad and shake their heads in confusion. The sailor says, "I could have given them the slip right there, but I stayed around to see the fun. The old boy's face was twisted up like a sour pickle." The chief takes off the chef's hat and scratches his head. The sailor continues, "Why, it was all I could do to keep meself from laughing out loud." But the chief suspects something is wrong and counts his cannibals on his fingers before lining me up for closer inspection. The sailor says, "He counted us and counted us and counted some more. But the number that he counted was neither two nor four. The fellow now was so hungry he didn't know what to do. He knew just that one of us belonged in that ruddy stew. So he held inspection and every bloke was found shipshape stem to stern, except me." The chief looks over the sailor and discovers a patch of white skin on his back. The game is up, so the sailor runs away, saying, "Their spears are out and the chase is on." The sailor hides in a coconut tree and then gets a another idea. He breaks open a coconut and smears some of the white juice on the chief's back. The other cannibals chase the chief while the sailor runs away laughing and says, "You should have heard what his pals called him in that cannibal gobble-gook." The cannibals catch the chief and throw him to the ground. The sailor runs back to the seashore and jumps into the soup pot, saying, "Me a goner. I always comes out on top, so I washes me hide off in the soup and I'm ready to say farewell. When I see those cannibals coming back, I made that pot my shell." He turns the pot over and climbs under it to hide. The chief and the cannibals arrive on the scene and can't find the sailor, so the disappointed chief sits down on the pot. The sailor says, "The chief was so broken up over my leaving that he sat down on me. When he got up, I crawled away like a giant tortoise. So he falls on his backside, which started a fight." The chief gets angry because the other cannibals laugh at him on the ground. The sailor says, "I had high hope they would slaughter each other. But when I moved again, they found me out." The cannibals tie them up, but the sailor manages to roll under a tiger skin lying nearby on the ground. The sailor puts on the tiger skin, and when the chief thinks he sees a tiger, he screams and runs away. Meanwhile the other two cannibals are busy washing the cooking pot in the ocean. When the sailor in the tiger skin arrives on the scene, they make a hasty departure. He says, "Like I said, you have to use your ingenuity in dealing with

the cannibals, just like old Robinson. And then what might have been a terrible, sad story turns out all right in the end." The sailor then pulls off the tiger skin, puts on his clothes and says, "And then I walk down to the shore and make a boat out of any old thing you find there and sail away for home." He sits in the cooking pot and uses two cannibal spears for oars to row away from the island. He stands up in the pot, smiles, tips his cap, looks back toward the island, and says, "Oh, the good ship Mary Ann was wrecked and the sole survivor was me. I sang and walked on the watery waves back to my own country" as the cartoon ends.

YOU'RE DRIVING ME CRAZY (1931)

Company: Dave Fleischer, Max Fleischer; distributed by Paramount Pictures
Type: Screen Song
Characters: Background music by Snooks and his Memphis Ramblers, black Africans

Story: There is not much of a story to this Screen Song, which begins with a rocket exploding in the air and the smoke from it forming the words *jungle festival* in the sky over a jungle below. The next scene shows a black African woman wearing a grass skirt. She has a face that resembles a dark-skinned Betty Boop. She sings the title song while another native charms a snake with the sound of the jazzy music. Next a giraffe scat sings the lyrics in the style of Louis Armstrong. His neck stretches and contracts in time with the beat. Soon all of the natives (some with long, flat lips) and all of the animals, including elephants, turtles, monkeys, lions, and an ostrich, are singing and dancing to the music. Suddenly the weather turns bad and it begins to rain. It rains so hard that a black fish jumps out of a pond, puts on a raincoat and hat, and jumps back in the water. Briefly the music changes to "Tiger Rag" as a lion and an elephant chase each other in circles under two palm trees that touch each other at the top. Suddenly the two trees transform into an ostrich that runs away before stopping and sticking its head in a hole. A bolt of lightning strikes the ostrich on its rear end as water pours down out of buckets in the clouds overhead. The music changes back to the title song, and the tempo increases. The animals become so excited that they run into each other and knock themselves down as the cartoon ends.

ZULA HULA (1937)

Company: Dave Fleischer, Max Fleischer, Paramount Pictures
Characters: Betty Boop, Grampy, black cannibals

Story: The cartoon opens as a small single-engine airplane is being tossed about in a storm while flying over the ocean. A lightning bolt tosses the plane upside down and then right side up again. Inside a frightened Betty Boop tells Grampy, "Oh Grampy. I'm sure there's something wrong with the altitude." Grampy says, "Oh no. It's just the engine's missin'." Betty says, "Well, why didn't you bring it along?" A great bolt of lightning crashes through the window, grabs the steering wheel out of Grampy's hands, and pulls it out of the plane. Betty screams and holds Grampy while another lightning bolt shaped like a pair of scissors cuts the tail and wing tips off the plane, sending it into a nosedive. But Grampy pulls a lever that releases a large umbrella. It allows the plane to float down gently. It comes to rest on the shore of a tropical island. Grampy and Betty look out of the cockpit and Betty says, "Oh Grampy, we're lost." Grampy says, "Don't worry, Betty. Everything will be hotsy topsy." Betty says, "Oh I hope so." Then they throw boxes of supplies out of the plane onto the beach. Betty says, "I hope they have a beauty parlor here because I need a shampoo." Betty and Grampy climb out of the plane. In no time Grampy, the inventor, using his tools and native flowage, constructs a house with all of the comforts of home in the city. After the work is completed, Betty and Grampy stand back and look at the house. Betty smiles and says, "Oh Grampy, you're just wonderful." Meanwhile they have been discovered by two black cannibals who peer at them from behind a tree. They have long, thick lips, and one wears a large bone tied to the hair on his head. They mumble to each other while Betty and Grampy sit down at a table and drink coconut milk. Grampy says, "How about a toast, Betty?" Betty says OK, and they click their coconut shells together. Meanwhile the hungry cannibals have become more agitated, whispering to each other and saying things like, "Oh, you mean it?" Other black cannibals have arrived, and they also look from behind trees at the two white strangers. Grampy says, "Well Betty, I have a surprise for you." Betty says, "Goody, goody." Grampy pulls on a rope, causing a palm-leaf fan, powered by two birds pulling on opposite ends of a fish, to cool them. Betty smiles and says, "All the comforts of home." Grampy smiles and says, "That's nothing. Look over there." He shows Betty a string of fish he has trapped with another of his inventions. They walk over and Grampy grabs the fish, saying, "Here ya are Betty. Look a' there." Betty is delighted and says, "Oh Grampy. You're a darling." Meanwhile the cannibals have grown more excited and begin to shout. Grampy and Betty hear them and turn around to see the cannibals. Grampy drops the fish and Betty screams. They are now surrounded by cannibals. They run to the plane but find that it is too damaged to fly. They duck behind the plane as spears fly over their heads. Betty says, "Oh Grampy, we'll be killed to death." But Grampy smiles and says, "Wait here, Betty. We'll be all right." Grampy crouches down and walks behind a rock, saying, "They can't see me behind here." The cannibals chant "ooh-lah-bo-lah . . ." Grampy puts on his thinking cap, which is a college graduation cap with a lightbulb mounted on the top. A spear flies by and breaks the bulb. Grampy replaces it by screwing in a new one. Finally Grampy's lightbulb turns on as he gets an idea. He dances around in circles with a smile on his face and says, "I'll get these fellows." He runs back to the plane and yanks on the propeller, pulling it off and taking the engine cover with it. He attaches bamboo tubes to the engine exhaust ports and then turns on the engine, saying "My, my, I'd better hurry," as the cannibals close in for the kill. All the cannibals carry spears except one who holds a long stick with a large barber's razor tied to the end of it. The engine exhaust gases blow through the tubes and make music. Hearing the music, the cannibals stop dead in their tracks, drop their spears, and begin to rock back and forth. Soon they are so excited that they jump up and down. Meanwhile Grampy has fashioned more musical instruments using jungle materials. Two cannibals keep time by beating each other on the head with the bones in their hair. Soon Betty and Grampy get in the spirit and join in dancing with the cannibals. A baby cannibal with a small bone in its hair jumps on top of a drum and tap dances. A fat female cannibal is playing with a bolo bat when two small baby cannibals pop their heads out of the woolly hair on her head. Two other female cannibals with long, flat lips dance under a tree where two monkeys are sitting. Each monkey reaches down and pulls on the bone in the hair of the female under him, which causes the cannibals' flat lips to slap together in time to the music. While the cannibals dance, Grampy constructs a crude helicopter that he and Betty use to escape the island. As they are taking off, they look down with smiles on their faces and wave at the dancing cannibals before flying back home as the cartoon ends.

Review: *Motion Picture Herald,* 15 January 1938

Miss Betty Boop and her grandfather are cast adrift on a desert isle when their plane crashes. As he is old, ingenious "Grampy" devises plans and means to make the unexpected stay in the unpleasant surroundings as comfortable as possible. The place is beginning to assume the aspects of home when the unwelcome presence of savage island cannibals threatens the castaways. Never at a loss for a suitable solution, the elderly gent renovates the wrecked air ship into a modern dance orchestra. Under a soothing spell of musical ministrations, the cannibals are diverted in their plans from making trouble to making rhythm. Finally, "Grampy" hatches up another "Rube Goldberg" invention which readies the plane to take off for home and a more assured state of safety. The whole of the business is detailed in an amusing and rapidly drawn vein of clever cartooning. (7 min)

Review: *Film Daily,* 11 January 1938

Betty Boop and her old pal Grampy are wrecked on a desert island. When the cannibals appear, things look pretty bad, but Grampy is resourceful, and succeeds in constructing an orchestra out of parts of their wrecked plane. The cannibals listen to the hotcha music and forget their eating designs on the two strangers. Finally Grampy ingeniously constructs an airplane of sorts, and then they fly away from their dangerous companions.

Review: *Boxoffice,* **29 January 1938**

Betty Boop and the inventive Grampy in another one of those sheer wacky cartoons that gather a fair share of laughs. Betty Boop and Grampy are forced down on a lonely island inhabited by savages. In his own inimitable manner, Grampy provides shelter and food. When attacked by the savages, Grampy constructs from the partially wrecked plane, a musical contraption that makes the natives go into a dance. His final stunt is a makeshift plane which transports Betty and him away from the island. (7 min)

Review: *Selected Motion Pictures,* **1 January 1938**

Grampy's ingenuity rescues Betty from desert island savages. Family.

Review: *Motion Picture Exhibitor,* **1 January 1938**

Grampy and Betty are flying, land in Zululand. Grampy, however, is equal to the occasion, inventing enough things to make their stay pleasant, eventually outwitting the natives by making them dance. Good.

Fig. 1. Sambo, a black stereotype, was featured in his own strip circa 1909. Also see p. 1.

Fig. 2. Black stereotypes such as the Gold Dust Twins were used to advertise popular household products, circa 1908. Also see p. 1.

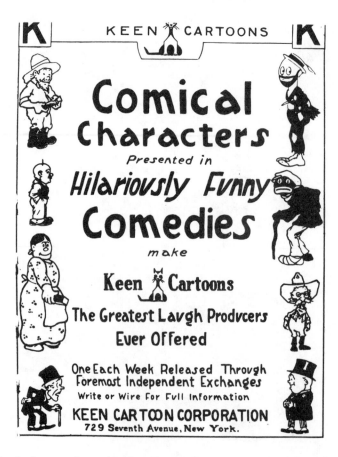

Fig. 3. Comic characters featured in Keen Cartoon Corp. cartoons, circa 1917. Also see p. 2.

Fig. 4. Illustration showing the popularity of black Jazz "Harlem" style and cartoon characters in France. Also see p. 2.

Fig. 5. Illustration showing the great appeal cartoons have to youngsters, circa 1940s. Also see p. 4.

Fig. 6. Advertisement introducing Bosko, Harman's and Ising's new cartoon character before their association with Warner Bros., circa 1929. Also see p. 11.

Fig. 7. Vitaphone/Warner Bros. trade ad announcing debut of the "Looney Tunes" cartoon series featuring Bosko and Honey, circa 1930. Also see p. 11.

Fig. 8. Bosko with his bag of cookies on board a pirate ship in BOSKO AND THE PIRATES, circa 1937. Also see p. 14. Courtesy of Turner Entertainment Company. All rights reserved.

Fig. 9. Bosko shows Honey his basket of colored eggs in BOSKO'S EASTER EGGS, circa 1937. Also see p. 18.

Fig. 10. Bosko and Honey as they appeared in YODELING YOKELS, circa 1931. Also see p. 26.

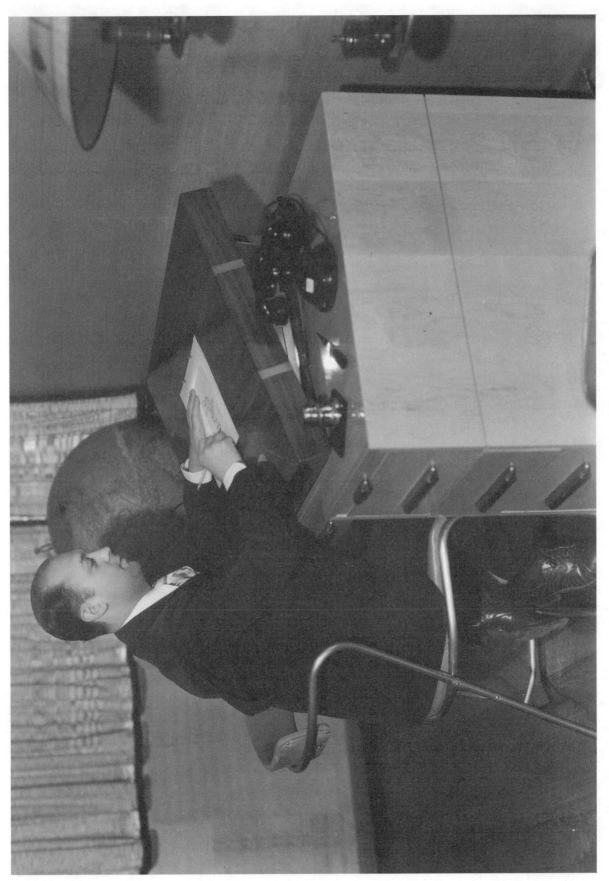

Fig. 11. Walter Lantz, creator of Li'l Eightball, circa 1944. Also see p. 27.

Fig. 12. George Pal with his cartoon creation Jasper, circa 1942. Also see p. 30.

Fig. 13. Trade ad introducing George Pal's new cartoon series *Madcap Models* in Technicolor featuring Jasper. Also see p. 30.

Fig. 14. Jasper, the Scarecrow, and Crow in JASPER IN A JAM, circa 1946. Also see p. 38.

Fig. 15. Scarecrow takes aim at an apple on Jasper's head in JASPER TELL, circa 1945. Also see p. 38.

Fig. 16. Jasper is tempted to eat a juicy watermelon in JASPER AND THE WATERMELONS, circa 1942. Also see p. 39.

Fig. 17. Minstrel Scarecrow performs on stage in JASPER'S MINSTRELS, circa 1945. Also see p. 43.

Fig. 18. The Scarecrow and Crow try to take Jasper's harmonica in PACKAGE FOR JASPER, circa 1944. Also see p. 48.

Fig. 19. Little Inki and the Minah bird as they appeared in INKI AT THE CIRCUS, circa 1947. Also see p. 54.

Osage Theatre

Osage Theatre

WEDNESDAY & THURSDAY, AUG. 16 & 17
(Both Sections)

SATURDAY, AUGUST 19
(Colored Section Fri. and Sat.)

YOUR BEST BET IS
BING'S BEST YET!

BING CROSBY
Coleen Gray
Charles Bickford
Frances Gifford
in
FRANK CAPRA'S
RIDING HIGH

Also WARNER BROS. NEWS
Cartoon "FOR SCENT-IMENTAL REASONS"

"ZINGIN'
LEAD!
Swingin'
rhythm!

CHARLES
STARRETT · BURNETTE
SMILEY
in
Trail OF THE
RUSTLERS

Gail DAVIS Tommy IVO
Eddie CLETRO
and his ROUNDUP BOYS

—Added—
Serial "JAMES BROTHERS OF MISSOURI" No. 5
Comedy "DUNKED IN THE DEEP"

FRIDAY, AUGUST 18
(White Section Only)

Sudden terror held the stage!

JANE MARLENE
WYMAN DIETRICH
MICHAEL
WILDING ALFRED
RICHARD HITCHCOCK'S
TODD "Stage
Fright!"

Also Cartoon "INKI AND THE MINA BIRD"

Fig. 20. Movie theater ad for racially segregated Osage Theatre, Plaquemine, Louisiana, where INKI cartoon was shown to white but not black patrons, circa 1943. Also see page 52.

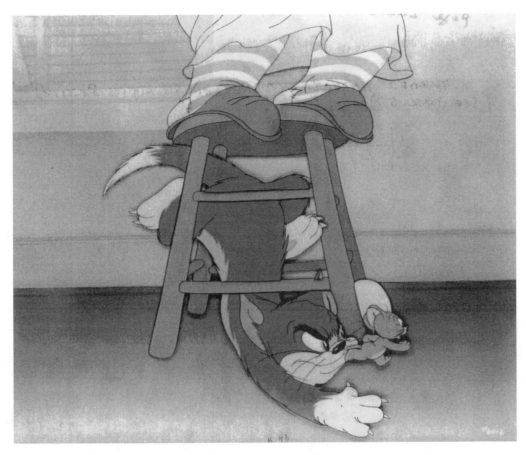

Fig. 21. Mammy Two-Shoes stands on stool while Tom chases Jerry in MIDNIGHT SNACK, circa 1940. Also see p. 57. Courtesy of Turner Entertainment Corporation. All rights reserved.

Fig. 22. Mammy Two-Shoes orders Tom to clean her kitchen as Jerry looks on in MOUSE CLEANING, circa 1948. Also see p. 58. Courtesy of Turner Entertainment Corporation. All rights reserved.

Fig. 23. Tom and his cat friend are about to paddle Mammy Two-Shoes in MOUSE IN THE HOUSE, circa 1947. Also see page 59. Courtesy of Turner Entertainment Corporation.

Fig. 24. Trade ad for a Famous Studios cartoon character, Buzzy the Crow, circa 1947. Also see p. 72.

Fig. 25. Katnip Cat prepares to eat Buzzy the Crow in CAT-CHOO, circa 1951. Also see p. 75.

Fig. 26. Col. Heeza Lair chases black cannibal in COL. HEEZA LIAR'S AFRICAN HUNT showing early appearance of black cannibals in animated cartoons, circa 1916. Also see p. 81.

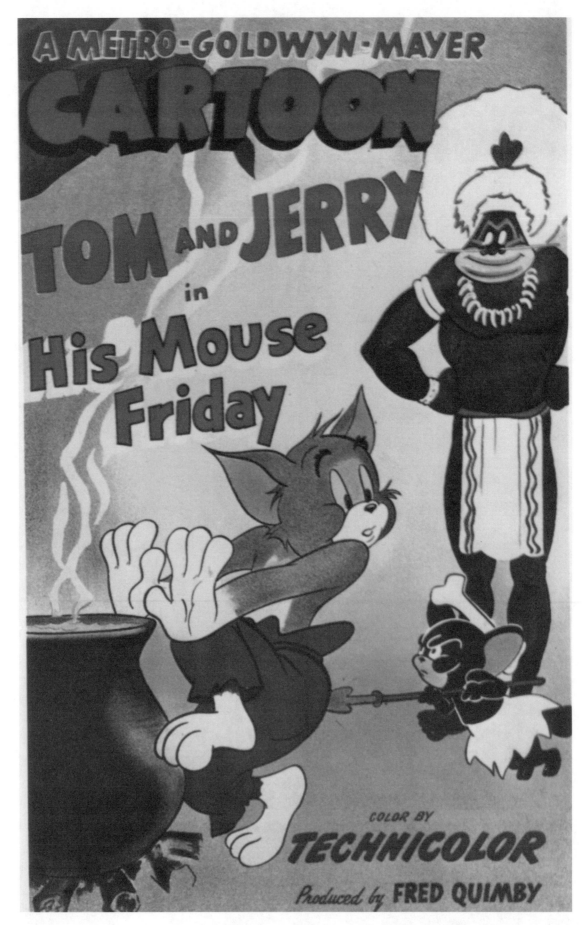

Fig. 27. Tom and Jerry as they appeared in HIS MOUSE FRIDAY, circa 1951. Also see p. 97. Courtesy of Turner Entertainment Corporation. All rights reserved.

Fig. 28. A black cannibal eyes his dinner in THE ISLE OF PINGO PONGO, circa 1938. Also see p. 100.

Fig. 29. Robinson Crusoe (Fred Allen) drives through the jungle with his man, Westchester ("Rochester"), and a tiger in IT HAPPENED TO CRUSOE, circa 1941. Also see p. 101.

Fig. 30. A black cannibal seasons his stew in JUNGLE JITTERS, circa 1938. Also see p. 105.

Fig. 31. Mammy and Little Black Sambo celebrate killing the tiger in LITTLE BLACK SAMBO, circa 1935. Also see p. 124.

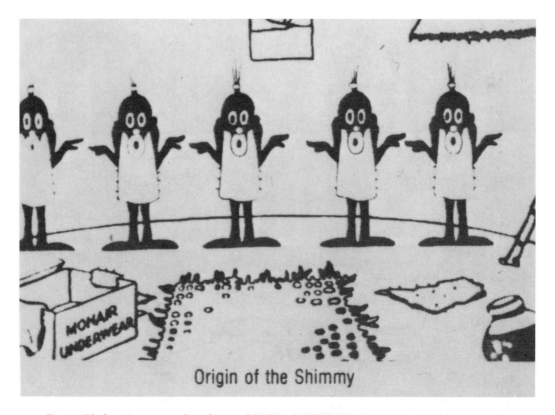

Fig. 32. Black natives wear mohair skirts in ORIGIN OF THE SHIMMY, circa 1919. Also see p. 115.

Fig. 33. An unsuspecting Popeye is about to become the cannibals' dinner in POP-PIE A LA MODE (foreign illustration). Also see p. 115.

Fig. 34. A black pygmy refuses to be captured by the Captain and the Inspector in PYGMY HUNT, circa 1938. Also see p. 119. Courtesy of Turner Entertainment Corporation. All rights reserved.

Fig. 35. A black cannibal crowns Felix the "King of the Cannibals" in TEE TIME, circa 1930. Also see p. 124.

Fig. 36. Uncle Tom and Topsy as they appeared in DIXIE DAYS, CIRCA 1930. Also see p. 132.

Fig. 37. Simon Legree and a humble Uncle Tom as they appeared in UNCLE TOM'S BUNGALOW, circa 1937. Also see p. 143.

Fig. 38. Uncle Tom and little Eva perform in their nightclub in UNCLE TOM's CABANA, circa 1947. Also see p. 144.

Fig. 39. Bob Clampett's characters form COAL BLACK AND DE SEBBEN DWARFS, circa 1943. Also see p. 147.

Fig. 40. Eddie Anderson (seated), whose voice was imitated in many animated cartoons as he appeared with the cast of the Jack Benny Radio Show. (Standing, left to right: Kenny Baker, tenor; Jack Benny, star; Don Wilson, announcer.) Also see p. 147.

Fig. 41. A scene from SWING WEDDING showing the Cab Calloway caricature that was frequently used by animators in the 1930s because of his unique and extremely popular style of singing and dancing. Also see p. 148. Courtesy of Turner Entertainment Corporation.

Fig. 42. Little Sambo stereotype captures Bugs Bunny in ALL THIS AND RABBIT STEW, circa 1941. Also see p. 150.

Fig. 43. Comic strip scenes from Walter Lantz's BOOGIE WOOGIE BUGLE BOY OF COMPANY B, circa 1941. Also see p. 158.

COAL BLACK AND DE SEBBEN DWARFS

IN TECHNICOLOR

A MERRIE MELODIE CARTOON

A LEON SCHLESINGER PRODUCTION

Fig. 44. Theater ad for COAL BLACK AND DE SEBBEN DWARFS, circa 1943, showing caricatures of black soldiers that initiated a protest from the NAACP when the cartoon was released during World War II. Also see p. 163.

Fig. 45. Duke Ellington with George Pal's crew filming DATE WITH DUKE. (Top: Duke Ellington seated at the piano with George Pal holding a puppet; bottom: Ellington and Pal take a close look at the main puppet character.) Also see p. 166.

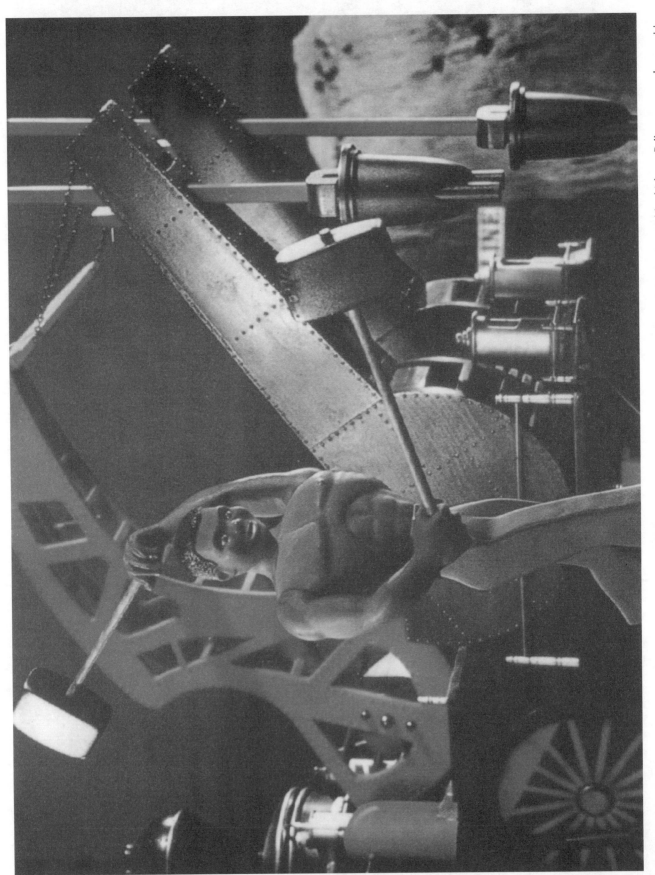

Fig. 46. The legendary John Henry, the steel-driving man, as he appeared in George Pal's JOHN HENRY AND THE INKY POO, circa 1946, which was Pal's attempt to show positive black images in his puppetoons. Also see p. 183.

Fig. 47. Borrah Minevitch (center) with his Harmonica Rascals as they appeared in Max Fleischer's LAZY BONES, circa 1934. Also see p. 186.

Fig. 48. Trade ad introducing Van Beuren's new Amos 'n' Andy cartoon series, circa 1934. Also see p. 186.

Fig. 49. Impy, the black cannibal, as he appeared in the LITTLE NEMO IN SLUMBERLAND cartoon (cover of children's book, circa 1941). Also see page 187.

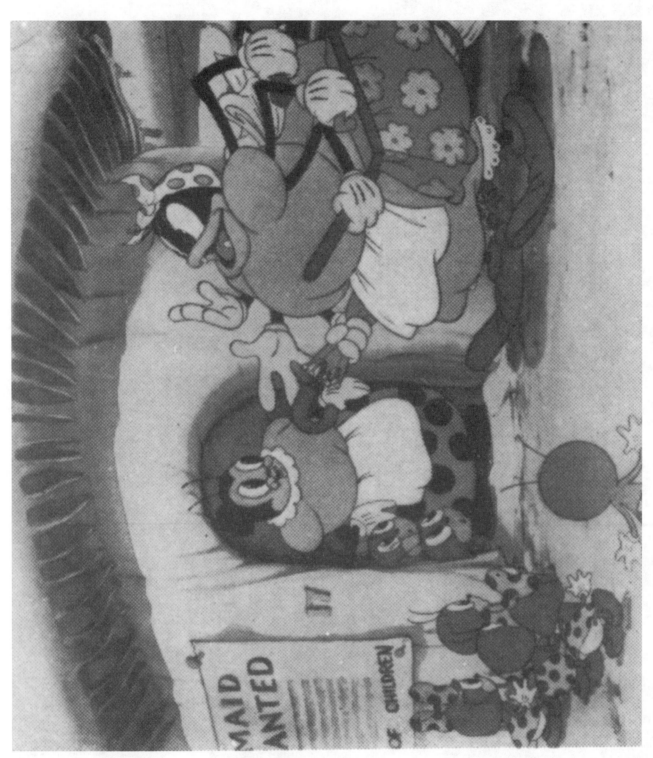

Fig. 50. Spider disguised as a black maid meets the bug family in a scene from MRS. LADY BUG. Also see p. 191. Courtesy of Turner Entertainment Corporation. All rights reserved.

Fig. 51. Trade ad showing Barney Google (right) and Snuffy Smith (left) and other main characters from PATCH MAH BRITCHES, circa 1935. Also see p. 197.

Fig. 52. Amos (left) tries to revive Andy from a scene in RASSLIN' MATCH, circa 1934. Also see p. 201.

Fig. 53. Romeo tries to elope with his Juliet in a scene from ROMEO IN RHYTHM, circa 1940. Also see p. 202.

Fig. 54. The black pig rescues Farmer Al Falfa's pigs in a scene from Paul Terry's THE RUNT, circa 1925. Also see p. 204.

Fig. 55. A stereotypical black resident of "Lazy Town" in a scene from Walter Lantz's SCRUB ME MAMMA WITH A BOOGIE BEAT, circa 1941. Also see p. 205.

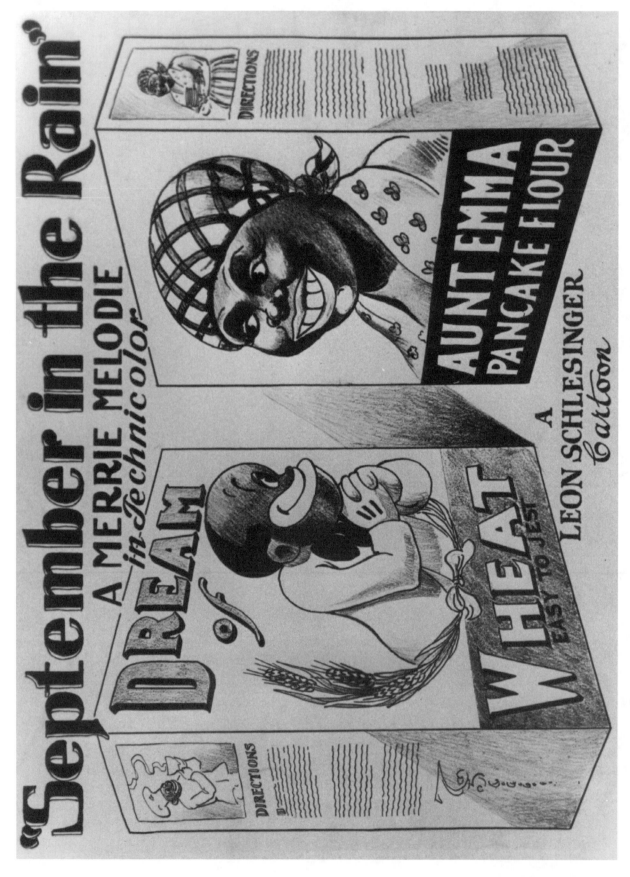

Fig. 56. A blackface Al Jolson caricature sings to a stereotypical black mammy in SEPTEMBER IN THE RAIN, circa 1937. Also see p. 205.

Fig. 57. Barney Google, Sambo, and Spark Plug the horse as they appeared in SPARK PLUG, circa 1936. Also see p. 208.

Fig. 58. Uncle Tom Bass standing in front of his FHA-approved cabin in SWING SOCIAL, circa 1940. Also see p. 210. Courtesy of Turner Entertainment Corporation. All rights reserved.

Fig. 59. Cab Calloway caricature (far left), Louis Armstrong caricature, fourth from left, and Stephin Fetchit caricature, far right, as they appeared in SWING WEDDING, circa 1937. Also see p. 211. Courtesy of Turner Entertainment Corporation. All rights reserved.

Chapter 4

Uncle Tom and Topsy: Animation on the Old Plantation

In 1851 Harriet Beecher Stowe wrote *Uncle Tom's Cabin,* one of the best known, most widely read, most influential novels ever published in the United States. In the years after the novel was published, the story was dramatized on the legitimate stage, in touring companies, and later in motion pictures. The main black characters—Uncle Tom, Topsy, Simon Legree, and Eliza—became well known throughout the world. Stowe also wrote *A Key to Uncle Tom's Cabin,* which was published by John Jewett in 1853. In it she explained how she researched and documented life on the slave plantations of the South. She explained that the main characters were based on true-to-life people. She states that the description of Eliza is based on a beautiful quadroon girl whom she observed tending to several white children in front of a church in Kentucky. Topsy was a composite character based on black slave children in general, as Stowe explained in the book:

> Topsy stands as the representative of a large class of the children who are growing up under the institution of slavery, quick, active, subtle and ingenious, apparently utterly devoid of principle and conscience, keenly penetrating, by an instinct which exists in the childish mind, the degradation of their condition, and the utter hopelessness of rising above it; feeling the black skin on them, like a mark of Cain, to be a sign of reprobation and infamy, and urged on by a kind of secret desperation to make their "calling and election" in sin sure.

As for Uncle Tom, Stowe responded to criticism that the character was improbable by arguing that she had "received more confirmation of that character, and from a greater variety of sources, than of any other in the book." She claimed she based her description of Tom on the numerous letters she had received from slave owners in the South describing their faithful and devoted male house slaves. She cites quotes from several accounts, such as the following:

> When on a visit to his his brother, in New Orleans, some years before, he found in his possession a most valuable negro man, of such remarkable probity and honesty that his brother literally trusted him with all he had. He had frequently seen him take out a handful of bills, without looking at them, and hand them to his servant, bidding him to go and provide what was necessary for the family, and bring him the change. He remonstrated with his brother on this imprudence; but the latter replied that he had such proof of his servant's impregnable conscientiousness that he felt safe to trust him to any extent.

In *Good-by to Uncle Tom,* published by William Sloane Associates in 1956, author J. C. Furnas provides a scholarly discussion of the Uncle Tom stageshows, which exaggerated Stowe's conception of life on the slave plantations. Motion pictures added another level of fantasy to the story of Uncle Tom in particular and in general presented to the public larger-than-

life, fanciful images of the happy, contented, and devoted plantation slaves. It was the animated cartoon, however, which changed the Uncle Tom story from high drama, as presented on the stage and in feature movies, to pure farce. The animators transformed the main characters—Uncle Tom, Simon Legree, Eva, and Topsy—into their corresponding caricatures. Dramatic scenes such as selling slaves at auction, the pursuit of runaway slaves by slave owners and their bloodhounds, picking cotton, and everyday life on the slave plantation, were depicted in burlesque fashion. Cartoons depicted the slaves as carefree people who are ready to dance at the sound of the first note from a banjo. They work hard picking cotton with a happy-go-lucky demeanor. But the animators usually throw in a lazy one who walks and talks like Stephin Fetchit.

It is remarkable that the American filmgoing public found such cartoons not only acceptable but also highly amusing. Why was there no outrage over the comic presentation of the unspeakable horror of human bondage, including the forced separation of families, beatings, torture, the human auction block, enforced illiteracy, forced labor, denial of citizenship, and rape? Why did the animators choose to select such a horrible subject upon which to base their cartoon humor? Why did the censor boards, theater managers, and distributors allow the theatrical exhibition of these cartoons? Why didn't the critics react with negative reviews? Was it ignorance? Indifference? Malice?" Answers to these questions could provide deeper insight into why racism remains so deeply embedded in the fabric of American society.

Plantation Stories and Reviews

BUDDY'S SHOWBOAT (1933)

Company:　Earl Duval, Vitaphone, Warner Bros.
Type:　Looney Tunes
Characters:　Buddy, Cookie, black minstrel quartet

Review: *Motion Picture Herald,* 10 February 1934

An amusing animated cartoon in which Buddy docks his showboat at a Mississippi town. He and Cookie entertain the natives until a rough deck hand captures the girl. Buddy goes into animated action, and hangs the villain over the paddle wheel, with disastrous results. Will fit any spot on the bill. (7 min)

CAMPTOWN RACES (1948)

Company:　Seymour Kneitel, Famous Studios; released by Paramount Pictures
Type:　Screen Song
Characters:　Blackface animal caricatures

Story: The opening scene shows an animal crowd packing a theater. They applaud as the curtain rises on a minstrel show. The cartoon opens with a group of blackface minstrels singing "Dixie." The elephant is the interlocutor. The next act shows a slowly walking kangaroo carrying a banjo. When he arrives at center stage, a small kangaroo pops out of the large kangaroo's pouch and plays "Camptown Races" on the banjo to the delight of the audience. The following act is a dog that plays a row of bottles. One bottle produces a sour note when struck. Puzzled, the dog reads the label on the bottle: Sour Cream. The next performance is given by a group of fleas singing "Dem Golden Slippers" to the delight of the audience. Then the band starts to play "Camptown Races" and the audience is invited to join in by following the bouncing ball as the lyrics to the song are flashed on the screen. In the background the story of the song is depicted, showing a slowly moving nag that gets stung by a group of bees. The nag becomes excited enough to come from behind and win the race. The closing sequence shows the minstrels as they parade out of town.

Review: *Motion Picture Herald*, 25 September 1948

A group of animals are attending an old time minstrel show, which provides some numerous and tuneful entertainment. The minstrels sing "Dixie," "Golden Slippers," and other favorites. Then they sing "Camptown Races," and the audience is invited to join in and follow the bouncing ball.

Review: *Boxoffice*, 23 October 1948

An entertaining cartoon short in the new Polacolor process. All of the animals who are attending an old time minstrel show seem to be enjoying it except for a big, sad Saint Bernard. The minstrels sing "Dixie," and "Golden Slippers" before going into the title song. The bouncing ball accompanies the lyrics of the latter, which are flashed on the screen for the audience.

CONFEDERATE HONEY (1940)

Company: I. Freleng, Warner Bros.
Type: Merrie Melodies
Characters: Elmer Fudd, southern blacks

Story: The cartoon opens to the music of "My Old Kentucky Home." The narrator says that the place is old Kentucky and the time is 1861 B.C. (before Sea Biscuit). The stately mansion of Col. O'Hair Oil is seen with the colonel sitting on the front porch. Behind the mansion is a group of cabins and a sign along the highway (U.S. 66) reads, "Uncle Tom's Bungalows—Rent $1.50 Night and Day." In an adjacent field black men and women are seen picking cotton with the music of "Old Black Joe" in the background. One man pushes a lawnmower that cuts the cotton and throws the balls into a sack on the man's back. Another man is lying with his back propped up against a tree. He is so lazy that he has a little boy picking cotton for him. He puts it in the lazy man's hand one ball at a time, and he then throws the cotton into a sack with one slow flip of his hand. When the little boy puts more than one cotton ball in the man's hand, the

man tells him, "Don't get too ambitious, son." Next the colonel's beautiful daughter, Crimson O'Hair Oil, tells the little black girl, Topsy, dressing her to hurry because her many suitors are coming to call on her. Topsy looks up and tells her, "Y'all sho' does look scrumptious, Missy." Crimson's many rich, handsome suitors come by, but she rejects them all until Ned Cutter (Elmer Fudd) comes on the scene riding his slow white horse. When Cutter arrives, he dismounts and gives his horse to a little black boy and tells him to hold it. The boy climbs on the horse and parks it like an automobile. Meanwhile Ned Cutler is on his knees before Crimson and is about to propose when the sounds of cannon fire are heard signaling the beginning of the Civil War. Ned hurries off to war to the sound of "Dixie," while the little black boy calls out after him that he forgot his horse. Crimson tells him that she will keep a light burning in her window until he returns. The scene shifts to the camp of the Union army where a colonel, pacing in front of his troops, tells them that they are facing a big battle. He tells them that Stone Ball Jackson, a southpaw, is pitching against them. He also informs them that if they win this one they will get to meet the South in the Cotton Bowl. In the Confederate army camp Ned is seen writing letters to Crimson. Meanwhile back on the plantation the colonel hears the news on the radio that the Yanks have won at Richmond. The little black boy is seen taking care of Ned's horse. Time passes, and it is 1865. The war is over and the boys are coming home. The flame in Crimon's window has burned out, and she is anxiously awaiting Ned. At last he shows up, falls on his knees, and asks her the question she has been waiting to hear all these years: "Will you, will you validate my parking ticket?" Crimson hits him on the head at the fade-out.

Review: *Motion Picture Exhibitor*, 17 April 1940

By far the slap-happiest and most laugh-provoking reel of color cartoon ever put out by Leon Schlesinger (and that takes in a lot of territory). This take-off on *Gone with the Wind* had a projection room audience doubled up with laughter. It concerns the sad tale of Elmer Cutter, who is called to the colors before he has an opportunity to propose to Crimson O'Hair Oil. He does return, however, but he doesn't get the gal who waited patiently for him. Ah, Woe! Excellent.

DIXIE DAYS (1930)

Company: John Foster, Van Beuren; distributed by RKO-
            Radio Pictures, Pathe Film Exchange
Type: Aesop's Sound Fable
Characters: Uncle Tom, Little Eva, Topsy, Liza and baby, Si-
            mon Legree

See fig. 36. Story: The cartoon scene opens on a paddle-wheel steamboat traveling up river. On board all the crew are happy, tap dancing and eating watermelon. The captain and other officers sing "Carry Me Back to Old Virginia." The scene shifts to the plantation where blacks are skipping along, singing as they pick cotton. In the next scene a larger watermelon opens to reveal the head of a black man. He opens his mouth in a wide grin to reveal two rows of big white teeth. They turn into piano keys as the background music plays "Dixie." Back in the cotton field, picked cotton is stuffed into the pants of one black man who is then picked up and carried on the back of another black man. Meanwhile old Uncle Tom is sitting in front of his small cabin and playing his horn. Before long Topsy, a small black girl with braided hair and a big grin on her face, skips into the scene. She is greeted by Uncle Tom who says, "Hello Topsy. Where is Little Eva?" Topsy points in the direction where Little Eva, a large white hippo dressed in a short dress, is seen skipping merrily along. After she arrives on the scene, she and Topsy dance to the tune of "Swanee River" played by Uncle Tom. But the happy scene is interrupted by Simon Legree, who arrives holding a long whip in his hands. He is unhappy with Uncle Tom, and before long Tom and Topsy are marched off to the slave auction. Meanwhile another band of smiling slaves, chained together and led by a black man playing a horn, march to the place where a sign reads, "Slave Auction Today." Uncle Tom is on the auction block doing a slow soft-shoe dance to the tune of "St. Louis Blues." The slave buyers are unhappy with his performance, and he is replaced by Topsy. Her dancing does not please the slave buyers either. They all shout, "We want Liza." Liza is in front of her cabin, giving her baby girl a bath in the washtub. When she hears the shouts from the slave auction, she becomes so frightened that she and her baby turn white. She grabs the baby in her arms and runs off the plantation in an attempt to escape. She is seen fleeing by Simon Legree. He calls for his pack of blood hounds, and they run off to capture Liza and her baby. Running on the frozen river, jumping from ice block to ice block, Liza frantically tries to elude the hounds but they catch up, closely followed by Simon Legree rowing a small boat. Meanwhile Uncle Tom is sitting in front of his cabin polishing a large iron ball that Legree has attached to his leg by a chain. An excited Topsy arrives and tells him that Liza and the baby are in big trouble. Pulling his ball and chain behind him, Uncle Tom runs with Topsy to help Liza, who is standing on a block of ice that is about to be carried over a waterfall in the river. Tom arrives in the nick of time and rescues her. But when Simon Legree arrives, Tom breaks his chain and throws the big iron ball into Legree's boat, sending him to his death over the falls. Later, back at the cabin, Uncle Tom, Liza and the baby, and Topsy are happy and singing "Way Down South in Dixie." When a chicken appears on the scene, they all suddenly stop singing. The chicken crows and runs away, and Uncle Tom, Liza, baby, and Topsy all chase after it as the cartoon ends.

Review: *Bioscope*, 28 May 1930

An excellent number of this series. The scene is laid in the cotton fields of the south, and the subject is a clever burlesque of Uncle Tom's cabin. For any audience. (679 ft)

Review: *Billboard*, 12 April 1930

One of the best animated cartoons seen to date. It is a burlesque on *Uncle Tom's Cabin,* and is done in such a manner as

to insure a lot of laughs from any kind of audience. The comedy is well done and the animation perfect.

Pathe short-subjects are rapidly reaching a stage of perfection that has been attained by few other companies. With the elimination of a lot of deadwood from other organization, the shorts are all improving and this year's product should be much sought after by exhibitors. (7 min)

Review: *Motion Picture News,* 5 April 1930

A sound cartoon take-off on "Uncle Tom's Cabin," done before in pen-and-ink style, but surely no more effectively than in this short in which many highly entertaining gags are pulled by Van Beuren.

Review: *Variety,* 21 May 1930

Amusing little cartoon and better than those usually turned out. Incorporated the tale of *Uncle Tom's Cabin* to be parodied by the cartoon characters. It is worked out entertainingly.

There's Liza, Topsy, Little Eva and Simon Legree and Uncle Tom, all done by the cartoon figures. Synchronization good. A number of Southern airs, some given a novel freak arrangement.

DOWN IN DIXIE (1932)

Company: John Foster, Harry Barleg, Van Beuren; released by Pathe-RKO Radio
Type: Jungle Jinks
Characters: Uncle Tom, Little Eva, Topsy, Simon Legree, Liza

Story: The cartoon opens on board a riverboat traveling down a southern river. On the boat, blacks are amusing themselves singing and dancing. One does a slow shuffle to the music of "Dark Town Strutter's Ball" played by a black using half a watermelon as a bass fiddle and another blowing a slice of melon like a harmonica. Meanwhile blacks are working on a cotton plantation. Several have have smiles on their faces as they skip along the rows planting cottonseeds. Another man picks cotton and puts it in a huge sack being carried on the back of another man who walks with a shuffling gait. Another man appears and picks up the man with the sack on his back and carries him off to the tune of "Swanee River." Uncle Tom, an old black man, is sitting in front of his small cabin playing "Swanee River" on a mouth harp when Topsy skips on the scene. She is a girl with braided hair that sticks straight out from her head. Uncle Tom stops playing and asks, "Where is Little Eva?" Topsy points off in the direction where Little Eva, a fat white hippo, is coming. After Eva arrives on the scene, Tom resumes playing and Eva and Topsy do a soft-shoe dance. Everybody is having fun, but the music stops when Simon Legree arrives on the scene. Legree beats Tom with his whip, and Topsy becomes angry. She kicks Legree in the shins, and Eva, Topsy, and Tom run off while Legree kneels and rubs his leg. Meanwhile Liza, a skinny black woman, is washing her baby outdoors in a large washtub of soapsuds. Tom and Topsy arrive on the scene to warn her that Legree is coming. She and her baby should run away with them. Liza quickly pulls her baby out of the tub, and they all run off the plantation. Legree calls out to his bloodhounds, and they chase the fleeing slaves, who hop onto blocks of ice while running across the frozen river. They eventually arrive at the North Pole where polar bears, penguins, and walruses are preparing to go to sleep for the night. But Uncle Tom quickly learns the the night is six months long. One walrus sets his alarm clock to ring on April 1. Uncle Tom, Topsy, and Liza with the baby in her arms lie down in the snow and go to sleep as the sun sets and the long winter night begins. But a strong icy wind awakens Uncle Tom, and he is frightened by a strange creature that is covered by white fur and walks on two legs. Shaking with fear, Uncle Tom begins to sing a prayer, "Lord, you made the river flow, flowers grow. You made the weak and the strong. But Lord, you made the night too long. You made the robins sing, and me you gave a lovely song. Oh Lord, is that why the night's so long?" Scary things are happening all around Uncle Tom, but he continues to sing. "I got a heart and I got a cabin. The door is open wide. What good's a heart and what good's a cabin if no love is inside?" Uncle Tom does not see two skeletons that are behind him. One takes a drink from a hot-water bottle and spits it out at Tom's feet. Uncle Tom jumps in the air in fear and then runs back, still singing, to rejoin Topsy and Liza. They all sing the conclusion of the song, "But Lord, you made the night too long." Meanwhile the riverboat, covered with ice and snow, sails onto the scene carrying Simon Legree. He smiles as he strokes his mustache because he has found his runaway slaves. The boat arrives at the shore, and Legree forces Uncle Tom, Liza and the baby, and Topsy to get on board. But before Legree can get back on board, he is confronted by a huge black walrus that knocks him to the ground and pushes the riverboat out to sea. Simon Legree having been vanquished, Uncle Tom, Liza and the baby, and Topsy smile and sing, "Goin' back to Dixie, hurray, hurray. We're goin' back to Dixie," as the boat sails away and the cartoon ends.

DOWN THE LEVEE (1933)

Company: Frank Moser, Paul Terry, Educational Pictures, 20th Century-Fox
Type: Terrytoons
Characters: Uncle Tom, Little Eva, Simon Legree, Topsy

Review: *Selected Motion Pictures,* April 1933

The animals all rush to the Show Boat coming down the river to attend a performance of "Little Eva."

ELIZA ON ICE (1944)

Company: Paul Terry, 20th Century-Fox
Type: Terrytoon (similar to *Eliza Runs Again* released in 1938)
Characters: Mighty Mouse, Uncle Tom, Eliza, Simon Legree, Topsy

Story: A big race is about to begin on the plantation. Uncle Tom stands at the starting line with the two participants, Eliza and her baby, and Simon Legree and his hounds. Uncle Tom rings the starting bell, and they are off. Eliza and her baby are in the lead, and she is about to cross a river. But there is no ice on it, so she runs over to an ice dispenser in the form of a slot machine. She puts in two coins, pulls the handle, and three cherries come up. Blocks of ice then roll out of the machine and into the river. Eliza runs on the ice, Legree and hounds in close pursuit. They all slide over a waterfall and land in a lake. Legree shoots his revolver at Eliza, but the bullets come out of the gun barrel as bubbles. They burst and release the bullets, which strike Legree. As he looks down the gun barrel to see what happened, a fish comes out and bites him on the nose. A swordfish sticks Legree in the rear end, and he leaps out of the lake. When he falls back in, he is immediately frozen into a block of ice. The hounds pull him out, ice and all, and they resume the race. Eliza and baby are running fast when Uncle Tom rings a bell signaling a time-out. Eliza is seen fanning her baby with a towel. Meanwhile Legree's hounds are fanning him. Uncle Tom rings the bell again, and Eliza and Legree resume the race. The hounds are catching up fast when Eliza tricks them by pulling a fire hydrant from behind a tree and placing it in the path of the hounds. They sniff the hydrant while Eliza keeps on running until she reaches the railroad tracks and jumps onto a moving train. Legree stays close behind, however, as he follows her by riding a hand-propelled railroad car. Eliza and baby throw watermelons into the coalburner, and they are propelled out of the smokestack and fly back and strike Legree. At this point we hear a voice say, "On, on comes the wicked Simon Legree. Liza can't hold out much longer. Isn't there a friend that can help her?" We next see little Eva in heaven looking at the doings down below through a spyglass. She then flies over to the next cloud to a telephone and calls Mighty Mouse at his home on a star. She tells Mighty Mouse that Simon Legree is up to his old tricks again. Mighty Mouse immediately flies off to the rescue. Meanwhile Legree, in a boat being rowed down river by his hounds, fires at Eliza on board a paddle-wheel riverboat. She dodges the bullets by diving into an exhaust stack. But when she comes out, she runs right into Legree. He chases her and tries to hit her with his whip. Eliza is trapped when she lands on the paddle wheels, but Mighty Mouse arrives in the nick of time. He puts the hounds out of action and then knocks Legree silly. At this point the steamboat falls over a waterfall and breaks into pieces. Eliza is riding a plank of wood approaching the falls. She and the baby go over the falls, but they are caught by Mighty Mouse before they hit bottom. He flies them back to the plantation, where they are welcomed by a happy Uncle Tom. The last scene shows Mighty Mouse and Little Eva sitting on the cloud smiling at a job well done.

Review: *Motion Picture Herald,* 10 June 1944

The familiar scene from *Uncle Tom's Cabin* is reenacted with a new hero. While Eliza is fleeing across the ice, trailed by bloodhounds and Simon Legree, the spirit of Little Eva calls on Mighty Mouse to insure her escape. Taking full advantage of the tricks of maneuvering on a slippery surface, he accomplishes his mission. (6 min)

Review: *Motion Picture Exhibitor,* 17 May 1944

Mighty Mouse, on request of the spirit of Little Eva, comes to the rescue of Eliza, who is having a tough time keeping ahead of Simon Legree. Fair.

Review: *Motion Picture Exhibitor,* 1 August 1938

A gagged version of the famous chase, the situation ends as a race with the narrator, spectators, Legree finally losing to Eliza. There are some funny gags, but animation draftsmanship do not do them justice. Legree loses because someone in the theatre audience throws a tomato at him. Good.

Review: *Besa Shorts Shorts,* 8 May 1944

The famed story of Uncle Tom and cabin, Little Eva, Simon Legree and hounds and poor little Liza gets a modern touch here in this Terrytoon. Uncle Tom is the starter for the race with Simon L. et al. They get on their marks, get set, and go—all over the icy countryside, hot after the fleeing Liza. She's awful smart and outwits the villain but you darn well know who actually saves her life. Mighty Mouse. And who do you think tipped him off? None other than Little Eva from her home in the clouds.

FELIX THE CAT IN UNCLE TOM'S CRABBIN (1927)

Company: Pat Sullivan; distributed by M. J. Winkler, Educational Pictures, Pathe Film Exchange
Characters: Felix the Cat, Uncle Tom, Topsy, Little Eva, Simon Legree, black mammy

Story: The cartoon opens on a plantation in the South where Uncle Tom, a partially bald old man, is sitting in front of his small cabin and playing his banjo. Topsy, a small, barefoot black girl with six strands of braided hair sticking straight out of her head, is dancing to the banjo music. Meanwhile Felix, who is in the cottonfield, hears the music and says to himself, "I'll warm up with Uncle Tom and Topsy!" He arrives on the scene and immediately starts to dance to the music. Meanwhile Simon Legree is sleeping in his bed with the sheets pulled over him. The music wakes him up, and he angrily jumps out of bed, grabs his long whip, and rushes out of the house to put a stop to the music. As Legree nears the scene, he stops and lashes out with his whip. He lassoes Uncle Tom while Felix and Topsy look on. Legree smashes the banjo to pieces with his whip then turns his attention to Uncle Tom, who is on his knees and wide-eyed with fear. Legree points his finger at Tom and orders him to "lay offa that banjo or I'll . . ." Tom trembles as he looks at his smashed banjo, and Felix is so sad that he lowers his head. But Topsy appears angry. When Tom starts to cry, Felix tells him not to worry and then walks away with an idea of how to get even with Legree. Felix walks back to the master's house. Through the window he sees Mammy cooking a pile of flapjacks in a frying pan over a wood-burning stove. Mammy is fat

and wears a bandanna on her head. Felix climbs through the window and grabs her frying pan. Then he returns to Uncle Tom and tells him that he can make the pan into a banjo, using the hairs from his face as the strings. Tom is so happy that he begins to dance as Felix plays the new banjo and Topsy joins in. Again the music wakes up Simon Legree, who grabs his whip and rushes out of his cabin. Tom and Topsy see him coming and run away, but Felix has his back turned and continues to play. Felix soon sees Legree and rides away after turning the banjo into a unicycle. As Legree chases Felix through the cotton fields, Felix looks back and thumbs his nose at him. Finally Felix stops, changes the unicycle into a bow, and then removes his tail and shoots it at Legree. The tail hits Legree in the face but does not stop him. Legree stops to throw stones at Felix but the cat uses the frying pan to bat them back at Legree. Legree then grabs his whip and again chases Felix, who runs to Little Eva and asks for her help. Eva is a little white girl who is neatly dressed and has long hair. Eva pulls a large bow from her hair and gives it to Felix. He uses it to make a propeller that lifts him off the ground. Legree sees Felix hovering in the air and uses his long whip to make stairsteps that he then runs up. But he still can't reach Felix. Felix then turns the bow into a parachute that lowers him gently back to the ground. Legree climbs down to the ground and changes his whip into a hound dog that he orders to chase Felix. Felix runs past a sign on the road that reads "100 Miles to Somewhere." Felix uses the zero and the one from the sign to make a pushcart that he climbs onto and rides away from Legree's dog. Felix comes to a stop at a covered ice wagon pulled by a horse. Felix jumps into the wagon, followed by the dog, and they run over large blocks of ice as the caption read, "Felix substitutes for Eliza crossing the ice!" Followed by the hound, Felix jumps out of the wagon. The hound jumps on Felix, and they disappear in a cloud of dust. When the dust clears, Felix holds a wire hoop that changes into Legree's whip. Felix smiles as the season changes to winter. With snow all around, Felix smiles and says, "The South is warm, but it ain't so hot with me" as the cartoon ends.

Review: *Moving Picture World,* 3 December 1927

This Pat Sullivan cartoon, *Felix the Cat in Uncle Tom's Crabbin,* is suggestive of *Uncle Tom's Cabin* with an acute comedy angle, and with snappy titles, has been rounded out into a charming little cartoon booking. (one reel)

Review: *Film Daily,* 4 December 1927

Felix the Cat does some good burlesque of the Uncle Tom's Cabin idea. Felix hikes to the sunny Southland and meets Uncle Tom and Topsy doing their stuff in front of the old cabin. Felix helps to jazz things up as Uncle Tom strums his old banjo. Then Simon Legree appears with his whip and starts to break up the party. The famous ice scene is burlesqued with Felix subbing for Eliza as Legree chases him over the cakes in the ice wagon. The comedy antics of Felix make this a lively number.

Review: *Motion Picture News,* 2 December 1927

The Sullivan Tomcat journeys down to Dixieland far away from the inclement weather of the north where Jack Frost holds forth. Down in the sunny Southland with its fields of cotton and fragment atmosphere Felix thought he could rest and dream and worry no more. But alas! The diabolical Simon Legree, his snarling whip and bloodthirsty hounds are on hand to make life miserable for the unoffending cat.

For you see when Felix went down South he probably unrolled the years back a bit and went to that particular locality where the name of Legree was something to be feared. Unaware of this, the cat blithely joins in the revelry of Uncle Tom and Topsy, dancing to the accompaniment of a banjo. The music arouses Legree and sends him into paroxysms of rage. After being chased by the mean Legree and that unworthy's whip, which has been changed into a whippet over an icy river, the cat decides that the North is his proper homeland.

This cartoon parody on *Uncle Tom's Cabin* is an appropriate release. In it you will find Uncle Tom, Topsy, Little Eva, and Felix, who much after the fashion of Eliza, crosses the ice to escape the terrible Legree.

GALLOPING FANNY (1933)

Company: Steve Muffati, Eddie Donnelly, Van Beuren; released RKO-Radio Pictures
Characters: Cubby the Bear, black porter

Story: The cartoon opens at a racetrack, where the jockeys and horses are getting ready for the race. The horses get rubdowns and are seen lifting weights. Cubby the Bear and the other jockeys are being weighed. The Kentucky colonel has engaged Cubby to ride his filly, Fanny Lou. When Cubby looks for her, he finds a note saying that she has decided to skip the race and go out on a date instead. At first Cubby is at loss, but then he gets an idea. He drags an old horse costume from the closet. He looks out of the window and pulls in a heavyset black man who is smoking a cigar and resembles Andy Brown of the *Amos 'n' Andy* radio show. He puts him in the tail of the horse. He reaches through the window again and catches a slow-walking black porter and puts him in the head end of the costume. They go to the starting line and get in line next to the favorite, a black horse ridden by a jockey who is determined to win by any means. The gates open and they are off, with the black horse ahead and Cubby in the rear. Using various tricks, such as changing road signs, the leading jockey is able to eliminate all the other riders except Cubby. But Cubby's horse is getting tired and begins to sag in the middle. Then two people riding a two-seat bicycle run into the mouth of Cubby's mount and ride off. Next the leading jockey pulls out a bomb and drops it in Cubby's path. The bomb explodes, and when the dust clears, Cubby and horse are riding a single-seat bicycle. There are only two contestants left, and he and Cubby are back on the track with Cubby catching up. As Cubby is about to pass, the leading horse kicks Cubby and his mount so hard they they fly off of the track, hit a tree, and bounce back and land on top of the leading horse and jockey. They get tangled up into a large ball that rolls toward the finish line but stops a few inches before crossing it. As the pile untangles, Cubby's horse stretches out its legs across the finish, making Cubby the victor. At the winner's circle, the colonel puts

a large wreath over the head of Cubby's horse. As the colonel leans forward to kiss the horse, the head of the black porter pops out, and the colonel kisses him instead. Cubby gets a laugh out of this as the picture ends.

THE GOOSE GOES SOUTH (1941)

Company: William Hanna, Joseph Barbera, M-G-M
Characters: Little Goose, southern blacks

Story: The carton opens with flocks of geese taking flight from their summer home on a lake. The offscreen narrator says, "Yes sir. These are wild geese and they're off for the sunny south. Each year at the very first sign of winter, these great flocks of birds fly southward, honking their way to southern marshes, there to bask in that warm tropical sun. It's their big annual trip and they all go—yes they all go but they don't all fly." A little goose is seen standing on U.S. Highway 1 south trying unsuccessfully to hitch a ride from passing motorists. The narrator says, "He'll arrive a little slow perhaps. But the road south takes us through the famous Blue Ridge mountains of Virginia," where a hillbilly farmer is trying to wake his lazy son and a revenue agent destroys a moonshine liquor still. Meanwhile the goose has stopped by the side of the road to eat a slice of watermelon but is chased away by an irate farmer. The goose runs all the way through Kentucky and Tennessee before stopping on the outskirts of Atlanta, Georgia, to take a rest. Then the scene changes to a southern plantation and the narrator says, "Here is a familiar sight—happy, carefree cotton pickers. In the cotton field two black women are picking cotton. One woman says to the other, "Oh, I hear you is havin' trouble with your chillun, Cindy Lou. The other woman responds, "I sho' is, gal. They all wants to grow up to be Rochester." Five black babies in a crib are making telephone calls, saying, "Hello Boss, hello Mr. Benny..." Meanwhile the goose still can't hitch a ride. He continues to be turned down by the motorist that he met at the beginning of his trip. Picking up the story, the narrator says, "Of great interest are the vast tobacco fields." Blacks are seen picking tobacco, and the narrator continues, "Of great interest are the tobacco workers. As we approach, we find that they have a strange new language of their own." Two black men are seen having a conversation. One talks as fast as a tobacco auctioneer. When he finishes, the other, a la Stephin Fetchit, scratches his head and attempts to give a slow version of the auctioneer's call. Next a southern swamp is seen as the narrator says, "The last leg of the goose's journey is through the everglades of Florida." Alligators are seen lurking in the shallow water, and the narrator says, "Hence very step is fraught with danger. Death lurks on every side. Look! Sitting there in the gaping mouth of an alligator is an innocent little child." A little black girl who has pigtails in her hair and eating a banana, is sitting between the jaws of a large alligator. The narrator shouts, "Quick, child, come out of that alligator's mouth! The little girl shakes her head no and says, "Dis ain't no alligator. Dis is a hollow tree." The narrator says, "Why, that's an alligator" and again the black girl replies, "Dis is a hollow tree," as the alligator slams its jaws shut. The narrator says, "It's an alligator," as the alligator's jaws open. The little black girl says, "I could be wrong," before the jaws close again. Meanwhile a tired goose has arrived at his destination and the narrator says, "At last the long journey is ended. And here by the sparkling waters of a winter's paradise, our little traveler stops for a well-earned rest." The goose hears a horn blowing and looks around to see the automobile of the driver who refused to give him a ride. He arrives and drives off the end of the pier and into the ocean as the cartoon ends.

Review: *Motion Picture Exhibitor,* 14 May 1941

The geese fly south when winter approaches, all except one little fellow who hitchhikes. Along the way he goes through the Blue Ridge Mountains, meets Hill-Billies, moonshiners, and "revenuers," encounters Georgia peaches, cotton-pickers, and tobacco auctioneers, alligators in the Everglades. Commenting and subject matter are quite amusing, even if this is similar to a technique used by another cartoon series. Good. (8 min)

HITTIN' THE TRAIL TO HALLELUJAH LAND (1930)

Company: Hugh Harman, Rudolph Ising, Vitaphone, Warner Bros.
Type: Merrie Melodies no. 4
Characters: Pigs playing *Uncle Tom's Cabin* characters, including Uncle Tom, Little Eva, Simon Legree

Story: The cartoon opens on a riverboat scene. Black musicians on deck are playing "Hittin' the Trail to Hallelujah Land" on a banjo, bones, and a Jew's harp. Several blacks are dancing, one of whom resembles the cartoon character Bosko. Meanwhile Little Eva and Uncle Tom are on a cart pulled by a donkey. Little Eva tells him to hurry so that they won't miss the boat. On board, the captain blows the whistle and docks the boat. The crowd at the pier cheers just as Uncle Tom and Eva drive up in the wagon. The captain helps Little Eva onto the boat and even carries her large trunk for her. She waves good-bye to Uncle Tom. He says, "Good-bye, Missie" as the boat moves off down the river. On the boat a black band starts to play some hot jazz music, and everybody has a good time. The captain entertains Little Eva by dancing on the stern, but he falls into the river. After nearly being eaten by an alligator, he manages to get back on board. Meanwhile Uncle Tom, asleep in his wagon, is going home. The donkey's tail keeps hitting him in the face and waking him up. He ties a big rock on the donkey's tail to keep it down, but the tail flies up anyway, hitting him on the head and knocking him off the wagon. He falls off into a cemetery where skeletons come to life. He says "holy mackerel" as he tries to run away. He finally manages to escape the graveyard through a hole in the fence. He does not stop running until he reaches a bottomless boat, which he tries to use to cross the river. But the boat sinks, and Uncle Tom cries out for help. On the boat the captain hears Uncle Tom and dives into the river. He swims over to Uncle Tom just as the old man is about to go under the water and swims with him back to dry land. Back on board the boat Little Eva is being attacked by Simon Legree. As she cries out for help, the captain runs along the shore until he comes upon a loading crane that has a hook on the end of a cable. As the riverboat passes, the captain lowers the hooks and catches Simon Legree holding Little Eva. The captain takes Little Eva from Legree and lowers him down so that his backside makes contact with the sawblade of a log cutter. Eva and the captain laugh as the cartoon ends.

Review: *Motion Picture Herald,* 19 December 1931

A New York Strand audience seemed to enjoy this number of the Merrie Melodies series in which popular song numbers accompany the animated cartoon figures. (7 min)

LAND O' COTTON (1929)

Company: Frank Moser, Paul Terry, Pathe Film Exchange
Type: Aesop's Fable
Characters: Black slave boy and black slave girl, Simon Legree

Review: *Motion Picture News,* 5 January 1929

There is some real good humor as well as a well executed story in this Aesop's Fable of Simon Legree and his slave boy and girl. Their purchase, incarceration and getaway from their brutal master provide more than the usual number of laughs found in these animated cartoons.

Simon, after buying the boy and girl on the auction block, locks them up in adjoining huts and they are aided in their getaway by a friendly mule. The chase for them is highly exciting and as they are about to be recaptured, the mule throws his two hind shoes with deadly accuracy and renders Simon null and void. (one reel)

MICKEY'S MELLERDRAMMER (1933)

Company: Wilford Jackson, Walt Disney, United Artists
Type: Shortened, silent version distributed by Hollywood Film Enterprises under the title *Mickey Mouse and Simon Legree*
Characters: Mickey Mouse (as Topsy and Uncle Tom), Minnie Mouse (as Little Eva), Goofy (as Eliza), Simon Legree

Story: The opening scene shows a posting for Mickey Mouse's production of *Uncle Tom's Cabin.* Inside the theater the animal audience is seen, and then the scene shifts backstage where the actors are making up. Minnie is putting on the Liza costume. Mickey is wearing the Topsy wig and explodes a firecracker in his mouth. The soot that is produced blackens his face, and he gets down on one knee and says, "mammy" a la Al Jolson. Simon Legree is seen just before the curtain rises on the first act, revealing Little Eva and several blacks singing "Dixie." Topsy comes out of the cabin, and she and Little Eva do a little soft-shoe routine. Simon Legree shows up on the scene, and Eva and topsy run into the cabin to hide. In the house Mickey changes into his Uncle Tom costume and goes outside to meet Simon Legree, who has summoned him to come out. Legree picks up Uncle Tom and says, "Bow down to your master. I own you, body and soul!" Uncle Tom replies, "You may own my body but my soul belongs to the Lord." This line brings loud applause from the audience. Legree pulls out his whip and is about to strike Uncle Tom, but the audience pelts him with all kinds of vegetables as the curtain falls on act 1. Then the curtain rises on act 2, which is entitled "Eliza on Ice." Eliza, played by Goofy in blackface, is seen running across the ice carrying a baby. Backstage Mickey and Minnie are providing the sound effects, which include rushing water, thunder, and lightning. For the bloodhounds they put dogs in costume but Legree, mischievously puts a cat in with the dogs. This creates a frantic scene with the dogs chasing the cat all over the place. They finally wind up on the stage with Eliza running across the ice, closely followed by the cat and the dogs. The audience loves it, and the curtain falls on the last act. Mickey and Minnie come out for a curtain call, greeted with applause and cheers. But when Legree comes out, he is pelted by vegetables. Next Goofy sticks his head out from behind the curtain and is immediately hit by an egg. He responds with a big grin at fadeout.

Review: *Selected Motion Pictures,* April 1933

Mickey, with the help of Minnie, Charley Horse and Pluto, presents an original version of *Uncle Tom's Cabin* to a delighted audience of animals, which cheers the hero and boos the villain in a most thorough manner.

Review: *Motion Picture Herald,* 1 July 1933

This time Mickey, the inimitable, stages an "Uncle Tom meller," with assorted animated mishaps in the accepted, and approved, Mickey fashion, while the antics of the animated audience contribute not a few of the laughs. It is good cartoon material, and the youngsters, old and young, should enjoy it. (8 min)

MISSISSIPPI SWING (1941)

Company: Connie Rasinski, Paul Terry, 20th Century-Fox Pictures
Type: Terrytoons
Characters: Southern blacks

Review: *Motion Picture Herald,* 22 February 1941

The carefree spirit of the Old South is pictured in this color cartoon and is enlivened by the music of Stephen Foster. Colored folks are shown gathering cotton in the fields and at home and rushing towards the docks when word comes that the Showboat is arriving. Aboard the boat, entertainment is the key word with the old time minstrel show proving most of the fun. (7 min)

Review: *Film Daily,* 6 February 1941

Filmed in Technicolor, this cartoon is a lively musical number. A showboat appears on the river and the Negroes assemble for the entertainment. Several Stephen Foster pieces are "swung" in approved fashion. The show on the showboat is good for some laughs. Reel is a Paul Terry production.

Review: *Boxoffice,* 6 March 1941

This cartoon takeoff on showboats and darkies having a high old musical time has a few smart comic moments. A good deal of animation detail, with varying degrees of humor, makes up for what is lacking. Generally it's tuneful and full of action.

Review: *Motion Picture Herald,* 25 March 1950

A combination of music, comedy and color is featured in this subject dealing with life in the deep South. To the tunes of Stephen Foster's melodies, colored folks sing the story of their life in the cotton fields. The high spot in the film is the arrival of the showboat with its oldtime minstrel show.

Review: *Motion Picture Exhibitor,* April 1941

A standard offering for the series, with the color well-used in picturing the Old South, this shows darkies cotton-picking and the excitement attendant on the arrival of the Show Boat. Bulk of the reel is devoted to singing, dancing, and comedy acts in the boat, and a tap dance number is outstanding. A swing version of "Jeannie with the Light Brown Hair" is well illustrated by colored comic characters burlesquing Scarlett O'Hara and Rhett Butler. Other Stephen Foster melodies are featured. Good.

MY OLD KENTUCKY HOME (1929)

Company: Dave Fleischer, Max Fleischer, Red Seal Pictures Film Company; released by Paramount Pictures
Type: Screen Song
Characters: Black cat, black girl, old black man; title song sung offscreen by the Metropolitan Quartet, with Jimmy Flora at the organ

Story: The cartoon opens as a black, catlike animal wearing a derby hat arrives home from work carrying a thermos and his jacket. He hangs his coat on a chair before filling his hat with water and washing his face. He dries his face with his coat, which turns into a tablecloth after he tosses it onto the dinner table. Next he pulls a large ham out of a box and places it on a platter on the table. He then uses a long knife to strip off all the meat. He throws it away because he only wants the bone. Next he pulls out his teeth and sharpens them on a grinding wheel before putting them back in his mouth. He then takes a bite from one end of the bone, which turns into a trombone. He plays "My Old Kentucky Home" on the trombone, but he stops playing and screws off the end of it, which turns into a small white ball. The animal then turns his face toward the audience and says,

"Now follow the ball and join in, everybody." The ball bounces on top of the following lyrics as they scroll on the screen:

The sun shines bright on my old Kentucky home.
     'Tis summer, the darkies are gay.
The corn-top's ripe and the meadows all in bloom.
     While the birds make music all day.
The young folks roll on the little cabin floor.
     All merry, all happy and bright.
By'n by hard times comes a-knockin' at the door.
     Then my old Kentucky home, good-night.

Weep no more my lady. Oh weep no more today.
We will sing one song for the old Kentucky home.
For the old Kentucky home, far away.

They hunt no more for the 'possum and 'coon.
     O're meadows, the hills and the shore.
They sing no more by the glimmer of the moon.
     On the bench by the old cabin door.
The day goes by like a shadow.
     O're the heart with sorrow where all was delight.
The time has come when the darkies have to part.
     Then my old Kentucky home good-night.

As the second chorus starts, the bouncing white ball is replaced by a little black girl with braided hair, who dances on top of the words. First she cries, her face covered by a white towel and her tearsdrops flying in the air. Then as she dances by, she pulls the clothes off a clothesline and puts them into a basket she is carrying. When she reaches the end of the line, the pants fly out of the basket and dance briefly over the words. After the song ends, she falls into a wagon that is attached by a rope to an old black man who has a partially bald head. The man does not pull the wagon, which makes the girl angry. She picks up a fishing pole from the back of the wagon and ties a large slice of watermelon to the end of the line. She uses the pole to dangle the watermelon in front of the face of the old man. As the juice drips from the watermelon, the man smiles and licks his lips with his tongue. He walks forward to grab the watermelon, pulling the wagon and the little girl behind him. The girl gives a big smile as the cartoon ends.

MY OLD KENTUCKY HOME (1926)

Company: Dave Fleischer, Max Fleischer, Red Seal Pictures
Characters: Ko-Ko the Clown, black girl, black man

Review: Film Daily, 28 March 1926

Ko-Ko and his quartet render this time the old southern classic, "My Old Kentucky Home," with the help of the audience of course. Fleischer has a new instruction for the opening, showing the quartet as a band marching and playing, and winding up on the stage of the theatre. There is always a humorous touch added to the chorus of the song. This time in the shape of a little pickaninny who dances along on top of the words.

Review: Motion Picture News, 23 March 1926

The old familiar favorite "My Old Kentucky Home" furnishes the subject for this Max Fleischer Song Car-Tune. The verses are shown in the usual manner and the comedy handling of the chorus shows a darky girl leaping from word to word doing stunts. Fleischer has provided a new opening. Instead of the Ko-Ko Kwartette leaping out of the ink bottle, a hand is shown drawing cartoons of a brass band which comes to life and marches into the theatre. This should prove one of the most popular of the series. (550 ft.)

Review: Motion Picture News, 5 October 1926

This ever-popular song has been decked out with cartoon ornamentation as well as synchronized score and vocal harmonizing by the Roxy Quartet. The number is a well balanced and developed one of the Inkwell cartoons, produced by S. Roy Luby and presented by Alfred Weiss. Good quality pervades it throughout.

There's no reason at all why these song cartoons can't successfully invade the foreign market, too. Cartoons and music make a good combination capable of breaking through the barrier of language. In this country this Biophone screen song should find a gratifying response.

OLD BLACK JOE (1929)

Company: Dave Fleischer, Max Fleischer, Red Seal Pictures Film Company; released by Paramount Pictures
Type: Ko-Ko Song Car-Tune
Characters: Blacks, Ko-Ko the Clown

Review: Motion Picture News, 23 March 1929

This is one of the Max Fleischer song novelties done in sound and released by Paramount. They have taken the old plantation ditty, that was the delight of the street corner quartets of the last fifty years, and worked it out effectively in cartoon and music. (4 min)

Review: Motion Picture News, 10 July 1929

This is the latest of the Ko-Ko Song Car-Tune series and will be found to have the same interest as the previous reels in this series. This is an amusing novelty and should be fully appreciated by every audience familiar with the antics of Ko-Ko in the earlier songs in this series.

Review: Billboard, 23 March 1929

Another cleverly executed song cartoon, animated by Max Fleischer and played with the idea of getting the audience to burst forth in song. The "Old Black Joe" number is done with song accompaniment and makes effective "filler" for all houses, highbrow or low.

Production A-1 and photography passes the acid test.

THE OLD PLANTATION (1935)

Company: Hugh Harmon, Rudolph Ising, M-G-M
Type: Happy Harmonies
Characters: Mammy, Uncle Tom, Topsy, Little Eva, Black
            Beauty

Story: The cartoon opens on a plantation setting in the deep South. A black quartet is singing "Old Black Joe" in front of a southern mansion. Mammy is in the field picking cotton with a big smile on her face and singing the "Rhythm Cotton Pickin'" song. At her side are three small black girls who dance and sing the chorus of the song. Finishing her work, she drops the sack of cotton and wipes her brow. She looks over toward the big house and says, "Well if that ain't Mammy's honey chile." She walks over to the house and lifts a little red-headed white girl, Little Eva, out of a cradle and into her arms. She sings her a lullaby as old Uncle Tom, walking slowly with the aid of a cane, comes on the scene to the music of "Old Black Joe." After Mammy finishes her song, Little Eva wakes up and says, "Oh, I don't want to miss Black Beauty running today." Mammy smiles and tells her, "Yuk, yuk, honey chile. Black Beauty better win that race today or we're sho' gonna lose the old Kentucky home." The evil Simon Legree comes on the scene and the blacks, with fear on their faces, move out of sight. Legree says, "Good day, pretty little Miss. Is old Colonel Julep about the plantation?" Eva tells him, "I don't like you," and she steps on his foot. Forcing a smile, Legree says, "Ha, ha, cute little thing," as he pats her on the head. Colonel Julep comes out the front door and asks Legree, "Well sir, what brings you here today?" Legree says, "Colonel Julep, sir, your mortgage must be paid today or your Kentucky home is mine." He holds up the mortgage paper for the colonel to read. The colonel orders Legree to leave. As he walks away, he looks over his shoulder and says, "You'll regret the day you insulted Simon Legree." The blacks moan at the thought of the colonel losing his home. The colonel tells Little Eva, "Black Beauty must win the race." It's race day at the track, and the crowd is excited as a black band parades around the oval. Dynamite, Simon Legree's horse and the favorite to win the race, is warming up by punching a bag as the crowd looks on. Meanwhile Topsy, the jockey, is preparing the colonel's horse, Black Beauty, for the race. Beauty is a mechanical horse, and Topsy is winding up its springs. When she leaves, Simon Legree tries to increase his chances of winning by tampering with Beauty. He removes the horse's springs and dumps them in a nearby pond. The trumpet signals post time, and the horses move to the starting gate. The gun is fired and they're off, with Legree and Dynamite taking the lead. Black Beauty remains at the starting line. Topsy wonders what's wrong until she looks inside the horse and finds that the springs are missing. Topsy is frantic, but then gets an idea. She stuffs several rockets inside Beauty, but has difficulty lighting them because the wind created by the other horses as they pass her keeps blowing out her match. Finally she gets the rockets lit, and Beauty is about to take off down the track. But then the rockets blow up, and Topsy and horse fall to the ground. Black Beauty is motionless, but Topsy is not discouraged and finds another rocket. After it is ignited, Beauty is propelled around the track and passes all the other horses. They pass Legree when he and Dynamite stop on the track to have their picture taken. Realizing he is behind, Legree rides off at top speed, but Topsy and Beauty manage to remain in front. Then Beauty's rocket burns out, and Topsy has to carry the horse on her back. Legree is about to pass her when Beauty's spring breaks, causing the horse's neck to stretch out and cross the finish line first. Beauty wins and the colonel gets to keep his plantation as the cartoon ends.

Review: *Motion Picture Reviews,* July 1935

The story is built around the characters in Uncle Tom's Cabin with accompanying songs by Stephen Foster. Good. Family.

Review: *Film Daily,* 18 October 1935

This creation of the Harman-Ising studios represents a lot of work, but its contents and action are a bit jumbled, resulting in just fair entertainment of its kind. It's a fast-moving execution of southern darky singing, cotton picking, Simon Legree melodramatics, etc., performed by a flock of toy characters, and done in Technicolor. (7 min)

Review: *Selected Motion Pictures,* 1 November 1935

Happy Harmony color cartoon, Black Beauty and characters from "Uncle Tom's Cabin" lift the mortgage. Amusing. Family and Junior Matinee.

Review: *National Exhibitor,* 5 November 1935

The scene is in toytown. The players are the Colonel of the plantation, Little Topsy, Eva, and Simon Legree, who holds the mortgage and whose horse will race the against the Colonel's, and the happy singing slaves. Of course, Legree fails to overcome the Colonel; and he fails to win the race the next day, in spite of his dirty work. Amusing race shots with marvelous use of color and ingenious ideas—this is first rate stuff. Good.

SOUTHERN FRIED RABBIT (1953)

Company: I. Freleng, Warner Bros.
Type: Looney Tunes
Characters: Bugs Bunny, Yosemite Sam as the colonel

Story: The cartoon opens on a farm where the carrot crop has been ruined by a drought. Bugs Bunny is standing in a field, pulls up a shriveled carrot, and says, "What carrots! What dried up specimens! I haven't seen a decent carrot for months around here." He picks up a copy of the September 3, 1952, edition of the "Daily Snooze" newspaper from the ground. The headline reads, "Record Carrot Crop in Alabama." Bugs smiles and says, "Alabama! Well, I'm Alabama bound." He walks down the highway singing "Dixie." After nearly collapsing from heat and thirst, he finally reaches the Mason-Dixon line. He finds the road blocked by Yosemite Sam as a southern colonel. Sam wears the uniform of a confederate officer and has a saber. Sam orders Bugs, "Step forward and be recognized. I have orders from General Lee to guard the whole Mason-Dixon line, and no Yankees are to cross." Bugs says, "General Lee? The war between the states ended almost ninety years ago." The colonel answers, "I'm no clock watcher. Until I hear from General Lee personally, I'm blasting any Yankee that sets foot on southern soil. Scram, Yankee." The colonel fires his pistol into the air. Bugs makes a hasty retreat as the colonel paces back and forth, guarding the line. The colonel stops, looks off in the distance, and smiles as he says, "Well, it's one of our boys." Bugs arrives back on the scene disguised as a black slave, wearing a long coat and a battered hat. He carries a banjo and sings "My Old Kentucky Home." The colonel says, "Hey there, Boy. How about givin' out somethin' more peppy on that there skin box." Bugs says, "Yes suh" and then starts to sing "Yankee Doodle Dandy." This makes the colonel furious and he calls Bugs a traitor. Bugs sinks to his knees, clasps his hands together, looks up at the colonel, and says, "Don't beat me, Massa. Please don't beat me. Don't beat this tired old body." The colonel stands in front of Bugs, who runs away before he can strike him with a long whip. Bugs returns, disguised as Abraham Lincoln, wearing a beard, a long coat, and a stovepipe hat. The colonel is shocked and Bugs says, "What's this I hear about you whipping slaves?" The colonel begins to stammer, and Bugs says, "Never mind. Here's my card. Look me up at my Gettysburg address." As he walks away, the colonel reads the card and then looks at Bugs. But then he sees his tail sticking out from under the coat Bugs is wearing. The colonel realizes that he has been tricked and runs after Bugs with his sword in his hand. Bugs strips off his disguise and then dives into a hole in the trunk of a tree. The colonel arrives and says, "OK you fur-bearing carpetbagger, I'm givin' you one second to come out or I'm blowing ya out." He strikes a match and prepares to light the fuse of a bomb he is holding. But Bugs sticks his head out of the tree and blows the match out. The colonel walks back a few feet from the tree and tries again, but Bugs sticks a long bamboo tube out of the tree and blows air through it, putting out the match again. The colonel walks further back from the tree and successfully lights the fuse. He runs back to the tree, but the bomb explodes in his hands before he can get there. As the smoke from the blast dissipates, the colonel is seen with his clothes partially blown off, saying, "I hate that rabbit." Meanwhile Bugs is now wearing the uniform of a confederate general with a saber that drags the ground as he walks to the colonel who says, "General Brickwall Jackson, suh," and salutes. Bugs is smoking a cigar and shouts, "Attention! Forward, march! To the left . . ." And after several more commands the colonel finds himself standing on the edge of a deep well, where Bugs has ordered him to halt. Bugs coolly manicures his fingernails while the colonel looks down in the well with sweat dripping

off his face. Bug shouts "forward" and the colonel falls into the well. The colonel climbs out with water dripping from his face as he sees Bugs walking away singing "Yankee Doodle Dandy." The colonel shouts "charge!" as the cartoon ends.

THE STEEPLE-CHASE (1933)

Company: Burt Gillett, Walt Disney, United Artists; later released in a silent version by Hollywood Film Enterprises under the title *Mickey's Trick Horse*
Characters: Mickey Mouse, Minnie Mouse, southern colonel, black stable boys

Story: The cartoon opens at a racetrack where the big steeple-chase is being held. Mickey, Minnie, and two black stable boys watch the colonel feeding his horse, Thunderbolt, who is happy and ready to race. After Mickey, Minnie, and the colonel leave, the two stable boys groom the horse for the race. They brush the horse and then shine the saddle like a pair of shoes, singing and smiling all the while. The horse eats hay and finds a bottle of moonshine whisky in it, which he drinks. He gets drunk and is in no shape to run the race when Mickey, who is the jockey, arrives. Mickey and the two black boys sit and wonder what to do next while Thunderbolt lies in a tub of water with a block of ice tied to his head. Mickey gets an idea and drags the two blacks to a costume shop. There he puts them into a horse costume. Meanwhile, back at the track, all of the the horses are at the starting gate. The colonel and Minnie wonder where Mickey and Thunderbolt are. Finally Mickey arrives at the gate riding his fake horse. The bell rings and the race is on. The other horses start quickly out of the gate, leaving Mickey and his horse behind. They trail the others by a long way until they are attacked by a swarm of angry bees. Mickey's horse is stung so many times on the rear end that it turns around and runs backward. Mickey and his horse win the race. As they cross the finish line, Mickey falls to the ground. Mickey's horse continues to run before splitting in two. The two black stable boys run their separate ways out of sight with the bees close behind them as the cartoon ends.

Review: *Motion Picture Herald*, 28 October 1933

Amusing and lively is the latest of the Mickey Mouse antics, as devised by Walt Disney and staff. Herein Mickey, the jockey, is all set to win the big race and save the colonel's money, when he discovers the horse to have achieved a jag—and what a jag. With the help of stable boys for a horse, he goes out to win in entertaining animated fashion. (7 min)

SUNNY SOUTH (1931)

Company: Walter Lantz; released by Universal Pictures
Characters: Oswald the rabbit, southern blacks

Story: (short version released by Castle Films for the home market): The cartoon opens as Oswald's girlfriend and his friends wait at the train station for his arrival in Dixieland. Oswald arrives as the band plays "Dixie." His arrival kicks off a celebration and Oswald and his girl start by doing a cakewalk dance down the main street. Meanwhile a small black boy with thick white lips shines the shoes of a tall black man wearing minstrel's attire. After he applies the polish, he straps a brush to the bottoms of his feet then finishes the shine by doing a soft-shoe dance on the man's shoes. Oswald and his girl play a brief saxophone duet, and then Oswald drops to one knee and says, "Mammy." Next the little black shoeshine boy eats a huge slice of watermelon as he dances on a pile of shoes while the farmer sleeps nearby. The farmer wakes up and is so the irate that he throws a watermelon at the little boy. He misses and the melon hits Oswald in the face. Oswald swallows the melon and then spits the seeds out of his mouth like machine-gun bullets, aiming them at the farmer. The seeds hit the farmer on his rear end. He leaps into the air before falling and landing on his rear end as the cartoon ends.

Review: *Variety*, 6 April 1931

Considerably below par for cartoons and plenty repetitious. Majority of the action centers around the animal character, Oswald the Rabbit, as the engineer of a train. But little happens. Last shots built around his welcome on coming back to mammy-land.

Photography under average in spots and drawing not as clear as in most cartoons.

THE SUNNY SOUTH (1933)

Company: Frank Moser, Paul Terry, Educational Pictures
Type: Terrytoon
Characters: Southern blacks

Review: *Film Daily*, 28 December 1933

Satisfactory vocal and musical accompaniment combined with a well-developed idea makes this a pleasant cartoon. Animation shows cotton picking scenes and then home a gay negro mammy and pickaninnies. Simon Legree is introduced and there follows a hot pursuit, including a chase over ice a la Uncle Tom, in which he first tries to seize one of the pickaninnies and then goes after mammy.

Review: *Motion Picture Herald*, 1 January 1934

An amusing and lively cartoon in the Terry Toon series, in which the animated Pickaninnies and their colored mammy are happy picking cotton until the dog chaser comes in pursuit. She escapes with one in her arms, Simon Legree after her. There is an amusing animated take-off of Eliza crossing the ice, which ends in the elimination of Legree and safety of the mammy. A good number. (6 min)

Review: *Selected Motion Pictures*, 1 January 1934

A Paul Terry-Toon. An inoffensive foolishness in Uncle Tom's Cabin that will fit any program.

SWANEE RIVER (1925)

Company: Dave Fleischer, Max Fleischer, Red Seal Pictures Film Company
Type: Song Car-Tune no. 1, Bouncing Ball
Characters: Ko-Ko the Clown, southern blacks; background music by the Metropolitan Quartet

Story: The cartoon opens with Ko-Ko jumping out of an ink bottle. He runs over to an asbestos screen and a lectern with sheet music on it. He makes a lightning change to a symphonic conductor. He whistles and a quartet comes out of the ink bottle. Ko-Ko then writes on the blackboard: "The Ko-Ko Kwartet will execute for your approval that old-time favorite—'Old Folks at Home'—better known to the old folks as 'Swanee River.' You remember that good old tune." The music begins, and the quartet starts to sing the title song. The screen changes to show the bouncing ball superimposed over a southern landscape near a river at night. Various distributive scenes involving southern blacks in silhouette flash across the screen, including an old man and woman sitting in their small cabin smoking corncob pipes, a hobo walking down the railroad track, and a black man with a huge sack full of cotton on his back. Sweat drips off his face as a small black girl stands behind him and helps him keep the sack from falling off his back. A man sits on the ground near a pot of boiling water on a campfire and eyes a chicken that walks by him. Next the screen changes to show a small black boy who dances on top of the words of the title song. Then the music stops, Ko-Ko jumps back into the ink bottle, and the cartoon ends.

Review: *Moving Picture World*, 25 April 1925

Max Fleischer's familiar character that makes his appearance out of an ink bottle essays a new role in this, the first of a series of Song Car-Tunes. Deftly changing his makeup himself, he calls a quartette out of the inkwell and they proceed to sing "Swanee River," the words being thrown on the screen and cleverly indicated by a traveling dot with the intention that the audience will sing them. The idea of familiar songs on the screen for the audience to sing is not new but Mr. Fleischer has given it new treatment and injected good comedy in his literal "play" upon words, for not only do the words themselves perform funny tricks but a little cartoon negro "plays" around all over them doing all sorts of funny stunts. A pleasing number that is novel and should please the average patron. (one reel)

SWEET JEANIE LEE (1932)

Company: Dave Fleischer, Max Fleischer; Paramount Pictures release
Type: Screen Song; combined live action and animation
Characters: Live musician, black cotton pickers

Story: The cartoon opens on the scene of an old-time southern plantation where lazy blacks are in the field picking cotton with the toes of their feet while lying on their backs as the background music plays "Dixie." Night falls, and the blacks gather around the cabin and sing the title song while the animals dance. A black girl, with her hair braided in pigtails, sings a solo while dancing a jig. A quartet sings a verse and invites the audience to sing along as the ball bounces over the words, which are displayed on the pages of the sheet music displayed on a piano being played by a live musician. The animation changes to a country road where a horse is pulling a cart carrying several pickaninnies who sing along with the driver. The little black girl eats a huge slice of watermelon and simultaneously plays it as a harmonica. She spits out the seeds as she dances above the words of the song as they scroll along the bottom of the screen. The black girl grins from ear to ear, displaying a row of big white teeth as the cartoon ends.

Review: *Film Daily,* 24 January 1932

Popular melody, southern plantation capers and animated cartoon work are effectively combined in this entertaining short. The tuneful "Sweet Jennie Lee" is the theme song of the skit, with the usual bouncing ball antics following the first rendition. At the introduction a group of Negro cotton pickers are shown doing their work and then doing their song and dance stuff under the moon. A very acceptable subject.

UNCLE TOM'S BUNGALOW (1937)

Company: Tex Avery, Vitaphone, Warner Bros.
Type: Merrie Melodies
Characters: *Uncle Tom's Cabin* characters, including Little Eva, Topsy, Uncle Tom, Liza, Simon Legree, Jr. (Uncle Tom voice characterization by Roy Glenn)

See fig. 37. Story: The cartoon is narrated by an offscreen voice. It opens on the banks of a river in the deep South. The musical background is "Swanee River." A small cabin comes into view followed by the front of the big white residence of the plantation's owner. The sounds of "Dixie" are heard and the narrator says, "Now let's introduce our characters, Now first, a little lady." Little Eva, with blond hair and wearing a long white dress, comes out of the front door and stands on the porch. The narrator says, "Now tell us your name." Little Eva tells him, "I live at 2415 First Street. I'm in the first grade and I can spell cat." Eva tries unsuccessfully to spell cat and says, "Well, anyway, I can spell dog, and I got a dolly and I got a teddy bear and I got lace on my [under] pants. Do you want to see?" She starts to pull up her dress and the narrator tells her, "Say, hold on. No, no. Remember you are a big girl. All we want to know is your name." Eva then shouts, "Little Eva, you dope!" The scene shifts to the front of a small plantation cabin. A little black girl is standing in the shadow of the doorway as the background music plays "Sweet Georgia Brown." The narrator says, "Hey girl, step out of that shadow and introduce yourself." The black girl, with plaited hair and bare feet, walks forward and says, "I's Topsy." The narrator chuckles and tells her, "Thanks. Here comes old Uncle Tom now." Uncle Tom is seen shuffling along

with his head bent low. The narrator says, "He's getting kind of feeble—just look at those knees shaking." Uncle Tom tells him, "Brother, my knees ain't shaking, I's trucking." Next a thin black woman is seen washing clothes in a tub outdoors. The narrator says, "Hey girl, give us the lowdown." She turns around and tells him, "My name is Liza and I'm from Dixie." The narrator asks, "Y'all from Dixie, Gal?" Liza says, "Are you from Dixie?" The narrator replies, "Yes, I's from Dixie." But Liza tells him, "Say, you lying fellow. I'm from the South." The narrator says, "So am I." Liza laughs so hard that she rolls on the ground. Next Simon Legree is seen and the narrator refers to him as a viper. Legree says, "Hello, hello everybody, everybody." Next on the scene is a pack of hounds fast asleep on the porch of a cabin. The narrator says, "Now, last but not least, the hounds." He says, "Say boys, say a word to the folks." One hound says hello and goes right back to sleep. The narrator says, "Oh well, now on with the show." He asks little Eva if she is ready and she responds, "Yes, dark, tall, and bowlegged." He asks Topsy the same question and she tells him, "Anytime y'all say, professor." Next the narrator asks Uncle Tom if he wants to be an actor. Uncle Tom tells him, "Oh sho', sho'." The narrator says, "How about you, Liza?" She answers, "Yeah man." Simon Legree says, "The sooner the better." Finally the narrator asks the hounds if they are ready and one says, "Yeah, I guess so. There ain't nothin' else to do." The narrator says, "Well, here we go," and the scene shifts to the front of Legree's office building. A sign reads, "Used Slaves Co. 6%." The door opens and Legree comes out. Legree's slaves, including Uncle Tom, are sleeping along the side of the building. The narrator warns Uncle Tom of Legree's approach as the music of "Old Black Joe" is heard in the background. Uncle Tom tells Legree, "My body might belong to you, but my soul belongs to Warner Bros." As Legree begins to beat Uncle Tom with the whip, Little Eva and Topsy show up on the scene. They offer to buy Uncle Tom, and Legree accepts. They go to Legree's office, and Little Eva signs the bill of sale. Legree warns them, "Here is your contract. But remember, if you fall behind in your payments, I'll take him back." Eva, Topsy, and Uncle Tom go back to Eva's house and are happy for a while, until winter comes and snow is on the ground. In his office Legree examines Topsy and Eva's contract and discovers that they are three months behind in their payments. When he starts out for Eva's house, the narrator warns Eva, Tom, and Topsy that he is coming. They hide Uncle Tom in a picture. Topsy and Eva refuse to tell Legree where Uncle Tom is hiding. He tells them that he will find him and then slithers along the floor like a snake. He reaches under a table to find Tom but accidently sticks his finger into an electrical outlet and lights up like a bulb. Angry Legree raises his whip to beat Topsy and Eva. They are so frightened that Topsy momentarily turns white and Eva turns black. At this moment Liza arrives on the scene, picks up the two girls, and runs out of the house. Legree calls to his hounds and the chase is on. It is called offscreen like a horse race. Liza runs to the river but finds that it is not covered by ice. She panics but the narrator tells her not to worry because there is an ice machine near her. Liza puts a nickel in the machine and hits the jackpot. Ice flows out of the machine and into the river. Liza crosses the river with Legree and his hounds in close pursuit. Liza reaches shore but stumbles, and she and Topsy and Eva fall into the snow. Legree arrives and is about to beat the girls with his whip, and the narrator is about to declare Legree the winner when Uncle Tom arrives on the scene driving a long limousine. Uncle Tom pays Legree the overdue payments. The narrator says, "It looks like the old boy has collected on his social security." After Legree leaves, Eva asks Uncle Tom where he got all that money. Uncle Tom pulls a pair of dice from his pocket, shakes them, and throws them on the ground, saying, "Come on dere, seven." The dice land on snake eyes but then turn over to show seven. The narrator says, "Now you have the story of Uncle Tom's bungalow—or do you?" as Uncle Tom picks up the dice and the cartoon ends.

Review: *Selected Motion Pictures,* 1 June 1937

An interesting travesty in Technicolor of the well-known story. Family and Junior Matinee.

Review: *National Board of Review of Motion Pictures,* 29 May 1937

A satire of *Uncle Tom's Cabin* Highly amusing and done in color.

UNCLE TOM'S CABANA (1947)

Company: Tex Avery, M-G-M
Characters: Uncle Tom, Little Eva, Simon Legree, black kids

See fig. 38. Story: The cartoon opens on a tranquil southern scene as the background music plays "My Old Kentucky Home." Uncle Tom, a partially bald man with white hair, sits on the steps of his little cabin with several children seated on the ground before him. Uncle Tom smokes his cigar and picks up one of the kids. He sits him on his lap and says (in a voice similar to Andy Brown of the *Amos 'n' Andy* Radio Show), "Well now, children, tonight ole Uncle Tom is gonna tell you the true story of Uncle Tom's cabin. Now this is the first one them Hollywood people got the straight dope on this Uncle Tom stuff. Dis is the way it really happened. Once upon a time in the big city . . ." The scene changes to a view of skyscrapers. Uncle Tom continues, ". . . lived a character named Simon Legree. He was sho' 'nuff a scoundrel." The front of a building is seen with a sign reading "Legree Building/Loans, Mortgages, and Crooked Deals/Widows Evicted, Dogs Kicked Out, Old Ladies Tripped, Kittens Drowned." Tom continues, "On top of that he was two-faced. But he sho' was powerful. Why, he owned dat whole town except one little spot. And that was your Uncle Tom's cabin." The scene shows Uncle Tom chopping cotton in the front yard of his cabin. Tom continues, "I was sho' happy, but Mr. Legree was figurin' on foreclosing the mortgage on my cabin so he could own de whole town. He was sho' a low-down snake." Legree is seen in his office slithering across the floor, which is covered with piles of money. Uncle Tom continues, "First thing he do, he go for dem bloodhounds but dey busy." Legree's hounds are seen in a blood bank

donating blood to the Red Cross. Legree flies to Uncle Tom's cabin in a helicopter and lands in Tom's front yard. Uncle Tom continues, "So he come after me personal. And he say iffin I don't have de mortgage money by twelve o'clock tonight, he gonna throw me out and take my little cabin." Legree is seen talking to Uncle Tom who stands at the door leaning on his walking stick. Uncle Tom's story continues, "Oh me? Worry, worry, worry. I didn't have a penny." He is seen pulling out his pockets as moths fly out of them. He continues his story, "Why starvation was starin' me in the face. But I got one last hope, my only friend—Little Eva." He walks to the telephone. His story continues. "She got the scrumptious southern penthouse, you know." The scene shows a southern mansion on the roof of a tall building. "And that ain't all, neither." Dressed as a southern belle of the old South, Little Eva answers Uncle Tom's phone call. Uncle Tom continues, "She say she come right over but we can't figure nothin' out." Eva and Tom sit in the cabin. Tom continues, "I's sittin' dere worrin', foolin' around with the piano." Tom is seen playing a boogie beat and Eva starts to dance. Uncle Tom continues, "All of a sudden it came to me, the big idea—Uncle Tom's Cabana." The scene shows Uncle Tom's nightclub with Eva billed as the star attraction. Uncle Tom continues, "We done turned dat cabin into a nightclub. The place was packed." Uncle Tom, the cashier, rakes in the money. "We was really gettin' the dough. Of course, Uncle Sam was gettin' his share." Uncle Sam stands beside him and collects the income tax. Tom continues, "But Legree wasn't gettin' his, and he gonna do somethin' about it. Next thing I know he got me tied on dat powder keg and lightin' de fuse." Uncle Tom is seen tied to a barrel of TNT. Legree lights the fuse and then takes the money. Uncle Tom continues, "And he done take every penny of dat money and get outta there. But he done forgot somethin'—Little Eva." As Legree is about to leave, Eva comes on stage and sings, "Carry Me Back to Old Virginia." Legree's eyes pop out when he sees Eva. As she finishes her number, he rushes to the stage and takes her into his arms. He opens the door to leave, but Uncle Tom hits him on the head with a club, knocking him flat as a pancake. Then the scene changes back to the cabin, and the boy on Tom's lap asks, "But Uncle Tom, how come you wasn't blowed up on dat powder keg?" Uncle Tom answers, "Why dat was nothin'. 'Dat sweat pourin' off me just naturally put dat fuse out. Den Legree come at me with dat machine gun . . ." The boy asks, "But Uncle Tom, didn't dem bullets kill ya?" Uncle Tom says, "Course not boy. I had my superduperman suit. Den he tie me on dem railroad tracks and the train run over me. Den he throw me in dat mill and dat saw cut me through . . ." The little boy interrupts, saying, "But Uncle Tom . . ." Tom says, "Don't bother me now, boy. I's really goin' den he shoved me off the top of dat cliff. Den I jumped on dat camel. He chased me with an elephant. Den dat alligator, den dere come dat steam roller and PT boat and den the rocket guns and dem dive bombers and dat machine gun. Den all of a sudden he chased me right up to the top of dat Empire State Building and pushed me right off the top. I fell down fourteen miles and hit on the pavement. And right then is where I get mad." The little boy shakes his head in disbelief as

Uncle Tom continues. "I grab dat Empire State Building with Legree up dere on top, and I throws him clear over the moon. And that was the end of Mr. Legree." Uncle Tom leans back and puffs his cigar, and the little boy says, "Uncle Tom is you all been tellin' us de truth?" Uncle Tom puts the boy on the ground and says, "Well now, wait a minute here boy. Iffin dis ain't the truth, I hope dat lightnin' come down and strike me dead." A lightning bolt comes down from a black cloud in the sky and strikes Uncle Tom dead. His angel rises slowly into the sky as the little boy says, "You know we lose more Uncle Toms dat way," as the cartoon ends.

Review: *Motion Picture Herald,* 30 August 1947

Uncle Tom's adventures with Simon Legree in a modern version with the emphasis on swing. Uncle has the kiddies wide-eyed with his tall yarns about his exploits. (8 min)

Review: *Film Daily,* 26 September 1947

Uncle Tom tells the kiddies about his adventures with Simon Legree which are short on fact but long on imagination. A modern version of the old tale, it is a real seller.

Review: *Motion Picture Herald,* 25 September 1954

Here is an up-to-date version of *Uncle Tom's Cabin* in which the old fellow tells the Kiddies about his adventures with Simon Legree and Liza. She's a singer and together they run a night club with Legree always looking for trouble.

Review: *Motion Picture Exhibitor,* 9 July 1947

Old Uncle Tom tells the little fellows his story of way back when wolf Simon Legree owned a big city metropolis with the exception of Uncle Tom's cabin. When Legree threatens to foreclose, Tom turns his place into a successful night club where Little Eva performs. Legree tries to put Tom out of the way by various fantastic means. Finally Tom rebels and tosses Legree and the Empire State Building over the moon. The kids don't believe the tale, and Tom wishes that he would drop dead if he is lying, which he promptly does. His spirit rises to heaven. This will appeal, especially to kids. Good.

Editorial: *Uncle Tom's Cabana Pittsburgh Courier,* 6 March 1954

"*Uncle Tom's Cabana*" Outrages Negro Audiences: What Price Brotherhood If Movies Play Up Handkerchief Heads?"

The damnedest thing in the world is to keep responsible Americans from writing dirty words on fences. The latest episode in this "ignorant compulsion" series is the motion picture cartoon *Uncle Tom's Cabana,* a base stereotype and an insult to Negroes. With the movies trying to buck television it is strange that a studio would distribute such a malodorous thing. What price brotherhood if movies play up handkerchief heads?

Even though there has been a general loosening of the Production Code in order to hype the box office, there is no reason why Negroes should continue to be ridiculed and jeered at in motion pictures. This medium reaches all levels of mentalities and feeds the flames of prejudice by projecting such canards as *Uncle Tom's Cabana.*

The uncommonly poor cartoon is showing in theatres all over America right now. Will it be shown in other countries where communism is battling for people's minds? Are ideas so lacking that movie short subjects must dredge up *Birth of a Nation?* Or was this thing called *Uncle Tom's Cabana* the result of thoughtlessness?

Motion pictures are designed to entertain, but the motion picture industry must face responsibilities to itself and the public it serves and seeks. The low buffoonery of Negroes on the screen is not appreciated. The callous depiction of Negroes as lackeys and cretins fresh out of cotton fields leaves everyone cold because people know better.

It does not require genius to point out that other racial and religious groups are never vilified on the screen. The pressure would almost wreck the movies. Negroes must rise in a mass and protest such antic foolishness as *Uncle Tom's Cabana,* and all other films of this type.

Now where were the state censors when this film was reviewed? Showing this insult during Brotherhood Week was a kick in the teeth to a fine effort to wipe out prejudice in America. With the world in ferment, *Uncle Tom's Cabana* set the movies back ten years. Withdraw the film immediately, huh?

Chapter 5

Who Dat Say Who Dat? The Animated Minstrel Show

In 1994 a group of distinguished historians of animation named the fifty greatest animated cartoons. Their selections were published in a book of the same title edited by Jerry Beck. *Coal Black and De Sebben Dwarfs* was ranked as one of the very best. This cartoon, which is a parody of the famous children's story "Snow White and the Seven Dwarfs," ranked twenty-first on the list. The selection included originality, artistry, animation, music, humor, and personality. Judging by these criteria, it is understandable why *Coal Black* was included in this select group of American cartoons. However this cartoon is packed from beginning to end with the most vicious stereotypes of black people ever depicted in an animated film. Unlike many other cartoons of this period, which also included negative images of blacks, this cartoon appears to be intentionally malicious in its treatment of black characters in general and black women in particular. For example, the character Queenie combines all of the stereotypes that have been applied to black women in feature films and in animated short subjects—fat, ugly, immoral, hedonistic, stupid. So White, although depicted as an attractive young black woman, is also shown involved in promiscuous sexual behavior. This is seen in a short sequence where she is captured by a gang of black male kidnappers, Murder, Inc. The men pull her into the car, and then it speeds off and bounces up and down and from side to side as it rolls down the highway. Suddenly the car screeches to a halt. So White, grinning from ear to ear, is lifted out of the car. Her male captors, clearly happy and satisfied, ride off into the night. If gang rape was involved, this sequence gives the clear impression that So White enjoyed the experience. This cartoon is unique in that it includes such a strong innuendo of illicit or immoral sexual behavior. It would not have passed the censor board, and certainly would have not been acceptable to moviegoing audiences of the period, if the female character involved had been a young attractive white woman. But Robert Clampett and other animators had learned that they could imbue black male and female characters with low morals without offending the majority of the general public (fig. 39).

During World War II almost all Hollywood films including animated shorts were screened for positive propaganda content. Although there was no official government censorship of movies during this period, the War Activities Committee in Hollywood encouraged producers to make films showing American society in a positive light and to employ less favorable depictions of Germans, Italians, and Japanese. Yet cartoons ridiculing black Americans continued to be produced throughout the war years. One Warner Bros. short cartoon featuring Bugs Bunny entitled *Any Bonds Today?* was shown in theaters across the country to promote the sale of U.S. war bonds. Yet even this cartoon ends with Bugs, in blackface, doing a stereotypical minstrel song and dance routine.

The prevailing thesis offered by animation historians appears to suggest that cartoons featuring black stereotypes conformed to existing norms. This view is expressed by Michael Shull and David Wilt in their book *Doing Their Bit: Wartime Animated Short Films, 1939–1945:*

> Contrary to what some may believe, there has never been a conscious effort on the part of the American film industry to stigmatize a particular racial or ethnic group. The adverse portrayals of blacks, Asians, Mexicans, Jews and the like result more from the industry's adoption of cultural stereotypes present in many other media than from actual dislike for a particular race or religion. Unpleasant as some movie stereotypes may be, they seem to have been included out of ignorance or laziness, rather than as part of a master plan to malign a certain group. The above argument may be valid when applied to some ethnic and religious groups.

But over fifty years of stereotypical negative cartoon images of blacks, combined with a lack of positive images, suggests that a more conscious motivation and intent was involved, which cannot be explained away as ignorance or laziness.

Caricatures of many of the famous black entertainers appeared in musical cartoons of the 1930s. But for brief gags the most popular black caricature used by animators was that of the comedian Lincoln Perry, aka. Stephin Fetchit. His drawling, shuffling, lazy, dim-witted screen persona was known and loved by movie audiences all over the world. The November 18, 1929, issue of *Film Weekly* was devoted to the "talkies," then the new rage in motion pictures. One article entitled "Who Who of Talking Pictures" provided biographical sketches of the most popular film stars of the period. The only black actor cited was Stephin Fetchit: "Musical comedy star, well known as the original singer of 'Old Man River' in *Showboat*. Talkies include *Fox Movietone Follies* and *Big Time.*"

Another article of the same issue included the following review of the film *Fox Movietone Follies:* "An ambitious revue held together by a very slight story. Some good turns here, but the demands of the revue show up the inexperience of the film stars in this kind of work. Stephin Fetchit, a negro comedian, is the most successful of the rather colourless artists."

Because of the popularity of Fetchit's on-screen character with the filmgoing public, animators used it to depict the quintessential black man in many cartoons.

Sight gags are an essential element of animated cartoons. One frequently used sight gag consisted of a sudden explosion that instantly transforms the face of the main character to a blackface racial stereotype usually depicted with big thick lips and one or more braids that stick out of the top of the head. The transformed character also spoke in Negro dialect. The background music for the blackface bit was usually "Swanee River," "Old Black Joe," "Dixie," or some other popular song associated with

BLACK ENTERTAINERS
Comparative Appearances

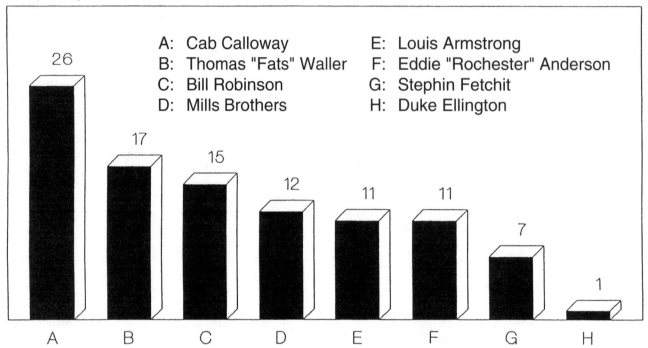

Frequency, %

A: Cab Calloway   E: Louis Armstrong
B: Thomas "Fats" Waller   F: Eddie "Rochester" Anderson
C: Bill Robinson   G: Stephin Fetchit
D: Mills Brothers   H: Duke Ellington

Fig. 5.1. Comparative appearances (live action, voice, animated caricatures) of black entertainers

black people or the old South. Eddie "Rochester" Anderson's voice was frequently imitated because of its instant public recognition. Anderson was heard as the featured character "Rochester" on the weekly national broadcasts of Jack Benny's radio and TV shows. The blackface gag was a particular favorite of Tex Avery when he was a director for M-G-M in the 1940s and 1950s. In several of his cartoons, such as *Droopy's Good Deed,* Avery used this gag twice in the same cartoon (fig. 40).

In the 1930s animators were significantly influenced by the national popularity of black entertainers on the vaudeville (and earlier minstrel) stage. Jazz and swing music, as well as black dance styles, were used as an integral part of the fast-paced action cartoon, especially by Fleischer, Iwerks, Van Beuren, and Disney (the first Silly Symphonies). In several cartoons Max Fleischer combined animation with live-action performances of such black stars as Louis Armstrong, Cab Calloway, the Mills Brothers, and Don Redman in his Screen Song series. *I'll Be Glad When You're Dead, You Rascal You* combined live action of Armstrong with an animated caricature of him as a cannibal who chases Betty Boop and friends through the jungle. The influence of black and blackface vaudeville is also evident in many of Disney's first black-and-white sound cartoons of the early 1930s. In *Blue Rhythm* starring Mickey Mouse, W. C. Handy's "St. Louis Blues" is the featured song, which is sung by Mickey and Minnie. In *Mickey Steps Out,* Mickey, Minnie, and Pluto do a blackface routine singing "Sweet Georgia Brown." In these films and others, such as the *Whoopie*

Party, the Disney characters perform tap, the shimmy, the charleston, and other dances. Some cartoons, like *Swing Wedding* and *Swing Social,* which featured black characters, were essentially black minstrel shows with a thin plot combined with plenty of hot music, jazz singing, and fast dancing. Many of these cartoons included the usual gags involving slow talking and walking, crap shooting, chicken stealing, and Uncle Tom. All of the color cartoons in the Bosko series produced at M-G-M by Harman and Ising follow this formula (fig. 41).

The story lines of several black cartoons of the 1930s were significantly influenced by the stage production (and later feature film) *The Green Pastures,* which featured an all-black cast but was written and produced by whites. This extremely successful play was based on a white man's conception of a mythical "Negro heaven," in which "de Lord" and his angels cooked fish and sang and danced all day. In other cartoons the featured character landed in "Negro hell" and was confronted by a black jive-talking devil and his helpers. Animators adapted these themes in such cartoons as *Clean Pastures, Goin' to Heaven on a Mule, Sunday Go to Meetin' Time* and *Tin Pan Alley Cats.* To varying degrees these cartoons burlesqued black religious customs for comic effect. Similar burlesquing of white religious customs was not considered funny.

In an effort to provide programming for cable TV networks, many of the 1930s and 1940s cartoons are being revived for public viewing. Those that include objectionable racial or ethnic stereotyping of minorities are generally not shown. However the owners of large cartoon libraries that supply the cable companies are attempting to edit out the objectional material. They have achieved varying degrees of success. Editing out gags in many cases has a negative impact on the continuity of the story line. Credibility is reduced when "white" voices are provided for obviously black characters. Editing a cartoon film requires skill to achieve complete success. One example of skillful editing is Disney's *Fantasia,* a feature-length cartoon released in 1942. Black stereotypes in the original version were removed with minimal impact on the continuity of the film.

Several of the cartoon stories presented in this chapter reflect a color prejudice that is ingrained in American society, as expressed in a well-known adage: If you're white, you're all right; if you're yellow, you're mellow; if you're brown, stick around; if you're black, get back. In these cartoons, the color of the character is important, not the racial identity. Animators used black to designate the oddball member of a homogeneous group of usually animal characters such chickens, pigs, or sheep. The oddball member of the family group was usually colored black. When others worked, the black one played and made trouble by being disobedient to parents. In other stories the black-colored member wants to be accepted but is rejected by the others because of his color. The black character may also be depicted as a slow learner. For example, a black duckling will be the only one that can't swim or the last one to learn to fly. In all cartoons of this type the black character must demonstrate some heroic action in order to be accepted and loved by the others. Before that, the character is subjected to scorn and hostility. In a relatively few cartoons, however, the black member is the hero and leader throughout the story.

Blackie the lamb is a cartoon series in which the black-colored character was depicted as being smarter and stronger than the white-colored lambs, and he usually bailed them out of trouble with the big bad wolf. But this black character was the exception rather than the general rule.

Black caricatures were too numerous in these early cartoons to be completely edited out, so many of them survive today in their original form, though rarely available for public viewing.

Animated Minstrel Show Stories and Reviews

A-LAD-IN BAGHDAD (1938)

Company: Cal Howard, Carl Dalton, Vitaphone, Warner Bros.
Type: Merrie Melodies
Characters: Egghead, black genie and slaves, Arab princess, and Arab sultan

Story: The cartoon opens as Egghead, down on his luck, walks along a crowded street in Baghdad. He is wearing patched pants and carrying a knapsack that contains all of his clothes. He comes upon an Arab who tries unsuccessfully to get a lamp prize in a nickel candy machine. Egghead puts in a coin, gets the lamp, and says, "Oh boy, am I lucky. What a pretty sugar bowl." He turns the lamp over and sees something written on the bottom: Directions—rub lamp three times. He rubs the lamp and in a puff of smoke a large black genie appears before him. Egghead is scared and tries to run away, but the genie grabs him and says, "Wait a minute, hey wait a minute. I ain't gonna hurt you. You is de mastah of de magic lamp. If you ever need anything, just give us a rub." Then he disappears back into the lamp in a puff of black smoke. Egghead looks at the lamp and says, "Let me see now. I wish I had some nice new clothes." He rubs the lamp, and immediately he is wearing a new outfit. Egghead says thank-you, and a black hand comes out of the lamp and pulls Egghead's nose, and a voice from inside the lamp says, "You are welcome." Meanwhile the mean-looking Arab who was unsuccessful in obtaining the lamp has been observing the proceedings and says, "That should be my lamp. And what's more, I shall get it." Meanwhile Egghead decides to follow a crowd of people who have stopped to read large sign: "I Want You! To the cleverest entertainer I will give my daughter's hand in marriage—The Sultan—Royal Palace—today." Egghead says, "With my magic lamp I will win the beautiful princess. He rubs his lamp saying, "I wish I had a magic carpet." In a puff of smoke the magic carpet appears before him. He climbs aboard and flies away. He lands at the front door of the sultan's palace, which is guarded by a large black slave and an Arab holding a whip. A sign reads, "Line forms to right," so Egghead goes to the end of the line and waits. Inside the palace the princess is crying as the sultan sits on his throne being fanned by a black slave. A smiling black boy carrying a sign announces the first act, which is "Ali Baabe Breen—the Strong Man." The sultan is not pleased and pulls a lever that opens a trapdoor through which Ali Baabe is dropped. The next two acts suffer the same fate. Outside the evil Arab sneaks behind Egghead and replaces his lamp with a plain teapot. Finally it's Egghead's turn, and he is announced as "Aladdin and His Wonderful Lamp." He enters the room and exchanges glances with the princess, and it is love at first sight. After a brief song and dance routine the sultan is about to pull the lever to the trapdoor, but Egghead says, "Wait a minute. Don't do that. I have my magic lamp. He rubs the teapot frantically, but nothing happens and the sultan pulls the lever. Egghead falls through the trapdoor and slides out of the palace, landing on the street. Looking through a window, he sees the Arab rub the lamp. A pile of gold and jewels is produced for the princess. The sultan is finally delighted, and he throws up his hands and proclaims, "Marvelous! Stupendous! Let the wedding begin." As a black slave blows the trumpet, Egghead runs back into the palace and interrupts the proceedings by knocking down the Arab thief, grabbing the lamp and the princess, exiting the palace, jumping on the magic carpet, and flying away while the angry sultan and his guards try in vain to stop him. With the beautiful princess at his side, Egghead is very happy. But the princess is not satisfied and wants more gifts. She rubs the magic lamp, and a handsome Arab genie appears. He takes her in his arms before they both disappear in a puff of white smoke back into the lamp. As Egghead looks on in disgust, the cartoon ends.

Review: *Motion Picture Exhibitor*, 1 September 1938

Another Schlesinger laff-hit. The boy, who talks like Joe Penner, secures the magic lamp, has it stolen from him as he competes for the Caliph's daughter, wins her anyway, recovers the lamp for her real desires—a composite Robert Taylor, Clark Gable. It's all very funny. Good.

ALL THIS AND RABBIT STEW (1941)

Company: Tex Avery, Warner Bros.
Type: Merrie Melodies
Characters: Little Sambo, Bugs Bunny

See fig. 42. Story: The cartoon opens with Little Sambo, a black boy who has the demeanor of Stephin Fetchit, on a hunting trip. He carries a shotgun that is so long it drags the ground as he walks. He says to himself, "I'm gonna catch me a rabbit." He sees rabbit tracks that he decides to follow. Meanwhile Bugs Bunny is relaxing in his hole in the ground eating carrots and tossing the stalks out of the hole. Sambo sees carrot stalks flying out of the hole and realizes that he has found a rabbit. He inserts the barrel of his gun into the hole and says, "All right Mr. Rabbit, I've got you covered. Put up your hands or I'll blitzkrieg you!" Bugs extends his hands out of the hole before climbing all the way out. Sambo orders Bugs to walk. As the rabbit does so, his hole follows him. Bugs bumps into a tree and quickly jumps into a hole in the trunk. Sambo sticks the barrel of his gun into the hole and fires a shot. When the smoke clears, Bugs, sitting on the barrel of Sambo's gun, says to him, "What's up, Doc?" Before Sambo can answer, Bugs pulls his hat down over his eyes and takes the gun away from him. Sambo lifts his hat so that he can see. Bugs gives him his gun back and tells him, "The rabbit ran that way." Sambo runs off in the direction that Bugs has indicated but stops when he realizes that Bugs has made a sucker of him. The image of a large lollypop appears over his head. Sambo returns to Bugs's hole and tries to suck him out with a toilet plunger. He pulls hard and is shocked to find that he has pulled out a skunk. Sambo says "Oh oh" and throws the skunk back in the hole and covers it with dirt. Bugs beckons for Sambo to follow him into a cave. Sambo enters the dark cave and sees a pair of eyes. He reaches out and grabs what he thinks is the bunny when he sees another pair of eyes and hears a voice say, "What's up, Doc?" This time Sambo has caught a bear, which chases him and Bugs out of the cave. Soon the hunt is on again with Bugs trying to escape the determined Sambo. Sambo fires his shotgun at Bugs, but the rabbit eludes the pellets by diving in and out of holes in the ground, finally ending up in the eighth hole of a golf course. Later Sambo thinks he has trapped the elusive rabbit inside a hollow log. He goes in one end of the log, but Bugs comes out the other end and turns the log in a half circle so that one end is over the edge of a high cliff. Sambo comes out of this end and runs on air until he realizes that he has been suckered again. Sambo manages to run back into the log, and every time he runs out Bugs turns the log so he winds up running on thin air. Finally Sambo runs out the wrong end and falls off the cliff to the ground below. Bugs, thinking that

he is rid of the pesky little hunter, turns to walk away but instead finds himself staring into the barrel of Sambo's shotgun. Sambo says, "Say your prayers, Rabbit." Bugs pleads, "Now wait a minute," as he pulls a pair of dice out of his pocket. Seeing this, Sambo says, "What y'all got dere, Man? It couldn't be a pair of dem . . ." as he pulls Bugs behind some bushes. Sounds of a dice game are heard before Bugs says, "All right Doc, shoot the works." Sambo is heard to say, "All right, dice, don't fail me now." Bugs is heard to say, "Sorry, Doc" before he emerges from the bushes wearing Sambo's clothes and carrying his shotgun. Sambo is next seen completely naked except for a fig leaf as the cartoon ends.

Review: *Motion Picture Herald*, 13 September 1941

The little colored Sambo decides to try his hand at capturing Bugs Bunny, but meets with the same success as his predecessors. Just as he has the screwy rabbit cornered, Bugs Bunny entices him into a craps game, and little Sambo winds up a sadder and wiser hunter. (7 min)

Review: *Boxoffice*, 14 September 1941

One big, long hand. That's what this Technicolor cartoon is. It shows unmistakable signs of extra effort, preparation and ingenuity in all departments. The central character, a little bitty colored Sambo, is a cinch to capture fun-loving audiences. Here he decides to go gunning for some rabbits. He meets up with a nimble-witted adversary that has little Sambo in a constant dither.

Review: *Motion Picture Exhibitor*, 17 September 1941

Sambo, a little negro boy, goes rabbit hunting, meets cynical Bugs Bunny, the screwy rabbit. The Bunny gives Sambo a beautiful chase for his money, making a sucker out of him any number of times. When the Bunny is finally cornered, he provides a pair of galloping dominoes and walks off with Sambo's clothes at the finish. This is a very funny reel in every respect—characters, situations, and story. If the feature is heavy or not so good, this will make the customers feel good anyhow. Excellent.

ALL'S WELL THAT ENDS WELL (1940)

Company: Mannie Davis, Paul Terry, Twentieth Century-Fox
Type: Terrytoons
Characters: Black kittens, dog

Review: *Motion Picture Exhibitor*, 20 March 1940

The four little kittens have no milk, so the black member of the quartet does his best to outwit the dog. The latter, seeing the plight of the kittens, relents, and brings them milk. Fair.

AMATEUR BROADCAST (1935)

Company: Walter Lantz, Universal Pictures
Characters: Caricatures of various radio stars, including Stephin Fetchit

Review: *Motion Picture Herald,* 29 June 1935

A good cartoon, this is a burlesque on the popular amateur nights on the radio, as the cartooned animals gather at the studio to hear the applicants, while others gather at their radio sets to hear the efforts. Burlesqued cleverly are Rudy Vallee, Stephin Fetchit, Bing Crosby, and the like. An entertaining cartoon number. (6 min)

ANY BONDS TODAY? (1943)

Company: Warner Bros.
Type: Commercial to promote the sale of U.S. war bonds
Characters: Bugs Bunny, Elmer Fudd, Porky Pig

Commercial: Bugs Bunny sells war bonds. Bugs tells the audience that "the tall man with the high hat and whiskers on his chin will soon be knocking at your door. And you ought to be in. Get your savings out when you hear him shout buy bonds today." Bugs then sings "Sammy, My Uncle Sammy" in blackface, imitating Al Jolson. He is joined by sailor Porky Pig and soldier Elmer Fudd, and they finish the commercial as a singing trio.

ANGEL PUSS (1944)

Company: Charles Jones, Warner Bros.
Type: Looney Tunes
Characters: Li'l Sambo, black cat

Story: The cartoon opens at night as Li'l Sambo walks to the end of a pier, carrying a large sack on his back. He is cheerful and sings "Shortnin' Bread." When he reaches the end of the pier, he puts down the sack, looks at the water, and says, "Dat sho' looks cold. He ain't gonna like dat a bit." He bends down and sticks his finger into the water to find out how cold it is. While his back is turned, a black cat crawls out of the bag. The cat then fills the bag with rocks. Sambo is about to throw it into the water, but has second thoughts about drowning the cat. Hiding behind him, the cat throws its voice through a length of drain pipe and says, "Go ahead, Sambo. Go ahead, boy. What's the matter with you? Getting cold feet? Remember the lady gave you four bits [fifty cents] to drown that kitty." When Sambo again hesitates to throw the bag in, the cat says, "Go ahead. The lady will take back the four bits if you don't." Reluctantly Sambo throws the bag in the water while the cat swallows some water to make gurgling sounds and says, "What have you done?" And Sambo says, "What is I gone and done?" Sambo lowers his head and slowly walks back home. Meanwhile the cat is already at his house making a white angel costume to wear to frighten Sambo. The cat covers its body with white talcum powder and then places a wire halo over its head before taking a harp and leaving the house to meet Sambo on the way home. As Sambo walks past the graveyard, he hears music and sees the cat playing the harp. Sambo is so frightened that his feet move and sound like a buzzsaw as he runs toward

his house. But the cat runs ahead of him and removes the fence and gate from in front of Sambo's house and places them in front of a haunted house next door. When Sambo arrives on the scene, he mistakenly runs into the haunted house and slams the door behind him. After he barricades the door with furniture, he feels safe and wipes the sweat from his brow. But he is shocked when he turns around and sees the cat standing behind him. Sambo dives out the window and is running away when the cat uses a magic force to pulls Sambo back inside. When they are facing each other, the cat shouts "Boo!" Sambo jumps off his feet before the cat chases him upstairs. Sambo and the cat run out of the second-floor window and fall into a pond behind the house. When they stick their heads out of the water, Sambo sees that the white powder has washed off of the cat. Then he realizes that he has been tricked. The cat does not realize that his disguise has been blown and says, "Boo!" Sambo is not frightened and follows the cat back into his house. Inside the cat again says, "Boo!" It realizes that the game is over after it sees itself in a mirror. Sambo picks up his shotgun and fires a shot through the front door at the cat, who has backed outside. Satisfied that the cat is now dead, Sambo is shocked to see nine white angel cats with wings floating through the door in single file. The cats tell Sambo, "This time, Brother, us ain't kidding," as the cartoon ends.

Reaction from the black press by Herman Hill: *"Angel Puss* vs. *Americans for All," Pittsburgh Courier,* 7 October 1944

Basis for the spontaneous protest by the long and patient suffering Negro theater-going public were the many forth-right expressions of condemnation made regarding Warner Brothers animated cartoon *Angel Puss.*

Almost in direct irony was the picture's showing in Los Angeles, in that it was sandwiched between the main feature and March of Time's *Americans For All,* which theme is directly aimed at the lessening of racisms.

It has since been learned that the Warner Brothers had ordered the somewhat considered controversial *Americans For All* to be shown in each of their theatres throughout the country as a contributory effort towards breaking down the evils of race prejudice.

In a further effort to throw light on the subject of caricatures, March of Time offices here were contacted.

A spokesman stated they had nothing to do with the placing of their film on the same program as *Angel Puss* or any other such picture.

It was admitted, however, that in consideration of the type of cartoon, poor taste was shown in the matter.

M. C. Pomerace, executive of the Screen Cartoonist Guild, AFL, expressed his approval of *The Courier's* stand and told the writer that in the past, certain of the membership of the local had expressed distinct dissatisfaction with the type of racial caricature material used in the making of animated film cartoons. At one time, he stated, the matter was brought to the attention of the Office of War Information for correction.

When the subject was bruited to Edward Staltzar, who heads Warner Brothers' cartoon department, he stated *Angel Puss* had been obtained when the company had purchased the Schlesinger interests.

Review: *Motion Picture Herald,* 24 June 1944

A cat out for mischief picks on a small Negro boy as his game. He first pretends that the youngster has drowned him and then proceeds to come back to haunt him. The boy had no intention of harming the cat and finds the appearance of the ghost as unreasonable as it is disturbing. (7 min)

Review: *Boxoffice,* 24 June 1944

A delectable bit of cartoon animation catches the natural aversion of a Colored boy to any form of supernatural suggestion as represented by a cat that was supposed to be drowned by the boy, but escaped. The cat makes life extremely miserable for the boy by dressing up as a spirit, but comes to an unfortunate end. There are lots of hearty chuckles in the reel.

Review: *Motion Picture Exhibitor,* 31 May 1944

The Negro lad thinks he has drowned the cat, but the latter placed bricks in the sack. Then the cat poses as a ghost and leads the lad on a merry chase until the latter kills him. The cat's nine lives come back to continue the job. Good.

Review: *Besa Shorts Shorts,* 19 June 1944

A Looney Tune in handsome color tells the story of small Sambo, who has been paid fo' bits to eradicate a black cat. Sambo gets cold feet when he gets right down to tossing the bag into the lake. As he mumbles about it, smart kitty lets himself out of the bag and eggs Sambo on to do the trick without Sambo knowing of his escape. He becomes a white cat via the paint bucket and haunts poor Sammy all over the place. They finally fall into the lake, off comes the disguise and Sammy finds that he has not committed murder.

ANOTHER TAIL (1914)

Company: Lubin Film Manufacturing Company
Type: Split reel with *The Tail of a Chicken* (black cast)
Characters: Sam Bug and Raskus Bug

Review: *Moving Picture World,* 25 April 1914

Sam Bug and Raskus Bug are suitors for Mandy Bug. Her attentions are strong for Sam, so she gives Raskus the "cold shoulder." Raskus Bug's blood is aroused and he loses no time in telling his troubles to his gang, the leader being no other than "Gyp the Bug." They cook up a scheme whereby they kill a silkworm, which is very much against the law in Bugland. They put the silkworm in the rain barrel near Sam Bug's sweetheart's home, then they get a Bug cop and Sam Bug is arrested. Mandy knows it is the work of the gang and gets Sherlock Bug, the

great detective, who gets on the trail, traps the gang by blowing up the gang's den, puts them all in jail and Sam Bug is released.

Review: *Moving Picture World,* 16 May 1914

On the same reel with *Tale of a Chicken.* An animated cartoon of "Bugdom." Senseless.

Review: *New York Dramatic Mirror,* 3 May 1914

This is a short length of the pen-magic pictures, a kind of "Adventures in Bugsville." The best part of the offering is that the pictures enacted are a rough burlesque on the part of the film that preceded it, *The Tail of a Chicken.* It holds an amused interest throughout the film.

ARTIST'S MODEL (1924)

Company: Earl Hurd, Educational Pictures
Type: Pen and Ink Vaudeville
Characters: Zulu jazz band, colored conductor

Review: *Moving Picture World,* 15 November 1924

This Pen and Ink Vaudeville by Earl Hurd portrays theatricals in which a briefly clad girl steps out of a poster, a wild Zulu Jazz Band is operated by means of the conductor's club, slack wire artists perform on a barrel. "Props" cleans out the Zulu group with the dice and the colored conductor seeks revenge. The sketching is well done but there is little novelty of idea, except, perhaps, where the piano player strips the keys in his contortions.

Review: *Film Daily,* 9 November 1924

Excellent results can in all probability be obtained by using this reel in connection with orchestral effects. The cartoon deals with a janitor-property man of a theater who forgets his cues for the different vaudeville performers in his dreams of a poster girl. The animal jazz band all play different instruments. The tight rope walkers have some trouble and there is a fine scrimmage between the janitor and the leader of the Zulu Jazz Band when the former wins the latter's grass-skirt. A funny musical accompaniment will do much toward making this very effective.

BAD LUCK BLACKIE (1949)

Company: Tex Avery, M-G-M
Characters: White kitten, black cat, bulldog

Story: The cartoon opens in a house where a big bulldog is having fun bullying a small white kitten. The bulldog pulls the kitten's tail and offers it a bowl of milk. When the kitten tries to take a drink, its nose is caught in a mousetrap. Finally the kitten tries to escape by running out of the house into the city streets, but the bulldog follows. The kitten manages to elude the dog and hides behind a trashcan. A black alley cat wearing a derby hat and smoking a cigar asks the kitten, "Hey Shorty, dog trouble?" The kitten nods its head yes and the black cat produces a business card: Black Cat Bad Luck Company. Paths Crossed. Guaranteed Bad Luck. He says, "What do you think? OK?" The kitten nods its head yes, and the black cat says, "That's great, Pal. I will now demonstrate." He peeks around the trashcan and sees the bulldog running down the sidewalk toward them. He says, "I just cross their path like this," as he coolly walks in front of the bulldog. Instantaneously a flowerpot falls from the sky and hits the dog on his head, knocking him silly. The black cat says, "And bingo they gets bad luck. And if you ever need me, just whistle." He gives the kitten a whistle before going on his way. The white kitten walks away, confident that its problem with the bulldog has been solved. Meanwhile the bulldog has recovered his senses and chases after the kitten. He is about to catch him, but the kitten blows the whistle, the black cat crosses the bulldog's path, and another flowerpot falls on the dog's head. The chase continues with the same bad result for the bulldog. By springing out of a box he manages to scare the kitten so badly that it drops the whistle before running off. Determined to get even with the black cat, the bulldog sets a trap. But when he blows the whistle to cause a safe to fall on the cat's head, the plan backfires and the safe falls on him. Then he paints the black cat white. Not realizing that his color has been changed to white, the black cat crosses the dog's path several times without results. Exhausted, the cat gives up and then realizes that his color is now white. Now frightened of the dog, the cat tries to run, but the bulldog catches him. Holding onto the cat's neck, the bulldog shakes him repeatedly while laughing and blowing the whistle in his face. The white kitten decides to help its friend and changes its color to black, using a can of black paint. The kitten then walks in front of the dog, causing an anvil to fall on his head. The dog is knocked silly and in the process also swallows the whistle. When he recovers, he finds that he has the hiccups. Each time he hiccups the whistle blows and in rapid succession a waterpot, a bathtub, a piano, a bulldozer, an airplane, a bus, and a battleship fall on him as he runs out of sight. Meanwhile the black cat, who is now white, shakes the hand of the kitten, who is now black, and places the derby hat on the kitten's head. They both smile as the cartoon ends.

Review: *Motion Picture Herald,* 7 May 1949

Blackie was a cat who had brought bad luck to everyone whose path he crossed. When he met Butch, the Bulldog, he found he could no longer rely on luck but had to substitute ingenuity. (7 min)

Review: *Film Daily,* 8 April 1949

Jet black Blackie brought bad luck to everyone who crossed his path until he met his match in large fanged bull-dog. Blackie turns white and not with age, as they work things out. This cartoon has lots of action and laughs.

Review: *Exhibitor's Servisection,* 16 February 1949

A small kitten is tormented by a huge bulldog, and gets protection from an infallible bad luck-bringing black cat. Each

time the kitten blows a whistle, the cat appears, and soon heavy objects fall upon the bulldog who almost breaks the spell for awhile. Good.

Review: *Boxoffice,* 5 February 1945

Very Good. Blackie, a jet black cat, befriends a white kitten being tormented by a bulldog. Every time the dog crosses Blackie's path, practically everything falls on him out of the sky, from bricks to pianos. When the dog finally removes the spell on him by painting Blackie white, the kitten goes in for black paint, and assorted articles as large as airplanes rain down on the dog. Well drawn and really funny.

BARNYARD FIVE (1936)

Company: Walter Lantz, Universal Pictures
Characters: Oswald the rabbit, black duckling

Review: *National Exhibitor,* 20 May 1936

The duck has five ducklings, one of them black. The quintet and parents are invited to Oswald's to eat. The quintet gets generally tangled up in the food with the gags average, ending weak. This is just filler. (9 min)

BEACH COMBERS (1936)

Company: Walter Lantz, Universal Pictures
Characters: Oswald the rabbit, his dog Elmer, the duck family, including four white ducklings and one black duckling

Story: The cartoon opens as the duck family arrives at the beach for a picnic. Walking behind Mamma and Papa are four white ducklings named Fee, Fi, Fo, and Fum. One black duckling named Fooey brings up the rear. They set-up the umbrella, and Mamma and Papa relax while the ducklings play in the sand. Oswald Rabbit arrives on the scene carrying his fishing pole and beach umbrella. His dog, Elmer, is carrying the lunch basket. Oswald sets up the umbrella and then picks up his fishing rod and heads for the shore as he tells Elmer, "Now you watch the lunch, Elmer, while I do a little fishing. And if you don't, I'll . . ." He makes a throat-cutting gesture. He is overheard by the ducklings, who put their heads together to figure out a plan to steal Oswald's food. As Elmer takes a nap, the ducklings send in the black duckling to climb into the basket and steal the food. But Elmer wakes up and kicks the black duckling on his backside. The black duckling rubs his rear end as the ducklings decide on their next plan of attack. This time they tie one end of a rope to a bone and the other end to the tail of the black duckling who walks past Elmer. The dog smells the sent and follows it with his nose to the ground. The black duckling stops and hits the dog on the head with the bone. Meanwhile the white ducklings have climbed into the basket and are eating the food when Elmer recovers his senses. Elmer chases the ducklings away, and they hide behind an overturned boat. While they are trying to think up another plan, the black duckling gets an idea. He sees an old shoe lying on the beach. The sole is half separated from the top, exposing the sharp points of nails. The black duck pulls the shoe over his head then joins his brothers and tells them the plan. He then bites a sleeping Elmer on the nose, and the shoe nails clamp tight on the dog's nose. Elmer barks in pain and runs off as the smiling black duckling watches him. By the time Elmer manages to get the shoe off his nose, he finds that the white ducklings are sailing across the water in the picnic basket and eating Oswald's food. Elmer is at first reluctant to go after them, but he remembers Oswald's warning and jumps into the water and swims after them. The black duckling, watching from the beach, decides to help his brothers. He swims under water and ties the black sail of a toy boat to Elmer's tail. He then surfaces in front of Elmer and shouts "shark, shark." Elmer thinks the black sail is a hungry shark about to attack and swims back to the beach. After he sees the sail and realizes that the black duckling has tricked him again, he pounds his hands in the sand and then puts his face in the sand and cries. Meanwhile a huge black octopus spots the white ducklings and grabs them in its tentacles. The ducklings' cries for help are heard by their parents on shore and Oswald in his boat, but no one can come to their rescue. Meanwhile the octopus carries the ducklings down to its home on the bottom of the ocean near a sunken ship and imprisons them in a clamshell. Reluctantly Elmer dives into the water, but when he arrives on the scene the octopus grabs him by the tail and flings him out of the water high into the air. Elmer lands back in the water and sinks to the bottom, where the octopus chases him again. But this time the octopus gets its tentacles tangled in the springs of an old mattress. Elmer rescues the ducklings, and they sail back to shore in the lunch basket. They are met by Oswald and the happy parents. Oswald, Elmer, the parents, and the white ducklings gather around the basket and Oswald says, "Now we will all eat." When Oswald pulls the sheet off the basket, he and the others are shocked and angry to see the black duckling lying inside, smiling and holding a half-eaten chicken leg. With a frown on his face Oswald asks, "Where is the lunch?" The black duckling says, "You really want to know?" and Oswald says yes. Fooey, the black duckling, turns to the audience and asks, "Should I tell him?" He winks his eye, smiles, and rubs his stomach as the cartoon ends.

THE BIRTHDAY PARTY (1937)

Company: Walter Lantz, Universal Pictures
Characters: Oswald the rabbit, black rabbit

Review: *National Exhibitor*, 20 April 1937

Oswald gives a birthday party for the quintuplet rabbits. One of the quintuplets is the "black sheep" causing a lot of commotion at the party. Oswald's dog comes in for most of the punishment. Fair.

THE BLACK DUCK (1929)

Company: Fable Pictures Inc.
Type: Fabletoons
Characters: Mouse, black duck

Story: The cartoon opens with a mouse (who resembles Disney's Mickey Mouse) leading a line of ducks on an outing. All of the ducks are white except one at the rear of the line that is having trouble keeping up with the group. The black duck wants to lead, and so he flies to the front of the line where he meets the angry mouse. "What are you doing here in front? Scram! Get back at the end of the line where you belong." The black duck obeys but before long flies to the front of the group. The mouse chases the black duck and says, "If I get hold of you I'll ring your black neck." The black duck tries to escape but the mouse catches him, ties a rope around his neck, and pulls him to a tree where he attaches the other end of the rope. As the mouse leaves to join the other ducks, he says, "What can you expect from a black duck?" The mouse leads his ducks to a pond. They all get in and take a swim while the mouse relaxes on the bank and watches over them. Meanwhile Butch is a black cat with a patch over one eye. He pulls a cart with a small cage containing a mouse. Butch sees the ducks and decides to capture them. He solicits the aid of a cat who is the manager of the Day and Night Club, where other cats dance to hot jazz music. Butch asks his friend, "Want to buy some ducks?" After agreeing to a deal Butch and his cat friend leave the club and put their scheme into action. Butch arrives back at the pond where he the greets the mouse. "Hi kid, I'm glad to meet you. I'm Butch cat from over the hill. I know you get tired of looking at dem ducks." Butch diverts the mouse's attention by giving him a book containing pictures of pretty girls in swimsuits. Butch leaves the scene and takes the little mouse out of the cage. He places the mouse in a duck decoy and instructs him to lure the ducks out of the pond and into a trap located nearby where his partner is waiting. The ducks are trapped and cry for help. They are heard by the black duck, who is still tied to the tree. Immediately the black duck breaks his bonds and flies away to tell the mouse, still reading the book, that his ducks are in trouble. The mouse jumps on the back of the black duck, and they fly to the rescue. They arrive in the nick of time to save one of the ducks from having his head chopped off by the cat. After a furious battle, the ducks are rescued and the black duck, with the mouse riding on his back, flies to the head of the line to lead the rest of the ducks as the cartoon ends.

Review: *Motion Picture News*, 16 March 1929

Raffles Cat and Woofus Wolf plot against Milton Mouse, who sedulously guards his troop of ducks. They beguile Milton with an attractive picture book while his ducks are lured away. But when disaster stares Milton in the face, his black duck, whom he has tied to a tree to voice his displeasure against his annoying manners, saves the day. He conveniently acts as Milton's airplane and carries him to where the ducks are kept captive by the mean Woofus Wolf. Milton immediately fights Mr. Woofus and beats him handily. Meanwhile the black duck again shows his incalculable worth by leading his fellows back to the pond.

More thrilling than Goldilocks and the three bears or the "huff and I'll puff 'til I blow your house down" story. The proper metier for these Fables is at a children's matinee, but a houseful of grown-ups derive enjoyment from them, too. (one reel)

BLACK PUPPY IN THE ARMY (1940)

Company: Produced and distributed in Japan
Type: Dialog in Japanese
Character: Black puppy

Story: The cartoon opens in the barracks of an army camp in Japan. The soldiers, all white puppies except for one black puppy, are sleeping. The bugle sounds and all the white puppies jump out of bed and run to assemble for roll call. But the black puppy is still asleep. When he finally wakes up, his cot carries him outside where the joins the others. When the drill sergeant calls his name, he jumps out of bed and stands at attention. The sergeant commands them to do calisthenics, including arm bends and push-ups. All the puppies exercise in synchronization, except the black puppy who gets tired and lies down to sleep. The sergeant shouts at him and orders him to scrub the floors of the barracks. The black puppy attempts to clean the floor, but makes a mess when he can't turn off a water hose. The barracks are flooded and he uses the wash pail as a boat. Meanwhile an alarm is sounded that a man-eating tiger is on the loose. The soldiers arm themselves and march off to capture the tiger, followed by tanks and heavy cannon. The black puppy rushes out of the barracks, grabs his rifle, and runs off to catch the other soldiers. They find the tiger asleep in a valley. The white puppies charge the tiger, who repulses them without even waking up. The commander, waving his sword, charges the tiger and hits him on is head. He only succeeds in waking up the tiger and making him angry. The tiger grabs the commander in his mouth, and the rest of the puppies charge the tiger. The tiger shakes off the puppies, and they run away. But the black puppy jumps on top of the tiger's head and jumps up and down. The tiger shakes the black puppy off his head and the black puppy runs for his life. The tiger gives chase, but the puppy is able to escape. Next the black puppy sees a pig who is painting a fence. The black puppy uses the white paint to cover himself with white stripes so that he resembles a small tiger. While the other puppies watch from a distance, the black puppy walks back to the tiger who is puzzled at what he sees. The black puppy throws some balls of candy in the tiger's mouth, and the tiger laughs so hard that he falls on his back. The tiger is captured by the puppies, who carry him back to the army camp in a cage. The black puppy is a hero. With a big smile on his face, he rides back to the camp on the top of a tank as the cartoon ends.

THE BLACK SHEEP (1924)

Company: Paul Terry; distributed by Pathe Film Exchange
Type: Aesop's Fable
Character: Black puppy

Review: *Moving Picture World*, 19 January 1924

When the puppy disgraces his family by smoking a pipe he is banished from the home. But his great chance to atone comes when the eagle snatches away the pet gosling and he rescues it by airplane, thus becoming a public hero. It is full of bright action and amusement—one of Paul Terry's best. (one reel)

Review: *Film Daily*, 13 January 1924

The Black Sheep is entirely up to the usual good standard of this cartoon series. The drawings are cute, the action amusing and the animation smooth. The little story deals with a pup who is considered the black sheep of his family kennel. However, he performs several brave deeds for which he is rewarded by a farmer with a medal and a huge plate of bones which he bears proudly home as a peace-offering.

THE BLACK SHEEP (1932)

Company: Charles Mintz, Samba Pictures; released by Columbia Pictures
Characters: Scrappy, black lamb, white sheep

Story: The cartoon opens as Scrappy, the sheepherder, leads his sheep as he skips along playing a fiddle. Trailing behind the other white lambs is a black lamb that has trouble keeping up with the others. He tries to skip but falls flat on his ground. The others turn and laugh at him. When the black lamb tries to sing to Scrappy's tune, the others throw stones at him. The lambs pair off and dance to the music while the lonely black lamb lowers his head and sobs. Two lambs dance close to him and jeer, but the black lamb is angered and zips up their mouths. The black lamb encounters a small white lamb that tries to pick a fight, but the black lamb chases it away. His action angers a huge ram that grabs the black lamb by the tail, slams him to the ground several times, and threatens him with a curved knife before walking away. The small lamb returns and the angry black lamb pounds him into the ground. The little lamb cries out, and Scrappy arrives on the scene. Scrappy grabs the black lamb by its ear and drags him to the gate and motions him to get out. The black lamb begs Scrappy not to throw him out, but Scrappy, the other sheep, and even a tree trunk turn their backs on him. While Scrappy has his back turned, the black lamb gives him a kick before turning to leave. As he walks away with tears flowing out of his eyes, a cow laughs at him—the last straw. The black lamb becomes angry and grabs a log and throws it at the cow, knocking her senseless. He then throws rocks at the other white lambs who become frightened and run into the barn and lock the door. The black sheep follows them and eventually cuts a hole in the door with the knife. Soon white fur is seen flying out of the barn. Scrappy arrives on the scene and runs into the barn, but he is tossed out and lands on his head. While Scrappy lies on the ground, knocked senseless, the barn door opens and the white sheep march out, shorn of their wool. Next the ram, who is also clean shaven, walks out pulling a cart with the black sheep riding in it. The black sheep removes the ram's large horns and puts them on his head. He smiles and holds the knife in the air as the cartoon ends.

THE BLACK SHEEP (1934)

Company: Frank Moser, Paul Terry, Educational Pictures, Twentieth Century-Fox
Type: Terrytoons
Characters: Black sheep, wolf

Review: *Film Daily,* **2 October 1934**

This is the fable of the black sheep whom the three little white sheep refused to play with. When he hollered "Wolf" they ran away until, having been fooled several times, they stayed on and one of them was seized. The black sheep effects a rescue and thus regains a white coat. Subject is splendidly animated and vocal score is amusing.

Review: *Motion Picture World,* **13 October 1934**

A cartoon reenactment of the fable which found a little black sheep crying "wolf" once too often. This is a fair animation. The black sheep, in retaliation for the manner in which he is snubbed, frightens the other sheep with his cry. Later they laugh when the wolf does appear and the black one rescues the wolf's captives, his deed restoring his natural color (he turns white). For youngsters especially. (6 min)

Review: *Motion Picture Reviews:* **November 1934**

An innocuous cartoon picturing a black sheep who called "wolf" too often. Only fair production. Family.

BLACK AND WHITE (1933)

Company: Amkio (Soviet Russia)
Characters: Cuban blacks

Review: *Film Daily,* **25 May 1933**

The musical cartoon based on a poem by Vladimir Maiakov depicts the oppression of Negroes by white men, and thereby smacks of social propaganda. Scene is laid in Cuba, where the white man makes the black slave serve him on plantations. When a colored bootblack, who is shown as a dreamy and puzzled fellow, asks a question of the plantation owner, who is characterized as a ferocious villain, the white man strikes the Negro down. Whether the cartoon, made in Russia by Mejhrabpomfilm, is intended to incite feeling against white men and sympathy for Negroes is an open question.

BLUES (1931)

Company: Frank Moser, Paul Terry, Twentieth Century-Fox Educational Pictures
Characters: Southern blacks

Review: *Motion Picture Herald,* **4 July 1931**

A Terry-Toon number with a setting in the South. Human and animal characters indulge in songs at every possible moment, which is quite frequently. (6 min)

Review: *Film Daily,* **7 June 1931**

A Terry-Toon cartoon with darkies as the animated figures, doing a typical Alabama Blues. The boy friend hotfoots it back to his mammy in the sunny south, with all the typical darky and the syn-copated jazz as musical accompaniment. A variation on the animal routine that should be somewhat of a novelty in the cartoon field.

BOBBY BUMPS IN THE GREAT "DIVIDE" (1917)

Company: Earl Hurd, J. R. Bray Studio, Paramount Pictures
Type: On split reel with Paramount-Bray Pictograms no. 54
Characters: Bobby Bumps, Dinah the black cook, Fido the pup

Review: *Moving Picture World,* **3 March 1917**

Equipped with a small boy's appetite for sweet things, Bobby Bumps steals into the region where Dinah holds forth bent on investigating the available supply of edibles and pleading his case with the dark skinned mistress ruling over the culinary department. Much to his surprise there rests in all of its white sugar frosted glory a wonderful cake, fresh from the ovens, and Dinah sits in her chair—fast asleep. But just as Bobby is about to get the prize, the dusky damsel wakes and Bobby beats a hasty retreat through the window.

But boys like Bobby consider obstacles only as incentives to the chase and with so wonderful a capture in sight he must consult his pal and chief adviser—Fido the pup. As usual, when two heads are put together, a means presents itself. A vacuum cleaning wagon and a lot of sewer pipes stand at the curbing. With the assistance of his enterprising pup, Bobby joins the pipes, pushes them through the window in touch with the cake, connects the vacuum hose, turns on the power, and the cake rests safely is his hands while Dinah, slumbering again, wakes only in time to see the two disappearing over the back-yard fence.

A chase follows in which Bobby and the pup make use of a friendly but excited goat and Dinah, the cook, an abandoned car, and no doubt it would still be on if a locomotive hadn't insisted that the tracks were built for it exclusively. After the dust settles the division of the cake is equally adjusted to the satisfaction of all—not to say the huge delight of Bobby and his pup.

BOBBY BUMPS LOSES HIS PUP (1916)

Company: Earl Hurd, J. R. Bray Studio; released by Paramount Pictures
Characters: Bobby Bumps, his mother, his father, his black friend, Choc'late, and his dog Fido

Story: The cartoon opens in Bobby's house as Bobby's pet dog, Fido, runs down the stairs, climbs onto a chair, and uses his mouth to grab Bobby's father's hat off the coatrack. He tosses it playfully until the brim comes off. He puts the brim on his head and then tosses it again. It comes down on Bobby's father's head. Father angrily looks at the brim and says to himself, "That pup is going to lose his happy home." Then he picks up Fido and carries him off. Meanwhile Bobby Bumps is in the kitchen, drying the dishes as his mother washes them. When she leaves for a moment, Bobby uses the plates to practice his juggling act. She returns to find Bobby juggling the dishes and admonishes him to get back to work. Just then Bobby hears the pup cry for help as his father carries him past the kitchen window. Bobby says to himself, "Gee, the pup's in bad fer somethin'! I better 'vestigage." Bobby's father doesn't see Bobby following him as he carries Fido to the house of a black man with thick white lips. Father gives Fido to the man and says, "And if a small boy with a white cap should try and claim him, don't give him back unless he gets my permission." Bobby overhears his father's instructions and develops a plan to get his pet back. He enlists the aid of his black friend, Choc'late. He dresses the black boy up to resemble Bobby's father in a two-piece costume. Choc'late stands in the bottom part of the costume while Bobby tells him, "It's the only way, Choc'late. And if it works, I'll set 'em up." Choc'late smiles as Bobby places the top of the costume on top of him. For his father's head, Bobby paints a glass vase to look like his face. Bobby takes Choc'late's hand and leads him back to the black man's house. Bobby tells the man, "Pa says I can have the pup now. Isn't that so, Pa?" As he looks back at Choc'late in costume, Choc'late says, "Yassah!" The black man falls for the trick and lets Bobby have his dog back. Bobby and Choc'late, still in costume, are walking back home when Bobby stops and laughs at Choc'late and says, "Jiggers." Just then Bobby sees his mother walking down the street toward them. Bobby says, "Gee, it's Ma," and hides behind Choc'late. Bobby's mother stops in front of her apparent husband and says, "What on earth ails you?" Choc'late doesn't respond, so she says, "Are you sick?" He remains silent, so she shakes her finger in his face and says, "You've been drinking!" Bobby whispers to Choc'late, "Say, 'no, I'm sick.' (you blamed idiot)." Choc'late tells her, "No, I'm sick, you blamed idiot!" His mother is so angry that she grabs the top part of the costume and pulls it off Choc'late. Bobby runs off followed by Choc'late in the bottom part of the costume. They run behind a fence and hide. Bobby angrily asks Choc'late, "Why ya wanta stand there like a big dummy fer?" Choc'late tells him, "Ain't dat wot I wuz s'posed to be?" He laughs. Meanwhile Bobby's mother is still holding the costume when Bobby's father arrives on the scene behind her. Thinking that she is holding another man, he becomes jealous and pulls out two pistols from his pocket and shoots them into the air. Bobby's mother turns and throws the dummy at him. Later he examines the dummy and sees Fido. Then he realizes that Bobby has played a trick on him. He reaches over the fence and grabs Bobby as Choc'late runs away. Later Bobby stands on a chair while he eats a bowel of soup that is on the mantelpiece. A pillow is tied to his rear end. Fido arrives on the scene, climbs up on the mantelpiece, and kisses Bobby on the face. Bobby smiles at him and says, "Thanks just the same, Fido. I've been licked enuf fer one day," as the cartoon ends.

BOBBY BUMPS AND THE SPECKLED DEATH (1918)

Company: Earl Hurd, J. R. Bray Studio; released by Paramount Pictures
Characters: Bobby Bumps, black lady

Story: The cartoon opens as a letter carrier arrives at a house and attempts to deliver a letter by throwing it into the mailbox. He misses and the letter falls on the porch. He blows a whistle and then walks away. A black woman wearing a long dress, an apron, and a bandanna on her head walks out of the front door at the sound of the whistle and looks in the mailbox. She doesn't see any letter, so she looks around before looking down and spotting it on the porch. She angrily picks it up and says, "I'll fix him." Then she walks back into the house and closes the door behind her. Bobby Bumps comes on the scene playing soldier as he marches in front of a black dog, a white dog, and a mouse who march in single file behind him. They march carrying sticks on their shoulders like rifles. Bobby calls out orders: "Halt! Right shoulder, arms! Hup! Attention! Left face! Attention! Left face! Mark time! Halt! 'Bout face! Salute! Forward, march! Fall in!" By the time the last order is given his friends are so confused that they are bumping into each other. They decide that they have had enough and jump over the fence. The black woman comes out of the front door carrying a sign that reads Mailbox Here. She nails it to the wall beside the mailbox and walks back into the house. Curious, Bobby walks over and reads the sign. Then he thinks of a trick to play on the black woman. He takes an inkpen from his pocket and changes the sign to read "Small Pox Here." He walks around to the side of the house, looks through the window, and sees the black woman sleeping in a chair. He leans through the window and paints white dots on her face and then pours the white paint into her mouth before leaving the scene. Meanwhile the letter carrier arrives and becomes excited when he sees the smallpox sign on the house. The black woman comes out of the house carrying a basket and is about to walk to the market. The letter carrier sees the white spots on her face and becomes so excited that his hat flies off and he drops the letter he is carrying before running down the street in fear. The black woman drops her basket, picks up the letter, and runs after him to give it back. Meanwhile Bobby and his dog are having fun watching the events. The black woman chases the letter carrier who runs away from her, letters flying out of his mail sack. Meanwhile Bobby stops the chief of police, who is riding a bicycle, and tells him, ". . . And now she's breaking quarantine." He points to the smallpox sign on the house. The chief rides off to catch the black woman who is chasing the letter carrier. He lassoes her with a rope, she falls flat on her face, and then he drags her down the street and into the jail. From outside, the building is seen to be shaking from side to side, indicating a fierce battle going on inside. Inside the black woman has freed herself from the rope and is using it to bind the chief's arms to his side. She is holding the chief by the top of his head with one hand while she punches him in the face with the other hand. She then bounces him off the wall. He manages to get the ropes off, but she catches him before he can escape. He pulls his pistol from his boot, but she takes it away from him and then shoots it at his feet while the chief dances to dodge the bullets. When she shoots the shoes off his feet, he holds up his hands and says "Kamerad!" She then turns her back on him to look in a mirror on the wall. She sees the white dots on her face and says, "By golly, I betcha I know who all done that." She immediately runs out of the jail and returns home. Meanwhile Bobby is playing mumblety-peg with his dog. Another boy is sitting with his back turned to Bobby. The boy turns around, and Bobby sees that he has black dots all over his face. The black woman arrives, pulls Bobby and his dog over the fence, takes them to the house, and puts them to bed. She then gives each a spoonful of medicine that they spit out of their mouths when she leaves the room. Meanwhile outside the house is a sign nailed to the wall that says Measles Here as the cartoon ends.

BOBBY BUMPS STARTS A LODGE (1916)

Company: Earl Hurd, J. R. Bray Studio, released by Paramount Pictures
Characters: Bobby Bumps, black boy

Story: The cartoon opens in a country village where clothes hang out to dry on clotheslines. Bobby Bumps arrives on the scene pulling one end of a long rope. He stops and eats an onion that he pulls out of his pocket. On the other end of the rope is Bobby's goat. It does not want to be pulled. When the goat smells the onion and runs toward Bobby, he grabs it by the horns but cannot push it into the barn. Finally Bobby manages to get the goat in the barn and closes and locks the door. Meanwhile a black boy with thick white lips and a clean-shaven head arrives on the scene. The black boy opens his mouth wide to yawn. Bobby pulls another onion from his pocket and throws it into the boy's open mouth. The black boy pulls the onion out of his mouth and looks angrily at the smiling Bobby, who pretends that he did not throw the onion. Bobby walks over and put his hands on the boy's shoulder, but the boy pushes his hand away. Bobby wants to make friends and asks the boy, "Wanta join a lodge?" Bobby pulls an apron out of his pocket that has the emblem of a goat on it. He tells the black boy, "This is the apron you wear. All regular lodges wear aprons." The boy looks at the apron, smiles, scratches his head, and says, "Yep, I'll jine!" Bobby ties the apron around the boy's waist so that the goat emblem is on the boy's back. The boy asks, "Ain't dat a kinda funny place to wear aprons? At de back?" Bobby tells him, "This lodge does everything 'zackly different. That's what makes it such a swell lodge." Bobby ties a blindfold over the boy's eyes and tells him, "You wait here while I get Third Degree." The black boy stands and waits while Bobby gets his goat. He positions him a few feet behind the black boy and tells the boy to bend over. The boy imagines that Bobby is about to paddle him and and says to himself, "I'll fool him." Bobby hits the goat, and it charges the boy. But the boy turns around and lowers his head. The goat runs into the boy's head and is knocked out flat on the ground. The boy pulls off the blindfold, looks at the goat, laughs, and dances a jig. But Bobby is mad that his trick did not work, and he chases the black boy. The black boy runs to the edge of a wide, deep canyon. He stops momentarily before jumping across to the other side, where he grabs onto a tree branch just before Bobby arrives on the scene. The boy stands on the limb and dances and smiles at Bobby on the other side. Bobby jumps up and warns the boy that a bear is under the tree where the boy is. The bear looks up at the boy, who trembles with fear. As the bear climbs the tree, the black boy walks out to the end of the limb, kneels, and starts to pray. He cries for help before kicking the bear

out of the tree. Bobby runs off and gets a rope and makes a lasso in one end. He tells the boy, "I'll save you. You will join the lodge, right?" Meanwhile the bear has climbed back into the tree. The boy kicks the bear again and then answers yes. Bobby tells him, "No fair turnin' 'round on the goat." By now the black boy is so scared of the bear that he turns white and starts to pray again. Bobby tosses the loop end of the rope to the other side of the canyon and lassoes the limb of the tree the boy is in. The boy slides on the rope across the canyon to the other side, where Bobby is standing. Then the bear tries to slide on the rope and pulls Bobby over the edge. Bobby holds onto one end of the rope as he dangles in the air. Bobby calls out for help, and the smiling black boy answers, "Is you all gwine let me 'nishiate you too?" Bobby cries yes, and the boy says, "How dat?" Bobby again says, "Yes, yes." The black boy then runs off and returns holding a large rock that he throws across the canyon. It hits the bear, knocking him into the canyon. Bobby swings on the rope back to the other side. Later Bobby and the black boy, both blindfolded, stand side by side at the end of a wooden plank over a barrel of water in front of them. The goat stands on the other end of plank behind them. The goat is tied with a rope that is near the flame of a candle. Bobby says, "When the candle burns down, it'll burn the rope up and let the goat loose and then we take the 'nishiation together. That's the 'greement, ain't it?" The black boy lifts the blindfold above his eyes, looks back at the rope, and then starts to walk away. But Bobby grabs him. The rope burns, but Bobby and the boy jump into the air as the goat charges them. The goat runs off the end of the plank and falls into the barrel of water. Both boys look at each other and laugh as the goat spits water out of his mouth. They say, "Well, I reckon I'm the goat all right," as the cartoon ends.

Review: *Moving Picture World,* 7 October 1916

This one-reel Bray cartoon shows Bobby, his pet goat and his little colored friend. Bobby starts a lodge of his own and invites Sambo to join. He expects to have great fun with the boy, and so does the goat, but the little negro fools them both, and Billy has to admit that he is the goat. Full of humor and good drawing.

Review: *Exhibitors Herald,* 7 October 1916

A pen and ink cartoon story of Bobby, who decides to start a lodge. He secures the services of a goat which makes things lively.

BOOGIE-WOOGIE BUGLE BOY OF COMPANY B (1941)

Company: Walter Lantz, Universal Pictures
Type: Nominated for Academy Award
Characters: Hot Breath Harry, black soldiers

See fig. 43. Story: The cartoon opens in the city. Hot Breath Harry is the star trumpet player in a band playing at a nightclub. Harry is producing some hot notes when another kind of note is put on his trumpet. It reads, "Official notice from the draft board—Little Boy Blue come blow your horn, or we'll come get you, as sure as you were born. Local Draft Board." Harry says, "Well, what do you know! I's been drafted. But I won't go. They can't do this to me. I's got influence . . ." Then a hand jerks him off the stage. Harry finds himself at an army camp where he is rapidly processed through the physical examination department, the fingerprinting department, and the uniform department, where he says, "I won't wear it. You can't put that stuff on me." Then he slides out the door of the unit assignment department. Harry looks around and says, "Where am I?" A short, fat, and tough-looking sergeant says, "Brother, you is in the army." Harry says, "They can't do this to me. I'm Hot Breath Harry, de hottest trumpet player in town." The sergeant tells him, "Well, Hot Breath, you is de new bugle boy of Company B" and gives Harry a bugle. Two soldiers walk by carrying a wounded soldier on a stretcher and Harry asks, "Who dat?" The soldier replies, "Dat wuz our last bugle boy." Harry says, "Bugle boy? I resign." He throws away the bugle and walks off. The bugle lands on the lips of the sergeant. He grabs Harry by the back of his shirt and asks him, "Did you lose a bugle?" Harry answers, "No, no man. I never had no bugle." The sergeant jams the bugle on Harry's face and tells him, "Well, you got one now. And remember, at 5 A.M. you blow reveille. So start practicin'." Harry blows one note on the horn before he is hit by many flying objects thrown by soldiers who prefer to sleep late. It's now early in the morning, and a nervous Harry paces back and forth. A clock indicates that it's almost 5 A.M. A large notice on the wall reads, Attention Buglers! Reveille Must Be Blown at *Exactly* 5 A.M. When the alarm goes off, Harry, with sweat running down his face, says, "So long." He begins to play, and a meat cleaver flies through the air and splits the bugle down the middle, coming to rest just before it hits Harry's face. The sergeant comes on the scene and says to Harry, "Well, do we get reveille or do you get canned?" Harry slowly backs away, runs into a wall, and knocks his trumpet off the shelf and into his hands. Harry smiles and starts to play the title song. The sergeant smiles, and lights come on in tents all over camp. The soldiers wake up with smiles on their faces and join in singing the title song. One soldier finishes brushing his teeth and grins, revealing two teeth shaped like dice. Another soldier strops a barber's razor that he uses to peel potatoes. A cook picks up two eggs, shakes them in his hand like a pair of dice, and throws them into the frying pan. Three shapely, light-skinned WACS show up on the scene and jitterbug with the happy soldiers. Another soldier beats a cannonshell like a drum and is blown up. He is next seen dressed in white with wings on his back, floating on a cloud while playing boogie-woogie on his harp. The soldiers go through their regular training routines while keeping perfect time with the boogie beat until it is dark and they all go to bed. Harry is still playing his trumpet by the light of a full moon as the cartoon ends.

Review: *Motion Picture Herald,* 23 August 1941

This Walter Lantz color cartoon features the boogie-woogie song popularized by the Andrews Sisters in the feature *Buck Privates.* It is jive music in cartoon style. (7 min)

Review: *Motion Picture Exhibitor,* 1 October 1941

The colored hot trumpeter is drafted, given the job of bugler, fears for his life, but when he puts swing into it, the boys get up without trouble. Topical, with some gags that will draw laughs. This is in the better cartoon division. Good.

BOOGIE-WOOGIE MAN (1943)

Company: Walter Lantz, Universal Pictures
Type: Swing Symphony
Characters: Black spooks from Harlem

Story: The cartoon opens at night at the city limits of Goose Pimple, Nevada, a ghosttown with a population of no living people. A strong wind turns into a whirlwind and moves down the road, pausing briefly at the city limits before entering the deserted town. It swirls down the main street and stops in front of a building with a large sign: Spook of the Month Club Welcomes You to the Swing Convention. The whirlwind blows into the building and moves directly to the front of the hall, where it changes into a ghost wearing a white sheet—the president of spooks. The ghost calls the meeting to order and announces to the other white spooks present that "the proceedings will be broadcast over a ghost-to-ghost network." This brings loud applause from the other spooks. The president then announces that "there will be a pause for a word from our sponsor." Three female spooks sing a commercial for "Ring 'Em White Soup." Next the president tells them, "We are beginning to slip and the sheet and haunting business is on the skids. We are on the brink of a catastrophe. The old nightmare ain't what it used to be." The spook audience shouts, "That man is right. Tooting a horn and rattling chains is strictly from corn. Let's get on the beam." However, not all the spooks agree. An old spook, the spirit of 1849, emerges out of a jar and says, "I disagree. What was good enough for my grandson is good enough for me." The other spooks shout him down, and the president says, "We will now have a word from the spooks from Lenox Avenue [Harlem]." Three black spooks appear on the scene wearing zoot sheets, burst into song, and dance to the tune of "The Boogie-Woogie Man Will Catch You If You Don't Watch Out." They do a wild boogie-woogie dance, jumping from table to table. Soon all of the other spooks are joining in the fun, dancing and singing. Even the old spook of 1849 gets the boogie spirit and does a boogie-woogie dance with the three shapely female spooks. The place goes wild until the clock strikes 5 A.M. The fun stops suddenly and all the spooks disappear. The president transforms back to a whirlwind, leaves the building, and whirls down the road out of town as the cartoon ends.

Review: *Motion Picture Exhibitor,* 6 October 1943

A desert ghost town is the scene of a ghost convention where the delegates seek to improve the ghost business by injecting swing and jive. Representatives from Harlem show how it is done until the entire convention is one great big mass of swing. The clock strikes the hour of dawn, and the ghosts disappear. Fair.

Review: *Besa Shorts Shorts,* 18 October 1943

In swell color and swell music the latest Swing Symphony concerns itself with the fabled nursery rhyme of the same title, but in this edition it is brought up to date with jive and such.

Released along about Halloween time, it quite naturally has to do with spooks and a spook convention at which all the boogies and woogies gather. Strictly jive talk prevails among the hep cats from Harlem and elsewhere. Spook Jones and his Creepy Crooners furnish the music and it's all pretty lively.

Review: *Boxoffice,* 17 June 1950

Good. A reissue of one of the more imaginative Lantz cartoons. A desert ghost town is the setting and the antics of the various shades is always amusing. At a ghost convention in an abandoned saloon, the delegates want to improve the spirit business by entertaining people with swing and the boogie woogie delegates from Harlem give out with shin-cracking jive in their zoot sheets. Everybody joins in until the clock strikes midnight.

Review: *Motion Picture Herald,* 25 September 1943

This is ghost town in swing time, as a meeting of the respected sheeted ones develops into an argument on the need for adopting new chills. A bearded delegate holds out for the old clutching hand, scream in the dark, table turning system, but boogie woogie wins the day after some dark spirits from Harlem stage a demonstration.

Review: *Film Daily,* 6 September 1943

Boogie-Woogie gets a good going over in this Technicolor cartoon. The action revolves around a convention of ghosts that is thrown into high by the jive antics of a delegation from Harlem. The subject has been well executed. The young folk should find this a booking to their taste. (7 min)

Review: *Boxoffice,* 16 October 1943

There's a plentiful supply of jive and comedy material in this cartoon. Ghosts hold a convention in a ghost town. Some of the delegates want to hype the ghost business by entertaining all sundry with swing and jive. Boogie woogie delegates from Harlem way garbed in their "zoot sheets" give out with their own particular brand, while everybody joins in the melee and dances until the clock strikes, then all vanish.

Review: *Motion Picture Herald,* 24 June 1950

A desert ghost town is the meeting place of a ghost convention. The Boogie Woogie delegates from Harlem give out with shin-cracking jive in their zoot sheets. Others join in and dance until the clock strikes and they disappear.

Review: *Film Daily,* 25 May 1950

A deserted ghost town is the rendezvous for a spook convention whose delegates want to improve their public relations by entertaining with swing and jive. Slightly weird but humorous. Not for very young kiddies.

BROKEN TOYS (1935)

Company: Ben Sharpsteen, Walt Disney, United Artists
Type: Silly Symphony

Characters: Doll caricatures of famous movie stars including W. C. Fields, and Stephin Fetchit, Aunt Jemima

Story: The cartoon opens on a winter's day at a rubbish dump where a lad of broken toys is being dumped. A toy sailor looks around and says, "Boy what a dump to land in." A Jack-in-the-Box character springs out and says, "You'll get use to it-I did" before popping inside. A sad looking female doll says, "Oh dear everyone loved us when we were new." Jack springs out of his box again and says, "But nobody wants us now—We're through." The sailor says, "I know a place where we'd be welcome." His words are heard by other broken toys who appear from their hiding places. The Sailor continues, "Winter is coming—It's gonna snow—Fix yourself up—Let's go." A black male puppet, with a Stephin Fetchit demeanor, slides out of a junk toilet bowl by pulling on a single hair on his head. W. C. Fields says, "Yes my worthy fellows—Let's not stand and mope—Where there's life there's hope." A blond girl doll with no eyes says, "With eyes—I'd be good as new." The black man pulls the string attached to one of his shoes and says, "I just needs to fix my feet." A black "Aunt Jemima" rag doll with thick white lips turns around to show her underpants through a large hole in the back of her dress. She turns her head and rolls her eyes as she says, "And I jest needs a brand new seat." The dolls help each other repair themselves. Meanwhile Aunt Jemima sings, "We're gonna get out of this dump" and ends doing some scat singing and jazz dancing. The black man tap dances on top of a tin washing board before falling off and landing back in the toilet bowl. Later the black man shines the top of his bald head using black shoe polish. He finishes by popping the rag on his head in a rhythm beat as he says, "Won't somebody take a shine to me." W. C. Fields finishes patching the hole in Aunt Jemima's dress saying, "Well there you are my little chocolate drop." The blond doll gets new eyes in the operating room where the black man is pumping oxygen to her through a hose as she lies on the operating table. But he falls asleep before the operation is over. W. C. Fields wakes him up and the black man says, "Yeh sah" and he pumps faster than before. Later the sailor leads the repaired toys as they march through the snow to the Orphanage. Arriving there they enter through the bars of the closed gate. W. C. Fields arrives driving a sled pulled by a stuffed elephant doll with the black man riding on the back. Fields drives through the gate but the black man's head hits one of the bars on the gate and he is knocked off and lands on the ground. Fields uses the curved end of his walking stick to hook the black man's neck and pull him through the gate saying, "Come on my Ethiopian." The black man says "Yeh Sah" as the cartoon ends.

BROTHERHOOD OF MAN (1946)

Company: United Film Productions, UAW-CIO
Characters: Races of man

Story: The cartoon opens on a dream sequence of people sailing around in chairs with propellers on their backs. The narrator says, "Everybody has his own special dream of what the world's going to be like in the future. But we all know it's steadily shrinking. One of these days we're going to wake up and find that people and places we used to just read about are practically in our own backyard." Meanwhile Henry, a white man, is awakened from sleep by the barking of his dog. He gets out of bed and sees the new world right in his own yard and says, "It's happened." He gets dressed and hurries downstairs and out of the house. He slips on the ice in front of an igloo, trips on the walk, and is thrown into a Chinese gong. But he gets up with a smile on his face and starts forward with his hand outstretched. Henry's ego appears as a green character and holds him back, saying, "I don't like the looks of this." Henry says, "Why not? It's going to be wonderful." His ego says, "It'll never work! You can't get along with those people. They're too different!" Henry says, "We'll get along, we've got to. The future of civilization depends on brotherhood." Again Henry starts forward to meet the other races, but again his ego catches him and pulls him back. At the same time Chinese, Negro, Mexican, and Turk egoes pull them back, and all of the races look at each other suspiciously. The egos then jump back into their respective races and before long the races are fighting each other. The narrator says, "Wait a minute. What about this business of brotherhood?" The fighting stops as the three races hold each other by the neck. Henry says, "But we're all different." The narrator replies, "Are you? Let's take a look at the facts—right from the start. The first people on earth knew only a very small section of it." Adam and Eve appear and then change into dots that move to the edge of the world map in three separate areas of color. The narrator continues, "They lived close together and looked alike. But pretty soon they started to spread out; and as they drifted further apart, little differences began to appear. Most of the people of the world kept the same in-between color as their ancestors—and still do—but three groups on the very edges of the world population developed distinct differences in color. These exceptional groups gave rise to our ideas of three separate races of mankind." Meanwhile the three guys with hands on each other's throats relax a little as Henry says, "Well, there are other differences in people besides their skin color." The narrator says, "Yes, you find all sorts of hair, eyes, nose shapes and sizes, but you find these same differences within each group. It's only color and a few other 'frills' that distinguishes our three races—the Caucasian, the Negroid, and the Mongoloid. There is no difference in physical strength." The scene changes to a diagram of a man's head. Different types of hair pop on. Different types of eyes and nose shapes pop on. The scene changes again to a group of white people of all sizes and shapes. The white dissolves into brown, and then the brown changes to yellow. The group then changes into three color shapes out of which appear outlines of Caucasian, Negro, and Mongoloid. Meanwhile Henry and the two others with hands on each other's throats all smile and release each other. Henry's ego jumps out again, hits Henry, and then jumps back in. Henry says, "Well strength, sure, but what about . . ." The ego jumps out again and says "brains!" The Chinese and Henry look at each other. The Chinese sulks, and Henry is embarrassed. The narrator says, "There are some variations. For instance, there is a difference of about 50 cubic centimeters in the size of the brain of the average American Negro and the brain of the average Amer-

ican white—both of which are smaller than the brain of the average Eskimo. And the largest brain on record was that of a imbecile. So it isn't the size of a brain that counts—it's what it can do. And tests have shown that average men are equal. If you take their skins off, there's no way to tell them apart. The heart, liver, lungs, blood—everything's the same." Meanwhile a hat bounces each head of the three men in turn. Then the imbecile puts on the hat and runs out. The scene shows the three characters figuring and ending up with the same answers. Then their skins dissolve to skeletons, showing blood and veins. Henry says, "Everything's the same—heart, liver, lungs, blood. Blood's different." The narrator says, "Well, there are four different types of blood—A, B, AB, and O," as a chart shows blood types. The scene changes to a hospital patient lying in bed and a voice saying, "Patient in room 216 needs a transfusion right away." A person says, "I'll give it to him—I'm his brother Stanley." His brother gives the transfusion, but the patient dies. Blood type A comes down from the chart and gives the transfusion. Then the patient sits up, fully recovered. The narrator says, "Yes, but he wouldn't be if we'd been more scientific about it. Brother or no brother, what he needs is type A. And the right blood donor for him could belong to any race, since the four blood types appear in all races." Henry says, "Say, we're not really so different at all. Like you say, it's just frills. Only wait a minute, I've got a question. How come we live like this?" Various scenes show the different civilizations, different families, a shot of a man working in his garage on a car, and then Eskimos fishing. The narrator says, "It wasn't always that way. For instance, at a stage of history, when the so-called pure whites of northern Europe were little better than savages, the darker skinned mixed peoples of the Near East and Africa had flourishing cultures, and the great civilization of northern China had begun to develop. All peoples contributed to civilization, reaching high levels at different times and each learning from the experience of the others. But there were certain basic ideas that were common to all branches of the human race: belief in a supreme being, the home, and the family. How civilized a person is depends on the surroundings in which he grows up. The differences in the way people behave are not inherited from their ancestors. They come from something called cultural experience or environment." The scene shows white and yellow mothers holding their children. The babies are switched and then they animate into grown men. The narrator says, "Suppose you could somehow switch two newborn infants from entirely different backgrounds. They would not inherit their real parents' cultural experience or ideas or mechanical aptitudes. Those things you acquire." The scene shows a yellow man raised as an American white who says, "Got a match, Bud?" A white man raised as Chinese answers in fluent Chinese. The scene shows all races sitting together with Henry on the porch. Henry says, "I get it. But now that we're living so close together, we can get used to each other's ways and work together peacefully." The crowd cheers and claps and Henry walks off, leaving his green ego sitting disconsolate. His ego then jumps up and leaves. As the group shakes hands, Henry's ego arrives and tries to jump into Henry but can't. Henry says, "All we need is a little real understanding and what I said before—brotherhood."

The races all shake hands, and all of their egos fall out of the scene. The narrator says, "Right! And we have to put those ideas into practice in certain very specific ways. We have to see to it that there's equal opportunity for everyone from the very beginning an equal start in life, equal chance for health and medical care and good education, and equal chance for a job. Then we can all go forward together." The scene shows all races. Then the group shrinks to babies in cribs, then to children running, then to people in caps and gowns, then to people in working clothes as they walk together as the cartoon ends.

Review: *Film Daily,* 5 March 1947

Cartoon technique is employed in an attempt to combat race prejudice with imagination and wit. The hero, Henry, dreams that the post-war world fits into his backyard. His first thought is to be friendly, but his devilish conscience interferes and he draws back suspiciously, as do the others. It explains most differences as result of historic development and environment variations. Quite novel. (10 min)

THE BULLDOG AND THE BABY (1942)

Company: Alec Geiss, Columbia Pictures
Type: Fable
Characters: Bulldog, black maid, white baby

Story: The cartoon opens on a city street where a black maid with shapely figure and legs (her face is not shown) pushes a baby in a stroller. She stops at a department store where there is a Sale sign in the window. She tells the bulldog, the family pet, "Now Butch, stay right here and don't let nothin' happen to the baby. Whatever you does, don't take yo' eyes offa dat chile. I'll be right back." Then she walks inside the store. Butch looks after the baby and tries to amuse it when it starts to cry. He turns flips to make the baby laugh and accidently kicks the stroller. It rolls down a hill, and Butch chases it through the crowded city streets, in and out of department stores, up and down buildings under construction before finally catching it and pushing it back to the place where the maid left it. The baby is fine but tired and lies down to take a rest. The maid walks out of the store, sees Butch sleeping and says, "Butch, you lazy, good fo' nothin' hound. Goodness knows what might have happened while you wuz asleep. Sleep, sleep all de day. I've got a good mind to whip ya . . ." Butch looks at her sheepishly as the cartoon ends.

CHILDREN'S CORNER (1931)

Company: Alfred Cortot (French); produced by Leslie Wink
Type: Combined live action and animation
Characters: Young white girl, animated dolls, golliwoggs
Note: A golliwogg is a grotesque black doll created by whites. It occurred frequently in illustrations by Florence K. Upton (1922) for a children's book series that was widely distributed in Europe and the United States.

Story: The film consists of a combination of live action and animation. It centers around a young white girl playing with her dolls and stuffed animals in her large playroom. The background music is furnished by a male musician playing selections from Claude Debussy on a piano. The second part of the film, entitled "Golliwogg's Cakewalk," deals with a female golliwogg doll that comes to life and dances, to the delight of the little white girl and her other stuffed dolls, including a male golliwogg. The female golliwogg doll is played by a white actress in blackface, and the male golliwogg is an animated doll.

CLEAN PASTURES (1937)

Company: I. Freleng Vitaphone, Warner Bros.
Characters: De Boss, Gabriel (Stephen Fetchit demeanor), and characterizations of Fats Waller, Bill Robinson, Cab Calloway, The Mills Brothers, and Louis Armstrong

Story: The opening scene is in Pair-O-Dice (heaven), where the angel Gabriel is trying unsuccessfully to play a musical note on his trumpet. Next down in Harlem (hades) good times are seen: Shooting craps, drinking, and fast-stepping chorus girls dancing to the tune of "Sweet Georgia Brown." Meanwhile back in Pair-O-Dice, De Boss is worried. A headline in the business section of the daily newspaper says, "Pair-O-Dice Preferred Stock Hits a New Low as Hades Inc. Soars." This news is confirmed by the stock tickertape, so he decides to send Gabriel down to Hades to see if he can drum up a little business for Pair-O-Dice. Gabriel sets up his stand on the street and tries unsuccessfully to catch the attention of each passersby, including Bill Robinson, who does a tap dance to the music of "Swanee River," and Al Jolson singing "Sonny Boy" in blackface. Meanwhile Fats Waller and some of the other angels look down from Pair-O-Dice and see that Gabriel has failed in his missionary endeavors. They convince De Boss that he must modernize his approach by adding plenty of swing music. De Boss is persuaded and sends the Pair-O-Dice jazz band, led by Cab Calloway, down to hades. In no time the band, with Cab singing "I Got Swing for Sale" in his famous hi-dee-ho style, attracts a huge crowd that readily joins in the fun. Fats Waller sings and plays two pianos as Louis Armstrong takes a vocal chorus and plays his trumpet. Even the Mills Brothers contribute as they sing a chorus of "Dem Golden Slippers" in their unique vocal style. Soon they have led all of the inhabitants of Hades up to Pair-O-Dice, where each one receives a pair of wings. De Boss is plenty happy when he hears a knock on the gate and a voice asking to come in. De Boss opens the door and in walks the devil with a smile on his face as the cartoon ends.

Review: *Boxoffice,* 12 June 1937

A clever cartoon satire on *The Green Pastures* with all the action taking place in the Heavenly land of "Pair-O-Dice." Saint Peter, worried about the decline in population, sends Gabriel (with a Stephin Fetchit demeanor) down to earth to attract some new visitors. The lazy Gabriel fails to use salesmanship, so the congress of angels (Cab Calloway, Fats Waller, etc.) start to pep up the heavenly music to such an extent that even Satan himself decides to return and join the fun. A lively number that will fit into any program. (9 min)

Review: Stanley Crouch, review of *Animated Coon Show, Village Voice,* 16–22 December 1981

Clean Pastures is really remarkable because it shows how much more attentive to skin tone cartoonists were then on Broadway, and how Al Jolson's blackface image had become. In short, heaven—known as Pair-O-Dice—is in trouble because Harlem Negroes (all Negroes live in Harlem) are too busy singing and dancing to listen to the gospel. They will not be lured by promises of watermelon and so on. The brainstorm solution is that the angels will have to swing the colored people into Pair-O-Dice. Appropriately skin-toned caricatures of Cab Calloway, Waller, Louis Armstrong, and a blacked-up Jolson (!) are the emissaries of heavy butt-shaking. Of course, the Negroes—all anonymous Negroes are dark—go to the Pair-O-Dice in droves.

COAL BLACK AND DE SEBBEN DWARFS (1943)

Company: Robert Clampett, Warner Bros.
Type: Merrie Melodies
Characters: Mammy (voice characterization by Lillian Randolph) So White (voice characterization by Vivian Dandridge), Queenie (voice characterization by Ruby Dandridge), Prince Charmin' (voice characterization by "Zoot" Watson), Sebben Dwarfs

See fig. 44. Story: The cartoon opens with Mammy holding her little girl in her lap in front a roaring fire in the fireplace. Mammy says, "Hey, hey, oh honey chile. What story would you have Mammy tell you, honey chile?" The little girl answers, "I would like to hear the story 'bout So White and the seven dwarfs." So Mammy opens the story by describing an old queen who lived in a gorgeous castle. The queen was just as rich as she was mean. To demonstrate that she had everything, the screen shows a room in the queen's castle full of rubber tires, sugar, and coffee (items that were rationed during World War II). The queen, a fat woman, is reclining on her throne wearing a long dress and polka-dot stockings. A bottle of gin is on a table, and a picture of the royal crest—crossed razors flanked by a pair of dice—is hanging on the wall behind her. She is tossing candy, Chattanooga Chew-Chews, into her mouth. The queen rises and walks over to her magic mirror and says, "Magic mirror on the wall, bring me a present about six feet tall." In the next instant a long limousine, with shoes as tires, pulls up at the castle. Out steps Prince Charmin' wearing a zoot suit and smoking a cigarette in a long holder. He says, "That mean ole queen, she sho's frightful but her girl So White is dynamite." He smiles broadly, revealing two teeth that are a pair of dice (adding up to seven). Meanwhile the shapely So White, wearing

short shorts with a patch on her rear end, is seen bending over a tub washing clothes. She sings, "My hair's coal black but my name is So White. I washes all day and I got de blues in the night. Some folks say I is kind of dumb, but I know some day my prince will come." She hangs one of the queen's polka-dot underpants on a line full of clothes that stretches out of sight. Prince Charmin' shows up on the scene and says, "So White, you're right for I has come." As So White and the prince do a jitterbug, the queen sees them out of her window and becomes very angry. She telephones Murder Inc. and tells them to blackout So White. The gang is seen leaving their hideout in a fast-moving black car. Their slogan is, "We rubs out anything. $1.00. Midgets half-price. Japs free." The prince and So White are still dancing when the black car drives up. So White is pulled in and and driven away. The car speeds along, but suddenly slows and begins to rock and roll. When the gang lifts So White out of the car, she is all smiles and says, "Well, thanks for the buggy ride." Four smiling faces peer out of the window and say, "Anytime, So White." So White tells them, "Well, all right." The car pulls away and So White starts to walk through the dark forest. She hears a hoot and lights a match to see what's making the noise. It is one of the seven dwarfs, the smallest, wearing a soldier's uniform and carrying a rifle that is longer than he is tall. He shouts, "Who goes there, friend or foe?" She tells him that her name is So White and then asks him where the other dwarfs are. The other six dwarfs show up wearing uniforms and singing, "We're in the Army Now." So White gives them all a kiss. Meanwhile back in the castle the evil queen is making a poisoned apple. She injects the fluid that is so potent it turns the red apple green. At the army camp the soldiers are asleep in their tents when reveille sounds. So White is in the cooking tent preparing breakfast and says, "Oh the five o'clock bugle, it just blew. I's frying eggs and pork chops too. Just joined up because the guys are good lookin'." The queen, disguised as a fruit peddler, arrives on the scene riding in an apple cart. She offers So White an apple, telling her, "So White, here's an apple just for you. It's from a friend, guess who." So White accepts the apple, and asks the queen, "You mean this apple's just for me?" The queen says, "Don't stand there blabbing, Woman, just try it and see." So White swallows the apple in one big gulp and immediately falls to the ground motionless. The little dwarf comes out of his tent just in time to see what happened to So White. He calls out to the other dwarfs and they all run out of the tent, grab their guns, and drive off in a jeep. They arrive at an artillery site and load the gun, with the smallest dwarf getting into the gun barrel. They fire the gun in the direction of the queen, who is standing on a hill laughing about what she has done to So White. The shell is about to land on the queen, when it stops in midair. The end opens and the little dwarf comes out and hits the queen on the head with a club, knocking her flat on her back. When they get back to camp, they try to figure out what is wrong with So White. One says, "She's got it bad and that ain't good." Another says, "There's only one thing that will remedy this. That's Prince Charmin' and his dynamite kiss." Prince Charmin' arrives on the scene and tells the dwarfs, "I'll give her a kiss and it won't be a dud." He gives So White a kiss, but nothing happens. He kisses her again and again, but nothing happens. He kisses her so much that he turns white and ages into an old man. The dwarfs says, "That didn't work." Then the smallest dwarf smiles and gets an idea. He kisses So White, and her eyes pop open immediately. She grabs him in her arms, and Prince Charmin' asks him, "Man, what you got that makes So White think that you so hot?" The little dwarf smiles and tells him, "Well, that's a military secret." He kisses So White, and her hair sticks straight out in braids with two flags attached as the cartoon ends.

Review: *Film Daily,* 28 January 1943

Set this one down as a rather amusing satire on *Snow White and the Seven Dwarfs.* All the characters in the latter are replaced by darkies. The satire sounds a timely note by placing the seven dwarfs in the Army. Coal Black has a deuce of a time keeping out of the clutches of the Enemy Queen, a terrifying villainess. The dwarfs come to the rescue in a way that makes for numerous laughs. The cartoon was produced by Leon Schlesinger in Technicolor. (7 min)

Review: *Motion Picture Exhibitor,* 13 January 1943

A satire on *Snow White* done in blackface, set in modern swing, this is the best in a long time. It's very funny. Excellent.

Review: *Besa Shorts Shorts,* 12 January 1943

This Merrie Melodie is a jig jamboree of joyous quality. A Mammy rocking her baby to sleep tells her version of *Snow White and the Seven Dwarfs.* It is authentic . . . just as *Green Pastures* is authentic Bible stories but this Prince Charming has a Zoot suit and a flashy smile that exposes two dice set in his front teeth for added glamour. The music is delightful and, of course, Coal Black is the heroine. The dwarfs we find are in the army and there is a patriotic twist that is good for an appreciative chuckle.

Review: Stanley Crouch, review of *Animated Coon Show, Village Voice,* 16–22 December 1981

Coal Black and de Sebben Dwarfs begins with a beautifully animated scene of a black mammy rocking a baby before a fireplace. It soon turns into a spoof of Disney's *Snow White* in which the evil queen is an FBI agent (fat, black, and indignant), and Prince Charmin is a zoot-suited spook with every tooth gold except for his two front ones, which are dice. Sometimes funny but usually contrived beyond the pale of sharp humor, it succeeds more as an example of eccentricity than anything else.

Review: David Rodowick, *Cinema Texas Program Note,* 6 February 1978

It is perhaps no surprise that a nation as steeped in a tradition of racism as America should have as its first bona fide classic a paean to the Ku Klux Klan, *Birth of a Nation.* It is also perhaps appropriate that one of the most beautifully animated and manically energetic masterpieces of American commercial animation, *Coal Black and De Sebben Dwarfs,* is virtually a catalog of Negro stereotypes. Despite this fact (and maybe because of it),

Coal Black is probably the most eclectic, the most inspired and most fully realized work of the madman Bob Clampett.

Combining a ridiculously cursory retelling of the *Snow White* story (with references to the Disney version, especially in the forest scene), the forties conception of black life-style and character type, and a war time obsession with army boot camp, Clampett creates a hodge-podge of gags and images from nowhere (or at least no logical place), bombarding the viewer with more activity than is to be found in any ten other Warners cartoons. The bizarrely diverse points of reference come together in the character of the Evil Queen, a fairy tale character played by a big black mama stereotype, who is so rich she can horde wartime luxuries such as tires and sugar.

The cartoon is most brilliant (as most of Clampett's ventures) when it is thrusting out totally irrelevant, unexpected, off-the-wall objects, sequences and references: the queen biting off the telephone mouthpiece, the dice caps on the Prince's teeth, the minuet step So White and the Prince do before breaking into the jitterbug, the sudden appearance of the Murder Inc. truck (advertising that they bump off Japs for free), the sun bopping over the horizon to a jazzed-up version of "Reveille," the face made out of bacon and eggs which seems to sing along with So White as it sizzles. Most bizarre (and an indication of the degree to which Clampett had lost his mind) is the reference to *Citizen Kane* when the Prince announces that he will wake So White with his special kiss: "Rosebud." Clampett shows us an enormous close-up of the Prince's lips as he pronounces the word, mimicking a similar shot of Orson Wells pronouncing the final word of Charles Foster Kane.

Energy bursts from each of the many situations, characters, gags and visual compositions of this cartoon. It is perhaps because of this nothing barred and nothing sacred attitude that the racial stereotypes are so vicious. But what makes the cartoon most amazing is the quality of the animation, filled with depth, shadows and carefully conceived, beautifully drawn compositions. Despite its bigotry, the cartoon presents that rare combination of great talent and unbridled inspiration which elevates it to the status of masterpiece.

It is impossible to ignore the blatant racial hyperpolarization of *Coal Black and De Sebben Dwarfs,* so it's not very likely that you'll get a repeat showing on *Cartoon Carnival.* I'm sure that the wave of parental protest would make the excitement over Disney's crows look pretty dim. Perhaps some children of the sixties are too sensitized to enjoy the subject, and perhaps some children of the seventies are too jaded to find it funny, but it is still one of the great Warner's cartoons worthy of Bob Clampett's signature, as well as being a genuine cultural artifact.

NAACP Protest: *New York Age,* 8 May 1943

The withdrawal from movie screens of an animated cartoon called *Coal Black and De Sebben Dwarfs* was sought this week by the NAACP in formal protest to Warner Brothers, distributors of the picture.

The cartoon is a Merrie Melody produced by Leon Schlesinger. In it the seven dwarfs represent seven miniature

Negro soldiers who are held up for ridicule by theatre-going audiences.

Ironically, the American flag floats over the camp in which the soldiers are quartered. Every established stereotype ever concocted to depict the Negro has been used in the picture.

COLONEL HEEZA LIAR AND THE GHOST (1923)

Company: Vernon Stallings, J. R. Bray Studio, distributed by Hodkinson and Selznick Pictures
Type: Animation combined with live action
Characters: Colonel Heeza Liar, black man (live action)

Story: This time Colonel Heeza Liar, the little animated cartoon cutout, has a scrap with the artist because he doesn't want to work at night. But the artist says that he must stay, so the Colonel tries to get revenge by dumping a jar of paint on him. Then when the boys are having a lunch the Colonel jumps into the prop room and climbing into a toy balloon which he has draped with chiffon he proceeds to scare the boys. One black man becomes so frightened that he shrinks in size and turns into a pair of dice and then rolls out of sight. How he succeeds in frightening them and also passing as a policeman provides the balance of the action. There is some very clever stuff in this one, which should prove a pleasing addition to almost any program.
*(Donald Crafton, *Before Mickey,* [MIT Press, 1987]).

Review: *Moving Picture World,* 10 February 1923

To get even with the cartoonist for a fancied slight, the Colonel by means of a toy balloon and a shroud poses as a ghost, resulting in badly scaring the cartoonist and his assistant.

COW COW BOOGIE (1943)

Company: Walter Lantz, Universal Pictures
Type: Swing Symphony
Characters: Black man, cowboys

Story: The cartoon opens on a cattle ranch way out west. One of the ranch hands is sitting on the porch of the ranch house playing his guitar and singing "Home on the Range." Meanwhile inside the ranch house the foreman is trying to concentrate on balancing the books, but the music distracts him. He walks outside, draws both of his six-guns, and fires them into the air. The music stops abruptly as the foreman says, "You boys spend more time at home than you do on the range. Just look at them cattle." All of the cows are playing various games, including gin rummy. The foreman continues, "You've got to stop singing that song. It's slowing down the industry." The foreman paces back and forth trying to decide what to do. He decides that they need a livelier song to sing, and just then he hears the sound of singing off in the distance. Meanwhile a black boy, who has a Stephin Fetchit demeanor, is riding his donkey while singing "Cow Cow Boogie." The donkey's legs are so short that the boy can walk on

the ground even though he is sitting on the donkey's back. The donkey stops to chew on some grass, but the black man keeps on singing and walking in a sitting position until his donkey catches up to him. Meanwhile the foreman grabs his rope, makes a loop, lassoes the black boy, and then yanks him so hard that he is pulled out of his clothes. Wearing only his underwear, the frightened black boy says, "Let me go! What y'all want with me?" The foreman tells him, "Pardner, all I want to hear is some of the boogie-woogie stuff." The black boy says, "Well, all right." He walks to a piano and begins to play "Cow Cow Boogie." After a few bars of the tune the piano starts to shake back and forth. Then the lid opens and several farm animals and a cowboy run out. The black boy plays so fast that the keys fly off the piano. He opens his mouth in a wide grin that shows teeth shaped like piano keys keeping up the hot beat. The music has the desired effect on the cowboys. They all run out of the bunkhouse, jump on their horses, and ride out on the range and round up the cattle. In no time they are herding the cattle up a ramp and loading them into cattlecars. All the while the black boy, sitting on top of the caboose, is still singing "Cow Cow Boogie." The name of the train is The Super Beef. As it pulls away, a group of smiling cows are seen in the caboose and the cartoon ends.

Review: *Motion Picture Exhibitor,* 24 February 1943

Lantz Swing Symphony. When the boys on the "Lazy S" refuse to do anything but sing, the foreman hires a colored boy to play the piano, the cows respond, and everything is right in the groove. Good.

Review: *Besa Shorts Shorts,* 16 February 1943

The ranch foreman is sick and tired of his cowhands just a settin' and singin' "Home On the Range" and a pickin' them gittars. He can't do nothing with 'em, so he aims to go look about for a new lament. Long about this time over the horizon comes a swing jig ridin' a burro and singing "Cow Cow Boogie." That does it the foreman gets the nig to teach the tune to the ornery cowhands who take on as lively as iffen an 'lectric prod had been given to 'em. Even the cattle go to carryn' on and a good time is had out where the west begins. It's a swell little cartoon and you can sell it to your swing fans. If you don't believe it contact your local music and record stores and hear them tell you that "Cow Cow Boogie" is the top tune of the day.

Review: *Boxoffice,* 5 November 1949

A plenty of melody and jive in this new release. The well known song "Cow Cow Boogie" is effectively used in boogie rhythm to get the cowboys and cattle of the Lazy "S" Ranch working.

Review: *Motion Picture Herald,* 20 February 1943

The farmer is having a hard time keeping the cows moving until a gay little colored boy rides by on a donkey singing "Cow-Cow Boogie." The rhythm is catching and the cows fall into line to be loaded up for "beef for the boys." (8 min)

Review: *Boxoffice,* **20 February 1943**

Plenty of music in the groove and good comedy situations in this cartoon. Cowhands and cows on the "Lazy S" ranch won't work, so the foreman gets the idea when a colored boy comes along singing "Cow Cow Boogie." The boy is assigned to playing boogie woogie on the piano. Everyone, including the bovine denizens, responds nobly to the stimulus of the jazz and everybody is happy.

Review: *Film Daily,* **7 December 1949**

A singer warbling "Cow Cow Boogie" has so much effect on the cows and cow-hands on the Lazy S ranch that the foreman hires him to continue his music making. Output more than doubles, and the ensuing action is quite funny. Pleasant cartoon.

Review: *Motion Picture Herald,* **14 January 1949**

The foreman of the "Lazy S" is having trouble getting his cowhands to work. Finally a colored boy comes along on a donkey singing "Cow Cow Boogie." The rhythm is just what the boys needed to pep them up, and the cows also respond to the pep music.

CROP CHASERS (1939)

Company: Ub Iwerks, Columbia Pictures
Type: Scrappy Color Rhapsody
Characters: Black crows, farmer, scarecrow

Review: *Motion Picture Exhibitor,* **18 October 1939**

One of the better Scrappy entries, *Crop Chasers,* starts off slowly and picks up speed and laughs as it goes along. It pleased a fairly large audience. Black crows raid a farmer's land until said farmer is forced to employ a couple of scarecrows, who are the acme of inefficiency. However the scarecrows come to the rescue of a baby crow, which almost drowns in a well. The black raiders make amends to the farmer and the farmer sets his scarecrows up in regal state. Good.

Review: *Boxoffice,* **21 June 1952**

When crows bedevil a farmer's crop, he hires a couple of animated scarecrows whose lives are made miserable by the birds as they continue to devastate the fields. Finally, a baby crow is rescued from a well by the scarecrows and its parents and friends in appreciation return every vegetable they have stolen. Well drawn and ingenious.

DAFFYDILLY DADDY (1945)

Company: Seymour Kneitel, Famous Studios, Paramount
            Pictures (film), U.M. & M. TV Corp. (television)
Characters: Little Lulu, Daddy, her dog

Story: The cartoon opens in Lulu's house where Lulu and her pet dog try to reel in a stuffed swordfish mounted on the wall. Her daddy rushes past her into another room and changes into a surgeon's uniform. As he walks past Lulu he says, "Lulu, pre-

pare for an emergency." Lulu drops the fishing line and follows her daddy into a room where he performs a successful operation. He removes a dead leaf from his prize flower. As her daddy is admiring his work, Lulu says, "It's getting late." Daddy says, "We have to be at the flower show in fifteen minutes, and I haven't shaved yet." He instructs Lulu to deliver his flower to the show, and he will meet her there later after he has dressed. Lulu and her dog are delivering the flower then it gets kidnapped by a mean bulldog that is guarding a private estate. Lulu tries various ways to get the flower back but is unsuccessful until she conceives another plan. Meanwhile the bulldog encases the flower in a brick enclosure and sits on top of it. He hears a voice say, "I'm powerful pleased to meet you, Mr. Watchdog." He turns to see Lulu in blackface and dressed in the costume of a stereotypical black maid. She wears a bandanna on her head and has thick red lips. Concealed under her wide and long dress is her pet dog. She arrives on the scene carrying a tray piled high with bones, which she sets on the ground. The bulldog jumps off of the brick enclosure and grabs the bones in his mouth. Lulu stands over the brick enclosure and says, "I'll bet dese here bones done chased dem strangers clean outah here. And when y'all slapped dat mutt, he done really jumped outta his skin." Meanwhile Lulu's dog removes bricks from around the flower before sticking his head out from under Lulu's dress and punching the bulldog in the face. The bulldog falls to the ground but gets up and charges Lulu. Lulu and pet manage to escape and arrive at the show floor a few minutes before her father. Before the judging begins, Lulu tries to shoot a hummingbird flying around the flower with her slingshot. She misses and hits the flower, which falls to the ground. The dog tries to bite the bird but bites the flower and destroys it. Lulu quickly finds a substitute flower, paints it the color of the original, and then picks up the blossoms of the original flower and hides them in a barrel of "Vitagrowth Plant Food." Daddy arrives on the scene and quickly discovers that the flower is a fake. He is heartbroken and cries as he rests his head on the lid of the barrel of Vitagrowth. Suddenly the top of the barrel lifts up to reveal a gigantic, rejuvenated version of Daddy's flower. Daddy is happy and is about to be awarded first prize when Lulu mistakenly destroys the giant flower with her slingshot as the cartoon ends.

DATE WITH DUKE (1947)

Company: George Pal, Paramount Pictures
Type: Puppetoons
Characters: Duke Ellington (as himself), perfume puppets

See fig. 45. Story: The cartoon opens with Duke Ellington playing a tune on the piano. Standing on a table across the room are four bottles of perfume. The cap comes off one of the bottles and the head of a perfume man pops out of the top. He looks around and says, "Oh, hey." He calls to his friends, and their heads pop out of their bottles. They ask him, "What's the matter?" He tells them, "Look, it's Duke. It's Duke Ellington." The others say, "Oh no!" The first perfume man says, "What heavenly music! If he would only conduct us," and the others say,

"Yes!" They persuade the first bottle to ask Duke. He says, "Oh Mr. Ellington, I thought, that is we thought, that if you wouldn't think that we are too presumptuous in asking, if you would conduct us in the 'Perfume Suite'?" The Duke answers, "Well, why not. Are you ready?" The perfume men answer, "Yes, any time." And the Duke replies, "Now." The perfume men pull out their horns and accompany Duke on the piano while he plays his composition. At the conclusion of the song one of the perfume men jumps out of his bottle and tells the others, "Well, I don't like it." Another perfume man says, "Be quiet! That's Duke Ellington," as Ellington looks over at them. The angry perfume man continues, "Ellington, Wellington, so what! I don't like music. I can't stand singing and I hate dancing." Ellington smiles and tells him, "Well, that's too bad. Here's a little tune that's just made for dancin'." He begins to play a jazz tune. The perfume man tells him, "You can tickle those ivories to death and wear your fingers to the bone, and I still wouldn't dance. No sir!" Duke continues to play and the perfume man's ears start to wiggle with the music. Then his toes begin to tap in time with the rhythm and soon he is dancing. He dances his way across the floor to the top of Duke's piano where he dances a few moments before he loses his balance and falls onto the keyboard. Duke picks him up and carries him back to the others and stuffs him back into his perfume bottle. Duke then walks back to his piano and resumes playing as the cartoon ends.

Review: *Exhibitor Servisection,* 12 November 1947

This features Duke Ellington on the piano and his band in the background to the accompaniment of a group of puppets cavorting in the foreground. Ellington and band play his famous "Perfume Suite." A rippling piano solo wraps up matters in a mirthful style. Excellent.

DIED IN THE WOOL (1927)

Company: Paul Terry; released by Pathe Film Exchange
Type: Aesop's Fable
Characters: Milton Mouse, black sheep

Review: *Moving Picture World,* 18 June 1927

Milton Mouse is a shepherd in this Aesop's Fable cartoon and he kicks a troublesome black sheep out of the fold. The cat conspires with a wolf and a camping mouse with the result that the flock is led into the wolf's corral, but the Black Sheep frees them and saves Milt. Up to the standard of the usual Paul Terry cartoons. (one reel)

Review: *Motion Picture News,* 17 June 1927

Paul Terry uncovers a new method of sheep-rustling in the current issue of Aesop's Fables which consists of diverting the attention of the guardian by soft music and spritely nymph-like dancing of a woodland elf, or perhaps it was a mouse made-up for the role. The plot succeeded, but the black-sheep proved he was "white" by effecting the rescue of the lambs and ewes, and peace once more reigned in the valley.

DINAH (1933)

Company: Dave Fleischer, Max Fleischer; distributed by Paramount Pictures
Type: Screen Song, live action and animation
Characters: Mills Brothers as themselves

Story: There is no plot to this cartoon. It opens with the famous Mills Brothers quartet being introduced by a sign that reads, "Presenting Radio's Greatest Sensation: The Mills Bros." Another on-screen note reads, "The music throughout this cartoon is furnished by the Mills Brothers quartet. They employ no musical instruments of any kind—except the guitar. There is no tuba, no trumpet, and no saxophone." The quartet sings a scat song as the cartoon shows a large steamship being loaded at the dock. The crew is keeping time with the music. The Mills Brothers appear on the screen again and invite the audience to sing "Dinah" along with them and to keep time with the bouncing ball and words as they roll from the top to the bottom of the screen. The cartoon sequence picks up again with the ship being tossed about on a stormy ocean. A bolt of lightning breaks off the ship's mast as the scene switches back to live action with the Mills Brothers finishing their song as the cartoon ends.

Review: *Film Daily,* 24 March 1933

In this Fleischer bouncing ball singing cartoon the Mills Brothers of radio serve very nicely as the headline attraction. Their appearances are interpolated among sequences of cartoon work, with the "Dinah" song as the musical background, and a nautical touch for the action. Makes a satisfying short of its kind.

Review: *Variety,* 5 March 1933

Semi-cartoon of 'A' novelty value has something for the box office through use of the Four Mills Bros. on the musical-singing end.

Mills quartet, using only a guitar, provide the instrumental accompaniment, and as the bouncing ball hops over the lyrics of "Dinah" they add their voices with effective results. Cartoon matter deals with a ship which loads up and gets under way, short cutting from the Mills boys to ship and storm and finish.

As the Mills are ahead of the camera, the lyrics of "Dinah" come up at their feet. In closeups the lyrics come close to their chins.

Well made short.

DINKY FINDS A HOME (1946)

Company: Eddie Donnelly, Paul Terry; released by Twentieth-Century-Fox
Type: Terrytoons
Characters: Dinky the black duckling, chicken family

Story: The cartoon opens as Dinky tries to join a group of ducks swimming in a pond but is rejected. When a hunter arrives on the scene and starts shooting, all of the other ducks fly away.

Dinky tries to escape by swimming out of danger as bullets fly all around him. Dinky gets out of the pond and hides near a chicken coop. Inside the mother hen is laying eggs, and outside Dinky is confronted by the rooster, which gives Dinky a hard kick that sends him flying before he crashes into the trunk of a tree, causing a beehive to fall down near Dinky. The angry bees chase Dinky away, and he crashes into the rooster as he is carrying boxes of eggs. The broken eggs fall on the rooster, covering him with egg yoke. Dinky brings the rooster a bucket of water to wash his face. But instead of thanking Dinky, the rooster spits water into his face. Still trying to please, Dinky takes a can of polish and shines the rooster's feet with a rag. Still the rooster is not pleased, and he chases Dinky away. Dejected Dinky walks to the edge of a river where he sits down and cries. Meanwhile mother hen takes her chicks out for a stroll and is caught in a storm. The wind blows and rain falls and lightning fills the sky. The hen tries to protect her chicks, but one is blown away from her and into the river, where he hangs onto a floating piece of wood. The hen is frantic, but the rooster is unable to save the baby chick. Dinky hears the mother's cry for help and dashes to the river where he dives in and manages to save the chick before it is carried over a waterfall. The chicken family is happy that the chick has been saved, but Dinky walks away with his head down, still feeling rejected. Seeing this, the rooster picks up Dinky in his arms and the grateful family gathers around him as the cartoon ends.

Review: *Boxoffice,* 20 July 1946

Little black duckling in a new version of his adventures with Rufus Rooster, the barnyard boss. There are plenty of laughs, and some sad moments, too, in duckling's search for a home. Separated from his family, duckling tries to find it with the chickens but is kicked out by the rooster. After adventures involving the heroic rescue of a baby chick, he is finally accepted by the barnyard family.

DINKY IN SINK OR SWIM (1952)

Company: Connie Rasinski, Paul Terry, Twentieth
            Century-Fox Pictures
Type: Terrytoons
Character: Dinky Duck

Review: *Exhibitor Servisection,* 10 September 1952

Dinky, the little black duck, can't swim, and the other little ducks make fun of him. He goes to Professor Owl who gives him a "sky hook" which helps him stay afloat, but Dinky is pursued by a huge alligator, and, swimming in desperation, he learns that he did not need the "sky hook." Good.

Review: *Boxoffice,* 13 December 1952

Dinky, the over grown duckling who is afraid of water, is the star of this laugh-provoking cartoon in Technicolor. While the other ducklings quickly take to the water, Dinky cringes on the shore. When he visits old Dr. Owl for advice, Dinky is told to

take a sky-hook (actually a crooked stick) and hang on to it while he floats. Then he does swim without realizing that the stick was a trick to give him confidence.

DISILLUSIONED BLUEBIRD (1944)

Company: Howard Swift, Columbia Pictures
Type: Color Rhapsody
Characters: Calypso Joe (as himself), bluebird, Sir Lancelot
            (as himself)

Review: *Film Daily,* 23 July 1944

Outstanding for its color and the Calypso music sung by the familiar voice of Sir Lancelot this one starts with a tough looking bluebird getting caught in an air raid. He hitches a ride on a cannon shell and lands on some distant isle where Calypso Joe, with choral support, gets off a set of verses to dissuade the bird from being disillusioned with the modern world. (7 min)

Review: *Motion Picture Herald,* 4 September 1954

Suffering from depression because of strife in the world, the bluebird is deeply despondent when this cartoon opens. But Calypso Joe and his friends, in little verse and song, point out to him that there are many things to be thankful for and the bluebird is full of life again at the fade out.

Review: *Boxoffice,* 8 July 1944

For those who enjoy the off-beat charm of calypso ballad singers, this reel should be a natural. The little bluebird gets caught in an air raid somewhere in Europe and winds up on a peaceful island in the Indies. His cynicism is dissolved by the calypsos and their clever lyrics, plus a vampy little charmer. A neat reel, done very well, with music as the highlight.

Review: *Motion Picture Herald,* 8 July 1944

Just what has disillusioned the bird is not quite clear. It may be that he put his faith in blockbusters and found himself rudely awakened in South America. Or it could even be that the Latin neighbors were more completion than he had bargained for. There's a crow singing to guitar accompaniment and an exotic character with the explosive singing style of Carmen Miranda. (7 min)

Review: *Motion Picture Exhibitor,* 25 June 1944

Caught in an air raid, the bluebird rides on a blockbuster shell, and lands somewhere in Latin America where he meets some singing natives, a guitar strumming crow, and a Carmen Miranda type of bird. Bad.

Review: *Besa Shorts Shorts,* 26 June 1944

A Color Rhapsody which presents a little bluebird who should be out caroling the world with songs of happiness, but who is forced to spend his time dodging shots and shells from all over the world. He finally lands in a South American Country where the black crows sing tuneful songs and chide him for having worries. Moreover, they introduce him to a little cup-cake and the bluebird decides that he really shouldn't be a sad bird anyhow.

DONALD'S LUCKY DAY (1938)

Company: Jack King, Walt Disney, RKO Radio Pictures
Characters: Donald Duck, black cat

Review: *Motion Picture Herald,* 11 October 1938

The fowl is a messenger boy this time, commissioned to deliver an infernal machine on Friday the 13th. His errand is stymied by a playful but very black cat which is unintentionally but most amusingly instrumental in preventing Donald's death by dynamite. Donald is less quarrelsome and a deal more understandable than commonly. It's one of his best appearances. (8 min)

THE EARLY BIRD AND THE WORM (1936)

Company: Rudolph Ising, M-G-M
Type: Happy Harmonies
Characters: Sonny worm, mother worm, the bird, two black
            crows

Story: The cartoon opens as a bluebird springs out of its nest high in a tree and flies off to look for a morning meal. A background choral group sings, "It's the early bird that gets the worm when it comes out to play, when it comes out to play." The bird lands behind the trunk of a tree where the worm family lives. The bird listens as the door of the house opens and Sonny worm walks out followed by his mother. Sonny wears a cap and carries his flute with him. The mother worm says, "Now run along and play, Sonny. And Sonny, be careful of the early bird. Be sure now. Now run along." Sonny smiles and says, "I'll be careful," as he skips away playing a tune on his flute. The bird follows him for a while before Sonny turns around and sees him. The bird chases Sonny, but he manages to escape by diving into a hole in the ground. While the bird looks into the hole, Sonny smiles and escapes through another hole. Sonny walks along but stops when he hears voices that come from two lazy black crows. A tall crow wearing a farmer's hat is lying on a hammock, and a short crow is lying on a bed of straw on the ground. Their voices are similar to those of Amos and Andy of the old *Amos 'n' Andy* radio program. The tall crow says, "Oh boy, I'm so hungry." The other crow says, "Well, just remember. The early bird catches the worm." The tall crow says, "The early bird catches what worm?" The short crow replies, "Any worm." Then the tall crow says, "Well, what of it? What about it?" The short crow says, "He catches it. That's all." And the tall crow says, "Well, let him have it. Who wants the worm anyhow?" The short crow says, "Well boy, I sure wouldn't mind having one, no sir."

After hearing the crow's conversation, Sonny slowly backs away but walks into the bird that is still looking for him in the hole. The chase is on again, and the worm and the bird run past the crows, who jump up and join the chase. Soon all of

them are chasing each other, running in circles around the trunk of a tree. The bird chases Sonny out of the circle, leaving the two crows running around the tree still believing that they are chasing the worm. The bird and the worm run past a rattlesnake (the snake has a baby rattle tied to the end of its tail). The snakes joins the chase and succeeds in casting a spell on the bird, which stops and stands in a trance. Sonny is about to escape but decides to rescue the bird by hypnotizing the snake with a tune that he plays on his flute. The music puts the snake in a trance as it stands on its tail, swaying back and forth and allowing the bird to escape. But when Sonny stops playing the music, the snake casts a spell on the worm. Now the bird decides to come to the worm's rescue. The snake coils itself to strike the bird, but only manages to tie itself up in a tight knot. The bird and the worm smile at each other and shake hands. They are now friends. As they walk away, they pass the two exhausted crows that are still chasing themselves in circles around the tree. The crows collapse in each other's arms. The tall crow says, "Who, who wants a worm anyhow," as the cartoon ends.

Review: *Film Daily,* 10 March 1936

Working out literally the adage that "the early bird catches the worm," the animators concoct a fairly amusing episode of a chase between a worm that walks on two legs and a bird that does more walking than flying. The bird, an extremely ethical bird, gives up the pursuit and shakes hands with "his breakfast" when the worm saves him from being devoured by a rattlesnake. Even a couple of lazy birds, with voices suspiciously like those of "Amos 'n' Andy," make an appearance. (9 min)

Review: *Motion Picture World,* 25 April 1936

An early bird and an earlier worm pursued by a serpent and two black crows that talk like Moran and Mack start out as enemies and wind up as friends in this brilliantly colored Harman-Ising fantasy. Music and dialog are used interchangeably to conduct the narrative. The two black crows afford the funniest element. The subject is about par for the series.

Review: *Boxoffice,* 16 May 1936

In plotting the course of their crackerjack cartoon subject, the Harmon-Ising combination have shown sparkling originality, deft humor and full control of the color brushes. The final result is a merry and excellent one. In less than a minute the early bird gleefully sets out to get the worm he discovers the task beyond his expectations, as does a rattlesnake and a pair of Amos 'n' Andy-ed crows. Suddenly the snake turns his attention to the bird and just when things look dark the worm plays a tune on his flute to save the day. Later the bird saves the worm from the hypnotic ministrations of the snake thus upsetting the age-old and popular adage, for a clever and funny a bit of draftsmanship as the animators have yet turned out. In other words, very Grade A.

THE EARLY WORM GETS THE BIRD (1940)

Company: Tex Avery, Warner Bros.
Type: Merrie Melodies
Characters: Blackbird family, Mammy and three baby birds, fox, worm

Story: The opening scene shows a blackbird family living in a small birdhouse at the top of a tall tree in the forest as "Swanee River" plays in the background. Inside three baby blackbirds are saying their prayers as they prepare to go to bed. Mammy says, "Good night, chillun," and leaves the room. One of the little birds decides he is not sleepy and pulls out a book entitled *The Early Bird Gets the Worm*. He wakes up one of his brothers and tells him that the early bird gets the worm. But his sleepy brother replies, "Who cares about dat?" Meanwhile Mammy decides to check the little ones before she turns in. When she opens the door, she sees the book and tells the little bird, "You all had better hand over that book. I declare, you is too young to be reading a book." She takes the book from the little bird and tosses it out the window. She adds, "And besides, if you try to catch the worm, the fox will catch you." They ask their mammy what a fox is. She tells them that the fox stands tall and has big round green eyes, a long pointed nose, and long sharp teeth that he uses to eat little birds just like them. She tells them to get to sleep and leaves the room. As soon as she leaves, the little bird tells his brothers that he is going to set the alarm clock so that he can get up early and look for the worm. The clock rings at 5 A.M. and the little bird gets out of bed, puts on his cap, and sneaks out the house backward, falling off the porch to the ground in the process. With his nose to the ground, he sets off to look for the worm. Meanwhile the little black worm is seen coming out of his hole in the ground and seeing the book that Mammy threw away. The worm decides to go off to find the early bird. With their noses to the ground, they bump into each other, look up, and are so surprised that they both run off and hide. Gaining courage, the bird comes out and finds the worm, who runs into his hole. While the little bird is looking into this hole, the worm comes out of another hole. Soon they square off to fight, but the chase is on again. The little bird is outwitted at each turn by the worm. At one point the worms hides in a flower blossom. When the bird reaches in after it, the worm makes so much noise that the bird runs away, but realizes he has been tricked. The next time he thinks the worm is in another flower so he climbs in after it. To his surprise the flower blossom is occupied by an angry bee that tosses him out. Meanwhile the worm is taunting the bird and the chase begins again. The fox has seen them and joins the chase. The little bird looks back, sees the fox, and asks him, "You all trying to catch him too? The fox replies in the affirmative. When they stop to rest, the bird tells the fox, "He sure is a tricky cuss, ain't he? But we'll git him, won't we?" The fox replies, "We will get him." The little bird says, "But there's one thing us early birds better watch out for around here—the fox." The fox says, "The Fox?" And the bird says, "My mammy done told me that he eats little birds. My mammy done told me that he is soooo tall with green eyes, just like you all." The little bird begins to look worried as he continues, "And a pointed nose just like yours." The bird looks in the fox's mouth and says, "And has long, sharp teeth, just like yours." The bird now realizes the danger and backs slowly away from the fox before starting to run. But the fox is too fast for him and catches the bird. A nearby worm sees the fox capture the bird and decides to help him escape. The worm taunts a bee that is buzzing around a flower blossom. The angry bee flies after the worm, who runs in the direction of the fox. He is preparing to make a sandwich as he slides the bird between two slices of bread. He is about to squeeze some ketchup on his sandwich when the worm, followed by the bee, arrives on the scene. The worm crawls onto the fox's back and then pulls up the fox's tail, offering the bee an excellent target. The bee takes aim and flies at the worm, who dodges the bee allowing it to sting the fox. The fox drops the sandwich and leaps into the air. When he hits the ground, the bottle of ketchup falls on his head and breaks, spilling red sauce all over his face. The fox wipes his face and then seeing the red stain on his hands cries out, "I've been stabbed." Then he runs off in search of a doctor. Meanwhile the little bird runs back home and climbs into his bed and under the covers just before the alarm clock rings. Mammy walks in the bedroom and asks her little babies, "Did you all sleep good?" Two of the baby birds answer, "Yes, Mammy." With sleepy eyes, the late little bird says, "Yes, Mammy." Mammy then says, "What do you all want for breakfast?" Two of the birds ask for worms and the other sleepy bird says, "I don't wants no worms fo' breakfast." Then the worm pops up from under the blankets and smiles and says, "Neither does I, Mammy," as the cartoon ends.

Review: *Motion Picture Herald,* 10 October 1943

A sidelight on the old adage, this Leon Schlesinger cartoon suggests that a bird can't be too careful. It reinforces, too, the primary lesson that Mama knows best. For the young one, "Butchie," was warned of the early rising habits of foxes and their interest in birds for breakfast. But he started out boldly and had to rely on his arch-enemy for protection. (7 min)

Review: *Motion Picture Herald,* 22 November 1952

A Mama Bird reads to her children the story of the early bird who got the worm. In the morning, one of the little fellows tries to do just that, but the worm is too smart for him. However, the bird then tangles with a fox who almost succeeds in eating him, but the worm saves his life. (7 min)

Review: *Motion Picture Exhibitor,* 24 January 1940

The little bird doesn't believe the story, wants to find out for himself, is caught by the bad fox, and then saved by the little worm, all of which is familiar, but made in the better Schlesinger vein. Good.

Review: *Besa Shorts Shorts,* 11 October 1943

A Blue Ribbon Merrie Melodie in reissue, which tells the story of a Mama Black Bird and her offsprings three. She tucks them in bed, warms them against the Fox, thinks they will behave, but she reckons not with the inquisitive one who has been reading the worm and early rising theory, where birds are concerned. He sneaks out of bed and he's off to see the worm. He does. He also sees the Fox, about which his mama done told him. After much scampering around he is all too happy to scamper back to his downy bed before his mother even misses him.

EATS ARE WEST (1925)

Company: Pat Sullivan, E. W. Hammond; distributed by Educational Film Exchange, Pathe Film Exchange
Characters: Felix the Cat, black mammy, Indians, cowboys

Story: The cartoon opens as a hungry Felix paces back and forth, wondering how to get something to eat. He sights a store with a sign that reads Tea Room. It is in the shape of a teakettle and hangs over the front door. He walks to the store but finds that his pockets are empty of money. He shakes his head and taps his foot in disgust as he wonders what to do next, symbolized by a large question mark that appears over his head. He reaches up and grabs the question mark and uses it to pull down the spout of the teapot, allowing tea to flow into his mouth. He is drinking tea when suddenly a teacup flies through the door and knocks him down. Felix looks inside the teahouse to find out who threw the cup at him, but he is hit by several other objects that knock him through the air. He lands on the ground outside the city and is still hungry. Nearby a man pastes a large billboard sign on a fence. The sign reads, "Try Mammy's Flapjack Flour." It includes the figure of a black mammy holding a stack of pancakes. She has thick white lips and wears a bandanna on her head. As the man walks away, Felix arrives on the scene. He runs to the sign and grabs the pancakes out of Mammy's hand and walks away smiling. But this makes Mammy angry, and she jumps off the sign and chases after Felix. In his haste to get away Felix drops the pancakes. Next he cleverly makes a pushcart using Mammy's pancakes as wheels and exclamation points as the frame. Felix jumps on the cart and rides off just before Mammy arrives on the scene. But he looks back to laugh at Mammy and crashes through a wooden fence. His cart falls apart as Mammy keeps coming. Again using his head, he uses exclamation points that appear over his head to make a propeller. He attaches it to a wooden fence plank to make a flying wing, which he boards and flies away. Smiling, he looks down at Mammy and thumbs his nose at her. This angers Mammy, and she looks up and shakes her fist at him. Next Felix puffs smoke from his pipe and maneuvers his plane to write a derogatory smoke message in the air, which angers Mammy even more. Felix flies west, as hungry as ever. He

looks down and sees a pony express rider carrying a sackful of sausages on his back as he rides his pony at top speed. Felix uses his umbrella to parachute down from his plane, landing in the sack on the man's back. Felix eats sausage after sausage before the rider finally arrives at a cowboy's house, where he jumps off his horse. Inside the hungry cowboys have been waiting for their meal to arrive. The rider drops the sack at the cowboys' feet, but they are shocked when Felix, his stomach full of sausages, climbs out. The cowboys are so angry that they pull their guns and shoot at Felix. After much commotion they finally chase him out of the house. Felix runs into the desert where he fashions a horse out of a rope. He jumps on the horse and rides it until it collapses and disappears. Meanwhile at an Indian village the cook holds up a pot of soup for the chief to smell. The chief is standing next to a teepee which, curiously, has a swastika on it. The chief frowns and knocks the pot out of the cook's hand and tells him, "Heap tired of soup. Chief want *meat*!" The cook bows to the chief and runs off carrying his bow and arrow to do his bidding. The cook is looking for fresh game when he sights Felix and shoots arrows at him. The cat dodges the arrows, but is soon surrounded by the chief and his angry Indian braves. Many arrows narrowly miss Felix before one gets caught in his tail. The arrow carries Felix through the air all the way back to the city where he lands at the feet of a wooden Indian standing by a cigar store. Felix pulls his two six-shooters and fires, making many bullet holes in the wooden statue. He finishes just as a policeman arrives on the scene and chases him away as the cartoon ends.

ESCAPADES OF ESTELLE (1916)

Company: Henry Palmer, Mutual Pictures; distributed by Gaumont American Film Co.
Type: Komic Kartoon
Character: Estelle

Story: The cartoon opens with a close-up of Estelle, a nicely dressed, heavyset black woman with thick white lips who wears a hat and carries an umbrella. She smiles, grins, rolls her eyes left and right, and says, "Ah hope yo don't draw no color line cause I's jes doin' black and white." Estelle walks down a city street and passes a department store where the latest fashions are displayed in a large window. One full-length dress with a striped pattern catches Estelle's eye and she says, "Dem bro'd stripes sho' make mah mouf water." She continues walking down the street, saying to herself, "Jes 'bout time dat rabbit's foot wo doin' sumfin' fo' dis Estelle." As she turns a corner, she looks up and sees a striped cloth 'awning on a window on the second story of a building. She stops and says, "Dem wide stripes am got me hypnotised. Fo' da lub of heben—dis am a spell of probedence. Here is where I reckkonoiter." She looks around to see if she is being watched, drops her umbrella, and says "Ah sees yeh, honey." She starts to climb a large pole in order to get to the striped cloth, but slips and falls to the ground. Trying again, she climbs nearly to the top before the pole wobbles from side to side and she falls off. Estelle says, "Don't weaken, Estelle. Don't weaken." On her third attempt she gets to the top where she reaches and removes the striped cloth from the window awning. Sliding back down to the street, she picks up her umbrella and walks away carrying the cloth. She is chased by two policemen but manages to escape by grabbing a ride on the electric trolly. In the next scene a policeman is leaning on a light pole with a horse standing nearby. Cries of "Police, Police" are heard. He looks down the street and says, "Holy sufferin' catfish. Call an ambulance. I'm passin' away." He and the horse faint and fall to the ground. Then Estelle walks into view with a broad grin on her face, holding her umbrella over her head and proudly wearing a new striped dress made from the stolen awning cloth as the cartoon ends.

EVERYBODY SING (1937)

Company: Walter Lantz, Universal Pictures
Characters: Oswald Rabbit, two black crows

Review: *Film Daily,* 2 January 1937

Oswald is in charge of the swing band at the summer hotel in Birdville. All the birds helped out in the song fest, till a bunch of black crows horned in and did the bandit act. They chased all the guests away, and took possession of the hotel. Oswald discovers a scarecrow in a field, and getting inside, comes back and cleans out the bandit crows. Then he gets the birds to assemble again and resume their swing show. (7 min)

Review: *Boxoffice,* 6 March 1937

A cleverly devised cartoon parody on the current craze for the community sing with the voices of the beasts, birds and bees sounding suspiciously similar to the groups of humans who enjoy joining their neighbors in song. In timely fashion, a Birdville swing band is also injected to give the short a touch of syncopation. Oswald, the comic rabbit, has an orchestra composed of robins, sparrows, and a gay chick-a-dee who play for the amusement of the animal guests. A couple of black crows break up the festivities temporarily until the rabbit finds a scarecrow who frightens the intruders. A gaily amusing cartoon.

Review: *Motion Picture World,* 30 January 1937

Under the musical ministrations of Maestro Oswald, everything is peace and song in the tuneful town of Birdville. But soon come sour notes and discord with a visitation by three terrible black crows. Oswald, though, is one smart rabbit and in a smash windup he gives the villains their due. Decidedly amusing, smartly concocted and rapidly paced, the whole tale is well worth a showing. (7 min)

Review: *National Exhibitor,* 5 February 1937

Oswald conducts a band in his Birdville nightclub till the three crows come along, terrorize the neighborhood. Oswald dresses as a scarecrow and scares them away. Good.

FAGIN'S FRESHMAN (1939)

Company: Ben Hardaway, Cal Dalton, Warner Bros.
Type: Merrie Melodies
Characters: Blackie the cat, his mother, other kittens

Story: The cartoon opens as Mother Cat is playing a piano and leading her kittens in a song. Blackie, her only black kitten, thinks that music is sissy stuff and prefers to listen to crime programs on the radio. He turns on the radio, and the sounds of sirens and gunshots disturb the music. His mother grabs him by the ear and says, "Enough of that, young man. You can march straight up to bed without your supper. I don't know whatever is to become of you. All you can think of is guns and shooting." Upstairs, she slaps him on his behind and pushes him into his room saying, "Now you get to bed and stay there until you can behave yourself." Blackie sits on the side of his bed and says, "Aw, I never get to do nothin'," before climbing into bed and going to sleep. He dreams that he has left home and is walking down a city street. He sees a sign posted on the side of a boarded-up house. The sign reads, "Boys Wanted. No experience necessary. Earn while you work." Blackie knocks on the door, and it opens. A black cat wearing a derby hat and smoking a cigar appears, and Blackie says, "I saw your sign and I . . ." The man says, "Sure thing. Come in. Fagin's my name. What's yours?" As they go in the house, Blackie says, "My real name is Wilber Scott. Most kids call me Blackie." Fagin says, "OK, Blackie, come in and meet the boys." They enter the back room, where several kittens are sitting on the floor playing craps. Fagin says, "This is recess and the boys like to relax. Fellows, this is Blackie, our new student." Blackie asks, "Do I have to go to school?" Fagin says, "Sure. You can't get any place nowadays without no education. Why just look at some of our graduates. They're in demand everywhere." He points to several wanted posters on the wall. Blackie says, "You mean you teach those boys to be criminals?" Fagin says, "Now you shouldn't have said that. All I do is teach them basic principles. Then they go out educated gentlemen. Well, the gold is where you find it. Hey fellas, let's run over our theme song for Blackie so he can kinda get the idea." After they sing the theme song, a knock on the door is heard. Fagin looks through the peephole in the door and says, "It's the cops!" Blackie says, "Are they real policemen?" Fagin says, "Well, if they ain't, they're a reasonable facsmile." Fagin refuses to let them in and soon there is a gun battle. Blackie is dodging bullets as he wakes up in his bed. It was all a dream. He jumps out of bed and runs downstairs where he joins his mother and the other kittens in song as the cartoon ends.

Review: *Motion Picture Exhibitor,* 29 November 1939

Blackie the Cat thinks his kid brothers and sisters are sissies on accounta they spend most of their spare time singing when they could be listening to gangster stories on the radio. Blackie dreams of enrolling in Fagin's School for Crime and joins his family in musical endeavors when he awakens. There are plenty of hearty laugh sequences. Good.

Review: *Motion Picture Herald,* 2 December 1939

The color composition lesson depicted in this newest Merrie Melody moment would seem to be that "be it ever so humble, there is no place like home," even if one of the household practices calls for familial community singing of nursery ditties. There's not so much as an irreverent nod to the Dickensian source, the nasty natured Fagin of "Oliver Twist" ill fame. The tale concerns a kitten by the name of Blackie who revolts against chiming in with his brothers and sisters in the family group's "sissy" songs. The business of the proceedings is nicely realized all along the picture, from comedy situations to color applications. (7 min)

Review: *Boxoffice,* 16 December 1939

Blackie is a little cat who does not like to sing nursery rhymes with his sisters. After being punished, he dreams that he enters Fagin's school which is attacked by the police. Fagin is a Lionel Stauder take-off and delivers the laughs. The cartoon is frisky and diverting.

Review: *Motion Picture Herald,* 30 December 1950

Blackie, a cat, refuses to sing nursery songs, so his mother sends him to bed. He dreams of a battle with the police, becomes afraid and jumps out the window. Just as he is falling toward the ground, wakes and finds himself in bed. (7 min)

FANTASIA (1940)

Company: Walt Disney, RKO-Radio Pictures
Broadcast: Uncensored "Pastoral Symphony" segment from *Fantasia* was included in "Magic and Music" segment of Walt Disney's weekly TV show *Disneyland,* broadcast in 1957 on the ABC television network and sponsored by Swift's Premium Meats and General Mills.
Characters: Mickey Mouse, black centaurettes

Story: The "Pastoral Symphony" opens with several beautiful white "centaurettes" (upper torso of a human female on the body of a horse) bathing in a small pond fed by a waterfall. A bare-breasted centaurette walks out of the pond, shakes the water off her body, and joins the other white centaurettes who are grooming themselves for the male centaurs who will arrive shortly. One blond centaurette is having her hoof shined by a small black centaurette that is sitting on her haunches. She has hair braided in pickaninny style with a bow tied to the end of each braid. The black centaurette smiles and rolls her eyes as she looks up at the white centaurette, who smiles back at her. The black centaurette spits on a reed of a water lily before using it to shine the hoof. Later in this sequence another black centaurette uses flower petals to decorate the tail of another white centaurette. This black centaurette has two strands of braided hair with a flower blossom tied to each strand. She wears a sunflower tied to the top of her head and wears earrings. The sound of a trumpet signals that the centaurs are on the way. The white centau-

rette becomes so excited that she shakes her tail, causing the flower blossoms to fly into the face of the black centaurette. The white centaurette runs to view the arrival with her friends, leaving the angry black centaurette standing with her hands on her hips. While the white centaurettes are standing together looking off in the distance, the black centaurette arrives on the scene and resumes decorating the tail of her mistress with flowers. The centaurs arrive to select their mates, and one by one the centaurettes parade in front of them. When it is the blond centaurette's turn, she wears a long strand of flowers looped around her waist, which her black servant has woven. As she walks past the centaurs, her black maid walks behind her, smiling and holding onto the other end of the loop. At one point the white centaurette also smiles as she looks back at her maid. After the white centaurs have selected their mates (there are no black centaurs for the maids to pair off with), the festivities begin with wine making. Later Bacchus, the god of wine, a fat white man dressed in a Roman toga and riding on the back of a small black donkey, arrives holding a goblet in his hand. He is flanked on one side by a black zebra centaurette who fans him with a fan of long feathers. Walking on the other side of him is another black zebra centaurette carrying a large bottle of wine on her head, which she uses to refill Bacchus's goblet. Meanwhile the other black "pickaninny" centaurette rolls a red carpet up the steps leading to Bacchus's throne, which is made from half a beer barrel. The black centaurette then dusts off the throne as Bacchus arrives. He is so drunk that the black centaurette and others have to drag him up the steps and push him onto his throne. Bacchus rolls back and forth, tips himself over, and rolls to the bottom of the stairs where the throne breaks apart, spilling him on the ground. The festivities continue, but the black centaurettes do not appear in the remaining parts of the "Pastoral" segment.

Comment: *Long Beach Press-Telegram,* 28 November 1991

The *Fantasia* recently released on video by Disney is not an exact copy of the animated classic as it first appeared in 1940. The 1991 version eliminates 51-year-old racial stereotypes—those of a servile, bare-breasted black "centaurette" who polishes the hooves of white centaurettes. The cutting task fell to John Carnochan, a Disney editor who got the job done between work on *The Little Mermaid* and *Beauty and the Beast, Entertainment Weekly* says. Four shots were reframed and others were simply eliminated. "It's sort of appalling to me that these stereotypes were ever put in," Carnochan says.

FARMER AL FALFA'S WATERMELON PATCH (1916)

Company: Paul Terry, J. R. Bray Studio, released by Pathe Film Exchange
Type: Released in London by the Commonwealth Co. under the title *First Prize*
Characters: Farmer Al Falfa, black man, mule

Story: The cartoon opens on Farmer Al Falfa's farm where he is out in the yard watering his crop of huge watermelons which are lined up in single file on the ground. After finishing he walks over to a billboard where a sign reads "Win a Prize at the County Fair—Come One—Come All—Best Watermelon $10.00. . . ." Meanwhile a black man, with thick white lips, wearing a derby hat, turtle neck sweater, and trousers, is walking down the road. When he passes Al Falfa's farm he stops short when he see's the farmer's ripe watermelons. He looks around to see if anyone is looking before he jumps over the fence and walks over to one of the melons. He smiles before pulling his long straight razor out of his pocket and sharpening it on the sole of his shoe. Then he quickly cuts the melon into several large slices. Smiling, he sits down on the ground and begins to eat a slice. Meanwhile the farmer is gently patting his prize melon which he pampers like a baby. The farmer places the nipple of a baby bottle full of milk into the mouth at one end of the melon, and then shakes powder on it's other end, before wrapping it with a diaper. Meanwhile the black man has finished eating one slice of melon and has started on his second when the farmer sees him from a distance. The angry farmer jumps up and down and shouts at the black man who is so busy eating that he does not hear him. The farmer gets his mule and orders him to walk over and kick the black man who has chewed his second slice down to the rind. The mule seems willing to obey but needs encouragement from the farmer. After a while the mule slowly moves towards the black man who is now eating the last slice of watermelon with all of the bare rinds scattered on the ground around him. Suddenly a small white rabbit jumps out of a hole in the ground and walks toward the black man. When he sees the rabbit, he is so frightened that he throws the watermelon away and quickly jumps to his feet and runs out of sight. Meanwhile the farmer pulls his mule back to the house where he loads his favorite watermelon on its back before they both leave for the fair. All the other animals are arriving at the exhibit hall but the farmer is delayed because the mule, full of pride, frequently pauses along the way to show off the watermelon he is carrying to the other animals and birds. Eventually they arrive at the exhibit hall where the farmer quickly enters, but the smiling mule stops at the entrance to bow to the other animals. When he lowers his head the watermelon rolls off his back and is smashed to pieces when it hits the ground. The irate farmer exits the hall carrying a huge club which he uses to beat his mule on his head for breaking his favorite melon. The farmer then drops the club and repeatedly punches the face of the mule with his fists as the cartoon ends.

Review: *Moving Picture World,* **15 July 1916**

Farmer Al Falfa, a negro with a keen taste for watermelons, and a mule are used to good purpose by Paul Terry in this comedy cartoon which occupies the greater part of a reel, concluding with Ashley Miller's Plastiques. This cartoon is cleverly drawn and is certain to excite laughter.

FELIX SAVES THE DAY (1922)

Company: Pat Sullivan; distributed by M. J. Winkler
Type: Live action and animation

Characters: Felix the Cat, Willie Brown, Tar Heels Nifty Nine

Story: Cartoon opens in the city where Felix is coaching the Nifty Nine, a white kid baseball team lead by their star catcher Willie Brown. Felix pitches but one kid just can't hit the ball and after a few swings, Willie Brown tells him "Wot a fat chance we've got of winnin' th' game this afternoon with you battin' like that!!—" Meanwhile, the Tar Heels, a black kid baseball team, sits on a curb and quietly watches them. (The Heels all resemble Sullivan's comic strip character "Sambo.") Felix decides to show the Nifty Nine how to hit and takes the bat and hits a fly ball so far that it knocks the hat off of a policeman before flying into the open mouth of a black street cleaner who is sitting on a curb sleeping. He has thick white lips and wakes up as his cap flies off his head. The policeman arrests Willie Brown and the judge sentences him to jail. Meanwhile elevated trains, loaded with fans, arrive at the stadium which is quickly filling with cheering fans. The fans root for the Nifty Nine but they trail the Tar Heels. Curious about the score, Felix climbs to the top of a light pole and looks over the stadium wall where the score board reads, Tar Heels 6, Nifty Nine 0. Felix quickly climbs down the pole and rushes to the jail where he tells Willie "They're putting it all over us!!—" Willie, who is dressed in a striped prison uniform, says, "You go and pinch—hit for us— We'll beat 'em yet!!—" Felix hails a taxi and tells the driver "Get to the polo grounds as quick as you can." On the way Felix sees the meter reach $2.00 so he jumps out of the taxi and then catches the elevated train. Felix arrives at the ball park, sees the score, and says, "There's no chance of winning—Our only hope is rain." The announcer shouts, "Felix is batting for Willie Brown." The Tar Heel pitches a curve. Felix swings and misses—Strike one." The pitcher throws another curve and again Felix misses the ball—Strike two. But when he throws Felix the third curve ball Felix hits it so high into the sky that it passes through the clouds where it hits the sleeping rain god, Jupiter Plavinis, on his head. Jupiter wakes up and is so angry that he looks down at the stadium and shouts, "Just for that— I'll spoil the game" and then he causes a rain storm. The game is called because of rain and a happy Felix runs back to the jail where he tells Willie Brown the good news. They both smile and dance around as the cartoon ends.

FISH FRY (1944)

Company: Walter Lantz; distributed by Universal Pictures
Characters: Andy Panda, black cat, fish

Story: The cartoon opens as Andy Panda is looking through the window of a pet store at a tank of goldfish. One of the fish swims in front of him and holds up a sign that reads Take Me Home—10 Cents. Andy buys the fish and takes him home in a jar of water. He passes by a black cat that is rummaging through a garbage can looking for a meal. The cat sees Andy's fish and decides that he has found his dinner. He sneaks up behind Andy, grabs the fish out of the bowl, and swallows it. But the little fish manages to pop out of the cat's mouth and get back into the fishbowl. The cat reaches into the bowl, but the fish bites the cat's paw. The fish pretends to be sympathetic to the cat's hurting paw, saying "poor little pussy cat" as it reaches into a medicine bag. But it takes out a huge pair of false teeth and uses them to bite the cat. Not discouraged, the cat goes to a hunting goods store, buys a safari hunter's hat, puts it on, and runs back to Andy. He collapses and falls to the sidewalk and pleads for water. Andy pours water from the fishbowl into the cat's mouth, but he fails to swallow the fish. The cat desperately tells Andy, "Now listen, Shorty, let's skip the frivolity and analyze the situation. In that bowl you have a fish—right. And in my stomach I got an appetite—right. My fish, my appetite—right." Then he grabs the fishbowl and runs away. As he looks back he says, "So long, Chum. It's been nice knowin' ya," and runs headlong into a Street Closed sign. The cat is knocked to the ground and the bowl falls to the sidewalk, spilling water and fish onto the street. The cat chases the fish as it swims along a pool of water and falls through the grating of a storm drain. The cat sticks his head through the grating and gets stuck. The fish uses the cat's head as a punching bag before hitting it with a large stick, which knocks it back through the grating. The fish swims away down the drain while the cat rushes to the end of the drainpipe to wait for him to come out. The fish comes out of the drain and falls into a frying pan, which the cat places on a barbeque grill. The fish is relaxing, but when he smells smoke he asks, "Who's cooking fish?" The cat says, "You're cooking, Fish." The fish leaps out of the frying pan high into the air and falls down into the the fishbowl held by Andy. Andy runs away with the bowl, and the cat chases them. Andy runs into the pet store, and the cat stands by the door holding a club and waiting for him to come out. When Andy leaves the store, the cat swings his club. He stops in midair when he sees that Andy, still holding the fishbowl, has bought another pet—a huge bulldog. The cat gives the dog a "sheepish" grin as he runs off and the cartoon ends.

Review: *Besa Shorts Shorts*, 19 June 1944

Andy Panda is the star of this latest Walter Lantz color cartoon. Andy is passing the pet shop when he notices their sign "For Father's Day—Give Pop A Pet." So in he goes and purchases a goldfish for the amount of 10 cents. Andy and the little fish are merrily on their way when they encounter the villain, a big black cat. Then it's a case of "fish bites cat." The old sly feline tries in every way to out-do Andy and the fish, but in the end he gets completely "slap-happy."

FLOP GOES THE WEASEL (1943)

Company: Charles Jones, Warner Bros.
Type: Merrie Melodies
Characters: Wiley Weasel, black chick, black mammy hen
            (voice characterization by Lillian Randolph)

Story: The cartoon opens with a long shot of a small cabin in the forest. With a closer view singing is heard coming from the hen-

house behind the cabin. Inside a black mammy hen is singing and knitting a baby sweater while sitting on an egg and waiting for it to hatch. Finally she hears a tapping sound coming from the egg. It's a message in Morse code, and the hen grabs a pencil to write down the translation. She writes, "Kill the fattened worm. Y'all is practically a mammy. P.S. Congratulations! Signed Junior." The excited hen runs out of the house to dig up a worm. Meanwhile Wiley Weasel appears on the scene. He sneaks into the henhouse, steals the egg, and takes it to his house. There Wiley decides to prepare himself a meal of Egg Delight Supreme. The recipe calls for one fresh egg. But the egg breaks itself open and a black chick rolls out. The chick takes one look at the weasel and shouts, "Mammy! Yo' is my mammy, ain't you? Yo' have a kind look in yo' eyes. Mammy, when do we eat?" Wiley likes the chick but is too hungry and fond of chicken to spare him from the cooking pot. He pretends to be the chick's mammy and puts a bandanna on his head. The chick asks Wiley, "What kind of animals are we? A turkey? A monkey? Wiley tells him that they are weasels. This makes the chick so happy and excited that he throws various objects that hit Wiley on the head and knock him down. The weasel is angry but quickly calms down and suggests that they play a game of hide and seek. While the little chick is counting to ten, the weasel puts him into a pot, closes the lid, and puts the pot in the oven. He turns on the heat but is given a hot foot by the chick, who was not in the pot after all. The weasel dunks his foot in a pail of water and is again very angry but calms down after the chick suggests they play a game of tag. The weasel hides behind the door, intending to hit the chick on the head with a club when he comes to find him. Instead the chick is waiting for the weasel and hits him on the head with an even larger club. While the weasel is still stunned from the blow, the chick suggests that the weasel sprinkle some salt on his tail as a way to catch him. But he gives the weasel a bottle of pepper. When the weasel tries to throw pepper on the chick, the chick turns on a fan that blows the pepper back into the weasel's face The weasel tries to catch the chick but is prevented by his sneezing. Finally the weasel gives up in exhaustion. While he is sitting down, the chick offers him some smelling salts—really more pepper. The weasel takes a deep breath, and the resultant sneeze sends him up to the ceiling, where he gets stuck. The chick then pushes a washing machine under him, and when the weasel lets go, he lands in the machine and its tossed around for a while. Finally we see a sign pop up out of the washer that reads, "I Surrender, Dear!" The next scene shows Mammy hen returning home with a very large worm. When she goes in the house, she find the chick, who proceeds to tell her how he vanquished the weasel. But he tells him, "Hush yo mouth, Chile, from telling all those lies." He says, "But I'm tell you the truth." Just then the weasel pops up all wrapped in bandages and says, "He ain't just whistling Dixie, Mama," followed by a big sneeze at the fadeout.

Review: *Motion Picture Herald*, 3 March 1943

The Weasel has stolen an egg from the hen only to have it hatch in his hands. The chick mistakes the Weasel for its mother, but still refuses to be persuaded into the frying pan in spite of the Weasel's tender words. (7 min)

Review: *Motion Picture Herald,* 4 June 1949

Wiley Weasel is about to eat an egg he has stolen from a barnyard hen. The egg hatches a small chick who mistakes the weasel for its mother. However, the weasel attempts to entice the chick into the roasting pan.

Review: *Motion Picture Exhibitor,* 24 March 1943

Wiley Weasel is about to prepare a meal with an egg he has just stolen from a barnyard hen. The egg suddenly hatches a small chick who mistakes the weasel for its mother. The weasel, taking the cue, pretends to play the game, and futilely attempts to entice the chick into the flying pan. Fair.

Review: *Boxoffice,* 30 July 1949

Very Good. The so-called Wiley Weasel is flabbergasted when an egg he has stolen from a barnyard hen for his meal, hatches out a small chick. The chick mistakes the weasel for its mother and the rodent is forced to play the game. He tries, without success, to lure the chick into the roasting pan.

THE FOOLISH DUCKLING (1952)

Company: Mannie Davis, Paul Terry, Twentieth Century-Fox Pictures
Type: Terrytoons
Characters: Dinky Duck, other ducks

Story: The cartoon opens on a lake where four white ducklings are learning to swim. An offscreen choral group sings, "Down on the pond where the weeping willows grow, swam a group of busy baby ducks learning what ducks should know. They followed the wake of a wise old drake to know how things were done. And every little duck was there, yes all 'cept one. He was a duck named Dinky. In a rubber tube he'd lie and spend his time composing rhymes as other ducks swam by." The little black duck, Dinky, relaxes on his inner tube and says, "Oh how I love to float upon the lake just like a boat." A little duck swims by and says, "You'd better stop spoutin' poetry and learn your lessons. Come on, come on." He tugs at Dinky's foot. Another duck pulls the plug on Dinky's inner tube, and the escaping air propels Dinky across the water like a jet. He hits the shore, flies through the air, and lands, suspended by the inner tube, on the limb of a tree. Dinky says, "I can't swim and they know it 'cause I'd rather be a poet." The leaves are turning color, and it is time for the ducks to take flying lessons in preparation for their flight south. All go except Dinky, who is sitting under a tree. One of the ducks asks him, "Hey Dink! Aren't you comin' for flying lessons?" Dinky says, "I'd much rather spend my time thinking up rhymes." The duck tells him, "You'll be sorry." All of the others graduate from flying school and tell Dinky, "We graduated and we have our diplomas." Dinky answers, "It doesn't mean a thing to me. I much prefer my poetry." Winter arrives, and all of the others fly south. Dinky sees them fly by and calls out, "Wait for me, wait for me." All along, Dinky is blown around by the cold winter wind before finding shelter is a hollow tree trunk. He says, "If I ever get out of this alive, I'll never

neglect my lessons." Just then the clouds part and a stork carrying a letter for Dinky lands near him and says, "A letter for Dinky Duck." Dinky opens the letter and reads, "Ducky Wucky Cereal Co. Dear Sir: The poem you submitted to our contest has been awarded first prize! Your prize is an airline trip to Florida—all expenses paid!" Dinky shouts "hooray" as he runs off to collect the prize. Meanwhile the other ducks are flying in formation south when they are passed by a DC-3 airliner. Dinky waves to them out of the window as the offscreen group sings, "It's nice to be a poet but it's better to learn to fly," as the cartoon ends.

Review: *Boxoffice,* 9 August 1952

A Dinky Duck cartoon which has a moral as well as a few laughs. Dinky is a lazy duck who spouts poetry instead of learning to fly like the other ducks. When winter comes, the others fly south and Dinky is left to cope with the snow and cold. However, a postman saves the day with a letter saying that Dinky has won a cereal rhyme contest with the prize being a free airplane trip south.

FRIED CHICKEN (1931)

Company: Frank, Moser, Paul Terry, Twentieth Century-Fox Pictures
Type: Terrytoons
Characters: Southern blacks

Review: *Variety,* 29 September 1931

Animals doing a Jolson and not too hot. One or two minor laughs, with most of the drawings ordinary.
Considerable vocalizing

Review: *Motion Picture Herald,* 3 October 1931

One of the commendably interesting angles of the Terry-Toon cartoons is that the music is not blatant or jarring. This particular issue has a Southern setting which is carried out in the singing. While there is no particular sequence to the cartooned events, at least the hero wins his sweetheart and that's sufficient.

FRIGHTDAY THE 13TH (1953)

Company: I. Sparber, Famous Studios, Paramount Pictures
Type: Noveltoons
Characters: Casper the friendly ghost, black kitten

Review: *Motion Picture Herald,* 7 February 1953

Casper the Ghost tries to bring good luck to a little black Kitten on Friday the 13th. Casper and the Kitten become fast friends and join in a search for good luck objects. In their treasure hunt they get into quite a bit of trouble but all works out well in the end. (7 min)

Review: *Exhibitor Servisection,* 11 March 1953

It's Friday the 13th and the local ghosts go about their mysterious duties, but Casper, unwilling to scare people, goes out to find a friend. Another outcast, a black cat, befriends him, and they join in a search for good luck objects. In the course of their search, however, they scare everyone. Fair. (7 min)

THE GINGERBREAD BOY (1934)

Company: Walter Lantz, Universal Pictures
Characters: Gingerbread boy, black cat

Review: *Film Daily,* 25 April 1934

Just a mildly amusing animated comedy based on a fairy tale. A childless old woman bakes herself a gingerbread boy, which comes to life and starts to cut up. A menacing black cat chases it around, but the wily imp outwits the feline.

GOIN' TO HEAVEN ON A MULE (1934)

Company: I. Freleng, Vitaphone, Warner Bros.
Type: Merrie Melodies
Characters: Southern blacks

Story: The cartoon opens on a southern plantation where black men, women, and children are happily picking cotton and loading the bales into a two-wheel horsedrawn wagon. One big black man picks cotton and puts it into a huge sack carried on the back of a small, gray-bearded black man. Another man picks the cotton by pushing a lawnmower through the field so that the cotton balls fly directly into a sack on his back. The next scene shows the cotton being placed in one end of a huge machine, as 100 percent wool suits come out of the other end. Meanwhile a lazy black man sleeps near a shed where a mule is feeding on a sack of grain. The man is attacked by an angry swarm of bees. He wakes up, scratches his head, and looks around before he decides to take a drink from a keg of gin. Before he can do so a little white angel appears and gestures to him not to take a drink. But then a little black devil also appears and urges him to take a drink. The angel and the devil get into a tussle, and in the meantime the man takes a big drink of gin that makes him dizzy. He imagines he has died and is riding to heaven on the back of a mule as he sings, "When I pass away on de judgment day, I's goin' to heaven on a mule, an old Missouri mule. And by and by I'll be ridin' high across the rainbow in the sky, goin' to heaven on a mule." He arrives at the gates of heaven and sees a sign reading Pair-O-Dice and a pair of dice on the top of each gatepost. He enters as the angels fly around singing to jazz music. One of them rolls a pair of dice. The Lord, an elderly man with a white beard, also greets him before he arrives at the front of the Milky Way Inn where he ties the ears of his mule to a lamppost. He is greeted by the doorman as he goes inside. A floor show is in progress as a male quartet sings and dances. He stops at a table where there is a large slice of watermelon. He eats it while humming a tune at the same time. He looks through a window and sees a gin orchard in which bottles of gin grow on trees. He climbs out of the window, ignoring the Keep Out and Hands Off signs. He picks a bottle of

gin off the tree and takes a long drink and becomes drunk. Then he turns around to find the angry Lord behind him, standing with his arms folded. The man tells the Lord, "Hi Ol' Boy. Oh, by the . . ." But the Lord interrupts him and says, "You'll be sorry for this." The man is not afraid of the Lord and laughs at him. Then the Lord claps his hands, and two burly men arrive on the scene. They obey the Lord's command to pick up the drunk and carry him to a door with a sign that reads Chute to to Hades. They open the doors and push him down the cute. They adjust the dial of the depth meter, which reads "70,000 Ft., 20,000 Ft., Sea Level, Below Sea Level, Way Below Sea Level, to Hades," to send him all of the way down to hades. But then he wakes up in front of the shed. It was all a dream. He grabs his bottle of gin and tosses it away, but changes his mind quickly and runs and catches the bottle before it hits the ground. He wipes his brow, smiles, and says, "Whew!" as the cartoon ends. Over the closing credits he says, "That's all, Folks."

Review: *Film Daily,* 9 July 1934

Based on the "Going to Heaven on a Mule" number in *Wonder Bar,* this animated cartoon produced by Leon Schlesinger fills its purpose very nicely. A lazy colored boy after taking a swig out of a jug falls into a nightmare in which the comical Negro Heaven action takes place, winding up with a crash that awakens him. (7 min)

Review: *Motion Picture Review: June 1934*

A darky whose taste for liquor is too much for him rides to his idea of heaven, where angels and the devil fight over him. Only fair and for adults only.

GOLDILOCKS AND THE JIVIN' BEARS (1944)

Company: I. Freleng, Warner Bros.
Type: Looney Tunes
Characters: Three black bears, Goldilocks, Red Ridin' Hood, wolf grandma; offscreen narration by Ernest Whitman

Story: The cartoon opens with a close-up of hands playing hot jazz on a piano. The offscreen narrator says, "Now let me tell a story that I heard of somewhere about Goldilocks and the three black bears. It was way down South in a forest where the three black bears lived in a tumbledown shack." The scene then shifts to a small shack in the woods. Inside the shack pictures of the three black bears hang on a wall. There is big-sized bear (a tall, skinny bear with a Stephin Fetchit demeanor), a middle-sized bear (a fat bear wearing a derby hat and smoking a cigar with the demeanor of Andy Brown of the *Amos 'n' Andy* show), and a wee, small bear. The narrator says, "Now these three bears, they never went to school. But when it comes to jivin' they was nobody's fool." The three bears pick up their musical instruments and begin to play a hot jazz. The middle-sized bear blows a clarinet. The big-sized bear plays the piano, and the wee bear plays a bass fiddle that is larger than he is. The middle-sized bear stops playing and says, "Man, you is crazy." He looks at the big-sized bear who is lying on the floor playing the piano with his toes. The big-sized bear says, "Naw, just lazy." The middle-sized bear stops playing and says, "My horn is too hot." The big-sized bear says, "My piano is all fired up" as flames and smoke pour out of the piano. The wee bear says, "Mine's runnin' a high temperature too." They all stop playing, and the big-sized bear says, "I'll tell you what we're gonna do. We'll take a nice walk through the woods, and when we get back the instruments will be all cooled off." But the other two look at him in disagreement. The big-sized bear pulls out a book entitled *Goldilocks and the Three Bears* and says, "But that's what it says here," as the other two read the book. The scene shifts to the woods where the three black bears are walking along in rhythm to the jive music playing in the background. The scene shifts to Grandma's house, which is next door to where the three black bears live. Inside the big bad wolf, dressed in Grandma's nightgown, lies in bed reading a newspaper. The narrator says, "Now if you've read your fairy tales just like you should, you've heard about the big bad wolf and Red Riding Hood." The wolf reads from a page in the paper: "Shopping News. Point Values: First little pig, 8 points; second little pig, 10 points; third little pig (lean), 12 points; Red Riding hood, 6 points; Goldilocks, no points." The wolf throws away the newspaper as the narrator says, "And there is that ole rascal in Grandma's bed." Just then a knock is heard on the front door. The door opens and there stands a black Western Union delivery boy in his bare feet, wearing his cap on backward and holding a telegram in his hands. He slowly reads the telegram (with a Stephin Fetchit demeanor), which says, "Telegram to grandmother, grandma's house, Hollywood, California, January 20, 1945. From Red. Quote. Sorry, Grandmother. Can't be there till later. Working at Lockheed as a riveter. Red Riding Hood." The wolf snatches the telegram from the delivery boy and says, "Well kill me dead." The delivery boy pulls out a gun and fires it at the wolf. The wolf dodges the bullet by jumping up in the air and grabbing onto a ceiling lamp. He says, "What's the matter with you, Puddin' Head?" The delivery boy answers, "Sorry sir, but that's what you said." Then he leaves the house. The narrator says, "But that wolf, he was hungry, mad, and sore until he heard a loud rapping at the front door." As the wolf paces the floor, Goldilocks, a shapely black woman wearing a short skirt and a red flower in her hair, knocks at the front door of the bears' house. The narrator says, "Well shut my mouth and ground me for corn! It's Goldilocks, just as sure as you were born." The wolf looks out of the window and says, "Goldilocks. When it's a food shortage, what am I waitin' for?" Meanwhile Goldilocks enters the house, stretches her arms, yawns, and walks upstairs as the narrator says, "Well now about this time, like the storybook said, Goldilocks was tired. She was goin' to bed." Goldilocks arrives in the bedroom, jumps on the bed of the big-sized bear, and bounces in the air. Goldilocks says, "This bed's too hard." She climbs into the bed of the middle-sized

bear and sinks into the mattress while saying, "This bed's too soft." Next she tries the bed of the wee bear and says, "I think that's just right," as the narrator says, "Good night." Goldilocks replies, "Goodnight," and the wolf (who is in bed with her) says, "Good night." Goldilocks says, "Who is you? You ain't de three old bears." The wolf says, "You bet I ain't, Honey. But lawdy, who cares?" Goldilocks screams and jumps out of bed and runs downstairs with the wolf close behind her. He chases her around the room before grabbing her and swinging her around and around. Meanwhile the three black bears arrive back home. The wee bear enters and says, "Well shut my mouth." The middle-sized bear enters next and says, "Well shut my mouth." The big-sized bear enters and says, "Well shut my mouth." They see the wolf holding Goldilocks, and they think that they are dancing the jitterbug. The bears say "jitterbug" as they grab their instruments and begin to play hot music. Goldilocks stops screaming and says, "Hit that jive, boys" as she grabs the wolf and they start to dance the jitterbug. As the music gets faster, the wolf becomes worn out and makes several unsuccessful attempts to get away from Goldilocks before he finally succeeds. He runs back to Grandma's house, puts on Grandma's nightgown, and jumps into bed. The narrator says, "This old wolf was pooped and was almost dead. He'd had more than enough, then along came Red." Red Riding Hood, a black girl dressed in red from head to foot and carrying a basket of food, walks over to the bed, looks at the wolf, and says, "Why Grandma, what big eyes you got." The wolf says, "Yeah, all the better to see you with. Now go away, leave it." Red Riding Hood then says, "Grandma, what big teeth you got." The wolf answers, "Yeah, the better to eat you up with." Red Riding Hood screams and jumps into the air. Her dress blows up over her head, revealing her white drawers. She also has a pigtail hair style. She runs to the door where she stops, turns around, and says, "What's the matter? Ain't you gonna chase me?" The wolf says, "What, with these?" He pulls up the sheets and shows her his red-hot feet. Suddenly the three black bears show up on the scene, look at the wolf, and say, "There's that jitterbug" before grabbing their musical instruments and starting to play hot jazz. The closet door opens and there is old Grandma wearing a bandanna and eyeglasses. She shouts out, "Jitterbugs! Well cut me loose." She runs to the wolf, pulls him out of bed, and starts to do a fast jitterbug with him. She laughs as the exhausted wolf looks around and says, with a Jimmy Durante demeanor, "Everybody wants to get into the act," as the cartoon ends.

Review: *Motion Picture Herald,* 7 October 1944

When hot swing hits the old nursery tales it cuts some strange capers. Here, three bears go to town in modern musical style leaving the way clear for a blackfaced Goldilocks who proceeds to sample the beds. In comes the wolf, weary of waiting for Little Riding Hood and on the prowl for other game. The bears return and Goldi gives the Wolf quite a workout, while Red Riding Hood and Grandma arrive in time to keep him on his feet. (7 1/2 min)

Review: *Motion Picture Herald,* 12 January 1952

When Red Riding Hood fails to show up, the wolf picks on Goldilocks instead. In his attempts to catch her, he gets mixed up with the three bears, who to the wolf's horror are a hot swing trio. Between Goldilocks, who is a rabid jitterbug, and the trio, the wolf almost goes mad.

Review: *Motion Picture Exhibitor,* 6 September 1944

This hilarious burlesque on fairy tales has the three Jivin' Black Bears going to town with some red hot music. They take a walk until their instruments can cool off. Goldilocks (in blackface) arrives and goes to bed. Meanwhile, at the Wolf's house the Wolf gets tired of waiting for Little Red Riding Hood and goes to the bear's house, where he tries to make Goldilocks. The bears return, go into jive sessions and Goldilocks, jitterbugging, wears the Wolf out, although they won't permit him to stop. He takes an awful beating, runs home and gets into bed to rest his tired feet. Red finally arrives, wants him to go through his usual routine. When he refuses, Grandmother, who was hiding in a closet, comes out and forces the Wolf to dance some more. With rhyme, colored dialect, swell music accompaniment, this is tops. Excellent.

Review: *Boxoffice,* 7 October 1944

The big bad wolf, Red Riding Hood and the Three Bears are spun merrily through this reel, and the wolf comes off a decided last. Seems he can't take the jitterbug proceedings, and everyone but him is a jivin' fool. It's a novelty to see a young girl chasing a wolf for a change.

Review: *Besa Shorts Shorts,* 18 September 1944

The Boogie version of Red and Granny and the three bears. The triple bruins are in this treatment a trio of red hot jive boys, Big Size, Middle Size, and Wee Size. The brand of boogie they play gives Red a chance to dance the feet almost off the old wolf and when Red finishes in comes Grandma to finish off the old grey who wishes he had never heard of any of these jive characters.

Review: Stanley Crouch, review of *Animated Coon Show, Village Voice,* 16–22 December 1981

We are given a version of the fairy tale told by a large, black piano player who trills blues or boogie-woogie figures between chuckles. The bears are Negro musicians and Goldilox [sic] is a vanilla-wafer tan sweetheart with a round backside, short dress, and high-heeled shoes of a sort that make the image extremely contemporary. When the big bad wolf commences chasing her, the bears fire up some music, and she dances him into sorefooted bad health. The scene seems a variation on Slim and Slam's appearance in "Hellzapoppin" and the kind of humor for which Waller was noted. And though it is sometimes amusing, one tires of its predictability, which is the bane of the stereotype.

HAPPY SCOUTS (1938)

Company: Walter Lantz, Universal Pictures
Characters: Oswald the rabbit, black duck

Story: The cartoon opens with scoutmaster Oswald Rabbit leading Duck Troop no. 13 on a hike. The little white ducks march along in single file but a little black duck trails behind. The black duck is having trouble keeping up his pants. Oswald decides it's time to make camp for the night. He tells the black duck to make a fire and cook dinner while he and the white ducks go fishing. Disappointed at being left behind, the black duck, with much effort, builds a fire near the shore of a lake by rubbing two sticks together. While he is not looking, however, a beaver comes out of the lake and puts it out by squirting water on it. The black duck is very angry, but an Indian comes out from behind a tree and restarts the fire, using a lighter. Meanwhile Oswald is teaching the other scouts how to fish. He hooks what he thinks is a big fish. But when he reels it in, he discovers that it is a turtle. The turtle is very angry and gives Oswald a kick in the pants. The ducks laugh. Back at the camp the black duck starts to prepare a meal of hot dogs. He opens a package of wieners and takes them out, putting each one on a skewer. To his surprise he has stuck the wieners on the quills of a porcupine that runs away and jumps into his den. The little black duck has lost his dinner, and all he has left is a can of beans—jumping beans. The can jumps up and down and makes the beaver laugh as he returns to put out the campfire again. This time the black duck grabs a club and jumps into the lake after him, but finds himself confronted by a large alligator. He flies across the lake just above the water with the snapping alligator close behind. Just as the little duck is about to be eaten, the beaver swims by. The duck grabs the beaver's tail and is pulled back to the dock. As they run into the dock, the black duck is knocked free of the beaver and lands in the lake. This time he is chased by the alligator as both swim under water. The black duck tries to hide in a sunken ship, but the alligator finds him. They swim in circles in and out of the ship. The duck swims free and grabs the ship's cannon and fires a ball at the alligator. The ball hits the alligator in the mouth, but he spits it out, and the chase is on again. The little black duck calls out for help as he swims along just ahead of the hungry alligator. Oswald hears his cries for help, drops his fishing rod, and picks up a duck decoy. He winds it up, pulls the black duck out of the water, and places the fake duck in the alligator's mouth. The alligator swallows the decoy, which starts to make loud sounds and jump around inside the alligator as it swims away. The last scene shows Oswald, followed by his duck troop, going back home singing "Be Prepared for Anything." The little black duck, as usual, is bringing up the rear and having trouble keeping his pants from falling down.

Review: *Motion Picture Herald,* 2 July 1938

Close on the trail blazed by Donald Duck's gay troop of "Good Scouts" comes Scoutmaster Oswald, the rabbit, and corps of camping ducks. Without the enhancing value of color and the personality of the inimitable Donald, Oswald's hiking expedition is passably good fare on its own activities. The unusual camp trials of opening a can of beans and building a fire are humorously caricatured. The finale of a black duckling scout with an alligator is a bit far fetched but still good for a laugh or two. The kids will find the whole affair much to their liking. (7 min)

Review: *Boxoffice*, 25 June 1938

Oswald, as a Scoutmaster, and his little troupe of ducks looking to him for inspiration while on a camping trip should provide a full measure of fun for the youngsters. A black duckling with a flair for getting into trouble is the springboard for most of the action. First a scrap with a beaver, then a hot can of beans, later an alligator, and so on until the seven minutes are up.

Review: *National Exhibitor*, 1 July 1938

Oswald scoutmasters a group of ducks on a camping trip that is effectively messed up by a beaver, alligator. Fair.

HAVE YOU GOT ANY CASTLES? (1938)

Company: Frank Tashlin, Warner Bros.
Type: Merrie Melodies
Characters: Various characters from classic adventure and mystery novels, as well as entertainers including Cab Calloway and his band, and Bill Robinson

Story: The cartoon opens in a bookstore, where various characters from famous novels come to life. Frankenstein, Mr. Hyde, the phantom of the opera, and Fu Manchu sing and dance. Then Bill Robinson does his famous stairstep tap dance on the cover of *The Thirty Nine Steps*. The other characters applaud, including Man Friday from *Robinson Crusoe*. Next a black angel, on the cover of *Green Pastures*, introduces a musical sequence from the cartoon *Clean Pastures* led by caricatures of Cab Calloway and his band. The band plays while Calloway dances and sings, "If the horns be too dreamy, and you like your trumpets screamy, that's when you should call to see me because I've got swing for sale." A trio of shapely black chorus girls from the Cotton Club dance as he sings. Cab continues, "If you think a war horse is horrid, and you like your rhythm torrid, and it makes you mop your forehead, I've got swing for sale." A trio of black angels sings, "Here's what this country needs. For years and years I've said it. If you buy it from me, it's C.O.D. I sell swings, but not for credit." After Calloway finishes, Heidi belts out her rendition of "Hi-dee-ho." Rip Van Winkle is angry when the music wakes him up. He grabs a pair of scissors from an Arab who is sewing on the cover of *The Valiant Tailor* and uses them to cut some hair from the head of Uncle Tom, who is on the cover of *Uncle Tom's Cabin*. He stuffs Tom's hair in his ears. When he tries the same trick again, he is beaten up by Uncle Tom, who uses the scissors to cut off some of Van Winkle's beard. Eventually Van Winkle becomes so angry that he blows everyone away using wind from the novel *Gone with the Wind* as the cartoon ends.

HE DABBLES IN THE POND (1917)

Company: Powers Film Company; distributed by Universal Film Co.
Characters: Mr. Fuller Pep, black man, and black woman

Review: *Bioscope* (London), 28 June 1917

"He Dabbles in the Pond," an admirable sub-title to this screamer. Fuller Pep bathes in a secluded nook, and to see his feet and legs tickled by fishes and turtles and then to see the expression on his face (his head only is out of the water) as he presumably writhes and itches is real humour. Pep gets into a barrel as a substitute for clothing, and hides in a dog kennel. A farmer fires at him, the nigger and his old mammy chase him, Pep falls into a dynamite crater and steals a fellow victim's clothes. Very funny cartoon. Animation great. (569 ft)

HE WHO GETS SOAKED (1925)

Company: Earl Hurd, Paul Terry, Educational Pictures, Pathe Film Exchange
Type: Pen and Ink Vaudeville
Characters: Black baby, Stork

Review: *Moving Picture World*, 7 February 1925

In this issue of Earl Hurd's "Pen and Ink Vaudeville" the familiar property man is called upon to take care of the strong man's infant son. This mischievous child escapes and is finally captured by a stork. Props boards an aeroplane, gives chase and runs into a whole flock of storks, each carrying an infant, and has a hard time. He picks a Negro, a Hebrew, a Chinese baby, etc., before he gets the right one, and awakens to find it all a dream. The action in this little cartoon is snappy and amusing and the interest well sustained. It is really the best of this series. (one reel)

HIS OFF DAY (1938)

Company: Connie Rasinski, Paul Terry, Twentieth Century-Fox Pictures
Type: Terrytoons
Characters: Puddy, Negro servant

Review: *National Exhibitor*, 1 February 1938

Puddy tries to make friends, but the cats, the organ grinder, and the old negro servant at the home, will have nothing to do with him. It is just Puddy's off day, nobody will play with him. This is just a cartoon filler. Fair.

HOLLYWOOD PICNIC (1937)

Company: Art Davis, Columbia Pictures
Type: Scrappy Color Rhapsody
Characters: Caricatures of various Hollywood stars, including Stephin Fetchit

Story: The cartoon opens as cars stream though the gate of the

Hollywood picnic grounds. All the stars have come out for a picnic, including W. C. Fields, the Marx Brothers, Abbot and Costello, The Three Stooges, Laurel and Hardy, Joe E. Brown, and Shirley Temple. A baseball game is in progress when Stephin Fetchit comes to the plate. He swings and misses the ball and scratches his head while saying, "I gets so tired playin' baseball . . ." The dinner bell rings, and it is time to eat. All the stars run to the table and take their seats. Meanwhile Stephin Fetchit, slowly walking along dragging the bat on the ground, says, "I don't know where the baseball is." He hears the dinner bell and runs to the table so fast that he leaves a cloud of dust behind him. He jumps into his seat at the table and devours a large slice of watermelon, pausing only briefly to spit the seeds out of his mouth like machine-gun bullets. When the meal is finished, Martha Raye jumps up on the table and sings, "Goin' up to Harlem to do some truckin' . . ." Soon everybody is doing the truckin' dance, including Stephin Fetchit, who is close to a pile of watermelons. Evening comes, and as the music plays in the background, a long line of cars with headlights on move out of the park as the cartoon ends.

A HOT TIME IN PUNKVILLE (1915)

Company: Lubin Film Manufacturing Company
Type: On the same reel with *Who Stole the Doggies?*
Character: Rastus

Review: *Moving Picture World*, 8 May 1915

This is a cartoon picture. Rastus lands in his native town from a boxcar after a pleasant trip. The first thing that attracts his attention is a wonderfully well developed chicken who greets him at the door of the baggage roon. Rastus resolves to capture the bird, but the chicken puts up a good fight and the robber has to content himself with an egg. Still pursuing his bent of crime, he turns his attention to a fine Jersey cow, but in this he is again disappointed, as the cow jumps over the moon. Rastus, pursuing, gets badly mixed up with the stars. He finally gets down to earth and intrudes himself into a humble domicile just as the mistress is preparing for a bath.

Review: *New York Dramatic Mirror*, 19 May 1915

Although hardly a complimentary caption, the short offering concerns itself with the attempts of the magic-loving darky to capture first a fowl, then milk a cow. The cartoon work is good.

THE HULA CABARET (1919)

Company: Bud Fisher; distributed by Fox Film Company
Characters: Mutt and Jeff, black Salome

Review: *Bioscope* (London), 27 March 1919

A whimsical pair now try their hands at running a cabaret; and at first all goes "merry as a marriage bell." The black Salome is in excellent form, and most fascinating in her poses and gestures, and Jeff at the bar is busy getting drinks for the thirsty. The beverage served is evidently full of "body" to judge by its effects on the champion, McPush, whose muscles are a sight to see, and whose extraordinary genius at the game furnishes excellent entertainment for himself as well as the audience, until Jeff comes to the rescue of his pal and soon proves himself the world's champion. (one reel)

HUMOROUS PHASES OF FUNNY FACES (1906)

Company: James Stuart Blackton, Vitagraph Company
Type: Live action and animation
Characters: J. Stuart Blackton, as himself; various characters, including black and Jewish stereotypes

Story: Blackton, as himself, draws sketches of various characters on a large sheet of white paper attached to a wall. The sketches come to life in a series of simplistic animated sequences. In one scene Blackton writes the word *coon* on the screen. Then he transforms the word into a sketch of the face of a black man using the *O*'s for eyes and the *C* and *N* for ears. Next he writes *Cohen* and transforms the word into a sketch of a sterotypical Jewish man.

I HEARD (1933)

Company: Dave Fleischer, Max Fleischer, Paramount Pictures
Type: Combined live action and animation
Characters: Betty Boop, Don Redman and his orchestra, Bimbo, Ko-Ko, waiter (voice characterization by Don Redman)

Story: The cartoon opens with live action of Don Redman and his band playing in front of a billboard for Betty Boop's Saloon. The scene changes to animation showing the Neva coal mine and the miners digging coal. When the lunch whistle blows, all of the miners come up to the surface and walk through a shower to clean themselves off before going into Betty Boop's tavern. Last to arrive are Bimbo and Ko-Ko, who also work in the mine. Inside the miners eat lunch served by a waiter who sings, "Now I know a gal named Betty Boop. Oh how she can boop-be-doop. She loves to dance and loves to sing and might take a chance on anything. Ain't every night right here in this hall just let that music play. And Betty will get on that floor. This is what she'll say . . ." Betty Boop walks down the stairs and sings, "How am I doin'? How am I doin'? Oh gee baby, oh shucks. Now I'm not braggin', but it's understood that everything I do is what should be dould." Meanwhile the waiter serves coffee while singing, "How am I doin'? Oh gee, puttin' on a show. Now I'll admit I'm not the best in town. But I'll be the best till the best comes 'round. How am I doin'? Oh gee, baby." As he serves Betty ice cream at her table, he continues singing, "Say, I only meant to do a little bit. You done made me like it and I just can't quit. How am I doin'?" He spills some food on several miners, who become angry and throw him down and jump on him. The whistle signals that lunch has ended, and the miners leave the tavern. They walk under a spray of coal dust before going back down into the mine. Bimbo arrives in the pit and breaks a hole through the rock wall. He puts his ear to the hole and listens before telling the other miners near him, "I heard . . ." Soon the word circulates throughout the mine, causing the miners to stop work and go to the surface. Bimbo finds a telephone and calls Betty Boop and tells her, "I heard, oh yes, I heard. Yes, it wasn't told to me, I only heard. How I heard, yes, I heard. Betty didn't buzz it to me. I only heard." Betty hangs up the phone and then tells the others in the tavern, "You know what he said, that he said. But he didn't say where he got it. But if he said what he said, then I think I'm gonna die. Yes, I heard. It wasn't told to me, I only heard." She climbs into a dumbwaiter that lowers her all the way down the mineshaft, where she lands on Bimbo and knocks her dress off. An embarrassed Bimbo looks away while Betty puts her dress back on. Then he tells her, "Come with me." Betty follows him to the hole in the rock wall. Betty looks through the hole and sees a group of ghosts playing baseball, using a bomb for the ball. The fuse on the bomb is lit before it is batted through the hole and is caught by Betty. Betty runs with the bomb before tossing it back to Bimbo, who throws it back to the ghosts who are now chasing them through the mineshaft. Betty and Bimbo climb on an elevator that carries them back to the surface. As the elevator begins to rise, the ghost throws the bomb back. It lands on top of the elevator that is carrying Betty and Bimbo up to the surface. They arrive at the top where Bimbo throws the bomb back into the mine before he and Betty run away. The bomb explodes, blowing up the mine and throwing chunks of coal and ghosts high into the air. The coal chunks land in the cars of a train where Betty is the engineer, while the miners all cheer. The ghosts land in the graveyard as Bimbo laughs and the cartoon ends.

IT'S A LIVING (1958)

Company: Win Hoskins, Twentieth Century-Fox Pictures
Type: Cinemascope Color Cartoon
Characters: Dinky Duck, other ducks

Review: *Motion Picture Exhibitor*, 30 April 1958

Tired of being chased by the other animals, Dinky, the little black duckling, decides to become an announcer for television commercials. His real troubles really start then. Fair.

JOHN HENRY (1957)

Company: Directed by Henry Pierpoint, Holt, Rinehart and Winston, Inc.
Type: Offscreen narration and singing, narration by Chuck Morgan, vocal by Bob Scott
Characters: John Henry, Polly Anne, the captain, the salesman

Story: The story of John Henry is told through animation and off-screen narration and singing. The narrator says: "Not long after Mr. Lincoln and the grand army of the republic put a finish to slavery, many black brothers were still in chains. Some were doing the menial chores they always did, only instead of slaves, they were called servants. Some were literally prisoners in the chain gangs of the South. They worked very hard. As they worked they sang. They sang of joy and heaven, of work and pain. In these songs are the roots of their heritage. One of these songs concerned a mighty black man, John Henry. He grew up to be a giant of a boy, John Henry did. Got his first job unloading cotton off the river queens in New Orleans. Oh yes, John Henry would be still working on that levee except for two things. First he met a gal. Some say she was named Polly, some say Anne. Some say she was sweet and delicate, some say she was strong as he was. Fact is, her name was Polly Anne and she was powerful strong and powerful sweet and the prettiest girl John Henry or any other man ever saw. Rightly enough John Henry took her to be his wife. Second reason John Henry left the levee was that he heard about the big money a man could make working on the railroad. Railroading was a special kind of job where who didn't count—who you was or what or where. Where you came from, where you was goin'. Only thing that mattered on the railroad was ifin'—Ifin' you had the muscle, ifin' you had the heart, ifin' you had the soul to stand the summer sun fittin' those railroad tracks together. You see, at this time the land was being knit together by great grasping fingers of steel—railroad steel—reaching westward, reaching southward. Soon those tracks stretched coast to coast. You could board a train in Sacramento, California, and ride it through to Salt Lake City—through Cheyenne, through Omaha, clear on into Chicago and from there all points east. Now all that steel rail had to be fastened to a million wooden crossties by the means of steel spikes. The man who swang the spike hammer was called the 'steel-drivin' man.' Well, that's the job John Henry got—steel driver. Now it was the custom of the spike setter to gently tap those spikes in place for the steel driver to drive. But John Henry spit them spikes into place. Then, using two hammers instead of one, he would leave them other steel drivers far behind. Whooee! Look at him, marveled the captain (a black man). There's a natural man. And they (John Henry and his wife) tasted life and it was sweet. Of all the railroads being constructed, the most difficult to build was the C&O, which went through the mountains of West Virginia. The surveyors could find but one way around Big Bend Mountain. That was to blast a hole right on through it. The best of the steel drivers came from all over—the Santa Fe, the seaboard—and of course the C&O. Ain't like drivin' steel into crossties, John Henry, the captain said. You gotta hammer the drill deep into that rock. Then put a jumper drill in on top of it and hammer that. The deeper we get the dynamite, the quicker we blast a hole through this mountain. And we gotta do it quick. Some folks thought it was an earthquake, some never did know what it was, but the word got around on the down-home grapevine that John Henry out in West Virginia was hammering a hole through Big Bend Mountain. John Henry and Polly found them a little house and life was as sweet as the smell of honeysuckle. What's that miserable monster, a man asked. Gentleman, the man said, the name's McBee and I'm here to introduce you to a genuine miracle of the age—the Acme two-ton, rock-eatin', gravel-splittin', six-week guaranteed, steam-powered, water-cooled rock drill. And this here drill is certified to do the work of twenty men. What do I need your steam drill for, sir, the captain said. Why, I got me John Henry. Hah! exclaimed the gentleman. In each of my hands I hold a genuine green back fifty-dollar bill. This hundred says my drill can beat John Henry and any ten–eleven men doin' a full day's work. Do I have any takers? Well, no one spoke up 'ceptin' John Henry, and he said, No ten men, no eleven men, me—John Henry. I'll take that bet slicker, the captain said. You ready, John Henry? John Henry nodded. Are you ready sir, he asked the drill operator. All right, gentlemen, you may proceed. Full steam ahead, shouted the salesman. When it was fixed, the steam drill started to gain on John Henry—it was gaining rapidly. John Henry hammered with two hands. Now brother John that day, he wearied more than any man ever wearied, but he went right ahead on like he was the machine. One minute to go, John Henry put every bit of himself in each stroke of that hammer. The pain was agonizing. Twenty seconds, ten seconds. Time! the captain called. Which one of them is ahead? John Henry by four whole feet! The workers cheered. Oh John Henry, Polly moaned, John Henry. He died with the hammer in his hand, just like he always said. John Henry was the man who said it. A man ain't nothing' but a man. He lives his time, he passes on. Folks came as far as New Orleans to pay their respects. John Henry lived a natural man and nobody who knew or heard tell of John Henry would ever think of him as anything else," and the cartoon ends.

JOHN HENRY AND THE INKY-POO (1946)

Company: George Pal, Paramount Pictures
Type: Puppetoons
Characters: John Henry, Rex Ingram (narrator) Luvenia Nash Singers (choral music)

See fig. 46. Story: The film is narrated by Rex Ingram, and it opens with a musical background by the Luvenia Nash Singers. The opening scene shows a cloudy, warm night that lasted forty-eight hours from evening to morning. The scene shifts to the inside of a small cabin by the railroad tracks where a woman is lying in bed. With a loud clap of thunder and a gust of wind that blows the window curtains open, a giant of a man appears. He is four feet wide and twelve feet high. He goes over to the bed and introduces himself as John Henry, who was fit to do work the moment he was born. The woman says, "I's yo' ma." Next John Henry is seen sitting on a hill by his shack, looking at the railroad tracks. When a train appears, he knows that working on the railroad will be his calling. He goes to the town and gets a job as a pile driver for the C&O Railroad, saying, "I have muscles of steel." He was three weeks old. At first he is happy working as a steel-driving man. Then the railroad buys a steam engine called

the Inky-Poo that can do the work of ten men. All the workers are worried and ask John Henry what they can do. John Henry tells them to leave everything to him, for he has a plan to show up that engine with his two bare hands and his thirty-pound hammers. He will challenge that engine to a race, declaring that "ain't no machine made that can beat a man if the man's got a mind that he can beat that machine." With the chorus singing "Camptown Races" in the background, a crowd is seen gathering at Big Ben Tunnel, the starting point for the race. The Inky-Poo is sitting on one track and John Henry is on the other with his two hammers in his hands. As the race begins, his mother pleads with him to stop, saying, "You'll be killed." But John Henry brushes her aside and the pace of the race gets faster. It is close, but John Henry crosses the finish line first, to the jubilation of all. Suddenly a scream rings out, and the crowd is seen standing over a fallen John Henry. Somebody says that he is dead. The next scene shows John Henry's funeral. The minister says, "A man can do anything that a machine can do if only he has a mind to do it. He didn't die, he just stopped living in his mammy's shack by the river beside the railroad track. But he is living in the hearts of men for forever and a day." As these words are spoken, John Henry is seen riding on an engine pulling a long train.

Review: *Motion Picture Herald,* 7 December 1946

John Henry, legendary figure of American folklore, goes to work for the C. & O. Railroad, which, shortly thereafter, buys an automatic steel-driving engine called the Inky-Poo. John Henry matches his strength against the Inky-Poo, saying that any man can beat a machine because a man has a mind. John Henry wins but drops at the finish line, never to rise again. Rex Ingram is the narrator and the voice of John Henry. The Luvenia Nash Singers provide the choral musical background. (7 min)

Review: *Boxoffice,* 9 December 1946

Excellent musical background is furnished by the Luvenia Nash Choral group in this take off on an American folk story. John Henry is the Negro hero of the short who was "four feet wide and twelve feet long" when he was born. Rex Ingram is the narrator. In lyrical ballad style he tells how John Henry matched his strength and mind against a machine that threatened to put the railroad men out of work. He dies after the battle of man against machine, but his memory lives on.

Review: *Film Daily,* 14 August 1946

In a departure from the fables dreamed up for the familiar scarecrow and the little pickaninny (Jasper) character, usually featured in this series. George Pal has produced an engaging Puppetoon version of the legendary figure, John Henry, drawn from the annals of American Folklore, who pitted his brawn and brains against the steam engine known as the Inky Poo in order to dispel the fear of his railroad coworkers that machines would eventually put them out of work. The Technicolor, Rex Ingram's narration, and the folk song delivered by the Luvenia Nash Singers are all standouts.

Review: *Motion Picture Exhibitor,* **21 August 1946**

Seen is the legendary figure of John Henry and the folklore story of his battle against the mighty machine, the Inky-Poo. John Henry battles the machine because it threatens to throw his friends out of their jobs, since it can do the work of 10 men. He succeeds in defeating the machine but dies at the finish. Rex Ingram is the narrator and voice of John Henry, while the Luvenia Nash Singers provide the choral musical background. Excellent.

JUNGLE JIVE (1944)

Company: Shamus Culhane, Walter Lantz, Universal Pictures
Type: Swing Symphony
Characters: Black natives

Story: The opening scene shows a map of the Sandwich Islands. Then the scene shifts to a close-up of several islands with familiar names, such as Deviled Eggs, Ham on Rye, Hot Dog, and Hamburger where there is a sign that reads Hold the Onions. Next the island of Tunaville is shown, which is inhabited by natives. One is shown in the boomerang field practicing his skill with the native hunting weapon. He throws it, and it travels in a wide circle. But to his surprise, it returns and hits him on the back of the head. Next a native is seen sitting at the top of a tall tree. He pulls out a telescope and sees a large box getting cast onto the beach by a large wave. The box is labeled "Musical Instruments." The sight of this makes him very excited. He climbs down the tree and beats out a message on a large drum that is shaped like a typewriter. Back at the village all the natives receive the message and hurry toward the beach. They open the box but are puzzled by what they see, not knowing anything about playing music. After using the instrument for a variety of things a crab climbs on a piano and crawls over the keys. After a short time it begins to play boogie-woogie music. This attracts a fat native who appears to be a caricature of the famous black artist and composer Fats Waller. At first the crab repulses the native as he tries to play the piano. But later the native gains the upper hand and pushes the crab off the piano. He continues to play the hot boogie-woogie music without missing a beat. Now the other natives have formed a band and join in playing boogie-woogie. The trumpet player is too close to the ocean, and a wave washes over him. After the water subsides, a large alligator is seen playing the trumpet. Shapely native girls are doing a rhythmic dance, and everybody is having a good time. The last scene shows the crab getting the best of the native and taking over the piano again as the cartoon ends.

Review: *Motion Picture Herald,* **8 April 1944**

Here's some native jive by the Sandwich Islanders, who start a jam session when a whole orchestra of instruments is washed ashore. They have little trouble mastering the horns, although their technique is a bit unusual, but their rhythm brings out the repressed ambitions of a sand crab, who crawls onto the piano keyboard. (7 min)

Review: *Boxoffice,* **29 April 1944**

When a crate of musical instruments—mostly percussion and brass—washes ashore on the Sandwich Islands, the hepcat natives gather round for an impromptu jam session which all but tears up the joint. The music is the thing here, with particular accent on the boogie woogie style. Exhibitors would do well to capitalize on this angle.

Review: *Motion Picture Herald,* **13 October 1951**

A visit to the Sandwich Islands reveals that they have a remarkable resemblance to the everyday delicatessen sandwiches ham on rye, tuna, hamburger, etc. Boogie Woogie is the native musical expression. There is jumpin' jive, as the locals and the native animals cut loose in accepted "real gone" fashion. (7 min)

Review: *Exhibitor Servisection,* **20 June 1951**

A gang of natives on a Pacific isle spot a crate of musical instruments floating in the ocean, and they gradually learn how to play. Bob Zurke does the off-screen piano playing, and the other natives join in until the entire island is jumping to the boogie woogie of the band. Good.

Review: *Besa Shorts Shorts,* **8 May 1944**

In color and located in the Sandwich Isles, where each island is designated as Ham on Rye and such, this story concerns a cargo of musical instruments adrift with a final landing on the island shore. The natives, both animal and mineral, take over to display their talents at jive. A gay lobster gets in the piano groove while the fuzzies wuzzies, guys and gals, do a swingeroo.

Review: *Boxoffice,* **23 June 1951**

A crate of musical instruments is washed on the shore of the Sandwich Islands and gives the natives a chance to improvise a band and give with some fast and furious music. Jam session fans should go for the hep piano playing by a crab and a huge native.

KO-KO SEES SPOOKS (1925)

Company: Dave Fleischer, Max Fleischer, Red Seal Pictures
Type: Out of the inkwell cartoon; combined live action and animation
Characters: Ko-Ko the Clown, black janitor (live action)

Review: *Motion Picture World,* **13 June 1925**

There is a clever touch at the beginning of this Out of the Inkwell Cartoon, when Mac Fleischer draws a number of "13s" and they dissolve into the little clown Ko-Ko. Fleischer then leaves Ko-Ko in charge of the negro porter and the clown proceeds to investigate a haunted house. He and his dog have some amusing experiences with the spooks. The humor in this one does not appear to be as snappy or spontaneous as usual, but it should please the "Inkwell" fans. (one reel)

Review: *Film Daily,* 7 June 1925

Ko-Ko, Max Fleischer's Inkwell Clown, has his share of thrills this time. The artist draws him from the numerals thirteen and the calendar shows the date as Friday the 13th. Then the colored porter who cleans the office draws a haunted house for the clown's background and throws his hat into it. In vain Ko-Ko tries to rescue his hat without going into the house, but in the end he has to enter it. Numerous incidents then occur with the ghosts chasing the clown and his dog, but he is finally rescued.

KO-KO'S HAREM SCAREM (1929)

Company: Dave Fleischer, Max Fleischer Inkwell Studio; distributed by Paramount Pictures
Type: Combination live action and animation
Characters: Ko-Ko the Clown, Fitz, black palace slaves

Story: Cartoon opens on live action as an Arabian sheik sits on his throne. He is agitated as he anxiously awaits a visitor. He picks his fingernails with his long knife and wonders to himself, "It's about time that boob was here with that treasure." Finally the man arrives carrying a chest under his arm. He tells the sheik, "I searched all over the world and finally found it in America." The sheik reaches out to take the box, but the man pulls it back, telling him to be patient. Then he sets the box on the floor and bows down before the sheik. Finally he places the box on a table and leaves. The sheik smiles, opens the lid of the box, and pulls out a bottle of black ink. He removes the cap from the bottle and sets it on the table. Ko-Ko the clown and his dog Fitz stick their heads out of the bottle. The sheik smiles, pulls them both out of the bottle, and lays them on flat on the bottle before using his knife to cut their heads off. Their heads fall to the floor, and the sheik smiles and leaves the room. The heads of Ko-Ko and the dog climb back onto the table and reattach themselves to their respective bodies. When Ko-Ko and the dog see a picture of an Arabian scene hanging on the wall, they climb up the wall and jump into the picture. The background changes to animation. They find themselves in front of a fakir who is charming a snake by playing music on a flute. The snake rises out of the vase and then disappears into it before the vase flies away. The fakir pulls out a cloth that he places on the floor before saying some magic words. When he takes up the cloth, Ko-Ko and the dog see that a mug of cold beer has materialized. Ko-Ko tries to grab the beer, but the fakir makes it disappear. Next the fakir beckons the dog to walk over to him, and then makes him disappear. Ko-Ko demands to know where his dog is, and the fakir points to the sultan's palace. Ko-Ko tries to enter the palace through the front door but finds that it is locked. Then the door changes into a huge mouth that sucks Ko-Ko inside the palace. Ko-Ko does not see anybody inside, but when he looks through a keyhole he sees a beautiful belly dancer. He does not notice as a black slave with thick white lips, who is carrying a large straight razor in his hand, walks up behind him. The slave yells at Ko-Ko, who is terrified when he turns around and sees him. Ko-Ko tries to run away, but the black man chases

him. Realizing he cannot get away, Ko-Ko stops and pulls out a pair of dice from his pocket. He holds them in front of the black man, who immediately stops in his tracks. The black slave's eyes bulge out of his head. He smiles and drops his razor. The black man kneels on the floor and bows to Ko-Ko, who stands above him as his new master. The black man rises and pulls the tassel from his cap and uses it to brush off Ko-Ko's clothes. Ko-Ko kicks him in the face, but the black man smiles as he shines Ko-Ko's shoes. As Ko-Ko leaves, the black man again bows down. Ko-Ko then enters another room where he sees a shoeshine stand. A black slave with a razor stuck in his belt shines the shoes of an Arab who is reading a newspaper. As he is about to finish the job, the black man finds that he has run out of black shoe polish. So he begins to sweat black sweat, which he uses to finish polishing the shoes. Next Ko-Ko peeps through the curtains to look in the sultan's harem. He sees his dog seated on the floor in front of the sultan. In order to rescue his dog, Ko-Ko disguises himself as a veiled dancing girl before entering the room and dancing before the sultan. The sultan is so pleased that he kisses Ko-Ko. The sultan laughs, but the kiss makes Ko-Ko so angry that he pulls off his costume. Then he and the dog run away. The sultan, his holy man, and one of his black slaves carrying a razor chase after Ko-Ko and the dog. They escape the cartoon scene by jumping out of the picture on the wall and climbing back into the ink bottle. Ko-Ko and the dog stick their heads out of the bottle and thumb their noses at the sultan and the black slave, who are still in the picture on the wall as the cartoon ends.

THE LATEST IN UNDERWEAR (1919)

Company: Frederick Burr Opper, J. D. Tippett
Type: Pussyfoot Cartoon Comedy
Characters: Hop Lee, Happy Holligan, black woman

Review: *Bioscope* (London), 27 November 1919

Hop Lee, the keeper of a laundry, is greatly perturbed at the disappearance of clothes off the line, especially as the big black woman tells him if he loses any of her underwear she will wring his neck. Hop advertises for a detective and Happy Holligan turns up to fill the job. Hooligan sits and watches the lingerie put out to dry, but is overcome by sleep. The goat, who is the criminal, seizes the opportunity to devour a pair of stockings. Hooligan wakes up, and decides that the birds are the thieves. He hides inside a pair of combinations, and gets bitten by the goat. Hooligan flies to the laundry, and the black woman turns up, and there is a great scrimmage. Extremely laughable and well-drawn pictures of an amusing subject. (459 ft.)

LAZY BONES (1934)

Company: Dave Fleischer, Max Fleischer; released by Paramount Pictures
Type: Screen Song, combined live action and animation

Characters: Borran Minevitch's Harmonica Rascals (Live action), Lazy Bones are horse

See fig. 47. Story: Lazy Bones is a very lazy horse that nevertheless manages to win a big race. The live action segment involves the Harmonica Rascals, who play the title song. The only black member of the group sings a verse solo and also plays the harmonica. The group is joined by Reese and Dunne, who sing a duet. The cartoon ends with a scene of Lazy Bones enjoying a nap in bed.

Review: *Boxoffice,* 12 January 1935

An entertaining short of the Screen Song series featuring the title song. Cartoon and reality are combined and the bouncing ball is featured when the words to the song appear. The reel opens with a horse, Lazybones, winning a race when he sees that a bed awaits him at the finish. The last part shows antics of Borran Minnevitch and his Harmonica Rascals in their rendition of the song. (7 min)

LET'S SING TOGETHER (1937)

Company: Arthur Price Productions
Type: Screen Song
Characters: Black boys, Mammy, doctor

Story: The cartoon is a Screen Song in four parts, including "Oh Susanna," "Carry On," "Pack Up Your Troubles," and "Shortnin' Bread." In the latter the animated characters tell the story of a mammy cooking shortnin' bread for four boys, one of whom steals the bread and is sent to jail. The song describes the action: "Put on de skillet, put on de lid. Mammy's goin' to make a little shortnin' bread. Mammy's goin' to make shortnin', shortnin', Mammy's gonna make shortnin' bread. Mammy's gonna make a little coffee too. Mammy's little baby loves shortnin', shortnin', Mammy's little baby loves shortnin' bread. Three little darkies lying in bed. Two was sick and the other 'most dead. Sent fo' de' doctor, and de doctor said, feed dose darkies some shortnin' bread. Ah slipped off de lid, filled my pockets full of shortnin' bread. Stole de skillet, stole de lid, stole dat gal makin' shortin' bread. Dey caught me with de lid, caught me with de gal makin' shortnin' bread. Paid six dollars fo' de skillet, paid six dollars fo' de lid, spent six months in jail eatin' shortnin' bread. Mammy's little baby loves shortnin', shortnin', Mammy's little baby loves shortnin' bread."

THE LION TAMER (1934)

Company: George Stallings, Van Beuren; distributed by RKO-Radio Pictures
Type: Characters based on the Amos 'n' Andy radio and television shows
Characters: Amos, Andy, Kingfish, Lightnin', Brother Crawford

See fig. 48. Story: Amos and Andy are riding in their taxi cab when they stop to pick up the Kingfish. Kingfish tells them to go to the carnival. He wants Brother Andy to tame a lion. Amos stops the cab and tells Andy that they should go back to the taxi office. But then Kingfish tells them that the lion is not real. It will be Brother Crawford and Lightnin' dressed in a lion costume. When they arrive at the carnival, Kingfish tells Amos and Andy to go inside the tent while he telephones Madame Queen to come over and see Andy tame the lion. In the tent the boys see a lion tied to a stake and wonder if it is the fake lion. The animal roars so loud that it scares the boys out of the tent. Kingfish tells them that they went in the wrong tent, and Amos says that it was the wrong lion also. Meanwhile Brother Crawford and Lightnin' flip a coin to see who will occupy the tail end of the lion costume. Lightnin' loses. Andy puts on his lion tamer's outfit and tells Amos that there's no lion that he can't tame. The fake lion enters the cage through a trapdoor, and the cage is pushed to the main tent where Andy is being introduced to the audience by Kingfish. Kingfish tells them that they will see the the wildest lion in captivity. Andy gets wild applause and enters the cage. He cracks his whip, and the boys inside the costume complain that the whip hurts. Andy puts the fake lion through its paces. Meanwhile the real lion has broken free of his chain and comes to the tent where Andy is performing. The lion opens the trapdoor of the cage, and Crawford and Lightnin's costume falls out. They take one look at the real lion and make a hasty getaway. Andy is inquiring about Madam Queen when the real lion crawls into the cage. Andy continues his act and doesn't hear Amos warn him of the danger. Andy tells the audience that he will now do the trick that he has been saving for the end of the performance. He will put his head into the lion's mouth. Andy pulls apart the lion's jaws, looks into his mouth, and calls out for Brother Crawford and Lightnin' before he realizes that he is in the cage with the real lion. Andy calls out for Amos to help him while the lion chases him around and around the cage. Amos opens the door of the cage and Andy escapes. The lion remains in the cage wearing Andy's hat and smoking Andy's big black cigar as the cartoon ends.

Review: *Selected Motion Pictures,* 1 April 1934

Featuring Amos 'n' Andy. A clever and funny animated cartoon of the famous characters, picturing a mix-up with the lions. The dialogue is synchronized with the voices of the comedians.

LITTLE BLUE BLACKBIRD (1938)

Company: Patrick Lenihan, Walter Lantz, Universal Pictures
Characters: Blackbird family

Review: *Motion Picture Herald,* 30 September 1938

Mama blackbird is a bit upset when she discovers in her latest batch of fledglings a little newcomer who is strangely off color. When a hawk seizes the brother blackbird, the pariah, compensating for his lack of flying equipment by a clever utilization of feathers from a duster, flies to the rescue of his bird brethren. (7 min)

Review: *Selected Motion Pictures*, 1 January 1939

Lantz Car-Tune. A brash blackbird outwits a hawk who has kidnapped his little brother. Family.

Review: *National Exhibitor*, 7 December 1938

Mother blackbird doesn't like the idea of hatching eggs which return three little birds, two black, and one blue. But the blue one is the black sheep, he will not fly or play. However, when his brothers are kidnapped by a hawk it is the blue blackbird that makes the rescue. Fair.

LITTLE NEMO IN SLUMBERLAND (1910)

Company: Winsor McCay, Vitagraph Company
Type: Combination of live action and animation
Characters: Winsor McCay (as himself), Impy the cannibal, Flip the dwarf, Little Nemo, the princess

See fig. 49. Opening credits: Winsor McCay, the famous cartoonist of the *New York Herald*, and his moving comics. The first artist to attempt drawing pictures that will move. Produced by the Vitagraph Company of America.

Story: The cartoon opens as McCay, playing cards with a group of friends at the club, bets them that he can create an animated cartoon from four thousand drawings of the characters appearing in his newspaper comic strip, "Little Nemo in Slumberland." The bet is on, and McCay produces his drawings at the Vitagraph Movie Studio, where they are photographed. Rolls of paper and kegs of black ink are shipped to the studio, where McCay is seen working. Finally he completes the work and exhibits the cartoon to his friends. The first character to come to life on the screen is Impy, the black cannibal. He is followed by Flip, the dwarf, and then by Little Nemo and the princess. All the characters change shape, stretching like rubber, before the cartoon ends. There is no story associated with the cartoon sequence.

Review: *Moving Picture World*, 6 April 1911

At the club, Winsor McCay with a party of boon friends is engaged in a friendly game, the subject of moving pictures is broached, the game is forgotten and the discussion becomes quite animated and interesting. One of the fellows asks Winsor why he has never been able to make moving pictures; he replies that he feels positive he can produce drawings that will move, and wagers that he will make four thousand pen drawings inside of one month as actively and as lifelike as anything ever reproduced by the camera, and surpass in their performance anything ever seen. His companions laugh at him and tell him he is getting foolish in his "noodle."

One month later, he has the four thousand drawings ready for the Vitagraph Company's camera and invites his club friends to come see him make good. They arrive and he shows them drawings of some of the leading characters of his "Little Nemo" series. The camera man turns the crank of the machine, and what these celebrated little cartoon characters do, would be more difficult to tell than what they do not do. The incredulous friends of McCay are surprised and puzzled.

Review: *Moving Picture World*, 22 April 1911

Here Little Nemo and his friends are made to do amusing and surprising stunts. Indeed, after watching these pictures for a while one is almost ready to believe that he has been transported to Dreamland along with Nemo and sharing his remarkable adventures. The film presents something like 4,000 drawings which "Winsor McCay" draws on a bet that he could make moving pictures, and it is an admirable piece of work. It should be popular everywhere. It is one of those films which have a natural advertising heritage in the great and wide popularity of its subject—Little Nemo is known everywhere.

THE LITTLE RED HEN (1934)

Company: Pat Powers, Ub Iwerks, Celebrity Pictures
Type: Comi-Color
Characters: Little red hen, three white chicks, black chick

Story: The cartoon opens as the Little Red Hen walks along looking for food. Walking behind her in single file are her three white chicks, and bringing up the rear is her black chick. She pulls a worm out of a hole and tosses it to her chicks to share but, it is swallowed by the black chick. Next she finds a pile of wheat on the ground next to a huge silo. Her hungry chicks want to eat the grain, but she tells them, "We'll sow this wheat." Then she hurries off to find help. She finds a pig sitting near a fence on which a small gray mouse and a white duck are standing. The hen asks, "Who will help me sow my wheat?" The pig laughs and says, "Not I—I'm much too fat." The duck says, "Not I—my feet are flat." The mouse says, "Go ask the cat." The hen turns in a huff, saying, "I'll sow it all myself." She finds an eggbeater and uses it to plow the ground while the three white chicks walk behind and plant the wheat. The black chick wants to play so he pulls out a blowgun, tosses some kernels of wheat into his mouth, and then blows them out, hitting his white brothers in front of him. The mother chick gathers the white chicks in her arms. Frowning, she shakes her finger at the black chick and tell him, "Now none of that." She then asks the pig, duck, and mouse, "Who will help me grow my wheat?" Again they refuse. So she tells them, "I'll grow it myself." She uses an empty hair oil bottle to water the wheat, which instantly grows up in tall stalks. Next she uses barber clippers to cut the wheat and then grinds it into flour using a coffee grinder. The three white chicks help her work while the black chick has fun dancing on top of the grinder. The hen then asks the three lazy animals, "Who will help me bake my bread?" Again they refuse her request. The hen then kneads the dough. Her little white chicks help her by rolling it flat with a huge rolling pin. The hen stuffs the dough into an empty mailbox and places it in a hot oven. Soon mother hen and her chicks are holding each other's hands while they dance in a circle around their large loaf of freshly baked bread. The hen picks up the bread and carries it to the others and asks them, "Who will help me eat my bread?" The pig, mouse, and duck answer, "I will." But the hen and her chicks run into the henhouse, slamming the door behind them. The other three try to follow them into the house, but they run into the closed door and fall to the ground. The hen then comes out of the house and says to the pig, the duck, and the mouse respectively, "Not you, you're much too fat." "Not you, your feet are flat." "Not you, I'll ask the cat." She then tells them, "I'll eat it myself" and then walks back into the house and slams the door. The little black chick crawls out through a hole in the wall carrying a Do Not Disturb sign. He nails the sign to the front door and then crawls back inside the house. He then sticks out his head and sticks out his tongue at the other three as the cartoon ends.

MAID IN CHINA (1938)

Company: Connie Rasinski, Paul Terry, Twentieth Century-Fox
Type: Terrytoons
Characters: Aladdin, black genie

Review: *Motion Picture Exhibitor,* 1 May 1938

Aladdin, with his magic lamp and a drawing of a coal-black genie, rescues the fair maiden from the fearsome villain. It's fast, and at times quite funny. Good.

MAKING STARS (1935)

Company: Dave Fleischer, Max Fleischer, Paramount Pictures
Characters: Betty Boop, white babies, oriental baby, three black babies, Mammy and her baby

Story: The cartoon opens in the city outside a theater where the marquee reads "Betty Boop in Making Stars." A subway train rolls up the stairs from the underground tunnel and stops on the sidewalk in front of the theater where the theater goers get out and enter. Inside the theater Betty Boop, dressed in formal attire and a top hat, dances on stage and sings, "Strike up the band. Get ready for something grand, a wonderful treat. You're going to meet the stars of the future. Wait 'til you see the ones who will make history. If you think that Jolson's great, Cantor and Jessel too, Mammy. Well folks, see right here today my stars outshine those to you. You'll see how they dance and sing—My stars of the future." She finishes and the audience applauds. Betty walks to a piano and announces the first two baby acts, a drummer and a Russian dancer. When they finish, Betty announces, "The next act is called "The Colorful Three," and the things they do—The Colorful Three." Three black babies

enter with their backs to the audience tap dancing. They are barefoot and have braided hair that sticks out from their heads. They turn around to reveal smiling faces with thick white lips. Each wears a white diaper that is pinned with the same huge safety pin, so the babies are tied together. They try to pull themselves apart but can't, so they sing "hi-dee-ho, hi-dee-hi" with tears rolling down their cheeks. Finally the stage manager reaches a large slice of watermelon out from the wings. The three babies' crying turns to smiling as they follow the watermelon as it is pulled off stage. The audience applauds them, including their mammy, a fat black woman who is in the audience. She is holding a small baby on her lap. The baby is smiling and licking her lips but then begins to cry and shout "hi-dee-ho." Her mammy tries to shush her, but the baby won't stop. Finally mammy reaches into a paper sack, pulls out a large slice of watermelon, and gives it to her baby. The baby immediately stops crying and smiles with one tooth showing. Then she eats the watermelon and spits the melon seeds out of her mouth like machine-gun bullets. They hit the bald head of a white man sitting in the row in front of them. Meanwhile Betty introduces two more baby acts, a juggler-marksman, and quintuplets before she ends the show by bringing all of the babies back on stage. They all lie in one huge crib and drink milk from a common large bottle using individual rubber tubes as the cartoon ends.

MIGHTY MOUSE IN CRYING WOLF (1947)

Company: Connie Rasinski, Paul Terry, Twentieth Century-Fox Pictures
Type: Terrytoons
Characters: Mighty Mouse, black sheep

Review: *Film Daily,* 16 April 1947

One black sheep can cause a lot of trouble to a slow-thinking sheep dog tending his flock, especially when he cries "Wolf, wolf." A scolding doesn't help, and the black one continues his mischief till he comes face to face with a real wolf. Thinking it another false alarm, the dog does nothing, the black sheep finds himself on a chopping block, and in a last minute effort Mighty Mouse is summoned. M. M. turns the table and saves the day.

Review: *Motion Picture Herald,* 22 March 1947

A Black sheep tired of just grazing contentedly with the other sheep, cries "wolf! Wolf!" He does this once too often, but through a prodigious feat of Mighty Mouse, this sheep is rescued from the wolf.

MINNIE THE MOOCHER (1932)

Company: Dave Fleischer, Max Fleischer, Paramount Pictures
Type: Talkartoons, combined live action and animation
Characters: Betty Boop, Bimbo, Cab Calloway and his band (live action)

Story: The opening shows the one and only Cab Calloway and his band performing one of his many hits of the period, "Minnie the Moocher." As the band plays, the scene changes to Betty Boop sitting at the dinner table. She is very unhappy because her parents are scolding her. She cannot finish her meal and gets up and sits on the stairs and cries before deciding to teach her parents a lesson by running away from home. She hurries upstairs to her room and packs and leaves a good-bye note pinned to the pillow on her bed. She telephones her boyfriend Bimbo and tells him that she is leaving. He tells her that he will go with her. They are seen leaving the city, and as night falls they are in the forest. They become frightened and take refuge in a large, dark cave. Suddenly a light goes on, revealing a large walrus. In Cab Calloway's voice he starts to sing "Minnie the Moocher" and mimics Calloway's dance routine. Betty and Bimbo try to escape but find the way blocked by dancing skeletons that join in on the hi-dee-ho chorus of the song. The skeletons dissolve into ghosts who don't miss a beat in their singing. Even a mother cat and her four kittens join in the singing chorus. Finally the walrus dissolves into a huge open mouth. This sight scares Betty and Bimbo out of the cave. They are chased by flying witches and goblins as they flee back home with Calloway and band playing a hot rendition of "Tiger Rag." When they arrive home, Bimbo dives into his doghouse and Betty rushes to her room where she jumps into bed and pulls the covers over her head. At the end Betty's hand is seen tearing up her old note and replacing it with one that reads, "Home Sweet Home."

Review: *Film Daily,* 10 January 1932

This Max Fleischer musical cartoon is one of the best turned out so far with the cute pen-and-ink star, Betty Boop, who seems to be getting more sexy and alluring each time, and her boyfriend, Bimbo. The musical portion is supplied by Cab Calloway and his orchestra, and what these boys can't do to the "Minnie the Moocher" number isn't worth mentioning. Cab and his boys are shown only for a brief moment at the opening. Then a cartoon character, a big walrus with serpentine hips, performs the gyrations to the tune of the "Minnie" song. The effect is short of a knockout, especially to those who are familiar with Cab's stuff on the radio or stage or night club. Betty Boop's part in the action concerns her running away from home because of her bad parents. With Bimbo she goes into a cave, where spooky figures and erie noise give them such a scare that they beat it back home.

MONKEY DOODLE (193?)

Company: Krazy Toons
Characters: Monkeys, black natives

Story: The cartoon opens in a jungle populated by weird-looking animals, black monkeys, and black natives. Except for their tails, the monkeys are indistinguishable from the natives. The cartoon includes a musical sequence that opens with a black boy dressed in a baby diaper playing a violin. He is standing close to

a black man wearing a derby hat and minstrel costume. The man, who is smoking a pipe, is resting on a log and listening to the boy play. Before long a monkey jazz band joins in the music, and a black native does a sexy shimmy dance with a brown-skinned native girl. She wears a very short skirt similar to the costumes worn by Cotton Club chorus girls. Soon two elephants and all of the jungle animals are dancing to the hot music. When the music ends, a monkey dressed in a frock coat asks the boy, "Where did you get that talent?" The boy answers, "The old man" and points to him. The monkey character climbs onto the back of his huge hound dog, and they spend the rest of the cartoon being chased by a Bengal tiger. They escape as the cartoon ends.

MORE KITTENS (1937)

Company: Wilford Jackson, Walt Disney, United Artists
Type: Silly Symphony
Characters: Three kittens—Blackie, Whitie, Calico, black mammy

Review: *Boxoffice, 30 January 1937*

Continuing the amazing adventures of the three little kittens who were introduced to picture fans in an earlier Silly Symphony, the cartoon is again quaintly laughable throughout although lacking somewhat in the originality and sparkle of the other recent Disney subjects. A great furry, slow moving St. Bernard proves a haven of refuge for the tiny creatures when they are chased out of the house by an indignant black mammy. From the protection of his long fur they gaily race along, encountering such objects as a big stone which turns out to be a turtle, a meddlesome bee and a pesky blue bird, none of which can quell their natural playfulness. But when real trouble comes their way, they run back to their dog pal, knowing they can rely on him for sympathy. Worthy of a spot on any bill.

Review: *Motion Picture Herald,* 9 January 1937

The antics of three playful kittens imbued with infectious gaiety serve to number this as one of the best of Walt Disney's animated Silly Symphonies. In the characteristic feline manner, scaled down to fit their size, the three kittens cavort from prank to prank, much to the conservation of a Negro servant. An indigent member of the canine family, though much abused by the kittens, in the time of stress becomes their benefactor.

Review: *Selected Motion Pictures,* 1 January 1937

Three little kittens do more than lose their mittens, for they scamper about and send everyone, including the dog, into panic. Family.

Review: *National Exhibitor,* 5 January 1937

Three cute kittens frolic amidst the huge jowls of a lazy St. Bernard. They annoy him, and a bluebird, and a fly, but when they're chased by an irritable housemaid, the great dog shelters them. The antics are amusing, especially when a bluebird torments the kittens. Good.

MOTHER GOOSE GOES HOLLYWOOD (1938)

Company: Wilford Jackson, Walt Disney, released by RKO-Radio Pictures
Type: Silly Symphony, Nominated for Academy Award
Characters: Katherine Hepburn caricature as Mother Goose and caricatures of many other Hollywood stars and black entertainers, including Cab Calloway and his band, Fats Waller, Stephin Fetchit

Story: The cartoon opens with a disclaimer: "Any resemblance of characters herein portrayed to persons living or dead, is purely coincidental." Katherine Hepburn, as Little Bo Peep, appears on the scene, looks around and says, "I'm Little Bo Peep. I've lost my sheep, really I have. I can't find them anywhere, really I can't." A series of scenes feature caricatures of Hollywood stars appearing as Mother Goose nursery rhyme characters, including Hugh Herbert (Old King Cole), Donald Duck as himself, the Marx Brothers (king's fiddlers), Charles Laughton (Captain Bligh), W. C. Fields (Humpty Dumpty), and Charlie McCarthy. The final scenes begin with Oliver Hardy baking a stack of blackberry pies while Stan Laurel fishes. Oliver offers Stan a pie, but he declines and pulls one out from the middle of the stack instead. When the stack does not fall over, Oliver tries the same trick. This time the stack falls over, crushing most of the pies. Oliver is so angry that he throws a pie at Stan. He ducks out of the way and the pie strikes Little Bo Peep, turning her face black. Little Bo Peep in blackface says, "Is any of you all folks seen any of my sheep anywhere?" Next Little Jack Horner (Eddie Cantor) steps from behind a huge blackbird pie, dances around, and sings, "Sing a song of six pence, a pocket full of rye. Four and twenty blackbirds backed in a pie." Cab Calloway's head (in blackface) pops out of the pie and sings "hidee-ho" followed by eight more heads of his band who sing "hidee-pie." Cantor then sings, "When the pie was opened, the birds began to sing." The pie opens up and Calloway and his band sing "sheeps in de meadow, cows in de corn" as Cab looks over and sees Little Boy Blue sleeping near a haystack while holding his horn. Cab says, "Come on Boy, play dat horn" as the band members clap their hands. Fats Waller's head sticks out of the pie, looks around, and says, "Where is dat boy?" Stephin Fetchit scratches his head and slowly says, "What boy?" Fats says, "You, Boy Blue! Come on, Boy Blue, blow dat horn." Boy Blue finally wakes up and plays hot jazz on his horn as the door of Old Mother Hubbard's house opens and out come all the characters who join in the music and dance. Meanwhile Fats Waller is playing his piano when two of the Marx Brothers show up and take over the keyboard. Fats pushes them away, saying, "Get away from here." He is puzzled as the piano continues to play. He asks, "What's d'matter with dat piano" as he opens the lid and looks inside to see the third Marx Brother playing the piano wires. Fats says, "The man is crazy." Meanwhile Fred Astair tap dances as Stephin Fetchit shuffles by

scratching his head and saying, "Git along . . . Little doggie." Meanwhile Cab Calloway sings and dances, circled by his band. Everybody is happy and Charles Laughton says, "It's mutiny, but I love it." Joe E. Brown sings a scat song and opens his huge mouth wide. The camera pans the inside of his mouth and finds Little Bo Peep in it. She says, "I lost my sheep. I can't find them anywhere, really I can't" as the cartoon ends.

Review: *Variety*, 2 July 1938

Mother Goose Goes Hollywood. Also haywire. She thinks she is Leo the Lion and opens the picture with that Metro college yell, three leonine rahs.

So in angles Katharine Hepburn Bo Peep with a Back Bay accent. She has lost her sheep on account of she looks hungry enough to eat a flock of mutton. While she is paging her sheep, up pops Hugh Herbert who looks more like a roast beef. He is dressed up like Old King Cole and calls for fiddlers three but all he gets is the Ritz Brothers.

Joe Penner asks if anybody wants to buy a Donald Duck, and Charles Laughton has a mutiny in a washtub while Manuel Tracy fishes the Bartholomew moppet out of the ocean just in time to escape Katherine Bo Peep who thinks he is a codfish.

That makes Garbo want to go home but she don't because her boy friend is Eddie Robinson, instead of Stokowski. So Little Jack Cantor sits in a corner eating his Christmas borsht and Little Boy Berry blows his horn while Mae West invites Clark Gable to come up and see her sometime.

Meanwhile, Humpty Dumpty Fields puts on a one-round duel with Charlie McCarthy and is all broken up when he falls off the wall. Joe E. Brown and Martha Raye give realistic impersonations of the Mammoth Cave and the Grand Canyon, respectively, and Simple Simon Laurel and Hardy the Pieman do a pastry juggling act. Three Marx Brothers, Fred Astaire and Stephin Fetchit are adequate in the supporting cast and Little Bo Hepburn is still hunting her mutton at the finish, looking hungrier then ever.

This is a preview of *Mother Goose Goes Hollywood* at the Pantages last night, and if you think the previewer is crazy, go and look at it yourself. A Walt Disney production for RKO-Radio release. Running time not long enough.

Review: *The Family Circle*, 18 November 1938

A sharp—at times painfully sharp—retelling of Mother Goose in terms of Hollywood personalities. The running gag is Katharine Hepburn as Little Bo Peep, always popping up in other tales, still looking for her lost sheep. It's a gem of a short.

MOUSE TRAPPED (1950)

Company: Alex Lovey, Walter Lantz; Universal Pictures
Characters: Hickory the boy mouse, Dickory the girl mouse, Doc the black cat

Story: The cartoon opens with Hickory and Dickory playing with a hula hoop. The radio announcer says, "We interrupt this program to bring you a special bulletin. It is Friday the thirteenth, and the police department asks your cooperation in removing all black cats from the streets." Hickory tells Dickory, "Gee whittigers, I wouldn't want to be a black cat." Meanwhile, Doc, a black cat wearing a top hat, is selecting his evening meal from the contents of a trash can. Not satisfied with the food selection, he decides to cross the street to try another can and is surrounded by police cars. He manages to escape by climbing up a telephone pole and looks down as all the police cars crash into each other. Doc says, "Sunday drivers—I'll report this to the police." He climbs down to the ground, looks around, and says, "When you need an officer, he's never around." Then he is surrounded again and one cop shouts, "Let him have it." They all shoot at Doc as he runs away. Hickory and Dickory, seeing what has happened, say, "Look at Doc. He's in trouble. We had better save him." They run over to Doc and tell him, "Hey Doc, the police are after all black cats because it's Friday the thirteenth. Doc trembles with fear as they tell him, "But you are our friend and we'll save you. Hide in here." They point to the house of Cecil the dog. Doc runs inside and then sticks his head out of the door and says, "Love those mice . . ." As a snapping sound is heard, Doc emerges from the house with his rear end clutched in the jaws of Cecil, a large bulldog. He yells and leaps out of the dog's jaws. Cecil tells him, "Stay out of my house." Hickory and Dickory, holding open the door of a storm cellar, call to Doc to hide in there. Doc runs over to the cellar and is about to jump in as the two mice slam the door closed and Doc crashes into it. Hickory and Dickory next appear near a hole in the fence and call, "Hey Doc, this way and step on it." Doc runs through the fence into a waiting patrol car where he finds himself seated between two large policemen. Doc escapes and the two mice direct him into the house. But when Doc runs inside, he finds himself in a dishwashing machine. The mice close the door and turn on the machine. Doc is put through the washing cycle before the door opens and he is thrown out. Over in the corner the two mice are laughing and Doc says to himself, "Methinks I have been getting the runaround." Hickory and Dickory call to him to follow them as they disappear around a corner in the house. Doc decides to take revenge and attaches a string to one end of a large mousetrap that he throws in the direction the mice have gone. He hears the trap snap shut and pulls it back, but he has caught Cecil. Cecil points to the trap and asks Doc, "Does this thing belong to you?" Doc smiles and nods yes and the dog stuffs the trap into Doc's mouth. The trap springs shut, clamping Doc's lips together. Doc is in so much pain that he leaps up crashing through the ceiling of the house, and falls crashing through the roof of the police car where he lands in the backseat with two large policemen, one on either side of him. Doc again escapes and tries to enter the house again but is stopped by Cecil. Next he tries to get rid of Cecil by tying one end of a rope to a cannonball and the other end to Cecil's leg. Doc fires the cannon before he realizes that Cecil has attached the rope to Doc's leg. Doc is pulled through the roof of a shed that he soon discovers is

surrounded by police cars and army tanks. They demand that he come out in ten seconds and begin to count. Finding a can of whitewash, Doc uses it to paint himself white. Then he comes out of the house and says, "Good evening, gentlemen. Looking for someone?" The cops are puzzled, but Hickory and Dickory turn on the lawn sprinkler and rinse the whitewash from Doc. The police capture him and, with their guns drawn, they march him to the police van. Doc goes in the back and comes out the front. The policemen go in the back and Doc says, "Take him away, Clancy." The van drives off and Doc stands on the sidewalk. Smiling, Doc says, "Friday the thirteenth—what nonsense." He walks under a ladder just before a large safe falls on him as the cartoon ends.

Review: *Motion Picture Exhibitor,* 3 February 1960

Doc, the black cat, is saved from the cops by two mice, Hickory and Dickory. They want to have some fun so they introduce Cecil, a huge bulldog, and the dog really gets rid of Doc, the mouse-eater, by sending him into a police stake-out. Fair. (6 min)

MRS. LADYBUG (1940)

Company: Rudolph Ising, M-G-M
Characters: Mrs. Ladybug and children, black spider

See fig. 50. Story: Four small birds sing the opening to the film and introduce a bug family. Mrs. Ladybug has a house full of baby bugs. She is seen spending her whole day cooking and cleaning with no time to rest. She decides to hire a maid and hangs out a Maid Wanted sign on her door. A big black spider sees the sign and decides to apply for the job, thinking that he can make a good meal of the children. He makes up like a black maid by putting a dress on and wrapping a bandanna around his head. Then he heads off to the Ladybug house while the music of "My Old Kentucky Home" plays in the background. He knocks on the door and when Mrs. Ladybug opens it, he says, "Ma'am, I's de new maid." Mrs. Ladybug asks him if he has taken care of children before. He tells her, "You just give me one day with these here kids and they won't bother you no more." He does not notice one of the clever baby bugs come up behind him as he is talking and pull up his dress, which reveals his true identity. His first job is washing the dishes. While he is working, the little baby bug comes by and eyes him suspiciously. He tries to catch several of the small bugs but each time he is foiled by the clever little bug. Finally he pretends to join a game of hide and seek and manages to trap several of the baby bugs in a trunk. He sits on it to keep them from getting out. While he is sitting there smoking his cigar, the clever little bug comes by. The spider tries to conceal his cigar by putting all of it into his mouth. The little bug walks by slowly, eyeing the spider. All the time the spider can barely contain the hot cigar in his mouth. Finally the bug asks him if he is hiding something in his mouth. The spider shakes his head in the negative. The little bugs asks him to open his mouth and prove it. The spider swallows the cigar, and when he opens his mouth, the light of a flame can be seen coming from deep in his throat. When the little bug leaves, the heat has become so intense that the spider grabs a large bottle of liquid and drinks it. He has a satisfied look on his face until he reads the label on the bottle—gasoline. At this instant a huge explosion blows the spider off the face of the earth. As the Ladybug family is happily rejoicing, they hear a knock on the door. Mrs. Ladybug opens the door and a little bug is seen who says, "I's de new maid" at the fade to end.

Description: *METRO-GOLDWYN-MAYER Short Story,* December 1940

In nature, claims Rudolph Ising, producer of cartoons for Metro-Goldwyn-Mayer, it is simple to find animals, birds and even insects whose personalities are closely aligned to the human species. Substitute a ladybug for any poor mother who strives conscientiously to raise her brood of a dozen or so children properly and then substitute a spider for the villain who tries to take advantage of her hopelessness and you will have the characters of Ising's latest Technicolor cartoon *Mrs. Ladybug*.

Opening with Mama Ladybug hanging out her wash, the cartoon goes on to show the kids tearing down the washline. This is the last straw. Mama decides that she can't manage her household work and children alone so she puts a sign up which reads: "Maid Wanted."

The sign is seen by no other than a big spider who has a particular appetite for little ladybugs. He disguises himself as a maid and applies for the job.

The kids play "hide-and-seek" in the same room in which the spider is working. One by one, as the children run past, he grabs them and shoves them into a trunk, closes the lid and sits on it.

When he thinks he has all, he lights a big cigar. As he puffs away happily, he hears a child's voice in the hall. Quickly he doubles the cigar inside his mouth. Soon wisps of smoke curl from the corner of his mouth and the drops of perspiration that fall on his nose turn to steam.

Meanwhile, the youngster becomes curious at this exhibition and asks the spider to open his mouth. To oblige, the spider swallows the cigar and, as he opens his mouth, smoke billows out from his throat. Now his stomach is afire. He grabs a nearby jug and drinks it down, but the jug is filled with gasoline. The spider turns pink, red then blue and finally explodes in a blinding flash. When the smoke clears away, all that can be seen is a bandanna floating lazily to the floor.

Review: *The Motion Picture Exhibitor,* 8 January 1941

Like the old woman in the shoe, this woman didn't know what to do, so she hired a maid to take care of her children. But the maid turned out to be a spider who is thwarted in his designs on the children. Fair.

A MULE'S DISPOSITION (1926)

Company: Walter Lantz, J. R. Bray Studio
Type: Unnatural History series
Characters: White kids, colored nurse

Review: *Moving Picture World,* 31 July 1926

Another of Bray's "Unnatural History Comedies" combining cartoon work and photography. A colored nurse, when the kids tease her, tells them about the mule which until the days of Noah had a sweet disposition. Noah, however, kept changing him to poorer quarters on the ark to please the animals that kicked. Finally the mule rebelled and wrecked the place. One of the most amusing and interesting of the series. (one reel)

NIGHT LIFE OF THE BUGS (1936)

Company: Richard Bickenbach, Jack Dunham, Walter Lantz, Universal Pictures
Characters: Oswald the rabbit, blackbird

Review: *Motion Picture Herald,* 3 October 1936

Oswald rescues the dragonfly princess from the clutches of a blackbird and as a reward is invited to attend the Bug Town Amusement Park. A reducing pill shrinks Oswald to the size of the priness. After trying all the amusements, the princess gives Oswald an enlarging pill but before he can swallow it the blackbird pounces on him. Oswald finally locates his pill and when full size turns on the blackbird, relieving the bird of several feathers. (8 min)

OLD BLACKOUT JOE (1942)

Company: Paul Sommer, Screen Gems; Columbia Pictures
Type: Phantasy Cartoon
Characters: Old Blackout Joe

Story: The cartoon opens on a close-up of the face of Old Blackout Joe, a World War II air-raid warden, as he cries, "Black out, black out!" Behind him is a sign that reads "Air-Raid Warden, Post 13, Harlem Branch." He calls out, "Black out! Put dem lights out" as he walks down the street. As he walks past the neon signs of the Onyx Room, the Shadrack, and other businesses and apartments, the lights go out. In an alley he sees three men shooting craps and tells them lights out. The lights go out and only the eyes of the men are seen. The dice are thrown and they land on seven. The teeth in the smiling face of one of the men fill the screen. Joe passes the Club Hoola Boola and shouts, "Hey, lights out up dere." Next he climbs to the roof of a tall building where he looks around and says, "My, my, de black out is done. As Longfellow says, 'The darkness falls from the wings of night like a feather fallin' down from an eagle in flight.'" He observes that all the lights are out except one gas streetlamp. He rushes down to the street and runs to the gaslamp and blows it out. But the flame comes back on. Joe sees his shadow and says, "Who dat?" Then he turns around to see if the light is out. Just as he does, the light goes out again. Each time he turns away, the light comes back on. But when he turns around, the light goes back out. Finally he walks around a corner and takes a peek back before sneaking back to the lamp and trying to blow out the flame, which refuses to go out. After several unsuccessful attempts he is out of breath. Finally he manages to blow the flame over to a stack of boxes of TNT. He runs to the flame and inhales, sucking the flame inside him. It lights up his insides so that his skeleton is seen. He blows the flame back out of his mouth and covers it with his hand. He starts to walk away, not realizing that the flame is still attached to his hand. He sees his shadow and can't figure out where the light is coming from. He pulls off his helmet and scratches his head. The flame comes off his hand and becomes attached to his head as he puts his helmet back on and walks off, smiling. A cloud of black smoke forms over his head, and he says, "Man, dis blackout sho' is totalitarian." As his head begins to burn, he pulls off his helmet and throws it on the ground. He attempts to stamp out the flame with his feet in front of a Loan Shop sign. The flame appears to go out and Joe says, "Dat double-crossin' lamp given' me more trouble . . ." as he screams and jumps into the air, realizing that the flame is now on the inside of his shoe. His head hits the balls on the pawn shop sign as he jumps around on one foot. He pulls off his shoe and picks up the flame, takes the cover off a manhole, and throws the flame down into the sewer. He is satisfied until he sees light coming out of all the sewers on his street. Frustrated, he takes several sticks of TNT and is about to throw them into the sewer when the all-clear signal is heard. All of the city lights come back on, which Joe observes, not realizing that he is still holding the TNT in his hand. As he walks away, he hears the hissing sound of the fuse and realizes the TNT is about to blow up. He screams, throws the TNT into an open sewer, and puts on the lid. The TNT explodes, sending a cloud of black smoke out of the sewer. As Joe runs down the street, all the other sewers blow up and the covers fall down on top of his head. Finally the flame also falls on his head, and he jumps up and down as the cartoon ends.

Review: *Boxoffice*, 12 September 1942

When old Black Joe, an air warden, is on duty in a blackout test, funny things can happen, particularly with a street light that disregards all conventions and orders. It's amusing and should get a couple of laughs.

Review: *Motion Picture Herald*, 12 September 1942

The problems of a Negro air-raid warden during a blackout are described in this short subject. His sector includes a street light without a sense of civic duty which keeps blinking on and off and other annoying problems. (6 min)

THE OLD MAN OF THE MOUNTAIN (1933)

Company: Dave Fleischer, Max Fleischer, Paramount Pictures
Type: Combination live action and animation
Characters: Betty Boop, Cab Calloway and his orchestra, old man of the mountain (Cab Calloway voice characterization)

Story: The cartoon opens on live action as Cab Calloway, wearing a white suit, fronts his orchestra and sings "hi-dee-ho . . ." The animation begins in a small village where a lion rolls down the mountain on skates to the village below where he shouts the alarm that

the old man of the mountain has appeared. All of the animals that inhabit the village pack their belongings and leave town. Wearing a short black skirt, Betty Boop walks out of the tourist house and asks an owl what's going on. The owl (Cab Calloway voice characterization) sings, "A long white beard and a crooked nose tramps along with the folks all scared. With a dingle in his eye he passes on by, the old man of the mountain. Though he wears long hair and his feet are bare, they say he's a mad and bad creature. His cares are bare and he fears no one, the old man of the mountain. He talks with the bears when he's lonely, he sleeps with the sky for a tent. And he will eat you up when he's hungry, and it wouldn't cost him a red cent. And he'll live as long as an old oak tree. He'll eat up fools like you and me. Oh, I often sigh and jump up and cry of the old man of the mountain." Betty says, "I'm goin' up to see that old man of the mountain." She climbs to the top of the mountain and arrives at the opening of a large cave. An old man with a long white beard suddenly jumps from behind the rocks and sings, "You got to ho-dee-ho, you got to heh-dee-heh to get along with me. You got to learn my song. If you do me wrong, you got to kick the gong around to get along with me." Betty asks, "What you gonna do now?" The old man backs away from her, saying, "I'm gonna do the best I can." Then he does a nifty Cab Calloway dance routine while singing, "You got to hi-dee-hi, you got to hi-dee-heh-dee-heh to get along with me." He then walks back toward Betty Boop, who runs out of the cave and down the mountain. The old man chases her and gets close enough to grab her dress. But Betty slips out of her dress and continues to run. Betty's dress jumps out of the old man's hands and then catches up to Betty and jumps back on her. Betty attempts to escape by climbing to the top of a tree, but the old man pulls the tree out of the ground and carries it with him while singing, "When your sweetie tells you everything will be OK, just keep up the bop-bob-dee. If you feel like shoutin', advertise it just this way, she-bob . . ." as Betty slides down the tree trunk and pinches the old man's nose. When the old man drops the tree, Betty jumps to the ground and runs away. The old man catches Betty again, but the other animals quickly surround him and rescue her. Several skunks tickle his chin with their tails while another ties his long nose into a knot as the cartoon ends.

Review: *Film Daily*, 24 July 1933

To the tune of Cab Calloway's music and vocalizing, this Max Fleischer animated unreels some amusing antics having to do with the kidnapping of Betty Boop by the old man of the mountain and her rescue by the forest animals. A nice subject of its kind, the Calloway musical background being distinctive and the cartoon stuff amusing.

THE OLD MILLPOND (1936)

Company: Hugh Harman, M-G-M
Type: Happy Harmonies, Nominated for Academy Award
Characters: Frog caricatures of Cab Calloway, Fats Waller, Stephin Fetchit, the Mills Brothers, Ethel Waters, Cotton Club girls

Story: The cartoon opens on a tranquil setting—an old millpond at dusk. In the background, "Down by the Old Millstream" is heard, and the frog inhabitants are resting quietly. The mood changes suddenly as Deacon Frog climbs on the top of a waterlily and tells his congregation, "Brethren (the crowd responds with "Yeah man"), my good teaching ain't been reaching you (the crowd says "Yeah man")." The deacon continues, "You should hark unto my plea and this is what you should do. Come dressed up in style. Start right down the aisle. No use talking . . . start shouting. Smile on brother, smile on." All the members of the frog congregation are dressed in their Sunday best. From under the water Cab Calloway frog and his band come to the surface and begin to play "Minnie the Moocher" while Cab sings and dances in the unique style that made him famous. Cab finishes with a hi-dee-ho just before the curtain rises on an Ethel Waters frog that sings a jungle tune accompanied by a chorus of dancing girls in native costumes. She finishes to a round of applause from the frog audience. Next the curtain rises to show Fats Waller sitting at a piano. He starts to play, but stops when he hears the sound of tapping feet. Fats Waller frog asks, "Who dat?" Bill Robinson frog, after a couple of taps, responds with, "Who dat?" Fats then says, "Who dat say who dat when I say who dat?" Fats then plays the piano and sings "Mississippi Is My Name" as Bill Robinson frog sings a chorus and tap dances. Next the Mills Brothers frog quartet sings a snappy tune, "Oh I Heard It." At the far end of the stage Stephin Fetchit frog dressed as a big-game hunter slowly shuffles in, saying, "Where did all the animals go?" He is followed by a big tiger and when Fetchit looks around and sees it, he runs and hides in a grass hut while the music makers play "Tiger Rag." Calloway, Louis Armstrong, Fats Waller, and the Cotton Club dancing chorus all join in the music making and dancing. As the music reaches a climax, it stops and all the frogs dive back into the water. The pond returns to normal with the music of "The Old Millpond" as the cartoon ends.

Review: *Film Daily,* 13 May 1936

This musical comedy cartoon is a knockout. Following the opening, which is the song "Down by the Old Mill Stream," the impersonations are Cab Calloway and his band doing "Minnie the Moocher" routine, "Fats" Waller doing his piano number, Bill Robinson his taps, the Mills Bros. their "Hold That Tiger," Stephin Fetchit is presented, and a dancing chorus does "Jungle Rhythm." The Technicolor is beautiful, especially in the water numbers. This short is just one load of entertainment all the way through. (10 min)

Review: *Film Daily,* 1 June 1936

In Technicolor, a swell interpretation by the frogs in the millpond of the famous colored artists of tap dance and orchestra. The leading lights among the colored entertainers are presented in fine imitations, the technique is very clever, and the entire production a real novelty in cartoon with beautiful color and catchy music.

Review: *Motion Picture Herald,* 6 June 1936

This Harman-Ising jazz fantasy combines brilliant pigmentation adroitly with swingingly syncopated orchestration to produce a rare consolidation of visible and audible impressions keynoted by a Cab Calloway band composed of frogs. Bill Robinson is another of several Negro personalities imitated with startling effect by the jump citizens of an old millpond gone rhythmic for a night. The total effect is swift, moderately stimulating, and briskly entertaining.

Review: *Boxoffice,* 4 July 1936

Delightful stretches of colored scenic views and an unusually brisk brand of animation serve as a background for this cartoon which depicts a group of frogs imitating some of the most famous colored characters of the entertainment world. Cab Calloway, Bill Robinson, Sleep 'N Ear, "Fats" Waller and many others do their stuff by means of a very clever technique with the result that there's never a dull moment. The popularity of the characters presented assures wide audience appeal.

Review: *National Exhibitor,* 6 June 1936

Cab Calloway, Fats Waller, Bill Robinson, Mills Bros., Stephin Fetchit are seen via the impersonation route and a dancing chorus is included as well, color is fine, with the result an above average short. Very good.

ONE NOTE TONY (1948)

Company: Connie Rasinski, Paul Terry, Twentieth Century-Fox Pictures
Type: Terrytoons
Characters: One Note Tony, an African boy

Review: *Motion Picture Herald,* 5 June 1948

Little Tony, the drummer in the Jungle Symphony Orchestra, can't master his solo. At a concert Tony continually does the wrong thing. Eventually the sedate concert becomes a riotous, rollicking jam session. The bewildered conductor yields to the popular decision that Tony, with his music, has become King of Swing. (7 min)

Review: *Film Daily,* 18 September 1947

Little Tony, the drummer in the Jungle Symphony orchestra, can't master his one-note solo and is heckled unmercifully by the conductor. A playful elephant takes matters into his own trunk and Tony, unwittingly, starts off a jam session which the sleepy audience digs, and crowns Tony King of Swing. Lots of fun.

Review: *Exhibitor Servisection,* 1 October 1947

Little Tony, the drummer in the Jungle Symphony Orchestra, has been practicing days on end for his big debut. The only thing that phases him is that he has only one note belonging to him in the entire symphony, and can't learn to get that note down pat. Finally, the night arrives, and he gets all set. However, he messes things up in grand style with his drumsticks as he transforms the band into a jazz band. The audience seems to like it though and everything turns out okay. Good.

THE ORPHAN DUCK (1939)

Company: Connie Rasinski, Paul Terry, Twentieth Century-Fox Pictures
Type: Terrytoons
Characters: Dinky Duck, family of chickens

Review: *Boxoffice,* 14 October 1939

A neat cartoon effort in Technicolor that rates as one of the funnier jobs turned out by this studio. It is all about a black duckling who attaches himself to a family of chicks. His presence is resented by the rooster until the duckling saves one of the chicks from drowning. (7 min)

Review: *Selected Motion Pictures,* 1 October 1939

Little Black Duck rescues a baby chick from drowning and finds a home for himself with a chicken family. Amusing. Family and Junior Matinee.

Review: *Motion Picture Exhibitor,* 4 October 1939

The orphan duck (black) succeeds in having himself adopted by a hen and rooster after he saves their chicks from drowning. This is one of Paul Terry's better Technicolor offerings, indicating a definite trend forward. Good.

Review: *Exhibitor Servisection,* 20 April 1950

The orphan duck succeeds in having himself adopted by a hen and rooster after he saves their chicks from drowning. This was first reviewed in the *Servisection* of October 1939. Good.

OTHELLO (1920)

Company: Anson Dyer, Hepworth Film Co. (London)
Character: Othello

Review: *Bioscope* (London), 29 July 1920

In the latest of Anson Dyer's delightful Shakespearean burlesque cartoons, the Moor of Venice becomes a seaside nigger minstrel, whilst Desdemona (known as "Mona" for short) is the lovely daughter of the local bathing machine proprietor. After many humorous adventures, in which the main points of the famous tragedy are ingeniously, if irreverently, introduced, Othello "smothers" Desdemona with kisses.

The animated cartoon has rightly won a permanent place as a feature of the modern cinema programme, where it supplies an element of unique variety. In the past the branch of film pro-

duction has been largely in the hands of foreign artists, whose work has not invariably proved best suited to British tastes. It is, therefore, gratifying to find a British artist, of the quality of Anson Dyer, devoting himself to the exploitation of the popular form of screen humour.

Already Mr. Dyer has gained considerable command of the complicated technique of the film cartoon through which he is accordingly able to give expression freely to his quaint humorous fancies. His draughmanship is invariably good, and the little landscapes, against which he makes his puppet players move, have great pictorial charm.

One of the best of the Shakespeare series, *Othello* will please all kinds of picture-goers, and should make a welcome addition to any programme. (one reel)

OUIJA BOARD (1919)

Company: Dave Fleischer, Max Fleischer, J. R. Bray Studio, Paramount Pictures
Type: Combination live action and animation, Inkwell Imp Cartoon
Characters: Max Fleischer (as himself), artist (as himself), black porter (as himself), Ko-Ko the Clown (animated)

Story: The cartoon opens with live action in a cartoon studio. A black porter is sweeping the floor while an artist sits at a drawing board studying a sketch. Max Fleischer, the boss, arrives and sits at his drawing board, where he makes a sketch of Ko-Ko the Clown. Ko-Ko becomes animated and dances around. Meanwhile the porter stops work and sits down to play with the ouija board with the artist. Fleischer draws a haunted house near Ko-Ko, who pretends that he is not afraid to go in it. Fleischer walks over to the other two and tells them that he does not believe in the ouija board. Ko-Ko walks into the haunted house but immediately runs out, followed by a series of ghosts that taunt him. Meanwhile Fleischer decides to sit down and play the ouija board with the artist. The ghosts all leave Ko-Ko and the haunted house hops away and dissolves into a spot of ink that disappears. Ko-Ko jumps off the drawing board and walks over to get a closer look at the ouija board while the others stand nearby and discuss it. Ko-Ko jumps onto the board and moves the pointer. The others wonder why the pointer appears to move by itself. The porter is so scared that he jumps back, knocking a statue off a stool. It breaks when it hits the floor. Ko-Ko moves the pointer on the board to spell a message that reads, "The fellow who looks like this is going on a journey where no man will return." Then it points to the face of a black man painted on the board. The porter's face turns white with fear and then turns black again. His eyes are wide open and his knees shake with fear as Ko-Ko crawls off the board. Fleischer and the artist examine the board while Ko-Ko climbs up on a hat rack where he gets inside a hat, causing it to fall to the floor. Ko-Ko crawls across the floor under the hat, the others wondering in fear why the hat appears to move by itself. Fleischer's hair stands on end, and the artist jumps back in fear. The porter falls to his knees in a corner and begins to pray before he pulls a pair of dice from his pocket and tosses them on the floor. They land on two sixes, which increases his fear. Fleischer suspects a trick and crushes the hat with his foot. The artist becomes angry at Fleischer for crushing his hat. While they argue, Ko-Ko climbs up on a shelf and laughs at them. They see him and are very angry. The porter picks up a ball of putty and throws it at the clown. It misses but hits a bottle of black ink, which breaks and splatters ink all over the wall. Ko-Ko jumps on the front of Fleischer's shirt and dissolves into a big spot of black ink as the others look on and the cartoon ends.

OUT OF THE INKWELL (1938)

Company: Dave Fleischer, Max Fleischer, Adolph Zukor, Paramount Pictures
Type: Combined live action and animation
Characters: Betty Boop, black janitor (live action)

Story: The cartoon begins with live action in the office of a cartoon studio as a black janitor sits and struggles to read a book entitled *The Art of Hypnotism*. It says that hypnosis can be achieved in four steps: (1) select a victim, (2) look victim in the eye, (3) manipulate hands in front of victim, and (4) then say "dunka-hunka-lunka." The janitor slowly says, in a Stephin Fetchit demeanor, "Dunka-hunka-lunka." He drops the dusting brush he is holding, puts down the book, and says, "I think I'm gonna try that." He points his fingers at an ink pen on the desk and says "dunka-hunka-lunka." The pen spins around and rolls across the desk. The janitor smiles and says, "Well look a here." The top of the pen comes off as the pen moves out of live action into an animated scene where it draws a spinning figure of Betty Boop. Betty stops spinning and falls down. The janitor laughs at her as Betty gets to her feet and points her finger at him. She angrily says, "Oh, so you think that's funny!" The smiling janitor puts another spell on her and tells her, "You is now a high diver." Betty stiffly climbs an imaginary ladder to the top where she dives off an imaginary diving board into an imaginary pool and swims around the room before landing again on the floor. She shakes the water off herself and says, "Look here, you better start working right now." But the janitor only laughs and puts another spell on her before telling her, "Now you is a rubber woman." Betty's body stretches and contracts and then she bounces like a rubber ball across the room. When she stops, she shakes her fist at the janitor, saying, "You stop this and get to work right this minute. You've rested long enough." The janitor frowns but obeys, getting up slowly and saying, "Why I was just readin' up on a little hypno-ma-la-tisn." He grabs his broom and begins to sweep the floor, saying, "I jus' works my head to the bone around heah. And I don't get no time off

fo' myself." Betty chuckles at him and walks away, saying, "Oh, you want your rest, huh? Well, I will read up on that." She climbs onto the desk and reads the instruction book on hypnotism, saying, "Here we go." Meanwhile the janitor stops sweeping, yawns, and goes to sleep standing while leaning on the broom. After reading the instructions Betty says, "I think I'll try that." First she puts a spell on a bisque figure of a dog, and it comes to life. Betty smiles and says "whoopee" before putting a spell on a typewriter, which types a few lines on a sheet of paper. Then she puts a spell on a pair of scissors, which open and close. Betty climbs down from the table, walks over to the sleeping janitor, and says, "So it's hypnotism you want. It's hypnotism you get." She puts a spell on the broom the janitor is leaning on, and it moves away and he falls to the floor and wakes up. Betty tells him, "Maybe some fresh air will pep you up" as she puts a spell on an electric fan. It plugs itself into the electric socket and then blows sheets of paper around the room. The bewildered janitor looks on and yells, "How am I gonna get all this stuff cleaned up around here?" Next Betty puts a spell on the broom, and it sweeps bits of paper under the rug on the floor. Betty puts a spell on some cigarette butts and they fly off the floor and into a spittoon. Betty's next spell causes a broken chair to repair itself and a dust brush to dust the furniture and the pictures hanging on the wall. Next she looks at the janitor and says, "Now you're goin' to work." She puts a spell on him, and his face turns white then back to black. He jumps up and in speeded-up action cleans the office in no time. Meanwhile Betty climbs on the desk and jumps into the ink bottle. She pulls half of her body out of the bottle and puts a spell on the cap, causing it to jump to the top of the bottle. Betty is heard to say "see you" as the cartoon ends.

Review: *Selected Motion Pictures,* 1 October 1938

A lazy office porter hypnotises Betty Boop out of the inkwell. Fair Family.

Review: *Motion Picture Exhibitor,* 1 May 1938

The Boops will not be distributed by Paramount next year. This entrant will do nothing to make any exhibitor regret the company's decision. It has novelty, true, but of the old days. A colored porter (human), reading a book on hypnotism, makes Betty come out of the bottle. In retaliation, Betty causes magic of her own, finally causing porter to work. Fair.

Review: *Boxoffice,* 24 March 1938

Mostly juvenile appeal. That popular Max Fleischer animated stunt is used here, but the results are far from effective. There is a colored porter, who picks up hypnotism from a book lying on a cartoonist's desk. He brings the pen to life with an unaided drawing of Betty Boop. Betty watches the porter tire at his work and then hypnotizes him into doing the work at a speedy clip.

PANTRY PIRATE (1940)

Company: Gerry Geronimi, Walt Disney, distributed by RKO Radio Pictures

Characters: Pluto, black maid (voice characterization by Lillian Randolph)

Story: Cartoon opens as the back door opens and the black maid says, "Come on Git outta heh Dog gone yah lazy Good for nothin'-No count hound" as she grabs Pluto's collar and drags him out of the house. She is seen from the waist down and is a big muscular woman wearing a dress, ankle high house slippers, and stripped stockings. Pluto frowns as he hears the maid say, "You let me catch you messin' 'round in my kitchen again and I'm gonna bust all the hide off 'n you." She drags Pluto to his house where she ties a rope around his neck, and then says, "I guess dis will hold you uumph Now you stay out of trouble" as Pluto frowns and tears roll down his face. She turns and walks away saying, "Never in my born days did I ever see such a low down heap of yellow dog trash." Pluto sulks while in the kitchen, the maid pulls a roast from the oven and says, "Ummm Ummm Dis roast sho' smells good heh heh." She sets the roast on the counter near an open window and sings, "Hallelujah-Bless the day ummmm-ummm." The scent of the roast wakes Pluto from his sleep and he slips his head out of the noose and sneaks into the house. He hides in a dirty clothes basket as the full-length shadow of the maid is seen walking by singing, "Hallelujah Bless the day Ummm Ummm." Pluto finds the roast but in the process he makes noise as he bumps into furniture. He is about to grab a bite but he slips off an ironing board and falls to the floor knocking over a box of "Super Sudsy Soap" which is next to a pail of water. He inhales the soap powder which makes him sneeze. He inhales more powder and also some water and is soon sneezing bubbles out of his mouth. Later the maid hears the sneezes and as she stands at the top of the stairs holding a broom in one hand and a dish pan in the other hand and says, "What's dat noise Who is dat." Pluto is silent and the maid turns to go back to work saying, "I swear I heard somthin'." Later Pluto again sneezes and breaks some cups and the noise brings the maid who rushes down the stairs saying, "What's goin' on down dere What in the name of goodness is dat yellow devil up to." The maid arrives down stairs and says, "Where did all dese bubbles come from It's dat dog." Pluto manages to escape out of the house, and he runs back to his house where he slips his head back in the noose and lies down pretending to sleep. The maid says, "Where is he, I'll tear him limb from limb" as she runs out of the house. She says, "Wait 'till I gets my hands on dat dog, I'll skin him alive" as she runs to Pluto's house where she finds him lying down with his eyes closed. She says, "Land sakes-Well I'll be, Look at him, Sleeping like a baby." "She holds Pluto's head in her hand and turns his smiling face toward her before she turns and walks away saying, "I could swear it was dat darn dog—Somethin' wrong—Somewhere." She walks into the house and slams the door as Pluto opens his eyes and sneezes. He smiles and bubbles flow out of his ears as the cartoon ends.

PATCH MAH BRITCHES (1935)

Company: Charles Mintz, Manny Gould, distributed by Columbia Pictures

Characters: Barney Google, Sparkplug the horse, Sambo the black jockey, black man, Ma, Snuffy Smith, Rudy the ostrich, Sully

See fig. 51. Story: The cartoon opens as Barney Google carries a huge roast turkey he has prepared for the dinner he is hosting for all his friends. He sets it down on the dining room table, which is set for a formal dinner. He is basting the turkey by pouring gravy on it when he hears his friends arrive. He pulls off his apron and walks outside to welcome them. As the car pulls to a stop at the curb, the first to emerge is Snuffy Smith, who breaks a window and climbs out. Snuffy, smoking his corncob pipe, then opens the door and helps the others out, including Sambo, Barney's little black jockey; Ma, who pushes a baby carriage with six sleeping babies; a large black man; Sparkplug the race horse; Rudy the ostrich; and many other strange-looking characters. They all go inside the house and seat themselves at the dinner table. In no time at all they are rapidly eating the food. They eat so fast that food is flying into the air. Barney gets hit in the face by gravy when he stands up to light his cigar. The large black man eats a huge slice of watermelon very politely European style, using knife and fork. Sitting across from him is Sambo, who eats his slice of watermelon with his hands. When Sambo finishes his slice, he reaches over the table, takes the black man's slice, and rapidly eats it. Sparkplug eats the straw stuffing from the couch. After they have consumed all the food, Barney's guests are still hungry and want more. They toss the dinner table into the air, sending empty dinner plates crashing down on Barney's head. The guests leave the house, climb back into the car, and drive away, leaving a disgusted Barney sitting on the floor littered with broken dishes. He picks up a leftover pie and smashes it on his face as the cartoon ends.

THE PENGUIN PARADE (1938)

Company: Tex Avery, Warner Bros.
Type: Merrie Melodies
Character: Fats Waller caricature

Review: *Motion Picture Exhibitor*, 15 April 1938

A musical revue at an Artie Penguin Night Club. "Fats Waller" pounds out music. There is an amusing little double talking M.C. Animation is very smooth, music is hot, tuneful. This constitutes a moderately funny cartoon for all classes. Good.

PHILIPS BROADCAST OF 1938

Company: George Pal Productions, Philips Corporation
Type: Puppetoons
Characters: Caricatures of Ambrose and his orchestra, black band and dancers

Story: This cartoon consists of a series of musical sequences with no plot. The middle sequence depicts a black band and dancers performing in Harlem. Included are several scenes showing men playing dice; Mammy and children playing trumpets; heads of two smiling black men under a sign that reads Great Watermelons; a fast-dancing female chorus that arrives on the "A" train; and a jazz band playing a hot tune.

THE PLAYFUL POLAR BEARS (1938)

Company: Dave Fleischer, Max Fleischer, Paramount Pictures
Type: Color Classic
Characters: Polar bears

Review: *Motion Picture Exhibitor,* 15 November 1938

Here's a natural for the kids. The Fleischers put Myron Waldman to work turning out one of the best shorts they have made. Three polar bears (one is naturally the "black sheep") cavort in the snow, are chased by hunters. The "black sheep" fails to run to safety, is kayoed by a falling icicle. Thinking him dead, an effective mourning chant follows. He comes to life, there's great celebration. Excellent. (7 min)

PLUTO'S DREAM HOUSE (1940)

Company: Gerry Geronimi, Walt Disney; distributed by RKO-Radio Pictures
Characters: Mickey Mouse, Pluto, black genie (voice only)

Story: The cartoon opens as Mickey and Pluto are looking at blueprints for Pluto's new home. Mickey tells Pluto, "It's your new dream house, Pluto." Pluto is excited and happy. Mickey picks up a shovel and says, "Hey, let's break ground." Mickey begins to dig a hole, but Pluto, using his paws, digs faster and deeper. Soon dirt and other objects fly out of the hole. Mickey picks up one of the objects, a lamp, and tells Pluto, "Hey look at this." He rubs dirt off the lamp and says, "Just an old teapot." Then a voice inside the lamp says, "Golden teapot!" Mickey looks around and says, "Who said that?" The voice replies, "I did." Mickey drops the lamp as he and Pluto jump to the other side of the fence. When the lamp hits the ground, the voice inside says, "Take it easy." Sticking his head over the fence, Mickey hears the voice of the genie inside the lamp say, "Well, what do you want?" Mickey answers, "Nothing." The genie says, "A man who don't want nothin' don't rub us magic lamps." Mickey responds, "A magic lamp?" The genie tells him, "Yes, sir, Boss. Anything you say you wants, I's does it." Mickey asks, "Can you build a doghouse?" The genie replies, "A dog house? Is you referrin' to a villa for a canine beast?" Mickey replies, "Yeah, for Pluto." The genie says, "Production is commencing." A puff of smoke from the lamp turns into a ghostlike hand that saws wood and nails planks. In no time the house is completed. When the house is painted, Pluto gets too close and comes away with paint all over his face. The genie puts a paint-brush wig on his head and then calls him "Mammy!" Finally the genie announces, "The production is completed." Mickey looks at Pluto and says, "Pluto, isn't it swell?" Pluto is so happy that he licks Mickey's face with his tongue. Mickey says, "Hey, you got paint on the lamp" and brushes the lamp to wipe it off. The genie then says, "Did you rub, Mr. Mickey?" Mickey answers, "Oh yes, lamp. I think I want . . ." He is interrupted by the genie, who says, "Now I specks you want me to give that dog a bath?" Mickey answers, "A bath! Say, that's a swell idea." The Genie says, "OK Boss. Here I go!" A puff of smoke that turns into a hand comes out of the lamp, grabs Pluto, and says, "Come here, dog. Yo' bath is ready." He drops Pluto into a tub of water and bathes him while Mickey relaxes on a couch. He tells the genie, "Now use plenty of soap and don't spare the brush." The genie responds, "OK Boss. This is a complete bath." Mickey turns on the radio and finds a number of programs that he does not like, including a cooking show and a boxing match, before deciding to listen to a program of soft music. He tells the genie, "Hey, don't forget to scrub his ears." The genie replies, "Yes sir, Boss" and Pluto gets his ears scrubbed with a washcloth. Pluto tries to pull the cloth away from the genie but it tears and sends Pluto flying across the room and crashing into a door. This action breaks Mickey's radio so he decides to fix it. In doing so he tunes in several radio stations. In the meantime the genie, hearing voices from the radio programs and thinking that they are commands from Mickey, begins mixing dough to bake a cherry pie using Pluto as the main ingredient. In the process Pluto is mixed, rolled flat, boxed about his head, and almost sliced before he wakes up on the floor beside Mickey, who is asleep in his bed. It was all a nightmare. The frightened Pluto jumps on the bed and wakes up Mickey, who tells him, "Why Pluto, you've been dreaming again." They both laugh as the cartoon ends.

Review: *Motion Picture Exhibitor,* 24 July 1940

Loaded with old fashioned belly-laughs, the latest Walt Disney cartoon adventure will keep audiences in high spirits through its entire eight minutes. Mickey Mouse has plans for building a new dog house for Pluto. Up pops a Rochester talking magic lantern to do the construction work by magic. Comes the house and then comes some rip-roaring situations where the lantern magically slaps Pluto around. It is a nightmare for Pluto but good fun for the audience. Excellent.

THE POLICE DOG GETS PIFFLES IN BAD (1915)

Company: C. T. Anderson, J. R. Bray Studios, distributed by Pathe Film Exchange
Type: On the same reel with *The Intimate Study of Birds*
Characters: Police dog, Officer Piffles, black butcher shop owner

Review: *New York Dramatic Mirror,* 28 July 1915

A well-drawn animated cartoon showing the ludicrous adventures of the police dog, in which he has devised a peculiar system of graft all his own, by forcing the owner of a negro butcher shop to keep him supplied with bones. A larger dog continuously steals them from him, and at last, becoming disgusted, the police dog sounds the S.O.S. on his police whistle. Officer Piffles comes hurrying to his assistance, and while he is receiving much the worst of it in a battle with the larger dog, the police dog calmly enjoys a meal from the pilfered soup bones.

Review: *Motography,* 7 August 1915

Animated cartoon by C. T. Anderson of the Bray Studios. The little dog pesters the butcher for bones. There is a limit to the butcher's patience and his pent-up anger, through an amusing circumstance, is vented upon Piffles, the brave, but bungling cop. There is some real fun in this picture.

THE POLICE DOG TO THE RESCUE (1915)

Company: J. R. Bray Studios; released by Pathe Film Exchange
Characters: Police dog, Mrs. Dingle (a black woman), Officer Piffles

Review: *Moving Picture World,* 25 September 1915

The Police Dog To the Rescue, an animated cartoon comedy from the Bray studios, is down for release at an early date on the Pathe program. It is fully up to the standard of its popular predecessors.

Mrs. Dingle, a dusky washerlady, goes to a funeral and leaves her baby behind ensconced in a washboiler and with nursing bottle conveniently near. A wandering calf spies the refreshment and helps itself to it, showing its gratitude by licking the baby's face with its rough tongue. The baby sets up such a shriek that the police dog rushes to the rescue, but is driven off by the belligerent calf. Officer Piffles is hastily summoned by the dog and then finds himself plunged into the midst of some extraordinary adventures.

PORKY AT THE CROCADERO (1938)

Company: Frank Tashlin, Warner Bros.
Type: Looney Tunes
Characters: Porky Pig, black porter

Story: The cartoon opens in front of the Club Crocadero where Porky is looking at a posted announcement that reads, "Tonite guest Nite. Famous orchestra leaders in person directing the Crocadero band. Hear them play 'Little Man You've Had a Busy Day,' 'In The Shade of the Old Apple Tree,' 'With the Lady Who Couldn't Be Loved.'" Porky says to himself, "H-H-H-Hot Diggity dog! All the big shots in person. Some day I'm gonna lead a band too, see." He pulls a diploma out of his pocket that reads, "This is to certify that Porky Pig has completed our course in Hi, dee, hi—do, do dee, do; poo, poo, pa, doop. And can he swing it? Yea man!" Porky then says, "Man, I'll be famous like Leopold Stokowski, Rudy Vallee, and Benny

Goodman." He imitates each one. He is about to enter the club when he sees a sign: Crocadero Deluxe Dinner $25.00 per plate (with food $25.50). Porky puts his hand in his pocket and pulls out a penny that has the imprint of a skunk on it. Disappointed, he turns and walks away. Then he sees a Boy Wanted sign posted on the club. Porky rushes into the club and in no time is washing a stack of dishes while his boss, a walrus, tells him if he does a good job with the dishes he may give him a chance to lead the band. But Porky ruins his chance when he accidently breaks a stack of dishes and the owner kicks him out of the club into the street. But the owner has a big problem. The animals in the audience are clapping their hands, pounding their fists on the tables, and stamping their feet, impatient for the music to start. But the band leaders are late arriving at the club. He receives a message that reads, "Western Bunnion To: Manager, Crocadero. Plane delayed forcing landing. We fall down and go boom. The Bandleaders." The owner remembers Porky and runs out of the club to find him. He drags him back to the club, dresses him in formal clothes and tells him, "Pull the wool over their eyes." The first band is called The Jazz King and Porky, with a pillow stuffed under his shirt, does his imitation of Paul Whiteman while the patrons dance to the music. Next Porky imitates Guy Lumbago and his Boiled Kanadians dressed in a uniform of the Mounted Police. The vocal is by Cryman Lumbago, an old man with a long white beard who leans on a cane. His singing is bad, and a black porter pushes him off the stage in a wheelchair. The next band is Cab Howlaway and his Absorbent Cotton Club Orchestra. Porky performs in blackface, doing a singing impersonation of the great Cab Calloway. Porky sings, "Hi-dee-hi-dee-hi—Hi-dee-ho-dee-ho." He is backed by a black singing quartet. Next Porky sings a red-hot version of "China Town" in the famous and unique Calloway style backed by the Crocadero band. The music ends, the audience applauds, and Porky takes a bow as the cartoon ends.

PORKY'S MOVING DAY (1936)

Company: Jack King, Warner Bros.
Type: Looney Tunes
Characters: Porky Pig, Dopey, Mrs. Cud

Story: The cartoon opens on Porky and his hired hand Dopey, a black, punch-drink ex-prize fighter. They are sleeping in Porky's moving van, a two-wheeled cart pulled by an ostrich. A kerosene lamp sits on a small table with Porky's moving diploma. Photographs of Dopey as a boxer hang on the walls. Meanwhile Mrs. Cud, a cow, is frantic as her house, which sits precariously on the edge of a cliff, is being rocked back and forth and lifted up and down by huge waves from the stormy ocean below. Finally she decides to have Porky move her furniture out of the house before it slides through the window and falls into the ocean. The telephone in the moving van rings and wakes up Dopey. He jumps to his feet and begins to shadowbox. When Porky hits him on the head with a large mallet, Dopey stops and says, "OK, Boss" as he waves his hand in front of his face. Porky answers the phone, and Mrs. Cud tells him to "come quick and save my furniture."

Porky, stammering, says, "Come on, Dopey. We gotta go." Dopey says, "OK, Boss." Porky hitches the ostrich to the van, and when they arrive at Mrs. Cud's house, she is standing on the front porch to greet them. Mrs. Cud tells Porky, "Hurry! There's no time to waste. We'll be washed out before you know it." She and Porky rush into the house, slamming the door behind them. Dopey tries to follow them but runs into the door, which knocks him on his backside. He gets up and rings the doorbell. When the bell rings, Dopey begins to shadowbox and hits Mrs. Cud in the face as she opens the door and looks out to find him. She gets up, goes back inside, and returns with a large mallet that she uses to hit Dopey on his head. Dopey stops and says, "OK, Boss" before walking inside. Meanwhile Porky is pushing furniture, including a huge piano, out of the second-floor window into the van below. A huge wave causes the house to tilt, and Porky falls on a child's toy cart. He rolls into the next room and runs into Dopey, knocking him down. Porky tells him, "Hurry up, Dopey. Snap out of it." Dopey says, "OK, Boss." Dopey gets up and decides to move a mantelpiece, but he pulls it so hard that he also pulls the fireplace and chimney down. Next Dopey places some dishes in a barrel, but when he lifts the barrel it has no bottom and the dishes remain stacked on the floor. Dopey picks up the dishes and walks into the next room where the ostrich has swallowed an alarm clock. When the clock rings, Dopey throws the dishes into the air and starts to shadowbox. All the dishes crash to the floor except one that falls on Dopey's head. He stops boxing and says, "OK, Boss." Later a huge wave comes through the window and washes Porky, the ostrich, Dopey, and the rest of the furniture out of the house through the front door and into the van. Inside the van, the ostrich pops his head out of a barrel and the clock in this throat rings again. Dopey starts to shadowbox and continues until Porky gets out of a dresser drawer and hits him on the head with a mallet. Dopey waves his hand and says, "OK, Boss" as the cartoon ends.

THE PRODIGAL PUP (1924)

Company: Paul Terry, Pathe Film Exchange
Type: Originally released in 1917 as *Farmer Al Falfa's Wayward Pup*
Characters: Farmer Al Falfa, black pup

Review: *Moving Picture World,* 23 August 1924

After getting in bad with the old farmer, Paul Terry's clever little cartoon pup wins forgiveness and praise by rescuing the farmer's son when he floats away on a balloon tire that has been inflated too much. The cartoonist's ingenuity shows to advantage especially in the airplane used by the pup, which is pulled by a bird with the pup dangling a piece of meat in front of his beak. It is an amusing offering, well up to his cartoonist's high standard as a laugh-getter.

PUPPET SHOW (1936)

Company: Walter Lantz, Universal Pictures
Characters: Oswald the rabbit, black puppet

Review: *Motion Picture Herald,* 17 October 1936

The outstanding feature in this edition of Oswald's adventures is the exhibition of some skillful puppet work. Used as a background for the antics of the comic rabbit, such delightful puppetry lends a novel note of entertainment. Knocked senseless in the course of his puppet show, Oswald is visited by a weird dream concerning the difficulties one of his rebellious subjects meets when the little figure would try to free himself of the strings that bind him to his master manipulator. Awakening, as usual, only proves that it was but a nasty dream. (8 1/2 min)

Review: *National Exhibitor,* 5 November 1936

The endeavor to do something different results this time in Oswald the cartoon character pulling cartoon strings of real photographed puppets, in the manner of Max Fleischer's old "Out of the Inkwell" series. The novelty is refreshing but the entertainment is so-so. Finally Oswald, stung by a bee, falls, is hit on his head, and dreams one of his puppets escapes and as cartoon character tries to become part of toyland. But the toys capture him, have him tied to a sawmill, and are about to execute him when Oswald wakes in time to gather strings and pull show to close. Fair. (8 min)

RAILROAD RHYTHM (1937)

Company: Manny Gould, Ben Harrison, Columbia Pictures
Characters: Krazy Kat, black Pullman porter

Story: The opening scene shows Krazy Kat as the engineer on an old coal-burning engine pulling a trainload of passengers. The Pullman porter is seen walking through the cars and listening to the passengers complain about the rough ride. He says, in the manner of Stephin Fetchit, "Every minute I git mo' and mo' convinced we is traveling on the ocean. My, my, we sho' is having a rough voyage." The porter is next seen saying to Krazy, "Mr. Chief, the passengers sho' feel bad about the way this train is travelin' round." The train stops at a station, and the passengers can't wait to get off. They all change to a sleek, streamlined train. As they leave, the porter says, "Boss, that sho' is a scrumptious train." Krazy wishes he had enough money to buy himself a new train. Krazy starts up the engine and they pull out of the station and are on their way. Meanwhile a villain has tied a wealthy young couple, handsome Harry and winsome Winnie, to the railroad tracks directly in the path of Krazy's train. As the train approaches the couple, the engine's eyes sight the couple. Krazy puts on the brakes so hard that the train burrows under the couple thus saving them the intense displeasure of the villain. Krazy and the porter get off the engine and untie the couple. They are so grateful that they give Krazy a large bag of money. Krazy says that now he can buy himself a new train, and the next scene shows him at the engine of his sleek, streamlined train. The train is full of passengers, including the young couple who have decided to get married on the train. There is a party with a band playing swing music. The porter does a mean shuffle. The couple is married in the chapel car and then retires to the honeymoon car. Meanwhile Krazy looks up and sees an airplane approaching. It is piloted by the villain, who tosses bombs at the train. They all miss but one, which destroys the honeymoon car but does not injure the young couple. Handsome Harry blows a bugle, and a tank that is on the last car fires its guns at the villain, blasting his plane out of the air. It lands in a lake. The train pulls off the tracks into the lake, goes under water, and surfaces as a battleship. Krazy commands, "ready, aim, fire," and the porter fires a cannon that sinks the villain at the fade-out.

Review: *Selected Motion Pictures,* 1 January 1938

Krazy Kat rescues his sweetheart from the villain in an old-time melodrama with a modern ending. Clever and amusing cartoon. Family.

Review: *Motion Picture Exhibitor,* 1 December 1937

The cat is engineer of an old train. The passengers are sick from the constant rocking and ride the new streamlined train. The cat and the porter (mimic of Stephin Fetchit) save a band leader and his girlfriend from death, receive as reward enough cash to buy a streamlined train. The animation is good but the gags are a little weak. Fair.

THE RASSLIN' MATCH (1934)

Company: George Stallings, Van Beuren; released by RKO-Radio Pictures
Type: Characters based on Amos 'n' Andy radio and television shows
Characters: Andy, Amos, Kingfish

See fig. 52. Story: As the cartoon opens, Amos is walking along the street singing "Is I Blue." He arrives at the office of the Fresh Air Taxi Company where he finds Andy sitting at the desk fast asleep. He wakes him up just before Kingfish arrives and tells the boys that he has got the greatest deal for them that they have ever had in their lives. He tells them that Andy will wrestle Bullface Moosehead for the world's championship. Amos tries to discourage Andy, telling him that he "don't know nothing about wrestling." Andy tells Amos to mind his own business and Kingfish carries them over to the gym to meet Andy's trainer, Hercules. Hercules shakes Andy's hand, throws him to the floor, and ties him up in a knot. He tells Andy that his opponent, Bullface Moosehead, has one weak spot—the top of his head. Andy does some shadowboxing, and his shadow makes a fool of him. Amos and Kingfish take Andy out for some roadwork. Kingfish and Amos ride in the taxi while Andy runs behind, continually falling into holes in the road. When they stop to rest, Amos tells Andy that they brought him along this road because of the building where Bullface does his secret training. The boys look through a window and see the huge wrestler beat up on his sparring partners, sending them to the hospital. Andy asks if that is the guy he is going to wrestle and then faints. On the night of the big match

the auditorium is full of people. When Andy arrives at ringside, Kingfish tells him that he will be awarded a gold-and-diamond watch for winning. Bullface arrives, and the two combatants are introduced in the ring. Bullface gets applause and cheers, and Andy gets boos. The match starts and as expected Andy is getting tossed all over the ring. The situation looks hopeless when Bullface bounces Andy off the ropes from one side of the ring to the other. Amos tells Andy to take off his hat. Then he and Bullface collide head to head. Bullface is knocked out and Andy wins. Amos tells him, "You is the winner, Andy. Your weak spot was harder than his" as the cartoon ends.

Review: *Film Daily,* 9 January 1934

This cartoon brings a new technique to the screen insofar as the actual voices of Amos and Andy have been synchronized with the drawn characters. It has been fairly well accomplished and should prove a good laugh number, especially for the followers of the two radio comedians. "The Kingfish" and "Bullneck Mooseface" are the only other characters included in the film. The story is taken from the radio episode where Andy and "Bullneck Mooseface" meet on the canvas and wrestle for the championship of "sumphin."

Review: *Selected Motion Pictures,* 1 February 1934

An Amos 'n' Andy cartoon-voice combination in which the voices of the comedians are synchronized with a cartoon of one of their radio episodes. Amusing and the new technique is interesting.

RASTUS' RABID RABBIT HUNT (1914)

Company: J. R. Bray Studio; distributed by Electric Company
Characters: Mr. and Mrs. Rastus Lazybones

Review: *Moving Picture World,* 2 January 1915

Mrs. Rastus Lazybones, seeing Christmas approaching and the larder empty, compels her shiftless blacker half to bestir himself and go out and shoot something. So Rastus grabs his "ole muzzle loader" and departs prepared to shoot anything that will grace the pot.

Lucy Cottontail, the rabbit, is scared up by old Ceasar, the darkie's "hound dawd," and decides that it's her move and move she does with speed. After a merry chase the rabbit seeks refuge in a hole. When Caesar, under the urging of his master, tries to dig her out, she promptly makes use of another entrance to her home and exits with rapidity.

Numerous funny adventures happen to Rastus and his dog, one of them being that he finds his head to be considerably harder than a hornet's nest and in consequence suffers from a swelled head.

Finally, after old Caesar is thoroughly disgusted, Rastus makes a wonderful shot which loads him down with game, insures a warm welcome from his spouse and a magnificent Christmas dinner.

Review: *Bioscope* **(London), 25 March 1915**

Another addition to this wonderfully clever and amusing series. It is not so good as some of its predecessors, perhaps, but it is nevertheless full of humour and ingenuity.

ROMEO IN RHYTHM (1940)

Company: Hugh Harman, M-G-M
Characters: Black Crow Opera Company

See fig. 53. Story: The cartoon opens at night on a farm in the country where several black crows are perched on tree branches. Two crows fly to a scarecrow and pull his coat aside to reveal a billboard that reads, "Romeo and Juliet performed by the Black Crow Opera Company." The story begins as the curtain is raised on a scene at the rear of an apartment building in the city. It is evening as a black crow arrives dressed in the costume of the character Romeo from Shakespeare's famous *Romeo and Juliet.* He is carrying a mandolin. As the background music plays "Darktown Strutters Ball," he looks up and sees the silhouette of his lover, Juliet, in a second-floor window of an apartment building. She is putting on her makeup to meet him. A fly buzzing around her face annoys her. She can't shoo it away so she sprays it with her perfume, and the fly falls out of the air dead. Romeo lets Juliet know that he is there by playing his mandolin. Juliet calls down, "Who is dat?" He answers, "It's Romeo, Honey. I wants to woo." Juliet responds, "I does too. I'll be right out." Romeo starts to play and sing a jazzy rendition of "You Were Meant for Me." Juliet walks out on the balcony and calls down to him, "Swing it for me." Juliet pulls a long-stemmed rose out of her bosom, smells it, and then drops it down to Romeo. It hits Romeo on his head and knocks him backward. He falls through the roof of a coal bin. Juliet can't see him and calls out, "Oh Romeo, Romeo. Where fo' is you Romeo?" Romeo climbs up from the coal bin, and he and Juliet sing a duet. However their duet is interrupted when a paperboy comes along and hits Romeo so hard in the face with a newspaper that Romeo swallows the paper. He is unable to sing until he spits the paper out of his mouth. Again Romeo and Juliet resume their love song and again they are interrupted, this time by the milkman, singing, "I'm an Old Cowhand from the Rio Grande." After he goes away, a small dog with tin cans tied to its tail runs by. Soon after this the sound of jungle drums is heard. Stanley and Africans carrying bags on their heads show up on the scene. Stanley says, "Dr. Livingstone, I presume." He takes one look and Romeo and says, "Pardon me," and is quickly on his way. Trailing behind Stanley's group is a small African boy carrying several large packages on his head. As he staggers past Romeo, he tells him, "I sure wish you was Dr. Livingstone. I'm tired." Romeo, frustrated by all the interruptions, angrily throws down his mandolin and kicks it to pieces. He says, "If you want to play the part of Romeo, all you got to have is seclusion from intrusion." Then various scenes show where not to look for seclusion, including Coney Island, a goldfish bowl, a subway car, and the last row in a movie theater. Finally Romeo and Juliet are seen parked in what appears to be a secluded spot, but lights come on

and it turns out to be the Hollywood Bowl. Returning to the apartment scene, Juliet looks down at Romeo and says, "Darlin', you is alone." Romeo is about to resume his wooing when a clock alarm rings. Juliet says, "I got to get to work, so long." She goes back into her bedroom, changes into her maid's uniform, and rushes off to catch her bus. She is in such a hurry that she knocks the ladder out from under Romeo's feet, leaving him hanging on the second story by his hands. As she goes out of sight, she tells Romeo, "Good-bye until we meet tomorrow. Parting is such sweet sorrow." Romeo replies, "Partin' is such sweet sorrow." He falls and hits the ground in a cloud of dust as the cartoon ends.

Review: *Motion Picture Herald,* **7 September 1940**

Hugh Harman has taken the story of unrequited love by William Shakespeare and through the medium of the Black Crow Opera Company presents *Romeo and Juliet.* In this the crows present a swing version of the Shakespearean play but with numerous interruptions from the milkman, an expedition in search of Dr. Livingston and others. In an effort to find seclusion for their romantic escapades the two crows try the subway, Coney Island, a fish bowl and other spots but without success. An amusing cartoon. (8 min)

Review: *Film Daily,* **9 May 1940**

Hugh Harman has succeeded in putting good humor into this one, which is a travesty on the famous "balcony scene" from *Romeo and Juliet.* The delineated principals are two enamored crows enacting roles in behalf of The Black Crow Opera Co. Reel is done in the spirit of torrid Harlem, even to the dialogue. Romeo warbles some hot swing numbers to Juliet, and, dolled up in the best manner of this cosmetic age, she goes stepping with him to find a quiet place to woo. Finding none, she leaves him flat.

Review: *Boxoffice,* **7 September 1940**

An acceptable cartoon, but not beyond. Free wheeling is applied to Shakespeare and *Romeo and Juliet,* with plenty of swing peppering the stew. The cartoon work is standard, which reminds that it is not Disney. With emphasis on that score. (8 min)

Review: *Motion Picture Exhibitor,* **18 September 1940**

The crows put on a show which turns out to be a swing version of "Romeo and Juliet" with the two crows as the protagonists. All sorts of interruptions plague Romeo who speaks with a colored dialect, and finally impatient Juliet goes off and leaves him flat. Fair.

Description: *Metro-Goldwyn-Mayer Short Story,* **July/August 1940**

When William Shakespeare wrote his important tragedy of unrequited love, it was probably beyond the scope of his imagination ever to envision the day when the "greatest love story of all time" would be presented as a comedy . . . and in swing, too. Yet, this is just what has been done in Hugh Harman's *Romeo In*

Rhythm. The film introduces the "Black Crow Opera Company." Two crow love birds are about to entertain a variety of cornfield crows with the famous balcony scene. The male bird, dressed in the traditional Romeo attire, quotes the bard. "But soft, what light from yonder window shines, 'tis Juliet." But from this point on, the classic scene has but little in common with the Shakespearean theme. It is switched to the mood of a deep South revival meeting and to the tempo of a "jive" session.

Juliet, far from being the innocent maid that Shakespeare depicted, goes in for atomizers and plucked eyebrows. When she hears the soft strain of Romeo's guitar, she doesn't address the stars or the moon in true Juliet fashion. Instead, she asks, "Who dat down dere snoopin' aroun'?" And Romeo shows the swing influence on the house of Montague when he answers, "It's Romeo, honey, an' I want to woo." Romeo has success with his courting until Juliet asks the famous question about what's in a name and in a rose. When she gets no answer, she lets fly with a flowerpot that knocks the gallant lover into an open cellar. When Romeo staggers out, he is covered with tin cans and looks like the "Tin Woodsman of Oz." Momentarily confused, he starts singing, "I'm off to see the Wizard, the Wonderful Wizard of Oz."

Thereafter, interruptions constantly interfere with the course of true love. The payoff comes when Stanley, as the head of an African safari, taps Romeo on the shoulder and says, "Pardon me, Dr. Livingston, I presume?"

Romeo, in disgust, then seeks seclusion to do his "wooin'." He tries Coney Island, a goldfish bowl, a subway, and a theater without success. Finally he finds seclusion in a parked car on a lonely, secluded road.

But just as he settles down for a serious session of woo with his gal friend, an alarm clock rings and Juliet has to go to work. This is too much for Romeo and when Juliet ends the scene with "parting is such sweet sorrow," the gallant swain holds his nose in disgust.

ROVER'S RIVAL (1937)

Company: Robert Clampett, Warner Bros.
Type: Looney Tunes
Characters: Porky Pig, Rover, black pup

Story: The cartoon opens as Porky sits in his easy chair in an upstairs room in his house reading a book entitled "New Tricks to Teach Your Dog." He says, "Boy, here is a lot of tricks to teach my pooch. Here's one and another . . ." Then he gets up and runs down the stairs. He grabs a loop and a ball before going out the door and running to Rover's doghouse. He calls out, "Rover ole boy, come on out!" Rover, a long, skinny hound dog with long ears and droopy eyes slowly walks out of his house as the background music plays "Old Black Joe." He is trembling as he sits down in front of Porky, who says, "Well, let's try a couple of easy ones to warm up." He commands Rover to "sit up," and Rover slowly sits up on his hind legs. Porky's next command is to roll over. Rover tries to roll over but gets stuck on his back. Meanwhile a little black pup arrives on the scene and observes what is happening before walking over to Rover and blowing him all the

way over. Porky gives a command to jump through the hoop as he holds the hoop up. Before Rover can move, the black pup jumps through the hoop. Porky lowers the hoop just as Rover jumps, and Rover crashes into the side of the house and then falls flat on the ground. The black pup looks down on him and says, "You old antique, you can't teach an old dog new tricks. Why don't you just give up?" Porky continues to issue commands, and each time the black pup humiliates Rover by doing the trick first. Rover is about ready to give up. With tears in his eyes he asks the black pup, "You mean to say I'm one of them has-beens?" The pup answers yes. But Porky won't give up and throws a stick for Rover to fetch. Again the black pup fetches the stick and brings it back to Porky. Porky says, "Now this time it's Rover's turn" and then throws the stick. Rover fetches the stick by grabbing it with his teeth but leaves his teeth and the stick on the ground when he returns to Porky. The black pup fetches the stick and Rover's teeth. Rover puts his teeth back into his mouth, and again Porky throws the stick for him to fetch. Rover runs to fetch the stick but it lands in a building where sticks of dynamite are stored. Instead of the stick, Rover fetches a stick of dynamite for Porky. The situation gets hectic as Porky tries to throw the stick of dynamite away, but the black pup keeps returning it. Meanwhile Rover cries "dynamite" and runs inside the house to look up the word in the dictionary. Eventually the black pup manages to confront Porky with more sticks of dynamite. Finally Rover learns that dynamite means explosive and he then runs outside where he grabs the dynamite from the black pup and runs off. Porky and the pup hear a loud explosion and run to investigate, fearing for Rover's safety. They find Rover stretched out on the ground, motionless. The black pup is very sorry as he leans over Rover and says, "Rover, don't blame me. I didn't mean to jump through the hoop first. Of course you can teach an old dog new tricks. You're not really washed up . . ." Rover opens his eyes, jumps up with a smile on his face, and asks the black pup, "Do you really mean it?" as the cartoon ends.

RUNAWAY BLACKIE (1933)

Company: Harry Bailey, Van Beuren, released by RKO-Radio Pictures
Type: Aesop's Fable
Characters: Black sheep

Review: *Motion Picture Reviews,* April 1933

In this animated cartoon the little black sheep lives up to his name, but finds that good behavior has its compensation. Recommended for all.

Review: *Film Daily,* 8 April 1933

This cartoon story of a little black lamb who ran away from home and experienced some very surprising adventures, finally winding up on the chain gang. He escapes and is being chased by bloodhounds, only to waken and find that it was all a nightmare. Just a fair cartoon. (7 min)

Review: *Motion Picture Herald,* **20 May 1933**

More than the mechanics of having a cartoon character turn to making orchestras out of tableware, typewriter keys and what not, is required in pen and ink comedy now that "everybody's doing it." In *Runaway Blackie,* Aesop's Fables, the one elevation above routine is the windup—and literally so—with the chained convicts wound up on a huge roller by the jailer, for their night's sleep.

THE RUNT (1925)

Company: Paul Terry, Pathe Film Exchange
Type: Terrytoon; later released by Educational Pictures with added sound track in 1936 as *Aesop's Fable*
Characters: Farmer Al Falfa, black pig

See fig. 54. Story: The cartoon opens in Farmer Al Falfa's barnyard where all of the big fat white pigs are smiling, singing, and dancing. One pig, a black runt, sits on a rock frowning. Inside the house Farmer Al Falfa is cooking a huge pot of spaghetti for them. Lying on the floor beside him is his little black cat. Farmer dishes out a spoonful that he gives to the cat before taking the pot off the stove and blowing a trumpet to call all the pigs to dinner. All of the pigs run to the house, picking up plates and forks on the way. The black pig brings up the rear and arrives as the Farmer is dishing out spaghetti to the pigs through the window of the house as they walk by in single file. The little black pig cuts to the front of the line, but the farmer reaches over him to put the food on another pig's plate. The little black pig makes several more attempts to cut into line, but he is kicked out of the way each time. When he tries again, the white pig grabs him by his tail jerks him out of line. Finally the black pig gives up and goes to the back of the line. As he reaches the window to get his food, he finds that it is closed. He will not be fed again today and will continue to be a runt. The black pig angrily throws his plate on the ground before going over to the dinner table where the other pigs are eating. He sits down at the table next to one pig who gives him some spaghetti before shoving him off the bench to the ground. The black pig slowly walks away with his head down, crying, and then sits down under a tree. Several frogs climb out of a nearby toadstool and swim in the pool of the black pig's tears. The black pig sings, "I'm unhappy, so unhappy. Never any food for me. No one ever thinks of me. Oh, I'm so unhappy, I'm as hungry as can be. No one thinks of me." Meanwhile the other pigs are enjoying their dinner as Honest Joe, the wholesale butcher, passes by in his horse-drawn delivery wagon. Joe sees the pigs, smiles, and licks his lips before saying, "Nice fat pigs." Joe stops his wagon and opens the side door of the meat locker before posting a Free Lunch sign. He then shouts "Oink! Oink!" The pigs come running and climb into the locker. When they are all inside, Joe locks the door. As usual the little black pig arrives late on the scene and sees that the others are captured. He tries to run away, but Joe catches him and then throws him down after weighing him and finding that he is too skinny to keep. Joe climbs aboard his wagon and heads for his butcher shop while the black pig runs

back to the farmhouse where he grabs Farmer Al Falfa and pulls him to the barn where the car is parked. The Farmer speeds after Joe with the black pig standing in the hood of the car pointing the way. They drive up behind Joe's wagon, and the black pig uses a rope to lasso the lock on the locker door. The little black pig walks across the rope from the car to the wagon where he uses his tail to unscrew the bolts holding the lock to the door. The door opens and the other pigs, one by one, walk across the rope to the car. After all of the other pigs are safely across, the black pig cuts the rope with a knife before he is pulled by the others back to the car. All are smiles as they drive back home with the little black pig riding in front of the car with the Farmer. Later all the pigs, including the little black pig, sit at the dinner table as the Farmer places a huge pot of hot spaghetti on the table. The little black pig eats while the other pigs sing, "Our hero is the runt" as the cartoon ends.

Review: *Moving Picture World,* **6 June 1925**

A little black pig that gets nosed out of his porridge by his bigger and fairer brethren becomes a hero when he rescues the crowd from the slaughter house in *The Runt.* The cartoon by Paul Terry is on the order of some familiar nursery stories and should tickle the youngsters and amuse their parents.

SANTA'S SURPRISE (1947)

Company: Seymour Kneitel, Famous Studios, Paramount Pictures
Type: Noveltoons
Characters: Santa Claus, Little Audrey, Audrey's friends, including a black boy

Story: The cartoon opens on Christmas Eve with Santa Claus, riding in his sleigh pulled by six reindeer. They deliver toys to children all over the world. His last delivery is to Little Audrey's house in New York City. He puts toys under the tree while Little Audrey lies in bed pretending to be asleep. Having finished a long night's work, a weary Santa arrives back home at the North Pole where he climbs into bed and is soon fast asleep. Meanwhile Little Audrey and her friends, including a black boy, a Russian boy, a Dutch boy, a Chinese boy, a Spanish girl, and a Hawaiian girl, are stowaways on Santa's sleigh. They climb out of the sleigh, wipe the frost from the window of Santa's house, and look inside. Little Audrey says, "Hey kids, I betcha he's asleep now, I betcha." They see that Santa's workshop is a mess. Dirty dishes are stacked in the kitchen sink, and Santa is snoring in his bed. Little Audrey lowers her head and says sadly, "I feel sorry for Santa." The black boy says, "Yeah, man. He sho' tired and worn." They all agree and the Spanish girl says, "Si si. He helps everyone at Christmas, but no one thinks of Santa Claus." Little Audrey says, "Well, we could tidy his house." The others agree and they all go inside. They work together to clean Santa's house. The Chinese boy does the laundry and the black boy smiles as he shines Santa's shoes and sings, "I shines his shoes with a boogie beat . . ." The boys use a rope, hoist, and sling to lift Santa off his bed while Audrey and the two other girls change the sheets. As they are about to lower him back down, he wakes up. They let go of the rope and then run and hide. Santa drops down on the bed and wakes up. He looks around and sees a clean, tidy house and says, "Oh, what's that?" He gets out of bed and walks over to the Christmas tree where he picks up a present and says, "A present for me." He opens his present and finds a music box. He sees the smiling faces of Little Audrey and her friends. He also finds a note. It is written on a calendar of December with the twenty-fifth day circled. It reads, "Don't forget us next year." Santa laughs and says "ho, ho, ho," as the cartoon ends.

THE SCARED CROWS (1939)

Company: Dave Fleischer, Max Fleischer, Paramount Pictures
Characters: Betty Boop, black crows, Pudgy, scarecrow

Review: *Motion Picture Exhibitor,* 31 May 1939

Betty is tormented by the crows, who annoy Pudgy and eat her provisions, but her friend the Scarecrow comes to her aid and the crows are routed. Fair.

SCRUB ME MAMMA WITH A BOOGIE BEAT (1941)

Company: Alex Louis, Frank Tipper, Walter Lantz, Universal Pictures
Characters: Harlem Honey, southern blacks

See fig. 55. Story: The cartoon opens in Lazytown, a little village in the South where all the people are lazy to the extreme. The background music is "Swanee River." Everybody in town is either sleeping or lazily going about their daily routines. The chickens are too lazy to lay eggs, and the dogs bark in a lazy manner. A cotton picker picks one cotton ball at a time. The whistle of a steamboat is heard and the black captain calls out, "Lazytown. One-hour stay for lunch." The only person getting off the boat is a Harlem honey walking to a boogie beat. She tells a woman slowly washing clothes, "Listen, Mammy. That ain't no way to wash clothes. What you all need is rhythm." The woman answers, "What you all mean, rhythm?" The Harlem swingster starts to sing "Scrub Me Mamma with a Boogie Beat." The music works wonders on the people of the town. The pace of their daily activities quickens as they all get caught up in the rhythm. Couples are jitterbugging in the streets, and children join in the singing. The hour is up, and it is time for the Harlem cutie to leave. As she gets back on the boat, the people in Lazytown continue to boogie. A woman washing clothes bends over, displaying "The End" on her underpants as the cartoon ends.

Review: *Motion Picture Herald,* 28 April 1941

In this color cartoon a lazy group of southern darkies awaken on the arrival of a Harlem miss and proceed to get rhythm in the modern manner. It is a subject of especial interest to swing devotees. (7 min)

Review: *Boxoffice,* 23 March 1941

To Lazytown, where all the colored folk are snoozing, comes a river boat and a gal. She wakes up everybody, and gets them in the mood with her rendition of the boogie woogie number. The action builds effectively. This one is for the under seat feet shufflers.

Review: *Film Daily,* 25 March 1941

A light brown gal arrives in Lazytown and wakes the locals to the tune of a rhythm number. The music is hot and the former sleeping inhabitants step right out to it in this fast color cartoon. A couple of skirt silhouette shots and some exaggerated body movements make this one questionable for kid matinees.

Review: *Motion Picture Exhibitor,* 14 May 1941

This will not only provoke laughs but it is worth extra selling effort. All the colored characters take off on this popular song but with a high-brown beauty shaking hips to all points while beating a song with every note. It is in the better cartoon sphere. Good.

Article: NAACP Protests Cartoon, *Pittsburgh Courier,* 12 February 1949

N. J. Blumberg, president of Universal Pictures Company, Inc., this week notified the National Association for the Advancement of Colored People that the film cartoon *Scrub Me Mama* has been withdrawn from circulation following NAACP protests of its exhibition.

The NAACP's national office and several of the association's branches had received complaints that the movie portrayed a vicious caricature of Negro life and that it was "insulting derogatory, and offensive." Members of the NAACP staff who discussed the picture with a Universal official submitted a memorandum requesting that the picture be withdrawn.

SEPTEMBER IN THE RAIN (1937)

Company: I. Freleng, Warner Bros.
Type: Merrie Melodies
Characters: Caricatures of Al Jolson in blackface, Aunt Emma, Fats Waller, Louis Armstrong, Ethel Waters, Fred Astaire, Ginger Rogers

See fig. 56. Story: The cartoon opens in a grocery store. Ethel Waters comes off a can of blueing to sing "Am I Blue." An Indian snake charmer charms a "snake" of Tootsie Tooth Paste. A Dutch girl steps off a can of Old Maid Cleanser and does a clog dance wearing wooden shoes. A rubber glove inflates itself into the shape of an octopus. The camels on packages of Camel Cigarettes walk along to the tune of the musical background of the title song. Two ladies jump off a bottle Good Oh' Scotch and dance a jig. A green worm crawls out of an apple and is attacked by four little chicks off cans of My Ami Cleaning Powder. The worm manages to escape after one of the chicks swallows him. A waterfall on a box of Threaded Wheat spills over onto a box of salt a little girl wearing a raincoat keeps dry with her umbrella.

She sings "By A Waterfall" while a little boy in a raincoat steps off a box of Uneedum Corks and joins her in a duet. Al Jolson, blackface, steps off a box of Dream of Cream Wheat and sings the title song. Midway through his song he does his famous "Mammy" routine to a black lady on a box of Aunt Emma's Pancake Flour. She throws out her arms and says "Sonny Boy." Jolson points to his old southern home, which is a can of Cabin Syrup. From a box of Domingo, Ginger Rogers joins Fred Astaire, who comes off a box of Tarrytown Cigarettes, and they do a ballroom dance routine. Next on a box of Gold Dust Washing Powder, Louis Armstrong and Fats Waller call out to a chef from a box of Bosko's Baking Powder to start the music. The chef beats drums on a mixing bowl, and Fats Waller hurries over to a piano on a can of piano wax and starts to play hot jazz while Louis Armstrong sings "Nagasaki." Two roosters on a box of chicken feed join in the chorus while Aunt Emma does a shimmy dance. The music is getting so good that Fats leans back and plays the piano with his feet. Louis Armstrong joins in with a trumpet solo as the cartoon ends.

Review: *Film Daily,* 12 December 1937

In this cartoon done in Technicolor, the scene is a grocery store after closing time, with the rain pouring down. The fantasy has all the trade-marked characters on the labels of boxes and cans come to life and join in a party staged to swing music. The musical revue is cleverly handled, with a lot of well known advertised goods thinly disguised getting a nice plug, intentional or otherwise. Who knows? Who cares? It is smartly done. Produced by Leon Schlesinger. Animation by Cal Dalton. (7 min)

Review: *Boxoffice,* 5 February 1938

A cheerful and pleasing little fantasy which takes place in a grocery store. The familiar trademarks and symbols on the various products come to life and participate in a musical revue set to swing music. The cartoon is conceived in a gay and light manner.

Review: *Motion Picture Herald,* 7 October 1944

Warner Bros., continuing its policy of reissuing popular shorts, brings back a musical fantasy in a grocery store. The performers are the familiar figures from the package and can labels who dance off to swing music.

Review: *Selected Motion Pictures,* 1 January 1938

The merchandise in a grocery store comes to life and gives clever impersonations. Amusing. Family and Junior Matinee.

Review: *Motion Picture Exhibitor,* 18 October 1944

This re-issue is a frolic of popular brands who come to life from off their package labels in a grocery store. There is a Jolson impersonation by the Cream of Wheat figure, a dance by the boy and girl from off cigarette packages, while the Gold Dust Twins swing it; Aunt Jemima hoofs, etc. Animation and idea is cute, drawings and color tops. Excellent.

Review: *Motion Picture Exhibitor,* 1 January 1938

No plot this time, just some take-offs on nationally advertized goods with slight variation. Animation is nice; a burlesque on Jolson is clever; gags are up to the usual high standard, but short lacks the sock quality of some of the series. Good.

Review: *Besa Shorts Shorts,* 23 October 1944

A Blue Ribbon Merrie Melodie located in the corner grocery store where all the labels come to life and do a gag or dance turn. Among these is Aunt Jemima and some other well-known pictures which includes Fats Waller and Louis Armstrong as well as Al Jolson singing a mammy tune.

THE SHANTY WHERE SANTA CLAUS LIVES (1933)

Company:	Hugh Harman, Rudolph Ising, Vitaphone, Warner Bros.
Type:	Merrie Melodies
Characters:	Santa Claus, little white boy, Sambo jazz band

Story: The cartoon opens on Christmas Eve as a small boy wearing a ragged coat and a cap walks slowly along the snow-covered street. His head is down as he passes a church where he hears sounds of a choir singing "Silent Night." He walks past a house where he looks through an open window and sees happy children inside dancing around a Christmas tree loaded with gifts. He finally arrives home and is disappointed when he finds an empty stocking hanging above a cold fireplace. He walks over to a chair, sits down, and starts to cry when he hears the sound of a sleigh outside. He runs to the window, looks out, smiles, and says, "Santa Claus." Santa enters the boy's house with a big smile on his face and wipes the tears from the boy's face. The boy tells him, "Oh boy, I'd like to go with you. Perhaps there will be a bunch of toys for me." Santa smiles and takes the boy with him. Soon they arrive at Santa's toy shop. The toys cheer and proceed to put on a musical show. The boy walks over to a black, four-piece Sambo wind-up jazz band. He winds them up and they play the title song. All the toys join in, including a white baby doll that falls into a coal box. The doll comes out covered with black coaldust, sees a black woman, and says "Mammy." The black woman, wearing a maid's apron and a bandanna on her head, grins and says "Sonny boy" as she takes the baby into her arms. Next a female doll trio sings the title song. One of the trio is a white girl with flowing curly hair. The other two girls are black and have hair that looks like wire springs sticking out of their heads. After the boy puts a Christmas tree fire, all have a good time. The boy has a happy Christmas after all as the cartoon ends.

SHIP AHOY (1930)

Company:	John Foster, Van Beuren; released by Pathe
Type:	Aesop Sound Fable
Characters:	Farmer, white boy, black girl

Story: At the conclusion of cartoons in the Aesop Sound Fable series, an animated character(s) speaks to the moral of the cartoon. At the conclusion of this cartoon a little smiling white boy appears next to a little girl who is standing next to him. Her back is turned and a large bonnet hides her face. The boy says, "Fools throw kisses, but wise men deliver them in person." He grabs the girl and gives her a kiss, but then stops suddenly and screams. The girl turns out to be a smiling black girl with thick white lips and braided hair sticking out of her head. The little white boy jumps out of his clothes and then runs away. The little black girl grins as the cartoon ends.

SHUFFLE OFF TO BUFFALO (1933)

Company: Rudolph Ising, Hugh Harman, Vitaphone, Warner Bros.
Type: Merrie Melodies
Characters: White and black babies

Story: "Shuffle Off to Buffalo" is the musical theme of this cartoon. The opening scene shows storks flying out of a baby factory and delivering new babies. Inside the factory an old man is seated at a desk taking orders for babies over the phone and recording them in his order book. He smiles at one order, which reads, "Send us twins. Signed, Mr. and Mrs. Nanook." He says, "What a man!" He goes to the deep freezer and retrieves two baby Eskimos and gives them to a stork, one in the upper berth and the other in the lower berth, to carry to the north pole. The old man has a hard time reading the next order, for it is written in Hebrew. He places it in a basket that is sent to the stock room, where a Jewish baby with curly hair and a big nose is retrieved. He stamps the words "Kosher for Passover" on the baby's bottom. The baby sings a chorus of "Shuffle Off to Buffalo" and is joined by a chorus of other babies. Meanwhile in the factory the baby assembly line is in full production. Babies are carried on a conveyor belt where they are washed, dried, powdered, diapered, and given milk. In the holding room the babies are noisy and restless. The attendant asks them what they want and they respond, "We want Cantor." An Eddie Cantor baby sings the title song and does an Ed Wynn impersonation. The black Gold Dust twin babies show up on the scene and shuffle off into the bathroom. They are all having a grand time as the cartoon ends.

S'MATTER PETE? (1920)

Company: Walter Lantz, J. R. Bray Studio
Type: Combination live action and animation
Characters: Pete the dog, a cartoonist-teacher (as himself), black girl, two white boys

Story: The cartoon opens with live action as a cartoonist is drawing a sketch on a large sheet of white paper attached to the wall. He pauses to sharpen the tips of his paintbrushes by putting them through a meat grinder. Then he completes his sketch of a small, one-room schoolhouse with a doghouse

standing nearby. After he finishes, he rings a school bell and a large white kid shows up in front of the school. The kid looks inside before moving away, revealing a black girl and a small white boy standing behind him. The black girl has thick white lips, and two braids, with a bow tied to each, stick out of her head. The black girl and the small boy enter the school, but the third boy is too fat to squeeze through the door and needs the small boy to push him from behind. Meanwhile the cartoonist looks at his watch as says to himself, "Pete the pup is missing." Impatiently he rings the bell again. Pete the pup runs out of his small doghouse and stops in front of the school. The artist scowls at the dog for being late and pushes him through the front door. The artist then brushes off one wall of the schoolhouse, revealing the four students seated at their desks. The artist then seats himself behind his desk and takes on his role as teacher of the class. The teacher begins the lesson by drawing a picture of a bull on the chalkboard and then asking his students, "Who can tell me what this is?" The black girl is chewing gum and doesn't know the answer. The dog answers "cow" and the teacher tells him he's incorrect. The small boy answers "one cup of coffee" before the fat boy answers "a cow's husband." Meanwhile the dog, who is sitting behind the black girl, ties her two braids into the shape of a sling shot. Then he uses it to shoot a ball that hits the sketch of the bull and causes it to run off the blackboard. The little boy laughs and shouts, "Bully." The teacher tells him to shut up and then turns his back to the class. The dog uses the black girl's slingshot hair to propel another ball, which hits the teacher on the back of his head. The teacher turns around to see who hit him, but only sees the students with books in front of their faces. The teacher says that "our next lesson will be on the frozen north" before drawing a sketch of the North Pole on the blackboard. The snow-covered mountains are so realistic that the students shiver with cold. He too is cold and looks over to see that the coal heater is covered with ice. He chops up a wooden box and places the pieces of wood in the stove. He steps on a piece of sticky flypaper that won't come off his shoe, so he takes his shoes off and throws them into the stove while the kids and Pete laugh at him. He has trouble lighting the stove but finally succeeds after pouring in some kerosene. The fire ignites in a puff of smoke, which covers the teacher's face as the students laugh. He tries to get the fire going by shoveling in some coal but mistakenly pours in water, which almost puts out the fire. While he is bending over to blow into the stove to get the fire going again, the small boy paints a bull's-eye target on his rear end. Two students shoot their blowguns at the target. The black girl throws her schoolbook at the teacher but misses, and the book knocks over a can of kerosene standing on the stove. The kerosene drips down on the teacher. The teacher stands up to admonish the children just as the fire ignites and sets his pants aflame. As the teacher dances around trying to put out the fire, Pete climbs to where a picture of a waterfall is hanging on the wall. The dog turns on the waterfall, and the room quickly fills with water. The teacher tries unsuccessfully to grab the dog as he floats by. Water fills the room, and the teacher's head goes under as the cartoon ends.

THE SNEEZING WEASEL (1938)

Company: Tex Avery, Warner Bros.
Type: Merry Melodies
Characters: Black chick, yellow chicks, weasel

Review: *Boxoffice,* **9 August 1947**

A lively cartoon about a naughty dark chick and his little yellow brothers. When the mother hen and brothers run into the house, the dark chick continues chasing a worm in the rain. The chick catches cold and a weasel disguises himself as a doctor and enters the house. The chicks gang up on him and chase him from the house when his identity is discovered. (7 min)

SNOW WHITE (1933)

Company: Dave Fleischer, Max Fleischer, Paramount Pictures
Characters: Betty Boop, Bimbo, Ko-Ko the Clown (Cab Calloway voice-over)

Story: The cartoon opens in a palace where the ugly queen sits on her throne looking into her magic mirror and asking it, "Who's the fairest in the land?" A black face in the mirror responds, "You are." Meanwhile Betty Boop, living in her modest home, decides to visit her step-aunt, the queen. She arrives at the castle and tells the queen, "I have heard of your magic looking glass." After seeing Betty, the queen decides to again ask the mirror who is the fairest. The face in the mirror takes one look at Betty and answers, "Betty is." The queen is furious and orders her guards to take Betty away to be beheaded. They obey, and Betty is tied to a tree while the executioners, Ko-Ko and Bimbo, dressed in suits of armor, sharpen their ax. When Betty begins to cry, her executioners feel sorry for her and decide to spare her life. They throw their ax and grinding wheel down a hole and jump in after them. They fall all the way to the bottom and land in a huge cave. Meanwhile Betty manages to free herself and runs away. But she trips and rolls down a snow-covered hill. As she rolls, she becomes covered by snow, and soon she is encased in a big snowball. The snowball reaches the bottom of the hill and it bounces off a tree. Betty finds herself trapped in a block of ice. The ice slides into a lake, out of the lake, and then through the front door of the seven dwarfs' house. The dwarfs befriend Betty and use their magic spell to transform the block of ice surrounding her into a beautiful sled. Then they push her to the entrance of the cave. Betty enters the cave and meets Ko-Ko and Bimbo. Meanwhile the evil queen again asks the mirror, "Who is the fairest?" This time the answer she receives is, "If I were you, I'd hide my face." Infuriated, the queen transforms herself into a witch and flies out the castle on her broomstick to the cave to find Betty. Betty, Bimbo, and Ko-Ko decide to explore the cave. Along the way Ko-Ko sings "St. James Infirmary" with the demeanor of the great Cab Calloway. The witch-queen arrives on the scene and uses one of her evil spells to transform Ko-Ko into a huge

white walrus. Nevertheless, he continues to dance and sing in the Calloway style. The witch-queen transforms herself back to the queen and confronts Betty and Bimbo before she casts a spell on them that leaves them frozen stiff. The queen asks the mirror the familiar question. The mirror responds by casting a magic spell on the queen, turning her into a huge dragon. The dragon chases Betty, Ko-Ko, and Bimbo, who are now in their natural bodies. Betty and Ko-Ko manage to escape from the cave, but Bimbo is swallowed by the dragon. Bimbo, from inside the dragon, grabs its tail and holds onto it as he runs out of the dragon's mouth. As a result, the dragon is turned inside out and then changes into a skeleton before running back into the cave. Betty, Bimbo, and Ko-Ko celebrate their escape as the cartoon ends.

SPARK PLUG (1936)

Company: Charles Mintz, distributed by Columbia Pictures
Characters: Spark Plug, Barney Google, Sambo, Rudy, Snuffy Smith, Maw

See fig. 57. Story: The cartoon opens at the racetrack as the horses are lining up at the starting gate. The stands are crowded with spectators, including Barney Google, Rudy the ostrich, Snuffy Smith wearing a farmer's straw hat and holding a shotgun, and Maw. The horses and jockeys are ready. Spark Plug is being ridden by the black jockey, Sambo, who is Barney's servant. Barney waves his hat at Spark Plug to wish him luck. They're off, and all the horses are out of the gate and well out in front of Spark Plug, who is running slowly in last place. Disgusted with his horse, Barney Google buries his face in his hands while still puffing on his cigar. Meanwhile Spark Plug walks slowly down the track with Sambo lying on his back fast asleep. The race is over, night falls, and the stands are empty except for Barney. He sits alone waiting for Spark Plug to reach the finish line. A rooster crows, signaling the dawn. Spark Plug finally reaches the finish line and jumps across, waking up Sambo. Barney is so angry at his horse that he throws rocks at him. Later, back at the stable, Barney shouts at Spark Plug, who lowers his head in shame. Barney pulls out a bottle of castor oil from his pocket and pours a spoonful of the liquid in Spark Plug's mouth, but the horse spits it out back into Barney's face. Spark Plug and Rudy laugh at Barney. Spark Plug is in love with Rudy and rubs his head on Rudy's shoulder. But Rudy rejects him and admonishes him for losing the race. Dejected, Spark Plug slowly walks away with his head down and tears flowing from his eyes. Meanwhile the racing form announces a "big match race today—Spark Plug vs Man-O-War." It's race day, and the stands are crowded as Man-O-War, a frisky black horse, and Spark Plug, again carrying Sambo, line up at the starting gate. The bell rings and the race starts. The black horse jumps out of the gate and is off to a big lead. Meanwhile Sambo frantically whips Spark Plug as he tries to get the horse out of the starting gate. Snuffy Smith shoots his gun at Spark Plug, and Barney is so angry that he jumps out of the stands and runs across the track to the gate, where he grabs Spark Plug and tries unsuccessfully to pull him out. Rudy arrives on the scene and pushes Barney away before smiling at the horse. Spark Plug runs out of the gate so fast that he creates a wind that blows the leaves off the trees. Spark Plug gains on the black horse while Barney sits in the stands and chews the brim of his hat. Beads of sweat drop from his face. As they round the turn to the home stretch, Spark Plug and Man-O-War are running neck and neck as Barney and Rudy cheer him on. Spark Plug passes Man-O-War and wins the race. Sambo pats Spark Plug on the head while Rudy and Barney Google close by with big smiles on their faces as the cartoon ends.

SUNDAY GO TO MEETIN' TIME (1936)

Company: I. Freleng, Vitaphone, Warner Bros.
Type: Merrie Melodies
Characters: Nicodemus, his wife, the preacher (voice characterization by Roy Glenn), the devil

Story: The cartoon opens in the colored section of a small town. Chickens walk in the middle of the street. It is Sunday morning, and the sound of a church bell is heard. Inside the church the organ is playing, and at the front door the pastor is greeting arriving members while singing, "Hear the congregation playin'. Hear the organ softly playin'. To this chapel come the sinners one and all. When the church bells ring their greetin', callin' us to go to meetin', on the good Lord we is goin' to make a call." The church bells are rung by a man on the first floor pulling a rope attached to a rocking chair on the second floor, in which a man sits with his head inside the bell. "Truckin'" while they walk arm in arm are a woman and her man wearing their Sunday best. The man sings, "Once a week I get dressed in my Sunday best and wear a great big smile as I take you down the aisle when it's Sunday-go-to-meeting time. Even though I ain't what you call a saint, when the church bells chime above, even sinners fall in love when it's Sunday-go-to meetin'-time. I read it in the good book there's heaven in view. And when I take a good look it seems my heaven is you. Maybe I'll be blue waitin' six days for you, the seventh day looks fine. We will meet in rain or shine, when its Sunday-go-to-meetin' time." Meanwhile all over town people are preparing to go to church. In one house a mother is rubbing black shoe polish on the top of the bald head of each of her boys before they put their heads on a shoeshine stand where the father shines each by rubbing it with a cloth. A mother walks down the street pushing her twin babies in a stroller and steals a woman's brassiere, which she uses to make twin bonnets for her babies to wear on their heads. Meanwhile a big woman dressed in her Sunday clothes, carrying her handbag in one hand and a man's straw hat in the other, is standing in the door of her small shack calling out, "Nicodemus, Nicodemus . . ." She continues calling her husband while walking, but stops when she hears the sound of a dice game on the other side of a fence. There is a Mammy's Barbecue Pit sign posted on the fence. When she hears a voice say, "Come on

dice, come to papa," she reaches over the fence, pulls Nicodemus to her, and drops him on the sidewalk. She puts the straw hat on his head and marches him off to church, saying, "You good fo' nothin'. You git yourself right on to church. The devil's gonna get you as sure as you were born. Nicodemus, who is a caricature of Stephin Fetchit, reluctantly walks along and says, "I don't wanna go to no church." His wife says, "Git along there now. Don't give me no lip. I never seen any man so lazy and shiftless in my whole life." Nicodemus stops and tells her, "Don't crowd me, woman," but she pulls him along. They arrive at the church and go inside as the choir is singing "Go Down Moses." After a brief moment, Nicodemus slips out the backdoor and runs as fast as he can down the street. He comes to a screeching halt when he hears the sound of chickens behind a fence. He smiles, picks up a club, enters the gate, and tries to steal a chicken. The chicken runs and stops at a fence. Posted on the side of a nearby building is a sign that reads, "Vote for Judge Jailem for Court Justice." The chicken ducks through a loose board on the fence, but when Nicodemus tries to follow, he hits his head on the fence, and is knocked senseless. He is dazed and the sign behind him now reads, "Hades Court of Justice." He falls down to hell, where he is greeted by the gatekeeper, "Well look at who's here. So you came at last. Just one look at my book and we will review your past." He opens his book to a page titled "Nicodemus." It says, "Shooting craps, stealing chickens, missing church, raisin' dickens, stealing watermelons." After reading Nicodmus his sins, he pulls a lever and Nicodemus falls down to a lower hell where the devil, sitting on his throne, sings to him, "Oh you got to give the devil his due. Up all night you always had your way, drank your gin and slept your life away. Now just for that you've got to pay. You got to give the devil his due." After finishing, the devil says, "All right boys, give him the works." The devil's helpers surround Nicodemus, knock him to the ground, and beat on his head. But it is all a nightmare. As Nicodemus wakes up by the fence, the chickens are pecking him on the head. He shoos away the chickens and then runs as fast as he can back to the church. He enters and takes his place in the choir as it sings "All God's Chillun' Got Shoes" as the cartoon ends.

Reaction from the Black press: *Pittsburgh Courier,* 16 March 1945

In a letter written to the editor of the theatrical magazine *Variety* recently, a white GI, "somewhere in the Pacific." took time from the few other beefs which he had, to protest against the treatment of the "color question" in motion pictures. By doing so, he was speaking for thousands of servicemen who feel the same way, and perhaps simply haven't gotten around to a written protest.

An excerpt from the letter follows ". . . one more growl while I am in the mood. The other night at the regimental bowl we saw a "Merrie Melody" cartoon called *Sunday Go to Meetin' Time* that was a perfect example of bad taste at its worst. A great many people now are working to bring around a better understanding between the white and colored people, but this cartoon, served only to make the colored race look ridiculous. Hollywood can make a great contribution toward a better understanding between all the peoples of the world. The money spent on this cartoon could have been spent on a short featuring some of the great colored acts in show business today. Several colored men have gained honor for themselves and their race in combat. Their stories would make great motion picture material. Why not use them? Sincerely Yours, Pfc. Bruce O. Bishop."

Review: *Motion Picture Herald,* 5 September 1936

An entertaining "Merrie Melody" cartoon in color, this concerns the trials and tribulations of Nicodemus, a black boy, who prefers to steal chickens than go to church. Nicodemus is shooting craps when the missus finds him and drags him off to church. Nicodemus sneaks out and heads for the rap game but on the way he stops to steal a chicken. The black boy runs headlong into a fence and while he is unconscious dreams that he is in Hades and being punished for his earthly missteps. On awaking Nicodemus makes a bee line for the church. (7 min).

Review: *Boxoffice,* 22 August 1936

When a cartoon arouses enthusiasm in a projection room of hard boiled critics, it denotes a hit. In Technicolor, this subject tells the story mostly in Negro rhythm and tuneful jazz. The main character is Nico Demus, a black boy who would rather shoot craps and steal chickens than go to church on Sunday. In the act of pilfering a fowl, he is knocked unconscious and dreams he is in Hades where he is being punished. Upon awakening he seems to have learned his lesson and runs to the church.

Review: *Motion Picture Herald,* 4 November 1944

Warner Bros. reissues the cartoon adventures of Nicodemus who thought he'd skip church and shoot craps. But his conscience troubles him and he sees himself in Hades faced with the sins he has committed and receiving appropriate punishment for each. When he gets back to earth he's quite eager to establish himself as a regular church-goer.

Review: *Selected Motion Pictures,* 1 July 1936

A dream encourages Nicodemus to mend his ways and go to church. Good. Family.

Review: *National Exhibitor,* 5 September 1936

One of the best in the series this, however, should not be played on the same bill with *Green Pastures.* The shiftless darky doesn't want to go to church on Sunday, escapes from his wife, runs away, is knocked out chasing a chicken, dreams he is in Hell where he is made the ball in a bagatelle (pinball) game with other things happening to him. Finally he wakes up, heads for church. Color, animation, gags are above average with the whole thing a stand out. Very Good.

Review: *Motion Picture Exhibitor,* 18 October 1944

The good folks, all dressed up in their best, and going to a colored church as the song of the same name as the title is heard. One crap shooting, chicken thief gets knocked out, and thinks he is in court in front of the Devil, imagines what happens down in Hades while the song "You Gotta Give the Devil His Due" is heard. When he comes to, he makes a bee line for church, where they are singing "Yo Gotta Walk All Over God's Heaven." Excellent.

Review: *Besa Shorts Shorts,* 27 October 1944

A Blue Ribbon Merrie Melodie that stories Sunday church going activities of down in colored town where Nicodemus lives. He's a crap shooting, chicken stealing darky whose wife has to drag him to church. He sneaks out of the meeting house to chase a fat hen only to get a bump on his head which sends him to dreaming about his sins. His dream takes him to Hades where he gets a good going over and you may well be sure he's glad to run back to church when he wakes up.

SWING SOCIAL (1940)

Company: William Hanna, Joseph Barbera, Rudolph Ising, M-G-M
Characters: Deacon, Chief Bass, Brother Brown Bass, Uncle Tom Bass

Description: *Metro-Goldwyn-Mayer Shorts Story,* April/May 1940

See fig. 58. In his famous "bathysphere," which descends hundreds of feet into the depths of the sea, William Beebe, noted ocean explorer, has seen many strange, almost unbelievable sights in the murky waters on the ocean's floor. But never in any of his subaqua prying will he witness a sight as strange as the one William Hanna and Joe Barbera depict in their first cartoon for Metro-Goldwyn-Mayer. The cartoon is titled *Swing Social.*

One Sunday morning, the film relates, way down South in the land of cotton, when all the folks are in the meeting hall, Brother Brown, a fugitive from the meeting, is sitting by the edge of the river fishing for bass. Deacon Black, who happens to be passing by, sees Brother Brown and stops to talk to him.

"Don't yo' know dat on a Sunday morn' yo' can't catch no black bass on accounta' de black basses has dere swing social evr'y Sunday. If yo' don' believe me, look down dere," Deacon Black says. So, the Brother and the good Deacon look into the river, and sure enough there are all the black bass in a terrific swing session.

Sister Finn is there, in her Sunday best, with Brother Gill, who is wearing his favorite checkered vest. Soon, Old Man Mose, who was thought to be dead, arrives. He has come to kick the bucket on this social Sunday morning. Uncle Tom is also there, all decked out in a new store-bought suit. Formerly, he had had trouble with a scaly Simon Legree, and no more trouble. In fact, Uncle Tom has just brought a new black bass cabin on the F. H. A. plan. Next to arrive is F. D. R. Jones, youngest member of the younger set.

Then, come the funny pickaninnies, to swing and sway with the older folks and to watch old Grandpa as he leads the singers while shimmying, jiving and rug-cutting.

"Whatcha doin' Grandpa?" one pickaninny asks.

"Ah'm doin' de voodoo," he replies. 'Dere's de polka, de waltz, and de Suzy-Q, but dey is all the same with a different name, but the voodoo is de only one dat's really different."

At this point, Deacon Black, who is watching the swing social with Brother Brown, looks up from the water and says, "Yo' see, dat's de reason why de black bass won't bite on Sunday."

Brother Brown, very sheepishly hangs his head and shuffles slowly down the road to join the rest of the Brother and Sisters at the meeting hall.

Review: *Motion Picture Herald*, 1 January 1940

Swing Social is one of the liveliest, funniest and most completely entertaining color cartoons to appear this season. It is all about black bass and the swing social they put on, on Sundays. The cartoon opens with a Negro, in his week day clothes, sitting on a wooden bridge, fishing. Along comes another Negro in his Sunday going-to-meeting clothes to tell the fisherman that the black bass never bite on Sundays because of the social. The scene shifts below the water where the black bass are gathered. Well known characters, such as Old Black Joe, have their counterpart in the gathering. The animation is superbly done and the humor very human. (8 min)

Review: *Boxoffice*, 8 June 1940

This cartoon belongs in the top rank of animated entertainment. In Technicolor the content is musical and pleasantly rhymed as it tells the doings at a Colored "go to meetin'" singing festival. It's sure fire entertainment comparable with the best and definitely worth while. (8 min)

Review: *Motion Picture Exhibitor*, 12 June 1940

The swing addicts have their day in this, with Deacon Brown describing to Brother Black, who fishes on Sunday, that the black bass have a swing social every Sunday, so there can't be good fishing that day. Whereupon the camera descends to the bottom of the sea where the fish go through their gyrations. This has some good gags, animation and should please anywhere. Good.

SWING WEDDING (1937)

Company: Hugh Harman, Rudolph Ising, M-G-M
Type: Happy Harmonies
Characters: Frog caricatures of Fats Waller, Bill Robinson, the Mills Brothers, Ethel Waters, Cab Calloway, Stephin Fetchit (Smokey Joe), Louis Armstrong

See fig. 59. Story: The cartoon opens on a peaceful evening near a frog pond while "Deep River" plays in the background. As three frogs hum a tune, another frog asks them, "What you ol' boys moanin' about?" The four of them (Mills Brothers

caricatures) sing, "When you beat your feet on that Mississippi mud . . ." and another frog says "Yeah man." The quartet continues, "What a dance do they do! Lawdy how I'm tellin' you. They don't need no band. They keep time by clapping their hands." A male and a female frog dance, and the male frog says, "Say how come you keep clapping yo' hands?" The female answers, "Why, that's what we call boogie, man." A female frog (Ethel Waters caricature) walks from behind the curtain and sings, "Just as happy as a cow chewin' on his cud we is . . ." The quartet sings, "Got to beat your feet on the Mississippi mud." The music stops and a frog preacher stands before the others and says, "Brotherettes and sisterettes! Whenever folks in Chinatown start actin' gay, there's somethin' in the air that makes them feel that way." The crowd answers, "Yeah man," and the minister says, "Did I hear someone say it's Minnie the Moocher's wedding day?" A shapely female chorus line dances and sings, "Smokey Joe's so happy he can hardly wait, payin' a million dollars for a weddin' cake." Minnie the Moocher comes through the curtains wearing her white wedding dress. She says, "I heard somebody say . . ." and the crowd sings "Minnie the Moocher's wedding day." Minnie sings, "You better come on down, down to Chinatown. Let me take you down to see them kick the gong around." The group sings, "Millions of couples singin' hi-dee-hi-dee-hay" as frog couples do the cakewalk. The song continues, "We gonna see the preacher give the bride away, yeah man. I heard somebody say it's Minnie the Moocher's wedding day." A frog holding a trumpet in his hand (Louis Armstrong caricature) blows a short trumpet solo and then sings, "Yeah, yeah, they're goin' to that old wedding. Yeah man, yeah . . . and do-by-do. See our sunburnt babes, how fine. They just fall in line. Oh baby, with those sweethearts on parade." Meanwhile another frog, Smokey Joe (Stephin Fetchit caricature), is shuffling along scratching his head and wearing a tuxedo suit and holding flowers in one hand. He says, "Oh goodness, I guess I don't care fo' that ol' matra-matra-allimony." Louis Armstrong tells him, "Well, Smokey Joe, where you goin' boy?" Smokey says, "I guess I's goin' to that ole weddin'." Armstrong says, "You guess you're goin'! Boy, you is de groom." Smokey pauses for a moment, scratches his head, then runs off in a cloud of dust. Then he stops and scratches his head and says, "Where is dat wedding anyhow?" Meanwhile Minnie is nervously tapping her feet, waiting for Smokey to arrive. She says, "Dat low-down, good-fo'-nothin' rascal. Where can he be?" Just then a band leader (Cab Calloway caricature) and his band rise from the pond and sing to Minnie, "Come on Minnie and swing with me—with the hi-dee-ho king." Minnie says, "Get away from here man. I's true to my Smokey Joe." As she swings her hips around, Cab looks at her and says, "Oh come on, take a plane with the man who can swing." Minnie follows Cab, saying, "Tell me more, tell me more. What is dat swing you talkin' 'bout?" Minnie and Cab are joined by the others, and they cakewalk together to see the minister. Meanwhile a fat frog wearing a derby hat (Fats Waller caricature) plays the piano while another frog tap dances (Bill Robinson caricature) and sings, "Oh here I am, the very best man, to make this wedding the best I can." Minnie and Cab stand before the preacher. He asks Minnie, "Do you take this man for your groom?" Minnie says, "Yes I do, a roota-tap-tap and a booda-dum too." The preacher asks Cab, "Do you take dis girl to be yo' wife?" Cab says yes in jive talk. The preacher asks, "Does you promise to honor and obey?" And Cab sings, "Hi-dee-hay-dee-hay, wash de dishes, do de washin', cook de roast, roast de cookin', bake de bakin' . . ." Fats Waller says, "What's the matter with him?" The preacher asks the people, "Is there any man here who can honestly say dat dis here couple can't be wed today?" Meanwhile Smokey Joe, still slowly walking along scratching his head, hears the preacher's question. His mouth drops open so wide that his lower lip touches the ground. He shouts, "Yow sah! I objects most strenuously." Fats Waller turns around and says, "Who dat?" Louis Armstrong repeats, "Who dat?" Waller says, "Who dat say who dat when I say who dat?" Armstrong pulls Smokey along with him and they stand in front of Cab and Minnie. He says, "You talk about rhythm, he's got rhythm" as he points to Smokey. Armstrong says "swing out now" and blows hot jazz on his trumpet. Smokey's feet start to move faster and faster. The tempo keeps increasing, and soon he is dancing all over the place. All the others join in, and soon the music gets so hot that the thermometer breaks. The dancing is so frantic that Armstrong falls into the pond. He smiles and says "sweet" as the background music plays "Swanee River" and the cartoon ends.

Review: *Boxoffice,* 10 April 1937

Against a background of riotous color, Harman-Ising studios have executed a clever satire on the current craze for swing music which is certain to add a bright note to any program. Such famous sepia stars as Cab Calloway, "Fats" Waller and Bill Robinson are caricatured as frogs and the resemblance to the millpond denizens is astounding. The musical accompaniment to the gay frog-pond wedding ceremony is delightfully swinging, although the basic tunes are easily recognizable. A distinctly novel color cartoon. (8 min)

Review: *Selected Motion Pictures,* 1 May 1937

A colorful fantasy of the wedding of two frogs. Fine musical syncopation. Amusing though noisy entertainment. Family and Junior Matinee.

Review: *National Board of Review of Motion Pictures,* 4 March 1937

A color cartoon in with frog caricatures, swing music and some of its stars. Clever and entertaining for swing addicts.

Review: *National Exhibitor,* 20 March 1937

The frogs put on a wedding to hot music. Caricatures are made of Negro mannerisms. There appear characters very much like Stephin Fetchit, Bill Robinson, Cab Calloway, Fats Waller.

This isn't up to the previous efforts from the Harman-Ising bunch. Fair.

SWING YOU SINNER! (1930)

Company: Dave Fleischer, Max Fleischer; released by Paramount Pictures
Type: Talkartoons
Character: Blackie

Story: The cartoon opens as Blackie, a black character, sees a chicken and decides to steal it, but it hides behind a fence. When Blackie reaches through a loose board in the fence to grab the chicken, he finds the arm of a policeman instead. The policeman eyes Blackie suspiciously as Blackie walks away, not realizing that the chicken is standing on top of his head. The policeman follows Blackie as Blackie tries to get rid of the chicken. The chicken finally jumps off Blackie's head just before he runs through the gate of a cemetery. The gate closes behind him and then turns into a solid wall. Blackie is surrounded by gravestones that become animated and begin to sing with the voices of a black choral group. "Good-bye, this is your finish, brother. You never gwine to get away. You'll never rob another henhouse. You sinned and now you must pay, otherwise, brother, you'll . . ." A grave opens, and a For Rent sign appears on the headstone. Blackie tries to run but is stopped by a ghost that sings, "Chickens you used to steal." Blackie says, "I don't steal no more." Another ghost sings, "Craps you used to shoot." And Blackie says, "I don't shoot no more." Another ghost sings, "Gals you used to chase." And Blackie says, "I don't chase no more." The ghosts, depicted as both black and Jewish stereotypes, sing, "Get ready, brother. Your time has come." Blackie jumps over the wall and runs to a haunted house where he tries to hide. Inside he sees a haystack. Then a voice says, "Stand up, you sinner. We got you at last. You can't get away. This time will be your last. Brothers and sisters, come on get hot. We'll help to take care of you. Voo-doo-doo and its time to get hot." All of the objects surrounding him grow in size and change shape. A huge chicken appears, and two black ghosts wearing top hats do a shimmy dance. Blackie tries to run, but the ghosts follow him, singing, "Brothers you sho' gonna get your face lifted, and a permanent shave, ha-ha." One of the ghosts swings a large razor at Blackie's head, but he ducks under it and runs out of the house. The door of the house becomes animated with black and Jewish faces who sing, "Where you want your body sent?" Another ghost, a Jewish stereotype with a long, crooked nose, sings, "Body? There ain't gonna be no body, ha-ha-ha." The ghosts follow Blackie as he runs, singing, "You can't make excuses. Swing, you sinner. Oh let your chickens loose. You're at the end of your rope, so just give up all hope. Swing, you sinner. We'll stretch you like a giraffe. Maybe cut you in half just for a laugh. Swing, you sinner." A large skull appears and swallows Blackie as the cartoon ends.

Review: *Motion Picture News,* 11 October 1930

The clever cartoon pen of Max Fleischer again demonstrates itself in this Talkartoon. An off-stage chorus sings the lyrics to the rhythm of the action and the result is usually diverting. The cartoon hero is this time taken into a grave-yard with the absurd results that you might well imagine. Worth a play. (9 min)

TAKING THE BLAME (1935)

Company: Dave Fleischer, Max Fleischer, Paramount Pictures
Characters: Pudgy the dog, black cat

Review: *Selected Motion Pictures,* 1 March 1935

Betty Boop cartoon. Wicked black cat piles up circumstantial evidence against Pudgy the dog. Amusing. Family and Junior Matinee.

THEM WERE THE HAPPY DAYS (1917)

Company: Pat Sullivan, Powers Film Company; distributed by Universal Pictures
Characters: Old man, black nurse
Type: On same reel with *Superstitions*

Review: *Moving Picture World,* 9 June 1917

The old man goes to sleep and dreams that he is a boy again. He finds a vacuum cleaner and plays with it. Every one who comes near him is sucked into it, including his darky nurse. After many other adventures, he wakes to regret his lost youth.

THREE ORPHAN KITTENS (1935)

Company: David Hand, Walt Disney, United Artists
Type: Silly Symphony, Academy Award winner
Characters: Black cook, three kittens (Blackie, Whitie, Calico)

Review: *Film Daily,* 31 October 1935

Looks as if Walt Disney has hit on something as entrancing as his three little pigs in these three kittens. They are lost on a snowy night and left out in the cold, till they find their way into a cellar of a fine house and sneak upstairs. Then their adventures begin, as they find their way into the kitchen in the cook's absence, and turn things topsy turvey. Then they continue their adventures into other rooms in the house, and when the colored mammy discovers them and is about to throw them out in the cold again, the little miss of the mansion adopts them and they supposedly live happily with her ever after. The three cute kittens will prove a wow—especially in that sequence where they go to bat with the automatic playing piano and come off second best. That piece of business is a laugh riot.

Review: *Boxoffice,* 7 December 1935

Walt Disney's latest Silly Symphony promises to attract the popularity of his *Three Little Pigs,* certainly one of finest cartoon subjects ever produced. The kittens of the title role are just as cute as the little porkies of the previous short, while their adventures are so delightfully amusing that the patrons will exit from the theatre singing its praises. Blackie, Whitie and Calico, lost in the snow, find an open window in a nice warm kitchen and creep in where they are blissfully happy until their curiosity gets the better of them and they go exploring during the cook's absence. From this point they get into every possible kind of mischief culminating in their discovering of an automatic player-piano which plays "Kittens on the Keys" as they scamper and tumble over it. This proves to be the picture's high spot and will keep audiences in a riot of laughter. Color work is again excellent, short is ideal for youngsters, perfect for adults, and will fit into any bill, any time, any where.

Review: *National Exhibitor,* 20 November 1935

The three kittens come in out of the snow storm, upset household, exploring in the kitchen and parlor, spilling pies, smashing furniture. Excellent color and appealing characterizations of kittens mark this. Excellent. (9 min)

THRU THICK AND THIN (1926)

Company: Paul Terry; distributed by Pathe Film Co.
Type: Aesop's Fable
Characters: Farmer Al Falfa, Al Jr. and his pet cat, Nigger

Review: *Motion Picture News,* 6 November 1926

Showing that friendship is worthy of the name will do and in the showing providing an unusual number of laughs; that is the latest Aesop's Fable. Al Jr. (this is the first I knew farmer Al was married) is a great pal with Nigger. He is always succoring his little playmate and drying his tears. But the cat gets in bad by falling into a milk pail and is banished by hard-hearted Al. But when Al, Jr. is kidnapped, who goes to his rescue? Of course our little feline friend. Over hill and dale, down a river filled with floating cakes of ice until the rescue is effected and the gypsy kidnapper gets his just desserts. Then the triumphant return with the child and naturally all is forgiven. With the fade-out Farmer Al has two children, the blood son, and the foster child, the cat.

The moral "Good friends like good glue stick" is doubtless correct, but they must be "good" otherwise the state of your finances is rather apt to be the determining factor.

TIN PAN ALLEY CATS (1943)

Company: Robert Clampett, Warner Bros.
Type: Merrie Melodies
Characters: Cat caricatures of Fats Waller, Louis Armstrong

Story: The cartoon opens on the street of a large city with music, "By the Light of the Silvery Moon," playing in the background. Fats Waller cat is walking on the sidewalk and stops to get his shoes shined. Next he follows a shapely girl walking ahead of him, but stops when he is confronted by the girl's burly boyfriend. Fats decides to visit the Kit Kat Club for some hot jazz music. Next door to the club is Uncle Tom's Mission, and the mission band is standing on the sidewalk playing "Gimme That Old Time Religion." One of the band members stops Fats and says, "Brother, don't go in that den of iniquity, or you'll be tempted by wine, women, and song." Fats smiles at her and says, "Well, what's the matter with that?" He enters the club and is soon sitting at the piano playing and singing "Nagasaki." He gets so caught up in the rhythm that he removes his shoes and plays the piano with the toes of his feet. Next Fats walks over to the bandstand and sings a duet with Louis Armstrong cat. They sing "We're Going to Send You out of This World." When Louis plays the trumpet solo, the music is so hot at it literally sends Fats "out of this world." Fats finds himself in a strange lower world inhabited by weird creatures that torture him with very loud music. He hears a voice say, "You're out of this world." Fats says, "Who dat?" The voice responds, "Who dat?" And Fats replies, "Who dat say who dat when I say who dat?" Fats is scared and shouts "let me out of here" as he tries unsuccessfully to climb aboard an elevator going to the upper world. He sees Joseph Stalin kicking Adolph Hitler before he is lifted up and transported to the club, where he lands on the bandstand. He gets off the floor, runs outside, and joins up with Uncle Tom's Mission Band. As Fats plays the drums, the others look on and ask each other, "What's the matter with him?" as the cartoon ends.

Review: *Motion Picture Herald,* 17 July 1943

The trumpet notes of a night club musician are a little too much for Leon Schlesinger's cat and like so many of the present-day jitterbugs, he's sent "out of this world." When he gets there, however, he's happy to return to earth's solid soil for the weird land of phantasy is not all it's cracked up to be. Music and laughs are combined in a pleasant Technicolor cartoon. (7 min)

Review: *Besa Shorts Shorts,* 2 August 1943

Opening quietly, down on the water front, a chorus hums "By the Light of the Silvery Moon," as the lights come up on a street scene in Harlem. Here a Fats Waller cat is dishing out hot tunes while right next door the Salvation Army sings out. They try to persuade the wicked cat, but he prefers the trumpeting of Louis Armstrong cat. He wants to be sent out of this world in jive time, and so the cartoonist obliges and takes him thru a series of weird situations. After a frenzied time, Fats is glad to get back and join with the Salvation Army.

Review: *Stanley Crouch, review of* Animated Coon Show, Village Voice, 16–22 December 1981

Tin Pan Alley Cats makes it obvious how popular Waller (Fats) must have been: a caricatured figure of the pianist is the hero of this very interesting cartoon in which good wins out over evil, "Guys and Dolls" style. On the way to the Kit Kat Klub, our hero passes a street revival held by a group known as Uncle Tom Cats. He spurns their offer and goes into the club, where a series of hot notes sends him into a surreal netherworld in which he's assaulted by nightmare variations on stereotypic

black American images. When he returns, the hero immediately joins the revivalists.

TOYLAND BROADCAST (1934)

Company:	Hugh Harman, Rudolph Ising, M-G-M
Type:	Happy Harmonies
Characters:	Caricatures of various radio personalities including Kate Smith, the Mills Brothers, Paul Whiteman, the Boswell Sisters, African dancers

Story: There is no plot to the story, which involves a radio broadcast of a vaudeville revue held in a toy shop. The cartoon opens with the announcer, a toy soldier, speaking into a microphone, saying, "This is station ABC, broadcasting a toyland revue." Paul Whiteman leads the black "Sambo Jazz Band" that provides music for the various acts. A black African with a ring through his nose beats a drum with a pair of bones while a black female trio dances in grass skirts. A quartet of black bellboys (Mills Brothers) sings "Congo Rhythm," the theme song: "That's my baby, darktown sweetheart. I'm comin' back to you, wild-eyed woman, nature's dream girl. Jungle fever is in my blood for you. Ever see the jungle in the middle of the night? Ever see the jungle with the animals in fright? Put me in the Congo, in the jungle, and I'm right. Got that fever, jungle fever. You know the route I long to go . . ." A black sterotypical mammy wearing a bandanna on her head joins in singing, "Oh baby, I've got jungle fever, yeah, yeah man . . ." The quartet continues singing, "Jungle fever is in my blood for you." All of the toys join in the singing and dancing as the announcer says, "This is ABC signing off. Good night, folks" as the cartoon ends.

Review: *Motion Picture Herald,* 10 November 1934

In this Harman-Ising musical cartoon in color, the inhabitants of a toy shop, on table and shelf, offer a broadcast featuring dancing, instrumental work, and singing, with a lively and tuneful zest. Little figures representing various personalities of the radio and stage "doing their stuff" to an enthusiastic response for the fellow toys. An entertaining subject. (9 min)

Review: *Motion Picture Herald,* 8 December 1934

This Happy Harmony cartooned Christmas fantasy is geared to a light and mirthful tune, and is done in Technicolor. Featuring comic caricatures of Kate Smith, Boswell Sisters, Bing Crosby, Rubinoff, Paul Whiteman, Mills Brothers and other noted radioites doing their stuff, the picture is highlighted by a dog crooning "Trees" to a pine tree. A Hugh Harman-Rudolph Ising production. It's a nice children's attraction for holiday programs, more cleverly constructed than the ordinary short picture.

TRAMP, TRAMP, TRAMP (1919)

Company:	John D. Tippett (London)
Type:	Pussyfoot Cartoon
Characters:	Happy Hooligan, Dusty Dan (black)

Review: *Bioscope* (London), 23 October 1919

"Happy's" sad tale to his children of the days when Ma-in-law invaded the house, and forces him to run away, makes delightful telling. He and his new pal, Dusty Dan, have to grapple for food, and eventually run for their lives, will make all the little folks laugh. The popularity of these new cartoons is assured. They are full of "pep" and "delightfully" original throughout. (400 ft.)

TWO LAZY CROWS (1936)

Company: Ub Iwerks, Columbia Pictures
Type: Color Rhapsodies
Characters: Two black crows

Review: *Exhibitor Servisection,* 14 September 1949

A pair of crows are extremely lazy, and are unwilling to work, but would rather live off of others. They laugh at the industrious who prepare for the winter by either stocking up on food or flying south. Finally winter does arrive, and they are forced to beg shelter off of an industrious squirrel and his wife, and they are put to work. They do until they think no one is watching, and then they take a nap whereupon they are thrown out as is Mr. Squirrel as he, too, catches the lazy bug. Fair.

THE UGLY DINO (1940)

Company: Dave Fleischer, Max Fleischer, Paramount Pictures
Type: Stone Age Cartoon
Characters: Black baby dinosaur, dinosaur family

Story: The cartoon opens in prehistoric times. A mother dinosaur is knitting as she sits on her eggs and waits for them to hatch. She stands up, sees that they haven't hatched yet, and says, "A clean pot never boils." Finally all the eggs except one hatch. Four little white dinosaurs greet each other by shaking hands and saying, "Glad to meet ya." Finally the last egg hatches, and a black baby dino arrives on the scene. He greets his brothers, saying, "Hi brothers. I'm sorry I'm late. Shake?" He holds out his hand, but his white brothers fall back into their mother's arms. The black dino says, "Hi ya, Mom" but she doesn't answer. Then she leads her white dinos off to play, ignoring the black dino. The black dino sees his brothers playing a game where three of them toss the other one high into the air and catch him on a blanket. The black dino says, "I want to play too." The others agree reluctantly but decide to play a trick on him. They toss him into the air and then pull the blanket away so that he falls hard on the ground as they walk away laughing. Not discouraged, the black dino tries to join his brothers in a game of hopscotch, but they kick him away. The black dino walks away crying. When he sees his reflection in a pond, he says, "Oh, what an ugly face. I'll end it all. Now is the chance." Then he picks up a rock and jumps into the water. But he pops right back onto shore as a fish sticks its head out of the water and says, "And stay out, you ugly goon." Meanwhile a large saber-toothed tiger has watched the white dinos play and decides

that they would make a good meal. He rubs his stomach and sharpens his long fangs. He walks toward them but is stopped by the black dino. He holds onto his tail and says, "Please eat me up." The tiger looks at him and says no. He walks to the other dinos and captures them one by one. Three are tied to a stake in the ground, and the other dino is tied to a rock. The tiger is sharpening his knife as he prepares to eat him. The black dino arrives on the scene and says, "Please eat me." But the tiger refuses even after the black dino sprinkles salt and ketchup on himself. Finally the black dino throws a rock at the tiger that hits him on the head. He becomes angry and ties the black dino to a tree, saying, "I don't want no more trouble from you." Meanwhile their mother hears the white dinos' cries for help and runs off to save them. The black dino slips out of his rope, and when the tiger tries to charge him, he gets his long fangs stuck in the tree trunk and is knocked silly. Meanwhile the mother dino arrives on the scene and releases the white dinos, who are very happy and tell her that the black dino saved them. Finally he is welcomed as a member of the happy family as the cartoon ends.

Review: *Boxoffice,* 13 July 1940

The Ugly Duckling cliche has been transferred to a prehistoric setting and a few variations from the routine animation procedure have been injected in this item. Mama dinosaur hatches a brood of five. Four are grey, the fifth is black. The usual happens, but this time the black one saves the others from a saber tooth tiger. It is effective entertainment. (7 min)

Review: *Motion Picture Herald,* 27 July 1940

The story of the Ugly Duckling has been supplanted by a baby Dino who is ignored by his own brothers and his mother. Not until he rescues them from the fangs of a ferocious tiger do they appreciate his loyalty as one of the family. (7 min)

Review: *Motion Picture Exhibitor,* 12 June 1940

Stone Age Cartoon. The ugly duckling idea with four white dinos born, one black, and the latter ridiculed until he saves the others, etc. Fair.

THE UGLY DUCKLING (1925)

Company: Paul Terry, Pathe Film Exchange
Type: Aesop's Fable
Company: Black duckling, chicken family

Story: As the cartoon opens, a mother hen is caring for her baby chicks. Then a black duckling arrives on the scene and tries to join the group but is rejected. Strong winds start to blow, and a tornado heads toward the farm. All the animals run for cover, including the hen and chicks, who run into the henhouse. When the black duckling tries to enter, he finds the door locked. So he digs a hole under the wall and enters just before the henhouse is blown away. The hen and her chicks are trapped in the henhouse as it is carried along by the tornado. Meanwhile the black duckling has been left behind. The hen is thrown free of the tornado and falls to the ground where she watches her chicks being blown away from her. The henhouse and chicks finally fall into a raging river, while on the bank the frantic hen cries for help. The black duck arrives on the scene and immediately jumps into the river. He manages to save the chicks before they are carried over a waterfall. Happy that her chicks are safe on shore, the hen picks up the black duckling in her arms and gives him a hug and a big kiss as the cartoon ends.

Review: *Moving Picture World,* 19 September 1925

Paul Terry in *The Ugly Duckling* makes a hen the proud mother of four chicks and the disgruntled guardian of a black duck. The homely one, however, rates aces high when he saves the favored children from the clutches of a cat. Terry handles this subject in his novel way which is sufficient assurance that it will be acclaimed a real funster behind any box office.

VOODOO IN HARLEM (1938)

Company: Frank Tipper, Merle Gibson, Walter Lantz; released by Universal Pictures
Type: Combination live action and animation
Characters: Cartoonist (live), black maid (live), black natives (animated)

Story: The cartoon opens with live action in a studio where a cartoonist is seated at his desk drawing cartoons. When the clock strikes ten, he leaves the studio. A storm is brewing, and the wind blows through an open window. It knocks over a bottle of black ink that drips to the floor and forms a puddle. Four black male natives wearing short grass skirts then emerge from the ink. One wears a derby (caricature of Andy Brown of the *Amos 'n' Andy* radio show). Another is a caricature of Stephin Fetchit, another looks like a black cannibal and has a bone tied to the hair on top of his head, and another takes shape from an eightball. The quartet sings the title song as they dance around the studio: "Voodoo in Harlem, black rendezvous. Be sure you take your rabbit's foot along. You gonna kneel and shout until it's dawn . . ." More black natives join them, and the song continues. "Voodoo in Harlem, nothin's taboo here on Lenox Avenue. Who catch who is confusin' you in a black rendezvous. There's a sayin' goin' 'round that new religion is found that's voodoo. Boys and girls down Haiti way throw away their clothes and say that voodoo. Take a tip and go uptown to Harlem. There you'll find they're playin' voodoo too. Take a rabbit's foot along, be prepared to kick the gong. Take a fool's advice and come along . . ." By now the natives are dancing on tables, desks, and the typewriter. The song continues, "Voodoo in Harlem, black rendezvous. Be sure you take a rabbit's foot along. You gotta kneel and shout and feel it strong, voodoo in Harlem. Nothin's taboo here on Lenox Avenue. Who catches who is confusin' in a black rendezvous." The musical beat gets faster and all the natives are "truckin'." Finally the sound of a rooster crowing signals that dawn has arrived. All of the natives dive back into the ink bottle moments before the scene changes back to live action. A black maid comes in, looks at the mess,

and says, "Look at dis here mess. Work, work, work and it doesn't do no good." She picks up papers from the floor and puts them in a wastebasket. She sees a large ink spot on one of the papers and says, "I wonder what dis here black spot is." She stuffs the trash into the incinerator, and dark smoke flows out the chimney as the cartoon ends.

Review: *Motion Picture Herald,* 9 July 1938

Reviving the effective cartoon technique of pouring drawings out of an inkwell and arranging them in their animated business against realistic backgrounds, this pen product produces some imaginative and entertaining moments. The miniature fantasy occurs when a bottle of indigo ink becomes upset and a crew of colored figures take form and growing atavistic indulge in a set of lively trucking steps. Comes the dawn and the charm is broken. A combination of good musical background and some atmosphere shots of wind and cloud effects create a subtly eerie mood for the ingenious cartooning. (7 min)

Review: *Film Daily,* 20 June 1938

Cartoonist's fantasy. The animator leaves his work room, and a storm comes up and blows his drawing paper around, and overturns the inkwell. Big blotches of ink fall on the sheets of paper, and become wild African warriors and Harlem jitterbugs who go into weird dances as the storm howls outside. As dawn comes, the storm subsides, and the inky figures go back into the inkwell again, as the maid comes in to clean up the room, and finds nothing but ink smudges on the scattered papers. A Walter Lantz production.

Review: *Boxoffice,* 25 June 1938

In a minor way this is a welcome departure from the usual run of animated offerings. It mixes real life action and scenic views that blend with the tunes of the material. An artist, on leaving his drawings on his desk, departs for the day. The winds blow the sketches to the floor, at the same time overturning an ink bottle. Much in the manner of the early cartoons, the drawings and the loose ink take on a life, turning into jungle natives singing and dancing in typical Harlem spirit. When the storm subsides the figures go back to the original state.

Review: *Selected Motion Pictures,* 1 October 1938

Oswald the Rabbit cartoon. Ink spots come to life and give a swing concert. Family.

Review: *National Exhibitor,* 1 July 1938

An artist's finished drawings come to life, offer various junglish dances to a storm-thunder music motif. Fair.

WHO KILLED COCK ROBIN? (1935)

Company: David Hand, Walt Disney, United Artists
Type: Nominated for 1935 Academy Award for Short Subjects

Characters: Bird caricatures of Mae West (Jenny Wren), Bing Crosby (Cock Robin), Stephin Fetchit (bar room porter)

Story: The cartoon opens in the forest where Cock Robin, perched on the limb of a tree, croons a love song to Miss Jenny Wren. He does not see a shadowy figure arrive on the scene who shoots him with an arrow. Robin falls from the tree, and lands on the ground where he lies still and appears to be dead. The patrons of the "Old Crow Bar" look through the window at Robin as the police and an ambulance arrive on the scene. The cops suspect the killer is in the bar so they enter and round up the patrons for questioning. A crow, dressed in a porter's uniform, with a Stephin' Fetchit demeanor, attempts to escape by crawling out underneath the swinging door but is pulled back inside. The cops drag the patrons out of the bar one by one including the porter who says, "I don't know nothin' 'bout it officer—I ain't done nothin'" as a cop beats him with his baton before pushing him into the patrol wagon with the other prisoners. The prisoners and Cock Robin are taken to court where Judge Owl calls for order. The prosecutor, a parrot, asks the porter, "Who killed Cock Robin?" The porter rises from the witness nest and says, "I don't know nothin'" before a cop standing behind knocks him back down in the nest. The prosecutor then walks to Cock Robin, pulls off the sheet covering him, points to the arrow sticking out of his chest and says to the porter, "There's the arrow—Where is the bow?—That's the question—Yes or no." The sight of the apparently dead body of Cock Robin frightens the porter and causes his eyes to bulge out of his face and he turns white before he scratches his head and answers, "I ain't done nothin'—I ain't seen nothin'—I don't know nothin' at all" before he is knocked out of the nest by the cops who carry him to jail where he is put in ball and chains with the other prisoners. Several other witnesses from the bar are questioned and clubbed but they all plead innocent. Jenny Wren arrives on the scene and declares, "These birds look guilty to me—Somebody ought to be hung." The judge is about to hang them all when an arrow, shot from tree, knocks his hat off. The judge looks up and sees a small white bird holding bow and asks, "Well who are you." The bird answers, "Say don't be stupid—I'm fair cupid—I shot Cock Robin—But Robin isn't dead—He fell for Miss Jenny Wren and landed on his head." Jenny looks and Robin, touches his wing and says, "Kiss me—tall dark and handsome." The sound of Jenny's voice wakes up Robin and he gets off of the stretcher and kisses Jenny behind her extended umbrella as the cartoon ends.

WOODLAND CAFE (1937)

Company: Wilford Jackson, Walt Disney, United Artists
Type: Silly Symphony
Characters: Black doorman, caricatures of Cab Calloway and his orchestra

Review: *Motion Picture Herald*, 26 June 1937

Gay and tuneful is this richly imaginative visit to a bug night club. Equal to the brightly tinted tones in which the comic business has been dressed is the sparkling mood of animated fun and nonsense which the subject creates. Simply as enumeration of some of the hilarious and musical moments that occur in this odd rendezvous of frolic and frivolity, the incidents depicted will perhaps have a stronger appeal for the adult and the teen-age spectator. An aged albeit willing host and his young, blond female companion, an amusing travesty of an apache dance executed by a spider and a fly, a "Cab Callowayish" orchestra playing some hot and low down tunes, a finale wherein an epidemic of "truckin'" sweeps the patrons and the entertainers off their feet supply cartoon moments that should hold small appeal value for the very young. Or, perhaps, the children of today are wiser in some respects than the children of yesterday. (one reel)

WOT A NIGHT (1931)

Company: George Stallings, John Foster, Van Beuren; distributed by RKO Radio Pictures
Characters: Tom and Jerry, black skeleton quartet

Story: The cartoon opens on a stormy night. It is raining hard, and the streets are flooded. Tom and Jerry, in their taxicab, ride to the train depot to await the arrival of the train and possible fares. The train finally arrives and two strange, bearded men, both wearing black suits and stovepipe hats, disembark. Tom and Jerry persuade them to take their cab, and they depart. Their destination turns out to be a castle. When they arrive, the two men quickly get out of the cab and go inside the castle. Tom and Jerry follow them, asking for their fare. Once inside, Tom and Jerry find themselves locked in. As they begin to explore the weird-looking place, a large black bat appears on the scene and flies off. Next they look into a room with a Private sign just outside the door. They see a skeleton taking a bath in a large bathtub. The skeleton starts to dry itself with a towel, turns, and sees them. Then it disappears quickly down the tub drain. At the same time a large number of ghosts in white sheets appear. Tom and Jerry become frightened and drop through a hole in the floor. They land in another room where they see a skeleton playing a piano. Another group of skeletons starts to dance, and a female skeleton flamenco dancer arrives. Tom and Jerry quickly depart. Next Tom finds an umbrella, picks it up, and uses it to play a snappy tune before a black skeleton quartet appears on the scene and begin to sing, "Can you learn what the good book says? Yes, dear Lord. When Daniel was in the lion's den, what did he do? He said unto those colored men, what did he say? You all want to get to heaven? Sho' do! Sho' do! Then cut out your crap shooting and put on your long white robes with the starry crowns and be ready when the great day comes. Good Lord, I'm ready, indeed I'm ready." At the end of the song Jerry pulls out a pair of dice and throws them on the floor. The black skeletons dive after the dice and dissolve. Next the bearded men show up. They point to Tom and Jerry and then nod at each other as if they know some secret. Tom and Jerry are puzzled until they look under their shirts, and discover that they have turned into skeletons. They run out of the castle terrified as the cartoon ends.

A YARN OF WOOL (1932)

Company: John Foster, Harry Bailey, Van Beuren, RKO Radio Pictures
Type: Aesop's Fable
Characters: Black sheep

Review: *Film Daily,* 4 March 1933

An enjoyable cartoon. A flock of sheep are being led to the pasture, and among them is a black one which is causing trouble. So the shepherd chases it away from the fold. Later, when some sheep thieves succeed in stealing the flock, the black outcast is instrumental in catching the culprits.

YE OLD TOY SHOP (1935)

Company: Frank Moser, Paul Terry, Educational Pictures
Type: Terrytoon
Characters: *Uncle Tom's Cabin* characters

Review: *Boxoffice,* 14 December 1935

Xmas draws near and the toy-shop cartoons are upon us. This one gets off to an auspicious start, with a fairly amusing degree of animation. After the proprietor leaves the store, the mechanical toys parade in a series of characterizations, such as Mary and her Little Lamb, Uncle Tom's cabin, etc. There's considerable fun until Simon Legree in the form of a spider interrupts with the inevitable counter attack and victory for the playthings. Good holiday stuff. (6 min)

Appendix

Cartoons Including Black Characters
Produced in the United States before 1960

*Synopsis included in this book.

*A-Haunting We Will Go. 1939. Burt Gillett, Walter Lantz, Universal Pictures. Characters: Li'l Eightball, ghosts.

*A-Lad-in Bagdad. 1938. Cal Howard, Cal Dalton, Vitaphone, Warner Bros. Characters: Egghead, black genie, black palace slaves.

A-Lad-in His Lamp. 1948. Warner Bros. Characters: Bugs Bunny, black palace guards. Opening scene has Bugs singing as he digs in his hole in the ground, "Dear ol' massa am sleeping, sleeping in the cold, cold ground." (A take-off on an old Negro spiritual).

The Ace of Spades. 1931. Dave Fleischer, Max Fleischer, Talkartoon, Paramount Pictures. Characters: Black vaudeville comedy track plus jazz music.

Adventures of Ranger Focus. 1917. African Film Productions, Ltd. (London). Characters: Ranger Focus, African natives.

The Adventures of Willie Woodbine and Lightning Larry: A Joy Ride to the Cannibal Islands. 1915. Sidney Aldridge, New Agency (London). Characters: Willie Woodbine, Lightning Larry, black women.

Africa. 1930. Bill Nolan, Walter Lantz, Universal Pictures. Characters: Oswald the rabbit, African natives. Dancing Africans scene in this cartoon was used in a animated segment of the feature film The King of Jazz (1930) featuring Paul Whiteman (white).

Africa before Dark. 1928. (released in 1930 with sound track), Walt Disney. Characters: Oswald the rabbit, African natives.

Africa Squawks. 1939. Connie Rasinski, Paul Terry, Terrytoon, Twentieth Century-Fox Pictures. Terrytoons. Characters: Africans.

*Africa Squeaks. 1932. Ub Iwerks, Celebrity Pictures, M-G-M. Characters: Flip the frog, black cannibals.

*Africa Squeaks. 1939. Robert Clampett, Looney Tunes, Warner Bros. Characters: Porky Pig, African natives.

African Daze. See The Lion Hunt.

African Diary. 1945. Jack Kinney, Walt Disney, RKO-Radio Pictures. Characters: Goofy, African natives.

*The African Hunt. 1915. Lubin Film Manufacturing Co., Characters: White hunter, black Africans.

*African Jungle Hunt. 1957. Paul Terry, Terrytoon. 20th-Century. Characters: Phoney Baloney, Africans.

*Ain't Nature Grand. 1931. Hugh Harman, Rudolph Ising, Vitaphone. Character: Bosko.

Aladdin's Lamp. 1935. Paul Terry, Frank Moser, Terrytoon. Character: Aladdin. Includes a gag in which a huge black genie with thick white lips comes out of Aladdin's magic lamp and says, "Are you Aladdin?" Then he holds out his hand andd says, "Shake." Aladdin says, "I am shaking" and the genie bows down and says, "Fear not—I am your slave."

Alaska. 1930. Walter Lantz; released by Universal. Characters: Oswald the rabbit. Includes gag by black cook in saloon.

Alaska Sweepstakes. 1936. Walter Lantz, Universal. Characters: Oswald the rabbit. Includes gag by Stephin Fetchit caricature.

*Alice Cans the Cannibals. 1925. Walt Disney; released by M. J. Winkler. Characters: Virginia Davis as Alice, black cannibals.

Alice Hunting in Africa. 1926. Walt Disney; released by M. J. Winkler. Characters: Alice and African native.

*All This and Rabbit Stew. 1941. Tex Avery, Warner Bros. Characters: Bugs Bunny, Little Black Sambo.

All Wet. 1927. Walt Disney, Universal Pictures. Characters: Oswald the rabbit, blacks.

*All's Well That Ends Well. 1940. Mannie Davis, Paul Terry, Terrytoon, 20th Century-Fox Pictures. Characters: Black kittens, dog.

*Amateur Broadcast. 1935. Walter Lantz, Universal. Characters: Includes gag by Stephin Fetchit caricature.

*Andy Panda Goes Fishing. 1940. Burt Gillett, Walter Lantz, Universal Pictures. Characters: Andy Panda, black cannibals.

*Angel Puss. 1944. Charles Jones, Looney Tunes, Warner Bros. Characters: Li'l Sambo, black cat.

*Another Tale. 1914. Lubin. Characters: Sam Bug, Raskus Bug.

*Any Bonds for Sale. 1943. Warner Bros. Characters: Bugs Bunny (in blackface), Elmer Fudd, Porky Pig.

*Aroma of the South Seas. 1926. Bud Fisher, Fox Films. Characters: Mutt and Jeff, black cannibals.

Art Gallery. 1939. Hugh Harman, M-G-M. Characters: Paintings of famous people come to life. Includes a gag in which Nero sets the gallery on fire and a painting of three white baby angels sing "He's Burning Rome." The angels turn black and sing "Way Down Upon De Swanee River."

*The Artist's Model. 1924. Earl Hurd, Educational Pictures. Characters: Zulu jazz band.

*As the Crow Lies. 1951. Seymour Kneitel, Famous Studios, Paramount Pictures. Characters: Buzzy crow, Katnip cat.

Audrey the Rainmaker. 1951. I. Sparber, Famous Studies; released by Paramount Pictures. Characters: Little Audrey, black maid.

*Aviation Vacation. 1941. Tex Avery, Warner Bros. Characters: White hunters, black cannibals.

*The Awful Tooth. 1952. Seymour Kneitel, Paramount Pictures. Characters: Buzzy the crow, Katnip the cat.

The Babysitter. 1947. Seymour Kneitel, Famous Studios; released by Paramount Pictures. Characters: Little Lulu. Includes gag in a dream sequence by a black baby swing band led by a baby Cab Calloway caricature who sings "hi-dee-hi-dee-hi-dee-ho." Later a black baby beats his drums as Lulu dives off a high diving board into a barrel of water, which wakes her up.

Baby Weems (included as animated sequence in *The Reluctant Dragon,* which also included live action of Robert Benchley touring the Disney studio). 1941. Walt Disney; released by RKO-Radio Pictures. Character: White Baby Weems. Includes gag of African native beating drums and another black native clapping using his long, flat lips.

**Bad Luck Blackie.* 1949. Tex Avery, M-G-M. Characters: Black cat, bulldog.

Baffled by Banjoes. 1924. Pat Sullivan, Winkler Films. Characters: Felix the Cat, black natives.

Barnyard Five. 1936. Walter Lantz, Universal. Characters: Oswald the rabbit, black duckling.

A Barnyard Mix-up. 1915. Lubin. Character: Rastus.

**Battling Bosko.* 1932. Hugh Harman, Rudolph Ising, Vitaphone. Characters: Bosko, Honey.

**Beach Combers.* 1936. Walter Lantz, Universal. Characters: Oswald the rabbit, his dog Elmer, a duck family including four white ducklings and one black duckling.

**Beau Bosko.* 1935. Hugh Harman, Rudolph Ising, Vitaphone. Characters: Bosko, Honey.

Becall to Arms. 1946. Robert Clampett, Warner Bros. Characters: Caricatures of Lauren Bacall (Laurie Becool) and Humphrey Bogart (Bogey Gocart). Includes gag where exploding cigarette butt turns Bogey's face into a blackface stereotype and he says, in a Rochester-like voice, "My oh my! I can work for Mr. Benny now!"

**Better Bait Than Never.* 1953. Seymour Kneitel, Famous Studios, Paramount Pictures. Characters: Buzzy the crow, Katnip the cat.

**Betty Boop's Bamboo Isle.* 1932. Dave Fleischer, Max Fleischer, Paramount Pictures. Characters: Betty Boop, Bimbo, black natives.

Betty Boop's Rise to Fame. 1934. Max Fleischer, Paramount Pictures. Characters: Betty Boop, Max Fleischer (as himself); gag appearance by the old man of the Mountain (Cab Calloway voice characterization).

**The Big Flood.* 1922. (released in 1929 by RKO-Radio Pictures with sound track under the title *Noah Knew His Ark*), Paul Terry, Aesop's Fable, Pathe Film Exchange. Characters: Farmer Al Falfa as Noah, black cannibal.

**Big-Hearted Bosko.* 1932. Hugh Harman, Vitaphone. Characters: Bosko, Bruno.

**Big Man from the North.* 1931. Hugh Harman, Rudolph Ising, Vitaphone. Characters: Bosko, Honey.

The Birth of Jazz. 1932. Charles Mintz, Samba Pictures; released by Columbia Pictures. Characters: Krazy Kat; Includes a gag of black Africans doing a jazz dance to the music of W. C. Handy's "St. Louis Blues," which is played in the background throughout the cartoon.

The Birthday Party. 1931. Walt Disney, Columbia Pictures. Characters: Mickey Mouse, Minnie Mouse. Includes a gag by Mickey and Minnie dancing to the tune of "Darktown Strutter's Ball" by the black composer Shelton Brooks.

**The Birthday Party.* 1937. Walter Lantz, Universal. Characters: Oswald the rabbit, black rabbit.

**The Black Duck.* 1929. Fabletoon, Fables Pictures. Characters: black duck, mouse.

**Black Puppy in the Army.* 1940. Japan. Characters: Black puppy, Japanese army.

**The Black Sheep.* 1924. Paul Terry, Terrytoon, Pathe Film Exchange. Characters: Black pup, eagle.

**Black Sheep.* 1932. Charles Mintz, Columbia Pictures. Characters: Scrappy, white sheep, black lamb.

**The Black Sheep.* 1934. Frank Moser, Paul Terry, 20th Century-Fox Educational Pictures. Characters: Black sheep, wolf.

**Black and White.* 1933. Amkino (Soviet Union). Characters: White plantation owner, black worker, black shoeshine man.

Blue Rhythm. 1931. Walt Disney, Columbia Pictures. Characters: Mickey Mouse, Minnie Mouse. The entire cartoon is played to the background music of W. C. Handy's "St. Louis Blues" and includes a segment in which Minnie dances and sings the title song and Mickey and Minnie tap dance.

**Blues.* 1931. Frank Moser, Paul Terry, Terrytoon, Educational Pictures. Characters: Southern blacks.

**Bobby Bumps in the Great "Divide".* 1917. Earl Hurd, J. R. Bray Studios; distributed by Paramount Pictures. Characters: Bobby Bumps, Dinah, black cook.

**Bobby Bumps Loses His Pup.* 1916. Earl Hurd, J. R. Bray Studios; released by Paramount Pictures. Characters: Bobby Bumps, his father, his mother, Choc'late, black man, Fido.

**Bobby Bumps and the Speckled Death.* 1918. Earl Hurd, J. R. Bray Studio; released by Paramount Pictures. Characters: Bobby Bumps, black woman.

**Bobby Bumps Starts a Lodge.* 1916. Earl Hurd, J. R. Bray Studio; distributed by Paramount Pictures. Characters: Bobby Bumps, black boy.

**Bola Mola Land.* 1939. Frank Tipper, Dick Marion, Walter Lantz, Universal Pictures. Characters: Black cannibals.

**Boogie-Woogie Bugle Boy of Company B.* 1941. Walter Lantz, Universal. Characters: Hot Breath Harry, black soldiers.

**Boogie-Woogie Man.* 1943. Walter Lantz, Universal. Characters: Dark spirits from Harlem.

Book Revue. 1946. Robert Clampett, Warner Bros. Characters: Daffy Duck, caricatures of popular big band entertainers including Frank Sinatra, Tommy Dorsey, and Benny Goodman as fictional characters from famous books. Includes gag with Daffy in blackface impersonating Uncle Tom. This gag was later edited out of this cartoon when it was released on laser disk by MGM/UA Home Video.

The Bookworm. 1939. I. Freleng, Hugh Harman, M-G-M. Characters: Bookworm, black raven. Includes sequence where Paul Revere jumps out of a book and then jumps into another book entitled *Black Beauty.* The sound of a horse's whinny is heard. Then Paul appears riding on the back of a fat black woman of the Aunt Jemima type. She carries him to a book entitled *Racket Busters.* Then she stops and a caricature of Thomas Dewey comes out.

Paul then hits the black woman on her backside with a cooking spatula. She jumps in the air and screams before carrying him off to summon characters from other books, including *Police Gazette, Robin Hood, Gabriel over the White House, Charge of the Light Brigade,* and *Heroes of Gettysburg.*

Booze Hangs High. 1930. Hugh Harman, Rudolph Ising, Vitaphone, Warner Bros. Character: Bosko.

Bosko and Bruno. 1932. Hugh Harman, Rudolph Ising, Vitaphone, Warner Bros. Characters: Bosko, Bruno.

Bosko and the Cannibals. 1937. Hugh Harman, M-G-M. Characters: Bosko, Mammy, cannibals, frog impersonations of Bill Robinson, Cab Calloway, Styme Byrd, Fats Waller, Louis Armstrong.

Bosko and Honey. 1932. Hugh Harman, Rudolph Ising, Vitaphone, Warner Bros. Characters: Bosko and Honey.

Bosko and the Pirates. 1937. M-G-M, Hugh Harman. Characters: Bosko, Mammy, frog pirates impersonating Cab Calloway, Bill Robinson, Louis Armstrong, Fats Waller.

Bosko at the Beach. 1932. Hugh Harman, Rudolph Ising, Vitaphone, Warner Bros. Characters: Bosko, Honey.

Bosko at the Zoo. 1932. Hugh Harman, Rudolph Ising, Vitaphone, Warner Bros. Characters: Bosko, Honey.

Bosko the Doughboy. 1931. Hugh Harman, Rudolph Ising, Vitaphone, Warner Bros. Character: Bosko.

Bosko the Drawback. 1933. Hugh Harman, Rudolph Ising, Vitaphone, Warner Bros. Character: Bosko.

Bosko in Baghdad. 1938. Hugh Harman, M-G-M. Characters: Bosko, Mammy, frog impersonations of Stephin Fetchit, Fats Waller, Bill Robinson, Cab Calloway, Louis Armstrong.

Bosko in Dutch. 1933. Hugh Harman, Rudolph Ising, Vitaphone, Warner Bros. Character: Bosko.

Bosko in Person. 1933. Hugh Harman, Rudolph Ising, Vitaphone, Warner Bros. Character: Bosko.

Bosko the Lumberjack. 1932. Hugh Harman, Rudolph Ising, Vitaphone, Warner Bros. Character: Bosko.

Bosko the Musketeer. 1933. Hugh Harman, Rudolph Ising, Vitaphone, Warner Bros. Character: Bosko.

Bosko the Sheepherder. 1933. Hugh Harman, Rudolph Ising, Vitaphone, Warner Bros. Character: Bosko.

Bosko Shipwrecked. 1931. Hugh Harman, Rudolph Ising, Vitaphone, Warner Bros. Characters: Bosko, black cannibals.

Bosko the Speed King. 1933. Hugh Harman, Rudolph Ising, Vitaphone, Warner Bros. Character: Bosko.

Bosko the Talk-Ink Kid. 1929. Hugh Harman Rudolph Ising Productions. Characters: Rudolph Ising as himself, Bosko (pilot film for Looney Tunes series).

Bosko's Dizzy Date. 1933. Hugh Harman, Rudolph Ising, Vitaphone, Warner Bros. Character: Bosko.

Bosko's Dog Race. 1932. Hugh Harman, Rudolph Ising, Vitaphone, Warner Bros. Character: Bosko.

Bosko's Easter Eggs. 1937. Hugh Harman, Happy Harmonies, M-G-M. Characters: Bosko, Mammy, Honey.

Bosko's Fox Hunt. 1931. Hugh Harman, Rudolph Ising, Vitaphone, Warner Bros. Character: Bosko.

Bosko's Holiday. 1931. Hugh Harman, Rudolph Ising, Vitaphone, Warner Bros. Character: Bosko.

Bosko's Knight-Mare. 1933. Hugh Harman, Rudolph Ising, Vitaphone, Warner Bros. Character: Bosko.

Bosko's Mechanical Man. 1933. Hugh Harman, Rudolph Ising, Vitaphone, Warner Bros. Character: Bosko.

Bosko's Orphans. 1932. Hugh Harman, Rudolph Ising, Vitaphone, Warner Bros. Character: Bosko.

Bosko's Parlor Pranks. 1934. Hugh Harman, Happy Harmonies, M-G-M. Character: Bosko.

Bosko's Party. 1932. Hugh Harman, Rudolph Ising, Vitaphone, Warner Bros. Character: Bosko.

Bosko's Picture Show. 1933. Hugh Harman, Rudolph Ising, Vitaphone, Warner Bros. Character: Bosko.

Bosko's Soda Fountain. 1931. Hugh Harman, Rudolph Ising, Vitaphone, Warner Bros. Characters: Bosko, Honey.

Bosko's Store. 1932. Hugh Harman, Rudolph Ising, Vitaphone, Warner Bros. Character: Bosko.

Bosko's Woodland Daze. 1933. Hugh Harman, Rudolph Ising, Vitaphone, Warner Bros. Character: Bosko.

Bosko's Zoo. 1932. Hugh Harman, Rudolph Ising, Vitaphone, Warner Bros. Character: Bosko.

Bottles. 1936. Hugh Harman, Rudolph Ising, Happy Harmonies, M-G-M. Characters: Characters from various bottled products in a drug store come to life. Includes gag in which three black characters from "Golliwogg Perfume" do a brief dance to the beat of jungle drums.

Box Car Blues. 1931. Hugh Harman, Rudolph Ising, Vitaphone, Warner Bros. Character: Bosko.

Boyhood Daze. 1957. Charles Jones, Warner Bros. Characters: Ralph Phillips, black cannibals.

Bring 'Em Back Alive Half Shot. 1932. RKO-Radio Pictures. Characters: Frank Buck's "Bring 'Em Back Alive" with African natives.

Broken Toys. 1935. Ben Sharpsteen, Walt Disney, United Artists. Characters: Various broken toy caricatures of famous movie stars including W. C. Fields, "Aunt Jemima" and Stephin Fetchit.

Brotherhood of Man. 1946. United Film Productions. UAW-CIO. Characters: The three races of mankind.

Buddy in Africa. 1935. Ben Hardaway Looney Toons, Vitaphone, Warner Bros. Characters: Buddy, black natives.

Buddy of the Apes. 1934. Ben Hardaway, Looney Tunes, Vitaphone, Warner Bros. Characters: Buddy, black cannibals.

Buddy of the Legion. 1935. Bob Clampett, Charles Jones, Vitaphone, Warner Bros. Character: Buddy. Includes gag involving black porter who is summoned by the queen and arrives pushing a mummy on a two-wheeled cart.

Buddy the Gee Man. 1935. Jack King, Looney Tunes, Warner Bros. Character: Buddy. Includes gag in "Sing Song Prison" where a black prisoner, with thick white lips, and wearing a porter's uniform, smiles as he shines the shoes of the other prisoners.

Buddy's Circus. 1934. Jack King, Looney Tunes, Vitaphone. Characters: Buddy, African stereotypes.

Buddy's Showboat. 1933. Earl Duvall, Looney Tunes, Vitaphone, Warner Bros. Characters: Buddy, cameo by black quartet.

The Bulldog and the Baby. 1942. Alec Geiss Columbia Pictures. Characters: Bulldog, baby, black maid.

Bullony. 1933. Ub Iwerks, Pat Powers, Celebrity Productions, Released by MGM. Characters: Flip the Frog. Includes gag where black trainer with thick white lips carries a towel and water bucket, as he follows Flip, who is dressed in a bull's costume, into a Spanish bull ring.

A Bully Romance. 1939. Paul Terry, Educational Pictures (later released in 16mm for home use by Castle Films). Character: Gandy Goose. Includes a gag by a black duck who says to Gandy at the end of the cartoon, "But, but Boss, yo' opportunity is heah" as Gandy is chased by a large bull. Then he smiles and says, "Some bull."

The Bum Bandit. 1931. Dave Fleischer, Max Fleischer, Paramount Pictures. Characters: Betty Boop, Bimbo. Includes a gag by a black chicken thief.

Bushy Hare. Robert McKimson Warner Bros. Characters: Bugs Bunny, black native.

Butterscotch and Soda. 1948. Seymour Kneitel, Famous Studios; released by Paramount Pictures. Characters: Little Audrey, black maid (voice characterization by Amanda Randolph).

Call to Arms. 1946. Robert Clampett, Warner Bros. Characters: caricatures of Lauren Bacall (Laurie Becool) and Humphrey Bogart (Bogey Gocart). Includes gag where exploding cigarette butt turns Bogey's face into a blackface stereotype and he says, in a Rochester-like voice, "My oh my! I can work for Mr. Benny now!"

Camptown Races. 1948. Seymour Kneitel, Famous Studios, Screen Song, Paramount Pictures. Characters: Blackface animal caricatures.

Cannibal Capers. 1930. Burt Gillett, Walt Disney, Columbia Pictures (silent version released under title *Zulu Jazz* by Hollywood Film Enterprises). Characters: Black cannibals.

The Cannibal Isle. 1916. J. R. Bray Studio. Characters: Black cannibals.

Cannibal Island. 1928. Kinex Studios. Characters: Snap the gingerbread man, Snap's dog, black cannibal.

Captain Grogg. 1920. Victor Bergdahl, Svenska Bio Co. (Sweden). Character: Captain Grogg. Includes a cameo by a gum-chewing black man who has thick white lips and bare feet. He wears overalls and a farmer's hat and gives his ostrich to Captain Grogg.

The Captain's Christmas. 1938. M-G-M. Characters: The captain and the kids. Includes gag by a dancing black male wind-up toy.

Cartoon of Mr. Paul Rainey's African Trip. 191?. Characters: Paul Rainey, black cannibals.

Cartoons Ain't Human. 1943. Seymour Kneitel, Paramount Pictures. Character: Popeye. Includes gag by a portrait of a smiling fat black woman that is entitled "Moana Lisa."

Casanova Cat. 1951. William Hanna, Joseph Barbera, M-G-M. Characters: Tom cat, Jerry mouse. Jerry does a blackface routine while he sings and tap dances to the tune of "Dixie."

Cat-Choo. 1951. Seymour Kneitel, Famous Studios, Paramount Pictures. Characters: Buzzy the crow, Katnip the cat.

Cat O' Nine Ails. 1948. Seymour Kneitel, Famous Studios, Paramount Pictures. Characters: Buzzy the crow, Sam the cat.

Caveman Inki. 1950. Charles Jones, Warner Bros. Characters: Inki, mynah bird.

Charlie Cuckoo. 1939. Elmer Perkins, Walter Lantz; released by Universal. Character: Charlie Cuckoo. Includes a gag by a black man with a Stephin Fetchit demeanor.

Charlie's African Quest. 1916. Pat Sullivan; distributed by *New York Herald,* later released by Empire Safety Film Company. Characters: Charlie Chaplin caricature, Africans (second of six animated one-reel cartoons produced by Sullivan.)

Chew Chew Baby. 1958. I. Sparber, Famous Studios, Paramount Pictures. Characters: Black pygmy cannibal, American visitor.

Chicken A La King. 1937. Dave Fleischer, Max Fleischer; released by Paramount. Character: Chicken sultan. Includes gag in which a black palace slave greets a chicken caricature of Mae West saying, "What ya'll want, Ma'am?"

The Chicken Thief. 1921. International Cartoon. Character: Black man.

Children's Corner. 193?. Alfred Cortot, Leslie Wink Production (French). Characters: Combined live action and animation, white girl, puppets, black golliwogg.

Chow Hound. 1951. Charles Jones, Merrie Melodies, Warner Bros. Characters: Cat, hungry dog (chow hound), cat. Includes gag: Mouse made up as black African native with thick white lips, wearing ring in nose, and carrying a spear in his hand and a cat on top of his head. The mouse says "how mortified" as he marches behind the dog, who is made up as a white hunter on safari.

Christmas in Toyland. 193?. (Includes sequences from *Midnight in a Toy Shop*), Winfred Jackson, Walt Disney. Characters: Santa Claus, children, includes sequence involving marching toys including a black band, and a black man driving a wagon full of barrels pulled by a donkey.

Christmas Night. 1934. Van Beuren, Distributed by RKO-Radio Pictures: Characters: Little King. Includes gag where little King looks through a window of a toy shop where he sees a blackface stereotype toy with thick white lips tap dancing like Bill Robinson. He ends his with a cartwheel which makes the Little King laugh.

Cinderella. 1930. Charles Mintz, Columbia Pictures. Characters: Cinderella, black caricatures.

The Circus. 1932. Ub Iwerks, M-G-M. Character: Flip the frog. Includes a gag by Willie Straight, a black rubber man.

Circus Capers. 1930. Aesop's Fables. Van Beuren; released by Pathe Film Exchange. Characters: Mice, black stereotypes.

Circus Comes to Clown. 1947. I. Sparber, Screen Song, Paramount Pictures. Characters: Includes gag by black Siamese twins. One eats a slice of watermelon while the other one spits out the seeds.

Circus Daze. 1937. Hugh Harman, Happy Harmonies, M-G-M. Characters: Bosko, Honey, Bruno.

*Clean Pastures. 1936. Isadore Freling, Warner Bros. Plot thinly based on the all-black cast movie *Green Pastures,* with De Lord, and Stephin Fetchit character as Gabriel, Bill Robinson, Cab Calloway, Bill Robinson, Fats Waller, Louis Armstrong, Mills Brothers.

*Coal Black and de Sebben Dwarfs. 1943. Robert Clampett, Merrie Melodies, Warner Bros. Black version of Snow White and the Seven Dwarfs.

*Cocoa the Trapper. 194?. Produced in London, England. Characters: Little Cocoa, a black boy.

*Col. Heeza Liar in Africa. 1913. J. R. Bray Studio; released by Hodkinson and Selznick Pictures. Characters: Col. Heeza Liar, African blacks.

*Col. Heeza Liar in the African Jungles. 1923. J. R. Bray Studio; released by Hodkinson and Selznick Pictures. Characters: Col. Heeza Liar, black cannibals.

*Col. Heeza Liar and the Ghost. 1923. J. R. Bray Studio; released by Hodkinson and Selznick Pictures. Characters: Col. Heeza Liar, black man (live action).

*Col. Heeza Liar in the Haunted House. 1915. J. R. Bray Studio; released by Hodkinson and Selznick Pictures; distributed by Pathe Film Exchange. Characters: Col. Heeza Liar, black man.

*Col. Heeza Liar in Uncle Tom's Cabin. 1923. J. R. Bray Studio; released by Hodkinson and Selznick Pictures. Characters: Col. Heeza Liar, Uncle Tom, Topsy, Little Eva, Liza.

*Col. Heeza Liar's Treasure Island. 1923. J. R. Bray Studio; distributed by Hodkinson & Selznick Pictures. Characters: Col. Heeza Liar, black cannibals.

*Confederate Honey. 1940. I. Freleng, Merrie Melodies, Warner Bros. Characters: No data.

*Congo Jazz. 1930. Hugh Harman, Rudolph Ising, Vitaphone, Warner Bros. Character: Bosko.

*The Cookie Carnival. 1935. Silly Symphony, Walt Disney, United Artists. Characters: Includes gag by black licorice sticks singing and dancing to jazz music.

*A Corny Concerto. 1943. Robert Clampett, Merrie Melodies, Warner Bros. Characters: Little black duck in the Blue Danube sequence.

*Cow Cow Boogie. 1943. Alex Lovy, Walter Lantz, Swing Symphonies, Universal Pictures. Characters: Little black boy, ranch cowboys.

*A Coy Decoy. 1941. Robert Clampett, Warner Bros. Characters: Daffy Duck, Porky Pig. Includes gag where Daffy puts on a ten-gallon cowboy hat and jumps into a book entitled *Black Beauty* and rides out of it on the back of a fat black woman of the Aunt Jemima stereotype who carries him on her back, running on all fours. She stops suddenly, and Daffy flies off her back and into a pond.

*Crack Pot Cruise. 1939. Alex Lovy, Walter Lantz, Universal. Characters: A round-the-world cruise, including Africa.

*Crazy Cruise. 1942. Tex Avery, Robert Clampett, Warner Bros. Characters: Travelog including black cannibals.

*Croon Crazy. 1933. Van Beuren; released by RKO-Radio Pictures. Character: Cubby Bear. Includes gag with Cubby in blackface singing "Mammy." Cameo appearance by Tom and Jerry.

*The Crop Chasers. 1939. Ub Iwerks, Columbia Pictures. Characters: Black crows, farmer.

*Cuckoo the Magician. 1933. Ub Iwerks, Celebrity Pictures; released by M-G-M. Characters: Flip the frog, black stereotypes.

*Cupid Gets Some New Dope. 1917. Pat Sullivan, Powers Film Company; distributed by Universal. Character: Sammy Johnsin.

*Curtain Razor. 1949. I. Freleng, Warner Bros. Character: Porky Pig. Includes gag where an Al Jolson caricature talks about his mammy and says "Not your mammy I'm talkin' about."

*Daffy Dilly Daddy. 1945. Seymour Kneitel, Famous Studios; released by Paramount Pictures; TV distribution by U.M. & M. Television Corporation. Characters: Little Lulu, Daddy, her pet dog.

*Dancing Shoes. 1950. Terrytoon, 20th-Fox, Characters: Talking magpies.

*Daredevil Droopy. 1951. Tex Avery, M-G-M. Characters: Droopy, Spike the bulldog. Includes gag in which a stick of dynamite blows up in Spike's face, turning it into a blackface stereotype with thick white lips and two braids of hair sticking out of his head.

*Darkest Africa. 1925. Paul Terry, Pathe Film Exchange. Characters: African natives.

*A Date to Skate. 1938. Max Fleischer, Adolph Zukor, Paramount Pictures. Characters: Popeye, Olive Oyl. Includes gag where a smoke from a car crash turns the face of a white man into a black face stereotype with thick white lips.

*A Date with Duke. 1947. George Pal, Puppetoon; released by Paramount Pictures. Characters: Duke Ellington (live action), perfume bottle puppets.

*A Day in the Life of a Dog. 1917. Pat Sullivan, Powers Film Company; distributed by Universal. Character: Sammy Johnsin.

*Detouring America. 1939. Tex Avery, Merrie Melodies, Warner Bros. Characters: Includes gag showing Eskimo man carrying a black man back to "Old Virginny." Nominated for Academy Award.

*Dick Wittington's Cat. 1934. Ub Iwerks, Pat Powers Celebrity Pictures; released by M-G-M. Characters: Dick Wittington, black butler.

*Died in the Wool. 1924. Paul Terry, Aesop's Fable, Pathe Film Exchange. Characters: Milton Mouse, black sheep.

*Dinah. 1933. Dave Fleischer, Max Fleischer, Screen Song, Paramount Pictures. Characters: Mills Brothers voices.

*Dinky Doodle in Uncle Tom's Cabin. 1926. J. R. Bray Studio, Standard Cinema Corporation. Characters: Dinky Doodle, Uncle Tom.

*Dinky Finds a Home. 1946. Eddie Donnelly Paul Terry, 20th-Century. Characters: Dinky Doodle, Chicken Family.

*Dinky in Sink or Swim. 1952. Connie Rasinski, Paul Terry, 20th-Century-Fox. Characters: Dinky Doodle, Professor Owl.

*Disillusioned Bluebird. 1944. Howard Swift, Color Rhapsody, Columbia Pictures. Characters: Sir Lancelot (live action), bluebird.

Dixie Days. 1930. John Foster Van Beuren, Pathe Film Exchange. Characters: Uncle Tom, Liza, Topsy Little Eva, Simon Legree.

Dr. Dolittle's Trip to Africa. 1928. Lotte Reinger, Deutcher Werkfilm (Berlin). Characters: Dr. Dolittle, black cannibals.

Dog Trouble. 1942. William Hanna, Joseph Barbera, M-G-M. Characters: Tom cat, Jerry mouse, Mammy Two-Shoes (voice characterization by Lillian Randolph).

Donald's Lucky Day. 1938. Jack King, Walt Disney, RKO-Radio Pictures. Characters: Donald Duck, black cat.

Don't You Believe It. 1917. African Film Productions (London). Characters: Ben Crocker (white hunter), black cannibals.

Down in Dixie. 1923. Bud Fisher Productions; released by Pathe Film Exchange. Characters: Mutt and Jeff, southern blacks.

Down in Dixie. 1932. John Foster, Harry Bailey, Van Beuren; released by Pathe RKO. Characters: Uncle Tom, Little Eva, Liza, Topsy, Simon Legree.

Down the Mississippi. 1919. Frank Moser, Paramount Magazine, Famous Players Lasky Co. Characters: Bud, Susie. Includes sequence where the cat decides to play a trick on the black maid. He approaches her while she is trying to read a book titled "Beauty Hints" and asks her to find a book entitled *Huckleberry Finn.* She says, "Walk this way," before shuffling off. The cat hesitates, scratches his head, then shuffles after her. She stops at the book case but can't read the titles, so the cat gets the book for her.

Down on the Levee. 1933. Frank Moser, Paul Terry, Terrytoons, Educational Pictures. Characters: Uncle Tom, Little Eva, Topsy.

Dreamy Dud in the African War Zone. 1916. Wallace Carlson; released by Essanay Film Company. Characters: Dreamy Dud, black cannibals, black washerwoman.

Dreamy Dud Joyriding with Princess Zlim. 1916. Wallace Carlson, Essanay Pictures. Characters: Dreamy Dud, African princess.

Dreamy Dud in King Koo Koo's Kingdom. 1915. Wallace Carlson; released by Essanay Film Company. Characters: Dreamy Dud, Princess Zlim (black princess).

Dreamy Dud in Lost in the Jungle. 1915. Wallace Carlson; released by Essanay Film Company. Characters: Dreamy Dud, African natives.

Drippy Mississippi. 1951. Seymour Kneitel, Famous Studios, Screen Song, Paramount Pictures. Characters: southern blacks.

Droopy's Good Deed. 1951. Tex Avery, M-G-M. Characters: Droopy, Spike. Includes one gag in which Spike turns into a blackface stereotype after being hit by a bolt of lightning while the background music plays "Swanee River" and another in which Spike gets caught in a burning cabin and turns black with thick white lips. Droopy opens the door and asks him, "Hey Blackie! Any more babes in there?"

A Drop in the Bucket. 1925. L. B. Cornwall. Character: Little Ebony.

The Ducktators. 1942. Norman McCabe, Looney Tunes, Warner Bros. Includes gag of Herr Hitler (duck) reviewing his soldiers (ducks) and one black duck says, "Sieg Heil, Boss. I'm from south Germany" in an Eddie "Rochester" Anderson voice as the background music plays "My Momma Done Told Me."

Duke Dolittle's Jungle Fizzle. 1917. Pat Sullivan, Powers Film Company. Characters: Duke Dolittle, blacks.

Dumb Bell of the Yukon. 1946. Jack King, Walt Disney, released by RKO Radio Pictures. Character: Donald Duck. Includes gag where Donald does black stereotype routine saying "Mammy."

The Dumb Patrol. 1931. Hugh Harman, Rudolph Ising, Vitaphone, Warner Bros. Character: Bosko.

The Early Bird and the Worm. 1936. Rudolph Ising, M-G-M. Characters: Two black crows, the worm, the early bird.

The Early Bird Dood It. 1942. Tex Avery, M-G-M. Characters: Blacks.

The Early Worm Gets the Bird. 1940. Tex Avery, Warner Bros. Characters: Blackbird, worm, fox.

Eatin' on the Cuff or the Moth Who Came to Dinner. 1942. Robert Clampett, Looney Tunes, Warner Bros. Characters: Live action piano player and narrator, moth, honey bee. Includes gag in which the moth eats the pants off a black man with long flat feet and skinny legs who is standing at a bar. Afterward he jumps up in the air and says, "my oh my" before running off.

Eats Are West. 1925. Pat Sullivan, E. W. Hammond, distributed by Educational Pictures and Pathe Film Exchange. Characters: Felix the Cat, black mammy, Indians, cowboys.

Ebony Cleans Up. 1925. L. B. Cornwall. Character: Little Ebony.

Eggs Don't Bounce. 1943. I. Sparber, Famous Studios; released by Paramount Pictures. Characters: Little Lulu, Mandy the black maid.

Eightball Bunny. 1950. Charles Jones, Warner Bros. Characters: Bugs Bunny, Penguin, black cannibals.

Eliza on Ice. 1944. Connie Rasinski, Paul Terry, Terrytoon, 20th-Century Fox. Characters: Mighty Mouse, Uncle Tom, Eliza, Topsy, Little Eva, Simon Legree.

Eliza Runs Again. 1938. Connie Rasinski, Paul Terry, Terrytoon, Educational Pictures, 20th-Fox released again in 1944 under the title *Eliza on Ice.* Characters: Mighty Mouse, Uncle Tom, Eliza, Topsy, Little Eva, Simon Legree.

English Channel Swim. 1925. Paul Terry, Aesop's Fable; released by Pathe Film Exchange. Characters: Includes gag by black stereotypes.

The Escapades of Estelle. 1916. Henry Palmer; released by Gaumont America Film Co. Character: Estelle.

Everybody Sing. 1933. Walter Lantz, Universal. Characters: Oswald the rabbit, two black crows.

Fagin's Freshmen. 1939. Ben Hardaway, Cal Dalton, Warner Bros. Character: Blackie the cat.

Family Album (Portraying the notable descendents of the Tel E. Phone). 1929. Paul Terry, Audio Cinema; distributed by Western Electric. Characters: Animated telephones. Includes gag by smiling girl pickaninny, with thick white lips, and seven braids sticking out of her head.

Fantasia. 1940. Walt Disney, RKO-Radio Pictures. Characters: Mickey Mouse, black centaurettes (characters edited out of later releases).

Farmer Al Falfa's Revenge. 1916. Paul Terry, J. R. Bray Studio, Pathe Film Exchange, Thomas Edison, Inc. Characters: Farmer Al Falfa, black porter, Sir Henry Bonehead.

Farmer Al Falfa's Watermelon Patch. 1916. Paul Terry, J. R. Bray Studio, released by Pathe Film Exchange. Characters: Farmer Alfalfa, black man, donkey.

Felix the Cat in Eats Are West. 1925. Pat Sullivan, M. J. Winkler; released by Educational and Pathe Film Exchange. Characters: Felix the Cat, black woman (Aunt Jemima caricature).

Felix the Cat in Futuritzy. 1928. Pat Sullivan, Jacques Kopfstein, Bijou Film Co.; distributed by Educational and Pathe Film Exchange. Characters: Felix the Cat. Includes gag by black chauffeur/airplane pilot.

Felix the Cat in Jungle Bungles. 1928. Pat Sullivan, M. J. Winkler; released by Educational Pictures. Characters: Felix the Cat, Africans.

Felix the Cat in Nonstop Fright. 1927. Pat Sullivan, Pathe Film Exchange. Characters: Felix the Cat, black cannibals.

Felix the Cat in Oceantics. 1930. Pat Sullivan, Jaques Kopfstein; released by Copley Pictures Corp. Character: Felix the Cat. Includes gag by black man playing a harmonica on the street. When he finishes his performance, coins are tossed into his hat as he smiles.

Felix the Cat in Stars and Stripes. 1927. Pat Sullivan, Pathe Film Exchange. Characters: Felix the Cat, convict, black porter.

Felix the Cat in Uncle Tom's Crabbin'. 1927. Pat Sullivan, M. J. Winkler; released by Educational and Pathe Film Exchange. Characters: Felix the Cat, Uncle Tom, Topsy, Little Eva, Simon Legree.

Felix the Cat Switches Witches. 1927. Pat Sullivan, M. J. Winkler; released by Educational and Pathe Film Exchange. Character: Felix the Cat. Includes gag in which Felix frightens a black man with a jack-o'-lantern. The man is so terrified that he jumps out of his clothes, which run off without him as Felix laughs.

Felix Dopes It Out. 1925. Pat Sullivan, released by M. J. Winkler; released by Educational and Pathe Film Exchange. Characters: Felix the Cat, black cannibals.

Felix Saves the Day. 1922. Pat Sullivan, Distributed by M. J. Winkler. Characters: Felix the Cat, Willie Brown, the Tar Heels (Black Kid Baseball Team).

Figaro and Cleo. 1943. Jack Kinney, Walt Disney, distributed by RKO-Radio Pictures. Characters: Figaro, Cleo. Includes scenes with Aunt Delilah, a large black maid with thick white lips, who snores while she sleeps. (Included in segment of the Mickey Mouse Club on ABC TV Network October 2, 1984.)

Fish Fry. 1944. James Culhane, Walter Lantz, Universal Pictures. Characters: Andy Panda, black cat.

The Fistic Mystic. 1947. Dave Fleischer, Max Fleischer, Famous Studios; released by Paramount Pictures. Characters: Popeye, black Africans.

Flying Elephant. 1920. Pathe Film Exchange, J. R. Bray Studio. Character: Little darky boy.

Flop Goes the Weasel. 1943. Charles Jones, Merrie Melodies, Warner Bros. Characters: Wiley Weasel, black chick, mammy hen, weasel.

The Foolish Duckling. 1952. Manny Davis, Paul Terry, 20th-Century. Character: Dinky Duck.

Foolish Follies. 1930. Paul Terry, Aesop's Fable, Pathe Film Exchange. Character: Bill Robinson.

Forbidden Fruit. 1923. J. R. Bray Studio; released by Hodkinson and Selznick Pictures. Characters: Col. Heeza Liar, black cannibals.

Fraidy Cat Mouse. 1942. William Hanna, Joseph Barbera, M-G-M. Characters: Tom cat, Jerry mouse, Mammy Two-Shoes (voice characterization by Lillian Randolph).

Framed Cat. 1950. Joseph Barbera, M-G-M. Characters: Tom cat, Jerry mouse. Includes gag by Mammy Two-Shoes (voice characterization by Lillian Randolph), who says, "Thomas is that you messin' 'round in the kitchen" and "Thomas come here and get dis chicken stealin' mouse."

Fresh Hair. 1942. I. Freleng, Warner Bros. Characters: Bugs Bunny, Elmer Fudd. Includes gag by black minstrel quartet singing "Camptown Races" joined by brief appearance of Elmer Fudd in blackface and Bugs Bunny playing a banjo.

Fried Chicken. 1931. Frank Moser, Paul Terry, Educational Pictures; 20th Century-Fox. Characters: Animal caricatures in blackface.

Frightday the 13th. 1953. I. Sparber, Paramount Pictures. Characters: Casper the friendly ghost, black kitten.

From Hand to Mouse. 1944. Charles Jones, Warner Bros. Characters: Lion, mouse. Includes gag of the mouse in blackface disguised as an African holding a spear who tells the lion that's chasing him, "He went that way, Boss" with a voice impersonating Eddie "Rochester" Anderson.

Funny Face. 1931. Ub Iwerks; released by M-G-M. Character: Flip the frog. Includes gag by stereotypical black man who sings, "I so handsome as you can see. The gals down south sho' go fo' me" and a Topsy-like black girl.

Galloping Fanny. 1933. Steve Muffati, Eddie Donnelly, Van Beuren; released through RKO-Radio Pictures. Characters: Cubby the Bear, black porter. Released by Official films in the 1940s under the title *Galloping Hoofs,* with Cubby Bear's name changed to Brownie Bear.

Garden Gopher. 1950. Tex Avery, M-G-M. Characters: Spike and Tyke, black stereotype.

The Gingerbread Boy. 1934. Walter Lantz, Universal. Characters: Gingerbread boy, black cat.

Goin' to Heaven on a Mule. 1934. I. Freleng, Merrie Melodies, Vitaphone, Warner Bros. Characters: Southern blacks.

Gold Diggers of '49. 1936. Tex Avery, Bob Clampett, Charles Jones, Warner Bros. Characters: Beans, Porky Pig. Includes gag in which the black exhaust smoke from Porky's car turns two Chinese gold prospectors into Kingfish and Amos stereotypes (*Amos 'n' Andy* radio show), and Kingfish says, "Now look heah, brother, as I was saying 'bout dis heah proposition and Amos says "Ah-Wah, Ah-Wha . . . "

Goldilocks and the Jivin' Bears. 1944. I. Freleng, Merry

Melodies, Warner Bros. Characters: Three Black Bears, Red Ridin' Hood; narrated by Ernest Whitman.

*A Good Liar. 1917. Pat Sullivan, Powers Film Company; distributed by Universal. Characters: Black kids, black army veteran.

The Good Little Monkeys. 1935. Hugh Harman, M-G-M. Characters: Includes gags by black African caricatures.

Goodrich Dirt in Darkest Africa. 1918. J. R. Bray Pictograph; released by Paramount Pictures. Characters: Goodrich Dirt, Africans.

Goodrich Dirt in King of Spades. 1918. J. R. Bray Pictograph; released by Paramount Pictures. Characters: Goodrich Dirt, blacks.

Goofy Groceries. 1941. Robert Clampett, Warner Bros. Character: Jack Benny. Includes a gag by the Gold Dust Twins and caricature of Eddie "Rochester" Anderson who says, "My, oh my! Tattletale gray."

*The Goose Goes South. 1941. William Hanna, Joseph Barbera, M-G-M. Characters: Little Goose, black cotton pickers.

Graduation Exercises. 1935. Charles Mintz, Ub Iwerks, Columbia Pictures. Character: Scrappy. Includes gag in which a white schoolboy gets a bottle of black ink poured over his head, which turns him into a blackfaced stereotype with thick white lips.

The Greatest Man in Siam. 1944. James Culhane, Walter Lantz, Swing Symphony, Universal. Character: King of Siam. Includes a gag by black palace slave.

The Grocery Boy. 1943. Winford Jackson, Walt Disney, distributed by United Artists. Character: Mickey Mouse. Includes gag where soot from a stove turns Mickey's face into a blackfaced stereotype with thick white lips.

Gulliver Mickey. 1934. Burt Gillett, Walt Disney, United Artists. Character: Mickey Mouse. Includes brief gag in which a white man gets ink squirted in his face, which turns him into a blackface stereotype with thick white lips.

*Hair Today, Gone Tomorrow. 1954. Seymour Keitel, Famous Studios, Paramount Pictures. Characters: Buzzy the crow, Katnip the cat.

*Half-Pint Pygmy. 1948. Tex Avery, M-G-M. Characters: George and Junior black pygmies.

Happy-Go-Nutty. 1944. Tex Avery, M-G-M. Characters: Screwy Squirrel, hound dog. Includes gag in which bomb explodes in the hand of the hound dog, turning his face into a black stereotype with thick red lips and two braids sticking out of his head. He says, "Oh, oh, he done it again" in a voice imitating that of Eddie "Rochester" Anderson.

Happy Birthdaze. 1943. Dave Fleischer, Max Fleischer, Famous Studios; released by Paramount Pictures. Characters: Popeye, Olive Oyl, Shorty. Includes gag where Olive slides down a chimney and lands in a coal furnace. When she comes out, she is a blackface stereotype.

*Happy Scouts. 1938. Walter Lantz, Universal. Characters: Oswald the rabbit, black duck.

Hare Trigger. 1945. I. Freleng, Warner Bros. Characters: Bugs Bunny, Yosemite Sam. Includes gag in which Bugs Bunny im-

personates black redcap on a train. He gives Sam several pieces of luggage as he says, "Last stop, all out! Grand Central Station. Watch yo' step, suh. Yes suh. Yes suh. Yuk, yuk. Thank-you."

Harem Scarem. 1927. Walter Lantz, Universal. Characters: Oswald the rabbit, black slaves.

*Have You Got Any Castles? 1938. Frank Tashlin Warner Bros. Characters: Caricatures of various performers, including Cab Calloway and Bill Robinson.

*A Haunting We Will Go. 1939. Burt Gillett, Walter Lantz, Universal. Character: Li'l Eightball.

*He Dabbles in the Pond. 1917. Pat Powers; distributed by Universal. Characters: Mr. Fuller Pep, black man, Mammy.

*He Who Gets Soaked. 1925. Earl Hurd, Educational Pictures, Pathe Film Exchange. Characters: black baby, stork.

Headless Horseman. 1934. Ub Iwerks, Famous Fairytale; released by Pat Powers and Commonwealth Films. Characters: Ichibod Crane, a black three-piece band. Includes a gag by black messenger boy who rides a mule and has a Stephin Fetchit demeanor.

Henpecked Hoboes. 1946. Tex Avery, M-G-M. Characters: George and Junior. Includes gag in which dynamite blows up and turns George into a blackface stereotype with thick pink lips and two braids sticking out of his head. George says, "OK Junior, bend over" while the background music plays "Swanee River."

Hero for a Day. 1953. Paul Terry, Terrytoon, 20th-Century Fox. Character: Mighty Mouse. Includes gag in which an explosion turns the face of a cat into a blackface stereotype.

*Hey, Hey Fever. 193?. Hugh Harman, M-G-M. Character: Bosko.

Highway Snobbery. 1936. Charles Mintz, Columbia Pictures. Character: Krazy Kat. Includes gag involving black stereotype.

His Artistical Temperature. 1937. Max Fleischer; released by Paramount Pictures. Character: Popeye. Includes a gag by large blackface man singing "Mammy."

*His Dark Past. 1919. William Noland, International Film Service; distributed in England by John D. Tippett (London) as a Pussyfoot Cartoon. Characters: Happy Hooligan, black cannibals.

*His Mouse Friday. 1951. William Hanna, Joseph Barbera, M-G-M. Characters: Tom cat, Jerry mouse, black cannibals.

*His Off Day. 1938. Connie Rasinski, Paul Terry, Terrytoon, Educational Pictures, Twentieth Century-Fox. Characters: Puddy the cat, black servant.

*Hitting the Trail to Halleluah Land. 1931. Rudolph Ising, Hugh Harman, Vitaphone, Warner Bros. Characters: Piggy, Uncle Tom, Litle Eva, Simon Legree.

*Hold Anything. 1930. Hugh Harman, Rudolph Ising, Vitaphone, Warner Bros. Characters: Bosko, Honey.

Hollywood Canine Canteen. 1946. Warner Bros. Characters: Caricatures of Hollywood stars including Carmen Miranda, Bing Crosby, Abbott and Costello, and Lionel Hambone (Lionel Hampton).

*Hollywood Picnic. 1937. Art Davis, Scrappy Color Rhapsody, Columbia Pictures. Characters: Caricatures of various movie stars, including Stephin Fetchit.

Hoola-Boola. 1941. George Pal, Puppetoon, Paramount Pictures. Characters: Jim Dandy, Sarong Sarong, black cannibals.

Horse Cops. 1931. Aesop's Fable, Van Beuren; released by Pathe Film Exchange. Characters: Includes gag involving black stereotype emerging from a tuba.

HotLips Jasper. 1944. George Pal, Puppetoons, Paramount Pictures. Characters: Jasper, Scarecrow (voice characterization by Roy Glenn), Crow.

A Hot Time in Punkville. 1915. Lubin Film Manufacturing Company. Character: Rastus.

House Cleaning. 1924. Paul Terry, Pathe Film Exchange. Character: Black cat.

How Do I Know It's Sunday. 1934. I. Freleng, Vitaphone, Warner Bros. Characters: Caricatures of various consumer goods, including Aunt Jemima and Uncle Tom.

The Hula Cabaret. 1919. Company: Bud Fisher, distributed by Fox Film Company. Characters: Mutt and Jeff, black Salome.

Humorous Phases of Funny Faces. 1906. J. S. Blackton, Vitagraph. Character: Black "coon."

I Ain't Got Nobody. 1932. Dave Fleischer, Max Fleischer, Screen Song, Paramount Pictures. Characters: Mills Brothers (live action), lion, black cannibals.

I Heard. 1933. Dave Fleischer, Max Fleischer, Paramount Pictures. Characters: Betty Boop, Don Redman and his band (live action).

I Love a Parade. 1932. Hugh Harman, Rudolph Ising, Warner Bros. Characters: Includes two gags by black characters. In one a black man is billed as "Jo Jo the Wild Man." He has two bones tied to the hair on his head, a ring in his nose, and a leopard skin on his body. He shakes the bars of his cage and growls. The other black man is billed as "Gumbo the Indian Rubber Man." He jumps up and down and changes his body into various shapes including an automobile tire, a Jew's harp, and a bouncing rubber ball.

I Taw A Putty Tat. 1948. I. Freleng, Warner Bros. Characters: Sylvester Cat, Tweety Bird. Includes gag where a stick of exploding dynamite turns Sylvester's face into a blackface stereotype maid who says, in a Rochester voice, "Uh! Oh! better git back to the kitchen—I smell somethin' burnin.'"

I'd Love to Take Orders from You. 1936. Tex Avery, Warner Bros. Characters: Black crow, scarecrow.

I'll Be Glad When You're Dead, You Rascal You. 1934. Dave Fleischer, Max Fleischer, Paramount Pictures. Characters: Betty Boop, Louis Armstrong (animation and live action), Ko-Ko, Bimbo, black cannibals.

In the Bag. 1932. Van Beuren; released by RKO-Radio Pictures. Characters: Tom and Jerry. Includes a gag by a stereotypical black man.

Inki and the Lion. 1941. Charles Jones, Warner Bros. Characters: Inki, minah bird, lion.

Inki and the Minah Bird. 1943. Charles Jones, Warner Bros. Characters: Inki, minah bird, lion.

Inki at the Circus. 1947. Charles Jones, Warner Bros. Characters: Inki, minah bird.

Insultin' the Sultin. 1934. Ub Iwerks, Celebrity Pictures; released by M-G-M. Characters: Willie Whopper, black slaves.

Into Your Dance. 1935. I. Freleng, Vitaphone, Warner Bros. Character: Captain Benny. Includes a gag by a black quartet that sings "Go into Your Dance."

The Island Fling. 1946. Bill Tytla, Paramount Pictures. Characters: Popeye, Olive Oyl, Bluto (as Robinson Crusoe), Friday (black slave), Friday's family (Saturday, Sunday, and Monday).

The Isle of Pingo-Pongo. 1938. Tex Avery, Vitaphone, Warner Bros. Characters: black natives.

It Happened to Crusoe. 1941. Charles Mintz, Columbia Pictures. Characters: Robinson Crusoe and cannibals. Voice impersonations of Jack Benny as Robinson Crusoe, Fred Allen as the cannibal king, and Eddie "Rochester" Anderson as Friday.

It's a Living. 1950. 20th Century-Fox. Character: Dinky Duck.

I've Got Rings on My Fingers. 1929. Dave Fleischer, Max Fleischer, Screen Song. Characters: Policeman, cannibals.

I've Got to Sing a Torch Song. 1933. Tom Palmer, Looney Tunes, Vitaphone, Warner Bros. Characters: Various Hollywood stars, black cannibal.

Jasper and the Beanstalk. 1945. George Pal, Puppetoons, Paramount Pictures. Characters: Jasper, Scarecrow (voice characterization by Roy Glenn), Crow.

Jasper and the Choo-Choo. 1943. George Pal, Madcap Models, Paramount Pictures. Characters: Jasper, Scarecrow (voice characterization by Roy Glenn), Crow, Mammy.

Jasper Derby. 1946. George Pal, Paramount Pictures. Characters: Jasper, Hi-Octane.

Jasper Goes Fishing. 1943. George Pal, Puppetoon, Paramount Pictures. Characters: Jasper, Scarecrow (voice characterization by Roy Glenn), Crow.

Jasper Goes Hunting. 1944. George Pal, Puppetoon, Paramount Pictures. Characters: Jasper, Mammy, Scarecrow (voice characterization by Roy Glenn), Crow, Bugs Bunny (cameo).

Jasper and the Haunted House. 1942. George Pal, Madcap Models, Paramount Pictures. Characters: Jasper, Scarecrow (voice characterization by Roy Glenn), Crow.

Jasper in a Jam. 1946. George Pal, Puppetoons, Paramount Pictures. Characters: Jasper, policeman (voice characterization by Roy Glenn), vocalist (Peggy Lee), orchestral music by Charlie Barnet and his orchestra.

Jasper Tell. 1945. George Pal, Puppetoons, Paramount Pictures. Characters: Jasper, Scarecrow (voice characterization by Roy Glenn), Crow, Mammy.

Jasper and the Watermelons. 1942. George Pal, Madcap Models, Paramount Pictures. Characters: Jasper, Scarecrow (voice characterization by Roy Glenn), Crow, Mammy.

Jasper's Booby Trap. 1945. George Pal, Puppetoons, Paramount Pictures. Characters: Jasper, Scarecrow (voice characterization by Roy Glenn), Crow.

Jasper's Close Shave. 1945. George Pal, Puppetoons, Paramount Pictures. Characters: Jasper, Scarecrow (voice characterization by Roy Glenn), Crow.

*Jasper's Minstrels. 1945. George Pal, Puppetoons, Paramount Pictures. Characters: Jasper, Scarecrow (voice characterization by Roy Glenn), Crow.

*Jasper's Music Lesson. 1943. George Pal, Madcap Models, Paramount Pictures. Characters: Jasper, Scarecrow (voice characterization by Roy Glenn), Crow, Mammy.

*Jasper's Paradise. 1944. George Pal, Puppetoon, Paramount Pictures. Characters: Jasper, Scarecrow (voice characterization by Roy Glenn), gingerbread man (voice characterization by Joel Fluellen), Crow.

Jazzbo Singer. 1932. Charles Mintz, Columbia Pictures. Characters: Al Jolson character in blackface.

Jeepers Creepers. 1939. Robert Clampett, Warner Bros. Character: Porky Pig. Includes a gag by a large blackface character who says, "My oh my! Tattletale gray."

*Jingle Jangle Jungle. 1950. Seymour Kneitel Famous Studios, Paramount Pictures. Characters: black cannibals.

Jitterbug Follies. 1939. Milt Gross, M-G-M. Characters: Count Screwball and J. R. Includes gag where a pie opens up and the blackberry filling turns into a black jazz band.

*John Henry. 1957. Henry Pierpoint, Holt Rinehart and Winston, Inc. Characters: John Henry, Polly Anne, the captain, salesman McBee.

*John Henry and the Inky-Poo. 1946. George Pal, Puppetoons, Paramount Pictures. Characters: John Henry, the legendary steel-drivin' man. Narrated by Rex Ingram. Voices: Rex Ingram as John Henry, Luvenia Nash Singers, Lillian Randolph.

Jungle Drums. 1943. Don Gordon, Paramount Pictures. Characters: Superman, Lois Lane, black natives, Nazis.

*Jungle Jam. 1931. John Foster, Van Beuren; released by RKO-Radio Pictures. Characters: Tom and Jerry, black cannibals.

*Jungle Jazz. 1930. John Foster, Harry Bailey, Van Beuren; released by Pathe Film Exchange. Characters: Waffles the cat, Don the dog, black cannibals.

Jungle Jitters. 1934. Ub Iwerks, M-G-M. Characters: Willie Whopper, black cannibals.

*Jungle Jitters. 1938. I. Freleng, Vitaphone, Warner Bros. Characters: Black cannibals, caricatures of Clark Gable, Robert Taylor.

*Jungle Jive. 1944. James Culhane, Walter Lantz, Universal. Characters: Black natives.

Jungle Jumble. 1919. International Film Service; released through Educational Pictures. Characters: Happy Hooligan, blacks.

A Jungle Jumble. 1932. Walter Lantz, Universal. Characters: Oswald the rabbit, blacks.

Jungle Rhythm. 1929. Ub Iwerks, Walt Disney. Characters: Mickey Mouse, cannibals.

*Kannibal Kapers. 1935. Manny Gould, Columbia Pictures. Characters: Krazy Kat and black cannibals.

*King Klunk. 1933. Bill Nolan, Walter Lantz, Universal Pictures. Characters: Pooch the pup, black natives.

King Zilch. 1933. Paul Terry, Frank Moser, Terrytoon, Educational Pictures. Includes gag with the stereotypical face of a smiling black man with thick white lips.

Kings Up. 1934. Walter Lantz, Universal Pictures. Character: Oswald Rabbit. Includes gag where Oswald is thrown into a stove pipe. When he sticks his head out, his face is a blackface stereotype with thick white lips as he shouts "Mammy."

*Ko-Ko Sees Spooks. 1925. Dave Fleischer, Max Fleischer, Red Seal Pictures. Characters: Ko-Ko the Clown, back porter.

*Ko-Ko's Harem Scarem. 1929. Dave Fleischer, Max Fleischer, Inkwell Studio; released by Paramount Pictures. Characters: Ko-Ko the Clown, black natives.

Ko-Ko's Thanksgiving. 1925. Dave Fleischer, Max Fleischer, Red Seal Pictures. Characters: Ko-Ko the Clown, black cook (live action).

*Kongo-Roo. 1946. Howard Swift, Columbia Pictures. Characters: Fuzzy-Wuzzy, black cannibals.

*Korn Plastered in Africa. 1932. Features Film Company. Characters: Kernel Korn (voice characterization by Uncle Don), black cannibals.

*Land O' Cotton. 1929. Frank Moser, Paul Terry, Pathe Film Exchange. Characters: Black slave boy, Simon Legree.

The Last Mail. 1933. Mannie Davis, Van Beuren; released by RKO-Radio Pictures. Characters: Cubby Bear, black stereotype.

*The Latest in Underwear. 1919. Pussyfoot Cartoon (England), International Film Service, released in the U.S. by Educational Films. Characters: Happy Holligan, black women.

Laughing Gas. 1931. Ub Iwerks, Celebrity Pictures, M-G-M release. Characters: Flip the Frog. Includes gag where Flip steals a stick of dynamite while a black Porter, with thick white lips, sleeps with his back propped up against the boxes.

*Lazy Bones. 1934. Dave Fleischer, Max Fleischer, Paramount Pictures. Characters: Lazy Bones (horse), Borran Minevitch's Harmonica Rascals, including black boy who sings the title song.

Let's Ring Doorbells. 1935. Ub Iwerks, Charles Mintz, Columbia Pictures. Characters: Scrappy, Oopie. Includes gag where black ink squirted through a key hole turns Scrappy's face into a black face stereotype with thick white lips. He sticks his head through a hole and finds himself a circus attraction where people throw baseballs at his head for "five shots for five cents." Oopie pulls his head out and Scrappy dances to the tune of the Negro spiritual "Old God's Children Got Wings" before bending to one knee and shouting "Mammy."

*Let's Sing Together. 1937. Arthur Price Production. Characters: Black boy and his mammy.

*The Lion Hunt. 1938. Paul Terry, Terrytoon, Educational Pictures. Characters: Mouse, lion, white hunter, black natives.

*The Lion Tamer. 1934. George Stallings, Van Beuren; distributed by RKO-Radio Pictures. Characters: Amos and Andy, Kingfish, Lightnin', Brother Crawford.

*The Lion's Friend. 1934. Frank Moser, Paul Terry, Twentieth

Century, Educational Pictures. Characters: Farmer Al Falfa, black cannibals.

Little Black Sambo. 1935. Ub Iwerks, Celebrity Pictures. Character: Little Black Sambo.

Little Blue Blackbird. 1938. Patrick Lenihan, Walter Lantz, Universal Pictures. Characters: Blackbird family.

The Little Broadcast. 1939. George Pal, Paramount Pictures. Characters: Jim Dandy, black cannibals.

Little Dutch Mill. 1934. Max Fleischer, Color Classic; released by Paramount Pictures. Character: Dutchman. Includes gag by a black boy who shines the wooden shoes of a white Dutchman.

The Little Goldfish. 1940. Rudolf Ising, M-G-M. Characters: Goldfish, black maid.

Little Lion Hunter. 1947. Warner Bros. Characters: Inki, mynah bird, lion.

Little Nemo in Slumberland. 1910. Winsor McCay, Vitagraph. Characters: Winsor McCay as himself, Impy the cannibal, Flip, Little Nemo, the princess.

Little Orphan. 1949. William Hanna, Joseph Barbera, M-G-M. Characters: Tom cat, Jerry mouse. Includes gag by Mammy Two-Shoes as she places a Thanksgiving turkey on the dinner table (voice characterization by Lillian Randolph) Academy Award Winning Cartoon.

Little Red Hen. 1934. Ub Iwerks, Pat Powers, Celebrity Pictures. Characters: Little red hen, three white chicks, black chick.

Little Tinker. 1948. Tex Avery, M-G-M. Includes gag by female rabbit in blackface and thick red lips saying, "I loves dat man."

The Lonesome Mouse. 1943. William Hanna, Joseph Barbera, M-G-M. Characters: Tom and Jerry, Mammy Two-Shoes (voice characterization by Lillian Randolph).

Loose in the Caboose. 1947. Dave Fleischer, Max Fleischer; released by Paramount Pictures. Characters: Little Lulu, black baggage porter. Includes two gags. A black redcap is slowly pushing a baggage cart and says, with a Stephin Fetchit demeanor, "Baggage—smash your baggage. Baggage—smash your baggage." Lulu, her face black with coaldust, says, "Yassuh Boss, she went thataway."

Lost in the Jungle. 1915. Wallace Carlson; released by Essanay Pictures. Characters: Dreamy Dud, African natives.

Lucky Ducky. 1948. Tex Avery, M-G-M. Characters: George and Junior. Includes two gags. A shotgun blows up and turns George into a blackface stereotype, and another shotgun blows up in the faces George and Junior, turning them into blackface stereotypes with thick red lips and three braids sticking out of their heads while the background music plays "Swanee River."

Lucky Lulu. 1944. Seymour Kneitel, Famous Studios, Paramount Pictures. Characters: Little Lulu, Mandy.

Lulu Gets the Birdie. 1944. Max Fleischer; distributed by Paramount Pictures. Characters: Little Lulu, Mandy, black crow.

Lulu Gets the Birdie. 1944. I. Sparber, Famous Studios; distributed by Paramount Pictures. Characters: Little Lulu, black maid.

Lulu's Birthday Party. 1944. I. Sparber, Paramount Pictures. Characters: Little Lulu, Mandy.

Lulu's Indoor Outing. 1944. I. Sparber, Famous Studios, Paramount Pictures. Characters: Little Lulu, black maid.

The Lunch House. 1927. Walter Lantz, Hot Dog Cartoons, J. R. Bray Studio. Characters: Walter Lantz (live action), Pete the pup. Includes gag involving a note from Sally, the black cook, which reads, "Dear Boss, Ah am leavin' dis place cause I done found mah self a bettah job." Also includes a cameo involving a sleeping black chauffeur and Pete.

Lyin' Hunter. 1937. Charles Mintz, Columbia Pictures. Characters: Krazy Kat, black cannibals.

A Mad House. 1934. Paul Terry, Terrytoon, Educational Pictures. Characters: Puddy the pup, mad scientist. Includes gag by a black skeleton that works as a porter for white skeletons.

Magazine Rack. 1933. Characters: Black baby, African natives with big lips.

Magic Art. 1932. John Foster, Harry Bailey, Aesop's Fable, Van Beuren; released by RKO-Pathe Film Exchange. Character: Dog artist. Includes musical number performed by a black girl who "scat" sings, with an Ethel Waters demeanor, "I Ain't Got Nobody."

Magical Maestro. 1952. Tex Avery, M-G-M. Character: Dog that is a concert singer. Includes a gag in which the dog sings an operatic selection. A man sitting in the balcony of the theater dislikes his performance so much that he squirts black ink from his ink pen into his face, turning the singer into a blackface caricature of Bill Kenney, the tenor and lead singer of the famous Ink Spots quartet, who sings, "Everything I have is yours." Then he throws an anvil that lands on the dog and squashes him into a short caricature of the bass singer of the Ink Spots, singing, "Yeah, honey chile, everything has is mine."

Maid in China. 1938. Connie Rasinski Paul Terry, 20th Century-Fox Educational. Characters: Black genie, Aladdin.

The Major Lied 'Til Dawn. 1938. Frank Tashlin Warner Bros. Characters: Major Twambe, little Freddie, black African natives.

Making Stars. 1935. Dave Fleischer, Max Fleischer, Paramount Pictures. Characters: Betty Boop, white baby performer, Japanese baby, three black baby performers, Mammy and her baby.

Malibu Beach Party. 1940. I. Freleng, Vitaphone, Warner Bros. Characters: Caricatures of Jack Benny and other radio stars. Includes gag by Eddie "Rochester" Anderson caricature.

Marty the Monk. 193?. Associated Films. Character: Marty the monk. Includes a gag where Marty puts on a long wig and does a brief imitation of Cab Calloway.

Mary's Little Lamb. 1935. Ub Iwerks, Comi Color, Celebrity Pictures. Characters: Mary, white lamb, lady teacher, school children, including black boy.

The Mascot. 193?. Ladislas Starwick, Gelma-Film (Paris). Characters: Combination live action and animated puppets including a black Zulu puppet that has thick white lips and wears a grass skirt.

Meet John Doughboy. 1941. Robert Clampett, Looney Tunes, Warner Bros. Character: Porky Pig. Includes a gag in which a white man, smoking a cigar, is being driven in a convertible automobile by a black chauffeur who has thick white lips. The white man says, "Hellow Jazzbo" (Jack Benny voice imitation) and the chauffeur answers, "Hold on to your britches, Boss" (Eddie "Rochester" Anderson voice imitation) as the car speeds off.

Mickey in Arabia. 1932. Wilford Jackson, Walt Disney, Columbia Pictures release. Characters: Mickey Mouse, Minnie Mouse. Includes scenes showing black female slaves with thick white lips who are chained together.

Mickey Steps Out. 1931. Burt Gillett, Walt Disney, released by Columbia Pictures. Characters: Mickey Mouse, Minnie Mouse, Pluto. Includes gag where soot from a stove turns Mickey, Minnie and Pluto into blackface stereotypes who dance and sing to the music of "Sweet Georgia Brown."

Mickey's Follies. 1929. (Also released as *Mickey's Vaudville Show* by Hollywood Film Enterprises), Wilfred Jackson, Walt Disney, Columbia Pictures. Character: Mickey Mouse. Includes gag by black stereotypes.

Mickey's Man Friday (Silent version released by Hollywood Film Enterprises under title Robinson Crusoe Mickey). 1935. David Hand, Walt Disney, United Artists. Characters: Mickey Mouse, Friday, black cannibals.

Mickey's Mellerdrammer (Also released by Hollywood Film Enterprises under the title *Mickey Mouse and Simon Legree*) 1933. Wilford Jackson, Walt Disney, United Artists. Characters: Mickey Mouse, Minnie Mouse, Little Eva, Eliza, Simon Legree.

Mickey's Nightmare. 1932. Burt Gillet, Walt Disney, United Artists. Characters: Mickey Mouse, Minnie Mouse, Pluto. Includes gag in which baby mouse paints the face of a bust of Venus, turning it into the face of a smiling black mammy with thick white lips.

Midnight in a Toy Shop. 1930. (*See also Christmas in Toyland*) Wilford Jackson, Walt Disney. Characters: Toys. Includes gag where two stereotypical black dolls dance and cry "Mammy."

Midnight Snack. 1940. William Hanna, Joseph Barbera, M-G-M. Characters: Tom and Jerry, Mammy Two-Shoes (voice characterization by Lillian Randolph).

Mighty Mouse in Crying Wolf. 1947. Connie Rasinski, Paul Terry, 20th Century-Fox. Characters: Mighty Mouse, black sheep.

Mighty Mouse in Swiss Cheese Robinson. 1948. Manny Davis, Paul Terry, Twentieth Century-Fox. Characters: Mighty Mouse, black cannibals.

Mild Cargo. 1934. George Stallings, Van Beuren; distributed by RKO-Radio Pictures. Characters: Cubby Bear, African natives. Released in a silent version by Official Films under the title *Brownie Bear Bucks the Jungle.*

Minnie the Moocher. 1932. Dave Fleischer, Max Fleischer, Paramount Pictures. Characters: Betty Boop, Bimbo, Cab Calloway and his band (live action).

The Minstrel Show. 1932. Charles Mintz, Columbia Pictures. Characters: Krazy Kat, blackface minstrels.

Mississippi Hare. 1949. Charles Jones, Warner Bros. Characters: Bugs Bunny, Yosemite Sam as Col. Shuffle. Includes cameo of black cotton pickers who mistake Bugs's tail for a cotton ball. Bugs is picked, baled, and loaded into the cargohold of a Mississippi paddle-wheel riverboat. Also includes gag of a cigar exploding in the face of Col. Shuffle, which turns him into a blackface minstrel who plays the banjo while Bugs dances and sings "Camptown Ladies."

Mississippi Mud. 1928. Walter Lantz, Universal Pictures. Characters: Southern blacks.

Mississippi Swing. 1941. Paul Terry, Terrytoon, Twentieth Century-Fox. Characters: Southern blacks.

Mr. Coon. 1917. Keen Cartoon Company, London. Characters: Blacks.

Mr. Jocko from Jungletown. 1916. Kartoon Komics, Gaumont, England; released through Mutual Film Exchange. Characters: Africans.

Molly Moo-Cow and Robinson Crusoe. 1936. Burt Gillett, Van Beuren; released by RKO-Radio Pictures. Characters: Molly Moo-Cow, black cannibals.

Monkey Doodle. 193?. Krazy Toons. Characters: Black monkeys, black natives.

More Kittens. 1936. Wilford Jackson, Walt Disney, Released by United Artists. Characters: Three Kittens (Blackie, Whitie, and Calico). Includes gag where black maid slips on a bar of soap and lands on her huge behind.

Morning, Noon and Night Club. 1937. Dave Fleischer, Max Fleischer, Fleischer Studios and Famous Studios; released by Paramount Pictures. Characters: Popeye, Olive Oyl, Bluto, Wimpy, black doorman at theater who opens door of taxicab for Olive.

Mother Goose Goes Hollywood. 1937. Wilford Jackson, Walt Disney; released by RKO-Radio Pictures. Characters: Caricatures of Hollywood stars, including Katherine Hepburn, Stephin Fetchit, Fats Waller, Cab Calloway and his band.

Mouse Cleaning. 1948. William Hanna, Joseph Barbera, M-G-M. Characters: Tom and Jerry, Mammy Two-Shoes (voice characterization by Lillian Randolph).

The Mouse Comes to Dinner. 1945. William Hanna, Joseph Barbera, M-G-M. Characters: Tom and Jerry, Mammy Two-Shoes. Includes gag by Mammy Two-Shoes (voice characterization by Lillian Randolph) who says, "Boy, dat's a beautiful table. Sho' hopes nothin' happens to it befo' the company gets heah."

Mouse for Sale. 1955. William Hanna, Joseph Barbera, M-G-M. Characters: Jerry mouse, Tom cat, Mammy Two-Shoes (voice characterization by Lillian Randolph).

A Mouse in the House. 1947. Joseph Barbera, William Hanna, M-G-M. Characters: Tom cat, Jerry mouse, Mammy Two-Shoes (voice characterization by Lillian Randolph).

Mouse-Merized Cat. 1946. Robert McKimson, Warner Bros. Characters: Catsello the short, fat mouse, Babbit the tall, skinny mouse (caricatures of Bud Abbott and Lou Costello), Caricatures of Bing Crosby, Jimmy Durante, Frank Sinatra.

Includes a gag by Catsello mouse in blackface and smoking a cigar (Eddie "Rochester" Anderson caricature) saying on the phone, "Hello Mr. Benny. I'm stuck over here in Harlem at my grandmother's house. Roll 'em out, Granny. You're faded" as the sound of clicking dice is heard in the background.

Mouse That Jack Built. 1959. Robert McKimson, Warner Bros. Characters: Mice with voices of Jack Benny and Rochester.

*Mouse Trapped. 1950. Alex Lovey, Walter Lantz, Universal Pictures. Characters: Black cat, Hickory, Dickory, Doc.

Movie Mad. 1931. Ub Iwerks, Celebrity Pictures; released by M-G-M. Characters: Flip the frog, black servant.

Movie Struck. 1933. Charles Mintz, Samba Pictures; released by Columbia Pictures. Character: Scrappy. Cartoon opens in a movie producer's office where a black porter, on his knees, sweeps dust off the floor into a dust pan.

*Mrs. Ladybug. 1940. Rudolph Ising, M-G-M. Characters: Bug family, black spider.

*A Mule's Disposition. 1926. F. O. B., J. R. Bray Studio. Character: Black nurse.

Musical Lulu. 1947. Dave Fleischer, Max Fleischer; released by Paramount Pictures. Characters: Little Lulu, black heads singing jazz music.

My Artistic Temperature. 1937. Dave Fleischer, Max Fleischer, Paramount Pictures. Characters: Popeye, Olive Oyl, Bluto. Includes gag in which Popeye, the artist, blows a blob of black paint on a painting depicting the shining sun. The paint hits the sun, which turns into the smiling face of a black man with thick white lips who shouts "Mammy!"

*My Man Jasper. 1945. George Pal, Puppetoons, Paramount Pictures. Characters: Jasper, Scarecrow (voice characterization by Roy Glenn), Crow, black cannibals.

*My Old Kentucky Home. 1926. Dave Fleischer, Max Fleischer, Red Seal Pictures Film Company. Characters: Ko-Ko the Clown, black female pickaninny, old black man.

*My Old Kentucky Home. 1929. Red Seal Film Company, Dave Fleischer, Max Fleischer, Paramount Pictures. Characters: Black cat, black female pickaninny, old black man.

Night Before Christmas. 1933. Wilford Jackson, Walt Disney. Character: Santa Claus. Has sequence of marching toys including a Black Sheep-herder pushing flat-bed chart which has white lamb standing on it, a little white baby whose face is turned into a blackfaced stereotype by soot falling from a chimney, and Amos and Andy in a truck-pulling trailer with three stereotypical black female dolls who sing "Mammy."

*Night Life of the Bugs. 1936. Richard Bickenbach, Jack Dunham, Walter Lantz, Universal Pictures. Characters: Oswald the rabbit, blackbird.

*Nit-Witty Kitty. 1951. William Hanna, Joseph Barbera, M-G-M. Characters: Tom cat, Jerry mouse, Mammy Two-Shoes (voice characterization by Lillian Randolph).

*No Ifs, Ands or Butts. 1954. I. Sparber, Famous Studios, Paramount Pictures. Characters: Buzzy the crow, Katnip the cat.

Off to China. 1936. Paul Terry, Terrytoon, 20th Century-Fox. Character: Cat. Includes scene where three stereotypical black drummers are sitting on the ground playing ukuleles and singing while four beautiful Hawaiian girls in grass skirts dance the Hula.

Off We Glow. 1952. I. Sparber, Famous Studios; released by Paramount Pictures. Includes gag in which a black pygmy fly wearing a bone in its hair lands on the bald head of a white man. The fly hits the man on the head with a large club, knocking him out, as the offscreen narrator says, " . . . Whose sting puts its victims to sleep."

*Old Black Joe. 1926. (released with sound track in 1929), Dave Fleischer, Max Fleischer, Red Seal Film Company, Paramount Pictures. Character: Ko-Ko the Clown.

*Old Blackout Joe. 1942. Paul Sommer Screen Gems, Columbia Pictures. Character: Black air-raid warden.

*The Old House. 1936. Hugh Harman, Happy Harmonies, M-G-M. Characters: Bosko, Honey, Bruno.

Old MacDonald Had a Farm. 1945. Seymour Kneitel, Famous Studios, Noveltoon, released by Paramount Pictures. Character: Farmer MacDonald. Includes gag where black smoke turns three white lambs into a female trio of blackface stereotypes, with thick white lips, who sing a jazzy version of "Mary Had A Little Lamb."

*Old Man of the Mountain. 1933. Dave Fleischer, Max Fleischer, Paramount Pictures. Characters: Betty Boop, Cab Calloway and his orchestra (live action).

*The Old Mill Pond. 1936. Hugh Harman, Rudolph Ising, Happy Harmonies, M-G-M. Characters: The old croaker and frog impersonations of Cab Calloway singing "Minnie the Moocher," Ethel Waters singing "Am I Blue?," Fats Waller, Bill Robinson, Mills Brothers, Stephin Fetchit.

Old Mother Hubbard. 1935. Ub Iwerks, Pat Powers, Comicolor, Celebrity Pictures. Characters: Old Mother Hubbard, her pet dog. Includes a sequence where the dog gets hit on the head by a spittoon which turns into a straw hat. The dog's lower lip protrudes and he sings, in "Negro" dialect, "Cheer up. Why do you look so sad. . . ."

*The Old Plantation. 1935. Hugh Harman, Rudolph Ising, Happy Harmonies, M-G-M. Characters: Mammy, Uncle Tom, Topsy, Little Eva, Black Beauty (the horse).

*Old Rockin' Chair Tom. 1948. William Hanna, Joseph Barbera, M-G-M. Characters: Tom cat, Jerry mouse, Mammy Two-Shoes (voice characterization by Lillian Randolph).

*Olio for Jasper. 1946. George Pal, Puppetoons, Paramount Pictures. Characters: Jasper, Scarecrow (voice characterization by Roy Glenn), Crow.

*On the Pan. 1933. Van Beuren; released by M-G-M (also released by Celebrity Pictures under the title *Little King in Darkest Africa*). Characters: Little king, black cannibals.

*100 Pygmies and Andy Panda. 1940. Alex Lovy, Walter Lantz, Universal Pictures. Characters: Andy Panda, Daddy Panda, black pygmies.

*One Note Tony. 1948. Connie Rasinski, Paul Terry, 20th Century-Fox. Characters: Tony, an African boy.

One Step Ahead of My Shadow. 1933. Rudolph Ising, Vitaphone, Warner Bros., Merrie Melodies. Characters: Includes gag by a Chinese man in blackface impersonating Amos and Andy.

The Opry House. 1929. (abbreviated version released by Hollywood Enterprises under the title *Mickey's Vaudeville.*) Walt Disney; released by Columbia Pictures. Characters: Mickey Mouse. Includes gag involving a blackface stereotype.

The Origin of the Shimmy. 1919. Pat Sullivan, Goldwyn-Bray Pictograph, Bray Studios. Characters: Reporter, sailor, black natives.

Othello. 1920. Anson Dyer, Hepworth (London). Character: Black Moor.

The Ouija Board. 1919. Dave Fleischer, Max Fleischer, J. R. Bray Studio. Characters: Max Fleischer (live action), Ko-Ko the Clown, an artist (live action), black porter (live action).

Out of the Inkwell. 1938. Dave Fleischer, Max Fleischer, Paramount Pictures. Characters: Black janitor (live action), Betty Boop.

Package for Jasper. 1944. George Pal, Puppetoon, Paramount Pictures. Characters: Jasper, Scarecrow (voice characterization by Roy Glenn), Crow.

Pantry Pirate. 1940. Gerry Geronimi, Walt Disney, Distributed by RKO Radio Pictures. Characters: Pluto, Black Maid.

Parade of the Wooden Soldiers. 1933. Dave Fleischer, Max Fleischer; distributed by Paramount Pictures. Character: Betty Boop. Includes gag of smiling black toy making music by eating a slice of watermelon.

Part Time Pal. 1947. William Hanna, Joseph Barbera, M-G-M. Characters: Tom cat, Jerry mouse, Mammy Two-Shoes (voice characterization by Lillian Randolph).

Patch Mah Britches. 1935. Charles Mintz Studio, Manny Gould; distributed by Columbia Pictures. Characters: Barney Google, Spark Plug, Sambo the black jockey, black man, Ma, Barney Google, Rudy the ostrich.

The Penguin Parade. 1938. Tex Avery, Warner Bros. Character: Fats Walrus (Fats Waller impersonation).

The Phantom Rocket. 1933. George Rufle, Van Beuren; released by RKO-Radio Pictures. Characters: Tom and Jerry. Includes gag in which three photographers fire their flashbulbs and turn into blackfaced stereotypes and sing, "We're the photographers away on the job. We can be found wherever there's a mob."

Philips Broadcast of 1938. George Pal, Philips Radio of Holland. Characters: Black band and dancers in Harlem.

Philips Cavalcade. 1940. George Pal. Character: Phlippa Ray. Includes short musical sequence where black man plays a trumpet while a black male and female choral group sing "Hallelujah—Oh Lordy—Because we've got those blues."

Pickaninny's G-String. 1913. Bud Fisher Productions; released by Pathe Film Exchange. Characters: Mutt and Jeff, blacks.

Pilgrim Porky. 1940. Robert Clampett, Warner Bros. Character: Porky Pig. Includes gag in which black cook catches fish by jumping into the ocean and then saying to Porky, "How's dis, Boss?"

The Pincushion Man. 193?. Castle Films (silent version). Character: Black balloon man.

Plane Dumb. 1932. George Rufle, Van Beuren; released by RKO-Radio Pictures. Characters: Tom and Jerry, black Africans.

The Playful Polar Bears. 1938. Dave Fleischer, Max Fleischer, Paramount Pictures. Characters: Polar Bears.

Pluto's Dream House. 1940. Gerry Geronimi, Walt Disney; released by RKO-Radio Pictures. Characters: Mickey Mouse, Pluto, black genie.

Pluto's Judgment Day. 1935. David Hand, Walt Disney, United Artists. Character: Pluto. Includes gag involving stereotypical black female cats.

Police Dog Gets Piffles in Bad. 1915. C. T. Anderson, J. R. Bray Studio, Pathe Film Exchange. Characters: Police dog, black butcher show owner.

The Police Dog to the Rescue. 1915. Pathe Film Exchange. Characters: Police dog, Mrs. Dingle—a black washerwoman.

Polka-Dot Puss. 1949. William Hanna, Joseph Barbera, M-G-M. Characters: Tom cat, Jerry mouse, Mammy Two-Shoes (voice characterization by Lillian Randolph).

Poor Little Me. 1935. Hugh Harman, Rudolph Ising, Happy Harmonies, M-G-M. Characters: Skunk family. Includes segment in which an alley cat with a Louis Armstrong demeanor chases the skunk while he sings "I'll Be Glad When You're Dead, You Rascal You."

Pop-Pie A La Mode. 1945. I. Sparber, Paramount Pictures. Characters: Popeye, black cannibals.

Popeye's Pappy. 1952. Seymour Kneitel, Famous Studios, Paramount Pictures. Characters: Popeye, his pappy, black cannibals.

Porky at the Crocadero. 1938. Frank Tashlin, Warner Bros. Character: Porky Pig. Includes a gag by Porky in blackface imitating Cab Calloway.

Porky in Egypt. 1938. Robert Clampett, Warner Bros. Character: Porky Pig. Includes a gag by two black men (similar to Amos and Andy) shooting craps.

Porky the Fireman. 1938. Frank Tashlin. Warner Bros. Character: Porky Pig. Includes a gag by a black man with a Stepin Fetchit demeanor, who says, "Catch me! I sho' hope yo' guys speed up" as he falls from the window of a burning house.

Porky in Wacky Land. 1938. Robert Clampett, Warner Bros. Characters: Porky Pig, black stereotypical caricature with wide lips saying "Mammy."

Porky's Ant. 1941. Charles Jones, Warner Bros. Characters: Porky Pig, black African pygmy, black pygmy ant.

Porky's Hero Agency. 1937. Robert Clampett, Looney Tunes, Warner Bros. Character: Porky Pig. Includes gag by black palace guard.

Porky's Midnight Matinee. 1941. Charles Jones, Warner Bros. Characters: Porky Pig, African pygmy ant.

Porky's Moving Day. 1936. Jack King, Warner Bros. Characters: Porky Pig, Dopey—a black prizefighter, Mrs. Cud the cow.

Porky's Poppa. 1938. Robert Clampett, Warner Bros. Character: Porky Pig. Includes where Old Bessie the Cow gives a

Porky a black bottle of chocolate milk while the music plays "Dixie."

Porky's Preview. 1941. Tex Avery, Warner Bros. Character: Porky Pig. Includes gag by Al Jolson caricature singing "September in the Rain" in blackface and doing his "mammy" routine on bended knee.

Postwar Inventions. 1945. Paul Terry, Twentieth Century Fox. Character: Grandy Goose. Includes gag by black smiling face with thick red lips and big white teeth saying, "Do you like bright, sparkling teeth? If you do, send us your teeth and we will clean them for you."

* The Prodigal Pup. (Originally released as *Farmer Al Falfa's Wayward Pup.*) 1924. Paul Terry, distributed by Pathe Film Exchange. Characters: Farmer Al Falfa, Black Pup.

* Professor Bonehead Is Shipwrecked. 1917. Emil Cohl, Released in U.S.A. by Gaumont America, Mutual Film Exchange. Characters: Professor Bonehead, black cannibals, black bear.

Prosperity Blues. 1932. Charles Mintz, Columbia Pictures, Characters: Krazy Kat, stereotypical black heads.

* The Puppet Show. 1936. Walter Lantz, Universal. Characters: Oswald the rabbit, black puppet.

* Push-Button Kitty. 1952. William Hanna, Joseph Barbera, M-G-M. Characters: Tom cat, Jerry mouse, Mammy Two-Shoes (voice characterization by Lillian Randolph).

* Puss Gets the Boot. 1940. Rudolph Ising, M-G-M. Characters: Jasper the cat, Pee-Wee the mouse, Mammy Two-Shoes (voice characterization by Lillian Randolph).

* Puss 'N' Toots. 1942. William Hanna, Joseph Barbera, M-G-M. Characters: Tom cat, Jerry mouse, Mammy Two-Shoes (voice characterization by Lillian Randolph).

* Pygmy Hunt. 1938. I. Freleng, M-G-M. Characters: Captain, the inspector, black pygmy.

* Pygmy Trouble. 1939. Walter Lantz, Universal Pictures. Characters: Andy Panda, his father, black pygmies.

* Railroad Rhythm. 1937. Manny Gould, Ben Harrison, Columbia Pictures. Characters: Krazy Kat, "Stephin Fetchit" Pullman porter.

* The Rasslin Match. 1934. George Stallings Van Beuren; distributed by RKO-Radio Pictures. Characters: Amos, Andy, Kingfish.

* Rastus' Rabid Rabbit Hunt. 1914. J. R. Bray Studio; released by Pathe Film Exchange. Characters: Mr. and Mrs Rastus Rabbit.

Rastus Runs Amuck. 1917. Kartoon Komics, Gaumont, England; released through Mutual Film Exchange. Character: Black man.

Red-Headed Baby. 1931. Rudolph Ising, Warner Bros. Character: Red-headed baby doll. Includes gag by two stereotypical black female singing dolls that have hair sticking out of their heads like coils of wire. Also shows Black "Sambo" dancing toy.

Ride Him Bosko. 1933. Hugh Harman, Rudolph Ising, Vitaphone, Warner Bros. Character: Bosko.

Robinson Crusoe. 1925. J. R. Bray Studio. Characters: Robinson Crusoe, black man.

* Robinson Crusoe. 1933. Paul Terry, Terrytoon; released by Educational Pictures. Characters: Farmer Al Falfa as Robinson Crusoe, Friday, black cannibals.

* Robinson Crusoe Isle. 1935. Walter Lantz, Universal. Characters: Robinson Crusoe, Oswald the rabbit, black cannibals.

* Robinson Crusoe Jr. 1941. Norman McCabe Warner Bros. Characters: Porky Pig, Friday, black cannibals.

Robinson Crusoe Limited. 1921. Gaumont (London). Characters: Ham, black cannibals.

Robinson Crusoe Returns on Friday. 1923. Red Head Comedy Company. Characters: Little red head, black man.

* Robinson Crusoe's Broadcast. 1938. Paul Terry, Terrytoon, Educational Pictures. Characters: Robinson Crusoe and cannibals.

Rolling Stones. 1936. Paus Terry, Frank Moser, Terrytoon. Characters: Two puppies. Includes a gag in which a fat black woman with thick white lips and wearing a fancy dress and house slippers walks to "The International Dog Show." She pulls five dogs on a leash, while another dog sits on her huge rear end.

* Romeo in Rhythm. 1940. Rudolph Ising, M-G-M. Characters: Black Crow Opera Company.

* Rover's Rival. 1937. Robert Clampett, Warner Bros. Characters: Porky Pig, Rover the dog, black pup.

A Royal Good Time. 1934. George Stallings, Van Beuren, RKO-Radio Pictures. Character: Little King. Includes gag in which Little King encounters African Rubber Man in a circus. He has thick white lips, and he becomes an "African dodger" who dodges baseballs thrown at his head, which is stuck through a hole in a sheet.

* Runaway Blackie. 1933. Harry Bailey, Van Beuren; released by RKO-Radio Pictures. Character: Black lamb.

* The Runt. 1925 (released in 1936 under the same title with added sound track by Educational Pictures). Paul Terry, Aesop's Fable, Pathe Film Exchange. Characters: Farmer Al Falfa, black pig.

Safari So Good. 1947. Dave Fleischer, Max Fleischer; released by Paramount Pictures. Characters: Popeye, African natives.

* Sammy Johnsin at the Seaside. 1916. Pat Sullivan, Powers Film Company; distributed by Universal Pictures. Character: Sammy Johnsin.

* Sammy Johnsin Gets a Job. 1916. Pat Sullivan, Powers Film Company; distributed by Universal. Character: Sammy Johnsin.

* Sammy Johnsin and His Wonderful Lamp. 1916. Pat Sullivan, Powers Film Company; distributed by Universal. Character: Sammy Johnsin.

* Sammy Johnsin—Hunter. 1916. Pat Sullivan, Powers Film Company; distributed by Universal Pictures. Character: Sammy Johnsin.

* Sammy Johnsin in Mexico. 1916. Pat Sullivan, Powers Film Company; distributed by Universal. Character: Sammy Johnsin.

* Sammy Johnsin—Magician. 1916. Pat Sullivan, Powers Film

Company; distributed by Universal Pictures. Character: Sammy Johnsin.

Sammy Johnsin Minds the Baby. 1916. Pat Sullivan, Powers Film Company; distributed by Universal Pictures. Character: Sammy Johnson.

Sammy Johnsin Slumbers Not. 1916. Pat Sullivan, Powers Film Company; distributed by Universal Pictures. Character: Sammy Johnsin.

Sammy Johnsin—Strong Man. 1916. Pat Sullivan, Powers Film Company; distributed by Universal Pictures. Character: Sammy Johnsin.

Sammy Johnsin's Love Affair. 1916. Pat Sullivan, Powers Film Company; distributed by Universal. Character: Sammy Johnsin.

Santa's Surprise. 1947. Seymour Kneitel, Famous Studios; released by Paramount Pictures. Characters: Little Audrey, black maid.

Santa's Workshop. 1932. Wilfred Jackson, Walt Disney, Silly Symphony, Distributed by United Artists. Character: Santa. Includes gag where Santa inspects the talking dolls as they come off the assembly line. He insists all the dolls say "Mamma" before he stamps "O.K." on their rear end. All the white dolls comply. A black doll, with a Topsy demeanor and thick red lips tumbles off the assembly line, smiles, then bends to one knee and says "Mammy." Santa laughs. She then does a somersault off of the conveyor belt and in mid air she pulls up the back of her dress before landing on her rear end on top of Santa's stamp. She bends over, so Santa can see "O.K." stamped on her underpants, which makes Santa laugh. Also as the toys march in a line into Santa's toy bag, a black man wearing a derby hat is seen riding on a donkey cart with a load of barrels in the back. The donkey stops a couple of times and kicks the cart with its rear hoofs, which makes the black dolls spring up and down (same sequence used in *Christmas in Toyland*).

Saturday Evening Puss. 1950. William Hanna, Joseph Barbera, M-G-M. Characters: Tom cat, Jerry mouse, Mammy Two-Shoes (voice characterization by Lillian Randolph).

Say Ah Jasper. 1945. George Pal, Puppetoon, Paramount Pictures. Characters: Jasper, Scarecrow (voice characterization by Roy Glenn), Crow, Mammy.

The Scared Crows. 1938. Dave Fleischer, Max Fleischer, Paramount Pictures. Characters: Betty Boop, black crows.

School Days. 1932. Ub Iwerks, Powers Film Company, Celebrity Pictures. Character: Flip the frog. Includes a gag by a black schoolboy.

Scrub Me Mama with a Boogie Beat. 1941. Alex Lovy, Frank Tipper, Walter Lantz, Universal Pictures. Characters: Southern blacks.

September in the Rain. 1937. I. Freleng, Vitaphone, Warner Bros. Characters: Al Jolson caricature in blackface, Aunt Ema, Gold Dust Twins.

The Shanty Where Santa Claus Lives. 1933. Hugh Harman, Rudolph Ising, Vitaphone, Warner Bros. Characters: Santa Claus, white boy, Sambo jazz band.

Sheepish Wolf. 1943. I. Freleng, Warner Bros. Character: Wolf, sheepdog. Includes gag involving a black lamb that says in a "Rochester" voice, "Boss, Boss, Oh Boss, I ain't the suspicious kind, but there's a wolf in sheep's clothing among us. And it don't look like he's going to no masquerade party."

Sherlock Hawshaw and Company. 1921. Bud Fisher Productions; released by Fox Films. Characters: Mutt and Jeff, black washerwoman.

Ship Ahoy. 1930. John Foster, Van Beuren; released by Pathe Film-RKO. Characters: Farmer Al Falfa, black girl.

Shoeshine Jasper. 1946. George Pal, Puppetoon, Paramount Pictures. Characters: Jasper, Scarecrow (voice characterization by Roy Glenn), Crow.

Shortnin' Bread. 193?. Arthur Price. Characters: Song cartoon with black kids, black doctor.

Shuffle Off to Buffalo. 1933. Hugh Harman, Rudolph Ising, Vitaphone, Warner Bros. Characters: Caricatures of Eddie Cantor, Ed Wynn, and other entertainers. Includes gag by the "Gold Dust Twins," two black babies with thick white lips and bald heads, who dance their way offstage and into the men's restroom.

Silly Superstitions. 1939. Walter Lantz, Universal Pictures. Characters: Li'l Eightball, his dog, Mammy.

Sing, Babies Sing. 1933. Dave Fleischer, Max Fleischer, Paramount Pictures. Characters: Stork, human and animal babies. Includes gags in which the stork sorts babies for delivery. He places a black baby with thick white lips and big round eyes next to a white baby who drinks black ink and turns into a black baby. Another gag has a black baby smiling as it shakes a rattle containing a pair of dice and who is placed in a bin labeled "Africa." Another gag has two black babies sharing one diaper, one eats a slice of watermelon and the other one spits out the seeds.

Sinkin' in the Bathtub. 1930. Hugh Harman, Rudolph Ising, Vitaphone, Warner Bros. Characters: Bosko and Honey.

Slap Happy Lion. 1947. Tex Avery, M-G-M. Includes gag of lion in blackface dressed like an African native.

Slap-Happy Pappy. 1940. Robert Clampett, Warner Bros. Characters: Porky Pig, caricatures of Hollywood stars including Bing Crosby, Eddie Cantor, Kay Kyser, Jack Benny. Includes a gag with Eddie "Rochester" Anderson hatching out of a black egg and saying "Hold it. My oh my, heaven can wait."

Sleepy-Time Tom. 1951. William Hanna, Joseph Barbera, M-G-M. Characters: Tom cat, Jerry mouse, Mammy Two-Shoes (voice characterization by Lillian Randolph).

S'Matter Pete? 1920. Walter Lantz, J. R. Bray Studio. Characters: Pete the dog, black girl, teacher (live action).

The Sneezing Weasel. 1938. Tex Avery, Warner Bros. Characters: Black chick, yellow chicks, weasel.

Snow White. 1933. Dave Fleischer, Max Fleischer, Paramount Pictures. Characters: Betty Boop, Ko-Ko the Clown, Bimbo, Cab Calloway (voice impersonation).

Sock-A-Bye Kitty. 1950. Seymour Kneitel, Famous Studios, Paramount Pictures. Characters: Buzzy the crow, Katnip the cat.

Somewhere in Egypt. 1943. Mannie Davis, Terrytoon, 20th

Century-Fox. Characters: Grandy Goose, black African palace guards.

Song of the Birds. 1949. Bill Tytla Famous Studios, Paramount Pictures. Characters: Little Audrey, black maid.

Sooty Sketches. 1909. Urban Trading Co. (London). Characters: Blackface minstrel man.

Southern Exposure. 1934. Charles Mintz, Columbia Pictures. Characters: Krazy Kat and southern Blacks.

Southern Fried Rabbit. 1957. I. Freleng, Warner Bros. Character: Bugs Bunny. Includes gag with Bugs in blackface saying, "Don't whip me, Massa," and singing "My Old Kentucky Home."

Southern Rhythm. 1932. Paul Terry, Terrytoon; released by Educational Pictures. Characters: Southern blacks.

Spare the Rod. 1954. Jack Hannah, Walt Disney, Distributed by RKO Radio Pictures. Character: Donald Duck. Includes gag where black Pigmy Cannibals boil Donald in a cooking pot. Included as a segment in "Donald's Week End," an episode of the Disneyland TV series shown on ABC TV Network (1957–1958).

Spark Plug. 1936. Charles Mintz Studio; distributed by Columbia Pictures. Characters: Barney Google, Snuffy Smith, Rudy the ostrich, Sambo the black jockey, Spark Plug the horse, Ma.

Speaking of the Weather. 1937. Frank Tashin, Warner Bros. Characters: Caricatures of movie stars, black cannibals.

Springtime. 1929. Ub Iwerks, Walt Disney; released by Columbia Pictures. Characters: Includes gag by singing blackface flowers.

Stars and Strips. 1927. Pat Sullivan, Pathe Film Exchange, Educational Pictures. Characters: Felix the Cat, black porter.

The Steeple-Chase. 1933. Burt Gillett, Walt Disney, Released by United Artists. Characters: Mickey Mouse, Minnie Mouse, The Southern Colonel, Black Stable Boys. Includes gag where Stable Boys say to Mickey, "Yes Boss."

The Stork Brought It. 1926. J. R. Bray Studios, Walter Lantz; distributed by Film Booking Office of America. Characters: Stork, black baby.

The Stowaway. 1925. L. B. Cornwall, London. Character: Little Ebony.

The Strange Adventures of Smiling Sambo. 1913. J. R. Bray Studios; released by Pathe Film Exchange. Character: Sambo.

Streamlined Gretta Green. 1937. I. Freleng, Vitaphone. Characters: Black quartet impersonating the Mills Brothers.

Streamlined Robinson Crusoe (shortened and silent version of Robinson Crusoe released by Castle Films in 1940).

Strong to the Finish. 1934. Dave Fleischer, Max Fleischer Studios; released by Paramount Pictures. Characters: Popeye, Olive Oyl, children including a black child who appears throughout the film but is not part of the main plot of the cartoon.

The Stubborn Mule. 1939. Walter Lantz, Universal Pictures. Characters: Li'l Eightball, the mule.

Stupidstitious Cat. 1947. Seymour Kneitel, Famous Studios, Paramount Pictures. Characters: Buzzy the crow, Katnip the cat.

Sunday Go to Meetin' Time. 1936. I. Freleng, Warner Bros. Character: Nicodemus, a lazy black man.

Sunny South. 1931. Walter Lantz, Universal. Characters: Oswald the rabbit, southern blacks.

The Sunny South. 1933. Frank Moser, Paul Terry, Terrytoon, Educational Pictures. Characters: Southern mammy, pickaninnies, Simon Legree.

Swanee River. 1925. Dave Fleischer, Max Fleischer, Song Cartune, Red Seal Film Company. Characters: Ko-Ko the Clown, black boy.

Sweet Jennie Lee. 1932. Dave Fleischer, Max Fleischer, Paramount Pictures. Characters: Black cotton pickers.

Swing, Monkey Swing. 1937. Manny Gould, Columbia Pictures. Characters: Scrappy, Negro choir in background music.

Swing Social. 1940. William Hanna, Joseph Barbera, M-G-M. Characters: Old Deacon Bass, Old Black Joe Bass.

Swing Wedding. 1937. Hugh Harman, Rudolph Ising, M-G-M. Characters: Frog impersonations of Cab Calloway, Bill Robinson, Fats Waller, Louis Armstrong, Stephin Fetchit. Songs: "Minnie the Moocher's Wedding Day," "Runnin' Wild."

Swing, You Sinner. 1930. Dave Fleischer, Max Fleischer, Paramount Pictures. Characters: Blackie, jazz musicians with black choral singers.

Swiss Cheese Family Robinson. 1948. Mannie Davis, Paul Terry, 20TH-Fox. Characters: Mighty Mouse, black cannibals.

The Swooner Crooner. 1944. Frank Tashlin, Warner Bros. Character: Porky Pig. Chicken caricatures of popular singers including Nelson Eddy, Al Jolson (who sings "September in the Rain" in blackface), Jimmy Durante, and Cab Calloway (who dances and sings "Blues in the Night").

Taking the Blame. 1935. Dave Fleischer, Max Fleischer, Paramount Pictures. Characters: Pudgy the dog, black cat.

A Tale That Knot. 1916. George Herriman, International Film Service, Hearst-Vitagraph News Pictorial. Characters: Krazy Kat, Ignatz mouse. In the last scene of the film Krazy Kat, lying in a bathtub, tells Ignatz Mouse, "Oh, oh. The nigger in the woodshed!"

Tea for Two Hundred. 1948. Jack Hannah, Walt Disney, Released by RKO Pictures. Characters: Donald Duck, Black Pygmy Ants. Shown January 1, 1997, on Disney Cable Channel as a black and white segment, narrated by Walt Disney, of the 1950's Disneyland TV Series.

Tee Time. 1927 (released with added sound track in 1930 by Copey Pictures Corporation). Pat Sullivan, M. J. Winkler, Pathe Film Exchange. Characters: Felix the Cat, black cannibals.

Ten Little Nigger Boys. 1912. Empire Films (London). Characters: Ten little black boys.

Tetched in the Head. 1935. Charles Mintz, Columbia Pictures. Characters: Barney Google, black man.

Them Were the Happy Days. 1917. Pat Sullivan, Powers Film Company; distributed by Universal Pictures. Characters: Old man, black nurse.

Those Beautiful Dames. 1935. I. Freleng, Vitaphone, Warner

Bros. Character: Little white girl. Includes gags by a wind-up black toy jazzbow singer who sings and dances while another black plays the piano and by two black girl dolls ("Topsy" types) who sing " . . . And we have made a chocolate cake for you . . ."

Three Orphan Kittens. 1935. David Hand, Walt Disney, Silly Symphony, Released by United Artists. Characters: Black Cook, Three Kittens (Blackie, Whitie, Calico). Includes gag where stereotypical black doll says, "Mammy."

Three's a Crowd. 1933. Hugh Harman, Rudolph Ising, Vitaphone, Warner Bros. Characters: Caricatures of various famous characters from popular literature, including bits involving Robinson Crusoe's Friday, a black boy with thick white lips, no shirt, and bare feet who does a Mills Brothers routine using his voice like a trumpet to play a jazzed-up version of the title song. Another bit involves Uncle Tom, an old, partially bald black man who slowly walks out of the book and sings, "When the dark night is comin', and the moon starts to glow. What is the thing that keeps callin'? It's the South in my soul. Let me live on that levee, let me burn black as coal. But my heart won't be happy with the South in my soul."

Thru Thick and Thin. 1926. Paul Terry, Aesop's Fable, Pathe Film Exchange. Characters: Farmer Al Falfa Jr., his black cat "Nigger."

Tightrope Tricks. 1933. John Foster, George Rulfo, Van Beuren; released by RKO-Radio Pictures. Characters: Tom and Jerry. Includes a gag by black rubber man circus performer.

Tin Pan Alley Cats. 1943. Robert Clampett, Merrie Melodies, Warner Bros. Characters: Caricatures of Fats Waller, Louis Armstrong.

Toby Tortoise Returns. 1936. Wilford Jackson, Silly Symphony, Walt Disney; released by United Artists. Characters: Toby Tortoise, hare. Includes gag by black rabbit who shines the white hare's paws.

Too Canny for the Cannibals. 1927. Pathe Film Exchange. Characters: Black cannibals.

Toot, Whistle, Plunk, and Boom. 1953. Jack Hannah, Walt Disney, distributed by RKO Radio Pictures. Includes musical segment with a black African cannibal wearing a bone in his hair who is playing a xylophone with human skulls held in each hand while a lion sits next to him. Also includes two blackface minstrel banjo players with thick white lips. Also shown on the "Walt Disney Presents-Disneyland" program directed by Wilford Jackson and narrated by Walt Disney. Broadcast on the ABC Television Network in 1959 and sponsored by Hills Bros Coffee, Reynolds Aluminum Co. and Mars Candy Co.

A Toyland Broadcast. 1934. Hugh Harman, Rudolph Ising, M-G-M. Characters: Caricatures of Kate Smith, Boswell Sisters, Bing Crosby, Rubinoff, Paul Whiteman, Mills Brothers.

Toyland Premiere. 1934. Walter Lantz, Universal. Characters: Toy caricatures of Hollywood stars, including Eddie Cantor, in blackface.

Toy Town Hall. 1936. I. Freleng, Warner Bros. Characters: Toy caricatures of radio stars including Fred Allen, Rudy Vallee, and a black wind-up band.

Toy Trouble. 1941. Charles Jones, Warner Bros. Characters: Sniffles, black jazzbo band.

Trader Mickey (silent version released by Hollywood Film Enterprises under the title *Cannibal Capers*). 1932. David Hand, Walt Disney, United Artists. Characters: Mickey Mouse, Pluto, black cannibals.

Tramp, Tramp, Tramp. 1919. John D. Tippett, Pussyfoot Cartoon Comedy (London). Characters: Happy Hooligan and Dusty Dan (a black man).

Travel Squawks. 1938. Harry Love, Louie Lilly, Columbia Pictures. Characters: Krazy Kat, black Africans.

Treasure Island. 1923. Hodkinson, J. R. Bray Studio. Characters: Col. Heeza Liar, African natives.

Tree's Knees. 1931. Hugh Harman, Rudolph Ising, Vitaphone, Warner Bros. Character: Bosko.

The Trials of Willie Winks. 1917. Pat Sullivan, Powers Film Company; distributed by Universal Pictures. Characters: Willie Winks, Sammy Johnsin.

Triplet Trouble. 1952. Joseph Barbera, William Hanna, M-G-M. Characters: Tom cat, Jerry mouse, Mammy Two-Shoes (voice characterization by Lillian Randolph).

Two Lazy Crows. 1936. Ub Iwerks, Columbia Pictures. Characters: Two black crows.

The Ugly Dino. 1940. Dave Fleischer, Max Fleischer, Paramount Pictures. Characters: Black baby dinosaur.

Ugly Duckling. 1925. Paul Terry, Aesop's Fable, Pathe Film Exchange. Characters: Black duckling, hen family.

Uncle Remus (nos. 1, 2, 3). 1919. Kine Komedy Films (London). Characters: Uncle Remus and his stories.

Uncle Tom and Little Eva. 193?. Jungle Jinks, Characters: Uncle Tom, Little Eva, Topsy.

Uncle Tom's Bungalow. 1937. Tex Avery, Merry Melodies, Warner Bros. Characters: Uncle Tom, Little Eva, Topsy, Liza, Simon Legree.

Uncle Tom's Cabana. 1947. Tex Avery, M-G-M. Characters: Uncle Tom, Simon Legree, Little Eva, black kids.

Ups 'N Downs. 1931. Hugh Harman, Rudolph Ising, Vitaphone, Warner Bros. Character: Bosko.

Voodoo in Harlem. 1938. Frank Tipper, Merle Gilson Walter Lantz, Universal. Characters: Black natives, cartoonist (live action), black maid.

We, the Animals Squeak. 1941. Robert Clampett, Warner Bros. Character: Porky Pig. Includes gag by mice in blackface.

When Yuba Plays the Rumba on the Tuba. 1933. Dave Fleischer, Max Heirchen; released by Paramount Pictures. Characters: Mills Brothers.

Which Is Witch. 1949. I. Freleng, Warner Bros. Characters: Bugs Bunny, black witch doctor.

Who Killed Cock Robin? 1935. David Hand, Walt Disney, Silly Symphony, United Artists. Characters: Cock Robin bird (Bing Crosby demeanor), Jennie Wren (Mae West demeanor), and Crow (Stephin Fetchit demeanor).

Wholly Smoke. 1938. Frank Tashin, Warner Bros. Character:

Porky Pig. Includes a gag where a pipe cleaner sticks his head into the bowl of a pipe and when he removes it, it has turned into the face of a caricature of Cab Calloway who sings "Little boys shouldn't smoke" in his own unique style.

The Whoopee Party. 1932. Wilford Jackson, Walt Disney, United Artists. Characters: Mickey Mouse, Minnie Mouse, Pluto. Includes gag in which the heads of four matches burn, turning them into blackface stereotypes with thick white lips who say "Mammy."

*Who's Cookin'. 194?. Canadian Production. Characters: Sailor, black cannibals.

Why Play Leapfrog? 1947. John Sutherland, Harding College. Characters: Various whites in business and the workforce. The only black person shown is a man in a barber shop who is smiling as he shines the hoofs of a bull being prepared for the meat market.

Winter Draws On. 1948. Seymour Kneitel, Famous Studios; released by Paramount Pictures. Includes gags by Buzzy the crow who says, "The ice man comin' and South us birds goin'," by black duckling who has an eightball painted on his head, by black Pullman porters singing "Alabamy Bound," and by black mammy.

Wise Quackers. 1949. I. Freleng, Warner Bros. Characters: Elmer Fudd, Daffy Duck. Includes gag with Daffy in blackface and "Uncle Tom" deameanor saying to Elmer, "Don't beat me, Massa. Don't whip this po' old body."

*Woodland Cafe. 1937. Wilford Jackson, Walt Disney, Silly Symphony, Released by United Artists. Includes stereotypical Black Doorman and Black Bugs, and also includes sequence with Cab Calloway caricature and Orchestra. Cab sings and dances "Everybody's Truckin'."

The Woods Are Full Of Cuckoos. 1937. Frank Tashlin, Warner Bros. Characters: Caricatures of famous entertainers including Fats Swallow (Fats Waller).

*Wot a Night. 1931. George Stallings, John Foster, Van Beuren; distributed by RKO-Radio Pictures. Characters: Tom and Jerry, black skeleton quartet.

Wotta Knight. 1947. I. Sparber, Paramount Pictures. Characters: Popeye the sailor, Olive Oyl, Bluto. Includes a gag in which a king tries to ring a bell held by a black boy who has thick lips and is dressed in a loincloth. The king hits the black boy on the top of his head, making his eyeballs spin around. The second time the king swings, he hits a skillet the boy has put on his head.

Yankee Doodle Mouse. 1943. William Hanna, Joseph Barbera, M-G-M. Characters: Tom cat, Jerry mouse. Includes a gag with Tom made up as a blackface stereotype.

*A Yarn of Wool. 1932. John Foster, Van Beuren, RKO-Radio Pictures. Character: Black sheep.

*Ye Old Toy Shop. 1935. Paul Terry, Frank Moser, Educational Pictures, 20th Century Fox. Characters: Santa, Black Dolls.

*Yodeling Yokels. 1931. Hugh Harman, Rudolph Ising, Vitaphone, Warner Bros. Characters: Bosko, Honey.

You Don't Know What You're Doin'. 1931. Isadore Freleng, Looney Tunes, Vitaphone, Warner Bros. Characters: Piggy and Fluffy (Pig characterizations of Bosko and Honey). Includes gag where the exhaust smoke from a motorcycle turns a white doorman into a blackface stereotype with thick white lips.

*You're an Education. 1938. Frank Tashlin, Warner Bros. Characters: Includes gag by black baby trio singing "Food's An Education."

*You're Driving Me Crazy. 1931. Dave Fleischer, Max Fleischer, Screen Song, Paramount Pictures. Characters: Snooks and his Memphis Ramblers, black Africans.

*Zula Hula. 1938. Dave Fleischer, Max Fleischer, Paramount Pictures. Characters: Betty Boop, black cannibals.

*Zulu Jazz. See *Cannibal Capers.*

INDEX

ABOUT THE AUTHOR

A native of Jackson, Mississippi, Henry T. Sampson (Morehouse College; B.S. Chemical Engineering, Purdue University; M.S. Engineering, UCLA; M.S., Ph.D. Nuclear Engineering, University of Illinois) is Senior Project Engineer, The Aerospace Corp. He holds patents for the Gamma-Electric Cell and solid rocket propellant case bonding, and has published numerous technical papers. He has written these books published by Scarecrow Press: *Blacks in Black and White: A Source Book on Black Films* (1977); *Blacks in Blackface: A Source Book on Early Black Musical Shows* (1980); *The Ghost Walks: A Chronological History of Blacks in Show Business* (1988); and *Blacks in Black and White: A Source Book On Films, 2nd edition* (1995). Dr. Sampson is a contributing author to the *New Grove Dictionary of Music in the United States,* consults and lectures on blacks in the motion picture industry and the performing arts, and owns an extensive collection of historic black films, theatrical material, animated cartoon shorts, and other entertainment memorabilia.